The Great American Mosaic

The Great American Mosaic

An Exploration of Diversity in Primary Documents

Gary Y. Okihiro, General Editor

Volume 2
American Indian Experience

James E. Seelye Jr., Volume Editor

GREENWOOD

AN IMPRINT OF ABC-CLIO, LLC
Santa Barbara, California • Denver, Colorado • Oxford, England

Library of Congress Cataloging-in-Publication Data

The great American mosaic: an exploration of diversity in primary documents/Gary Y. Okihiro, general editor.
   volumes cm
Contents: Volume 1. African American Experience/Lionel C. Bascom, volume editor.
ISBN 978-1-61069-612-8 (hardback : acid-free paper)—ISBN
978-1-61069-613-5 (ebook) 1. Cultural pluralism—United States—History—Sources. 2. United States—Race relations—History—Sources. 3. United States—Ethnic relations—History—Sources. 4. Minorities—United States—History—Sources. 5. United States—History—Sources. I. Okihiro, Gary Y., 1945- II. Bascom, Lionel C.
E184.A1G826 2014
305.800973—dc23   2014007428

ISBN: 978-1-61069-612-8
EISBN: 978-1-61069-613-5

18 17 16 15 14   1 2 3 4 5

This book is also available on the World Wide Web as an eBook.
Visit www.abc-clio.com for details.

Greenwood
An Imprint of ABC-CLIO, LLC

ABC-CLIO, LLC
130 Cremona Drive, P.O. Box 1911
Santa Barbara, California 93116-1911

This book is printed on acid-free paper ∞
Manufactured in the United States of America

Contents

Volume 2: American Indian Experience

Creation Stories and First Contact to 1715

Imperial Crisis (1716–1826)

Fighting the United States: Winning and Losing (1827–1877)

Attempt to Regain the Past (1878–1920)

The Indian New Deal and a Turn to the Militant (1921–1973)

Coexistence (1974–Present)

General Introduction

Peoples of color—African Americans, Asian and Pacific Islander Americans, Latinas/Latinos, and Native Americans—were not always included within the American mosaic. In fact, throughout much of the nation's history, peoples of color were not members or citizens of these United States. In 1787, John Jay, a Founding Father and a leading designer of the nation-state, declared in "Concerning the Dangers from Foreign Force and Influence," essays that were part of *The Federalist* papers, that Americans are "one united people—a people descended from the same ancestors, speaking the same language, professing the same religion, attached to the same principles of government, very similar in their manners and customs."

Jay's "one united people" were Europeans, foreigners, who called themselves "persons" and "whites" in the new nation's Constitution, laws, and census. Those not included within that racialized, nationalized category or "the citizen race" in the words of U.S. Supreme Court chief justice Roger Taney in *Dred Scott v. Sandford* (1857), were of "another and different class of persons" and they represented "foreign dangers," threatening disunity and conflict. It is the experiences of those peoples that *The Great American Mosaic: An Exploration of Diversity in Primary Documents* covers in its four volumes. Volume 1 provides a collection of documents exploring the African American experience; Volume 2, the American Indian experience; Volume 3, the Asian American and Pacific Islander experience; and Volume 4, the Latino experience.

Standard narratives of the nation routinely excluded peoples of color. Only around the mid-20th century did U.S. history textbooks reflect more fully the nation's diversity, highlighting especially the presence of African Americans. Still, the architecture of American history remains white at its core; Native Americans, including American Indians and Pacific Islanders, formed the environment and background for white expansion and settlement, and African and Asian Americans and Latinas/Latinos played minor notes in an anthem devoted to the European nation.

Indeed, the nation, since the English invasion and colonization of America in the 17th century, systematically excluded peoples of color from the privileges and protections accorded Taney's "citizen race." "We, the people" of the U.S. Constitution was never intended to embrace nonwhites; that exclusion is the foundational premise upon which the nation was conceived. Conversely, the inclusion of peoples of color democratized the nation and was truly revolutionary. The American Revolution, by contrast, was not transformative in that the new nation was an extension of the original white settler colonialism that infringed upon these shores.

American Indians

To the invaders, American Indians were impediments to their freedom, especially embodied in the concept of "free" land. Conquest and expulsion were the means of American Indian alienation whereby English foreigners became natives on their sovereign estates, and the land's natives became aliens. The English-drawn border of 1763, despite its porous nature, was indicative of that demarcation, that segregation of "citizens" from "aliens."

The postcolonial nation acknowledged that arrangement in the Treaty of Greenville (1795), which recognized Indian sovereignty in territories not claimed by the United States. In *Worcester v. Georgia* (1832), the U.S. Supreme Court declared the Cherokee nation to be a "foreign state," a condition reaffirmed by Chief Justice Taney in his *Dred Scott* (1857) majority opinion. As Taney wrote, the United States signed treaties with American Indian nations, "under subjection to the white race," and, accordingly, in the United States whites were the "citizen race" and American Indians were "aliens."

That exclusion shifted with the white flood, which by the late 19th century had engulfed the entire continent from sea to shining sea. Following the final bloody wars of conquest waged mainly against Indians of the Great Plains, the U.S. census of 1890 declared in that year, which saw the massacre of Indian men, women, and children at Wounded Knee, that the entire continent had been filled (by whites). President Theodore Roosevelt called those lands, memorably, the "red wastes," and other men called them "virgin land." There were no more frontiers for manly probing and capture.

Conquest achieved, the Dawes Act (1887) sought to dissolve Indian nations and assimilate American Indians as individuals. Soon thereafter, the U.S. Supreme Court affirmed, in *Lone Wolf v. Hitchcock* (1903), the plenary powers of Congress over Indian nations because they constituted "domestic dependent nations." The assimilation continued with U.S. citizenship bestowed in 1924 on those born after that year, and, in 1940, on all American Indians.

Following a brief interlude during the New Deal of the 1930s, the attempt to absorb American Indians politically and culturally continued into the 1950s, when Dillon Myer, as chief of the Bureau of Indian Affairs, pursued the policy called appropriately "termination." Myer had experience with termination, having administered the concentration camps for Japanese Americans as the War Relocation Authority's director during World War II.

American Indians, thus, were at first excluded as "foreign" nations and peoples, and, after conquest, were assimilated and rendered domestic dependencies and dependents.

African Americans

Like American Indians, African Americans were "aliens" excluded from community membership. In 1669, a Virginia colony jury ruled that Anthony Johnson was "a Negroe and by consequence an alien." Race determined citizenship. The postcolonial nation and its founding Constitution (1787) specified that African Americans were not "persons" but "three fifths of all other Persons" and thereby failed to qualify for full representation in the Congress.

In fact, as Chief Justice Taney held in *Dred Scott* (1857): "Negroes of the African race" and their descendants "are not included, and were not intended to be included, under the word 'citizens' in the Constitution, and can therefore claim none of the rights and privileges which that instrument provides for and secures to citizens of the United States." Moreover, Taney pointed out, from the republic's founding, the 1790 Naturalization Act limited citizenship to "free white persons," making clear the distinction between the "citizen race" or whites and "persons of color" or those "not included in the word citizens."

That separation dissolved with the Thirteenth (1865), Fourteenth (1868), and Fifteenth (1870) Amendments to the U.S. Constitution, which, respectively, ended slavery, extended citizenship to all persons born in the United States, and enfranchised men regardless of "race, color, or previous condition of servitude." In 1870, Congress extended to Africans the right of naturalization. African American citizens, although without full equality under Jim Crow, transformed the complexion of the "citizen race" and, thus, the nation. The change was a radical break with the past; it was, in fact, revolutionary.

Still, racial segregation was the primary instrument of the state to secure African American political and economic dependency, and Jim Crow, as was affirmed by *Plessy v. Ferguson* (1896), ruled the land until *Brown v. Board of Education* (1954), which integrated public schools. In *Plessy*, the U.S. Supreme Court ruled that racial segregation in private businesses, conducted under the doctrine of "separate but equal," fulfilled the Fourteenth Amendment's equal protection clause. States routinely denied African American men and, after 1920, women access to the ballot through property and literacy requirements from the end of Reconstruction in the 1870s to the Voting Rights Act of 1965.

Latinas/Latinos

Mexican Americans were a people made through conquest, much like American Indians. In the 1820s and 1830s, Americans, many of them owning slaves, settled in the Mexican province of Texas. These white Protestant settlers, never comfortable in a Catholic republic that sought to end slavery, shook off Mexican control in 1836. In 1845, the United States admitted Texas as a state, an action that helped precipitate the Mexican American War (1846–1848). Driven by Manifest Destiny, an expansionist doctrine that proclaimed the God-given right of the United States to expand across the North American continent, the U.S. government, after defeating Mexico, demanded the cession of almost half of Mexico's territory, land that later formed the entire states of California, Nevada, and Utah, as well as portions of Colorado, Wyoming, Arizona, and New Mexico. The Treaty of Guadalupe Hidalgo (1848), which ended the war, granted U.S. citizenship to Mexican residents of the ceded lands, and Mexicans were thus rendered "white" by treaty. At the same time, many Mexican Americans lost their farms and land, like American Indians, and were widely denied equality in employment, housing, and education on the basis of race, class, and culture.

Judicial decisions commonly cited the contradiction between Mexican whiteness by treaty and Mexicans as a mestizo and "mongrel" race by scientific and common opinion. Further, courts decided, in accordance with the one-drop rule, that is, one drop of nonwhite blood meant a person was considered nonwhite, that children of whites and nonwhites were "colored." This principle was applied in such cases as *In re Camille* (1880), involving a white father and American Indian mother, and *In re Young* (1912), involving a white father and Japanese mother. Still, as *In re Rodriguez* (1897), the courts were compelled to rule that Mexican Americans were white and thus citizens. At the same time, whiteness in theory disallowed Mexican American claims of racial discrimination in practice, such as the right to a trial of their peers, which, if granted, would end instances of all-Anglo juries ruling on Mexican Americans.

The state segregated Mexican American children in inferior schools on the basis of language and "migrant farming patterns," as was affirmed by a Texas court in *Independent School District v. Salvatierra* (1930). Mexicans emerged from the white race in the 1930 U.S. census and appeared as "Mexicans." The enumeration facilitated the expulsion to Mexico of about half a million Mexican and Mexican Americans from the United States during the Great Depression, when their labor was no longer required. That removal complemented the 1935 Filipino Repatriation Act, which offered Filipino Americans, like Mexican American migrant laborers, free passage to the Philippines.

Asian and Pacific Islander Americans

The 1790 Naturalization Act, which limited U.S. citizenship to "free white persons," excluded Pacific Islanders and Asians, like American Indians and African Americans, from the "citizen race." In the 1850s, California's supreme court chief judge Hugh Murray affirmed the distinction between "a free white citizen of this State" and American Indians, Africans, Pacific Islanders, and Asians, those "not of white blood," in Murray's words. Unlike Native Americans, including American Indians and Pacific Islanders, whose utility to the nation involved mainly their land, Asians were employed, like African and Mexican Americans, as laborers.

As persons "not of white blood," Pacific Islander and Asian men served as slaves and servants to whites; appealed to whites and antislavery societies for manumission; married American Indian, African American, and Mexican women; were counted in the U.S. census as colored and mulatto; fought in African American units in the Civil War; and were buried in colored cemeteries. Like Mexicans, Asians and Pacific Islanders served employers as migrant laborers, mainly in agriculture but also in mines and on railroads; formed unions irrespective of race; and married and produced bicultural children.

Unique among people of color in the United States was the persistent condition of Asians as "aliens ineligible to citizenship" under the 1790 Naturalization Act. Mexicans by treaty and African Americans and American Indians through law acquired U.S. citizenship, albeit absent its full rights and privileges. Unable to naturalize, Asians and Pacific Islanders gained U.S. citizenship by birth under the Fourteenth Amendment. Chinese acquired the right to naturalization in 1943, South Asians and Filipinos in 1946, and Japanese and Koreans not until 1952. Accordingly, the United States denied Asians naturalization rights for more than 160 years, from 1790 to 1952.

Tempering those acts of inclusion were immigration quotas imposed on Asians and Pacific Islanders. Starting in 1929, under the Johnson-Reed Immigrant Act (1924), Congress assigned an annual quota of 100 each to those immigrating from Australia and Melanesia, Bhutan, China, India, Iran, Iraq, Japan, Micronesia, Nepal, New Zealand, Oman, Sāmoa, and Thailand.

The law gave to Turkey, straddling Europe and Asia, a quota of 226. Likewise, the law assigned to African nations, from Egypt to South Africa, annual quotas of 100.

European countries, by contrast, which supplied the "citizen race," received quotas of 1,181 (Denmark), 2,377 (Norway), 3,153 (Netherlands), 5,802 (Italy), 17,853 (Irish Free State), 25,957 (Germany), and 65,721 (Great Britain and Northern Ireland). In force until 1965, the Johnson-Reed Act established the nation's first comprehensive, restrictive immigration policy. The act also served to define the nation, its citizens, and its peoples—called a race—by excluding those who were deemed unworthy or even dangerous. In that sense, immigration is a matter of national defense and homeland security.

Imperialism

Conquest did not end with the filling of the continent. The nation, in the late 19th century, extended its imperial reach overseas to the Caribbean and Pacific. Peoples indigenous to and settled upon those territories thereby became Americans, though not fully. After the Spanish-American War of 1898, Puerto Ricans and Filipinos, natives of unincorporated territories, followed divergent paths; Puerto Ricans became U.S. citizens in 1917, and Filipino nationals became Asian aliens in 1934. Contrarily, Hawaiians and Alaska's indigenous peoples, natives of incorporated territories, became U.S. citizens, whereas those in the unincorporated territories of Guam, where "America's day begins," are U.S. citizens while those in American Sāmoa are nationals.

American Mosaic

Founding Father John Jay's "one united people" diversified with the nation's expansion. European immigration during the late 19th century was unlike the usual flow from Great Britain and northern Europe. These new immigrants came from southern and eastern Europe and brought with them different religions, languages, and cultures. Nonetheless, most, through Americanization and assimilation, became members of the white, citizen race.

Peoples of color were not counted among that number at first, and when they became Americans and citizens, they transformed the nation and its peoples from a people descended from the same ancestors to an American mosaic. Racism and segregation, nonetheless, deferred dreams and attenuated the achievement of that revolution. As the documents in these four volumes testify, however, peoples of color are more than minor figures in the nation's narrative; they are central to it, and the documents collected in these volumes shed new light on that history, revealing a more complex, diverse, and troubled American past.

These documents expand upon the standard narratives of nation, which have, for the most part, excluded and marginalized peoples of color. They offer a fuller, more comprehensive understanding of these United States, and are of great consequence for all Americans. They are also important for peoples of color. As Frantz Fanon pointed out in his *The Wretched of the Earth* (1961), colonization denies a people their past, leading to "estrangement" from their history and culture. Freedom requires a recuperation of "the whole body of efforts made by a people in the sphere of thought to describe, justify, and praise the action through which that people has created itself and keeps itself in existence" (p. 233).

We, the people, and descendants of the nation's branching genealogy possess the ability and share the responsibility to shape a more inclusive, equitable, and democratic future.

Gary Y. Okihiro

Volume Introduction

American and Indian Experience, volume 2 *of The Great American Mosaic: An Exploration of Diversity in Primary Document*s, is a collection of documents that epitomize many different kinds of voices from within Native American cultures and societies. The documents in this volume were created during the past 400 years following contact with European colonists. The collection provides an indigenous perspective on the creation of the universe and the origins of humanity, treaties, speeches, laws, court decisions, and many other documents that represent the contemporary effort to incorporate an American Indian perspective into the writing of history. Until recently, the historiography on Native Americans and American history in general reflected a belief in certain myths about the tragedy of the Indian experience. According to these powerful myths, Native Americans were fated to disappear as Americans expanded across the continent and made full use of the land. Among the many writers, artists, and poets who embraced and advanced this myth was a historian from Wisconsin, Frederick Jackson Turner, whose ideas helped to enshrine these myths as an accepted part of America's growth and development from a colony to a world power.

In July 1893, Turner delivered his famous address, "The Significance of the Frontier in American History," at the World's Columbian Exposition in Chicago. Once published, this address helped to establish a master narrative not only for America's development but also for its future. Turner argued that a unique American identity was created during the westward migrations from the Atlantic to the Pacific Ocean. Initiative, informality, democracy, and strength were some of the characteristics of the American identity forged through interaction with a wild and hostile environment. Native Americans, where they appeared in Turner's narrative, were part of the environment that needed to be tamed for American institutions to put down roots and flower. Turner's work greatly influenced the writing of American history for several generations, and even today his ideas continue to attract attention.

Turner's master narrative depicted Native Americans as an obstacle to be overcome for the United States to be successful; conquest was therefore deemed both necessary and beneficial. Americans believed that when the first Europeans arrived in the 15th century, North America was a savage wilderness, inhabited by ignorant and barbaric tribes. By the late 19th century, when Turner first published his thesis, Americans were experiencing the difficult transformation to an industrialized economy, and waves of immigrants threatened to alter the American identity. For these Americans, Turner's essay was a source of reassurance moving forward. His thesis provided many Americans with a sense of historic purpose. Americans of the late 19th century would absorb immigrants in the same way that their ancestors conquered this continent's indigenous inhabitants. Turner's thesis was American exceptionalism, a powerful myth about our past and future; this myth gave Americans direction and purpose because it allowed them to know where they came from and where they were going.

Not until the 1980s was Turner's myth sufficiently challenged in academia to begin the process of rewriting American history to include an indigenous perspective. This process started much earlier, however, at the moment of contact between Europeans and American Indians. The Native American experience described by the documents in this collection has been characterized by conquest, colonization, and displacement. It has also seen the fracturing of indigenous economic, cultural, and social structures; yet, the entire process has also been one of survival, adaptation, resistance, and perseverance.

The Native American experience presented by these documents begins with the period of contact with Europeans, a time of great social, cultural, and economic transformation for both groups. Two worlds, separated by water for thousands of years, were suddenly reunited during the period of European exploration beginning with Columbus's first voyage to the Western Hemisphere in 1492. The introduction of new technologies, as well as new plants, animals, and diseases, set off profound demographic changes, often well in advance of contact with Europeans.

A period of colonization and conquest usually followed contact, although in some cases the three occurred simultaneously. The displacement of many Eastern Woodlands groups by European colonists set the pattern for future interactions between Native peoples and Euro-Americans, events that accelerated throughout the 19th century.

In 1851, the U.S. government passed the Indian Appropriations Act, which allowed for the establishment of reservations in Indian Territory, present-day Oklahoma. Many indigenous groups, especially those living on the Great Plains, resisted the transition from traditional lifestyles to the reservation system. During the Indian Wars period, which lasted roughly from the end of the Civil War to the 1890s, the U.S. military engaged in a series of conflicts with the indigenous inhabitants of the region west of the Mississippi River. One of the most well-known conflicts, the Great Sioux War of 1876, occurred while the United States celebrated its centennial in Philadelphia. These celebrations marked 100 years of sovereign status and freedom, freedom from the control of another nation that dictated how American social, economic, and political institutions would function. At the same time these celebrations were under way, the rights of Plains Indians (including the Lakota and Cheyenne) to these same freedoms were being violated by American military forces.

The end of the 19th century saw many Native American groups adjusting to life on reservations. Native peoples continued to adapt to the reservation system and persevered through the boarding-school period, the suppression of traditional religious practices, and the adoption of new economic systems (e.g., agriculture). Many Native Americans entered the 20th century attempting to adjust to the same types of transformations that the shift to an industrial economy forced white Americans to endure.

One of the most significant events to affect the lives of Native Americans during the 20th century was the passage of House Concurrent Resolution 108 in 1953, which established a policy of termination in which Indian reservations and federal services would come to an end.

At the same time, Natives would become citizens of this nation, subject to the same laws and responsibilities as other citizens. Public Law 280, which gave state governments authority over reservations, was also passed in 1953 and signaled an official end to the special relationship between some tribes and the federal government.

In many ways, the federal termination policy instituted a period of transformation for tribes. Without federal services such as health care, housing assistance, and other necessary programs, Native Americans began leaving their traditional territories and moving to urban areas to find work. For the first time, the phenomenon of the urban Indian came into existence. Groups of Native Americans from various tribes lived side by side, a long distance from their traditional homelands, to find work in cities like Chicago, Minneapolis-St. Paul, San Francisco, Los Angeles, Denver, and Seattle.

Many of these urban Indian enclaves established Indian centers for the protection and practice of traditions, cultural and religious ceremonies, and a sense of community. Eventually, a Pan-Indian identity sprang from these nascent meetings and led to the formation of the Red Power movement and groups like the American Indian Movement (AIM). This movement would successfully demand the repeal of the federal termination policy and become a voice for other Native issues throughout the rest of the 20th century and into the new millennium. The Red Power movement has also played a role in instilling pride in indigenous culture and language.

Awareness and empathy toward the Native American experience grew in the last four decades of the 20th century as the Red Power movement attracted attention to the voices and actions of American Indians. An example of this is the reinterpretation of the meaning of the Little Bighorn Battlefield National Monument (known as the Custer Battlefield until 1991). The victory experienced by the Lakota and Cheyenne peoples at the site in 1876 during the Great Sioux War had for nearly a century been interpreted to visitors as a terrible loss of heroic U.S. cavalrymen at the hands of bloodthirsty warriors. Movies, art, books, and poetry elevated George Custer and his men to the status of martyrs, men who paid the ultimate price to expand the frontier further west. Although Native Americans had protested this interpretation for decades, during the late 1960s they were joined by an American public who saw similarities between what Custer was ordered to do on the plains of southeastern Montana Territory and what the U.S. military was doing in Vietnam. Through the work of Native Americans like Vine Deloria, Russell Means, and members of AIM, not only were American Indians successful in changing the name of the battlefield to reflect sensitivity to indigenous groups, but they were also able to force the National Park Service to change the way the site is interpreted to visitors.

Since the 1970s, the movement for American Indian rights has achieved many advances. In 1978, passage of the American Indian Religious Freedom Act offered new protections for the religious rights and cultural practices of Native Americans, and enactment of the Indian Child Welfare Act halted the widespread removal of Indian children from their families by state agencies that misunderstood the importance of extended families to Native Americans and gave to white foster parents children they thought abandoned. In 1990, the Native American Graves Protection and Repatriation Act provided new protections for the cultural artifacts of Native Americans, which had for years been carried away by archaeologists, tourists, and looters seeking their own profit. Executive Order 13007, issued by President Bill Clinton in May 1996, ordered federal agencies to assist Native Americans in conducting religious rituals and ceremonies at sites they deemed sacred. In 2005, passage of Title IX of the Violence Against

Women Act focused on the protection of Indian women against domestic violence, sexual assault, and murder, all of which they suffered at high rates. In 2009, the *Cobell v. Salazar* court decision addressed the lax management of hundreds of thousands of Native American trust accounts by the Bureau of Indian Affairs, while Congress designated the Friday after Thanksgiving as Native American Heritage Day and apologized to Native American peoples for the injustices committed against them throughout the country's history. Finally, in 2013, the U.S. Supreme Court case *Adoptive Couple v. Baby Girl* addressed issues arising from the controversial abrogation of Native American parental rights.

In 1969, N. Scott Momaday won the Pulitzer Prize for his book, *House Made of Dawn*. Subsequently, publishers began to seek out Native American writers, which led, in part, to what has become known as the Native American Renaissance. At the time of Momaday's Pulitzer Prize ceremony, few Native Americans were published authors within the genre of fiction and poetry. Today, many more American Indians have added their voices to the field, including Sherman Alexie, Paula Gunn Allen, Joy Harjo, Leslie Marmon Silko, and Simon Ortiz, among others. Through their writings in the fields of poetry, fiction, and nonfiction, and their work as artists, directors, musicians, and actors or actresses, indigenous peoples are adding new voices to the chorus of the Native American experience.

James E. Seelye Jr.

Brief Guide to Primary Sources

Primary sources are original, direct, firsthand stories, personal experiences, testimony, and viewpoints that are created during the time period involved. They may include such forms as diaries, journals, letters, personal narratives, government records, graffiti, laws, court cases, plays, novels, poems, architectural plans, maps, memoirs, autobiographies, sound recordings, songs, advertisements, photographs, paintings, prints, speeches, and other material objects. The sources become the raw material that historians, or other scholars, use to create their works in book or article form. Secondary sources are interpretations, which are often made using myriad primary sources.

Primary sources provide readers with a wealth of firsthand information that gets them close to the actual experiences of the historical time period, people, and events. Firsthand material offers a window to a particular time and place, viewpoints, and eyewitness accounts that supplement information and facts typically provided in textbooks and other secondary sources. Primary sources offer readers the raw material of history that has not been analyzed and interpreted.

How to Read and Reflect on Primary Documents

Primary sources in written form, as illustrated by the document selections included in *The Great American Mosaic: An Exploration of Diversity in Primary Documents*, were produced at a particular historical moment and for a particular purpose. These volumes are intended to provide an outlet for the voices of people of color whose experiences and viewpoints are often overlooked or downplayed in the larger American history narrative. Some of these documents were written by an author conscious of a larger audience or with the expectation that they would be published; others were written for personal reasons without the expectation that others would read them. Some documents were intended to persuade, inform, or entertain. Note that documents are based on the particular viewpoints, experiences, and memories of the writer and can reflect selective memories, mistaken information, or deception. The reader is left to evaluate the relevance, reliability, and value of the information and to take into account the analysis and interpretations of secondary sources. The documents in *The Great American Mosaic* provide readers with a variety of firsthand content, ranging from creation myths to legislation to reflections on historical events that provide insights into the experiences of people of color in the United States.

What Questions Should You Ask as You Read?

- Who wrote or produced the document, and what do we know about him or her?
- When and where was the source written or produced, and how does it fit into the timeline of the events and period described?
- Where was the source written or produced? Does that material portray cultural, social, or religious values? What form did it take originally?
- Why was the source material written or produced? What was its creator's intention or purpose? What is the overall tone of the source material?
- Who was the intended audience? How was the document used, and how widely distributed or read was it?
- Overall, how do we evaluate the relevance, reliability, and value of the content? What might the author have left out, intentionally or not?

Anishinabe Creation Story

An Algonquian-speaking people, the Anishinabe, sometimes called Ojibwa or Chippewa, live in the Great Lakes area of what is now the United States and Canada. Anishinabe means "the people." Their mythology often features the culture-hero/trickster/spirit figure, Nanabozho, (Manbhozo, Michabo, Mishaabooz, the Great Hare). Their creation story tells how a broken world was re-created by the Kitchi-Manitou—the Great Spirit—with the help of Nanabozho. The central figure in the Anishinabe myth is Nanabhozo, who, as a culture hero, initiates the process of re-creation, acting, like other culture heroes, as the representative on Earth of the ultimate creator Great Spirit. In the earth-diver myths, humans and animals are typically left to achieve the elements of creation themselves rather than through divine intervention. The message of this cultural dream is that the creative act, whenever and wherever it takes place in human life, requires the participation of humans. The Great Spirit can conceive of creation but it is the beings of creation—the little Muskrat, symbolically, like the seemingly insignificant little human—who makes it real.

The original world and its original people, the Anishinabe, were created, like all things, by the greatest of spirits (manitou), the Kitchi-Manitou (Gitchi Manito, the Great Spirit). The world was beautiful, but gradually the people became evil and destructive, upsetting the balance among themselves and their environment. The Great Spirit put an end to the mess by sending a great flood to destroy everything and everyone—everyone except Nanabozho, sent to the world by the Kitchi-Manitou, and a few flying and swimming creatures. Nanabhozo and some of the animals survived by floating on a log.

After a time, Nanabhozo announced that he would dive to the bottom of the waters to retrieve enough earth to begin a new world. The dive lasted for a very long time, but eventually Nanabhozo surfaced without any earth. The waters are too deep, he said. Several of the animals more experienced in diving tried to accomplish Nanabhozo's goal for him. The Loon tried and failed, as did the helldiver, the mink, and the turtle. All returned, more dead than alive, without retrieving any earth. Just as everyone was about to give up, the muskrat asked to be allowed to dive. The other animals jeered at his suggestion but Nonabhozo insisted that the little animal be given his chance.

So it was that little Muskrat dove into the depths. When after many hours he floated back to the surface, Nanabhozo pulled him onto the log and sadly announced that he was dead. But in the dead animal's closed paw was a bit of earth. The muskrat had reached the bottom of the waters after all. Now the turtle volunteered his back and his life as a surface for the ball of earth, and the animals called on Kitchi-Manitou for help. Help came in the form of winds from the Four Directions, winds that caused the little ball of earth to grow gradually into an island on the now dead turtle's back. Nanabhozo and the animals danced and chanted to help the process along, and finally the world we know was formed, thanks to the Kitchi-Manitou and especially to the sacrificial act of the turtle and muskrat.

Source: Spence, Lewis. *The Myths of the North American Indians.* London: George G. Harrap and Company, 1914.

Aztec (Mexica) Creation Story

The people who in about 1350 founded the city of Tenochtitlan, which is now Mexico City, are generally known as Aztec, but, more accurately, were the Mexica. With the decline of the great Mesoamerican classical period city of Teotihuacan in the eighth century, various peoples emerged and achieved periods of dominance in the valley of Mexico. The Nahuatl-speaking Toltec dominated beginning in the 10th century, but in the 13th century the area was invaded by various other less sophisticated Nahuatl-speaking peoples known as the Chichimec, and among whom were the Mexica. The Mexica settled around Lake Texoco and gave their name not only to the area but also to the culture that eventually emerged through a combination of Mexica and Toltec traditions. The Mexica dominated the area with a vast empire built on alliances until their conquest by the Spanish, led by Hernán Cortés, in 1521. The creation stories that we associate with the Aztec-Mexica are deeply influenced by the earlier Toltec culture, itself in all likelihood influenced by the traditions of the much earlier pre-classical Olmec and classical Teotihuacán cultures; the figure of the Feathered Serpent, for example, who eventually became known as Quetzalcóatl, the most popular of the Mesoamerican deities, has roots in the earlier cultures. When we speak of Aztec or Mexica deities and creation stories, then, we are really referring to a culmination of myths that emerged from the Nahuatl past. The two stories here are examples of this combined heritage.

Quetzalcoatl and his dark brother Tezcatlipoca took note from Heaven of a giant goddess floating on the primordial waters down below. The goddess was devouring everything that came near her, so rather than allow the destruction of all creation, the gods decided to act. Becoming two gigantic serpents, they dove into the water and tore the goddess apart. The two parts of the dismembered goddess became our world—one part the earth, the other the sky. The violence of the dismemberment disturbed the other deities so they compensated by making the rendered goddess the sources of Earth's beauties. Her hair became plant life, her eyes became water, her mouth rivers, her shoulders hills and mountains.

Coatlicue was at once the birth-giver—the one whose womb provided the moon and stars and the sun, personified by the great warrior god

Huitzilopochtli—and the one who takes life back into herself; she gives life and brings death. Coatlicue is the center of one of the world's many miraculous conception stories. The myth about the dismemberment of the primal goddess provides narrative justification for the Toltec-Aztec tradition of human sacrifice. Like the Indian goddess Kali, the Aztec goddess demands human blood as payment for nurturing human life. The Aztecs, and those who came before them, recognized and were deeply concerned with the fact that the Earth provides for life but that part of life's cycle is turmoil, disintegration, death, and a return to earth.

It was said that Coatlicue was somehow impregnated by an obsidian knife and that, as a result, she gave birth to Coyolxanuhqui and the stars. As she was sweeping a temple one day a ball of feathers somehow entered her and soon she gave birth to Quetzalcoatl and Xolotl. Her other children became angry and decapitated her, only to be attacked in turn by the great Huizilopochtli, who descended fully armed from Coatlicue's womb. Some say that Huizilopochtli prevented the decapitation of his mother. In any case, Huizilopochtli was especially enraged by his sister Coyolxauhqui who had led the charge against their mother and, as an act of revenge, he decapitated Coyolxauhqui and hurled her head into the sky to become the moon. Others say he threw her whole body into a mountain gorge where it remains to this day.

Source: Leeming, David A. *Creation Myths of the World: An Encyclopedia.* 2nd ed. Santa Barbara, CA: ABC-CLIO, 2009.

Luiseño Creation Story

The Luiseño people of the Southern California coast are the southernmost group of the Shoshoneans, who were once powerful in Utah, Nevada, and California. These Native Americans, like all others in the area, came under the influence of Spanish missions. Some of the Temecula Valley–based Pechanga band of the Luiseño tell a complex creation story that contains many familiar motifs, beginning with creation from chaos and including a world parent aspect. It is a story that shares similarities with the Hawaiian myth of the gradual coming of light.

In the beginning there was only Kevish-Atakvish (space void) or Omai-Yamal (nothingness). Then things began to fall into forms. Time came, and the Milky Way. There was no light yet, but there was a creative stirring. Kevish-Atakvish made a man, Tukmit, who was the sky, and a woman, Tomaiyovit, who was the earth. They could not see each other, but brother and sister knew each other and they conceived and gave birth to the first elements of creation. They produced the valleys, mountains, stones, streams, and all things that would be necessary for worship, ceremonies, and cooking. From the earth came Takwish, the terrifying meteor, and his son, Towish, who is the immortal soul of humans. Wiyot also came forth, and from Wiyot came the people. It was still dark.

The Earth Mother made a sun, but it was too bright and had to be hidden away since it frightened the people. The people made more people and they followed the growing Earth as it stretched southward. They came to Temecula, where the Earth Mother brought out the sun again. The people raised it up to the sky, where it followed a regular path and was not so frightening. At Temecula, it is said by some, the father of the people, Wiyot, died. Because Frog hated him for the legs he had made for her, she spit poison into his water. After drinking the poison, Wiyot announced that he would die in the spring. Before he left, he taught the people what they needed to know. When he died, a great oak tree grew from his ashes, an axis mundi for the people.

Now Wiyot visits the people each night; he has become the moon and is the center of their celebrations: "Wiyot rises," the people cry as they dance for him.

Source: Leeming, David A. *Creation Myths of the World: An Encyclopedia.* 2nd ed. Santa Barbara, CA: ABC-CLIO, 2009.

"The Creation of Beginning" (Navajo/Dine)

Creation myths are some of the most important cultural stories because they deal with the life-shaping questions of "Who are we?," "Why are we here?," and "Where did we come from?" Such stories provide key insights into the way that the people of a culture see and understand the world around them. For the Navajo, this story addresses such themes as gender roles, the relationship of humans to nature, and the consequences of behaving in an unseemly manner. The story features a number of characters, both human and nonhuman, all of whom have specific roles that become increasingly defined over the course of the tale.

THE FIRST WORLD

These stories were told to Sandoval, Hastin tlo'tsihee, by his grandmother, Esdzan Hosh kige. Her ancestor was Esdzan at a', the medicine woman who had the Calendar Stone in her keeping. Here are the stories of the Four Worlds that had no sun, and of the fifth, the world we live in, which some call the Changeable World.

The First World, Ni'hodilqil, was black as black wool. It had four corners and over these appeared four clouds. These four clouds contained within themselves the elements of the First World. They were in color, black, white, blue, and yellow.

The Black Cloud represented the Female Being or Substance. For as a child sleeps when being nursed, so life slept in the darkness of the Female Being. The White Cloud represented the Male Being or Substance. He was the Dawn, the Light-Which-Awakens, of the First World.

In the East, at the place where the Black Cloud and the White Cloud met, First Man, Atse'hastqin was formed; and with him was formed the white corn, perfect in shape, with kernels covering the whole ear. Dohonot i'ni is the name of this first seed corn, and it is also the name of the place where the Black Cloud and the White Cloud met.

The First World was small in size, a floating island in mist or water. On it there grew one tree, a pine tree, which was later brought to the present world for firewood.

Man was not, however, in his present form. The conception was of a male and a female being who were to become man and woman. The creatures of the First World are thought of as the Mist People; they had no definite form, but were to change to men, beasts, birds, and reptiles of this world.

Now on the western side of the First World, in a place that later was to become the Land of Sunset, there appeared the Blue Cloud, and opposite it there appeared the Yellow Cloud. Where they came together First Woman was formed, and with her the yellow corn. This ear of corn was also perfect.

With First Woman there came the white shell and the turquoise and the yucca.

First Man stood on the eastern side of the First World. He represented the Dawn and was the Life Giver. First Woman stood opposite in the West. She represented Darkness and Death.

First Man burned a crystal for a fire. The crystal belonged to the male and was the symbol of the mind and of clear seeing. When First Man burned it, it was the mind's awakening. First Woman burned her turquoise for a fire. They saw each other's lights in the distance. When the Black Cloud and the White Cloud rose higher in the sky First Man set out to find the turquoise light. He went twice without success, and again a third time; then he broke a forked branch from his tree, and, looking through the fork, he marked the place where the light burned. And the fourth time he walked to it and found smoke coming from a house.

"Here is the home I could not find," First Man said.

First Woman answered: "Oh, it is you. I saw you walking around and I wondered why you did not come."

Again the same thing happened when the Blue Cloud and the Yellow Cloud rose higher in the sky. First Woman saw a light and she went out to find it. Three times she was unsuccessful, but the fourth time she saw the smoke and she found the home of First Man.

"I wondered what this thing could be," she said.

"I saw you walking and I wondered why you did not come to me," First Man answered.

First Woman saw that First Man had a crystal for a fire, and she saw that it was stronger than her turquoise fire. And as she was thinking, First Man spoke to her. "Why do you not come with your fire and we will live together." The woman agreed to this. So instead of man going to the woman, as is the custom now, the woman went to the man.

About this time there came another person. The-Great-Coyote-Who-Was-Formed-in-the-Water, and he was in the form of a male being. He told the two he had been hatched from an egg. He knew all that was under the water and all that was in the skies. First Man placed this person ahead of himself in all things. The three began to plan what was to come to pass, and while they were thus occupied another being came to them. He also had the form of a man, but he wore a hairy coat, lined with white fur, that fell to his knees and was belted in at the waist. His name was Atse'hashke', First Angry or Coyote. He said to the three: "You believe that you were the first persons. You are mistaken. I was living when you were formed."

Then four beings came together. They were yellow in color and were called the *tsts' na* or wasp people. They knew the secret of shooting evil and could harm others. They were very powerful.

Four more beings came. They were small in size and wore red shirts and had little black eyes. They were the *naazo'zi* or spider ants. They knew how to sting, and were a great people.

After these came a whole crowd of beings. Dark colored they were, with thick lips and dark, protruding eyes. They were the *wolazhi'ni,* the black ants. They also knew the secrets of shooting evil and were powerful; but they killed each other steadily.

By this time there were many people. Then came a multitude of little creatures. They were peaceful and harmless, but the odor from them was unpleasant. They were called the wolazhi'ni nlchu nigi, meaning that which emits an odor.

And after the wasps and the different ant people there came the beetles, dragonflies, bat people, the Spider Man and Woman, and the Salt Man and Woman, and others that rightfully had no definite form but were among those people who peopled the First World. And this world, being small in size, became crowded, and the people quarreled and fought among themselves, and in all ways made living very unhappy.

THE SECOND WORLD

Because of the strife on the First World, First Man, First Woman, The-Great-Coyote-Who-Was-Formed-in-the-Water, and the Coyote called First

Angry, followed by all the others climbed up from the World of Darkness and Dampness to the Second or Blue World.

They found a number of people already living there; blue-birds, blue hawks, bluejays, blue herons, and all the blue-feathered beings. The powerful swallow people lived there also, and these people made the Second World unpleasant for those who had come from the First World. There was fighting and killing.

The First Four found an opening in the World of Blue Haze; and they climbed through this and led the people up into the Third or Yellow World.

THE THIRD WORLD

The bluebird was the first to reach the Third or Yellow World. After him came the First Four and all the others.

A great river crossed this land from north to south. It was the Female River. There was another river crossing it from east and west, it was the Male River. This Male River flowed through the Female River and on; and the name of this place is tqo alna'osdli, the Crossing of the Waters.

There were six mountains in the Third World. In the East was Sis najin, the Standing Black Sash. Its ceremonial name was Yol gai'dzil, the Dawn or White Shell Mountain. In the South stood Tso'dzil, the Great Mountain, also called Mountain Tongue. Its ceremonial name is Yodolt i'zhi dzil, the Blue Bead or Turquoise Mountain. In the West stood Dook'oslid, the meaning of this name is forgotten. Its ceremonial name is Dichi'li dzil, the Abalone Shell Mountain. In the North stood Debe'ntsa, Many Sheep Mountain. Its ceremonial name is Bash'zhini dzil, Obsidian Mountain. Then there was Dzil na'odili, the Upper Mountain. It was very sacred; and its name means also the Center Place, and the people moved around it. Its ceremonial name is Ntl'is dzil, Precious Stone or Banded Rock Mountain. There was still another mountain called Chol'i'i or Dzil na'odili choli, and it was also a sacred mountain.

There was no sun in this land, only the two rivers and the six mountains. And these rivers and mountains were not in their present form, but rather the substance of mountains and rivers as were First Man, First Woman, and the others.

Now beyond Sis na'jin, in the east, there lived the Turquoise Hermaphrodite, Ashon nutli'. He was also known as the Turquoise Boy. And near this person grew the male reed. Beyond, still farther in the east, there lived a people called the Hadahuneya'nigi, the Mirage or Agate People. Still farther in the east there lived twelve beings called the Naaskiddi. And beyond the home of these beings there lived four others—the Holy Man, the Holy Woman, the Holy Boy, and the Holy Girl.

In the West there lived the White Shell Hermaphrodite or Girl, and with her was a big female reed which grew at the water's edge. It had no tassel. Beyond her in the West there lived another stone people called the Hadahunes'tqin, the Ground Heat People. Still further on there lived another twelve beings, but these were all females. And again, in the Far West, there lived four Holy Ones.

Within this land there lived the Kisa'ni, the ancients of the Pueblo People. On the six mountains there lived the Cave Dwellers or Great Swallow People. On the mountains lived also the light and dark squirrels, chipmunks, mice, rats, the turkey people, the deer and cat people, the spider people, and the lizards and snakes. The beaver people lived along the rivers, and the frogs and the turtles and all the underwater people in the water. So far all the people were similar. They had no definite form, but they had been given different names because of different characteristics.

Now the plan was to plant.

First Man called the people together. He brought forth the white corn which had been formed with him. First Woman brought the yellow corn. They laid the perfect ears side by side; then they asked one person from among the many to come and help them. The Turkey stepped forward. They asked him where he had come from, and he said that he had come from Grey Mountain. He danced back and forth four times, then he shook his feather coat and there dropped from his clothing four kernels of corn, one grey, one blue, one black, and one red. Another person was asked to help in the plan of the planting. The Big Snake came forward. He likewise brought forth four seeds, the pumpkin, the watermelon, the cantaloupe, and the muskmelon. His plants all crawl on the ground.

They planted the seeds, and their harvest was great.

After the harvest the Turquoise Boy from the East came and visited First Woman. When First Man returned to his home he found his wife with this boy. First Woman told her husband that Ashon nutli' was of her flesh and not of his flesh. She said that she had used her own fire, the turquoise, and had ground her own yellow corn into meal. This corn she had planted and cared for herself.

Now at this time there were four chiefs: Big Snake, Mountain Lion, Otter, and Bear. And it was the custom when the Black Cloud rose in the morning for First Man to come out of his dwelling and speak to the people. After First Man had spoken the four chiefs told them what they should do that day. They also spoke of the past and of the future. But after First Man found his wife with another he would not come out to speak to the people. The Black Cloud rose higher, but First Man would not leave his dwelling; neither would he eat or drink. No one spoke to the people for four days. All during this time First Man remained silent, and would not touch food or water. Four times the White Cloud rose. Then the four chiefs went to First Man and demanded to know why he would not speak to the people. The chiefs asked the question three times, and a fourth, before First Man would answer them.

He told them to bring him an emetic. This he took and purified himself. First Man then asked them to send the hermaphrodite to him. When he came First Man asked him if the *metate* and brush were his. He said that they were. First Man asked him if he could cook and prepare food like a woman, if he could weave, and brush the hair. And when he had assured First Man that he could do all manner of woman's work First Man said: "Go and

prepare food and bring it to me." After he had eaten, First Man told the four chiefs what he had seen, and what his wife had said.

At this time The-Great-Coyote-Who-Was-Formed-in-the-Water came to First Man and told him to cross the river. They made a big raft and crossed at the place where the Male River flowed through the Female River. And all the male beings left the female beings on the river bank; and as they rowed across the river they looked back and saw that First Woman and the female beings were laughing. They were also behaving very wickedly.

In the beginning the women did not mind being alone. They cleared and planted a small field. On the other side of the river First Man and the chiefs hunted and planted their seeds. They had a good harvest. Nadle ground the corn and cooked the food. Four seasons passed. The men continued to have plenty and were happy; but the women became lazy, and only weeds grew on their land. The women wanted fresh meat. Some of them tried to join the men and were drowned in the river.

First Woman made a plan. As the women had no way to satisfy their passions, some fashioned long narrow rocks, some used the feathers of the turkey, and some used strange plants (cactus). First Woman told them to use these things. One woman brought forth a big stone. Another woman brought forth the Big Birds of Tsa bida'hi; and others gave birth to the giants and monsters who later destroyed many people.

On the opposite side of the river the same conditions existed. The men, wishing to satisfy their passions, killed the females of mountain sheep, lion, and antelope. Lightning struck these men. When First Man learned of this he warned his men that they would all be killed. He told them that they were indulging in a dangerous practice. Then the second chief spoke: he said that life was hard and that it was a pity to see women drowned. He asked why they should not bring the women across the river and all live together again.

"Now we can see for ourselves what comes from our wrong doings," he said. "We will know how to act in the future." The three other chiefs of the animals agreed with him, so First Man told them to go and bring the women.

After the women had been brought over the river First Man spoke: "We must be purified," he said. "Everyone must bathe. The men must dry themselves with white corn meal and the women with yellow."

This they did, living apart for four days. After the fourth day First Woman came and threw her arms around her husband. She spoke to the others and said that she could see her mistakes, but with her husband's help she would henceforth lead a good life. Then all the male and female beings came and lived with each other again.

The people moved to different parts of the land. Some time passed; the First Woman became troubled by the monotony of life. She made a plan. She went to Atse'hashke', the Coyote called First Angry, and giving him the rainbow she said: "I have suffered greatly in the past. I had suffered from want of meat and corn and clothing. Many of my maidens have died. I have suffered many things. Take the rainbow and go to the place where the rivers cross. Bring me the two pretty children of Tqo holt sodi, the Water Buffalo, a boy and a girl."

The Coyote agreed to do this. He walked over the rainbow. He entered the home of the Water Buffalo and stole the two children; and these he hid in his big skin coat with the white fur lining. And when he returned he refused to take off his coat, but pulled it around himself and looked very wise.

After this happened the people saw white light in the East and in the South and West and North. One of the deer people ran to the East, and returning, said that the white light was a great sheet of water. The sparrow hawk flew to the South, the great hawk to the West, and the kingfisher to the North. They returned and said that a flood was coming. The kingfisher said that the water was greater in the North, and that it was near.

The flood was coming and the Earth was sinking. And all this happened because the Coyote had stolen the two children of the Water Buffalo, and only First Woman and the Coyote knew the truth.

When First Man learned of the coming of the water he sent word to all the people, and he told them to come to the mountain called Sis na'jin. He told them to bring with them all the seeds of the plants used for food. All living beings were to gather on the top of Sis na'jin. First Man traveled to the six sacred mountains, and, gathered earth from them, he put them in his medicine bag.

The water rose steadily.

When all the people were halfway up Sis na'jin, First Man discovered that he had forgotten his medicine bag. Now this bag contained not only the earth from the six mountains, but his magic, the medicine he used to call the rain down upon the earth and to make things grow. He could not live without his medicine bag, and he wished to jump into the rising water; but the others begged him not to do this. They went to the kingfisher and asked him to dive into the water and recover the bag. This the bird did. When First Man had his medicine bag again in his possession he breathed on it four times and thanked his people.

When they had all arrived it was found that the Turquoise Boy had brought with him the big Male Reed; and the White Shell Girl had brought with her the big Female Reed. Another person brought poison ivy; and another, cotton, which was later used for cloth. This person was the spider. First Man had with him his spruce tree which he planted on the top of Sis na'jin. He used his fox medicine to make it grow; but the spruce tree began to send out branches and to taper at the top, so First Man planted the big male Reed. All the people blew on it, and it grew and grew until it reached the canopy of the sky. They tried to blow inside the reed, but it was solid. They asked the woodpecker to drill out the hard heart. Soon they were able to peek through the opening, but they had to blow and blow before it was large enough to climb through. They climbed up inside the big male reed, and after them the water continued to rise.

THE FOURTH WORLD

When the people reached the Fourth World they saw that it was not a very large place. Some say that it was called the White World; but not all medicine men agree that this is so.

The last person to crawl through the reed was the Turkey from Grey Mountain. His feather coat was flecked with foam, for after him came the water. And with the water came the female Water Buffalo who pushed her head through the opening in the reed. She had a great quantity of curly hair which floated on the water, and she had two horns, half black and half yellow. From the tips of the horns the lightning flashed.

First Man asked the Water Buffalo why she had come and why she had sent the flood. She said nothing. Then the Coyote drew the two babies from his coat and said that it was, perhaps, because of them.

The Turquoise Boy took a basket and filled it with turquoise. On top of the turquoise he placed the blue pollen, tha'di'thee do tlij, from the blue flowers, and the yellow pollen from the corn; and on top of these he placed the pollen from the water flags, tquel aga'di din; and again on top of these he placed the crystal, which is river pollen. This basket he gave to the Coyote who put it between the horns of the Water Buffalo. He said that the male child would be known as the Black Cloud or Male Rain, and that he would bring the thunder and lightning. The female child he would keep. She would be known as the Blue, Yellow, and White Clouds or Female Rain. She would be the gentle rain that would moisten the earth and help them to live. So he kept the female child, and he placed the male child on the sacred basket between the horns of the Water Buffalo. And the Water Buffalo disappeared, and the waters with her.

After the water sank there appeared another person. They did not know him, and they asked him where he had come from. He told them that he was the badger, nahashch'id, and that he had been formed where the Yellow Cloud had touched the Earth. Afterward this Yellow Cloud turned out to be a sunbeam.

THE FIFTH WORLD

First Man was not satisfied with the Fourth World. It was a small, barren land; and the great water had soaked the earth and made the sowing of seeds impossible. He planted the big Female Reed and it grew up to the vaulted roof of this Fourth World. First Man sent the newcomer, the badger, up inside the reed, but before he reached the upper world water began to drip, so he returned and said that he was frightened.

At this time there came another strange being. First Man asked him where he had been formed, and he told him that he had come from the Earth itself. This was the locust. He said that it was now his turn to do something, and he offered to climb up the reed.

The locust made a headband of a little reed, and on his forehead he crossed two arrows. These arrows were dressed with yellow tail feathers. With this sacred headdress and the help of all the Holy Beings the locust climbed up to the Fifth World. He dug his way through the reed as he digs the earth now. He then pushed through mud until he came to water. When he emerged he saw a black water bird swimming toward him. He had arrows crossed on the back of his head and big eyes.

The bird said: "What are you doing here? This is not your country." And continuing, he told the locust that unless he could make magic he would not allow him to remain.

The black water bird drew an arrow from his head, and shoving it into his mouth drew it out of his nether extremity. He inserted it underneath his body and drew it out of his mouth.

"This is nothing," said the locust. He took the arrows from his headband and pulled them both ways through his body, between his shell and his heart. The bird believed that the locust possessed great medicine, and he swam away to the East, taking the water with him.

Then came the blue water bird from the South, and the yellow water bird from the West, and the white water bird from the North, and everything happened as before. The locust performed the magic with his arrows; and when the last water bird had gone he found himself sitting on land.

The locust returned to the lower world and told the people that the beings above had strong medicine, and that he had great difficulty getting the best of them.

Now two dark clouds and two white clouds rose, and this meant that two nights and two days had passed, for there was still no sun. First Man again sent the badger to the upper world, and he returned covered in mud, terrible mud. First Man gathered chips of turquoise which he offered to the five Chiefs of the Winds who lived in the uppermost world of all. They were pleased with the gift, and they sent down the winds and dried the Fifth World.

First Man and his people saw four dark clouds and four white clouds pass, and then they sent the badger up the reed. This time when the badger returned he said that he had come out on solid earth. So First Man and First Woman led the people to the Fifth World, which some call the Many-Colored Earth and some the Changeable Earth. They emerged through a lake surrounded by four mountains. The water bubbles in this lake when anyone goes near.

Now after all the people had emerged from the lower worlds First Man and First Woman dressed the Mountain Lion with yellow, black, white, and grayish corn and placed him on one side. They dressed the Wolf with white tail feathers and placed him on the other side. They divided the people into two groups. The first group was told to choose whichever chief they wished. They made their choice, and, although they thought they had chosen the Mountain Lion, they found that they had taken the Wolf for their chief. The Mountain Lion was the chief for the other side. And these people who had the Mountain Lion for their chief turned out to be the people of the Earth. They were to plant seeds and harvest corn. The followers of the Wolf chief became the animals and birds; they turned into all the creatures that fly and crawl and run and swim.

And after all the beings were divided, and each had his own form, they went their ways.

This is the story of the four Dark Worlds and the Fifth, the World we live in. Some medicine men tell us that there are two worlds above us, the first is the World of the Spirits of Living Things, the second is the Place of Melting into One.

Source: O'Bryan, Aileen. "The Dine: Origin Myths of the Navaho." Bulletin 163. Bureau of American Ethnology, Smithsonian Institution, 4–11. Washington, DC: United States Government Printing Office, 1956.

Onondaga Creation Story

One of the Six Nations that form the Iroquois Confederation—the Haudenosaunee (People of the Longhouse)—the Onondaga (People on the Hilltop) live in the northeast on both sides of the New York/Canada border. They are a matrilineal culture; their clans are led by clan mothers. The Onondagan creation story has developed over the centuries, and continues to develop, as creation myths must take into account the way things are as well as the way they once may have been. This myth contains elements of the earth-diver and sky woman motifs so common to Iroquoian speakers and other northeastern Native Americans. This myth is almost the same as the Iroquoian Mohawk creation myth. The dominance of the Sky Woman is appropriate for matrilineal cultures such as those of the Iroquoian tribes. Sky Woman and her daughter become true culture heroes, teaching their people how to live. They are the first clan mothers. The fact that an evil child is born of the daughter's armpit rather than in the usual manner suggests the abnormality that the child brings into an otherwise stable world.

They say that there were once man-beings who lived in the sky of the world above this one, and that a woman-being went there with a comb and began straightening out the hair of one of the man-beings. Soon she became pregnant and the man-being became the first to experience the mystery of death, for with birth must come death. The man-being was placed by his mother in a coffin.

When the woman-being gave birth to a girl, her mother (the Ancient One) asked the woman-being who would be the child's father, but the woman-being did not answer. The child grew, and one day she began crying and would not stop. It was the Ancient One who told her daughter to take the child to the male-being's coffin. When the child saw the coffin she was happy. The corpse of the man-being gave her instructions on the right way to be until she married.

When the girl child herself had a baby called Zephyrs, her husband, a chief, became ill. He sang a song, telling the other man-beings to pull the tree called Tooth that grew near his hut. Through the hole left by the tree, he threw his wife and Zephyrs down to the world below—our world.

The woman-being, Sky Woman, fell and fell and saw only water beneath her. The animals below saw Sky Woman and Zephyrs falling and decided to make land for them. Many animals tried to dive below the waters to get earth, but only Muskrat succeeded, and he died in the process. With the earth he brought up, however, the animals made land on the Turtle's back. Then the flying creatures formed themselves into a huge net in which they caught the falling women, and they brought them safely to the new earth.

Sky Woman and her daughter brought fire and taught the people the art of hunting. When the daughter had grown she was visited in the night and she soon became pregnant. Just before she gave birth, she heard two male-beings talking inside her body, arguing about how to be born. One came out by the normal way, the other by an arm-pit. This armpit child killed his mother and told his grandmother the other son had done the deed. Thus, there are good and evil people. These were the first man-beings on Earth.

Source: Leeming, David A. *Creation Myths of the World: An Encyclopedia.* 2nd ed. Santa Barbara, CA: ABC- CLIO, 2009.

Oneida Creation Story

Like the Onondaga, the Oneida (People of the Standing Stone) of New York are members of the Iroquois Confederation. Like the other Iroquois, the Oneida are led culturally by clan mothers and their Sky Woman. Their earth-diver creation story has many elements that are present in the creation myths of the other members of the group.

In the beginning the earth was covered in water and every place was dark. Only water animals lived down here. The spirits lived in the world above with the Great Spirit. There was a huge apple tree there with deep roots. It happened that one day the Great Spirit uprooted the tree, leaving a great hole in the ground of the upper world. He ordered his daughter to look down through the hole at the dark, water-covered lower world and he asked her to go there. He picked his daughter up and dropped her through the hole. Slowly Sky Woman, as she was now called, floated down towards the world below, shining like a star. The water animals looked up, afraid. At first they hid under the water, but then they came back up and decided they would need a dry place on which Sky Woman could land. Beaver dove into the depths to find soil but drowned in the process. The loon and others failed, too. Finally the muskrat dove, and though he resurfaced dead, he had some mud in his paw. The animals placed the bit of mud on the turtle's back and immediately the turtle and the earth on his back grew into what is now North America. Meanwhile, swans flew up to catch the falling Sky Woman and they brought her safely to the new earth. Almost immediately she gave birth to twins; one was good and the other was so bad that his mother died trying to give birth to him.

The Good Twin, or Good Spirit, as he is called, hung his mother's head in the sky as the Sun. He also used parts of her body to become the Moon and Stars. The rest of her body he buried, making the earth itself sacred and fertile. But for every good thing the Good Spirit did, his evil brother, the Bad Spirit, did the opposite. The Good Spirit made beautiful plants and the Evil Spirit put thorns and knots on them. The Evil Spirit countered his brother's deer and bear with poisonous snakes, his beautiful rivers with rocks to cause dangerous rapids. Finally, the Good Spirit made humans out of clay, and the Evil Spirit mocked that creation by creating monkeys.

The Good Spirit now placed a protective power over his whole creation and ordered his brother to respect the protection. When the Evil Spirit refused, the Good Spirit challenged him to a fight; the winner to rule the world. After many days of brutal fighting, the Good Spirit prevailed and condemned his brother to a dark underground cave. Unfortunately, however, the Evil Spirit's servants come up to this world and cause problems, especially by making humans do evil things. This is why all of us can be evil as well as good.

Source: Leeming, David A. *Creation Myths of the World: An Encyclopedia.* 2nd ed. Santa Barbara, CA: ABC-CLIO, 2009.

Thompson River Indians Creation Story

The Thompson River Native North Americans of British Columbia are related to the Salishan, who live further south. Their creation story, however, seems to be very much their own. This retelling is based on a story told by an old shaman named Nkamtcine'lx at the turn of the century. The shaman said he had heard the myth from his grandfather.

In the beginning of time there was only water everywhere. Old One got tired of looking at all the water, so he came down on a cloud, determined to create something new. When the cloud—now fog—reached the waters, Old One plucked five hairs from his head (some say from his pubic area) and threw them down, and they became five perfect young women, already able to speak, see, and hear. Then he asked the women what they would like to do with their lives.

The first woman said she would like to have many children, be wicked, and pursue her own pleasure. She wanted her descendants to be fighters, murderers, adulterers, thieves, and liars. Old One was sorry for this answer.

The second woman said she too would like to bear children, but that she and her descendants would be good and true people—wise, honest, peaceful, and chaste. Old One praised the second woman and pointed out that in the end her way would triumph over the first woman's.

The third woman said she wanted to be the earth, the place where her sisters and their descendants would live. She would allow the people to take life from her, and she promised to give abundantly of herself. Old One was well pleased with new Earth Mother. He foresaw that she would nurture the world and then take the dead back to herself and keep them warm. She would give forth beautiful trees and plants.

The fourth woman said she planned to be fire, that she would give warmth to the people and help them make their food better. Old One was more than satisfied with this plan.

The fifth woman simply wished to be water.

Then Old One changed the women into their wishes for themselves. The third woman lay down in the waters and became the Earth Mother on which we live. The fifth woman became the waters within Earth, the fourth woman became the spirit of fire in all things that burn. As for the first and second women, Old One placed them on Earth and immediately impregnated them. "You will be the first people," he said, "and from you will come all the people of the earth—male and female." Old One foresaw that at first the evil woman's children would dominate but that eventually the good woman's children would prevail. Old One said he would bring together the five sisters and all of the people—good and evil, dead and alive—at the end of the world.

All of this explains why there are good and bad people on Earth. It also explains how all of us are directly related to earth, fire, and water.

Source: Leeming, David A. *Creation Myths of the World: An Encyclopedia.* 2nd ed. Santa Barbara, CA: ABC-CLIO, 2009.

White Mountain Apache Creation Story

Creation stories offer important insights into a culture's values, as well as the way they see their place in the world. These stories explore the concept of origins, the how and why of the earth's existence. The people in the following story play an important role in constructing the world, which is described in anthropomorphic terms—it has bones and blood, and it breathes, like any living thing. The story offers important insights into the culture of the Apache of the American Southwest, offering a window for understanding the Native American relationship to the earth.

Four people started to work on the earth. When they set it up, the wind blew it off again. It was weak like an old woman. They talked together about the earth among themselves. "What shall we do about this earth, my friends? We don't know what to do about it." Then one person said, "Pull it from four different sides." They did this, and the piece they pulled out on each side they made like a foot. After they did this the earth stood all right. Then on the east side of the earth they put big black cane, covered with black metal thorns. On the south side of the earth they put big blue cane covered with blue metal thorns. Then on the west side of the earth they put big yellow cane covered with yellow metal thorns. Then on the north side of the earth they put big white cane covered with white metal thorns.

After they did this the earth was almost steady, but it was still soft and mixed with water. It moved back and forth. After they had worked on the earth this way Black Wind Old Man came to this place. He threw himself against the earth. The earth was strong now and it did not move. Then Black Water Old Man threw himself against the earth. When he threw himself against the earth, thunder started in the four directions. Now the earth was steady, and it was as if born already.

But the earth was shivering. They talked about it: "My friends, what's the matter with this earth?

It is cold and freezing. We better give it some hair." Then they started to make hair on the earth. They made all these grasses and bushes and trees to grow on the earth. This is its hair.

But the earth was still too weak. They started to talk about it: "My friends, let's make bones for the earth." This way they made rocky mountains and rocks sticking out of the earth. These are the earth's bones.

Then they talked about the earth again: "How will it breathe, this earth?" Then came Black Thunder to that place, and he gave the earth veins. He whipped the earth with lightning and made water start to come out. For this reason all the water runs to the west. This way the earth's head lies to the east, and its water goes to the west.

They made the sun so it traveled close over the earth from east to west. They made the sun too close to the earth and it got too hot. The people living on it were crawling around, because it was too hot. Then they talked about it: "My friends, we might as well set the sun a little further off. It is too close." So they moved the sun a little higher. But it was still too close to the earth and too hot. They talked about it again. "The sun is too close to the earth, so we better move it back." Then they moved it a little higher up. Now it was all right. This last place they set the sun is just where it is now.

Then they set the moon so it traveled close over the earth from east to west. The moon was too close to the earth and it was like daytime at night. Then they talked about it: "My friends, we better move the moon back, it is like day." So they moved it back a way, but it was still like daylight. They talked about it again: "It is no good this way, we better move the moon higher up." So they moved it higher up, but it was still a little light. They talked about it again and moved it a little further away. Now it was just right, and that is the way the moon is today. It was night time.

This is the way they made the earth for us. This is the way all these wild fruits and foods were raised for us, and this is why we have to use them because they grow here.

Source: Goodwin, Granville. *Myths and Tales of the White Mountain Apache.* Memoirs of the American Folklore Society. New York: J. J. Augustin, for the American Folklore Society, 1939, 33: 1–2.

A Legend of Crater Lake

Nearly 8,000 years ago, a volcano named Mount Mazama collapsed in what is now south-central Oregon. Crater Lake formed as a result. The lake fills a caldera that is more than 2,000 feet deep. The Klamath Indians hold Crater Lake in a deep spiritual regard, and the site is sacred to them. Like many other American Indians, they have a story about how it was created. The story also provides a moral lesson.

Wimawita [grizzly bear] was the pride of his family and tribe [Shasta]. He could kill the grizzly bear, and his prowess in the fight was renowned even among those fierce braves who controlled the entrance to the Lake of the Big Medicine, where the black obsidian arrowheads are found. But the chase no longer had pleasure for him, and he wandered far up the slopes of the Shasta, where the elk and deer abound, and they passed slowly by him, down into the heavy growth of murmuring pines, as if knowing that his mission was of peace. Above was the line of perpetual snow, where the tamarack was striving hard for existence in the barren rock. From this great height Wimawita gazed upon the lodges in the prairie, among the huge trees far below, and then suddenly descending, disappeared in the forest, advancing to the east, where springs the great, gushing sawul [large spring], the source of the Wini-mim [McCloud River]. There in a little hut dwelt old Winnishuya [Forethought]. "Tell me, O mother," he cried, "what can I do to regain the love of Tculucul [The lark]?" She laughs at me, and the dog Tsileu [Red Flicker] wanders with her over the snowclad mountain.

"'Tis well; Tculucul still loves you, but since your brave deeds among the Klarnaths, your thoughts are far away, and you long for further peril, to chant your great exploits in the councils of the brave. Tculucul has noticed your neglect and distaste for the exploits in which you formerly took pleasure. Why, O Wimawita, do you not seek for greater glory? Know you not of the great lake far away and deep down in the mountaintop. The way is long and difficult, and but few reach its rocky slopes. If you have the strength and courage to climb down and bathe in its crystal waters, you will acquire great and marvelous wisdom. Tculucul will look upon you with favor, and none will equal you among your people. The Lalos (children of the Great Spirit) guard the lake, and far in the past one of our own tribe reached it, but not propitiating the spirits, they killed him, and his body was sunk in the depths of the blue water." As she spoke the old woman's strength increased. Wimawita, listening, caught her energy.

"'Tis well, my mother; tomorrow, while all sleep, will I start upon this journey to the river where the Klamaths dwell. Then will I find the way to the wondrous lake and bathe in the deep water."

While speaking, he noted not the parting of the brush, where Tculucul was concealed, and who in her fright almost betrayed her presence. Nor was Tsileu visible behind the granite rocks near by, eagerly watching and hearing all that happened.

At dawn the following day, when even the dogs were still, Wimawita stole quietly away. Close behind him, clad in the raiment of a young brave, followed Tculucul, and after a short interval, gliding stealthily in the tracks of the others, came Tsileu. Thus they marched for several long and weary days, over the prairies of Shasta and the dreary lava fields of Modoc, until Wimawita reached the great river of the Klamaths. Then Tculucul came forth and accosted him.

"Whither goest thou, Wimawita, and why are you alone in this desolate place?"

"I seek the great lake in the top of the mountain, to bathe in its limpid waters."

"'Tis well, and I will reward your faith in me."

Tsileu, inwardly raging, cast a look of hate upon them, and sped northward through the land of the Klamaths.

The next day Wimawita and Tculucul journeyed up the river. They came to a large lake, and after some distance this gradually narrowed to a small but rapid stream. After a course for some distance through a deep ravine, the water again spread out into a lake, and far north could be seen the prairies of the Klamaths. Towards the east was a succession of rolling hills, with scanty vegetation, clear cut in the rarified atmosphere. On the west high mountains rose up precipitously, while here and there a snow-clad peak towered in the sky.

"'Tis there," said Wimawita, "where we must seek for the deep mountain lake." At last, after many weary days, they reached the lake and made camp close to the precipice. All night Wimawita changed his song, and when the sun was just lighting up the circular wall across the lake, he clambered down the steep and rocky walls, and plunged into the deep, clear water. His spirit seemed to sour from him: but it required all his strength to climb back to the rim of the crater. Next day he bathed again, and on returning said, "Once more only, Tculucul, will I have to bathe in the crystal water, then wisdom and strength will be mine, our tribe will be the grandest in the land, and you will be the greatest squaw of all. Thus will your faith and help to me be rewarded."

On the third morning he started, but, just as he reached the last descent, he beheld Tsileu.

"Dog of Wimawita, we will here find who is the greater man."

Like two great whirlwinds they came together, then struggled on the edge of the cliff, advancing, retreating, swaying far out over the dizzy height, watched by Tculucul from above, powerless to aid. Suddenly Wimawita slipped on the mossy rock, and Tsileu, exerting all his strength, raised and hurled him far out into the lake. Then the Llaos arose in their wrath, tore Tsileu's body in pieces and cast them on the lake. As they disappeared the waters parted and lava burst out with a mighty noise. The island of Llao Nous [Wizard Island] arose as the gasp of a dying crater, and here it is said dwells the spirit of Wimawita, the brave, and Tculucul, the lark.

Source: Kerr, Mark Brickell. "Wimawita—A Legend of Crater Lake." *The Pacific Monthly* 6, no. 5 (1901): 190–191.

The Great Law of Peace (Gayanashagowa) (Iroquois Nation)

The Great Law of Peace of the Iroquois Nation that binds together the Seneca, Mohawk, Cayuga, Oneida, Onondaga, and (later) Tuscarora dates to perhaps as early as the 11th century. In the following excerpt from the Great Law of Peace, Dekanawidah, the Great Peacemaker, discusses the planting of the Tree of Great Peace and the unification of the former enemy tribes into a confederacy.

1. I am Dekanawidah and with the Five Nations' Confederate Lords I plant the Tree of Great Peace. I plant it in your territory, Adodarhoh, and the Onondaga Nation, in the territory of you who are Firekeepers.

   I name the tree the Tree of the Great Long Leaves. Under the shade of this Tree of the Great Peace we spread the soft white feathery down of the globe thistle as seats for you, Adodarhoh, and your cousin Lords.

   We place you upon those seats, spread soft with the feathery down of the globe thistle, there beneath the shade of the spreading branches of the Tree of Peace. There shall you sit and watch the Council Fire of the Confederacy of the Five Nations, and all the affairs of the Five Nations shall be transacted at this place before you, Adodarhoh, and your cousin Lords, by the Confederate Lords of the Five Nations.

2. Roots have spread out from the Tree of the Great Peace, one to the north, one to the east, one to the south and one to the west. The name of these roots is The Great White Roots and their nature is Peace and Strength.

   If any man or any nation outside the Five Nations shall obey the laws of the Great Peace and make known their disposition to the Lords of the Confederacy, they may trace the Roots to the Tree and if their minds are clean and they are obedient and promise to obey the wishes of the Confederate Council, they shall be welcomed to take shelter beneath the Tree of the Long Leaves.

   We place at the top of the Tree of the Long Leaves an Eagle who is able to see afar. If he sees in the distance any evil approaching or any danger threatening he will at once warn the people of the Confederacy.

3. To you Adodarhoh, the Onondaga cousin Lords, I and the other Confederate Lords have entrusted the caretaking and the watching of the Five Nations Council Fire.

   When there is any business to be transacted and the Confederate Council is not in session, a messenger shall be dispatched either to Adodarhoh, Hononwirehtonh or Skanawatih, Fire Keepers, or to their War Chiefs with a full statement of the case desired to be considered. Then shall Adodarhoh call his cousin (associate) Lords together and consider whether or not the case is of sufficient importance to demand the attention of the Confederate Council. If so, Adodarhoh shall dispatch messengers to summon all the Confederate Lords to assemble beneath the Tree of the Long Leaves.

When the Lords are assembled the Council Fire shall be kindled, but not with chestnut wood, and Adodarhoh shall formally open the Council.

Then shall Adodarhoh and his cousin Lords, the Fire Keepers, announce the subject for discussion.

The Smoke of the Confederate Council Fire shall ever ascend and pierce the sky so that other nations who may be allies may see the Council Fire of the Great Peace.

Adodarhoh and his cousin Lords are entrusted with the Keeping of the Council Fire.

4. You, Adodarhoh, and your thirteen cousin Lords, shall faithfully keep the space about the Council Fire clean and you shall allow neither dust nor dirt to accumulate. I lay a Long Wing before you as a broom. As a weapon against a crawling creature I lay a staff with you so that you may thrust it away from the Council Fire. If you fail to cast it out then call the rest of the United Lords to your aid.

5. The Council of the Mohawk shall be divided into three parties as follows: Tekarihoken, Ayonhwhathah and Shadekariwade are the first party; Sharenhowaneh, Deyoenhegwenh and Oghrenghrehgowah are the second party, and Dehennakrineh, Aghstawenserenthah and Shoskoharowaneh are the third party. The third party is to listen only to the discussion of the first and second parties and if an error is made or the proceeding is irregular they are to call attention to it, and when the case is right and properly decided by the two parties they shall confirm the decision of the two parties and refer the case to the Seneca Lords for their decision. When the Seneca Lords have decided in accord with the Mohawk Lords, the case or question shall be referred to the Cayuga and Oneida Lords on the opposite side of the house.

6. I, Dekanawidah, appoint the Mohawk Lords the heads and the leaders of the Five Nations Confederacy. The Mohawk Lords are the foundation of the Great Peace and it shall, therefore, be against the Great Binding Law to pass measures in the Confederate Council after the Mohawk Lords have protested against them.

No council of the Confederate Lords shall be legal unless all the Mohawk Lords are present.

7. Whenever the Confederate Lords shall assemble for the purpose of holding a council, the Onondaga Lords shall open it by expressing their gratitude to their cousin Lords and greeting them, and they shall make an address and offer thanks to the earth where men dwell, to the streams of water, the pools, the springs and the lakes, to the maize and the fruits, to the medicinal herbs and trees, to the forest trees for their usefulness, to the animals that serve as food and give their pelts for clothing, to the great winds and the lesser winds, to the Thunderers, to the Sun, the mighty warrior, to the moon, to the messengers of the Creator who reveal his wishes and to the Great Creator who dwells in the heavens above, who gives all the things useful to men, and who is the source and the ruler of health and life.

Then shall the Onondaga Lords declare the council open.

The council shall not sit after darkness has set in.

8. The Firekeepers shall formally open and close all councils of the Confederate Lords, and they shall pass upon all matters deliberated upon by the two sides and render their decision.

Every Onondaga Lord (or his deputy) must be present at every Confederate Council and must agree with the majority without unwarrantable dissent, so that a unanimous decision may be rendered.

If Adodarhoh or any of his cousin Lords are absent from a Confederate Council, any other Firekeeper may open and close the Council, but the Firekeepers present may not give any decisions, unless the matter is of small importance.

9. All the business of the Five Nations Confederate Council shall be conducted by the two combined bodies of Confederate Lords. First the question shall be passed upon by the Mohawk and Seneca Lords, then it shall be discussed and passed by the Oneida and Cayuga Lords. Their decisions shall then be referred to the Onondaga Lords (Fire Keepers) for final judgment.

The same process shall obtain when a question is brought before the council by an individual or a War Chief.

10. In all cases the procedure must be as follows: when the Mohawk and Seneca Lords have unanimously agreed upon a question, they shall report their decision to the Cayuga and Oneida Lords who shall deliberate upon the question and report a unanimous decision to the Mohawk Lords. The Mohawk Lords will then report the standing of the case to the Fire-keepers, who shall render a decision as they see fit in case of a disagreement by the two bodies, or confirm the decisions of the two bodies if they are identical. The Fire Keepers shall then report their decision to the Mohawk Lords who shall announce it to the open council.

11. If through any misunderstanding or obstinacy on the part of the Fire Keepers, they render a decision at variance with that of the Two Sides, the Two Sides shall reconsider the matter and if their decisions are jointly the same as before they shall report to the Fire Keepers who are then compelled to confirm their joint decision.

12. When a case comes before the Onondaga Lords (Fire Keepers) for discussion and decision, Adodarho shall introduce the matter to his comrade Lords who shall then discuss it in their two bodies. Every Onondaga Lord except Hononwiretonh shall deliberate and he shall listen only. When a unanimous decision shall have been reached by the two bodies of Fire Keepers, Adodarho shall notify Hononwiretonh of the fact when he shall confirm it. He shall refuse to confirm a decision if it is not unanimously agreed upon by both sides of the Fire Keepers.

13. No Lord shall ask a question of the body of Confederate Lords when they are discussing a case, question or proposition. He may only deliberate in a low tone with the separate body of which he is a member.

14. When the Council of the Five Nation Lords shall convene they shall appoint a speaker for the day. He shall be a Lord of either the Mohawk, Onondaga or Seneca Nation.

   The next day the Council shall appoint another speaker, but the first speaker may be reappointed if there is no objection, but a speaker's term shall not be regarded more than for the day.

15. No individual or foreign nation interested in a case, question or proposition shall have any voice in the Confederate Council except to answer a question put to him or them by the speaker for the Lords.

16. If the conditions which shall arise at any future time call for an addition to or change of this law, the case shall be carefully considered and if a new beam seems necessary or beneficial, the proposed change shall be voted upon and if adopted it shall be called, "Added to the Rafters."

Source: Parker, Arthur C. The Constitution of the Five Nations. Albany: University of the State of New York, 1916, 30–34.

Response to the Spanish by Aztec Priests
(1524)

A large majority of missionaries, whether Spanish, French, English, or other, believed their religion—Christianity—was much better than that of the American Indians. In fact, many missionaries did not believe American Indians had any religion at all. Sometimes, missionaries faced an uphill battle in their search for souls,

and those they proselytized to often questioned what they heard, as in this case from Mexico during 1524, when Aztec priests discussed religion with Spanish priests.

You say that we do not recognize the being who is everywhere, lord of heaven and earth. You say our gods are not true gods. The new words that you utter are what confuse us; due to them we feel foreboding. Our makers [our ancestors] who came to live on earth never uttered such words. They gave us *their* laws, their ways of doing things. They believed in the gods, served them and honored them. They were the ones who taught us everything, the gods' being served and respected.

Before them we eat earth [kiss the ground]; we bleed; we pay our debts to the gods, offer incense, make sacrifice . . . indeed, we live by the grace of those gods. They rightly made us out of the time, the place where it was still dark . . . They give us what we go to sleep with, what we get up with [our daily sustenance], all that is drunk, all that is eaten, the produce, corn beans, green maize, chia. We beg from them the water, the rain, so that things grow upon the earth.

The gods are happy in their prosperity, in what they have, always and forever. Everything sprouts and turns green in their home. What kind of place is the land of Tlaloc [the god of rain]? Never is there any famine there, nor any illness, nor suffering. And they [the gods] give people virility, bravery, success in the hunt, [bejeweled] lip rings, blankets, breeches, cloaks, flowers, tobacco, jade, feathers, and gold.

Since time immemorial they have been addressed, prayed to, taken as gods. It has been a very long time that they have been revered, since once upon a time in Tula, in Huapalcalco, Xochitlapan, Tlamohuanchan, in Teotihuacan, the home of the night. These gods are the ones who established the mats and thrones [that is, the inherited chieftainships], who gave people nobility, and kingship, renown and respect.

Will we be the ones to destroy the ancient traditions of the Chichimec, the Tolteca, the Colhuaca, the Tepaneca? [No!] It is our opinion that there is life, that people are born, people are nurtured, people grow up, [only] by the gods' being called upon, prayed to. Alas, o our lords, beware lest you make the common people do something bad. How will the poor old men, the poor old women, forget or erase their upbringing, their education? May the gods not be angry with us. Let us not move toward their anger. And let us not agitate the commoners, raise a riot, lest they rebel for this reason, because of our saying to them: address the gods no longer, pray to them no longer. Look quietly, calmly, o our lords, at what is needed. Our hearts cannot be at ease as long as we cannot understand each other. We do not admit as true [what you say]. We will cause you pain. Here are the towns, the rulers and kings who carry the world. It is enough that we have lost political power, that it was taken from us, that we were made to abandon the mats and thrones. We will not budge; we will just end [this conversation]. Do to us whatever you want. This is all with which we return, we answer, your breath, your words, o our lords.

Source: Townsend, Camilla, ed. *American Indian History: A Documentary Reader.* Malden, MA: Wiley-Blackwell, 2009, 29–30. © 2009 Camilla Townsend. Reproduced with permission of Blackwell Publishing Ltd.

Powhatan, "Why Should You Destroy Us, Who Have Provided You with Food?"

(1609)

Powhatan was the leader of the eponymous tribe that the English first encountered upon their arrival in Virginia in 1607. At first, the interactions between the Indians and the English seemed benign enough. However, as pressures on land, food, and other resources mounted, and the English decided to steal provisions, relations quickly soured. In this speech to the English, the aging leader elaborates his concerns over the treatment of the Powhatan at the hands of the English.

I am now grown old, and must soon die; and the succession must descend, in order, to my brothers, Opitchapan, Opekankanough, and Catataugh, and then to my two sisters, and their two daughters. I wish that their experience was equal to mine; and that your love to us might now be less than ours to you. Why should you take by force that from us which you can have by love? Why should you destroy us, who have provided you with food? What can you get by war? We can hide our provisions, and fly into the woods; and then you must consequently famish by wronging your friends. What is the cause of your jealousy? You see us unarmed, and willing to supply your wants, if you will come in a friendly manner, and not with swords and guns, as to invade an enemy. I am not so simple, as not to know it is better to eat good meat, lie well, and sleep quietly with my women and children; to laugh and be merry with the English; and, being their friend, to have copper, hatchets, and whatever else I want, than to fly from all, to lie cold in the woods, feed upon acorns, roots, and such trash, and to be so hunted, that I cannot rest, eat, or sleep. In such circumstances, my men must watch, and if a twig should but break, all would cry out, "Here comes Capt. Smith," and so, in this miserable manner, to end my miserable life; and, Capt. Smith, this might be soon your fate too, through your rashness and unadvisedness. I, therefore, exhort you to peaceable councils; and, above all, I insist that the guns and swords, the cause of all our jealousy and uneasiness, be removed and sent away.

Source: Drake, Samuel Gardner, and J.W. O'Neill. *The Aboriginal Races of North America.* Philadelphia: Charles DeSilver, 1859, 353.

Miantinomo, "Brother, We Must Be One as the English Are, or We Shall Soon All Be Destroyed"
(1642–1643)

American Indians are not a homogeneous group, even within tribes. As time progressed, all European groups took advantage of this and tried to do as much as possible to create divisiveness among the Indians. Early on, long before Tecumseh in the early 19th century, many Indians realized the importance of working together. This brief speech by Miantinomo, given in New England in the wake of the Pequot War of the late 1630s, illustrates this.

Brothers, we must be one as the English are, or we shall soon all be destroyed. You know our fathers had plenty of deer and skins, and our plains were full of deer and of turkeys, and our coves and rivers were full of fish. But, brothers, since these English have seized upon our country, they cut down the grass with scythes, and the trees with axes. Their cows and horses eat up the grass, and their hogs spoil our beds of clams; and finally we shall starve to death! Therefore, stand not in your own light, I beseech you, but resolve with us to act like men. All the sachems both to the east and west have joined with us, and we are all resolved to fall upon them, at a day appointed, and therefore I come secretly to you, because you can persuade the Indians to do what you will. Brothers, I will send over fifty

Indians to Manisses, and thirty to you from thence, and take a hundred of Southampton Indians, with a hundred of your own here. And, when you see the three fires that will be made at the end of forty days hence, in a clear night, then act as we act, and the next day fall on and kill men, women, and children, but no cows; they must [not] be killed as we need them for provisions, till the deer come again.

Source: Drake, Samuel G. *Biography and History of the Indians of North America, from Its First Discovery.* Boston: Benjamin B. Mussey & Co., 1851, 353.

Dialogue between Piumbukhou and His Unconverted Relatives (ca. 1671)

Compared with their French and Spanish brethren, the English never enjoyed much success in the search for Indian souls. One Englishman who was somewhat successful, and perhaps the most well known, was John Eliot. He arrived in the New World in 1631 and devoted the rest of his life to proselytizing among the Indians. He learned their language—often a great advantage for a missionary—wrote a dictionary of their language, and translated the Bible into their language.

He gathered many of his converts into Praying Towns to quarantine them from harmful and detrimental contact with nonbelievers. As the following exchange between a convert named Piumbukhou and his kinsfolk illustrates, the missionary's message was not always a popular one, and those who chose to believe in it could have a difficult time convincing their kinsfolk that they should embrace the white man's religion.

KINSMAN: I had rather that my actions of love should testify how welcome you are, and how glad I am of this your kind visitation, than that I should say it in a multitude of words. But in one word, you are very welcome into my heart, and I account it among the best of the joys of this day, that I see your face, and enjoy your company in my habitation.

KINSWOMAN: It is an addition to the joys of this day, to see the face of my loving kinsman. And I wish you had come a little earlier, that you might have taken part with us in the joys of this day, wherein we have had all the delights that could be desired, in our merry meeting, and dancing.

And I pray cousin, how doth your wife, my loving kinswoman, is she yet living? And is she not yet weary of your new way of praying to God? And what pleasure have you in those ways?

PIUMBUKHOU: My wife doth remember her love to you. She is in good health of body, and her soul is in a good condition. She is entered into the light of the knowledge of God, and of Christ. She is entered into the narrow way of heavenly joys, and she doth greatly desire that you would turn from these ways of darkness in which you so much delight, and come taste and see how good the Lord is.

And whereas you wish I had come sooner, to have shared with you in your delights of this day. Alas, they are no delights, but griefs to me, to see that you do still delight in them. I am like a man that have tasted of sweet wine and honey, which have so altered the taste of my mouth, that I abhor the taste of your sinful and foolish pleasures, as the mouth doth abhor to taste the most filthy and stinking dung, the most sour grapes, or most bitter gall. Our joys in the knowledge of God, and of Jesus Christ, which we are taught in the Book of God, and feel in our heart, is sweeter to our soul, than honey is unto the mouth and taste.

KINSWOMAN: We have all the delights that the flesh and blood of man can devise and delight in, and we taste and feel the delights of them, and would you make us believe that you have found out new joys and delights, in comparison of which all our delights do stink like dung? Would you make us believe that we have neither eyes to see, nor ears to hear, nor mouth to taste? Ha, ha, he! I appeal to the sense and sight and feeling of the company present, whether this be so.

ALL: You say very true. Ha, ha, he!

PIUMBUKHOU: Hearken to me, my friends, and see if I do not give a clear answer unto this seeming difficulty. Your dogs take as much delight in these meetings, and the same kinds of delight as you do. They delight in each others company. They provoke each other to lust, and enjoy the pleasures of lust as you do. They eat and play and sleep as you do. What joys have you more than dogs have to delight the body of flesh and blood?

But all mankind have a higher and better part than the body. We have a soul, and that soul shall never die. Our soul is to converse with God, and to converse in such things as do concern God, and heaven, and an eternal estate, either in happiness with God, if we walk with him and serve him in this life, or in misery and torment with the Devil, if we serve him in this life. The service of God doth

consist in virtue, and wisdom, and delights of the soul, which will reach to heaven, and abide forever.

But the service of the Devil is in committing sins of the flesh, which defile both body and soul, and reach to hell, and will turn all to fire and flame to torment your souls and bodies in all eternity.

Now consider, all your pleasures and delights are such as defile you with sin, and will turn to flame, to burn and torment you. They provoke God to wrath, who hath created the prison of hell to torment you, and the more you have took pleasure in sin, the greater are your offences against God, and the greater shall be your torments.

But we that pray to God repent of our old sins, and by faith in Christ we seek for, and find a pardon for what is past, and grace and strength to reform for time to come. So that our joys are soul joys in godliness, and virtue, and hope of glory in another world when we die.

Your joys are bodily, fleshly, such as dogs have, and will all turn to flames in hell to torment you.

KINSMAN: If these things be so, we had need to cease laughing, and fall to weeping, and see if we can draw water from our mournful eyes to quench these tormenting flames. My heart trembles to hear these things. I never heard so much before, nor have I any thing to say to the contrary, but that these things may be so. But how shall I know that you say true? Our forefathers were (many of them) wise men, and we have wise men now living. They all delight in these our delights. They have taught us nothing about our soul, and God, and heaven, and hell, and joy and torment in the life to come. Are you wiser than our fathers? May not we rather think that *English* men have invented these stories to amaze us and fear us out of our old customs, and bring us to stand in awe of them, that they might wipe us of our lands, and drive us into corners, to seek new ways of living, and new places too? And be beholding to them for that which is our own, and was ours, before we knew them?

ALL: You say right.

PIUMBUKHOU: The Book of God is no invention of Englishmen. It is the holy law of God himself, which was given unto man by God, before Englishmen had any knowledge of God; and all the knowledge which they have, they have it out of the Book of God; and all the knowledge which they have, they have it out of the Book of God. And this book is given to us as well as to them, and it is as free for us to search the scriptures as for them. So that we have our instruction from a higher hand, than the hand of man. It is the great Lord God of heaven and earth, who teacheth us these great things of which we speak. Yet this is also true, that we have great cause to be thankful to the English, and to thank God for them. For they had a good country of their own, but by ships sailing into these parts of the world, they heard of us, and of our country, and of our nakedness, ignorance of God, and wild condition. God put it into their hearts to desire to come hither, and teach us the good knowledge of God; and their King gave them leave so to do, and in our country to have their liberty to serve God according to the word of God. And being come hither, we gave them leave freely to live among us. They have purchased of us a great part of those lands which they possess. They love us, they do us right, and no wrong willingly. If any do us wrong, it is without the consent of their rulers, and upon our complaints our wrongs are righted. They are (many of them, especially the ruling part) good men, and desire to do us good. God put it into the heart of one of their ministers (as you all know) to teach us the knowledge of God, by the word of God, and hath translated the holy Book of God into our language, so that we can perfectly know the mind and counsel of God. And out of this book have I learned all that I say unto you, and therefore you need no more doubt of the truth of it, than you have cause to doubt that the heaven is over our head, the sun shineth, the earth is under our feet, we walk and live upon it, and breathe in the air. For as we see with our eyes these things to be so, so we read with our own eyes these things which I speak of, to be written in God's own book, and we feel the truth thereof in our own hearts.

KINSWOMAN: Cousin, you have wearied your legs this day with a long journey to come and visit us, and you weary your tongue with long discourses. I am willing to comfort and refresh you with a short supper.

ALL: Ha, ha, he. Though short, if sweet that has good favor to a man that is weary. Ha, ha, he.

KINSWOMAN: You make long and learned discourses to us which we do not well understand. I think our best answer is to stop your mouth, and fill your belly with a good supper, and when your belly is full you will be content to take rest yourself, and give us leave to be at rest from these gastering and heart-trembling discourses. We are well as we are, and desire not to be troubled with these new wise sayings.

Source: Eliot, John. *Indian Dialogues, for Their Instruction in That Great Service of Christ, in Calling Home Their Country-Men to the Knowledge of God, and of Themselves and of Jesus Christ.* Cambridge, MA: M. Johnson, 1671.

The Conversion of Daniel Garakontié, an Onondaga
(1671–1672)

Possibly more than other Europeans, the French quickly realized that to be successful in their New World experiments, they needed Indian allies. Although other European nations also came to that realization, the French were perhaps quicker at figuring out that their way in the New World would be easier with Indian allies. French Jesuit missionaries were at the front lines of that effort. From time to time, their conversions had unintended consequences, such as when an Onondaga Indian named Garakontié converted. Taking the name Daniel, he quickly became an intermediary between the French and the other Indians. The following description of Garakontié and his importance to the French was written by a Jesuit missionary, the Reverend Claude Dablon.

The other circumstance that must give much joy to all who desire to see God glorified in the conversion of these Peoples, is the constancy of their Chief, Daniel Garakontié, in his high opinion of the faith, and in his fidelity in everywhere making open profession of Christianity. He did this with all solemnity two years ago when, after being baptized at Quebec, he declared upon his return, in a public meeting, that he intended thenceforward to discharge no function of his Office except so far as it should be in conformity with God's commandments. This declaration he repeated in a more courageous manner in New Holland, before the Europeans who hold command in that country, and the chief men of all the five Iroquois Nations, who had been summoned for the purpose of concluding a peace with the Loup Nations. The Father informs us in his last letter that Garakontié showed a truly Christian courage, the past Winter, in an illness that brought him to death's door. His relatives and all the village, seeing themselves in danger of losing him, urged him with great importunity to permit, for the sake of being cured, the employment of the usual juggler's arts, which pass for remedies in that country. To this he made constant and strenuous resistance. Nevertheless, a superstitious ceremony was executed in his cabin, after the custom of jugglers when they undertake to cure some ailment. The Father, hearing of it, felt some suspicion that it had received the sick man's consent. He went to visit him toward evening, and found with him all the elders,—who, believing his death to be near at hand, had come in a body to do him honor, and bid him a last Farewell. The sick man spoke first and said to him: "My Father, I was much distressed to-day on account of the ceremony which was performed, without my knowledge and out of my sight, at the other end of my cabin. 'Alas!' said I to myself, 'what will Teharonhiagannra'"—Father Millet's name—"'think and say of me? He will believe me to be a hypocrite and dissembler.' No, my Father, I have not changed my mind since my baptism, nor am I any longer the man to consent to such follies. I merely suffered myself to be scarified, and a little blood to be drawn from my head; but I do not think that I thereby offended God to keep his holy law all my life, to resume like a coward the old practices that I have renounced, and now once more renounce, with all my heart. No, my Father, I will never break my promise, even though my life should be at stake." The Father strengthened him in these good resolutions, which afforded the company great edification.

Subsequently our Neophyte, having recovered his health, went down to Mon-real as Ambassador from all the Iroquois Nations, to hold council with the Algonquin tribes known as the Outaouaks,—who held their rendezvous there for the arrangement of their affairs with one another, as well as for the sale of their furs. Now in this assembly of a hundred and fifty canoes,—that is, of more than five hundred Savages of various Nations,—in the presence of Monsieur de Courcelles, Governor of the country, for whom all these Tribes have a very marked veneration, Garakontié displayed his intelligence and good sense, and especially his Faith and zeal. For, after they had finished their negotiations, and ratified the treaty of peace by fresh protestations of friendship and an exchange of presents, he raised his voice to tell them now he was a Christian and was living a happy life, obeying God's commandments and hoping for a life eternal. He concluded his harangue by exhorting them, with his wonted eloquence, to imitate and follow him.

Such a speech, from the mouth of a Savage who thus frankly declares the feelings of his heart, often produces more effect upon these people's minds than the words of the most zealous Missionary,— as is shown by two very recent instances. This same Daniel Garakontié, says Father de Lamberville in his letter of September 23rd, "having on his homeward journey, encountered a kinswoman of his who was mortally ill, sought me out, and asked me for some remedy for her. 'My brother,' said I to him, 'the sole remedy that can avail her in her present state is Baptism, to save her from hell. But she is utterly averse to receiving this Sacrament, being obstinately bent on dying like her Ancestors, who she wishes to go and find in the so-called "land of souls." If thou hast a true affection for her, exert all thy efforts to render her more docile; but make haste, for she has only a little longer to live.' No sooner had I made this proposition to him"—these are the Father's words— "than that genuine Christian, who possesses no

attribute of the Iroquois Savage but his birth and name, went to visit her; and wrought on her so admirably by his zeal that she was thereupon sufficiently instructed to receive holy Baptism—to the great satisfaction of all the family." The Father was still unable to gain access to another poor dying creature, for the purpose of speaking to her concerning her salvation, because she showed an intense aversion for such themes, as well as an incredible attachment to the native superstitions. In this difficulty, he had recourse to a woman who was a friend of that family; she was not yet a Catechumen, and did not even attend prayers, but she had some knowledge of our mysteries and was well-intentioned. She met with such success from the very first time when she spoke to the sick woman about becoming a Christian, and cleverly contrived to predispose the latter so favorably toward the Father, that he was made most welcome in her cabin, and she never refused him a hearing thereafter. Being then sufficiently instructed, she was baptized; and, soon after her Baptism, she died a very Christian death. "Thus it is"—says the Father in closing his letter—"that, in spite of intemperance, which reigns here to the greatest excess, and the other obstacles that hell is constantly opposing to the advancement of the faith, we are continually finding souls to win, and fruits of the Blood of Jesus Christ to gather."

Source: Thwaites, Reuben Gold, ed. *The Jesuit Relations and Allied Documents, 73 vols.* Cleveland: Burrows Brothers Company, 1893–1901, 56: 41–47.

Metacom's Grievances

(ca. 1675)

Like the Powhatan and other American Indian tribes in Virginia, the Wampanoag of New England faced intense pressure with the arrival of Separatists from England in 1620. The English

brought disease with them—as well as an insatiable desire for land. Furthermore, many Puritans loathed the Indians and thought them to be in league with the devil. Therefore, hostilities occurred, as was the case with the Pequot War of 1636.

War broke out again in 1676. Metacom was chief of the Wampanoag. Known as King Philip to the English, he received an official from Rhode Island named John Eastman before fighting actually commenced. The following is Eastman's report of the meeting.

For forty years' time reports and jealousies of war had been very frequent that we did not think that a war was breaking forth, but about a week before it did we had cause to think it would. Then to endeavor to prevent it, we sent a man to Philip that if he would come to the ferry we would come over to speak with him. About four miles we had to come thither. Our messenger come to them, they not aware of it behaved themselves as furious but suddenly appeased when they understood who he was and what he came for he called his council and agreed to come to us himself unarmed and about forty of his men armed. Then five of us went over. Three were magistrates. We sat very friendly together. We told him our business was to endeavor that they might not receive or do wrong. They said that was well they had done no wrong, the English wronged them, we said we knew the English said they [the Indians] wronged them and the Indians said the English wronged them but our desire was the quarrel might rightly be decided in the best way, and not as dogs decided their quarrels. The Indians owned that fighting was the worst way then they propounded how right might take place, we said by arbitration. They said all English agreed against them and so by arbitration they had had much wrong, many square miles of land so taken from them for English would have English Arbitrators, and once they were persuaded to give in their arms, that thereby jealousy might be removed and the English having their arms would not deliver them as they had promised, until they consented to pay 100 pounds, and now they had not so much land or money, that they were as good be killed as leave all their livelihood. We said they might choose a [*sic*] Indian king, and the English might choose the

governor of New York that neither had cause to say either were parties of the difference. They said they had not heard of that way and said we honestly spoke so we were persuaded that if to hear their complaints, said it was not convenient for us now to consider of, but to endeavor to prevent war, said to them when in war against English [if] blood was spilled that engages all Englishmen for we were to be all under one king. We knew what their complaints would be, and in our colony had removed some of them in sending for Indian rulers in what the crime concerned Indian lives which they very lovingly accepted and agreed with us to their execution and said they were able to satisfy their subjects when they knew an Indian suffered duly, but said in what was only between their Indians and not in townships that we had purchased, they would not have us prosecute and that they had a great fear . . . and of their Indians should be called or forced to be Christian Indians. They said that such were in everything more mischievous, only dissemblers and then the English made them not subject to their kings, and by their lying to wrong their government to Indians all should be alike and that we knew it was our king's will it should be so, that although we were weaker than other colonies, they having submitted to our king to protect them others dated not otherwise to molest them. So they expressed they took that to be well, that we had little cause to doubt but that to us under the king they would have yielded to our determinations in what any should have complained to us against them, but Philip charged it to be dishonesty in us to put off the hearing of the complaints; therefore we consented to hear them. They said they had been the first in doing good to the English, and the English the first in doing wrong, said when the English first came their king's father [Massasoit] was as a great man and the English as a little child, he constrained other Indians from wronging the English and gave them corn and showed them how to plant and was free to do them any good and had let them have 100 times more land, than now the king had for his own people, but their king's brother when he was king came miserably to die by being forced to court as they judged poisoned, and another grievance was if 20 of their honest Indians testified that a Englishman had done them wrong, it was as nothing, and if but one of their worst Indians testified against any Indian or their king when it pleased the English that was sufficient. Another grievance was when their kings sold land the English would say it was more than they agreed to and a writing must be proof against all of them, and some of their kings had done wrong to sell so much. He left his people none and some being given to drunkenness the English made them drunk and then cheated them in bargains, but now their kings were forewarned not to part with land for nothing in comparison to the value thereof. Now whom the English had owned for king or queen they would disinherit, and make another king that would give or sell them their land, that now they had no hopes left to keep any land. Another grievance that English cattle and horses still increased that when they removed 30 miles from where the English had anything to do, they could not keep their corn from being spoiled, they never being used to fence, and thought when the English bought land of them that they would have kept their cattle upon their own land. Another grievance the English were so eager to sell the Indians liquors that most of the Indians spend all

in drunkenness and then ravened upon the sober Indians and they did believe often did hurt the English cattle, and their kings could not prevent it. We knew before these were their grand complaints that might be righted without war, but could have no other answer but that they had not heard of that way for the Governor of York and an Indian king to have the hearing of it. We had cause to think if that had been tendered it would have even accepted. We endeavored that however they should lay down their arms for the English were too strong for them. They said then the English should do to them as they did when they were too strong for the English. So we departed without any discourteousness, and suddenly had letter [that is, received word], from Plimouth Governor they intended in arms to conform Philip [make him submit], but no information what that was they required or what terms he refused to have their quarrel decided, and in a week's time after we had been with the Indians the war thus begun.

Source: Eastman, John. "A Relacion of the Indyan Warre" (1675). In *Narratives of the Indian Wars, 1675–1699,* edited by Charles H. Lincoln, 8–12. New York: Scribner's Sons, 1913. As edited and reproduced in Salisbury, Neal, ed. *The Sovereignty and Goodness of God by Mary Rowlandson.* Boston: Bedford/St. Martin's, 1997, 115–118.

A Micmac Questions French "Civilization"
(ca. 1677)

Many early explorers of the New World received a rude awakening at the difficulties they encountered when they reached a foreign land. Many travelers complained that the Indians lived mean and miserable lives, but, as interlopers, the Europeans had to rely on the Indians for food and shelter on occasion. No matter how horribly Europeans thought the Indians lived, most Indians were thoroughly content with their way of living and their material culture. In the following

document, a Micmac Indian from the Gaspé Peninsula, located on the south shore of the St. Lawrence River in what is now Quebec, Canada, critiques French conceptions of civilization and often wittily puts down what the French consider civilized living.

I am greatly astonished that the French have so little cleverness, as they seem to exhibit in the matter of which thou hast told me on their behalf, in the effort to persuade us to convert our poles, our barks, and our wigwams into those houses of stone and of wood which are tall and lofty, according to their account, as these trees. Very well! But why now, . . . do men of five to six feet in height need houses which are sixty to eighty? For, in fact, as thou knowest very well thyself, Patriarch—do we not find in our own all the conveniences and the advantages that you have with yours, such as reposing, drinking, sleeping, eating, and amusing ourselves with our friends when we wish? This is not all, . . . my brother, hast thou as much ingenuity and cleverness as the Indians, who carry their houses and their wigwams with them so that they may lodge wheresoever they please, independently of any seignior whatsoever? Thou art not as bold nor as stout as we, because when thou goest on a voyage thou canst not carry upon thy shoulders thy buildings and edifices. Therefore it is necessary that thou preparest as many lodgings as thou makest changes of residence, or else thou lodgest in a hired house which does not belong to thee. As for us, we find ourselves secure from all these inconveniences, and we can always say, more truly than thou, that we are at home everywhere, because we set up our wigwams with ease wheresoever we go, and without asking permission of anybody. Thou reproachest us, very inappropriately, that our country is a little hell in contrast with France, which thou comparest to a terrestrial paradise, inasmuch as it yields thee, so thou sayest, every kind of provision in abundance. Thou sayest of us also that we are the most miserable and most unhappy of all men, living without religion, without manners, without honour, without social order, and, in a word, without any rules, like beasts in our woods and our forests, lacking bread, wine, and a thousand other comforts which thou hast in superfluity in Europe. Well, my brother, if thou dost not yet know the real feelings which our Indians have towards thy country and towards all thy nation, it is proper that I inform thee at once. I beg thee now to believe that, all miserable as we seem in thine eyes, we consider ourselves nevertheless much happier than thou in this, that we are very content with the

little that we have; and believe also once for all, I pray, that thou deceivest thyself greatly if thou thinkest to persuade us that thy country is better than ours. For if France, as thou sayest, is a little terrestrial paradise, art thou sensible to leave it? And why abandon wives, children, relatives, and friends? Why risk thy life and thy property every year, and why venture thyself with such risk, in any season whatsoever, to the storms and tempests of the sea in order to come to a strange and barbarous country which thou considerest the poorest and least fortunate of the world? Besides, wince we are wholly convinced of the contrary, we scarcely take the trouble to go to France, because we fear, with good reason, lest we find little satisfaction there, seeing, in our own experience, that those who are native thereof leave it every year in order to enrich themselves on our shores. We believe, further, that you are also incomparably poorer than we, and that you are only simple journeymen, valets, servants, and slaves, all masters and grand captains though you may appear, seeing that you glory in our old rags and in our miserable suits of beaver which can no longer be of use to us, and that you find among us, in the fishery for cod which you make in these parts, the wherewithal to comfort your misery and the poverty which oppresses you. As to us, we find all our riches and all our conveniences among ourselves, without trouble and without exposing our lives to the dangers in which you find yourselves constantly through your long voyages. And, whilst feeling compassion for you in the sweetness of our repose, we wonder at the anxieties and cares which you give yourselves night and day in order to load your ship. We see also that all your people live, as a rule, only upon cod which you catch among us. It is everlastingly nothing but cod—cod in the morning, cod at midday, cod at evening, and always cod, until things come to such a pass that if you wish some good morsels, it is at our expense; and you are obliged to have recourse to the Indians, whom you despise so much, and to beg them to go a-hunting that you may be regaled. Now tell me this one little thing, if thou hast any sense: Which of these two is the wisest and happiest—he who labours without ceasing and only obtains, and that with great trouble, enough to live on, or he who rests in comfort and finds all that he needs in the pleasure of hunting and fishing? It is true, . . . that we have not always had the use of bread and of wine which your France produces; but, in fact, before the arrival of the French in these parts, did not the Gaspesians live much longer than now? And if we have not any longer among us any of those old men of a hundred and thirty to forty years, it is only because we are gradually adopting your manner of living, for experience is making it very plain that those of us live longest who, despising your bread, your wine, and your brandy, are content with their natural food of beaver, of moose, of waterfowl, and fish, in accord with the custom of our ancestors and of all the Gaspesian nation. Learn now, my brother, once for all, because I must open to thee my heart: there is no Indian who does not consider himself infinitely more happy and more powerful than the French.

Source: Ganong, William F, trans. and ed. *New Relation of Gaspesia, with the Customs and Religion of the Gaspesian Indians.* Toronto: Champlain Society, 1910, 104–106.

An Indian's Decision to Become a Christian
(1679)

Missionaries worked hard in their efforts to proselytize American Indians. They met with varying degrees of success. Many French Jesuit missionaries achieved some amount of success, and they recorded stories of their work that were published as the Jesuit Relations. *The works are an excellent source of what missionaries went through, their thoughts about those they worked with and lived among, and how they went about their work as missionaries. In the following document, the story of one Indian convert named Gandeaktena is related.*

The Queen of virtues has been wonderfully displayed in the person of a poor slave, taken prisoner by the Iroquois from the Chat nation. We shall undoubtedly be touched by the graces that God was pleased to confer upon this Captive, and by the singular virtues—and, above all, the Charity toward God and her neighbor—that she displayed before the eyes of the savages and the French at la prairie de la magdelaine. Here is the narrative:

God having permitted that Gentaienton, a village of the Chat nation, should be taken and sacked by the Iroquois, Gandeaktena, which is the name of the one of whom we are speaking, was taken into slavery together with her mother and brought to Onniout. There the misfortune of her country proved the blessing of our Captive; and her slavery was the Cause of her preparing herself to receive through baptism the liberty of the children of God. The innocency in which she had lived, even before intending to become a Christian, seemed to have prepared her to receive this grace; and it is an astonishing fact that, in the midst of the extreme Corruption of the Iroquois, she was able, before being illumined by the light of the gospel, to keep herself from participating in their debaucheries, although was their slave.

Some years after her coming to Onneiout, father Bruyas also came thither to preach the gospel. On the day after his arrival, he made known in public the reason of his coming. Our slave was at once Inwardly influenced by God, and so keenly affected with the desire of paradise and the fear of hell, that she Immediately resolved to spare no pains in acquiring the one and avoiding the other. She showed no less Constancy in the prosecution of her purpose than promptitude in forming it; and although she encountered great obstacles, there was none that she did not succeed in overcoming. Her extreme modesty, which would not permit her to visit the father all alone; the refusal of all whom she asked to bear her company; the determination, sudden and unexpected, of her husband to take her with him to the war; the work assigned to her by the woman whose slave she was,—that of going to the fishery, after her husband had sent her back from the expedition,—served only to bring to view the power of the spirit by which she was urged forward. This spirit, rendering her careful to Seek the favorable opportunity of corresponding to the divine inspiration, prevailed upon her to embrace at last what the providence of God rather than chance placed in her way. For, on her return from the fishery, she met one of her Companions who was on her way to the prayers. She went with her; and on arriving at the Cabin of the father, she repeated the prayers. The father noticed her, and judged from her modest countenance that there was something about this Young woman that was quite out of the common; this determined him to address to her some words of encouragement in private. From that time she never failed to come to pray to God in the Chapel. She learned in a very short time the prayers, and the mysteries of our faith; but, reflecting on the Corrupt morals and licentiousness of the Iroquois, and wisely Concluding that she would experience much difficultly in securing her salvation if she lived among them, she resolved to leave them and come to live with the French. She commended the matter to God, and spoke of her plan to her mother, to her father-in-law, and to her husband, after his return

from the war. She won them all over, as well as certain others of her neighbors, and came with them to Monseigneur Bishop of Canada, who, after they had been instructed, baptized them all. These blessed successes with which God had accompanied the Conversion of our Catherine— for that is the name she received at baptism—and that little band of persons whom she had attracted to the faith, and the train of events, made it apparent that he had from that time appointed her, and was Directing her, to become Instrumental in the salvation of many Iroquois; for he gave her the thought of going to dwell at la prairie de la magdelaine, where, two months ago, a settlement had been Started. She went there, in fact, together with those with whom she had been baptized—12 in number,—and gave the first Impulse to the mission which is now so flourishing.

No advance was made in these small beginnings for 2 or 3 years; but, at length they attained much renown, especially among the Iroquois nations, so that more than 200 Iroquois have come since that time to establish themselves at la prairie de la magdelaine, in order to live there as good Christians. And it is a surprising Thing that God should have willed that they [the Iroquois] should Spare the life of Catherine in order that, afterward, she might obtain for them eternal salvation, and that thus their slave might become their Conversion, but all the remainder of her life, through the rare examples of virtue which she furnished them.

Source: Thwaites, Reuben Gold, ed. *The Jesuit Relations and Allied Documents.* Cleveland: Burrows Brothers Company, 1893–1901, 61: 195–199.

Pedro Naranjo, "As They Had Been in Ancient Times," an Account of the Pueblo Revolt

(1680)

In the late 17th century, the boundaries of Spain's empire in North America had been pushed north into New Mexico, Texas, Arizona, and California.

The empire was little more than a string of small, hard-to-defend communities that had been settled by a mixture of Spanish soldiers, colonists, and missionaries. The arrival of the Spanish heralded many changes for the indigenous inhabitants of northern New Mexico, including large-scale changes to their religious and economic institutions. Pueblo Indians were forbidden from practicing their religion, and they were forced to work in the encomienda system of their new Spanish masters. These changes led to a latent hostility among the Pueblo Indians that would erupt in 1680 in the form of a massive rebellion, led by the highly charismatic Popé. During the rebellion, the Pueblo succeeded in pushing back Spanish colonization for a decade and reinstituting their traditional religion and economic systems. In the narrative that follows, Pedro Naranjo, a Keresan Pueblo man, presents his view of the causes of the rebellion.

Declaration of Pedro Naranjo of the Queres Nation. [Place of the Rio del Norte, December 19, 1681.]

In the said plaza de armas on the said day, month, and year, for the prosecution of the judicial proceedings of this case his lordship caused to appear before him an Indian prisoner named Pedro Naranjo, a native of the pueblo of San Felipe, of the Queres nation, who was captured in the advance and attack upon the pueblo of La Isleta. He makes himself understood very well in the Castilian language and speaks his mother tongue and the Tegua. He took the oath in due legal form in the name of God, our Lord, and a sign of the cross, under charge of which he promised to tell the truth concerning what he knows and as he might be questioned, and having understood the seriousness of the oath and so signified through the interpreters, he spoke as indicated by the contents of the autos.

Asked whether he knows the reason or motives which the Indians of this kingdom had for rebelling, forsaking the law of God and obedience to his Majesty, and committing such grave and atrocious crimes, and who were the leaders and principal movers, and by whom and how it was ordered; and why they burned the images, temples, crosses, rosaries, and things of divine worship, committing such atrocities as killing priests, Spaniards, women, and children, and the rest that he might

know touching the question, he said that since the government of Señor General Hernando Ugarte y la Concha they have planned to rebel on various occasions through conspiracies of the Indian sorcerers, and that although in some pueblos the messages were accepted, in other parts they would not agree to it; and that it is true that during the government of the said senor general seven or eight Indians were hanged for this same cause, whereupon the unrest subsided. Some time thereafter they [the conspirators] sent from the pueblo of Los Taos through the pueblos of the custodia two deerskins with some pictures on them signifying conspiracy after their manner, in order to convoke the people to a new rebellion, and the said deerskins passed to the province of Moqui, where they refused to accept them. The pact which they had been forming ceased for the time being, but they always kept in their hearts the desire to carry it out, so as to live as they are living today. Finally, in the past years, at the summons of an Indian named Popé who is said to have communication with the devil, it happened that in an estufa of the pueblo of Los Taos there appeared to the said Popé three figures of Indians who never came out of the estufa. They gave the said Popé to understand that they were going underground to the lake of Copala. He saw these figures emit fire from all the extremities of their bodies, and that one of them was called Caudi, another Tilini, and the other Tleume; and these three beings spoke to the said Popé, who was in hiding from the secretary, Francisco Xavier, who wished to punish him as a sorcerer. They told him to make a cord of maguey fiber and tie some knots in it which would signify the number of days that they must wait before the rebellion. He said that the cord was passed through all the pueblos of the kingdom so that the ones which agreed to it [the rebellion] might untie one knot in sign of obedience, and by the other knots they would know the days which were lacking; and this was to be done on pain of death to those who refused to agree to it. As a sign of agreement and notice of having concurred in the treason and perfidy they were to send up smoke signals to that effect in each one of the pueblos singly. The said cord was taken from pueblo to pueblo by the swiftest youths under the penalty of death if they revealed the secret. Everything being thus arranged, two days before the time set for its execution, because his lordship had learned of it and had imprisoned two Indian accomplices from the pueblo of Tesuque, it was carried out prematurely that night, because it seemed to them that they were now discovered; and they killed religious, Spaniards, women, and children. This being done, it was proclaimed in all the pueblos that everyone in common should obey the commands of their father whom they did not know, which would be given through El Caydi or El Popé. This was heard by Alonso Catití, who came to the pueblo of this declarant to say that everyone must unite to go to the villa to kill the governor and the Spaniards who had remained with him, and that he who did not obey would, on their return, be beheaded; and in fear of this they agreed to it. Finally the senor governor and those who were with him escaped from the siege, and later this declarant saw that as soon as the Spaniards had left the kingdom an order came from the said Indian, Popé, in which he commanded all the Indians to break the lands and enlarge their cultivated fields, saying that now they were as they had been in ancient times, free from the labor they had performed for the religious and the Spaniards, who could not now be alive. He said that this is the legitimate cause and the reason they had for rebelling, because they had always desired to live as they had when they came out of the lake of Copala. Thus he replies to the question.

Asked for what reason they so blindly burned the images, temples, crosses, and other things of divine worship, he stated that the said Indian, Popé, came down in person, and with him El Saca and El Chato from the pueblo of Los Taos, and other captains and leaders and many people who were in his train, and he ordered in all the pueblos through which he passed that they instantly break up and burn the images of the holy Christ, the Virgin Mary and the other saints, the crosses, and everything pertaining to Christianity, and that they burn the temples, break up the bells, and separate from the wives whom God had given them in marriage and take those whom they desired. In order to take away their baptismal names, the water, and the holy oils, they were to plunge into the rivers and wash themselves with amole, which is a root native to the country, washing even their clothing, with the understanding that there would thus be taken from them the character of the holy sacraments. They did this, and also many other things which he does not recall, given to understand that this mandate had come from the Caydi and the other two who emitted fire from their extremities in the said estufa of Taos, and that they thereby returned to the state of their antiquity, as when they came from the lake of Copala; that this was the better life and the one they desired, because the God of the Spaniards was worth nothing and theirs was very strong, the Spaniard's God being rotten wood. These things were observed and obeyed by all except some who, moved by the zeal of Christians, opposed it, and such persons the said Popé caused to be killed immediately. He saw to it that they at once erected and rebuilt their houses of idolatry which they call estufas, and made very ugly masks in imitation of the devil in order to dance the dance of the cacina; and he said likewise that the devil had given them to understand that living thus in accordance with the law of their ancestors, they would harvest a great deal of maize, many beans, a great abundance of cotton, calabashes, and very large watermelons and cantaloupes; and that they could erect their houses and enjoy abundant health and leisure. As he has said, the people were very much pleased, living at their ease in this life of their antiquity, which was the chief cause of their falling into such laxity. Following what has already been stated, in order to terrorize them further and cause them to observe the diabolical commands, there came to them a pronouncement from the three demons already described, and from El Popé, to the effect that he who might still keep in his heart a regard for the priests, the governor, and the Spaniards would be known from his unclean face and clothes, and would be punished. And he stated that the said four persons stopped at nothing to have their commands obeyed. Thus he replies to the question.

Asked what arrangements and plans they had made for the contingency of the Spaniards' return, he said that what he knows concerning the question is that they were always saying they would have to fight to the death, for they do not wish to live in any other way than they are living at present; and the demons in the estufa of Taos had given them to understand that as soon as the Spaniards began to move toward this kingdom they would warn them so that they might unite, and none of them would be caught. He having been questioned further and repeatedly touching the case, he said that he has nothing more to say except that they should be always on the alert, because the said Indians were continually planning to follow the Spaniards and fight with them by night, in order to drive off the horses and catch them afoot, although they might have to follow them for many leagues. What he has said is the truth, and what happened, on the word of a Christian who confesses his guilt. He said that he has come to the pueblos through fear to lead in idolatrous dances,

in which he greatly fears in his heart that he may have offended God, and that now having been absolved and returned to the fold of the church, he has spoken the truth in everything he has been asked. His declaration being read to him, he affirmed and ratified all of it. He declared himself to be eighty years of age, and he signed it with his lordship and the interpreters and assisting witnesses, before me, the secretary. ANTONIO DE OTERMÍN; PEDRO NARANJO; NICOLÁS RODRIGUEZ REY; JUAN LUCERO DE GODOY; JUAN Ruiz DE CASARES; PEDRO DE LEIVA; SEBASTÍAN DE HERRERA; JUAN DE NORIEGA GARCÍA; Luis DE GRANILLO; JUAN DE LUNA Y PADILLA. Before me, FRANCISCO XAVIER, secretary of government and war (rubric).

Source: Hackett, Charles Wilson, ed. *Revolt of the Pueblo Indians of New Mexico and Otermin's Attempted Reconquest, 1680–1682.* Vol 2. Albuquerque: University of New Mexico, 1942, 245–249.

Declaration of a Rebellious Christian Indian in the Pueblo Revolt
(1680)

The Pueblo revolt took place in 1680 in New Mexico. For nearly a century, the Indians of that area were controlled as much as possible by the Spanish, and especially by the Franciscan missionaries. The Pueblo were forced to abandon their traditional beliefs and practices and worship as Christians. Furthermore, they were forced to work for the priests, which included building churches. An organized revolt took place in August 1680. Hundreds of Spanish settlers were killed, and 21 of the 33 priests in the colony were killed. What follows is the response of one of the participants to Spanish questioning.

In the place of El Alamillo, jurisdiction of El Socorro, on the 6th day of the month of September, 1680 for the prosecution of this case, and so that an Indian who was captured on the road as the camp was marching may be examined, in order to ascertain the plans, designs, and motives of the rebellious enemy, his lordship, the senor-gobernador and captain-general, caused the said Indian to appear before him. He received the oath from him in due legal form, in the name of God, our Lord, and on a sign of the cross, under charge of which he promised to tell the truth concerning what he might know and as he might be questioned. Having been asked his name and of what place he is a native, his condition, and age, he said that his name is don Pedro Nanboa, that he is a native of the pueblo of Alameda, a widower, and somewhat more than eighty years of age. Asked for what reason the Indians of this kingdom have rebelled, forsaking their obedience to his Majesty and failing in their obligations as Christians, he said that for a long time, because the Spaniards punished sorcerers and idolators, the nations of the Teguas, Tao, Pecuries, Pecos and Jemez had been plotting to rebel and kill the Spaniards and the religious [Franciscans], and that they had been planning constantly to carry it out, down to the present occasion. Asked what he learned, saw and heard in the juntas and parleys that the Indians have held, what they have plotted among themselves, and why the Indians have burned the church and profaned the images of the pueblo of Sandia, he said that he has not taken part in any junta, nor has he harmed any one; that what he has heard is that the Indians do not want religious [friars] or Spaniards. Because he is so old he was in the cornfield when he learned from the Indian rebels who come from the sierra that they had killed the Spaniards of the jurisdiction and robbed all their haciendas, sacking their houses. Asked whether he knows about the Spaniards and religious who were gathered in the pueblo of La Isleta he said that it is true that some days ago there assembled in the said pueblo of La Isleta the religious of Sandia, Jemez, and Zia, and that they set out to leave the kingdom with those of the said pueblo of la Isleta and the Spaniards—not one of whom remained—taking along their property. The Indians did not fight with them because all the men had gone with the other nations to fight at the villa [in the capital] and destroy the governor and captain-general and all the people who were with him. He declared that the resentment which all the Indians have in their hearts has been so strong, from the time this kingdom was discovered, because the religious and the Spaniards took away their idols and forbade their sorceries and idolatries; that they have inherited successively from their old men the things pertaining to their ancient customs; and that he has heard this resentment spoken of since he was of an age to understand. What he has said is the truth and what he knows, under the oath taken, and he signs and ratifies it, it being read and explained to him in his language through the interpretation of Captain Sebastian Montano, who signed it with his lordship, as the said Indian does not know how, before me, the present secretary. Antonia de Oternin (rubric); Sebastian Montano (rubric); Juan Lucero de Godoy (rubric); Luis de Quintana (rubric). Before me, Francisco Xavier, secretary of government and war (rubric).

Source: Hackett, Charles Wilson, ed. *Revolt of the Pueblo Indians of New Mexico and Oternin's Attempted Reconquest, 1680–1682.* Vol. 1. Albuquerque: University of New Mexico Press, 1942, 60–62.

Chekilli, Origin of the Creek Confederacy

(1735)

Like many American Indian peoples, the Creek have traditional stories that describe their origins and how they came to occupy a particular region. In 1735, Creek chief Chekilli told an audience in Georgia the following story about how his people arrived and how various tribes united to form a confederacy. His speech was recorded on a buffalo skin and was first published in Germany four years after its delivery.

At a certain time the Earth opened in the West, where its mouth is. The Earth opened and the Kasihtas came out of its mouth, and settled nearby. But the Earth became angry and ate up their children; therefore they moved farther West. A part of them, however, turned back, and came again to the same place where they had been, and settled there. The greater number remained behind, because they thought it best to do so. Their children, nevertheless, were eaten by the Earth, so that, full of dissatisfaction, they journeyed toward the sunrise.

They came to a thick, muddy, slimy river—came there, camped there, rested there, and stayed overnight there. The next day they continued their journey and came, in one day, to a red, bloody river. They lived by this river, and ate of its fishes for two years; but there were low springs there; and it did not please them to remain. They went toward the end of this bloody river, and heard a noise of thunder. They approached to see whence the noise came. At first they perceived a red smoke, and then a mountain which thundered; and on the mountain was a sound as of singing. They went to see what this was; and it was a great fire which blazed upward, and made this singing noise. This mountain they named the King of Mountains. It thunders to this day; and men are very much afraid of it.

They here met a people of three different Nations. They had taken and saved some of the fire from the mountain; and, at this place, they also obtained a knowledge of herbs and of other things.

From the East, a white fire came to them; which, however, they would not use. From the South came a fire which was blue, neither did they use it. From the West, came a fire which was black; nor would they use it. At last, came a fire from the North, which was red and yellow. This they mingled with the fire they had taken from the mountain; and this is the fire they use today; and this, too, sometimes sings. On the mountain was a pole which was very restless and made a noise, nor could any one say how it could be quieted. At length they took a motherless child, and struck it against the pole; and thus killed the child. They then took the pole, and carry it with them when they go to war. It was like a wooden tomahawk, such as they now use, and of the same wood.

Here they also found four herbs or roots, which sang and disclosed their virtues: first, Pasaw, the rattlesnake root; second Micoweanochaw, red-root; third Sowatchko, which grows like wild fennel; and fourth, Eschalapootchke, little tobacco. These herbs, especially the first and third, they use as the best medicine to purify themselves at their Busk. At this Busk, which is held yearly, they fast, and make offerings of the first fruits. Since they have learned the virtues of these herbs, their women, at certain times, have a separate fire, and remain apart from the men five, six, and seven days, for the sake of purification. If they neglected this, the power of the herbs would depart; and the women would not be healthy.

About this time a dispute arose, as to which was the oldest, and which should rule; and they agreed, as they were four Nations, they would set up four poles, and make them red with clay which is yellow at first, but becomes red by burning. They would go to war; and whichever Nation should first cover its pole, from top to bottom, with the scalps of their enemies, should be oldest.

They all tried, but the Kasihtas covered their pole first, and so thickly that it was hidden from sight. Therefore, they were looked upon, by the whole Nation, as the oldest. The Chickasaws covered their pole next; then the Alabamas; then the Abihkas did not cover their pole higher than to the knee.

At that time there was a bird of large size, blue in color, with a long tail, and swifter than an eagle, which came every day and killed and ate their people. They made an image in the shape of a woman, and placed it in the way of this bird. The bird carried it off, and kept it a long time, and then brought it back. They left it alone, hoping it would bring something forth. After a long time, a red rat came forth from it, and they believed the bird was the father of the rat. They took council with the rat how to destroy its father. Now the bird had a bow and arrows; and the rat gnawed the bowstring, so that the bird could not defend itself, and the people killed it. They called this bird the King of Birds. They think the eagle is a great King; and they carry its feathers when they go to War or make Peace; the red means War; the white, Peace. If an enemy approaches with white feathers and a white mouth, and cries like an eagle, they dare not kill him.

After this they left that place, and came to a white footpath. The grass and everything around were white; and they plainly perceived that people had been there. They crossed the path, and slept near there. Afterward they turned back to see what sort of path that was, and who the people were who had been there, in the belief that it might be better for them to follow that path. They went along it to a creek called Coloose-hutche, that is, Coloose-creek, because it was rocky there and smoked.

They crossed it, going toward the sunrise, and came to a people and a town named Coosa. Here they remained for years. The Coosas complained that they were preyed upon by a wild beast, which they called man-eater or lion, which lived in a rock.

The Kasihtas said they would try to kill the beast. They dug a pit and stretch over it a net made of hickory-bark. They then laid a number of branches, crosswise, so that the lion could not follow them, and, going to the place where he lay, they threw a rattle into his den. The lion rushed forth in great anger, and pursued them through the branches. Then they thought it better that one should die rather than all; so they took a motherless child, and threw it before the lion as he came near the pit. The lion rushed at it, and fell in the pit, over which they threw the net, and killed him with blazing pinewood. His bones, however, they keep to this day; on one side, they are red, on the other blue.

The lion used to come every seventh day to kill the people; therefore, they remained there seven days after they had killed him. In remembrance of him, when they prepare for War, they fast six days and start on the seventh. If they take his bones with them, they have good fortune.

After four years they left the Coosas, and came to a river which they called Nowphawpe, now Callasi-hutche. There they tarried two years; and, as they had no corn, they lived on roots and fishes, and made bows, pointing the arrows with beaver teeth and flint-stones, and for knives they used split canes.

They left this place, and came to a creek, called Wattoola-hawka-hutche, Whooping-creek, so called from the whooping of cranes, a great many being there; they slept there one night. They next came to a river, in which there was a waterfall; this they named the Owatunka-river. The next day they reached another river, which they called the Aphoosa pheeskaw.

The following day they crossed it, and came to a high mountain, where were people who, they believed, were the same who made the white path. They, therefore, made white arrows and shot at them, to see if they were good people. But the people took their white arrows, painted them red, and shot them back. When they showed these to their chief, he said that it was not a good sign; if the arrows returned had been white, they could have gone there and brought food for their children, but as they were red they must not go. Nevertheless, some of them went to see what sort of people they were; and found their houses deserted. They also saw a trail which led into the river; and, as they could not see the trail on the opposite bank, they believed that the people had gone into the river, and would not again come forth.

At that place is a mountain, called Moterelo, which makes a noise like beating on a drum; and they think this people live there. They hear this noise on all sides when they go to war.

They went along the river, till they came to a waterfall, where they saw great rocks, and on the rocks were bows lying; and they believed the people who made the white path had been there.

They always have, on their journeys, two scouts who go before the main body. These scouts ascended a high mountain and saw a town. They shot white arrows into the town; but the people of the town shot back red arrows. Then the Kasihtas became angry, and determined to attack the town, and each one have a house when it was captured.

They threw stones into the river until they could cross it, and took the town (the people had flattened heads) and killed all but two persons. In pursuing these they found a white dog, which they slew. They followed the two who escaped, until they came again to the white path, and saw the smoke of a town, and thought that this must be the people they had so long been seeking. This is the place where now the tribe of Apalachicolas live, from whom Tomochichi is descended.

The Kasihtas continued bloody-minded; but the Apalachicolas gave them black drink, as a sign of friendship, and said to them: "Our hearts are white, and yours must be white, and you must lay down the bloody tomahawk, and show your bodies as proof that they shall be white." Nevertheless, they were for the tomahawk; but the Apalachicolas got it by persuasion, and buried it under their beds. The Apalachicolas likewise gave them white feathers, and asked to have a chief in common. Since then they have always lived together.

Some settled on one side of the river, some on the other. Those on one side are called Kasihtas, those on the other, Cowetas; yet they are one people, and the principle [sic] towns of the Upper and Lower Creeks. Nevertheless, as the Kasihtas first saw the red smoke and the red fire, and make bloody towns, they cannot yet leave their red hearts, which, though white on one side, are red on the other. They now know that the white path was the best for them: for, although Tomochichi was a stranger, they see he has done them good; because he went to see the great King with Esquire Oglethorpe, and hear his talk, and had related it to them, and they had listened to it, and believed it.

Source: Gatschet, Albert S. *A Migration Legend of the Creek Indians.* Philadelphia: D. G. Brinton, 1884, 244–251.

Atiwaneto Resists Colonial Expansion
(1752)

The Abenaki lived in present-day Maine. They previously held territory further south, but were pushed north by English colonists. They eventually aligned themselves with the French, which gave them access to firearms and ammunition. As a result, they gained more power, which they showed in the following statement to the English.

Propositions of the Abenakis of St. Francis to Captain Phineas Stevens, delegate from the governor of Boston, in presence of the Baron de Longeuil, governor of Montreal, commandant of Canada and of the Iroquois of the Sault Saint Louis and of the Lake of the Two Mountains, July 5, 1752.

ATIWANETO, CHIEF SPEAKER

1. Brother, We speak to you as if we spoke to your Governor of Boston. We hear on all sides that this Governor and the Bostonians say that the Abenakis are bad people. 'Tis in vain that we are taxed with having a bad heart; it is you, brother, that always attack us; your mouth is of sugar but your heart of gall; in truth, the moment you begin we are on our guard.

2. Brothers, We tell you that we seek not war, we ask nothing better than to be quiet, and it depends, Brothers, only on you English, to have peace with us.

3. We have not yet sold the lands we inhabit, we wish to keep the possession of them. Our elders have been willing to tolerate you, brothers Englishmen, on the seaboard as far as Sawakwato; as that has been so decided, we wish it to be so.

4. But we will not cede one single inch of the lands we inhabit beyond what has been decided formerly by our fathers.

5. You have the sea for your share from the place where you reside; you can trade there; but we expressly forbid you to kill a single Beaver, or to take a single stick of timber on the lands we inhabit; if you want timber we'll sell you some, but you shall not take it without our permission.

6. Brothers, Who hath authorized you to have those lands surveyed? We request our brother, the Governor of Boston, to have these Surveyors punished, as we cannot imagine that they have acted by his authority.

7. Brother, You are therefore masters of the peace that we are to have with you; on condition that you will not encroach on those lands we will be at peace, as the King of France is with the King of Great Britain.

8. By a Belt

    I repeat to you, Brothers, by this Belt, that it depends on yourselves to be at peace with the Abenakis.

9. Our [political] Father [the French governor] who is here present has nothing to do with what we say to you; we speak to you of our own accord, and in the name of all our allies; we regard our Father, in this instance, only as a witness of our words.

10. We acknowledge no other boundaries of yours than your settlements whereon you have built, and we will not [that is, do not desire], under any pretext whatsoever, that you pass beyond them. The lands we possess have been given to us by the master of Life. We acknowledge to hold only from him.

11. We are entirely free; we are allies of the King of France, from whom we have received the Faith and all sorts of assistance in our necessities; we love that Monarch, and we are strongly attached to his interests.

12. Let us have an answer to the propositions we address you, as soon as possible; take this message in writing to give to your Governor; we, also, shall keep a copy of it to use in case of need.

    Without stirring a step it is easy for your Governor to transmit his answer to us; he will have merely to address it to our [French] Father who will have the goodness to send it to us.

13. [Phineas Stevens speaks.] Brothers, I shall report your Message to my Governor, and in order that it may not suffer any alternation I shall take it in writing. He will transmit his answer to the Baron de Longeuil as you desire.

THE ENGLISH DEMAND OF THE ABENAKIS

1. Brothers Abenakis, I ask you if the attack which your Nation has made these two years [past] on the English is in consequence of encroachments by the latter on your hands?

2. Are you satisfied with the death of your people on account of your attacks on the English?

3. I know that it is not permitted to go on your lands; those who have been there are young fools, without any character.

THE ANSWER OF THE ABENAKIS

1. Brothers, When peace was concluded we hoped to enjoy it, like the French, but we learned at the same time, that you English had killed one of our people, and had hid him under the ice.

   We asked wherefore you killed us? You answered that you would give us satisfaction, but your ill-will having been sensibly indicated by your inaction, pending seven months, we resolved to avenge ourselves, and to pull down one house.

   Since when we have missed one man and one woman belonging to our village; we learned their sad fate only from an Englishwoman, who is at present at our place, who assured us that man and woman were killed in her presence by Englishmen, and in order to afford us a convincing proof thereof, she gave us a bag which we perfectly recognized as having belonged to those unfortunate people. We felt, as we ought to do, this murder, and avenged it last year.

   The two Englishmen that we killed this year on the head waters of our river, and the two others that we have taken prisoners, must attribute their misfortunes to themselves, because they hunted Beaver on our lands, and on this point we repeat to you, with all the firmness we are capable of, that we will kill all the Englishmen we shall find on the lands in our possession.

2. Our heart is good, and since we struck the blow our thirst for vengeance is extinguished.

3. Listen, Brothers Englishmen, to what is our Indian custom among ourselves, with persons we would find on the lands we possess? We should take their game, and if they made any resistance, we would knock them on the head.

   How can you suppose, Brothers, that we should suffer you on those lands?

   You have only to excite fear in your houses. We are not capable of offering the least insult, but should any of you be found on our lands, they shall die.

THE IROQUOIS TO THE ABENAKIS

We have heard, with pleasure, what you said to the English deputy; we are charmed that you have vigorously maintained your rights. We exhort you to keep your word with the English; should the case require it, we oblige ourselves to aid you with all our might.

Source: O'Callaghan, Edward, ed. *Documents Relative to the Colonial History of the State of New York.* Vol. 10 of *Transcripts of Documents in the Archives of the Ministere de la Marine et des Colonies.* Paris: Weed, Parsons and Co., 1858, 252–254.

Minavavana, "Englishman!—You Know that the French King Is Our Father" (1761)

To British trader Alexander Henry, who recorded this speech, Minavavana identified himself as a Chippewa. However, there is some evidence that he was in fact the Ottawa Pontiac, who was instrumental in the rebellion against the British in the wake of the French and Indian War in 1763. In this speech, the speaker rails against the British and urges the Indians listening to him to maintain their relationship with the French.

Englishman!—It is to you that I speak, and I demand your attention!

Englishman!—You know that the French king is our father. He promised to be such; and we, in return, promised to be his children. This promise we have kept.

Englishman!—It is you that have made war with this our father. You are his enemy; and how then could you have the boldness to venture among us, his children? You know that his enemies are ours.

Englishman!—We are informed that our father, the king of France, is old and infirm; and that being fatigued with making war upon your nation, he is fallen asleep. During his sleep, you have taken advantage of him, and possessed yourselves of Canada. But his nap is almost at an end. I think I hear him already stirring, and inquiring for his children the Indians—and, when he does awake, what must become of you? He will destroy you utterly!

Englishman!—Although you have conquered the French, you have not yet conquered us! We are not your slaves. These lakes, these woods and mountains were left to us by our ancestors. They are our inheritance, and we will part with them to none. Your nation supposes that we, like the white people, cannot live without bread, and pork, and beef! But, you ought to know, that He—the Great Spirit and Master of Life—has provided food for us in these broad lakes and upon these mountains.

Englishman!—Our father, the King of France, employed our young men to make war upon your nation. In this warfare, many of them have been killed; and it is our custom to retaliate, until such time as the spirits of the slain are satisfied. Now the spirits of the slain are to be satisfied in either of two ways. The first is by the spilling of the blood of the nation by which they fell; the other, by *covering the bodies of the dead,* and thus allaying the resentment of their relations. This is done by making presents.

Englishmen!—Your king has never sent us any presents, nor entered into any treaty with us. Wherefore he and we are still at war; and, until he does these things, we must consider that we have no other father, nor friend, among the white men, than the king of France. But, for you, we have taken into consideration that you have ventured your life among us in the expectation that we should not molest you. You do not come armed, with the intention to make war. You come in peace, to trade with us, and supply us with necessaries, of which we are much in want. We shall regard you, therefore, as a brother; and you may sleep tranquilly without fear of the Chippewas [*sic*]. As a token of friendship, we present you with this pipe, to smoke.

Source: Thatcher, B. B. *Indian Life and Battles.* Akron, OH: New Werner Company, 1910, 78–80.

Pontiac Describes Neolin's Vision
(1763)

As the 18th century progressed, a group of Indians known as the Prophets emerged among various tribes. Although their messages differed somewhat, they all had similar themes. In addition, one can see the influence of Christianity on traditional Indian religious practices. In this document, French trader Robert Navarre, who lived in Detroit and spoke the Ottawa language, recorded Pontiac's account of the Delaware prophet Neolin's vision. Neolin was not a traditionalist and did not advocate a strict return to traditional Delaware practices; he borrowed freely and heavily from Christianity, Nevertheless, certain themes appear, such as an overreliance on the whites, which has angered the Great Spirit.

Suddenly, he saw before him what appeared to be a mountain of marvelous whiteness and he stopped, overwhelmed with astonishment. Nevertheless, he again advanced, firmly determined to see what this mountain could be, but when he arrived at the foot of it he no longer saw any road and was sad. At this juncture, not knowing what to do to continue his way, he looked around in all directions and finally saw a woman of this mountain, of radiant beauty, whose garments dimmed the whiteness of the snow. And she was seated.

This woman addressed him in his own tongue: "Thou appearest to me to be surprised to find any road to lead thee where thou wishes to go. I know that for a long while thou hast been desirous of seeing the Master of Life and of speaking with him; that is why thou hast undertaken this journey to see him. The road which leads to his abode is over the mountain, and to ascend it thou must foresake [sic] all thou hast with thee, and disrobe completely, and leave all thy trappings and clothing at the foot of the mountain. No one shall harm thee; go and bathe thyself in a river which I shall show thee, and then thou shalt ascend."

The Wolf [Neolin, a reference to his clan affiliation] was careful to obey the words of the woman, but one difficulty yet confronted him, namely, to know how to reach the top of the mountain which was perpendicular, pathless, and smooth as ice. He questioned this woman how one should go about climbing up, and she replied that if he was really anxious to see the Master of Life, he would have to ascend, helping himself only with his hand and his left foot. This appeared to him impossible, but encouraged by the woman he set about it and succeeded by dint of effort.

When he reached the top he was greatly astonished not to see anyone; the woman had disappeared, and he found himself alone without a guide. At his right were three villages . . . he did not know them for they seemed of different construction from his own, prettier and more orderly in appearance. After he had pondered some time over what he ought to do, he set out toward the village which seemed to him the most attractive, and covered half the distance from the top of the mountain before he remembered that he was naked. He was afraid to go further, but he heard a voice telling him to continue and that he ought not to fear, because having bathed as he had, he could go on in assurance. He had no more difficulty in continuing up to a spot which seemed to him to be the gate of the village, and here he stopped, waiting for it to open so he could enter. While he was observing the outward beauty of this village the gate opened, and he saw coming toward him a handsome man, clothed all in white, who took him by the hand and told him he was going to satisfy him and let him talk with the Master of Life. The Wolf permitted the man to conduct him, and both came to a place of surpassing beauty which the Indian could not admire enough. Here he saw the Master of Life who took him by the hand and gave him a hat all bordered with gold to sit down upon. The Wolf hesitated to do this for fear of spoiling the hat, but he was ordered to do so, and obeyed without reply.

After the Indian was seated the Lord said to him: "I am the Master of Life, and since I know what thou desirest to know, and to whom thou wishest to speak, listen well to what I am going to say to thee and to all the Indians:

'I am He who hath created the heavens and the earth, the trees, lakes, rivers, all men, and all thou seest upon the earth. Because I love you, ye must do what I say and love, and not do what I hate. I do not love that ye should drink to the point of madness, as ye do; I do not like it that ye should fight one another. Ye take two wives, or run after the wives of others. . . . I hate that. Ye ought to have but one wife, and keep her till death. When ye wish to go to war, ye conjure and resort to the medicine dance, believing that ye speak to me; ye are mistaken—it is to the Manitou that ye speak, an evil spirit who prompts you to nothing but wrong, and who listens to you out of ignorance to me.'

'This land where ye dwell I have made for you and not for others. Whence comes it that ye permit the Whites upon your lands? Can ye not live without them? I know that those whom ye call the children of your Great Father supply your needs, but if ye were not evil, as ye are, ye could surely do without them. Ye could live as ye did live before those whom ye call your brothers came upon your lands. Did ye not live by bow and arrow? Ye had no need of gun or powder, or anything else, and nevertheless ye caught animals to live upon and to dress yourselves with their skins. But when I saw that ye were given up to evil, I led the wild animals to the depths of the forests so that ye had to depend upon your brothers [the whites] to feed and shelter you. Ye have only to become good again and do what I wish, and I will send back the animals for your food. I do not forbid you to permit among you the children of your Father [a reference to the French]; I love them. They know me and pray to me, and I supply their wants and all they give you. But as to those who trouble your lands,—drive them out, make war upon them. I do not love them at all; they know me not, and are my enemies, and the enemies of your brothers. Send them back to the lands which I have created for them and let them stay there . . . drive off your lands those dogs clothed in red [the British] who will do you nothing but harm.'"

Source: Navarre, Robert. *Journal of Pontiac's Conspiracy.* Translated by R. Clyde Ford. Detroit: Clarence Monroe Burton, 1910, 22–30.

Dragging Canoe, "We Will Have Our Lands!"
(1775)

Dragging Canoe was a member of the Lower, or Chickamauga, Cherokee. He fought against white encroachment on his people's lands from the American Revolution until his death in 1792. In the document that follows, Dragging Canoe discusses the fate of his people after the Treaty of Sycamore Shoals. This treaty (illegally) transferred ownership of Cherokee lands in the present-day state of Kentucky to Richard Henderson, who attempted to create the colony of Transylvania out of these newly acquired territories. Dragging Canoe left the treaty council without signing the document and took with him members of the Lower Cherokee who shared his way of thinking. Over the decades that followed, Dragging Canoe worked tirelessly to resist white encroachment and to establish a successful resistance to American expansionist activities.

We had hoped that the white men would not be willing to travel beyond the mountains. Now that hope is gone. They have passed the mountains, and have settled upon Cherokee land. They wish to have that usurpation sanctioned by treaty. When that is gained, the same encroaching spirit will lead them upon other land of the Cherokees. New cessions will be asked. Finally the whole country, which the Cherokees and their fathers have so long occupied, will be demanded, and the remnant of Ani-Yunwiya, the Real People, once so great and formidable, will be compelled to seek refuge in some distant wilderness. There they will be permitted to stay only a short while, until they again behold the advancing banners of the same greedy host. Not being able to point out any further retreat for the miserable Cherokees, the extinction of the whole race will be proclaimed. Should we not therefore run all risks, and incur all consequences, rather than submit to further loss of our country? Such treaties may be alright for men who are too old to hunt or fight. As for me, I have my young warriors about me. We will have our lands. I have spoken.

Source: Alderman, Pat. *Nancy Ward/Dragging Canoe: Cherokee Chieftainess/Cherokee-Chickamauga War Chief.* Johnson City, TN: Overmountain Press, 1990, 38.

Corn Tassel, Speech about the Treaty of Long Island

(1777)

This particular treaty does not refer to Long Island, New York. Long Island, also known as Long Island of Holston, is an island in the Holston River of eastern Tennessee. It is a site that the Cherokee tenaciously guarded and felt connected to spiritually. Colonial settlers believed the area held strategic importance, and because the Cherokee refused to sell the land, they launched a punitive raid against them. The settlers felt justified in doing so because many Cherokee aligned themselves with the British during the American Revolution. After two months of fighting, the Cherokee agreed to the Treaty of Long Island, whereupon they relinquished their claims to land occupied by whites in eastern Tennessee. In the following speech, Cherokee chief Corn Tassel, or Old Tassel, discusses the fact that the preservation of Cherokee lands was essential to his people's survival.

Now the beloved men of North Carolina shall hear my reply to what they said to me last night.

The talks you gave me came from the Governor to make a path from your Country and was very good till you came to talk of the boundary line. My beloved man and the beloved man of Virginia have taken hold of each other fast high up the arm.

It may be the same by my brothers of North Carolina. But by their asking so much land it seems as if they want to see what we would say, that we might refuse something, and they might catch us in a trap for an excuse. I left people both at home and in the woods far beyond there, who are waiting and listening to hear what I do. As you are talking of much land I don't know how they would like that part of your proposal. As I said before the beloved men are here together. My beloved Man has been to see the Great beloved man of Virginia who I suppose wrote to your Great beloved man to send you here, and talk about making Peace. I want to know whether he wrote anything to him to require so much land as you seem to do. I am talking to my Brothers so I call you all. As to land I did not expect any thing on that subject; but only concerning peace. The man above hath ordered it so that the white benches shall be set down for us, and I hope nothing will enter either of our hearts but good thoughts. I would leave it to the beloved man of Virginia to settle all things (about Lands) between us. I am talking with my elder Brothers on a subject I cannot clearly comprehend. I did not expect it would have been put to me at this time; for my elder Brothers have imposed much on me in the land way. If this and another house was packed full of goods they would not make satisfaction. But I will leave the difference between us to the great Warrior of all America. It seems mysterious to me why you should ask so much land so near me. I am sensible that if we give up these lands they will bring you more a great deal than hundreds of pounds. It spoils our hunting ground; but always remains good to you to raise families and stocks on, when the goods we receive of you are rotten and gone to nothing.

Your stocks are tame and marked; but we don't know ours they are wild. Hunting is our principle [sic] way of living. I hope you will consider this and pity me. Here is my old friend the Elk [Col. Preston] and two particular from Virginia hearing the answer I make to my brothers of North Carolina. You require a thing I cannot do, for which reason I return you the string of Beads to consider upon again.

In my talks at Chote Town house there shall be nothing bad towards my elder Brothers. I will hold them fast and strong. I have been often told that my elder Brothers were naked and had nothing. I said if so I will be naked also. I looked for nothing but to raise my children in peace and safety. My former friend who is now my Brothers enemy told me if I listened to you I should wear hickory bark shirts; but that Talk I do not mind.

Source: North Carolina Historical Review 8 (1931): 90–91.

Chickasaw Chief's Message to Congress
(1783)

The American Revolution and the ensuing peace treaty turned the world upside down for many American Indians. Old allies were gone, and new neighbors appeared where previously there had been no one. An example of this was the Mississippi Valley. Spain won West Florida from the British, and the geopolitical landscape of the region changed dramatically. The Chickasaw lost their British allies and found themselves friendless and surrounded by the Spanish, the U.S. government, and many different American states. As was often the case in such confusing situations, factionalism developed, which further hindered the cause of the Chickasaw. In the following document, the Chickasaw prudently realized it was time to put their former tenacity aside and reach out to the new United States.

To His Excellency the President of the Honorable Congress of the United American States

Friend & Brother,

This is the first talk we ever sent you—we hope it will not be the last. We desire you to open your Ears to hear, and your heart to understand us, as we shall always be ready to do to your talks, which we expect will be good, as you are a great and wise man.

Brother,

When our great father the King of England called away his warriors, he told us to take your People by the hand as friends and brothers. Our hearts were always inclined to do so & as far as our circumstances permitted us, we evinced our good intentions as Brothers the Virginians can testify—It makes our hearts rejoice to find that our great father, and his children the Americans have at length made peace, which we wish may continue as long as the Sun and Moon. And to find that our Brothers the Americans are inclined to take us by the hand, and Smoke with us at the great Fire, which we hope will never be extinguished.

Brother,

Notwithstanding the Satisfaction all these things give us we are yet in confusion & uncertainty. The Spaniards are sending talks amongst us, and inviting our young Men to trade with them. We also receive talks from the Governor of Georgia to the same effect—We have had Speeches from the Illinois inviting us to a Trade and Intercourse with them—Our Brothers, the Virginians Call upon us to a Treaty, and want part of our land, and we expect our Neighbors who live on Cumberland River, will in a Little time Demand, if not forcibly take part of it from us, also as we are informed they have been marking Lines through our hunting grounds: we are daily receiving Talks from one Place or other, and from People we Know nothing about. We Know not who to mind or who to neglect. We are told that the Americans have 13 Councils Compos'd of Chiefs and Warriors. We Know not which of them we are to Listen to, or if we are to hear some, and Reject others, we are at a loss to Distinguish those we are to hear. We are told that you are the head Chief of the Grand Council, which is above these 13 Councils: if so why have we not had Talks from you,—We are head men and Chiefs and Warriors also: and have always been accustomed to speak with great Chiefs & warriors—We are Likewise told that you and the Great men of your Council are Very Wise—we are glad to hear it, being assured that you will not do us any Wrong, and therefore we wish to Speak with you and your Council, or if you Do not approve of our so Doing, as you are wise, you will tell us who shall speak with us, in behalf of all our Brothers the Americans, and from where and whom we are to be supplied with necessaries in the manner our great father supplied us—we hope you

will also put a stop to any encroachments on our lands, without our consent, and silence all those People who send us Such Talks as inflame & exasperate our Young Men, as it is our earnest desire to remain in peace and friendship with our Br: the Americans for ever.

Brother,

The King our Common father always left one of his beloved Men among us, to whom we told anything we had to say, and he soon obtained an answer—and by him our great Father, his Chiefs & headmen spoke to us.

Our great father always gave him goods to cover the nakedness of our old men who could not hunt, our women and our children, and he was as one mouth, and one tongue between us, and was beloved of us all. Such a man living among us particularly at this time, would rescue us from the darkness and confusion we are in. By directing us to whom we should speak, and putting us in the right Path that we should not go wrong.

We have desired our Br. Mr. Donne, who brought talks from General Clark, and has been some time among us, to deliver this talk to you, and speak it in our behalf to your Grand Council, that you may know our want, and as you are wise, that you may direct us what to do for the best. He has Promised, at our desire to take it to your great council fire & bring as your answer, that you may be no more in the dark—believe what he tells you from us; we have told him all that is in our hearts.

Brothers, we are very poor for necessaries, for Ammunition particularly. We can supply ourselves from the Spaniards but we are averse to hold any intercourse with them, as our hearts are always with our Brothers the Americans. We have advised our young men to wait with patience for the answer to this talk, when we rest assured of having supplies, and every thing so regulated that no further confusion may ensue. We wish that this land may never again be stained with the blood of either white or Red men, that piece may last forever and that both our women and children may sit down in safety under their own shade to enjoy without fear or apprehension the Blessing which the good Spirit enriches them with. Brother, we again desire you and your chiefs to Listen to what we say that we shall not have to Repeat it again, and as you are all Wise, you will know what to do.

Done at Chuck-ul-issah our Great Town the 28th Day of July, 1783.

Minghoma,
Pyamathahaw,
Kushthaputhasa,
Pyamingoe of Christautra,
Pyamingo of Chuckaferah.

Source: "To His Excellency the President of the Honorable Congress of the United American States." In *Calendar of Virginia State Papers and Other Manuscripts*, edited by William P. Palmer, Preserved in the Capitol at Richmond. Volume 3: from January 1, 1782, to December 31, 1784. Richmond, VA: James E. Goode, 1883, 515–517.

Joseph Brant, Message to Governor Frederick Haldimand
(1783)

The 1783 Treaty of Paris ended the war between the American colonies and Great Britain. In it, Great Britain recognized the independence of its former 13 colonies and acknowledged the United States. The treaty failed, however, to even mention American Indians. Furthermore, Great Britain ceded the territory between the Appalachian Mountains and the Mississippi River to the United States. Indians who had lived there for generations occupied much of that land. As word of the peace treaty spread throughout Indian country, many Indians understandably were quite distressed to learn that not only were they not recognized in the peace treaty but that their lands had been given away as well. In the following message, renowned Mohawk leader Joseph Brant reminds Frederick Haldimand, governor of Quebec, of the long-standing alliance between his people and the British.

Brother Asharekowa and Representatives of the King, the sachems and War Chieftains of the Six United Nations of Indians and their Allies have heard that the King, their Father, has made peace with his children the Bostonians. The Indians distinguish by Bostonians, the Americans in Rebellion, as it first began in Boston, and when they heard of it, they found that they were forgot and no mention made of them in said Peace, wherefore they have now sent me to inform themselves before you of the real truth, whether it is so or not, that they are not partakers of that Peace with the King and Bostonians.

Brother, listen with great attention to our words, we were greatly alarmed and cast down when we heard that news, and it occasions great discontent and surprise with our People; wherefore tell us the real truth from your heart, we beg that the King will be put in mind by you and recollect what we have been when his people first saw us, and what we have since done for him and his subjects.

Brother, we the Mohawks, were the first Indian Nation that took you by the hand like friends and brothers, and invited you to live amongst us, treating you with kindness upon your debarkation in small parties. The Oneidas, our neighbors, were equally well disposed towards you and as a mark of our sincerity and love towards you we fastened your ship to a great mountain at Onondaga, the Center of our Confederacy, the rest of the Five Nations approving of it. We were then a great people, conquering all Indian Nations round about us, and you in a manner but a handful, after which you increased by degrees and we continued your friends and allies, joining you from time to time against your enemies, sacrificing numbers of our people and leaving their bones scattered in your enemies' country. At last we assisted you in conquering all Canada, and then again, for joining you so firmly and faithfully, you renewed your assurances of protecting and defending ourselves, lands and possessions against any encroachment whatsoever, procuring for us the enjoyment of fair and plentiful trade of your people, and sat contented under the shade of the Tree of Peace, tasting the favour and friendship of a great Nation bound to us by Treaty, and able to protect us against all the world.

Brother, you have books and records of our mutual Treaties and Engagements, which will confirm the truth of what I have been telling, and as we are unacquainted with the art of writing, we keep it fresh in our memory by Belts of Wampum deposited in our Council House at Onondaga. We have also received an ornament for the Head, i.e. a crown, from her late Majesty, Queen Ann, as a token of her mutual and unalterable friendship and alliance with us and our Confederacy. Wherefore, we on our side have maintained an uninterrupted attachment towards you, in confidence and expectation of a Reciprocity, and to establish a Perpetual Friendship and Alliance between us, of which we can give you several instances, to wit, when a few years after the Conquest of Canada, your people in this country thought themselves confined on account of their numbers with regard to a Scarcity of Land, we were applied to for giving up some of ours, and fix a Line or mark between them and Us. We considered upon it, and relinquished a great Territory to the King for the use of his Subjects, for a Trifling consideration, merely as a Confirmation of said Act, and as a proof of our sincere Regards towards them. This happened so late as the year 1768 at Fort Stanwix, and was gratefully Accepted and Ratified by the different Governors and Great men of the respective Colonies on the Sea Side, in presence of our Late Worthy Friend and Superintendent, Sir William Johnson, when we expected a Permanent, Brotherly Love and Amity, would be the Consequence, but in vain. The insatiable thirst for Power and the next Object of dissatisfaction to the King's Subjects on the Sea Coast, and they to blind our Eyes, Sent Priests from New England amongst us, whom we took for Messengers of Peace, but we were

Surprisingly undeceived when we found soon after, that they came to sow the Seeds of discord among our People, in order to alienate our ancient attachments and Alliance from the King our Father, and join them in Rebellion against him, and when they stood up against him, they first endeavored to ensnare us, the Mohawks, and the Indians of the Six Nations living on the Susquehanna River, and the Oneidas, by which division they imagined the remainder of the Confederacy would soon follow, but to not the Least effect.

About this Sad Period we lost our Greatest Friend, Sir William Johnson, notwithstanding we were unalterably determined to stick to our Ancient Treaties with the Crown of England and when the Rebels attempted to insult the Families and Descendents of our late Superintendent, on whom the management of our affairs devolved, we stuck to them and Protected them as much as in our Power, conducting them to Canada with a determined Resolution inviolably to adhere to our Alliance at the Risque of our Lives Families and Property, the rest of the Six Nations finding the Firmness and Steadiness of us, the Mohawks and Aughuagos, followed our Example and espoused the King's cause to this Present Instant.

It is as I tell you, Brother, and would be too tedious to repeat on this Pressing Occasion the many Proofs of Fidelity we have given the King our Father.

Wherefore Brother, I am now Sent in behalf of all the King's Indian Allies to receive a decisive answer from you, and to know whether they are included in the Treaty with the Americans, as faithful Allies should be or not, and whether those Lands which the Great Being above has pointed out for Our Ancestors, and their descendants, and Placed them there from the beginning and where the Bones of our forefathers are laid, is secure to them, or whether the Blood of their Grand Children is to be mingled with their Bones, thro' the means of Our Allies for whom we have often so freely Bled.

Source: Johnson, Charles M., ed. *Valley of the Six Nations.* Toronto: Champlain Society, 1964, 38–41. Reprinted with permission.

United Indian Nations, Speech at the Confederate Council (1786)

After the United States won its independence from Great Britain in 1783, the new nation almost immediately set about expanding westward. In doing so, the Americans brought themselves into direct contact, and often conflict, with various Indian nations. To avoid war, the United States tried to convince Indians to cede their land in treaties. The problem that existed, however, is that often some of the land a particular group of Indians ceded did not necessarily belong to them, or those gathered at the treaty negotiations did not have the power to cede land. To combat this, several Indian nations attempted to put together a confederacy and present a united front to the Americans. In the following speech, the United Indian Nations present this front to the U.S. Congress.

Present:—The Five Nations, the Hurons, Delawares, Shawanese, Ottawas, Chippewas, Powtewatimies, Twichtwees, Cherokees, and the Wabash confederates

To the Congress of the United States of America:

Brethren of the United States of America: It is now more than three years since peace was made between the King of Great Britain and you, but we, the Indians, were disappointed, finding ourselves not included in that peace, according to our expectations: for we thought that its conclusion would have promoted a friendship between the United States and the Indians, and that we might enjoy that happiness that formerly subsisted between us and our elder brethren. We have received two very agreeable messages from the thirteen United States. We also received a message from the King, whose war we were engaged in, desiring us to remain quiet, which we accordingly complied with. During the time of this tranquility, we were deliberating the best method we could to form a lasting reconciliation with the thirteen United States. Pleased at the same time, we thought we were entering upon a reconciliation and friendship with a set of people born on the same continent with ourselves, certain that the quarrel between us was not of our own making. In the course of our councils, we imagined we hit upon an expedient that would promote a lasting peace between us.

Brothers: We still are of the same opinion as to the means which may tend to reconcile us to each other; and we are sorry to find, although we had the best thoughts in our minds, during the beforementioned period, mischief has, nevertheless, happened between you and us. We are still anxious of putting our plan of accommodation into execution, and we shall briefly inform you of the means that seem most probable to us of effecting a firm and lasting peace and reconciliation: the first step towards which should, in our opinion, be, that all treaties carried on with the United States, on our parts, should be with the general voice of the whole confederacy, and carried on in the most open manner, without any restraint on either side; and especially as landed matters are often the subject of our councils with you, a matter of the greatest importance and of general concern to us, in this case we hold it indispensably necessary that any cession of our lands should be made in the most public manner, and by the united voice of the confederacy; holding all partial treaties as void and of no effect.

Brothers: We think it is owing to you that the tranquility which, since the peace between us, has not lasted, and that the essential good has been followed by mischief and confusion, having managed every thing respecting us your own way. You kindled your council fires where you thought proper, without consulting us, at which you held separate treaties, and have entirely neglected our plan of having a general conference with the different nations of the confederacy. Had this happened, we have reason to believe every thing would now have been settled between us in a most friendly manner. We did every thing in our power, at the treaty of fort Stanwix, to induce you to follow this plan, as our real intentions were, at that very time, to promote peace and concord between us, and that we might look upon each other as friends, having given you no cause or provocation to be otherwise.

Brothers: Notwithstanding the mischief that has happened, we are still sincere in our wishes to have peace and tranquility established between us, earnestly hoping to find the same inclination in you. We wish, therefore, you would take it into serious consideration, and let us speak to you in the manner we proposed. Let us have a treaty with you early in the spring; let us pursue reasonable steps; let us meet half ways, for our mutual convenience; we shall then bring [bury] in oblivion the misfortunes that have happened, and meet each other on a footing of friendship.

Brothers: We say let us meet half way, and let us pursue such steps as become upright and honest men. We beg that you will prevent your surveyors and other people from coming upon our side of the Ohio river. We have told you before, we wished to pursue just steps, and we are determined they shall appear just and reasonable in the eyes of the world. This is the determination of all the chiefs of our confederacy now assembled here, notwithstanding the accidents that have happened in our villages, even when in council, where several innocent chiefs were killed when absolutely engaged in promoting a peace with you, the thirteen United States.

Although then interrupted, the chiefs here present still wish to meet you in the spring, for the beforementioned good purpose, when we hope to speak to each other without either haughtiness or menaces.

Brothers: We again request of you, in the most earnest manner, to order your surveyors and others, that mark out lands, to cease from crossing the Ohio, until we shall have spoken to you, because the mischief that has recently happened has originated in that quarter; we shall likewise prevent our people from going over until that time.

Brothers: It shall not be our faults if the plans which we have suggested to you should not be carried into execution; in that case the event will be very precarious, and if fresh ruptures ensue, we hope to be able to exculpate ourselves, and shall most assuredly, with our united force, be obliged to defend those rights and privileges which have been transmitted to us by our ancestors; and if we should be thereby reduced to misfortunes, the world will pity us when they think of the amicable proposals we now make to prevent the unnecessary effusion of blood. These are our thoughts and firm resolves, and we earnestly desire that you will transmit to us, as soon as possible, your answer, be it what it may.

Done at our Confederated Council Fire, at the Huron village, near the mouth of the Detroit river, December 18th, 1786.
The Five Nations,
Hurons, Ottawas, Twichtwees, Shawanese,
Chippewas, Cherokees, Delawares,
Powtewatimies, The Wabash Confederates

Source: American State Papers, Class II: Indian Affairs. Washington DC: U.S. Government Printing Office, 1832, 8–9.

Saukamappee, Memories of War and Smallpox
(1787–1788)

Most scholars agree that within approximately 100 years of the first contact with Europeans, 90 to 95 percent of the indigenous population of North America had perished due to violence and disease. Smallpox had a horrific effect on

American Indians because they had no natural immunity to it. In the following narrative, Saukamappee, a Cree living among the Blackfeet, told fur trader David Thompson about how the Blackfeet first encountered horses, about how he used firearms in battle, and about the horrors of smallpox.

The Peeagans [Piegans] were always the frontier Tribe, and upon whom the Snake Indians made their attacks, these latter were very numerous, even without their allies; and the Peegans had to send messengers among us to procure help. Two of them came to the camp of my father, and I was then about his age (pointing to a Lad of about sixteen years) he promised to come and bring some of his people, the Nahathaways with him, for I am myself of that people, and not of those with whom I am. My father brought about twenty warriors with him. There were a few guns amongst us, but very little ammunition, and they were left to hunt for the families; Our weapons was a Lance, mostly pointed with iron, some few of stone, A Bow and a quiver of Arrows; the Bows were of Larch, the length came to the chin; the quiver had about fifty arrows, of which ten had iron points, the others were headed with stone. He carried his knife on his breast and his axe in his belt.

Such was my father's weapons, and those with him had much the same weapons. I had a Bow and Arrows and a knife, of which I was very proud. We came to the Peeagans and their allies. They were camped in the Plains on the left bank of the River (the north side) and were a great many. We were feasted, a great War Tent was made, and a few days passed in speeches, feasting, and dances. A war chief was elected by the chiefs, and we got ready to march. Our spies had been out and had seen a large camp of the Snake Indians on the Plains of the Eagle Hill, and we had to cross the River in canoes, and on rafts, which we carefully secured for our retreat. When we had crossed and numbered our men, we were about 350 warriors (this he showed by counting every finger to be ten, and holding up both hands three times and then one hand) they had their scouts out, and came to meet us. Both parties made a great show of their numbers, and I thought that they were more numerous than ourselves.

After some singing and dancing, they sat down on the ground, and placed their large shields before them, which covered them: We did the same, but our shields were not so many, and some of our shields had to shelter two men. Theirs were all placed touching each other; their Bows were not so long as ours, but of better wood, and the back covered with the sinews of the Bisons which made them very elastic, and their arrows went a long way and whizzed about us as balls do from guns. They were all headed with a sharp, smooth, black stone (flint) which broke when it struck anything. Our iron headed arrows did not go through their shields, but stuck in them; On both sides several were wounded, but none lay on the ground; and night put an end to the battle, without a scalp being taken on either side, and in those days such was the result, unless one party was more numerous than the other. The great mischief of war then, was as now, by attacking and destroying small camps of ten to thirty tents, which are obliged to separate for hunting: I grew to be a man, became a skilful and fortunate hunter, and my relations procured me a Wife. She was young and handsome and we were fond of each other. We had passed a winter together, when Messengers came from our allies to claim assistance.

By this time the affairs of both parties had much changed; we had more guns and iron headed arrows than before; but our enemies the Snake Indians and their allies had Misstutim (Big Dogs, that is Horses) on which they rode, swift as the Deer, on which they dashed at the Peeagans, and with their stone Pukamoggan knocked them on the head, and they had thus lost several of their best men. This news we did not well comprehend and it alarmed us, for we had no idea of Horses and could not make out what they were. Only three of us went and I should not have gone, had not my wife's relations frequently intimated, that her father's medicine bag would be honored by the scalp of a Snake Indian. When we came to our allies, the great War Tent [was made] with speeches, feasting, and dances as before; and when the War Chief had viewed us all it was found between us and the Stone Indians we had ten guns and each of us about thirty balls, and powder for the war, and we were considered the strength of the battle. After a few days march our scouts brought us word that the enemy was near in a large war party, but had no Horses with them, for at that time they had very few of them. When we came to meet each other, as usual, each displayed their numbers, weapons and shields in all which they were superior to us, except our guns which were not shown, but kept in their leather cases, and if we had shown [them], they would have taken them for long clubs. For a long time they held us in suspense; a tall Chief was forming a strong party to make an attack on our centre, and the others to enter into combat with those opposite to them; We prepared for the battle the best we could. Those of us who had guns stood in the front line, and each of us [had] two balls in his mouth, and a load of powder in his left hand to reload.

We noticed they had a great many short stone clubs for close combat, which is a dangerous weapon, and had they made a bold attack on us, we must have been defeated as they were more numerous and better armed than we were, for we could have fired our guns no more than twice; and were at a loss what to do on the wide plain, and each Chief encouraged his men to stand firm. Our eyes were all on the tall Chief and his motions, which appeared to be contrary to the advice of several old Chiefs, all this time we were about the strong flight of an arrow from each other. At length the tall chief retired and they formed their long usual line by placing their shields on the ground to touch each other, the shield having a breadth of full three feet or more. We sat down opposite to them and most of us waited for the night to make a hasty retreat. The War Chief was close to us, anxious to see the effect of our guns. The lines were too far asunder for us to make a sure shot, and we requested him to close the line to about sixty yards, which was gradually done, and lying flat on the ground behind the shields, we watched our opportunity when they drew their bows to shoot at us, their bodies were then exposed and each of us, as opportunity offered, fired with deadly aim, and either killed, or severely wounded, every one we aimed at.

The War Chief was highly pleased, and the Snake Indians finding so many killed and wounded kept themselves behind their shields; the War Chief then desired we would spread ourselves by twos throughout the line, which we did, and our shots caused consternation and dismay along their whole line. The battle had begun about Noon, and the Sun was not yet half down, when we perceived some of them had crawled away from their shields, and were taking to flight. The War Chief seeing this went along the line and spoke to every Chief to keep his Men ready for a charge of the whole line of the enemy, of which he would give the signal; this was done by himself stepping in front with his Spear, and calling on them to follow him as he rushed on their line, and in an instant the whole of us followed him, the greater part of the enemy took to flight, but some fought bravely and we lost more than ten killed and many wounded; Part of us pursued, and killed a few, but the chase had soon to be given over, for at the body of every Snake Indian killed, there were five or six of us trying to get his scalp, or part of his clothing, his weapons, or something as a trophy of the battle. As there were only three of us, and seven of our friends, the Stone Indians, we did not interfere, and got nothing. . . .

The terror of that battle and of our guns has prevented any more general battles, and our wars have since been carried by ambuscade and surprise, of small camps, in which we have greatly the advantage, from the Guns, arrow shods of iron, long knives, flat bayonets, and axes from the Traders. While we have these weapons, the Snake Indians have none, but what few they sometimes take from one of our small camps which they have destroyed, and they have no Traders among them. We thus continued to advance through the fine plains to the Stag River when death came over us all, and swept away more than half of us by the Small pox, of which we knew nothing until it brought death among us. We caught it from the Snake Indians. Our Scouts were out for our security, when some returned and informed us of a considerable camp which was too large to attack and something very suspicious about it; from a high knowl they had a good view of the camp, but saw none of the men hunting, or going about; there were a few Horses, but no one came to them, and a herd of Bison [were] feeding close to the camp with other herds near. This somewhat alarmed us as a stratagem of War; and our Warriors thought this camp had a larger not far off; so that if this camp was attacked which was strong enough to offer a desperate resistance, the other would come to their assistance and overpower us as had been once done by them, and in which we lost many of our men.

The council ordered the Scouts to return and go beyond this camp, and be sure there was no other. In the mean time we advanced our camp; The scouts returned and said no other tents were near, and the camp appeared as in the same state as before. Our Scouts had been going too much about their camp and were seen; they expected what would follow, and all those that could walk, as soon as night came on, went away. Next morning at the dawn of day, we attacked the Tents, and with our sharp flat daggers and knives, cut through the tents and entered for the fight; but our war whoop instantly stopped, our eyes were appalled with terror; there was no one to fight with but the dead and dying, each a mass of corruption. We did not touch them, but left the tents, and held a council on what was to be done. We all thought the Bad Spirit had made himself master of the camp and destroyed them. It was agreed to take some of the best of the tents, and any plunder that was clean and good,

which we did, and also took away the few Horses they had, and returned to our camp.

The second day after this dreadful disease broke out in our camp, and spread from one tent to another as if the Bad Spirit carried it. We had no belief that one Man could give it to another, any more than a wounded Man could give his wound to another. We did not suffer so much as those that were near the river, into which they rushed and died. We had only a little brook, and about one third of us died, but in some of the other camps there were tents in which every one died. When at length it left us, and we moved about to find our people, it was no longer with the song and the dance; but with tears, shrieks, and the howlings of despair for those that would never return to us. War was no longer thought of, and we had enough to do to hunt and make provisions for our families, for in our sickness we had consumed all of our dried provisions; but the Bisons and the Red Deer were also gone, we did not see one half of what was before, whither they had gone we could not tell, we believe the Good Spirit had forsaken us, and allowed the Bad Spirit to become our Master. What little we could spare we offered to the Bad Spirit to let us alone and go to our enemies. The Good Spirit we offered feathers, branches of trees, and sweet smelling grass. Our hearts were low and dejected, and we shall never again be the same people.

Source: Glover, Richard, ed. *David Thompson's Narrative, 1784–1812.* Toronto: Champlain Society, 1962, 240–247. Reprinted with permission.

Cornplanter, Half Town, and Big Tree Remind President George Washington of the Iroquois's Role in the American Revolution

(1790)

Both the Americans and the British sought American Indian assistance during the American Revolution. As the war went on, more and more

Indians joined the British because they saw the Americans as land-hungry usurpers. In addition, at one point during the conflict, George

Washington felt compelled to declare total war against the Iroquois of New York and ordered his men to indiscriminately murder the Iroquois and burn their homes and crops. However, some Iroquois, particularly the Seneca, aligned themselves more with the Americans. In this speech, three of those Indians remind President Washington of their role in the American Revolution and implore the president to respect Indian land rights.

Father, the voice of the Seneca Nations speaks to you, the great counselor, in whose heart the wise men of all the Thirteen Fires have placed in their wisdom; it may be very small in your ears, and we therefore entreat you to hearken with attention, for we are about to speak of things which are to us very great.

When your army entered the country of the Six Nations, we called you the town-destroyer; and to this day, when your name is heard, our women look behind them and turn pale, and our children cling close to the necks of their mothers. Our counselors and warriors are men, and cannot be afraid; but their hearts are grieved with the fears of our women and children, and desire that it may be buried so deep as to be heard no more.

When you gave us peace we called you father, because you promised to secure us in the possession of our lands. Do this, and so long as the land shall remain, that beloved name shall be in the heart of every Seneca.

Father, we mean to open our hearts before you, and we earnestly desire that you will let us clearly understand what you resolve to do.

When our chiefs returned from the treaty at Fort Stanwix, and laid before our council what had been done there, our nation was surprised to hear how great a country you had compelled them to give up to you, without your paying to us anything for it. Everyone said that your hearts were yet swelled with resentment against us for what had happened during the war, but that one day you would consider it with more kindness. We asked each other, what have we done to deserve such severe chastisement?

Father, when you kindled your Thirteen Fires separately, the wise men assembled at them told us that you were all brothers, the children of one great father, who regarded the red people as his children. They called us brothers, and invited us to his protection. They told us that he resided beyond the great water where the sun first rises; that he was a king whose power no people could resist, and that his goodness was as bright as the sun: what they said went to our hearts. We accepted the invitation, and promised to obey him. What the Seneca Nation promises they faithfully perform; and when you refused obedience to that king, he commanded us to assist his beloved men in making you sober. In obeying him, we did no more than yourselves had led us to promise. The men who claimed this promise told us that you were children and had no guns; that when they had shaken you, you would submit. We hearkened unto them, and were deceived until your army approached our towns. We were deceived, but your people teaching us to confide in that king had helped to deceive us, and we now appeal to your heart, is all the blame ours?

Father, when we saw that we had been deceived, and heard the invitation which you gave us to draw near to the fire you had kindled and talk with you concerning peace, we made haste toward it. You then told us you could crush us to nothing, and you demanded from us a great country at the price of that peace which you had offered to us; as if our want of strength had destroyed our rights. Our chiefs had felt your power and were unable to contend rights against you, and they therefore gave up that country. What they agreed to has bound our nation; but your anger against us must by this time be cooled, and although our strength is not increased, nor your power become less, we ask you to consider calmly: Were the terms dictated to us by your commissioners reasonable and just?

Father, your commissioners, when they drew the line which separated the land then given up to you from that which you agreed should remain to be ours, did most solemnly promise that we should be secured in the peaceable possession of the land which we inhabited, east and north of that line.— Does that promise bind you?

Hear now, we entreat you, what has since happened concerning that land. On the day we finished the treaty of Fort Stanwix, commissioners from Pennsylvania told our chiefs that they had come there to purchase within lines of their state; and they told us that all the lands belonging to us within the line would strike the river Susquehanna below Tioga branch. They then left us to consider of the bargain until next day. The next day we let them know that we were unwilling to sell all the land within their state, and proposed to let them have a part of it, which we pointed out to them in their map. They told us that they must have the whole, that it was already ceded to them by the great king at the time of making peace with you, and was then their own; but they said that they would not take advantage of that, and were willing to pay us for it, after the manner of their ancestors. Our chiefs were unable to contend at that time, and therefore they sold the lands up to the line, which was then shown them as the line of that state. What the commissioners had said about the land having been ceded to them at the peace, they considered as intended only to lessen the price, and they passed it by with very little notice; but since that time we have heard so much from others about the right to our lands which the king gave when you made peace with him, that it is our earnest desire that you will tell us what it means.

Our nation empowered J.L. to let out a part of our lands; he told us that he was sent by Congress to do this for us, and we fear he has deceived us in the writing he obtained from us; for since the time of our giving that power, a man named P has come and claimed our whole country northward of the line of Pennsylvania, under a purchase from that J.L. to whom he said he had paid twenty thousand dollars for it; he also said, that he had bought it from the council of the Thirteen Fires, and paid them twenty thousand more for the same; and he also said that it did not belong to us, for that the great king had ceded the whole of it, when you made peace with him. Thus he claimed the whole country north of Pennsylvania, and west of the lands belonging to the Cayugas. He demanded it;

he insisted on his demand, and declared to us that he would have it all. It was impossible for us to grant him this, and we immediately refused it. After some days he proposed to run a line a small distance eastward of our western boundary, which we also refused to agree to. He then threatened us with immediate war if we did not comply.

Upon this threat our chiefs held a council, and they agreed that no event of war could be worse than to be driven, with our wives and children, from the only country which we had any right to; and therefore, weak as our nation was, they determined to take the chance of war rather than submit to such unjust demands, which seemed to have no bounds. Mr. Street, the great trader at Niagara, was then with us, having come at the request of P; and as he had always professed to be our great friend, we consulted him on this subject. He also told us that our lands had been ceded by the king, and that we must give them up. Astonished at what we heard from every quarter, with hearts aching with compassion for our women and children, we were thus compelled to give up all our country north of the line of Pennsylvania, and east of the Chenesee river up to the great forks, and east of a south-line drawn from that fork to the line of Pennsylvania. For this land P agreed to pay us ten thousand dollars in hand, and one thousand dollars a year for ever. He paid us two thousand five hundred dollars, and he sent for us to come last spring and receive our money; but instead of paying us the residue (or remainder) of the ten thousand dollars, and the one thousand dollars due for the first year, he offered only five hundred dollars, and insisted that he had agreed with us for that sum to be paid yearly.

We debated with him for six days, during all which time he persisted in refusing to pay us for our just demand; and he insisted that we should receive the five hundred dollars; and Street from Niagara also insisted on our receiving the money as it was offered us. The last reason which he assigned for continuing to refuse paying us was—that the king had ceded the land to the Thirteen Fires, and that he had bought them from you and paid you for them.

Father, we could bear this confusion no longer and determined to press through every difficulty, and lift up our voice so that you might hear us, and to claim that security in the possession of our lands, which your commissioners so solemnly promised us; and we now entreat you to inquire into our complaints, and to redress our wrongs.

Father, our writings were lodged in the hands of Street of Niagara, as we supposed him to be our friend; but when we saw P consulting Street on every occasion, we doubted of his honesty towards us; and we have since heard that he was to receive for his endeavours to deceive us a piece of land ten miles in width west of the Chenesee river; and near forty miles in length extending to Lake Ontario; and the lines of this tract have been run accordingly, although no part of it is within the bounds which limit this purchase.

Father, you have said that we were in your hand, and that by closing it you could crush us to nothing. Are you then determined to crush us? If you are, tell us so, that those of our nation who have become your children, and have determined to die so, may know what to do. In this case one chief has said he would ask you to put him out of his pain. Another, who will not think of dying by the hand of his father, or of his brother, has said he will retire to the Chataughque, eat of the fatal root, and sleep with his fathers in peace.

Before you determine a measure so unjust, look up to God, who made us as well as you; we hope he will not permit you to destroy the whole of our nation.

Father, hear our case: Many nations inhabited this country, but they had no wisdom, therefore they warred together; the Six Nations were powerful and compelled them to peace. The land for a great extent was given up to them, but the nations which were not destroyed all continued on those lands: and claimed the protection of the Six Nations, as brothers of their fathers. They were men, and when at peace had a right to live upon the earth.

The French came among us, and built Niagara; they became our fathers, and took care of us. Sir William Johnson came, and took that fort from the French; he became our father, and promised to take care of us, and he did not until you were too strong for his king. To him we gave four miles round Niagara, as a place of trade. We have already said how we came to join against you; we saw that we were wrong, we wished for peace, you demanded a great country to be given up to you, it was surrendered to you as the price of peace, and we ought to have peace and possession of the little land which you then left us.

Father, when that great country was given up to you there were but few chiefs present, and they were compelled to give it up. And it is not the Six Nations only that reproach those chiefs with having given up that country. The Chippewas, and all the nations who lived on these lands westward, call to us, and ask us, "Brothers of our fathers, where is the place which you have reserved for us to lie down upon?"

Father, you have compelled us to do that which makes us ashamed. We have nothing to answer to the children of the brothers of our fathers. When last spring they called upon us to go to war to secure them a bed to lie down upon, the Senecas entreated them to be quiet until we had spoken to you; but on our way down, we heard that your army had gone towards the country which those nations inhabited; and if they meet together, the best blood on both sides will stain the ground.

Father, we will not conceal from you that the great God, and not men, has preserved Cornplanter from the hands of his own nation. For they ask continually, "Where is the land on which our children, and their children after them, are to lie down upon? You told us," say they, "that the line drawn from Pennsylvania to Lake Ontario would mark it forever on the east, and the line running from Beaver Creek to Pennsylvania would mark it on the west, and we see that it is not so; for first one, and then another, come and take it away by order of that people which you tell us promised to secure it to us." He is silent, for he has nothing to answer. When the sun goes down he opens his heart before God; and earlier than the sun appears again upon the hills he gives thanks for his protection during the night; for he feels that among men, become desperate by the injuries they sustain, it is God only that can preserve him. He loves peace, and all he had in store he has given to those who have been robbed by your people, lest they should plunder the innocent to repay themselves. The whole season, which others have employed in providing for their families, he has spent in endeavours to preserve peace; and this moment his wife and children are lying on the ground, and in want of food: his heart is in pain for them, but he perceives that the Great Spirit will try his firmness in doing what is right.

Father, the game which the Great Spirit sent into our country for us to eat is going from among us. We thought he intended we should till the ground with the plough as the white people do, and we talked to one another about it. But before we speak to you concerning this, we must know from you whether you mean to leave us and our children any land to till. Speak plainly to us concerning this great business.

All the land we have been speaking of belonged to the Six Nations: no part of it ever belonged to the King of England, and he could not give it up to you. The land we live on our fathers received from God, and they transmitted it to us for our children, and we cannot part with it.

Father, we told you that we would open our hearts to you: hear us once more. At Fort Stanwix we agreed to deliver up those of our people who should do you any wrong, and that you might try them accordingly; but instead of trying them according to your law, the lowest of your people took them from your magistrate, and put them immediately to death. It is just to punish the murderer with death, but the Senecas will not deliver up their people to men who disregard the treaties of their own nation.

Father, innocent men of our nation are killed, one after another, and of our best families; but none of your people who have committed those murders have been punished. We recollect that you did promise to punish those who killed our people; and we ask, was it intended that your people should kill the Senecas, and not only remain unpunished, but be protected from the next of kin?

Father, these are to us very great things; we know that you are very strong, and we have heard that you are wise, and we shall wait to hear your answer that we may know that you are just.

Source: Buchanan, James. *Sketches of the History, Manners, and Customs of the North American Indians with a Plan for Their Amelioration.* New York: William Borradaile, 1824, 108–116.

Red Jacket, "You Have Got Our Country, But Are Not Satisfied; You Want to Force Your Religion upon Us"

(1805)

Red Jacket was a Seneca, and chief of the Wolf clan. He was born around 1750 and lived in New York until his death in 1830. In this document, he shrewdly compares Christianity with traditional Seneca beliefs. In particular, he questions the Bible, and the fact that missionaries always tell Indians that the Christian way of worshiping is the only proper way. Red Jacket then wonders why, if that is the case—one true way of worshipping—are there so many differences among Christians? Here again, Indians prove their agency and ability to dictate at least some aspects of their lives with white Americans.

Friend and Brother: It was the will of the Great Spirit that we should meet together this day. He orders all things, and has given us a fine day for our council. He has taken his garment from before the sun and caused it to shine with brightness upon us. For all these things we thank the Great Ruler, and Him *only*.

Brother, this council-fire was kindled by you. It was at your request that we came together at this time. We have listened with joy to what you have said. You requested us to speak our minds freely. This gives us great joy, for we now consider that we stand upright before you and can speak what we think. All have heard your voice and can speak to you as one man. Our minds are agreed.

Brothers, listen to what we say. There was a time when our forefathers owned this great island. Their seats extended from the rising to the setting sun. The Great Spirit had made it for the use of the Indians. He had created the buffalo, the deer and other animals for food. He had made the bear and the beaver. Their skins served us for clothing. He had scattered them over the country and taught us how to take them. He had caused the earth to produce corn for bread. All this he had done for his red children because he loved them. If we had some disputes about our hunting-ground, they were generally settled without the shedding of much blood. But an evil day came upon us. Your forefathers crossed the great water and landed upon this island. Their numbers were small. They found us friends and not enemies. They told us they had fled from their own country on account of wicked men, and had come here to enjoy their religion. They asked for a small seat. We took pity on them and granted their request, and they sat down amongst us. We gave them corn and meat; they gave us poison [rum] in return.

The white people, brother, had now found our country. Tidings were carried back, and more came amongst us. Yet we did not fear them. We took them to be friends. They called us brothers; we believed them, and gave them a larger seat. At length their numbers had greatly increased. They wanted more land; they wanted our country. Our eyes were opened, and our minds became uneasy. Wars took place. Indians were hired to fight against Indians, and many of our people were destroyed. They also brought strong liquor amongst us. It was strong and powerful and has slain thousands.

Brother, our seats were once large, and yours were small. You have now become a great people, and we have scarcely a place left to spread our blankets. You have got our country, but are not satisfied; you want to force your religion upon us.

Brother, continue to listen. You say that you are sent to instruct us how to worship the Great Spirit agreeable to his mind; and if we do not take hold of the religion which you white people teach, we shall be unhappy hereafter. You say that you are right, and we are lost. How do we know this to be true? We understand that your religion is written in a book. If it was intended for us as well as you, why has not the Great Spirit given to us—and not only to us, but to our forefathers—the knowledge of that book, with the means of understanding it rightly? We only know what you tell us about it. How shall we know when to believe, being so often deceived by the white people?

Brother, you say there is but one way to worship and serve the Great Spirit. If there is but one religion, why do you white people differ so much about it? Why not all agree, as you can all read the book?

Brother, we do not understand these things. We are told that your religion was given to your forefathers, and has been handed down from father to son. We, also, have a religion which was given to our forefathers, and has been handed down to us, their children. We worship in that way. It teaches us to be thankful for all the favors we receive; to love each other, and be united. We never quarrel about religion, because it is a matter which concerns each man and the Great Spirit.

Brother, we do not wish to destroy your religion or take it away from you; we only want to enjoy our own.

Brother, we have been told that you have been preaching to the white people in this place. These people are our neighbors. We are acquainted with them. We will wait a little while and see what effect your preaching has upon them. If we find it does them good, makes them honest and less disposed to cheat Indians, we will consider again of what you have said.

Brother, you have now heard our talk, and this is all we have to say at present. As we are going to part, we will come and take you by the hand, and hope the Great Spirit will protect you on your journey, and return you safely to your friends.

Source: Wood, Norman B. *Lives of Famous Indian Chiefs.* Aurora, IL: American Indian Historical Publishing Co., 1906, 254–256.

Tenkswatawa, the Shawnee Prophet, Speech to Indiana Territory Governor William Henry Harrison

(1808)

Tecumseh's brother was born around 1770 and given the name Lalawethika. Once he had his religious vision in 1805, he changed his name to Tenkswatawa, meaning "Open Door." Like Neolin before him, the Shawnee prophet's religion preached a return to traditional practices with less reliance on whites. William Henry Harrison, future president of the United States, was governor of the Indiana Territory while Tecumseh and his brother lived at Prophetstown. Harrison considered them both major threats. In the speech that follows, the Shawnee Prophet tries to placate Harrison's fears by speaking a message of peace and mutual trust. His message eventually fell upon deaf ears; Harrison attacked and destroyed Prophetstown during the Battle of Tippecanoe in 1811.

Father, it is three years since I first began that system of religion which I now practice. The white people and some of the Indians were against me; but I had no other intention but to introduce among the Indians those good principles of religion which the white people profess. I was spoken badly of by the white people, who reproached me with misleading the Indians; but I defy them to say I did anything amiss.

Father, I was told that you intended to hang me. When I heard this, I intended to remember it, and tell my father, when I went to see him, and relate the truth.

I heard, when I settled on the Wabash, that my father, the Governor, had declared that all the land between Vincennes and Fort Wayne was the property of the Seventeen Fires. I also heard that you wanted to know, my father, whether I was God or man; and that you said if I was the former, I should not steal horses. I heard this from Mr. Wells, but I believed it originated from himself.

The Great Spirit told me to tell the Indians that he had made them, and made the world—that he had placed them on it to do good and not evil.

I told all the red-skins that the way they were in was not good, and that they ought to abandon it.

That we ought to consider for ourselves as one man; but we ought to live agreeably to our several customs, the red people after their mode, and the white people after theirs; particularly, that they should not drink whiskey; that it was not made for them, but the white people, who alone knew how to use it; and that is the cause of all the mischiefs which the Indians suffer; and that they must always follow the directions of the Great Spirit, and we must listen to him, as it was He that made us;

determine to listen to nothing that is bad; do not take up the tomahawk, should it be offered by the British, or by the Long-Knives; do not meddle with any thing that does not belong to you, but mind your own business, and cultivate the ground, that your women and your children may have enough to live on.

I now inform you that it is our intention to live in peace with our father and his people forever.

My father, I have informed you what we mean to do, and I call the Great Spirit to witness the truth of my declaration. The religion which I have established for the last three years has been attended to by the different tribes of Indians in this part of the world. These Indians were once different people; they are now but one; they are all determined to practice what I have communicated to them that has come immediately from the Great Spirit through me.

Brother, I speak to you as a warrior. You are one. But let us lay aside this character, and attend to the care of our children, that they may live in comfort and peace. We desire that you will join us for the preservation of both red and white people. Formerly, when we lived in ignorance, we were foolish; but now, since we listen to the voice of the Great Spirit, we are happy.

I have listened to what you have said to us. You have promised to assist us. I now request you, on behalf of all the red people, to use your exertions to prevent the sale of liquor to us. We are all well pleased to hear you say that you will endeavor to promote our happiness. We give you every assurance that we will follow the dictates of the Great Spirit.

We are all well pleased with the attention you have showed us; also with the good intentions of our father, the President. If you give us a few articles, such as needles, flints, hoes, powder, etc., we will take the animals that afford us meat, with powder and ball.

Source: Brice, William A. *History of Fort Wayne.* Fort Wayne, IN: D. W. Jones and Son, 1868, 178–179.

Shawnee Chief Tecumseh, Address to William Henry Harrison

(ca. 1810)

In the following document, Shawnee chief Tecumseh confronts William Henry Harrison regarding land cessions brought about by the Treaty of Fort Wayne in 1809. According to Tecumseh, no single tribe had the right to sell land to the Americans because land was equally owned for the use of all Indians. In the speech that follows, Tecumseh demands that Harrison destroy the Treaty of Fort Wayne; he also warns the governor against permitting settlers to inhabit Native lands. Harrison's refusal to meet Tecumseh's demands was a major cause of Tecumseh's War, pushing the Shawnee leader and his pan-Indian confederacy firmly into the British sphere of influence during the War of 1812.

SHAWNEE CHIEF TECUMSEH'S ADDRESS TO WILLIAM HENRY HARRISON

Houses are built for you to hold councils in. The Indians hold theirs in the open air. I am a Shawnee. My forefathers were warriors. Their son is a warrior. From them I take my only existence. From my tribe I take nothing. I have made myself what I am. And I would that I could make the red people as great as the conceptions of my own mind, when I think of the Great Spirit that rules over us all. I would not then come to Governor Harrison to ask him to tear up the treaty [the 1809 Treaty of Fort Wayne].

But I would say to him, "Brother, you have the liberty to return to your own country." You wish to prevent the Indians from doing as we wish them, to unite and let them consider their lands as a common property of the whole. You take the tribes aside and advise them not to come into this measure. You want by your distinctions of Indian tribes, in allotting to each a particular, to make them war with each other. You never see an Indian endeavor to make the white people do this. You are continually driving the red people, when at last you will drive them into the great lake [Lake Michigan], where they can neither stand nor work.

Since my residence at Tippecanoe, we have endeavored to level all distinctions, to destroy village chiefs, by whom all mischiefs are done. It is they who sell the land to the Americans. Brother, this land that was sold, and the goods that was [sic] given for it, was only done by a few. In the future we are prepared to punish those who propose to sell land to the Americans. If you continue to purchase them, it will make war among the different tribes, and, at last I do not know what will be the consequences among the white people.

Brother, I wish you would take pity on the red people and do as I have requested. If you will not give up the land and do cross the boundary of our present settlement, it will be very hard and produce great trouble between us.

The way, the only way to stop this evil, is for the red people to unite in claiming a common and equal right in the land, as it was at first, and should be now—for it was never divided, but belongs to all.

No tribe has the right to sell, even to each other, much less to strangers.

Sell a country?! Why not sell the air, the great sea, as well as the earth? Did not the Great Spirit make them all for the use of his children?

How can we have confidence in the white people? We have good and just reasons to believe we have ample grounds to accuse the Americans of injustice, especially when such great acts of injustice have been committed by them upon our race, of which they seem to have no manner of regard, or even to reflect. When Jesus Christ came upon the earth you killed him and nailed him to the cross. You thought he was dead, and you were mistaken. You have the Shakers among you, and you laugh and make light of their worship. Everything I have told you is the truth. The Great Spirit has inspired me.

Source: Gunn, Giles, ed. *New World Metaphysics: Readings on the Religious Meaning of the American Experience.* Cambridge: Oxford University Press, 1981, 279–280. By permission of Oxford University Press, Inc.

Tecumseh, "Sleep Not Longer, O Choctaws and Chickasaws" (1811)

In the years after the United States won independence from Great Britain, Americans flooded over the Appalachian Mountains and constantly encroached upon Indian lands. Many Indians resisted, including the Shawnee. In the early years of the 19th century, the Shawnee leader Tecumseh attempted to rally Indians across the Ohio Valley and the southeastern portions of the country to making common cause against whites. Although his success varied, his passion and eloquence were undeniable. This speech was given to the Choctaw and

Chickasaw in an attempt to get them to enter into an alliance with other tribes against the Americans.

In view of questions of vast importance, have we met together in solemn council tonight. Nor should we here debate whether we have been wronged and injured, but by what measures we should avenge ourselves; for our merciless oppressors, having long since planned out their proceedings, are not about to make, but have and are still making attacks upon those of our race who have as yet come to no resolution. Nor are we ignorant by what steps, and by what gradual advances, the whites break in upon our neighbors. Imagining themselves to be still undiscovered, they show themselves the less audacious because you are insensible. The whites are already nearly a match for us all united, and too strong for any one tribe alone to resist; so that unless we support one another with our collective and united forces; unless every tribe unanimously combines to give a check to the ambition and avarice of the whites, they will soon conquer us apart and disunited, and we will be driven away from our native country and scattered as autumnal leaves before the wind.

But have we not courage enough remaining to defend our country and maintain our ancient independence? Will we calmly suffer the white intruders and tyrants to enslave us? Shall it be said of our race that we knew not how to extricate ourselves from the three most to be dreaded calamities—folly, inactivity, and cowardice? But what need is there to speak of the past? It speaks for itself and asks, "Where today is the Pequot? Where are the Narragansetts, the Mohawks, Pocanokets, and many other once powerful tribes of our race?" They have vanished before the avarice and oppression of the white men, as snow before a summer sun. In the vain hope of alone defending their ancient possessions, they have fallen in the wars with the white men. Look abroad over their once beautiful country, and what see you now? Naught but the ravages of the pale-face destroyers meet your eyes. So it will be with you Choctaws and Chickasaws! Soon your mighty forest trees, under the shade of whose wide spreading branches you have played in infancy, sported in boyhood, and now rest your wearied limbs after the fatigue of the chase, will be cut down to fence in the land which the white intruders dare to call their own. Soon their broad roads will pass over the graves of your fathers, and the place of their rest will be blotted forever. The annihilation of our race is at hand unless we unite in one common cause against the common foe. Think not, brave Choctaws and Chickasaws, that you can remain passive and indifferent to the common danger, and thus escape the common fate. Your people too will soon be as falling leaves and scattering clouds before their blighting breath. You too will be driven away from your native land and ancient domains as leaves are driven before the wintry storms.

Sleep not longer, O Choctaws and Chickasaws, in false security and delusive hopes. Our broad domains are fast escaping from our grasp. Every year our white intruders become more greedy, exacting oppressive and overbearing. Every year contentions spring up between them and our people and when blood is shed we have to make atonement whether right or wrong, at the cost of the lives of our greatest chiefs, and the yielding up of large tracts of our lands. Before the pale-faces come among us, we enjoyed the happiness of unbounded freedom, and were acquainted with neither riches, wants, nor oppression. How is it now? Wants and oppressions are our lot; for are we not controlled in everything, and dare we move without asking, by your leave? Are we not being stripped day by day of the little that remains of our ancient liberty? Do they not even now kick and strike us as they do their black-faces? How long will it be before they will tie us to a post and whip us, and make us work for them in their corn fields as they do them? Shall we wait for that moment or shall we die fighting before submitting to such ignominy?

Have we not for years had before our eyes a sample of their designs, and are they not sufficient harbingers of their future determinations? Will we not soon be driven from our respective countries and the graves of our ancestors? Will not the bones of our dead be plowed up, and their graves be turned into fields? Shall we calmly wait until they become so numerous that we will no longer be able to resist oppression? Will we wait to be destroyed in our turn, without making an effort worthy of our race? Shall we give up our homes, our country, bequeathed to us by the Great Spirit, the graves of our dead, and everything that is dear and sacred to us, without a struggle? I know you will cry with me. Never! Never! Then let us by unity of action destroy them all, which we now can do, or drive them back whence they came. War or extermination is now our only choice. Which do you choose? I know your answer. Therefore, I now call on you, brave Choctaws and Chickasaws, to assist in the just cause of liberating our race from the grasp of our faithless invaders and heartless oppressors. The white usurpation in our common country must be stopped, or we, its rightful owners, be forever destroyed and wiped out as a race of people. I am now at the head of many warriors backed by the strong arm of English soldiers. Choctaws and Chickasaws, you have too long borne with grievous usurpation inflicted by the arrogant Americans. Be no longer their dupes. If there be one here tonight who believes that his rights will not sooner or later be taken from him by the avaricious American pale-faces, his ignorance ought to excite pity, for he knows little of the character of our common foe. And if there be one among you mad enough to undervalue the growing power of the white race among us, let him tremble in considering the fearful woes he will bring down upon our entire race, if by his criminal indifference he assists the designs of our common enemy against our common country. Then listen to the voice of duty, of honor, of nature and your endangered country. Let us form one body, one heart, and defend to the last warrior our country, our homes, our liberty, and the graves of our fathers.

Choctaws and Chickasaws, you are among the few of our race who sit indolently at ease. You have indeed enjoyed the reputation of being brave, but will you be indebted for it more from report than fact? Will you let the whites encroach upon your domains even to your very door before you will assert your rights in resistance? Let no one in this council imagine that I speak more from malice against the pale-face Americans than just grounds of complaint. Complaint is just toward friends who have failed in their duty; accusation is against enemies guilty of injustice. And surely, if any people ever had, we have good and just reasons to believe we have ample grounds to accuse the Americans of injustice; especially when such great acts of injustice have been committed by them upon our race, of which they seem to have no manner of regard, or even to reflect. They are a people fond of innovations, quick to contrive and quick to put their schemes into effectual execution, no matter how great the wrong and injury to us; while we are content to preserve what we already have. Their design [is] to enlarge their possessions by taking yours in turn; and will you, can you longer dally, O Choctaws and Chickasaws? Do you imagine that people will not continue longest in the enjoyment of peace who timely prepare to vindicate themselves, and manifest a determined resolution to do themselves right whenever they are wronged? Far otherwise. Then haste to the relief of our common cause, as by consanguinity of blood you are bound; lest the day be not far distant when you will be left single-handed and alone to the cruel mercy of our most inveterate foe.

Source: Cushman, H. B. *History of the Choctaw, Chickasaw and Natchez Indians.* Greenville, TX: Headlight Printing House, 1899.

Tecumseh, "Let the White Race Perish"
(1811)

Shawnee leader Tecumseh may not have originally felt militant toward white Americans. However, as the following speech shows, events eventually nudged him closer to open warfare with whites. In addition, he appears to have had little patience for those who chose to question or ignore his point of view. Tecumseh delivered this speech to the Muscogee in the southeastern United States in 1811.

In defiance of the white men of Ohio and Kentucky, I have traveled through their settlements—once our favorite hunting grounds. No war-whoop was sounded, but there is blood upon our knives. The pale-faces felt the blow, but knew not from whence it came. Accursed be the race that has seized on our country, and made women of our warriors. Our fathers, from their tombs, reproach us as slaves and cowards. I hear them now in the wailing winds. The Muscogee were once a mighty people. The Georgians trembled at our war-whoop; and the maidens of my tribe, in the distant lakes, sung the prowess of your warriors, and sighed for their embraces. Now, your very blood is white, your tomahawks have no edges, your bows and arrows were buried with your fathers. My Muscogees, brethren of my mother! Brush from your eyelids the sleep of slavery; once more strike for vengeance—once more for your country. The spirits of the mighty dead complain. The tears drop from the skies. Let the white race perish! They seize your land, they corrupt your women, they trample on your dead! Back! Whence they came, upon a trail of blood, they must be driven! Back! Back—ay, into the great water whose accursed waves brought them to our shores! Burn their dwellings! Destroy their stock! Slay their wives and children! The red man owns the country, and the pale-face must never enjoy it! War now! War forever! War upon the living! War upon the dead! Dig their very corpses from the graves! Our country must give no rest to a white man's bones. All the tribes of the North are dancing the war-dance. Two mighty warriors across the seas will send us arms.

Tecumseh will soon return to his country. My prophets shall tarry with you. They will stand between you and your enemies. When the white man approaches you the earth shall swallow him up. Soon shall you see my arm of fire stretched athwart the sky. I will stamp my foot at Tippecanoe, and the very earth shall shake.

Source: Brice, Wallace A. *History of Fort Wayne.* Fort Wayne, IN: D. W. Jones and Son, 1868, 193–194.

Pushmatah, "We Do Not Take Up the Warpath without a Just Cause and Honest Purpose"
(1811)

The following speech, delivered by the Choctaw leader Pushmatah in 1811, offers a different perspective from Tecumseh's speech to the Osages (see the next entry). Pushmatah's strategic response to Tecumseh's plea for an Indian alliance stems from the fact that the Choctaw experience with European Americans differed greatly from that of the Shawnees and their allies.

White Americans, Pushmatah argues, are their neighbors, who play a fundamental role within the Choctaw economy by purchasing skins, corn, and other Choctaw products. Additionally, the Choctaw benefited in other ways from their relationship with Americans, a fact that led Pushmatah and other members of his tribe to reject Tecumseh's plea.

Attention, my good red warriors! Hear ye my brief remarks.

The great Shawnee orator has portrayed in vivid picture the wrongs inflicted on his and other tribes by the ravages of the paleface. The candor and fervor of his eloquent appeal breathe the conviction of truth and sincerity, and, as kindred tribes, naturally we sympathize with the misfortunes of his people. I do not come before you in any disputation either for or against these charges. It is not my purpose to contradict any of these allegations against the white man, but neither am I here to indulge in any indiscreet denunciation of him which might bring down on my people unnecessary difficulty and embarrassment.

The distinguished Shawnee sums up his eloquent appeal to us with this direct question:

"Will you sit idly by, supinely awaiting complete and abject submission, or will you die fighting beside your brethren, the Shawnees, rather than submit to such ignominy?"

These are plain words and it is well they have been spoken, for they bring the issue squarely before us. Mistake not, this language means war. And war with whom, pray? War with some band of marauders who have committed there depredations against the Shawnees? War with some alien host seeking the destruction of the Choctaws and the Chickasaws? Nay, my fellow tribesmen. None of these are the enemy we will be called on to meet. If we take up arms against the Americans we must of necessity meet in deadly combat our daily neighbors and associates in this part of the country near our homes.

If Tecumseh's words be true, and we doubt them not, then the Shawnee's experience with the whites has not been the same as that of the Choctaws. These white Americans buy our skins, our corn, our cotton, our surplus game, our baskets and other wares, and they give us in fair exchange their cloth, their guns, their tools, implements, and other things which the Choctaws need but do not make. It is true we have befriended them, but who will deny that these acts of friendship have been abundantly reciprocated? They have given us cotton gins, which simplify the spinning and sale of our cotton; they have encouraged and helped us in the production of our crops; they have taken many of our wives into their homes to teach them useful things, and pay them for their work while learning; they teach our children to read and write from their books. You all remember the dreadful epidemic visited upon us last winter. During its darkest hours these neighbors whom we are now urged to attack responded generously to our needs. They doctored our sick; they clothed our suffering; they fed our hungry; and where is the Choctaw or Chickasaw delegation who has ever gone to St. Stephens with a worthy cause and been sent away empty handed? So, in marked contrast with the experiences of the Shawnees, it will be seen that the whites and Indians in this section are living on friendly and mutually beneficial terms.

Forget not, O Choctaws and Chickasaws, that we are bound in peace to the Great White Father at Washington by a sacred treaty and the Great Spirit will punish those who break their word. The Great White Father has never violated that treaty and the Choctaws have never been driven to the necessity of taking up the tomahawk against him or his children. Therefore the question before us tonight is not the avenging of any wrongs perpetrated against us by the whites, for the Choctaws and the Chickasaws have no such cause, either real or imaginary, but rather it is a question of carrying on that record of fidelity and justice for which our forefathers ever proudly stood, and doing that which is best calculated to promote the welfare of our own people. Yea, my fellow tribesmen, we are a just people. We do not take up the warpath without a just cause and honest purpose. Have we that just cause against our white neighbors, who have taken nothing from us except by fair bargain and exchange? Is this a just recompense for their assistance to us in our agricultural and other pursuits? Is this to be their gracious reward for teaching our children from their books? Shall this be considered the Choctaw's compensation for feeding our hungry, clothing our needy, and administering to our sick? Have we, O Choctaws and Chickasaws, descended to the low estate of ruthlessly breaking the faith of a sacred treaty? Shall our forefathers look back from the happy hunting grounds only to see their unbroken record for justice, gratitude, and fidelity thus rudely repudiated and abruptly abandoned by an unworthy offspring?

We Choctaws and Chickasaws are a peaceful people, making our subsistence by honest toil; but mistake not, my Shawnee brethren, we are not afraid of war. Neither are we strangers to war, as those who have undertaken to encroach upon our rights in the past may abundantly testify. We are thoroughly familiar with war in all its details and we know full well all its horrible consequences. It is unnecessary for me to remind you, O Choctaws and Chickasaws, veteran braves of many fierce conflicts in the past, that war is an awful thing. If we go into this war against the Americans, we must be prepared to accept its inevitable results. Not only will it foretoken deadly conflict with neighbors and death to warriors, but it will mean suffering for our women, hunger and starvation for our children, grief for our loved ones, and devastation of our beloved homes. Notwithstanding these difficulties, if the cause be just, we should not hesitate to defend our rights to the last man, but before that fatal step is irrevocably taken, it is well that we fully understand and seriously consider the full portent and consequences of the act.

Hear me, O Choctaws and Chickasaws, for I speak truly for your welfare. It is not the province of your chiefs to settle these important questions. As a people, it is your prerogative to have either peace or war, and as one of your chiefs, it is mine simply to counsel and advise. Therefore, let me admonish you that this critical period is no time to cast aside your wits and let blind impulse sway; be not driven like dumb brutes by the frenzied harangue of this wonderful Shawnee orator; let your good judgment rule and ponder seriously before breaking bonds that have served you well and ere you change conditions which have brought peace and happiness to your wives, your sisters, and your children. I would not undertake to dictate the course of one single Choctaw warrior. Permit me to speak for the moment, not as your chief, but as a Choctaw warrior, weighing this question beside you. As such I shall exercise my calm, deliberate judgment in behalf of those most dear to me and dependent on me, and I shall not suffer my reason to be swept away by this eloquent recital of alleged wrongs which I know naught of. I deplore this war, I earnestly hope it may be averted, but if it be forced upon us I shall take my stand with those who have stood by my people in the past and will be found fighting beside our good friends of St. Stephens and surrounding country. I have finished. I call on all Choctaws and Chickasaws indorsing my sentiments to rest their tomahawks on this side of the council fire with me.

Source: Indiana Magazine of History (Indiana University) 17, no. 1 (1921): 320–322.

Tecumseh, Speech to the Osages
(Winter 1811–1812)

During the fall and winter of 1811–1812, Tecumseh, a member of the Shawnee Nation, visited many Native American tribes in an attempt to build a pan-Indian confederacy to resist

American encroachment on Indian lands. According to Tecumseh, white encroachment was a common cause that should unite all tribes, regardless of differences or past animosities. In the following speech, Tecumseh pleads with the Osages to join a confederacy to resist the expansion of the United States. Although his plea failed to arouse the Osages, Tecumseh did convince many Indian nations to join his confederacy. Abandoned by his British allies, Tecumseh was killed on October 5, 1813, at the Battle of the Thames during the War of 1812.

Brothers we all belong to one family; we are all children of the Great Spirit; we walk in the same path; slake our thirst at the same spring; and now affairs of the greatest concern lead us to smoke the pipe around the same council fire!

Brothers,—We are friends; we must assist each other to bear our burdens. The blood of many of our fathers and brothers has run like water on the ground, to satisfy the avarice of the white men. We, ourselves, are threatened with a great evil; nothing will pacify them but the destruction of all the red men.

Brothers,—When the white men first set foot on our grounds, they were hungry; they had no place on which to spread their blankets, or to kindle their fires. They were feeble; they could do nothing for themselves. Our father commiserated their distress, and shared freely with them whatever the Great Spirit had given his red children. They gave them food when hungry, medicine when sick, spread skins for them to sleep on, and gave them grounds, that they might hunt and raise corn.

Brothers the white people came among us feeble, and now we have made them strong, they wish to kill us, or drive us back, as they would wolves and panthers.

Brothers,—The white men are not friends to the Indians: at first, they only asked for land sufficient for a wigwam; now, nothing will satisfy them but the whole of our hunting grounds, from the rising to the setting sun.

Brothers,—The white men want more than our hunting grounds; they wish to kill our warriors; they would even kill our old men, women and little ones.

Brothers,—Many winters ago, there was no land; the sun did not rise and set: all was darkness. The Great Spirit made all things. He gave the white people a home beyond the great waters. He supplied these grounds with game, and gave them to his red children; and he gave them strength and courage to defend them.

Brothers,—My people wish for peace; the red men all wish for peace; but where the white people are, there is no peace for them, except it be the bosom of our mother.

Brothers,—The white men despise and cheat the Indians; they abuse and insult them; they do not think the red men sufficiently good to live.

The red men have borne many and great injuries; they ought to suffer them no longer. My people will not; they are determined on vengeance; they will drink the blood of the white people.

Brothers,—My people are brave and numerous; but the white people are too strong for them alone. I wish you to take up the tomahawk with them. If we all unite, we will cause the rivers to stain the great waters with their blood.

Brothers,—if you do not unite with us, they will first destroy us, and then you will be an easy prey to them. They have destroyed many nations of red men because they were not united, because they were not friends to each other.

Brothers,—The white people send runners amongst us; they wish to make us enemies that they may sweep over and desolate our hunting grounds, like devastating winds, or rushing waters.

Brothers,—Our Great Father, over the great waters, is angry with the white people, our enemies. He will send his brave warriors against them; he will send us rifles, and whatever else we want— he is our friend, and we are his children.

Brothers,—Who are the white people that we should fear them? They cannot run fast, and are good marks to shoot at: they are only men; our fathers have killed many of them; we are not squaws, and we will stain the earth red with blood.

Brothers,—The Great Spirit is angry with our enemies; he speaks in thunder, and the earth swallows up villages, and drinks up the Mississippi.

The great waters will cover their lowlands; their corn cannot grow; and the Great Spirit will sweep those who escape to the hills from the earth with his terrible breath.

Brothers,—We must be united; we must smoke the same pipe; we must fight each other's battles; and more than all, we must love the Great Spirit; he is for us; he will destroy our enemies, and make all his red children happy.

Source: Hunter, John D. *Memoirs of a Captivity among the Indians.* London: Longman, Hurst, Rees, Orane, Brown and Green, 1823, 45–48.

Cherokee Women's Petitions
(1817, 1818, and 1831)

While the crisis over removal proceeded, the main voices of American Indian opposition were male. However, Cherokee women protested as well. On three separate occasions they presented themselves before councils comprised entirely of men and made their concerns heard. The three petitions that follow come from 1817, 1818, and 1831. The third petition is labeled here as 1821, as it is on the original. However, the current editor agrees with the editors of the volume in which these petitions were found that the evidence shows that the petition labeled as 1821 almost certainly was written in 1831.

1817 PETITION

The Cherokee ladys now being present at the meeting of the chiefs and warriors in council have thought it their duty as mothers to address their beloved chiefs and warriors now assembled.

Our beloved children and head men of the Cherokee Nation, we address you warriors in council. We have raised all of you on the land which we now have, which God gave us to inhabit and raise provisions. We know that our country has once been extensive, but by repeated sales has become circumscribed to a small track, and never thought it our duty to interfere in the disposition of it till now. If a father or mother was to sell all their lands which they had to depend on, which their children had to raise their living on, which would be indeed bad & to be removed to another country. We do not wish to go to an unknown country which we have understood some of our children wish to go over the Mississippi, but this act of our children would be like destroying your mothers.

Your mothers, your sisters ask and beg of you not to part with any more of our land. We say ours. You are our descendants; take pity on our request. But keep it for our growing children, for it was the good will of our creator to place us here, and you know our father, the great president, will not allow his white children to take our country away. Only keep your hands off of paper talks for its own country. For it was not, they would not ask you to put your hands to paper, for it would be impossible to remove us all. For as soon as one child is raised, we have others in our arms, for such is our situation & will consider our circumstance.

Therefore, children, don't part with any more of our lands but continue on it & enlarge your farms. Cultivate and raise corn & cotton and your mothers and sisters will make clothing for you which our father the president has recommended to us all. We don't charge any body for selling lands, but we have heard such intentions of our children. But your talks become true at last; it was our desire to forwarn you all not to part with our lands.

Nancy Ward to her children: Warriors to take pity and listen to the talks of your sisters. Although I am very old yet cannot but pity the situation in which you will hear of their minds. I have great many grand children which wish them to do well on our land.

1818 PETITION

Beloved Children,

We have called a meeting among ourselves to consult on the different points now before the council, relating to our national affairs. We have heard with painful feelings that the bounds of the land we now possess are to be drawn into very narrow limits. The land was given to us by the Great Spirit above as our common right, to raise our children upon, & to make support for our rising generations. We therefore humbly petition our beloved children, the head men & warriors, to hold out to the last in support of our common rights, as the Cherokee nation have been the first settlers of this land; we therefore claim the right of the soil.

We will remember that our country was formerly very extensive, but by repeated sales it has become circumscribed to the very narrow limits we have at present.

Our Father the President advised us to become farmers, to manufacture our own cloths, & to have our children instructed. To this advice we have attended in every thing as far as we are able. Now the thought of being compelled to remove the other side of the Mississippi is dreadful to us, because it appears to us that we, by this removal, shall be brought to a savage state again, for we have, by the endeavor of our Father the President, become too much enlightened to throw aside the privileges of a civilized life.

We therefore unanimously join in our meeting to hold our country in common as hitherto.

Some of our children have become Christians. We have missionary schools among us. We have heard the gospel in our nation. We have become civilized & enlightened, & are in hopes that in a few years our nation will be prepared for instruction in other branches of sciences & arts, which are both useful & necessary in civilized society.

There are some white men among us who have been raised in this country from their youth, are connected with us by marriage, & have considerable families, who are very active in encouraging the emigration of our nation. These ought to be our truest friends but prove our worst enemies. They seem to be only concerned how to increase their riches, but do not care what becomes of our Nation, nor even of their own wives and children.

1821 [1831?] PETITION

To the Committee and Council,

We the females, residing in Salequoree and Pine Log, believing that the present difficulties and embarrassments under which this nation is placed demands a full expression of the mind of every individual, on the subject of emigrating to Arkansas, would take upon ourselves to address you. Although it is not common for our sex to take part in public measures, we nevertheless feel justified in expressing our sentiments on any subject where our interest is as much at stake as any other part of the community.

We believe the present plan of the General Government to effect our removal West of the Mississippi, and thus obtain our lands for the use of the State of Georgia, to be highly oppressive, cruel and unjust. And we sincerely hope there is no consideration which can induce our citizens to forsake the land of our fathers of which they have been in possession from time immemorial, and thus compel us, against our will, to undergo the toils and difficulties of removing with our helpless families hundreds of miles to unhealthy and unproductive country. We hope therefore the Committee and Council will take into deep consideration our deplorable situation, and do everything in their power to avert such a state of things. And we trust by a prudent course their transactions with the General Government will enlist in our behalf the sympathies of the good people of the United States.

Source: Andrew Jackson Presidential Papers microfilm, series 1, reel 22. Washington, DC, 1961.

Metea, "You Are Never Satisfied," an Address to U.S. Government Officials

(1821)

A council of Potawatomie, Ojibwa, and Ottawa gathered in Chicago in 1821 for a council with the U.S. government. Although these tribes had sold massive amounts of land to the United States previously, the Americans wanted more. These three tribes, along with most others, believed the United States had taken enough land, by force, coercion, or negotiation, from the Indians. In this speech, Chief Metea expresses this fact and hopes the United States can peacefully and honorably respect the wishes of the gathered Indians.

My father, we have listened to what you have said. We shall now retire to our camps and consult upon it. You will hear nothing more from us at present. [When the council was again convened, Metea continued.] We meet you here today, because we had promised it, to tell you our minds, and what we have agreed upon among ourselves. You will listen to us with a good mind, and believe what we say. You know that we first came to this country, a long time ago, and when we sat ourselves down upon it, we met with a great many hardships and difficulties. Our country was then very large; but it has dwindled away to a small spot, and you wish to purchase that! This has caused us to reflect much upon what you have told us; and we have; therefore, brought all the chiefs and warriors, and the young men and women and children of our tribe, that one part may not do what the others object to, and that all may be witness of what is going forward.

You know your children. Since you first came among them, they have listened to your words with an attentive ear, and have always hearkened to your counsels. Whenever you have had a proposal to make to us, whenever you have had a favor to ask of us, we have always lent a favorable ear, and our invariable answer has been "yes." This you know!

A long time has passed since we first came upon our lands, and our old people have all sunk into their graves. They had sense. We are all young and foolish, and do not wish to do anything that they would not approve, were they living. We are fearful we shall offend their spirits if we sell our lands; and we are fearful we shall offend you, if we do *not* sell them. This has caused us great perplexity of thought, because we have counseled among ourselves, and do not know how we can part with the land. Our country was given to us by the Great Spirit, who gave it to us to hunt upon, to make our cornfields upon, to live upon, and to make down our beds upon when we die. And he would never forgive us, should we bargain it away. When you first spoke to us for lands at St. Mary's, we said we had a little, and agreed to sell you a piece of it; but we told you we could spare no more. Now you ask us again. You are never satisfied! We have sold you a great tract of land, already; but it is not enough! We sold it to you for the benefit of your children, to farm and to live upon. We have now but little left. We shall want it all for ourselves. We know not how long we may live, and we wish to have some lands for our children to hunt upon. You are gradually taking away our hunting grounds. Your children are driving us before them. We are growing uneasy. What lands you have, you may retain forever; but we shall sell no more.

You think, perhaps, that I speak in passion; but my heart is good towards you. I speak like one of your own children. I am an Indian, a red-skin, and live by hunting and fishing, but my country is already too small; and I do not know how to bring up my children if I give it all away. We sold you a fine tract of land at St. Mary's. We said to you then it was enough to satisfy your children, and the last we should sell: and we thought it would be the last you would ask for. We have now told you what we had to say. It was what was determined on, in a council among ourselves; and what I have spoken is the voice of my nation. On this account, all our people have come here to listen to me; but do not think we have a bad opinion of you. Where should we get a bad opinion of you? We speak to you with a good heart, and the feelings of a friend.

You are acquainted with this piece of land—the country we live in. Shall we give it up? Take notice, it is a small piece of land, and if we give it away, what will become of us? The Great Spirit, who has provided it for our use, allows us to keep it, to bring up our young men and support our families. We should incur his anger if we bartered it away. If we had more land, you should get more; but our land has been wasting away ever since the white people became our neighbors, and we have now hardly enough left to cover the bones of our tribe.

You are in the midst of your red children. What is due to us in money, we wish, and will receive at this place; and we want nothing more. We all shake hands with you. Behold our warriors, our women, and children. Take pity on us and on our words.

Source: Drake, Samuel G. *Biography and History of the Indians of North America, from Its First Discovery.* Boston: Benjamin B. Mussey & Co., 1851, 635–636.

Sharitarish, Address to President James Monroe
(1822)

By the time James Monroe was elected president in 1816, the Pawnee strongly felt the pressures of white civilization encroaching upon them. In later years, a smallpox epidemic killed nearly half the tribe, which also faced pressure from other Indian nations, including the Lakota. In the following address to President Monroe, Pawnee chief Sharitarish informed the president that, although the Pawnee people were in grave danger, they still tenaciously held on to their traditions and ways of life.

My Great Father.—I have travelled a great distance to see you. I have seen you, and my heart rejoices; I have heard your words; they have entered one ear, and shall not escape the other; and I will carry them to my people as pure, as they came from your mouth.

My Great Father.—I am going to speak the truth. The Great Spirit looks down upon us, and I call Him to witness all that may pass between us on this occasion. If I am here now, and have seen your people, your houses, your vessels on the big lake, and a great many wonderful things, far beyond my comprehension, which appear to have been made by the Great Spirit, and placed in your hands, I am indebted to my father here, who invited me from home, under whose wings I have been protected. Yes, my Great Father, I have travelled with your chief. I have followed him, and trod in his tracks; but there is still another Great Father, to whom I am much indebted—it is the Father of us all. Him who made us and placed us on this earth. I feel grateful to the Great Spirit for strengthening my heart for such an undertaking, and for preserving the life which he gave me. The Great Spirit made us all—he made my skin red, and yours white. He placed us on this earth, and intended that we should live differently from each other. He made the whites to cultivate the earth, and feed on domestic animals; but he made us red skins, to rove through the uncultivated woods and plains, to feed on wild animals, and to dress in their skins. He also intended that we should go to war to take scalps—steal horses, and triumph over our enemies—cultivate peace at home, and promote the happiness of each other. I believe there are no people, of any color, on this earth, who do not believe in the Great Spirit—in rewards and in punishments. We worship him, but we worship him not as you do. We differ from you in appearance and manners, as well as in our customs; and we differ from you in our religion. We have no large houses, as you have, to worship the Great Spirit in; if we had them today, we should want others tomorrow, for we have not, like you, a fixed habitation—we have no settled home, except our villages, where we remain but two moons in twelve; we, like animals rove through the country, whilst you whites reside between us and heaven; but still my Great Father, we love the Great Spirit—we acknowledge his supreme power—our peace, our health, and our happiness depend upon him; and our lives belong to him—he made us, and he can destroy us.

My Great Father.—Some of your good chiefs, or, as they are called, *Missionaries,* have proposed to send of their good people among us to change our habits, to make us work, and live like the white people. I will not tell a lie, I am going to tell the truth. You love our country; you love your people; you love the manner in which they live, and you think your people brave. I am like you, my Great Father, I love my country; I love my people; I love the manner in which we live, and think myself and warriors brave; spare me then, my Father, let me enjoy my country, and pursue the buffaloe, and the beaver, and the other wild animals of our wilderness, and I will trade the skins with your people. I have grown up and lived thus long without work; I am in hopes you will suffer me to die without it. We have yet plenty of buffaloe, beaver, deer, and other wild animals; we have also an abundance of horses. We have every thing we want. We have plenty of land, *if you will keep your people off of it.*

My Father has a piece on which he lives (Council Bluffs) and we wish him to enjoy it. We have enough without it; but we wish him to live near us to give us good counsel; to keep our ears and eyes open, that we may continue to pursue the right road; the road to happiness. He settles all differences between us and the whites, and between the red skins themselves—He makes the whites do justice to the red skins, and he makes the red skins do justice to the whites. He saves the effusion of human blood, and restores peace and happiness in the land. You have already sent us a father; it is enough, he knows us, and we know him. We have confidence in him. We keep our eye constantly upon him, and since we have heard *your* words, we will listen more attentively to *his.*

It is too soon, my Great Father, to send those good men among us. We are not starving yet. We wish you to permit us to enjoy the chase, until the game of our country is exhausted; until the wild animals become extinct. Let us exhaust our present resources, before you make us toil, and interrupt our happiness. Let me continue to live as I have done, and after I have passed to the Good or Evil Spirit from the wilderness of my present life the subsistence of *my children* may become so precarious, as to need and embrace the offered assistance of those good people.

There was a time when we did not know the whites. Our wants were then fewer than they are now. They were always within our control. We had then seen nothing which we could not get. But since our intercourse with the *whites,* who have caused such a destruction of our game, our situation is changed. We could lie down to sleep, and when we awoke, we found the buffaloe feeding around our camp; but now we are killing them for their skins, and feeding the wolves with their flesh, to make our children cry over their bones.

Here my Great Father, is a pipe which I present you, as I am accustomed to present pipes to all red skins in peace with us. It is filled with such tobacco as we were accustomed to smoke, before we knew the white people. I know that the robes, leggings, moccasins, bear's claws, &c. are of little value to you, but we wish you to have them deposited and preserved in some conspicuous part of your lodge, so that when we are gone, and the sod turned over our bones, if our children should visit this place, as we do now, they may see and recognize with pleasure the deposits of their fathers, and reflect on the times that are past.

Source: Morse, Jedediah. *A Report to the Secretary of War of the United States on Indian Affairs.* New Haven, CT: S. Converse, 1822, 242–245.

Elias Boudinot, "An Address to the Whites Delivered in the First Presbyterian Church on the 26th of May, 1826"

On May 26, 1826, Elias Boudinot, a Cherokee missionary, delivered a speech in Philadelphia as part of a fund-raising effort for the establishment of a printing press in the Cherokee Nation. In the following speech, Boudinot declares that the traditionally negative image of the American Indian was untrue, using his own people as an example. The Cherokee, he argues, have been progressing toward civilization since the encroachment of white settlers forced them to give up hunting wild game. He uses the creation of a written Cherokee language and the influence of Christian missionaries as further evidence of the Cherokees' continuing advancement. Boudinot would eventually become an editor of the Cherokee Phoenix *newspaper.*

To those who are unacquainted with the manners, habits and improvements of the Aborigines of this country, the term Indian is pregnant with ideas the most repelling and degrading. But such impressions, originating as they frequently do, from infant prejudices although they hold too true when applied to some, do great injustice to many of this race of beings.

Some there are, perhaps even in this enlightened assembly, who at the bare sight of an Indian, or at the mention of the name, would throw back their imaginations to ancient times, to the savages of savage warfare, to the yells pronounced over the mangled bodies of women and children, thus creating an opinion, inapplicable and highly injurious to those for whose temporal interest and eternal welfare, I come to plead.

What is an Indian? Is he not formed of the same materials with yourself? For "Of one blood God created all the nations that dwell on the face of the earth." Though it be true that he is ignorant, that he is a heathen, that he is a savage; yet he is no more than all others have been under similar circumstances. Eighteen centuries ago what were the inhabitants of Great Britain?

You here behold an Indian, my kindred are Indians, and my fathers sleeping in the wilderness grave—they too were Indians.

But I am not as my fathers were—broader means and nobler influences have fallen upon me. Yet I was not born as thousands are, in a stately dome and amid the congratulations of the great, for on a little hill, in a lonely cabin, overspread by the forest oak I first drew my breath; and in a language unknown to learned and polished nations, I learnt to lisp my fond mother's name. In after days, I have had greater advantages than most of my race; and I now stand before you delegated by my native country to seek her interest, to labour for her respectability, and by my public efforts to assist in raising her to an equal standing with other nations of the earth.

The time has arrived when speculations and conjectures as to the practicability of civilizing the Indians must forever cease. A period is fast approaching when the stale remark—"Do what you will, an Indian will still be an Indian," must be placed no more in speech. With whatever plausibility this popular objection may have heretofore been made, every candid mind must now be sensible that it can no longer be uttered, except by those who are uninformed with respect to us, who are strongly prejudiced against us, or who are filled with vindictive feelings towards us; for the present history of the Indians, particularly of that nation to which I belong, most incontrovertibly establishes the fallacy of this remark. I am aware of the difficulties which have ever existed to Indian civilization, I do not deny the almost insurmountable obstacles which we ourselves have thrown in the way of this improvement, nor do I say that difficulties no longer remain; but facts will permit me to declare that there are none which may not easily be overcome, by strong and continued exertions. It needs not abstract reasoning to prove this position. It needs not the display of language to prove to the minds of good men, that Indians are susceptible of attainments necessary to the formation of polished society. It needs not the power of argument on the nature of man, to silence forever the remark that "[i]t is the purpose of the Almighty that the Indians should be exterminated." It needs only that the world should know what we have done in the few last years, to foresee what yet we may do with the assistance of our white brethren, and that of the common Parent of us all.

It is not necessary to present to you a detailed account of the various aborigined [aboriginal] tribes, who have been known to you only on the pages of history, and there but obscurely known. They have gone; and to revert back to their days, would be only to disturb their oblivious sleep; to darken these walls with deeds at which humanity must shudder; to place before your eyes the scenes of Muskingum Sahtagoo and the plains of Mexico, to call up the crimes of the bloody Cortes and his infernal host; and to describe the animosity and vengeance which have overthrown, and hurried into the shades of death those numerous tribes. But here let me say, that however guilty these unhappy nations may have been, yet many and unreasonable were the wrongs they suffered, many the hardships they endured, and many their wanderings through the trackless wilderness. Yes "Notwithstanding the obloquy which the early historians of the colonies have overshadowed the character of the ignorant and unfortunate natives, some bright gleams will occasionally break through, that throw a melancholy lustre on their memories. Facts are occasionally to be met with in their rude annals, which though recorded with all the colouring of prejudice and bigotry, yet speak for themselves, and will be dwelt upon with applause and sympathy when prejudice shall have passed away."

Nor is it my purpose to enter largely into the consideration of the remnants, of those who have fled with time and are no more. They stand as monuments of the Indian's fate. And should they ever become extinct, they must move off the earth, as did their fathers. My design is to offer a few disconnected facts relative to the present improved state, and to the ultimate prospects of that particular tribe called Cherokees to which I belong.

The Cherokee nation lies within the charted limits of the states of Georgia, Tennessee, and Alabama. Its extent as defined by treaties is about 200 miles in length from East to West, and about 120 in breadth. This country which is supposed to contain about 10,000,000 of acres exhibits great varieties of surface, the most part being hilly and mountainous, affording soil of no value. The vallies [valleys] however, are well watered and afford excellent land, in many parts particularly on the large streams, that of the first quality. The climate is temperate and healthy, indeed I would not be guilty of exaggeration were I to say, that the advantages which this country possesses to render it salubrious, are many and superior. Those lofty and barren mountains, defying the labour and ingenuity of man, and supposed by some as placed there only to exhibit omnipotence, contribute to the healthiness and beauty of the surrounding plains, and give us to that free air and pure water which distinguish our country. These advantages, calculated to make the inhabitants healthy, vigorous, and intelligent, cannot fail to cause this country to become interesting. And there can be no doubt that the Cherokee Nation however obscure and trifling it may now appear, will finally become, if not under its present occupants, one of the Garden spots of America. And here, let me be indulged in the fond wish, that she may thus become under those who now possess her; and ever be fostered, regulated and protected by the generous government of the United States.

The population of the Cherokee Nation increased for the year 1810 to that of 1824, 2,000 exclusive of those who emigrated in 1818 and 19 to the west of the Mississippi—of those who reside on the Arkansas the number is supposed to be about 5,000.

The rise of these people in their movement toward civilization, may be traced as far back as the relinquishment of their towns; when game became incompetent to their support, by reason of the surrounding white population. They then betook themselves to the woods commenced the opening of small clearings, and the raising of stock; still however following the chase. Game has since become so scarce that little dependence for subsist-ence [subsistence] can be placed upon it. They have gradually and I could almost say universally forsaken their ancient employment. In fact, there is not a single family in the nation, that can be said to subsist on the slender support which the wilderness would afford. The love and the practice of hunting are not now carried to a higher degree, than among all frontier people whether white or red. It cannot be doubted, however, that there are many who have commenced a life of agricultural labor from mere necessity, and if they could, would gladly resume their former course of living. But these are indi-vidual failings and ought to be passed over.

On the other hand it cannot be doubted that the nation is improving, rapidly improving in all those particulars which must finally constitute the inhab-itants an industrious and intelligent people.

It is a matter of surprise to me, and must be to all those who are properly acquainted with the condi-tion of the Aborigines of this country, that the Cherokees have advanced so far and so rapidly in civilization. But there are yet powerful obstacles, both within and without, to be surmounted in the march of improvement. The prejudices in regard to them in the general community are strong and last-ing. The evil effects of their intercourse with their immediate white neighbours, who differ from them chiefly in name, are easily to be seen, and it is evident that from this intercourse proceed those demoralizing practices which in order to surmount, peculiar and unremitting efforts are necessary. In defiance, however, of these obstacles the Cherokees have improved and are still rapidly improving. To give you a further view of their condition, I will here repeat some of the articles of the two statisti-cal tables taken at different periods.

In 1810 There were 19,500 cattle; 6,100 horses; 19,600 swine; 1,037 sheep; 467 looms; 1600 spin-ning wheels; 30 wagons; 500 ploughs; 3 saw-mills; 13 grist-mills &c. [et cetera] At this time there are

22,000 cattle; 7,600 Horses; 46,000 swine; 2,500 sheep; 762 looms; 2488 spinning wheels; 172 wagons; 2,943 ploughs; 10 saw-mills; 31 grist-mills; 62 Blacksmith-shops; 8 cotton machines; 18 schools; 18 ferries; and a number of public roads. In one district there were, last winter, upwards of 1,000 volumes of good books; and 11 different periodical papers both religious and political, which were taken and read. On the public roads there are many decent Inns, and few houses for convenience, &c. [et cetera], would disgrace any country. Most of the schools are under the care and tuition of Christian missionaries, of different denominations, who have been of great service to the nation, by inculcating moral and religious prin-ciples into the minds of the rising generation. In many places the word of God is regularly preached and explained, both by missionaries and natives; and there are numbers who have publicly professed their belief in the merits of the great Savior of the world. It is worthy of remark, that in no ignorant country have the missionaries undergone less trou-ble and difficulty, in spreading a knowledge of the Bible than in this. Here, they have been welcomed and encouraged by the proper authorities of the nation, their persons have been protected, and in very few instances have some individual vaga-bonds threatened violence to them. Indeed it may be said with truth, that among no heathen people has the faithful minister of God experienced greater success, greater reward for his labour, than in this. He is surrounded by attentive bearers, the words which flow from his lips are not spent in vain. The Cherokees have had no established religion of, their own, and perhaps to this circumstance we may attribute, in part, the facilities with which mis-sionaries have pursued their ends. They cannot be called idolators; for they never worshipped Images. They believed in a Supreme Being, the Creator of all, the God of the white, the red, and the black man. They also believed in the existence of an evil spirit who resided, as they thought, in the setting sun, the future place of all who in their life time had done iniquitously. Their prayers were addressed alone to the Supreme Being, and which if written would fill a large volume, and display much sincerity beauty and sublimity. When the ancient customs of the Cherokees were in their full force, no warrior thought himself secure, unless he had addressed his guardian angel; no hunter could hope for success, unless before the rising sun he had asked the assistance of his God, and on his return at eve he had offered his sacrifice to him.

There are three things of late occurrence, which must certainly place the Cherokee Nation in a fair light, and act as powerful argument in favor of Indian improvement.

First. The invention of letters.

Second. The translation of the New Testament into Cherokee.

And third. The organization of a Government.

The Cherokee mode of writing lately invented by George Guest, who could not read any language nor speak any other than his own, consists of eighty-six characters, principally syllabic, the combinations of which form all the words of the language. Their terms may be greatly simplified, yet they answer all the purposes of writing, and already many natives use them.

The translation of the New Testament, together with Guest's mode of writing, has swept away that barrier which has long existed, and opened a spacious channel for the instruction of adult Cherokees. Persons of all ages and classes may now read the precepts of the Almighty in their own language. Before it is long, there will scarcely be an individual in the nation who can say, "I know not God neither understand I what thou sayest," for all shall know him from the greatest to the least. The aged warrior over whom has rolled three score and ten years of savage life, will grace the temple of God with his hoary head; and the little child yet on the breast of its pious mothr [mother] shall learn to lisp its Maker's name.

The shrill sound of the Savage yell shall die away as the roaring of far distant thunder; and Heaven wrought music will gladden the affrighted wilderness. "The solitary place will be glad for them, and the desert shall rejoice and blossom as a rose." Already do we see the morning star,

forerunner of approaching dawn, rising over the tops of deep forests in which for ages have echoed the warrior's whoop. But has not God said it, and will he not do it? The Almighty decrees his purposes, and man cannot with all his ingenuity and device countervail them. They are more fixed in their course than the rolling sun—more durable than the everlasting mountains.

The Government, though defective in many respects, is well suited to the condition of the inhabitants. As they rise in information and refinement, changes in it must follow, until they arrive at that state of advancement, when I trust they will be admitted into all the privileges of the American family.

The Cherokee Nation is divided into eight districts, in each of which are established courts of justice, where all disputed cases are decided by a jury, under the direction of a circuit Judge, who has jurisdiction over two districts. Sheriffs and other public officers are appointed to execute the decisions of the courts, collect debts, and arrest thieves and other criminals. Appeals may be taken to the Superior Court, held annually at the seat of Government. The Legislative authority is vested in General Court, which consists of the National Committee and Council. The National Committee consist of thirteen members who are generally men of sound sense and fine talents. The National Council consists of thirty-two members, beside the speaker, who acts as the representatives of the people. Every bill passing these two bodies, becomes the law of the land. Clerks are appointed to do the writings, and record the proceedings of the Council. The executive power is vested in two principal chiefs, who hold their office during good behaviour, and sanction all the decisions of the legislative council. Many of the laws display some degree of civilization, and establish the respectability of the nation.

Polygamy is abolished. Female chastity and honor are protected by law. The Sabbath is respected by the Council during session. Mechanics are encouraged by law. The practice of putting aged persons to death for witchcraft is abolished and murder has now become a governmental crime.

From what I have said, you will form but a faint opinion of the true state and prospects of the Cherokees. You will, however, be convinced of three important truths.

First, that the means which have been employed for the christianization and civilization of this tribe, have been greatly blessed. Second, that the increase of these means will meet with final success. Third, that it has now become necessary, that efficient and more than ordinary means should be employed.

Sensible of this last point, and wishing to do something for themselves, the Cherokees have thought it advisable that there should be established, a Printing Press and a Seminary of respectable character; and for these purposes your aid and patronage are now solicited. They wish the types, as expressed in their resolution, to be composed of English letters and Cherokee characters. Those characters have now become extensively used in the nation; their religious songs are written in them; there is an astonishing eagerness in people of all classes and ages to acquire a knowledge of them; and the New Testament has been translated into their language. All this impresses on them the immediate necessity of procuring types. The most informed and judicious of our nation, believe that such a press would go further to remove ignorance, and her offspring superstition and prejudice, than all other means. The adult part of the nation will probably grovel on in ignorance and die in ignorance, without any fair trial upon them, unless the proposed means are carried into effect. The simplicity of this method of writing, and the eagerness to obtain a knowledge of it, are evinced by the astonishing rapidity with which it is acquired, and by the numbers who do so. It is about two years since its introduction, and already there are a great many who can read it. In the neighbourhood in which I live, I do not recollect a male Cherokee, between the ages of fifteen and twenty-five, who is ignorant of this mode of writing. But in connexion with those for Cherokee characters, it is necessary to have type for English letters. There are many who already speak and read the English language,

and can appreciate the advantages which would result from the publication of their laws and transactions in a well-conducted newspaper. Such a paper, comprising a summary of religious and political events, &c. [et cetera] on the one hand; and on the other, exhibiting the feelings, disposition, improvements, and prospects of the Indians; their traditions, their true character, as it once was and as it now is; the ways and means most likely to throw the mantle of civilization over all tribes; and such other matter as will tend to diffuse proper and correct impressions in regard to their condition— such a paper could not fail to create much interest in the American community, favourable to the aborigines, and to have a powerful influence, on the advancement of the Indians themselves. How can the patriot or the philanthropist devise efficient means, without full and correct information as to the subjects of their labour. And I am inclined to think, after all that has been said of the aborigines, after all that has been written in narratives, professedly to elucidate the leading traits of their character, that the public knows little of that character. To obtain a correct and complete knowledge of these people, there must exist a vehicle of Indian intelligence, altogether different from those which have heretofore been employed. Will not a paper published in an Indian country, under proper and judicious regulations, have the desired effect? I do not say that Indians will produce learned and elaborate dissertations in explanation and vindication of their own character; but they may exhibit specimens of their intellectual efforts, of their eloquence, of their moral, civil and physical advancement, which will do quite as much to remove prejudice and to give profitable information.

The Cherokees wish to establish their Seminary, upon a footing which will insure to it all the advantages, that belong to such institutions in the state. Need I spend one moment in arguments, in favor of such an institution; need I speak one word of the utility, of the necessity, of an institution of learning; need I do more than simply to ask the patronage of benevolent hearts, to obtain that patronage.

When before did a nation of Indians step forward and ask for the means of civilization? The Cherokee authorities have adopted the measures already stated, with a sincere desire to make their nation an intelligent and a virtuous people, and with a full hope that those who have already pointed out to them the road of happiness, will now assist them to pursue it. With that assistance, what are the prospects of the Cherokees? Are they not indeed glorious, compared to that deep darkness in which the nobler qualities of their souls have slept? Yes, methinks I can view my native country, rising from the ashes of her degradation, wearing her purified and beautiful garments, and taking her seat with the nations of the earth. I can behold her sons bursting the fetters of ignorance and unshackling her from the voice of heathenism. She is at this instant, risen like the first morning sun, which grows brighter and brighter, until it reaches its fullness of glory.

She will become not a great, but a faithful ally of the United States. In time of peace she will plead the common liberties of America. In time of war her intrepid sons will sacrifice their lives in your defence. And because she will be useful to you in coming time, she asks you to assist her in her present struggles. She asks not for greatness; she seeks not wealth; she pleads only for assistance to become respectable as a nation, to enlighten and ennoble her sons, and to ornament her daughters with modesty and virtue. She pleads for this assistance, too, because on her destiny hangs that of many nations. If she completes her civilization— then may we hope that all our nations will—then, indeed, may true patriots be encouraged in their efforts to make this world of the West, one continuous abode of enlightened, free, and happy people.

But if the Cherokee Nation fail in her struggle, if she die away, then all hopes are blasted, and falls the fabric of Indian civilization. Their fathers were born in darkness, and have fled in darkness; without your assistance so will their sons. You see, however, where the probability rests. Is there a soul whose narrowness will not permit the exercise of charity on such an occasion? Where is he that

can hold his mite from an object so noble. Who can prefer a little of his silver and gold, to the welfare of nations of his fellow beings? Human wealth perishes with our clay, but that wealth gained in charity still remains on earth, to enrich our names, when we are gone, and will be remembered in Heaven, when the miser and his coffers have mouldered together in their kindred earth. The works of a generous mind sweeten the cup of affliction; they enlighten the dreary way to the cold tomb; they blunt the sting of death, and smooth his passage to the unknown world. When all the kingdoms of this earth shall die away and their beauty and power shall perish, his name shall live and shine as a twinkling star; those for whose benefit he did his deeds of charity shall call him blessed, and they shall add honor to his immortal head.

There are, with regard to the Cherokees and other tribes, two alternatives; they must either become civilized and happy, or sharing the fate of many kindred nations, become extinct. If the General Government continue its protection, and the American people assist them in their humble efforts, they will, they must rise. Yes, under such protection, and with such assistance, the Indian must rise like the Phoenix, after having wallowed for ages in ignorant barbarity. But should this Government withdraw its care, and the American people their aid, then, to use the words of a writer, "They will go the way that so many tribes have gone before them; for the hordes that still linger about the shores of Huron, and the tributary streams of the Mississippi, will share the fate of those tribes that once lorded it along the proud banks of the Hudson; of that gigantic race that said to have existed on the borders of the Susquehanna; of those various nations that flourished about the Potomac and the Rhappahannoc, and that peopled the forests of the vast valley of Shenandoah. They will vanish like a vapour from the face of the earth their very history will be lost in forgetfulness, and the places that now know them will know them no more."

There is, in Indian history, something very meloncholy [melancholy], and which seems to establish a mournful precedent for the future events of the few sons of the forest, now scattered over this vast continent. We have seen every where the poor aborigines melt away before the white population. I merely speak of the fact, without at all referring to the cause. We have seen, I say, one family after another, one tribe after another, nation after nation pass away; until only a few solitary creatures are left to tell the sad story of extinction.

Shall this precedent be followed? I ask you, shall red men live, or shall they be swept from the earth? With you and this public at large, the decision chiefly rests. Must they perish? Must they all, like the unfortunate Creeks (victims of the unchristian policy of certain persons,) go down in sorrow to their graves.

They hang upon your mercy as to a garment. Will you push them from you, or will you save them? Let humanity answer.

Source: Boudinot, Elias. *An address to the whites delivered in the First Presbyterian Church on the 26th of May, 1826.* Philadelphia: William F. Geddes, 1826, 1–15.

Fighting the United States: Winning and Losing

(1827–1877)

Constitution of the Cherokee Nation

(1827)

In 1826, the Cherokee National Council voted to call a constitutional convention for the following year. The Constitution of the Cherokee Nation follows in its entirety. It is a notable document because the Cherokee modeled their own constitution after the Constitution of the United States.

We the Representatives of the people of the Cherokee Nation, in Convention assembled in order to establish justice ensure tranquility, promote our common welfare, and secure to ourselves and our posterity the blessings of liberty, acknowledging with humility and gratitude the goodness of the sovereign ruler of the Universe affording us an opportunity so favorable to the design and imploring his aid and direction in its accomplishments do ordain and establish this Constitution for the Government of the Cherokee Nation.

Article 1st. The boundaries of this nation embracing the lands solemnly guaranteed and reserved forever to the Cherokee Nation by the treaties concluded with the United States is as follows, and which shall forever hereafter remain unalterably the same; To wit: Beginning on the north bank of Tennessee River at the upper part of the Chickasaw Old.

Fields thence along the main Channel of said River including all the islands therein to the mouth of Hiwassee River thence up the main channel of said river including Islands to the first Hill which closes in on said river about two miles above Highwassee Old Town, thence along the ridge which divides the waters of the Highwassee Little Tellico, to the Tennessee river at Tallasee, thence along the main channel including Islands to the junction of Cowee & Nanteyalee, thence along the ridge in the fork of said river to the top of the blue ridge, thence along the blue ridge to the Unicoy Turnpike road thence a straight line to the nearest main source of the Chestatee; thence along its main channel, including Islands to the Chatahoochie and thence down the same to the Creek boundary at Buzzard roost; thence along the boundary line which separates this and the Creek Nation, to a point on the Coosa river opposite the mouth of

Wills Creek, thence down along the South Bank of the same to a point, opposite Fort Strother, thence up the river to the mouth of Wills Creek, thence up along the east Bank of said Creek to the west branch, thereof and up the same to its source, & thence along the ridge which separates the Tombigby & Tennessee waters, to a point on top of said ridge, thence a due north Course to Camp Coffee, on Tennessee which is opposite the Chickasaw Island, thence to a place of beginning.

Section 2. The sovereignty & jurisdiction of this Government shall extend over the country within the boundaries above described, and the lands therein is & shall remain the common property of the nation; but the improvements made thereon, and in possession of the citizens of the nation, are the exclusive & indefeasible property of the citizens respectively who made or may rightfully be in possession of them provided that the citizens of the nation possessing exclusive and indefeasable rights to their respective improvements, as expressed in this article, shall possess no rights nor power to dispose of their improvements in any manner whatever to the United States individual states, nor to individual citizens thereof and that whenever any such citizen or citizens shall remove with their effects out of the limits of this nation and become Citizens of any other government all their rights and privileges as citizens of this nation cease, Provided nevertheless the legislature shall have power to readmit by law, all the rights of Citizen Ship to any such person or persons who may at any time desire to return to this nation by memorializing the General Council for such an admission— Moreover, the Legislature shall have power to adopt such laws & regulations as its wisdom may deem expedient and proper to prevent the citizens from monopolizing improvements with the view of speculation.

Article 2. The power of this Government shall be divided into three distinct departments, the legislative, Executive, and Judicial.

Section 2. No person or persons belonging to one of these departments, shall exercise any of the powers properly belonging to either of the others; except in cases herein after expressly directed or permitted.

Article 3. The Legislative power shall be vested in two distinct branches, a Committee and a council each to have a negative on the other, and both to be styled the General Council of the Cherokee nation, and the style of their acts and laws shall be: "Resolved by the Committee and Council in General Council convened."

Section 2. The Cherokee Nation as laid off into eight Districts, shall remain so.

Section 3. The committee shall consist of two members from each district and the council shall consist of three members from each district, to be chosen by the qualified electors of their respective districts for two years, and the elections to be held in every district on the first Monday in august for the year 1828, and every succeeding two years thereafter. And the Genl. Council shall be held once a year to be convened on the second Monday of October in each year at New Echota.

Section 4. No person shall be eligible to a seat in the general Council but a free Cherokee male citizen who shall have attained to the age of twenty-five years. The descendants of Cherokee men by all free women (except the African race) whose parents may be or may have been living together as man and wife according to the customs & laws of this nation & shall be entitled to all the rights and privileges of this Nation, as well as the posterity of Cherokee woman by all freemen, no person who is of a negro or mulato parentage either by the father or mother side, shall be eligible to hold any office of profit or honor or trust under this Government.

Section 5. The electors and members to the General Council shall in all cases except in those of treason, felony, or breach of the peace be privileged from arrest during their attendance at elections and the General Council, and in going to or returning from the same.

Section 6. In all elections by the people the electors shall vote Vi-Va-Voce. Elections for members to the General Council for 1828 shall be held at the place of holding their several courts & at the other two precincts in each Districts which are designated by the law under which the members of this convention were elected, and that the district Judges shall superintend the elections within the precinct of their respective Court Houses, and the Marshalls & Sheriffs to superintend the precincts which may be assigned them by the Circuit Judges of their respective Districts together with one other person who shall be appointed by the circuit Judges for each precinct within the District of their respective Circuits, and the Circuit Judges shall also appoint a Clerk to each precinct. The superintendent & Clerks shall on the Wednesday morning preceding the elections assemble at their respective Court Houses and proceed to examine and ascertain the true state of the polls and shall Issue to each member duly elected a certificate and also make an official return of the State of the polls of election to the Principal Chief and it shall be the duty of the Sheriffs to deliver the same to the executive office provided nevertheless the Genl. Council shall have power after the election of 1828 to regulate by law the precincts & superintendents & clerks of elections in the several Districts.

Section 7. All free male citizens (excepting negroes and descendants of white & Indian men by Negro women who may have been set free) who shall have attained to the age of 18 years shall be equally entitled to vote at all public elections.

Section 8. Each house of the General Council shall judge of the qualifications, elections & returns of its own members.

Section 9. Each house of the Genl. Council may determine the rules of its proceedings punish a member for disorderly behaviour and with the concurrence of two thirds expel a member, but not a second time for the same cause.

Section 10. Each House of the Genl. Council when assembled shall choose its own officers, a majority of each House shall constitute a quorum to do business, but a smaller number may adjourn from day to day, and compel the attendance of absent members, in such manner and under such penalties as each House may prescribe.

Section 11. The members of the Committee shall each receive from the public Treasury a compensation for their services, which shall be, two dollars and fifty cents per day, during their attendance at the general Council, and the members of the Council, shall each receive, Two dollars per day for their Services during their attendance at the General Council provided that the same, may be increased or diminished, by law; but no alteration shall take effect, during the period of service of the members of the General Council, by whom such alterations shall have been made.

Section 12. The General Council, shall regulate by law, by whom, and in what manner, Writs of election shall be issued, to fill the vacancies which may happen, in either branch thereof.

Section 13. Each member of the General Council before he takes his seat, shall take the following oath or affirmation, to wit—I A. B. do solemnly swear or affirm, as the case may be, that I have not obtained my election by bribery, treats or any undue, and unlawful means, used by myself or others, by my desire, or approbation for that purpose, that I consider myself constitutionally qualified as a member of and that in all questions, and measures which may come, before me, I will give my vote, and so conduct myself, as may in my judgment appear most conducive to the interest and prosperity of this nation, and that I will bear, true faith and allegiance to the same and to the utmost of my ability, and power observe, conform to support and defend the constitution thereof.

Section 14. No person who may be convicted of felony before any Court of this nation, shall be eligible to any office or appointment, of honor profit or trust, within this nation.

Section 15. The General Council shall have power to make, all laws and regulations, which they shall deem necessary and proper, for the good of the nation, which shall not be contrary to his constitution.

Section 16. It shall be the duty of the General Council to pass such laws, as may be necessary and proper, to decide differences, by arbitrators to be appointed by the parties, who may choose that summary mode of adjustment.

Section 17. No power of suspending the laws of this nation Shall be exercised unless by the Legislature or its authority.

Section 18. That no retrospective laws nor any law, impairing the obligation of contracts shall be passed.

Section 19. The Legislature shall have power to make laws for laying & collecting taxes for the purpose of raising a revenue.

Section 20. All bills making appropriations shall originate in the Committee; but the Council may propose amendments or reject the same.

Section 21. All other Bills may originate in either House, Subject to the concurrence, or rejection of the other.

Section 22. All acknowledged treaties shall be the Supreme law of the land.

Section 23. The General Council shall have the sole power of deciding on the construction of all treaty stipulations.

Section 24. The Council shall have the sole power of impeaching.

Section 25. All impeachments shall be tried by the Committee when sitting for that purpose the members shall be upon oath or affirmation no person shall be convicted without the concurrence of two thirds of the members present.

Section 26. The principal Chief, assistant principal Chief and all civil officers under this nation shall be liable to impeachments for any misdemeanors in office, but judgment in such cases, shall not extend further than removal from office, and disqualification to hold any office of honor, trust, or profit, under this nation the party whether convicted or acquitted, shall nevertheless be liable to indictment trial judgment & punishment according to law.

Article 4

Section 1. The supreme executive power of this nation, shall be vested in a Principal Chief who shall be chosen by the Genl. Council and shall hold his office four years to be elected as follows: the Genl. Council by a joint vote shall at their second annual session after the rising of this convention and at every fourth annual session thereafter on the second day after the two houses shall be organized and competent to proceed to business elect a Principal Chief.

Section 2. No person except a natural born citizen shall be eligible to the office of principal Chief neither shall any person be eligible to that office who shall have not attained to the age of thirty five years.

Section 3. There shall also be chosen at the same time by General Council in the same manner for four years an assistant Principal Chief.

Section 4. In case of the removal of the Principal Chief from office or of his death resignation or inability to discharge the powers and duties of the said office the same shall devolve on the assistant Principal Chief until the inability be removed or vacancy filled by the General Council.

Section 5. The General Council may by law provide for the case of removal, death, resignation, or inability both of the principal and assistant principal Chiefs declaring what officer shall then act as Principal Chief until the disability be removed or a principal Chief shall be elected.

Section 6. The Principal Chief and assistant Principal Chief shall at stated times receive for their services a compensation which shall neither be increased or diminished during the period for which they shall have been elected. And they shall not receive within that period any other emolument from the Cherokee nation or any other government.

Section 7. Before the Principal Chief enters on the execution of his office he shall take the following oath or affirmation: "I do solemnly swear or (affirm) that I will faithfully execute the office of Principal Chief of the Cherokee Nation and will to the best of my ability preserve, protect & defend the Constitution of the Cherokee Nation."

Section 8. He may on extraordinary occasions convene the Genl. Council at the seat of government.

Section 9. He shall from time to time give to the general Council information of the State of the Government and recommend to their consideration such measures as he may think expedient.

Section 10. He shall take care that the laws be faithfully executed.

Section 11. It shall be his duty to visit the different Districts at least once in two years to inform himself of the general condition of the country.

Section 12. The assistant Principal Chief shall by virtue of his office aid & advise the principal Chief in the administration of the Government at all times during his continuance in office.

Section 13. Vacancies that may happen in offices the appointment of which is vested in the general council, shall be filled by the principal Chief during the recess of the General Council by granting commissions which shall expire at the end of next session.

Section 14. Every bill which shall have passed both houses of the General Council shall before it becomes a law be presented to the Principal Chief of the Cherokee Nation. If he approves it he shall sign it, but if not he shall return it with his objections to that house in which it shall have originated, who shall enter the objections at large on their journals and proceed to reconsider it. If after such reconsideration two thirds of that house shall agree to pass the Bill, it shall be sent together with the objection to the other House by which it shall likewise be reconsidered and if approved of by two thirds of that house it shall become a law. If any Bill shall not be returned by the Principal Chief within five days (Sundays excepted) after it shall have been presented to him the same shall be a law in like manner as if he had signed it unless the General Council by their adjournment prevents its return in which case it shall be a law unless sent back within three days after their next meeting.

Section 15. Members of the General Council and all officers Executive & Judicial shall be bound by oath to support the Constitution of this Nation and to perform the duties of their respective offices with fidelity.

Section 16. In case of disagreement between the two Houses with respect to the time of adjournment the principal Chief shall have power to adjourn the Genl. Council to such a time as he thinks proper, provided it be not to a period beyond the next constitutional meeting of the same.

Section 17. The Principal Chief shall during the sitting of the Genl. Council attend at the seat of government.

Section 18. There shall be a council to consist of three men to be appointed by the joint vote of both Houses to advise the principal Chief in the executive part of the Government whom the principal Chief shall have full power at his discretion to assemble and he together with the assistant Principal Chief and Counsellors or a majority of them may from time to time hold and keep a council for ordering and directing the affairs of the nation according to law.

Section 19. The members of the Council shall be chosen for the term of one year.

Section 20. The Resolutions and advice of the Council shall be recorded in a Register and signed by the members agreeing thereto, which may be called for, by either House of the General Council, and any Counselor may enter his dissent, to the Resolution of the majority.

Section 21. The Treasurer of the Cherokee Nation shall be chosen by the joint vote of each House of the General Council for the term of two years.

Section 22. The Treasurer shall before entering on the duties of his office give bond to the Nation with Securities to the satisfaction of the Legislature,—for the faithful discharge of his trust.

Section 23. No money shall be drawn from the Treasury but by warrant from the principal Chief, and in consequence of appropriation made by law.

Section 24. It shall be the duty of the Treasurer to receive all public monies, and to make a regular Statement and account of the receipts and expenditures of all public monies to the annual Session of the General Council.

Article 5

Section 1. The Judicial powers shall be vested in a Supreme Court, and such Circuit and Inferior Courts as the General Council may from time to time ordain and establish.

Section 2. The Supreme Court, shall consist of three Judges, any two of whom, shall be a quorum.

Section 3. The Judges of each shall hold their commissions four years, but any of them may be removed, from office, on the address of two thirds of each House of the General Council, to the principal Chief, for that purpose.

Section 4. The Judges of the Supreme and Circuit Courts, shall at stated times receive a compensation which shall not be diminished during their continuance in office but they, shall receive no fees or perquisites of office—nor hold any other office, of profit or trust, under this nation or any other power.

Section 5. No person shall be appointed a Judge of any of the Courts, before he shall have attained to the age of thirty years, nor shall any person continue to exercise the duties of any of the said offices after he shall have attained, to the age of seventy years.

Section 6. The Judges of the Supreme and Circuit Courts, shall be appointed by joint vote of each House, of the General Council.

Section 7. There shall be appointed in each district under the Legislative authority as many Justices of the Peace as may be deemed the public good require—and whose powers; duties and duration in office shall be clearly designated.

Section 8. The Judges of the Supreme Court. and Circuit Court shall have complete criminal Jurisdiction in such cases, and in such manner, as may be pointed out, by law.

Section 9. Each Court shall choose its own clerk for the term of four years, but such clerks shall not be continued in office unless their qualifications, shall be adjudged and approved of by the Judges— of the Supreme Court, and they shall be removable for breach of good behaviour, at any time by the Judges of the respective Courts.

Section 10. No Judge shall sit on the trial of any cause, where the parties shall be connected with him by affinity, or consanguinity, except by consent of the parties. In case all the Judges of the Supreme Court, shall be entrusted in the event, if any cause, or related to all or either of the parties, the legislature may provide by law for the selection of three men of good Character, and

knowledge for the determination of thereof who shall be specially commissioned by the principal Chief for the case.

Section 11. All writs and other process shall run in the name of the Cherokee nation, and be as test, and be signed by the respective Clerk.

Section 12. Indictments shall conclude "against" the peace and dignity of the Cherokee nation.

Section 13. The Supreme Court shall hold its Session annually at the seat of Government to be convened on the Second Monday of October in each year.

Section 14. In all criminal prosecutions the accused shall have the right of being heard of demanding the nature and cause, of the accusation against him, of meeting the witnesses face to face of having compulsory process for obtaining witnesses in his favor—and in prosecutions by indictments or information, a speedy public trial by an impartial Jury of the vicinage nor shall he be compelled to give evidence against himself.

Section 15. That the people shall be secure in their persons, houses, papers, and possessions from unreasonable seizures and searches & that no warrant to search any place or to seize any person or things shall issue without describing them as nearly as may be, nor without good cause, supported by oath or affirmation. All prisoners shall be bailable, by sufficient securities unless for capital offences, when the proof is evident or presumption great.

Article 4

Section 1. Whereas the Ministers of the Gospel are by their profession dedicated to the service of God "and care of souls" and ought not to be divested from the great duty of their functions— Therefore no minister of the Gospel, or public preacher of any Religious persuasion, whilst he continues in the exercise of his pastoral functions, shall be eligible to the office of Principal Chief or a seat in either House of the General Council.

Section 2. No person who denies the being of God, of future state of rewards and punishments, shall hold any office in the civil department of this nation.

Section 3. The free exercise of religious worship and serving God without distinction, Shall forever be allowed within this Nation, provided that this liberty of conscience, shall not be so construed, as to excuse acts of licentiousness, or Justify practices inconsistent with the peace and safety of this Nation.

Section 4. Whenever the General Council shall determine, the expediency of appointing Delegators, or other public agents, for the purpose of transacting business with the government of the United States, the principal Chief shall have power, to recommend, and by the advice and consent of the committee shall appoint and commission such delegates or public agents accordingly, and on all matters of interest touching the rights of the citizens of this nation, which may require attention of the United States Government. The principal Chief shall keep a friendly correspondence with government through the medium of the proper officers.

Section 5. All commissions shall be the name and by the authority of the Cherokee Nation and be sealed with the Seal of the Nation and be signed by the Principal Chief. The principal Chief shall make use of his private Seal until a national Seal shall be provided.

Section 6. A Sheriff shall be elected in each district by the qualified electors thereof who shall hold his office for the term of two years unless sooner removed. Should a vacancy occur subsequent to an election, it shall be filled, by the principal Chief, as in other cases and the person so appointed, shall continue in office, until the next General election when such vacancies, shall be filled, by the qualified electors, and the sheriff then elected shall continue in for two years.

Section 7. There shall be a Marshall appointed by a joint vote of both Houses of the General Council for the term of four years, whom compensation and duty shall be regulated by law, and whose jurisdiction shall extend over the Cherokee Nation.

Section 8. No person shall for the same offence be twice put in jeopardy of life or limb. Nor shall any person's property be taken or applied to public use, without his consent provided that nothing shall be so construed in this clause as to impair the right and power of the General Council to lay and collect taxes. That all courts, shall be open and every person for an injury done him in his property, person, or reputation, shall have remedy by due course of law.

Section 9. The right of trial by Jury shall remain inviolate.

Section 10. Religion, Morality, and knowledge being necessary to good government and the preservation of liberty, and the happiness of mankind Schools and the means of education, shall forever, be encouraged in this nation.

Section 11. The appointment of all officers not otherwise directed by this constitution, shall be vested in the legislature.

Section 12. All laws in force in this nation at the passing of this constitution shall so continue until altered or repealed by the Legislature except when they are temporary in which case they shall expire at the times respectively limited for their duration if not continued by acts of the Legislature.

Section 13. The General Council may at any time propose such amendments to this Constitution as two thirds of each House shall deem expedient and the Principal Chief shall issue a Proclamation directing all the civil officers of the several Districts to promulgate the same as extensively as possible within their respective Districts at least nine months previous to the next general election and if at the first session of the General Council after such general election two thirds of each House shall be yeas and nay ratify such proposed amendments they shall be valid to all intents and purposes as parts of this Constitution provided that such proposed amendments shall be read on three several days in each house as well when the same are proposed as when they are finally ratified.

Done in Convention at New Echota, this twenty-sixth day of July, in the year of our Lord, one thousand eight hundred and twenty-seven; In testimony thereof, we have each of us, hereunto subscribed our names.

JNO. ROSS, *Pres't Con.*

Jno. Baldrige, Geo. Lowrey, Jno. Brown, Edward Gunter, John Martin, Joseph Vann, Kelechulee, Lewis Ross, Thomas Foreman, Hair Conrad, James Daniel, John Duncan, Joseph Vann, Thomas Petitt, John Beamer, Ooclenota,

Wm. Boling, John Timson, Situwakee, Richard Walker,

A. McCOY, *Sec'y to Con.*

Source: Laws of the Cherokee Nation: Adopted by the Council at Various Periods. Tahlequah, Cherokee Nation: Cherokee Advocate Printing Office, 1852.

Black Hawk Discusses the Institution of Slavery

(1833)

Black Hawk was a prominent figure in the Sauk Tribe in the early 19th century. He had a reputation as a fierce warrior and frequently fought against the encroachment of white American settlers. He fought with the British in the War of 1812 and during the Black Hawk War of 1832. He was captured, along with several other Native American leaders, and taken on a tour of the East, where the Indian leaders met with large curious crowds. In 1833, he sat down with interpreter Antoine Leclair, who wrote down Black Hawk's life story.

The book, The Autobiography of Black Hawk, *was the first Native American biography in the United States, and it was a best seller. The following excerpt from this story describes Black Hawk's opinion regarding another colonized people—African Americans. Slavery was a hot-button political issue during his lifetime, and Black Hawk offers a unique perspective on the situation.*

During my travels, my opinions were asked on different subjects—but for want of a good interpreter, were very seldom given. Presuming that they would be equally acceptable now, I have thought it a part of my duty, to lay the most important before the public.

The subject of colonizing the *negroes* was introduced, and my opinion asked, as to the best method of getting clear of these people. I was not fully prepared at the time, to answer—as I knew but little about their situation. I have since made many inquiries on the subject—and find that a number of states admit no slaves, whilst the balance hold these negroes as slaves, and are anxious, but do not know, how to get clear of them. I will now give my plan, which, when understood, I hope will be adopted.

Let the free states remove all the *male* negroes within their limits, to the slave states—then let our Great Father buy all the *female* negroes in the slave states, between the ages of twelve and twenty, and sell them to the people of the free states, for a term of years—say, those under fifteen, until they are twenty-one—and those of, and over fifteen, for five years—and continue to buy all the females in the slave states, as soon as they arrive at the age of twelve, and take them to the free states, and dispose of them in the same way as the first—and it will not be long before the country is clear of the *blackskins*, about which, I am told, they have been talking, for a long time; and for which they have expended a large amount of money.

I have no doubt but our Great Father would willingly do his part in accomplishing this object for his children—as he could not lose much by it, and would make them all happy. If the free states did not want them all for servants, we would take the balance in our nation to help our women make corn.

I have not time now, nor is it necessary, to enter more into detail about my travels through the United States. The white people know all about them, and my people have started to their hunting grounds, and I am anxious to follow them.

Source: Black Hawk, and J. B. Patterson. *Life of Ma-ka-tai-me-she-kia-kiak or Black Hawk.* Boston: Russell, Odiorne, & Metcalf, 1834, 152–154.

Black Hawk Talks about the Coming of the Americans
(1833)

In the following excerpt from his autobiography, Black Hawk, a Sauk leader, discusses an encounter with the famous American explorer Zebulon Pike in 1804. Pike's expedition to discover the source of the Mississippi River led him through territory controlled by Black Hawk and his people. His arrival in Sauk territory came just after the U.S. purchase of Louisiana from the French and thus represented an important event in American–Indian relations. As Black Hawk states in this excerpt, he and his people desired to have two fathers. The Sauk leader understood the value of playing off European American rivals against one another. Black Hawk even goes so far as to assist the expedition by sending out runners ahead of Pike to ensure his friendly treatment by neighboring Fox Indian villages.

We generally paid a visit to St. Louis every summer, but in consequence of the protracted war in which we had been engaged, I had not been there for some years. Our difficulties having all been settled, I concluded to take a small party that summer and go down to see our Spanish father [Charles Dehault Delassus]. We went and on our arrival, put up our lodges where the market house now stands. After painting and dressing, we called to see our Spanish father, and were well received. He gave us a variety of presents and plenty of provisions. We danced through the town as usual, and its inhabitants all seemed to be well pleased. They appeared to us like brothers, and always gave us good advice.

On my next and last visit to my Spanish father, I discovered on landing that all was not right—everyone seemed sad and gloomy! I asked the cause, and was informed that the Americans were coming to take possession of the town and country, and that we should then lose our Spanish father. This news made me and my band sad, because we had always heard bad accounts of the Americans from Indians who had lived near them and we were sorry to lose our Spanish father, who had always treated us with great friendship.

A few days afterwards [on 9 March 1804] the Americans [commanded by Captain Amos Stoddard] arrived. I took my band, and went to take leave, for the last time, of our father. The Americans came to see him also. Seeing them approach, we passed out at one door—as they entered another—and immediately started, in canoes, for our village on Rock River, not liking the change at St. Louis any more than our friends appeared to.

On arriving at our village, we gave the news that strange people had taken St. Louis and that we should never see our Spanish father again. This information made all our people sorry.

Some time afterwards, a boat came up the river, with a young American chief [General Zebulon Pike, then a lieutenant] and a small party of soldiers. We heard of him (by runners) soon after he had passed Salt River. Some of our young braves watched him every day to see what sort of people he had on board. The boat, at length, arrived at Rock River, and the young chief came on shore with his interpreter, made a speech, and gave us some presents. We, in return, presented him with meat, and such provisions as we could spare.

We were all well pleased with the speech of the young chief. He gave us good advice, and said our American father would treat us well. He presented us an American flag, which was hoisted. He then requested us to pull down our British flags and give him our British medals, promising to send us others on his return to St. Louis. This we declined, as we wished to have two Fathers!

When the young chief started, we sent runners to the Fox village some miles distant to direct them to treat him well as he passed, which they did. He went to the head of the Mississippi, and then returned to St. Louis. We did not see any Americans again for some time, being supplied with goods by British traders.

We were fortunate in not giving up our medals for we learned afterwards, from our traders, that the chiefs high up on the Mississippi, who gave theirs, never received any in exchange for them. But the fault was not with the young American chief. He was a good man, and a great brave—he died in his country's service [in 1813 during the War of 1812].

Some moons after this young chief descended the Mississippi, one of our people killed an American and was confined in the prison at St. Louis for the offense. We held a council at our village to see what could be done for him, which determined that Quash-qua-me, Pa-she-pa-ho, Ou-che-qua-ka, and Ha-she-quar-hi-qua should go down to St. Louis, see our American father, and do all they could to have our friend released by paying for the person killed, thus covering the blood and satisfying the relations of the man murdered. This being the only means with us of saving a person who had killed another, we then thought it was the same way with the whites!

The party started with the good wishes of the whole nation, hoping they would accomplish the object of their mission. The relatives of the prisoner blacked their faces, and fasted hoping the Great Spirit would take pity on them, and return the husband and father to his wife and children.

Quash-qua-me and party remained a long time absent. They at length returned, and camped a short distance below the village but did not come up that day—nor did any person approach their camp! They appeared to be dressed in fine coats and had medals. From these circumstances, we were in hopes that they had brought good news.

Early the next morning, the council lodge was crowded—Quash-qua-me and party came up, and gave us an account of their mission: "On their arrival at St. Louis, they met their American father [William Henry Harrison], and explained to him their business, and urged the release of their friend. The American chief told them he wanted land and they had agreed to give him some on the west side of the Mississippi, and some on the Illinois side opposite the Jefferson. When the business was all arranged, they expected to have their friend released to come home with them. But about the time they were ready to start, their friend was let out of prison, who ran a short distance and was shot dead! This is all they could recollect of what was said and done. They had been drunk the greater part of the time they were in St. Louis."

This is all I or my nation knew of the treaty of 1804. It has been explained to me since. I find, by that treaty, all our country, east of the Mississippi, and south of the Jefferson, was ceded to the United States for $1,000 a year! I will leave it to the people of the United States to say whether our nation was properly represented in this treaty, or whether we received a fair compensation for the extent of country ceded by those four individuals? I could say much about this treaty, but I will not at this time. It has been the origin of all our difficulties.

Source: Black Hawk. *Black Hawk: An Autobiography.* Minneapolis: Filiquarian Publishing, 2006, 13–16.

William Apess, Narrative
(1836)

William Apess was born in Massachusetts during the late 18th century. As a child, he was indentured to several white families who provided him with an education. In 1829, Apess was ordained as a Methodist preacher, being convinced that God wanted him to follow this vocation. During the course of his literary career, Apess authored several books. The excerpt that follows is one of the last things he is known to have written before his death in 1839. Apess was an early advocate for Indian rights, preaching through his writing for fair treatment and respect for Native Americans.

December 1620, the Pilgrims landed at Plymouth, and without asking liberty from anyone they possessed themselves of a portion of the country, and built themselves houses, and then made a treaty, and commanded them to accede to it. This, if now done, it would be called an insult, and every white man would be called to go out and act the part of a patriot, to defend their country's rights; and if every intruder were butchered, it would be sung upon every hilltop in the Union that victory and patriotism was the order of the day. And yet the Indians (though many were dissatisfied), without the shedding of blood or imprisoning anyone, bore it. And yet for their kindness and resignation towards the whites they were called savages and made by God on purpose for them to destroy. We might say, God understood his work better than this. But to proceed: It appears that a treaty was made by the Pilgrims and the Indians, which treaty was kept during forty years; the young chiefs during this time was showing the Pilgrims how to live in the country and find support for their wives and little ones; and for all this, they were receiving the applause of being savages. The two gentleman chiefs were Squanto and Samoset, that were so good to the Pilgrims.

The next we present before you are things very appalling. We turn our attention to the dates 1623, January and March, when Mr. Weston's colony came very near starving to death; some of them were obliged to hire themselves to the Indians, to become their servants, in order that they might live. Their principle [sic] work was to bring wood and water; but, not being contented with this, many of the whites sought to steal the Indians' corn; and because the Indians complained of it, and through their complaint, some one of their number being punished, as they say, to appease the savages. Now let us see who the greatest savages were; the person that stole the corn was a stout athletic man, and because of this they wished to spare him and take an old man who was lame and sickly and that used to get his living by weaving, and because they thought he would not be of so much use to them, he was, although innocent of any crime, hung in his stead. O savage, where art thou, to weep over the Christian's crimes? Another act of humanity for Christians, as they call themselves, that one Captain Standish, gathering some fruit and provisions, goes forward with a black and hypocritical heart and pretends to prepare a feast for the Indians; and when they sit down to eat, they seize the Indians' knives hanging about their necks, and stab them to the heart. The white people call this stabbing, feasting the savages. We suppose it might well mean themselves, their conduct being more like savages than Christians. They took one Wittumumet, the chief's head, and put it upon a pole in their fort and, for aught we know, gave praise to their God for success in murdering a poor Indian; for we know it was their usual course to give praise to God for this kind of victory, believing it was God's will and command for them to do so. We wonder if these same Christians do not think it the command of God that they should lie, steal, and get drunk, commit fornication and adultery. The one is as consistent as the other. What say you, judges, is it not so, and was it not according as they did? Indians think it is.

But we will proceed to show another inhuman act. The whites robbed the Indian graves, and their corn, about the year 1632, which caused Chicataubut to be displeased, who was chief, and also son to the woman that was dead. And according to the Indian custom, it was a righteous act to be avenged of the dead. Accordingly, he called all his men together and addressed them thus: "When last the glorious light of the sky was underneath this globe, and birds grew silent, I began to settle, as is my custom, to take repose. Before my eyes were fast closed, methought I saw a vision, at which my spirit was much troubled. A spirit cried aloud, 'Behold, my son, whom I have cherished, see the paps that gave thee suck, the hands that clasped thee warm, and fed thee oft. Can thou forget to take revenge of those wild people that have my monument defaced in a despiteful manner, disdaining our ancient antiquities and honorable customs? See, now, the sachem's grave lies, like unto the common people of ignoble race, defaced. Thy mother doth complain and implores thy aid against these thievish people, now come hither. If this be suffered, I shall not rest quiet within my everlasting habitation.'" War was the result. And where is there a people in the world that would see their friends robbed of their common property, their nearest and dearest friends; robbed, after their last respects to them? I appeal to you, who value your friends and affectionate mothers, you would have robbed them of their fine marble, and your storehouses broken open, without calling to account who did it. I trust not; and if another nation would come to these regions and begin to rob and plunder all that came in their way, would not the orators of the day be called to address the people and arouse them to war for such insults? And, for all this, would they not be called Christians and patriots? Yes, it would be rung from Georgia to Maine, from the ocean to the lakes, what fine men and Christians there were in the land. But when a few red children attempt to defend their rights, they are condemned as savages by those, if possible, who have indulged in wrongs more cruel than the Indians.

But there is still more. In 1619 a number of Indians went on board of a ship, by order of their chief, and the whites set upon them and murdered them without mercy; says Mr. Dermer, "without the Indians giving them the least provocation whatever." Is this insult to be borne, and not a word to be said? Truly, Christians would never bear it; why, then, think it strange that the denominated savages do not? O thou white Christian, look at acts that honored your country men, to the destruction of thousands, for much less insults than that. And who, my dear sirs, were wanting of the name of savages—whites or Indians? Let justice answer.

Source: Reprinted from *A Son of the Forest and Other Writings* by William Apess, a Pequot. © The University of Massachusetts Press by Barry O'Connell and published by the University of Massachusetts Press, 1997, 108–111.

Chief John Ross, "To the Senate and House of Representatives" (1836)

The Treaty of New Echota was signed on December 29, 1835, and was ratified by Congress in March 1836. This treaty, signed by a faction of the Cherokee Nation that supported removal to *Indian Territory, led to the forced removal of many tribal members, an event now known as the Trail of Tears. In the letter that follows, John Ross, principal chief of the Cherokee Nation, argues against ratification of the Treaty of New Echota on the grounds that a minority faction negotiated and signed the document.*

[Red Clay Council Ground, Cherokee Nation, September 28, 1836]

It is well known that for a number of years past we have been harassed by a series of vexations, which it is deemed unnecessary to recite in detail, but the evidence of which our delegation will be prepared to furnish. With a view to bringing our troubles to a close, a delegation was appointed on the 23rd of October, 1835, by the General Council of the nation, clothed with full powers to enter into arrangements with the Government of the United States, for the final adjustment of all our existing difficulties. The delegation failing to effect an arrangement with the United States commissioner, then in the nation, proceeded, agreeably to their instructions in that case, to Washington City, for the purpose of negotiating a treaty with the authorities of the United States.

After the departure of the Delegation, a contract was made by the Rev. John F. Schermerhorn, and certain individual Cherokees, purporting to be a "treaty, concluded at New Echota, in the State of Georgia, on the 29th day of December, 1835, by General William Carroll and John F. Schermerhorn, commissioners on the part of the United States, and the chiefs, headmen, and people of the Cherokee tribes of Indians." A spurious Delegation, in violation of a special injunction of the general council of the nation, proceeded to Washington City with this pretended treaty, and by false and fraudulent representations supplanted in the favor of the Government the legal and accredited Delegation of the Cherokee people, and obtained for this instrument, after making important alterations in its provisions, the recognition of the United States Government. And now it is presented to us as a treaty, ratified by the Senate, and approved by the President [Andrew Jackson], and our acquiescence in its requirements demanded, under the sanction of the displeasure of the United States, and the threat of summary compulsion, in case of

refusal. It comes to us, not through our legitimate authorities, the known and usual medium of communication between the Government of the United States and our nation, but through the agency of a complication of powers, civil and military.

By the stipulations of this instrument, we are despoiled of our private possessions, the indefeasible property of individuals. We are stripped of every attribute of freedom and eligibility for legal self-defence. Our property may be plundered before our eyes; violence may be committed on our persons; even our lives may be taken away, and there is none to regard our complaints. We are denationalized; we are disfranchised. We are deprived of membership in the human family! We have neither land nor home, nor resting place that can be called our own. And this is effected by the provisions of a compact which assumes the venerated, the sacred appellation of treaty.

We are overwhelmed! Our hearts are sickened, our utterance is paralized, when we reflect on the condition in which we are placed, by the audacious practices of unprincipled men, who have managed their stratagems with so much dexterity as to impose on the Government of the United States, in the face of our earnest, solemn, and reiterated protestations.

The instrument in question is not the act of our Nation; we are not parties to its covenants; it has not received the sanction of our people. The makers of it sustain no office nor appointment in our Nation, under the designation of Chiefs, Head men, or any other title, by which they hold, or could acquire, authority to assume the reins of Government, and to make bargain and sale of our rights, our possessions, and our common country. And we are constrained solemnly to declare, that we cannot but contemplate the enforcement of the stipulations of this instrument on us, against our consent, as an act of injustice and oppression, which, we are well persuaded, can never knowingly be countenanced by the Government and people of the United States; nor can we believe it to be the design of these honorable and high-minded individuals, who stand at the head of the

Govt., to bind a whole Nation, by the acts of a few unauthorized individuals. And, therefore, we, the parties to be affected by the result, appeal with confidence to the justice, the magnanimity, the compassion, of your honorable bodies, against the enforcement, on us, of the provisions of a compact, in the formation of which we have had no agency.

Source: Ross, John. *Letter from John Ross, Principal Chief of the Cherokee Nation of Indians, in Answer to Inquires from a Friend Regarding the Cherokee Affairs with the United States.* Washington, DC, 1836, 22–24.

Memorial of Protest of the Cherokee Nation
(1836)

As the Trail of Tears continued through the 1830s, many Cherokees tried desperately to convince the U.S. government to end removal. Numerous protests were lodged, including the following, which was submitted to Congress in 1836.

To the honourable the Senate and House of Representatives of the United States of North America, in Congress assembled:

The undersigned representatives of the Cherokee nation, east of the river Mississippi, impelled by duty, would respectfully submit, for the consideration of your honourable body, the following statement of facts: It will be seen, from the numerous subsisting treaties between the Cherokee nation and the United States, that from the earliest existence of this Government, the United States, in Congress assembled, received the Cherokees and their nation into favour and protection; and that the chiefs and warriors, for themselves and all parts of the Cherokee nation, acknowledged themselves and the said Cherokee nation to be under the protection of the United States of America, and of no other sovereign whatsoever; they also stipulated, that the said Cherokee nation will not hold any treaty with any foreign power, individual State, or with individuals of any States: that for, and in consideration of, valuable concessions made by the Cherokee nation, the United States solemnly guaranteed to said nation all their lands not ceded, and pledged the faith of the Government, that "all white people who have intruded, or may hereafter intrude on the lands reserved for the Cherokees, shall be removed by the United States, and proceeded against, according to the provisions of the act, passed 30th March, 1802," entitled "An act to regulate trade and intercourse with the Indian tribes, and to preserve peace on the frontiers." It would be useless to recapitulate the numerous provisions for the security and protection of the rights of the Cherokees, to be found in the various treaties between their nation and the United States. The Cherokees were happy and prosperous under a scrupulous observance of treaty stipulations by the Government of the United States, and from the fostering hand extended over them, they made rapid advances in civilization, morals, and in the arts and sciences. Little did they anticipate, that when taught to think and feel as the American citizen, and to have with him a common interest, they were to be *despoiled by their guardian,* to become strangers and wanderers in the land of their fathers, forced to return to the savage life, and to seek a new home in the wilds of the far west, and that without their consent. An instrument purporting to be a treaty with the Cherokee people, has recently been made public by the President of the United States, that will have such an operation, if carried into effect. This instrument, the delegation aver before the civilized world, and in the presence of

Almighty God, is fraudulent, false upon its face, made by unauthorized individuals, without the sanction, and against the wishes, of the great body of the Cherokee people. Upwards of fifteen thousand of those people have protested against it, solemnly declaring they will never acquiesce. The delegation would respectfully call the attention of your honourable body to their memorial and protest, with the accompanying documents, submitted to the Senate of the United States, on the subject of the alleged treaty, which are herewith transmitted.

If it be said that the Cherokees have lost their national character and political existence, as a nation or tribe, by State legislation, then the President and Senate can make no treaty with them; but if they have not, then no treaty can be made for them, binding, without and against their will. Such is the fact, in reference to the instrument entered into at New Echota, in December last. If treaties are to be thus made and enforced, deceptive to the Indians and to the world, purporting to be a contract, when, in truth, wanting the assent of one of the pretended parties, what security would there be for any nation or tribe to retain confidence in the United States? If interest or policy require that the Cherokees be removed, without their consent, from their lands, surely the President and Senate have no constitutional power to accomplish that object. They cannot do it under the power to make treaties, which are contracts, not rules prescribed by a superior, and therefore binding only by the assent of the parties. In the present instance, the assent of the Cherokee nation has not been given, but expressly denied. The President and Senate cannot do it under the power to regulate commerce with the Indian tribes, or intercourse with them, because that belongs to Congress, and so declared by the President, in his message to the Senate of February 22, 1831, relative to the execution of the act to regulate trade and intercourse with the Indian tribes, &c. passed 30th of March, 1802. They cannot do it under any subsisting treaty stipulation with the Cherokee nation. Nor does the peculiar situation of the Cherokees, in reference to the States, their necessities and distresses, confer

any power upon the President and Senate to alienate their legal rights, or to prescribe the manner and time of their removal.

Without a decision of what ought to be done, under existing circumstances, the question recurs, is the instrument under consideration a contract between the United States and the Cherokee nation? It so purports upon its face, and that falsely. Is that statement so sacred and conclusive that the Cherokee people cannot be heard to deny the fact? They have denied it under their own signatures, as the documents herein before referred to will show, and protested against the acts of the unauthorized few, who have arrogated to themselves the right to speak for the nation. The Cherokees have said they will not be bound thereby. The documents submitted to the Senate show, that when the vote was taken upon considering the propositions of the commissioner, there were but seventy-nine for so doing. Then it comes to this: could this small number of persons attending the New Echota meeting, acting in their individual capacity, dispose of the rights and interests of the Cherokee nation, or by any instrument they might sign, confer such power upon the President and Senate.

If the United States are to act as the guardian of the Cherokees, and to treat them as incapable of managing their own affairs, and blind to their true interests, yet this would not furnish power or authority to the President and Senate, as the treaty making power to prescribe the rule for managing their affairs. It may afford a pretence for the legislation of Congress, but none for the ratification of an instrument as a treaty made by a small faction against the protest of the Cherokee people.

That the Cherokees are a distinct people, sovereign to some extent, have a separate political existence as a society, or body politic, and a capability of being contracted within a national capacity, stands admitted by the uniform practice of the United States from 1785, down to the present day. With them have treaties been made through their chiefs, and distinguished men in primary assemblies, as also with their constituted agents or representatives. That they have not the right to manage their own internal affairs, and to regulate, by treaty, their intercourse with other nations, is a doctrine of modern date. In 1793, Mr. Jefferson said, "I consider our right of pre-emption of the Indian lands, not as amounting to any dominion, or jurisdiction, or paramountship whatever, but merely in the nature of a remainder, after the extinguishment of a present right, which gives us no present right whatever, but of preventing other nations from taking possession, and so defeating our expectancy. That the Indians *have the full, undivided, and independent sovereignty as long as they choose to keep it, and that this may be forever.*" This opinion was recognised and practised upon, by the Government of the United States, through several successive administrations, also recognised by the Supreme Court of the United States, and the several States, when the question has arisen. It has not been the opinion only of jurists, but of politicians, as may be seen from various reports of Secretaries of War—beginning with Gen. Knox, also the correspondence between the British and American ministers at Ghent in the year 1814. If the Cherokees have power to judge of their own interests, and to make treaties, which, it is presumed, will be denied by none, then to make a contract valid, the assent of a majority must be had, expressed by themselves or through their representatives, and the President and Senate have no power to say what their will shall be, for from the laws of nations we learn that "though a nation be obliged to promote, as far as lies in its power, the perfection of others, it is not entitled forcibly to obtrude these good offices on them." Such an attempt would be to violate their natural liberty. Those ambitious Europeans who attacked the American nations, and subjected them to their insatiable avidity of dominion, in order, as they pretended, for civilizing them, and causing them to be instructed in the true religion, (as in the present instance to preserve the Cherokees as a distinct people,) these usurpers grounded themselves on a pretence equally unjust and ridiculous. It is the expressed wish of the Government of the United States to remove the Cherokees to a place west of the Mississippi. That wish is said to be founded in humanity to the Indians. To make their situation more comfortable, and to preserve them as a distinct people. Let facts show how this *benevolent* design has been prosecuted, and how faithfully to the spirit and letter has the promise of the President of the United States to the Cherokees been fulfilled—that "*those who remain may be assured of our patronage, our aid, and good neighborhood.*" The delegation are not deceived by empty professions, and fear their race is to be destroyed by the mercenary policy of the present day, and their lands wrested from them by physical force; as proof, they will refer to the preamble of an act of the General Assembly of Georgia, in reference to the Cherokees, passed the 2d of December, 1835, where it is said, "from a knowledge of the Indian character, and from the present feelings of these Indians, it is confidently believed, that the right of occupancy of the lands in their possession should be withdrawn, that it would be a strong inducement to them to treat with the General Government, and consent to a removal to the west; and whereas, the present Legislature openly avow that their primary object in the measures intended to be pursued, *are founded on real humanity to these Indians,* and with a view, in a distant region, to perpetuate them with their old identity of character, *under the paternal care of the Government of the United States*; at the same time frankly disavowing *any selfish or sinister motives towards them in their present legislation.*" This is the profession. Let us turn to the practice of *humanity,* to the Cherokees, by the State of Georgia. In violation of the treaties between the United States and the Cherokee nation, that State passed a law requiring all white men, residing in that part of the Cherokee country, in her limits, to take an oath of allegiance to the State of Georgia. For a violation of this law, some of the ministers of Christ, missionaries among the Cherokees, were tried, convicted, and sentenced to hard labor in the penitentiary. Their case may be seen by reference to the records of the Supreme Court of the United States.

Valuable gold mines were discovered upon the Cherokee lands, within the chartered limits of Georgia, and the Cherokees commenced working them, and the Legislature of that State interfered by passing an act, making it penal for an Indian to dig for gold within Georgia, no doubt *"frankly disavowing any selfish or sinister motives towards them."* Under this law many Cherokees were arrested, tried, imprisoned, and otherwise abused. Some were even shot in attempting to avoid an arrest; yet the Cherokee people used no violence, but humbly petitioned the Government of the United States for a fulfilment of treaty engagements, to protect them, which was not done, and the answer given that the United States could not interfere. Georgia discovered she was not to be obstructed in carrying out her measures, *"founded on real humanity to these Indians,"* she passed an act directing the Indian country to be surveyed into districts. This excited some alarm, but the Cherokees were quieted with the assurance it would do no harm to survey the country. Another act was shortly after passed, to lay off the country into lots. As yet there was no authority to take possession, but it was not long before a law was made, authorizing a lottery for the lands laid off into lots. In this act the Indians were secured in possession of all the lots touched by their improvements, and the balance of the country allowed to be occupied by white men. This was a direct violation of the 5th article of the treaty of the 27th of February, 1819. The Cherokees made no resistance, still petitioned the United States for protection, and received the same answer that the President could not interpose. After the country was parcelled out by lottery, a horde of speculators made their appearance, and purchased of the "fortunate drawers," lots touched by Indian improvements, at reduced prices, declaring it was uncertain when the Cherokees would surrender their rights, and that the lots were encumbered by their claims. The consequence of this speculation was that, at the next session of the Legislature, an act was passed limiting the Indian right of occupancy to the lot upon which he resided, and his actual improvements adjoining. Many of

the Cherokees filed bills, and obtained injunctions against dispossession, and would have found relief in the courts of the country, if the judiciary had not been prostrated at the feet of legislative power. For the opinion of a judge, on this subject, there was an attempt to impeach him, then to limit his circuit to one county, and when all this failed, equity jurisdiction was taken from the courts, in Cherokee cases, by acts passed in years 1833 and 1834. The Cherokees were then left at the mercy of an interested agent. This agent, under the act of 1834, was the notorious William N. Bishop, the captain of the Georgia Guard, aid to the Governor, clerk of a court, postmaster, &c. and his mode of trying Indian rights is here submitted;

Table 1 Memorial of Protest of the Cherokee Nation (1836)

No. 95	25 District	2nd Section
86	25"	2"
93	25"	2"
89	25"	2"
57	25"	2"

MURRAY COUNTY, GEORGIA, January 20, 1835.

MR. JOHN MARTIN:

SIR:

The legal representative of lots of land, has called on me, as State's agent, to give him possession of the above described lots of land, and informs me that you are the occupant upon them. Under the laws of the State of Georgia, passed in the years 1833 and 1834, it is made my duty to comply with his request, you will, therefore, prepare yourself to give entire possession of said premises, on or before the 20th day of February next, fail not under the penalty of the law.

WM. N. BISHOP, State's Agent

Mr. Martin, a Cherokee, was a man of wealth, had an extensive farm; large fields of wheat growing;

and was turned out of house and home, and compelled, in the month of February, to seek a new residence within the limits of Tennessee. Thus Mr. Bishop settled his rights according to the notice he had given. The same summary process was used towards Mr. John Ross, the principal chief of the Cherokee nation. He was at Washington city, on the business of his nation. When he returned, he travelled till about 10 o'clock at night, to reach his family; rode up to the gate; saw a servant, believed to be his own; dismounted, ordered his horse taken; went in, and to his utter astonishment, found himself a stranger in his own house, his family having been, some days before driven out to seek a new home. A thought then flitted across his mind, that he could not, under all the circumstances of his situation, reconcile it to himself to tarry all night under the roof of his own house as a stranger, the new host of that house being the tenant of that mercenary band of Georgia speculators, at whose instance his helpless family had been turned out and made homeless.

Upon reflecting, however, that "man is born unto trouble," Mr. Ross at once concluded to take up lodgings there for the night, and to console himself under the conviction of having met his afflictions and trials in a manner consistent with every principle of moral obligation towards himself and family, his country and his God. On the next morning he arose early, and went out into the yard, and saw some straggling herds of his cattle and sheep browsing about the place. His crop of corn undisposed of. In casting a look up into the wide spread branches of a majestic oak, standing within the enclosure of the garden, and which overshadows the spot where lies the remains of his dear babe, and most beloved and affectionate father, he there saw, perched upon its boughs, that flock of beautiful pea-fowls, once the matron's care and delight, but now left to destruction and never more to be seen. He ordered his horse, paid his bill, and departed in search of his family, after travelling amid heavy rains, had the happiness of overtaking them on the road, bound for some place of refuge within the limits of Tennessee. Thus have his

houses, farm, public ferries and other property, been seized and wrested from him. Mr. Richard Taylor was, also, at Washington, and in his absence, his family was threatened with expulsion, and compelled to give two hundred dollars for leave to remain at home for a few months only. This is the "*real humanity*" the Cherokees were shown by the real or pretended authorities of Georgia, "disavowing any selfish or sinister motives towards them."

Mr. Joseph Vann, also, a native Cherokee, was a man of great wealth, had about eight hundred acres of land in cultivation; had made extensive improvements, consisting, in part, of a brick house, costing about ten thousand dollars, mills, kitchens, negro houses, and other buildings. He had fine gardens, and extensive apple and peach orchards. His business was so extensive, he was compelled to employ an overseer and other agents. In the fall of 1833, he was called from home, but before leaving, made a conditional contract with a Mr. Howell, a white man, to oversee for him in the year 1834, to commence on the first of January of that year. He returned about the 28th or 29th of December 1833, and learning Georgia had prohibited any Cherokee from hiring a white man, told Mr. Howell he did not want his services. Yet Mr. Bishop, the State's agent, represented to the authorities of Georgia, that Mr. Vann had violated the laws of that State, by hiring a white man, had forfeited his right of occupancy, and that a grant ought to issue for his lands. There were conflicting claims under Georgia for his possessions. A Mr. Riley pretended a claim, and took possession of the upper part of the dwelling house, armed for battle. Mr. Bishop, the State's agent, and his party, came to take possession, and between them and Riley, a fight commenced, and from twenty to fifty guns were fired in the house. While this was going on, Mr. Vann gathered his trembling wife and children into a room for safety. Riley could not be dislodged from his position up stairs, even after being wounded, and Bishop's party finally set fire to the house. Riley surrendered and the fire was extinguished.

Mr. Vann and his family were then driven out, unprepared, in the dead of winter, and snow upon the ground, through which they were compelled to wade, and take shelter within the limits of Tennessee, in an open log cabin, upon a dirt floor, and Bishop put his brother Absalom in possession of Mr. Vann's house. This Mr. Vann is the same, who, when a boy, volunteered as a private soldier in the Cherokee regiment, in the service of the United States, in the Creek war, periled his life in crossing the river at the battle of the Horse Shoe. What has been his reward?

Hundreds of other cases might be added. In fact, near all the Cherokees in Georgia, who had improvements of any value, except the favourites of the United States agents, under one pretext or other, have been driven from their homes. Amid the process of expulsion, the Rev. John F. Schermerhorn, the United States commissioner, visited the legislatures of Tennessee and Alabama, and importuned those bodies to pass laws, prohibiting the Cherokees who might be turned out of their possessions from within the Georgia limits, taking up a residence in the limits of those States.

In the month of May, 1835, the general council of the Cherokee nation passed a resolution, appointing agents to ascertain the value of improvements, taken by white men, and also the amount of all claims against the United States for spoliations upon the Cherokees. It was believed full justice could not be done in a treaty, otherwise than by ascertaining the injuries they had sustained. This resolution looked to a treaty with the United States, so soon as arrangements therefore could be made. Numbers of Cherokees had been forced from their houses and farms, particularly by the authorities of Georgia, and the citizens of the U. States being in possession of the improvements, if they were not valued in a short time, daily undergoing alterations and additions, they could not be identified as Cherokee improvements. These agents were required to register all claims for improvements and spoliations, in books to be kept for that purpose. To proceed forth with and to report to the principal chief, to be submitted to the next general council of the nation, which was to commence in October following, when the commissioner of the United States was to appear for the purpose of making a treaty. Messrs J. J. Trott, Robert Rogers, Elijah Hicks, Walter S. Adair, and Thomas F. Taylor, were appointed as agents, and in the latter part of July proceeded to the duties assigned them. After having made some progress, Messrs Trott and Hicks were arrested by a part of the Georgia guard. The officer commanding deprived them of all their books and papers, marched them off sixty miles, tied with ropes, to Spring Place, the station of the guard, and there kept them, with Messrs Taylor and Adair, who had also been arrested, in close confinement, in a guard-house, built to keep Indians in, for nine or ten days. A writ of *habeas corpus* was obtained, to bring the prisoners before a judge, but the guard evaded the service of the writ, by running the prisoners from place to place. The prisoners were required by Bishop, the captain of the guard, to give bond and surety to the State of Georgia, in the sum of one thousand dollars each, to appear at court, and to desist from valuing Cherokee improvements. They appeared at court, but no further steps were taken against them. Their books and papers have never been returned. This arrest was stated to be at the instance of Messrs Schermerhorn and Currey, agents for the United States, who, it is said, corresponded with the Governor of Georgia and the Secretary of War on the subject, and that a part of this correspondence may be seen in the War Department.

Joseph M. Lynch, an officer in the Cherokee nation, for executing the laws of the nation, was arrested by the Georgia guard, lodged in jail, and bail for his appearance at a court of justice refused. His negroes were also seized and committed to jail, and there continued until they broke jail and made their escape. Not less barbarity has been practised towards the Cherokees, by Benjamin F. Currey, the agent of the United States for Cherokee emigration, openly alleging it to be the policy of the United States to make the situation of the Indians so miserable as to drive them into a treaty, or an abandonment of their country, as may be seen by his letter to Messrs Brazleton and Kennedy, of 14th September, 1835. A few instances will be given as illustration of his mode of operation and general conduct.

Wahka and his wife were natives of, and residents in, the Cherokee nation east of the Mississippi. The agents of the United States prevailed upon the wife to enrol for emigration, against the remonstrances of the husband, and they afterwards, by force, separated her from her husband, and took her and the children to Arkansas, leaving the husband and father behind, because he would not enrol. The improvements upon which he resided, were valued in the name of the wife, and her turned out of possession.

Atalah Anosta was prevailed upon to enrol when drunk, contrary to the wish and will of his wife and children; when the time arrived for him to leave for Arkansas, he absconded. A guard was sent after him by B. F. Currey, which arrested the woman and children, and brought them to the agency about dark, in a cold rain, shivering and hungry. They were detained under guard all night and part of the next day, and until the woman agreed to enrol her name as an emigrant. The husband then came in, and he and his wife and their children were put on board a boat, and taken to Arkansas. There they soon lost two or three of their children, and then returned on foot to the Cherokee nation east of the Mississippi.

Sconatachee, when drunk, was enrolled by Benjamin F. Currey; when the emigrants were collecting, he did not appear, and Currey and John Miller, the interpreter, went after him. Currey drew a pistol, and attempted to drive the old man to the agency, who presented his gun and refused to go. Currey and Miller returned without him. He made the facts known to Hugh Montgomery, the Cherokee agent, who gave him a certificate that he should not be forced away against his will. So the matter rested till the emigrants were collected the next year, and then Currey sent a wagon and guard for him. He was arrested, tied, and hauled to the agency, leaving some of his children behind in the woods, where they had fled on the approach of the guard. Richard Cheek enrolled for emigration, but before the time of departure, he hired to work on the Tuscumbia rail-road, in Alabama. When the emigrants started, Currey had Cheek's wife taken, put on board a boat, and started, to Arkansas. She was even denied the privilege of visiting her husband as she descended the river. He was left behind, and never saw her more. She died on the way.

Such outrages, and violations of treaty stipulations, have been the subject of complaint to the Government of the United States, on the part of the Cherokees for years past; and the delegation are not surprised, that the American people are not now startled at those wrongs, so long continued, for by habit men are brought to look with indifference upon death itself. If the government of the United States has determined to take the Cherokee lands without their consent, the power is with them; and the American people can "reap the field that is not their own, and gather the vintage of his vineyard whom by violence they have oppressed."

There is no ground for the pretended necessity under which the authorities of the United States have acted, for at the time of the formation, and ratification of the pretended treaty, the Cherokee people had their delegation and representatives in Washington city, with instructions and full powers to negotiate a treaty. This delegation were importuning the Government for an opportunity to do so, as their correspondence with the War Department will show. It will further show, they were at first received and recognised as the proper party with which to make a treaty, and then rejected, unless they would adopt the act of the faction at New Echota, which, in them, would have been a violation of the express will of their constituents. They were willing to act under their authority for the Cherokee people, but the opportunity to do so was refused. Then there is no force in the argument for the ratification of a fraudulent treaty, that it was necessary something should be done. There is as little in the assertion, that the Cherokees were in a distressed and starving condition, and that it was therefore necessary to ratify the New Echota instrument, as a treaty for their benefit and preservation, as the best that could be done. This position denies to the Cherokees the right to think for themselves.

Their distresses have not been denied, but the argument comes with a bad grace from the agents of the United States, who have produced them avowedly for the purpose of forcing a treaty. The Cherokees have not asked, but refused the proffered relief, and are surely the best judges of their own true situation, can properly appreciate the motives for the offer, as also the expressed sympathy for their misfortunes, and the avowed benevolence towards the Indian race, all of which amounts simply to this: "we want, and intend to take your lands, and are sorry you are unwilling for us to do so in our own way."

The delegation will call to the recollection of the members of the House, the arguments and predictions of the opponents to the passage of "An act to provide for an exchange of lands with the Indians, residing in any of the States or Territories, and for their removal west of the Mississippi." While that measure was under discussion in the House of Representatives in 1830, the members opposed insisted its passage would be an encouragement to the States to press upon the Indians, and to force them from their homes; that it was the secret design to make their situation so wretched and intolerable, that they would be forced to abandon their country. This was expressly denied by the friends of the measure, by none more earnestly than the members from Georgia, who insisted the measure was founded in humanity to the Indians. Who was right, let subsequent facts decide. That law, though not so designed by Congress, has been the source from which much of the Cherokee sufferings has come. Immediately after its passage, Georgia commenced her oppressive legislation over Indian territory, and the payment of Cherokee annuities was suspended, and elections ordered, under the authority and direction of Government agents, for deciding to whom they were to be paid.

The present is the third attempt to make a treaty with a few unauthorized Cherokees, against the will of their nation. In the year 1834 a treaty was made at Washington with Andrew Ross, James Starr, Thomas J. Pack, and John West, which the Senate refused to ratify. Andrew Ross and James Starr have also signed the New Echota instrument. On the 14th of March, 1835, another was concluded with John Ridge, Archilla Smith, Elias Boudinot, S. W. Bell, John West, William A. Davis, and Ezekiel West. It was never submitted to the Senate, but by the President directed to be submitted to the Cherokees for their consideration and approbation, which was done, with an address from the President himself. The propositions were rejected with great unanimity by the Cherokee people. It will be observed that John Ridge, Archilla Smith, and Elias Boudinot, have also signed the New Echota instrument.

On the 23d of October, 1835, the general council of the Cherokee nation appointed a delegation of twenty, and vested in them full power to enter into a treaty with the United States, among them was John Ridge and Elias Boudinot. If they failed to make a treaty in the nation, with a commissioner, they were to go to Washington City, there to negotiate finally with the General Government of the United States. On the next day the matter was submitted to the people, when they declared, "we approve of, and confirm the nomination and appointment of John Ross, &c. as our representatives to the United States Government; also, of the powers in them vested, under the resolutions of the general council annexed; and we unite with the committee and council in forbidding any delegation to treat with the Government of the United States of North America, excepting the delegation now formally and openly confirmed by us, the people of the Cherokee nation." Signed by one thousand and seventy six individuals then present, and among them near every man who signed the New Echota treaty. The delegation thus appointed, opened a negotiation with John F. Schermerhorn, U. States commissioner, but could effect nothing; and in their letter of the 28th October, 1835, they say they are "the delegation chosen from and appointed by the Cherokee nation." Again they say, "upon examining the articles you have submitted as the basis of the treaty you have to propose, they can find in them no real variation from those against which the Cherokee nation have already openly and formally protested." "As a reference must be had, even by yourself to the Senate, when it convenes, under any circumstances, it will be necessary for us to conclude at Washington, and, therefore, we think it would only be trifling with your time to encourage any further negotiation here." This letter was signed by the delegation, including John Ridge and Elias Boudinot, and addressed to John F. Schermerhorn, United States commissioner. On the 31st of the same month, they addressed Mr. Schermerhorn another letter, declining a further negotiation with him and say, "in reference to another council at New Echota, we cannot enter into your views, as the people have already made their election upon the course they wish pursued. We, in their name, protest against any future meeting being called, under the name of a council, in the way you proposed, as an unnecessary agitation of the public mind, and as an act which will never be recognised by the Cherokee nation." This was the language of the delegation, with Ridge and Boudinot inclusive, in the month of October last. Before the delegation started to Washington, Boudinot resigned, and recommended that Stand Watie, his brother, should be appointed in his place, which was done, and he and Ridge came with the delegation to Washington, and remained with them till the month of February, when they left, and wrote a letter, through John F. Schermerhorn, to the Government of the United States, urging the ratification of the treaty made at New Echota, and abusing the authority under which they came to Washington, saying "all the members of the delegations for a number of years past, he, John Ross, had nominated to his council, who confirm them, always adding to their number John Ross himself," yet they say in the same letter, that they were appointed "by the people at Red Clay council."

They further say, "John Ross and his friends wished to get all the funds of the nation in their hands, and this accounted for their repugnance to make a treaty at home in open council." This assertion is false and gratuitous, and who showed a greater repugnance than John Ridge and Elias Boudinot? They have succeeded in having ratified an instrument constituting themselves and other friends a committee to manage all Cherokee affairs. A new way of making Indian chiefs, but it goes to show their original design. Their repugnance to make a treaty in the nation was founded in a desire to get the delegation out of the nation, when they and their friends could meet the commissioner, and make a treaty giving them all power and control of the funds of the nation, which they could never obtain by the consent of the Cherokee people. In another letter of the 25th March, 1836, they say, "the council (meeting at Red Clay) was called by Ross to *dodge* the commissioner to come to Washington." Now this council was not called, but was the regular annual meeting. Notwithstanding their own letters, they have the effrontery to say, "Ross drew up the papers granting full powers to twenty persons to treat there or elsewhere. To this instrument he added a protest against the acceptance of the five millions," that the people did not understand what was done. Let this be compared with their letters of the 28th and 31st of October, 1835, and their hypocrisy will be apparent. When Mr. Schermerhorn got them to Washington, they were prepared to certify any thing he might desire. In the New Echota treaty he had provided an office for himself, the propriety of which was questioned, and notwithstanding at the time of its formation, Ridge and Watie were at Washington, as members of what they called the Ross delegation. On the 25th March, 1836, they certified for Mr Schermerhorn in these words: "we must also do you the justice to say, that your name, and that of Governor Carroll, as commissioners to settle the affairs of our people under the treaty, was inserted in it according to our wishes and request," &c. They further say, "the constituted authorities of the Cherokees have defamed the high officers of the Government of the United States, and treated the friendship and kindness of the honorable Messrs Frelinghuysen and Everett, and Judge McLean, with contempt." The same is repeated by Mr Schermerhorn in his letter of the 29th of March, 1836, to the Secretary of War. These statements have no foundation in fact, and it is to be regretted Mr. Schermerhorn has given such implicit credence to his interested witnesses as to give their falsehoods the sanction of his name.

The charge has been made to excite prejudice against this delegation. They are attacked by naked assertion, to which, in duty to themselves, they give a positive denial, and feel assured their friends will not be found ready to believe every evil report.

Shortly after the Cherokee delegation arrived in Washington, they visited the Secretary of War, who told them Mr. Schermerhorn had an idea of bringing some Cherokees with him, but that he had been instructed not to bring one; yet he did bring them, and about the time they arrived the Commissioner of Indian Affairs was seen hunting a place and making arrangements for their board. Shortly after this, he wrote to the Cherokee delegation that those individuals had not come to make a treaty but to secure the ratification of that made at New Echota. Thus it seems they were brought as witnesses for Mr. Schermerhorn and themselves, to establish, by their evidence, whatever might be necessary to secure the ratification of the fraudulent treaty, and they have, from time to time, as circumstances required, addressed letters to Mr. Schermerhorn, to be submitted, through the Secretary of War, to the Senate. From the letters procured by Mr. Schermerhorn, and submitted to the Senate, it seems to have been the design to create an impression that the members of the committee and council, and also the principal chief, had lost the confidence of the Cherokee people. This is not new. It has been asserted for years, particularly by John Ridge, Elias Boudinot, and their associates, but let facts speak for themselves. In 1831, the payment of the Cherokee annuities to the treasurer of the nation was suspended, and so remained till 1834, when, under the idea that the authorities of the nation were self-constituted, and not sanctioned by the Cherokee people, an election was ordered to be held at the agency, to decide whether the annuities should be paid to the treasurer of the nation, or to the individual Cherokees. Every vote, save one, was given that they be paid to the

treasurer. Again, in 1835, another election for the same purpose, under authority of the United States' agents, was had, near the house of John Ridge. He and his associates exerted all their influence, and when the votes were taken, there appeared, two thousand two hundred and twenty-five for paying the treasurer, and one hundred and fourteen opposed; and among them many Creeks and Arkansas emigrants, having no interest in the matter. This is evidence more to be relied on, than the declarations of interested individuals.

The Cherokee delegation have thus considered it their duty to exhibit before your honorable body a brief view of the Cherokee case, by a short statement of facts. A detailed narrative would form a history too voluminous to be presented, in a memorial and protest. They have, therefore, contented themselves with a brief recital, and will add, that in reviewing the past, they have done it alone for the purpose of showing what glaring oppressions and sufferings the peaceful and unoffending Cherokees have been doomed to witness and endure. Also, to tell your honourable body, in sincerity, that owing to the intelligence of the Cherokee people, they have a correct knowledge of their own rights, and they well know the illegality of those oppressive measures which have been adopted for their expulsion, by State authority. Their devoted attachment to their native country has not been, nor ever can be, eradicated from their breast. This, together with the implicit confidence, they have been taught to cherish, in the *justice, good faith, and magnanimity of the United States,* also, their firm reliance on the generosity and friendship of the American people have formed the anchor of their hope and upon which alone they have been induced and influenced to shape their peaceful and manly course, under some of the most trying circumstances any people have been called to witness and endure. For more than *seven long years* have the Cherokee people been driven into the necessity of contending for their just rights, and they have struggled against fearful odds. Their means of defence being altogether within the grasp and control of their competitors, they have at last been trampled under foot.

Their resources and means of defence, have been seized and withheld. The treaties, laws, and constitution of the United States, their bulwark, and only citadel of refuge, put beyond their reach; unfortunately for them, the protecting arm of the commander-in-chief of these fortresses has been withdrawn from them. The judgments of the judiciary branch of the government, in support of their rights, have been disregarded and prostrated; and their petitions for relief, from time to time before Congress, been unheeded. Their annuities withheld; their printing press, affording the only clarion through which to proclaim their wrongs before the American people and the civilized world, has been seized and detained, at the instance of an agent of the United States.

An attorney at law, employed by them to defend the rights of the suffering Cherokees, before the courts of Georgia, has been induced to desert his clients' cause, under expectations of being better paid, at their expense, by taking sides against them. Some of their own citizens, seduced and prompted by officers of the United States Government to assume upon themselves the powers of the nation, unconferred, have been brought to negotiate a treaty, over the heads and remonstrances of the nation. Is there to be found in the annals of history, a parallel case to this? By this treaty all the lands, rights, interests, and claims, of whatsoever nature, of the Cherokee people east of the Mississippi, are pretended to be ceded to the United States for the pittance of $5,600,000. Let us take a cursory view of the country and other rights of the Cherokees professed to be surrendered to the United States, under the provisions of this fraudulent treaty. The Cherokee Territory, within the limits of North Carolina, Georgia, Tennessee and Alabama, is estimated to contain *ten millions of acres*. It embraces a large portion of the finest lands to be found in any of the States; and a salubrity of climate unsurpassed by any; possessing superior advantages in reference to water power; owing to the numerous rills, brooks and rivers, which flow from and through it; some of these streams afford good navigation, others are susceptible of being easily improved and made navigable. On the routes where roads have been opened by the Cherokees, through this country, there must necessarily pass some of the most important public roads and other internal improvements, which at no distant day will be constructed.

The entire country is covered with a dense forest of valuable timber, also abounding in inexhaustible quarries of marble and limestone. Above all, it possesses the most extensive regions of the precious metal known in the United States. The riches of the gold mines are incalculable, some of the lots of *forty acres* of land, embracing gold mines, which have been surveyed and disposed of by lottery, under the authority of Georgia, with the encumbrance of the Indian title, have been sold for *upwards of thirty thousand dollars!*

There are also extensive banks of iron ore interspersed throughout the country. Mineralogists who have travelled over a portion of this territory, are fully persuaded, from what they have seen, that lead and silver mines will also be found in the mountain regions. Independent of all these natural advantages and invaluable resources, there are many extensive and valuable improvements made upon the lands by the native Cherokee inhabitants, and those adopted as Cherokee citizens, by intermarriages.

The Cherokee population has recently been reported by the War Department to be 18,000, according to a census taken by agents appointed by the Government. This people have become civilized, and adopted the Christian religion. Their pursuits are pastoral and agricultural, and in some degree, mechanical. Their stocks of cattle, however, have become greatly reduced in numbers within the few past years, owing to the unfortunate policy which has thrown upon this territory a class of white and irresponsible settlers, who, disregarding all laws and treaties, so far as the rights of the Cherokees are concerned, and who have been actuated more from the sordid impulses of avarice, than by any principle of moral obligation or of justice, have by fraud and force made Cherokee property their own.

The possessions of the Cherokee inhabitants, consist of houses, which cost generally from fifty dollars, one hundred to one thousand dollars, and in many instances up to five thousand dollars; some few as high as six, eight, and ten thousand dollars, with corresponding out buildings, consisting of kitchens, meat houses, dairies, granaries or corn cribs, barns, stables, &c., grist and saw mills: connected with these are gardens for culinary vegetables; also peach and apple orchards; lots of enclosed ground for horses, black cattle, &c. The farms of the Cherokees contain from ten, twenty, thirty, forty, fifty, sixty, to one hundred and fifty, and two hundred acres of land under cultivation, and enclosed with good rail fences. Among the most wealthy there are farms of three and four hundred acres, and in one instance perhaps about eight hundred acres in cultivation. Some of the most extensive and valuable farms and possessions have been forcibly wrested from the proprietors by the Georgia guard and agents, and citizens of Georgia put into possession of them, whilst the Cherokee owners have been thrust out to seek shelter in a camp, or under the roof of a log hut in the woods, within the limits of North Carolina, Tennessee, and Alabama. There are many valuable public ferries also owned by the Cherokees, the incomes of some of them amount to from five hundred to one thousand, fifteen hundred and two thousand dollar per annum. Several public roads opened at private expense, were also kept up by companies under regulations of the national council, and toll gates were erected on them. These regulations have all been prostrated by State Legislation, and the Cherokee proprietors thus deprived of their rights, privileges, and property. Besides all this, there are various important interests and claims which are secured by the provisions of the former subsisting treaties, to the Cherokees, and for which the United States is justice bound to allow indemnification. For the surrender then of a territory containing about ten millions of acres, together with the various interests and claims spoken of, and the amount that will be required to cover these claims, no man, without

data, can form any estimate. The sum of five millions, six hundred thousand dollars only, is proposed to be paid: the price given for the lands at this rate would not exceed thirty cents per acre. Will Georgia accept the whole amount, for that portion within her limits?

The faith of the United States being solemnly pledged to the Cherokee nation for the guarantee of the quiet and uninterrupted protection of their territorial possessions forever; and it being an unquestionable fact, that the Cherokees love their country; that no amount of money could induce them voluntarily to yield their assent to a cession of the same. But, when under all the circumstances of their peculiar situation and unhappy condition, the nation see the necessity of negotiating a treaty for their security and future welfare, and having appointed a delegation with full powers for that purpose, is it liberal, humane, or just, that a fraudulent treaty, containing principles and stipulations altogether objectionable, and obnoxious to their own sense of propriety and justice, should be enforced upon them? The basis of the instrument, the sum fixed upon, the commutation of annuities, and the general provisions of the various articles it contains, are all objectionable. Justice and equity demand, that in any final treaty for the adjustment of the Cherokee difficulties, that their rights, interests, and wishes should be consulted; and that the individual rights of the Cherokee citizens, in their possessions and claims, should be amply secured; and as freemen, they should be left at liberty to stay or remove where they please. Also, that the territory to be ceded by the United States to the Cherokee nation west of the Mississippi, should be granted to them by a patent in fee simple, and not clogged with the conditions of the act of 1830; and the national funds of the Cherokees should be placed under the control of their national council.

The delegation must repeat, the instrument entered into at New Echota, purporting to be a treaty, is deceptive to the world, and a fraud upon the Cherokee people. If a doubt exists as to the truth of their statement, a committee of investigation can learn the facts, and it may also learn that if the Cherokees are removed under that instrument, it will be by force. This declaration they make in sincerity, with hearts sickening at the scenes they may be doomed to witness; they have toiled to avert such calamity; it is now with Congress, and beyond their control; they hope they are mistaken, but it is hope against a sad and almost certain reality. It would be uncandid to conceal their opinions, and they have no motive for expressing them but a solemn sense of duty. The Cherokees cannot resist the power of the United States, and should they be driven from their native land, then will they look in melancholy sadness upon the golden chain presented by President Washington to the Cherokee people as emblematical of the brightness and purity of the friendship between the United States and the Cherokee nation.

JNO. ROSS

JOHN MARTIN

JAMES BROWN

JOSEPH VANN

JOHN BENGE

LEWIS ROSS

ELIJAH HICKS

RICH'D FIELDS

Source: Memorial of Protest of the Cherokee Nation, 1836. United States Congressional Serial Set, House Document 286, 24th Cong., 1st session.

George Copway, Narrative

(1850)

In the following narrative, George Copway, a member of the Ojibwa Nation, discusses the causes for the decline in Native American population numbers. This excerpt offers an interesting counterargument to the then contemporary belief expressed by many whites that Indians were fated to disappear. Copway provides an informed perspective on the causes for shrinking Native American populations, including the use and effects of alcohol, disease, broken spirits, and dismal prospects for the future.

I was born in *nature's wide domain!* The trees were all that sheltered my infant limbs—the blue heavens all that covered me. I am one of Nature's children; I have always admired her; she shall be my glory; her features—her robes, and the wreath about her brow—the seasons—her stately oaks and the evergreen—her hair—ringlets of the earth, all contribute to my enduring love of her; and wherever I see her, emotions of pleasure roll in my breast, and swell and burst like waves on the shores of the ocean, in prayer and praise to Him who has placed me in her hand. It is though great to be born in palaces, surrounded with wealth—but to be born in nature's wide domain is greater still!

I have often been asked the question, "What is the reason that the Indians are diminishing in numbers in the midst of their white neighbors?" To state all that might be said in replying to this question, would require almost a separate volume. But the following are a few of the principle [sic] reasons:

1. The introduction of King Alcohol among them.
2. The introduction of new diseases, produced by their intercourse with the whites; and by adopting their intemperate habits.

3. Their inability to pursue that course of living, after abandoning their wigwams, which tends to health and old age.

4. Their spirits are broken down in consequence of seeing that their *race* are becoming homeless, friendless, moneyless, and trodden down by the whites.

5. Their future prospects are gloomy and cheerless—enough to break down the noblest spirits.

There are many other reasons which could be assigned for their diminution. But are not these sufficient of themselves to crush and exterminate even any *white* race, if not protected and defended by friends and wholesome laws? Our people have been driven from their homes, and have been cajoled out of the few sacred spots where the bones of their ancestors and children lie; and where they themselves expected to lie, when released from the trials and troubles of life. Were it possible to reverse the order of things, by placing the whites in the same condition, how long would it be endured? There is not a white man, who deserves the name of *man,* that would not rather die than be deprived of his home, and driven from the graves of his relatives. "Oh shame, where is thy blush!"

With all the wholesome and enlightened laws; with all the advantages and privileges of the glorious Gospel, that shines so richly and brightly all around the white man; the poor ignorant Indians are compelled, at the point of the bayonet, to forsake the sepulchres of those most dear to them, and to retire to a strange land, where there is no inhabitant to welcome them!!! May the day soon dawn, when Justice will take her seat upon the throne.

If I did not think that there were some who are alive to the interests of my people, and often shed a tear for them; if I did not think that I could discover a gleam of light and hope in the future, "I should of all men be most miserable." "Surely the bitterness of death" would be "past." I look

then to the Gospel and to education as my only hope.

I will now state, in a very brief manner, what I think ought to be done, by those whose benevolent feelings lead them to commiserate the condition of the Aborigines in America.

1. They should establish missions and high schools wherever the whites have frequent intercourse with them.

2. They should use their influence, as soon as the Indians are well educated, and understand the laws of the land, to have them placed on the same footing as the whites.

3. They should try to procure for them a territorial or district government, so they may represent their own nation.

4. They should obtain for them, deeds of their own lands; and, if qualified, according to law, urge their right to vote.

The Indians will be sure to waste and squander whatever they may receive from the American or British Government, unless *some,* at least, of the above suggestions, shall have been put into practice.

The Council was not dissolved. The President, Chief Sawyer, proceeded to His Excellency, the Governor General, and presented the petitions, in the name of the General Council. These petitions, as we learned afterwards, were received with a simple *nod!* Of the head. O mercy! Is this for ever to be our destiny? Common humanity, at least, might have induced his Lordship to speak a few consolary words, if nothing else. Our reception was both discouraging and chilling. When we have a press of our own, we shall, perhaps, be able to plead our own cause. Give us but the *Bible,* and the influence of a *Press,* and we ask no more. (pp. 150–152)

Source: Copway, George. *The Life, Letters and Speeches of Kah-ge-ga-gah-bowh, or, G. Copway, Chief Ojibway Nation.* New York: S. W. Benedict, 1850, 17, 139–141.

Big Eagle, Account of the Dakota War
(1862)

In June 1894, Jerome Big Eagle, a warrior and band leader of the Dakota Indians in Minnesota, provided the following account of the causes of the Dakota War of 1862. Big Eagle's account provides a counter explanation to the white narrative of this conflict, in which 400 to 800 white settlers and as many as 100 Native Americans lost their lives. Big Eagle argues that unhappiness about treaty agreements, mistreatment of Native Americans, and a belief that Minnesota residents were vulnerable to attack were some of the causes that ultimately led to the conflict.

Interestingly, although Big Eagle argues for a more complex understanding of the causes of the war, he also uses the trope of the vanishing, or doomed, Indian in this narrative, stating that he knows the United States will eventually overpower and defeat his people. This is exactly the kind of message many 19th-century Americans wanted to hear. The period from 1890 to 1920 represented the nadir of American race relations and was characterized by the restriction of civil rights, violence, and other forms of discrimination. Americans were afraid that immigrants and minorities would affect white social and cultural institutions if left unchecked. Big Eagle's narrative, therefore, served a dual purpose when originally published. It broadened the nation's understanding of the Dakota uprising while simultaneously reassuring fin de siècle United States of past victories in which white communities resisted attacks from different racial groups.

I was born in the Indian village of my father near Mendota, in 1827, and am now sixty-seven years old. My father was Grey Iron, a sub-chief of the Midawa-xanton Sioux. When he died I succeeded him as chief of the band and adopted the name of his father, Wambdetonka, which, as is commonly called, means the Big Eagle. When I was a young man I often went with war parties against the Chippewa and other enemies of my nation, and the six feathers shown in the headdress of my picture in the historical society at St. Paul stand for six Chippewa scalps that I took when on the warpath. By the terms of the treaties of Traverse des Sioux and Mendota in 1851, the Sioux sold all of their lands in Minnesota, except a strip ten miles wide on each side of the Minnesota river from near Fort Ridgely to the Big Stone lake. The Medawakantons and Wacoutas had their reservation up to the Yellow Medicine. In 1858 the ten miles of this strip belonging to the Medawakanton and Wacouta bands, and lying north of the river were sold, mainly through the influence of Little Crow. That year, with some other chiefs, I went to Washington on business connected with the treaty. The selling of that strip north of the Minnesota caused great dissatisfaction among the Sioux, and Little Crow was always blamed for the part he took in the sale. It caused us all to move to the south side of the river, where there was but very little game, and many of our people, under the treaty, were induced to give up the old life and go to work like white men, which was very distasteful to many.

Of the causes that led to the outbreak of August, 1862, much has been said. Of course it was wrong, as we all know now, but there were not many Christians among the Indians then, and they did not understand things as they should. There was great dissatisfaction among the Indians over many things the whites did. The whites would not let them go to war against their enemies. This was right, but the Indians did not then know it. Then the whites were always trying to make the Indians give up their life and live like white men—go to farming, work hard and do as they did—and the Indians did not know how to do that, and did not want to anyway. It seemed too sudden to make such a change. If the Indians had tried to make the whites live like them, the whites would have resisted, and it was the same way with many Indians. The Indians wanted to live as they did before the treaty of Traverse des Sioux—go where they pleased and when they pleased; hunt game wherever they could find it, sell their furs to the traders and live as they could.

Then the Indians did not think the traders had done right. The Indians bought goods of them on credit, and when the government payments came the traders were on hand with their books, which showed that the Indians owed so much and so much, and as the Indians kept no books they could not deny their accounts, but had to pay them, and sometimes the traders got all their money. I do not say that the traders always cheated and lied about these accounts. I know many of them were honest men and kind and accommodating, but since I have been a citizen I know that many white men, when they go to pay their accounts, often think them too large and refuse to pay them, and they go to law about them and there is much bad feeling. The Indians could not go to law, but there was always trouble over their credits. Under the treaty of Traverse des Sioux (1851) the Indians had to pay a very large sum of money to the traders for old debts, some of which ran back fifteen years, and many of those who had got the goods were dead and others were not present, and the trader's books had to be received as to the amounts, and the money was taken from the tribe to pay them. Of course the traders often were of great service to the Indians in letting them have goods on credit, but the Indians seemed to think the traders ought not to be too hard on them about the payments, but do as the Indians did among one another, and put off the payment until they were better able to make it.

Then many of the white men often abused the Indians and treated them unkindly. Perhaps they had excuse, but the Indians did not think so. Many of the whites always seemed to say by their manner when they saw an Indian, "I am much better than you," and the Indians did not like this. There was excuse for this, but the Dakotas did not believe there were better men in the world than they. Then some of the white men abused the Indian women in a certain way and disgraced them, and surely there was no excuse for that.

All these things made many Indians dislike the whites. Then a little while before the outbreak there was trouble among the Indians themselves. Some of the Indians took a sensible course and began to live like white men. The government built them houses, furnished them tools, seed, etc., and taught them to farm. At the two agencies, Yellow Medicine and Redwood, there were several hundred acres of land in cultivation that summer. Others staid in their teepees. There was a white man's party and an Indian party. We had politics among us and there was much feeling. A new chief speaker for the tribe was to be elected. There were three candidates—Little Crow, myself and Wa-sui-hi-ya-ye-dan (Traveling Hail). After an exciting contest Traveling Hail was elected. Little Crow felt sore over his defeat. Many of our tribe believed him responsible for the sale of the north ten-mile strip, and I think this was why he was defeated. I did not care much about it. Many whites think that Little Crow was the principal chief of the Kakotas at this time, but he was not. Wabasha was the principal chief, and he was of the white man's party; so was I; so was old Shakopee, whose band was very large. Many think if old Shakopee had lived there would have been no war, for he was for the white men and had great influence. But he died that summer, and was succeeded by his son, whose real name was Ea-to-ka, but when he became chief he took his father's name, and was afterwards called Little Shakopee, or Little Six, for in the Sioux language Shakopee means six. This Shakopee was against the white men. He took part in the outbreak, murdering women and children, but I never saw him in a battle, and he was caught in Manitoba and hanged in 1864. My brother, Medicine Bottle, was hanged with him.

As the summer advanced, there was great trouble among the Sioux—troubles among themselves, troubles with the whites, and [one] thing and another. The war with the South was going on then, and a great many men had left the state and gone down there to fight. A few weeks before the outbreak the president called for many more men, and a great many of the white men of Minnesota and some half-breeds enlisted and went to Fort Snelling to be sent South. We understood that the South was getting the best of the fight, and it was said that the North would be whipped. The year before the new president had turned out Major Brown and Major Cullen, the Indian agents, and put in their places Major Galbraith and Mr. Clark Thompson, and they had turned out the men under them and put in others of their own party. There were a great many changes. An Indian named Shonka-sha (White Dog), who had been hired to teach the Indians to farm, was removed and another Indian named Ta-opi (The Wounded Man), a son of old Betsy, of St. Paul, put in his place. Nearly all of the men who were turned out were dissatisfied, and the most of the Indians did not like the new men. At last Major Galbraith went to work about the agencies and recruited a company of soldiers to go south. His men were nearly all half-breeds. This was the company called the Renville Rangers, for they were mostly from Renville County. The Indians now thought the whites must be pretty hard up for men to fight the South, or they would not come so far out on the frontier and take half-breeds or anything to help them.

It began to be whispered about that now would be a good time to go to war with the whites and get back the lands. It was believed that the men who had enlisted last had all left the state, and that before help could be sent the Indians could clean out the country, and that the Winnebagoes, and even the Chippewas, would assist the Sioux. It was also thought that a war with the whites would cause the Sioux to forget the troubles among themselves and enable many of them to pay off some old scores. Though I took part in the war, I was against it. I knew there was no good cause for it, and I had been to Washington and knew the power of the whites and that they would finally conquer us. We might succeed for a time, but we would be overpowered and defeated at last. I said

all this and many more things to my people, but many of my own bands were against me, and some of the other chiefs put words in their mouths to say to me. When the outbreak came Little Crow told some of my band that if I refused to lead them to shoot me as a traitor who would not stand up for his nation, and then select another leader in my place.

But after the first talk of war the counsels of the peace Indians prevailed, and many of us thought the danger had all blown over. The time of the government payment was near at hand, and this may have had something to do with it. There was another thing that helped to stop the war talk. The crops that had been put in by the "farmer" Indians were looking well, and there seemed to be a good prospect for a plentiful supply of provisions for them the coming winter without having to depend on the game of the country or without going far out to the west on the plains for buffalo. It seemed as if the white men's way was certainly the best. Many of the Indians had been short of provisions that summer and had exhausted their credits and were in bad condition. "Now," said the farmer Indians, "if you had worked last season you would not be starving now and begging for food." The "farmers" were favored by the government in every way. They had houses built for them, some of them even had brick houses, and they were not allowed to suffer. The other Indians did not like this. They were envious of them and jealous, and disliked them because they were favored. They called them "farmers," as if it was disgraceful to be a farmer. They called them "cut-hairs," because they had given up the Indian fashion of wearing the hair, and "breeches men," because they wore pantaloons, and "Dutchmen," because so many of the settlers on the north side of the river and elsewhere in the country were Germans. I have heard that there was a secret organization of the Indians called the "Soldiers' Lodge," whose object was to declare war against the whites, but I knew nothing of it.

At last the time for the payment came and the Indians came in to the agencies to get their money.

But the paymaster did not come, and week after week went by and still he did not come. The payment was to be in gold. Somebody told the Indians that the payment would never be made. The government was in a great war, and gold was scarce, and paper money had taken its place, and it was said the gold could not be had to pay us. Then the trouble began again and the war talk started up. Many of the Indians who had gathered about the agencies were out of provisions and were easily made angry. Still, most of us thought the trouble would pass, and we said nothing about it. I thought there might be trouble, but I had no idea there would be such a war. Little Crow and other chiefs did not think so. But it seems some of the tribe were getting ready for it.

Source: Jerome Big Eagle. "A Sioux Story of the War." *Collections of the Minnesota Historical Society* 6 (1894): 382–400.

Little Bear, Account of the Sand Creek Massacre
(1864)

While the nation fought the Civil War, troubles in Indian Territory continued. In 1862, the so-called Sioux Uprising erupted in Minnesota, scaring many frontier Americans. Tensions between whites and Indians rose in the western region of the United States, especially as whites continued to encroach on Indian lands. In 1864, some Indians in Colorado killed a family. In retaliation, cavalry under Colonel John Chivington raided a village. Most, if not all, of the Indians gathered at that village because they thought they were safe. Word had spread from white authorities to Indians that if they were friendly they should gather at certain places so they would not be accidently labeled hostile. Unfortunately, treachery prevailed, and the Indians killed at Sand Creek were friendly. The soldiers not only killed men, women, and children but mutilated their bodies as well. In this document, Little Bear, who survived the massacre, related his memories of November 29, 1864, to his friend George Bent.

I got up before daylight to go out to where my brother-in-law Tomahawk had left our pony herd the evening before. He told me where he had left the ponies and said he did not think they would stray far from that place. As soon as I was dressed I went out of the lodge and crossed the creek; but as I was going up on the hill I saw Kingfisher running back toward the camp. He shouted to me that white men were driving off the herds. I looked forward to the Fort Lyon Trail and saw a long line of little black objects to the south, moving toward the camp across the bare brown plain. There was some snow on the ground, but only in the hollows. I ran back to the side of the creek as fast as I could, but soldiers had already come up on the other side of the creek and were firing in among the lodges. As I came into camp the people were running up the creek. As I passed Black Kettle's lodge I saw that he had a flag tied to the end of the pole and was standing there holding the pole. I ran to our lodge to get my bow, quiver, shield, and war bonnet. My father, Bear Tongue, had just recently given me these things. I was very young then and had just become a warrior.

By this time the soldiers were shooting into the camp from two sides, and as I put on my war bonnet and took up my shield and weapons, the bullets were hitting the lodge cover with heavy thumps like big hailstones. When I went out again I ran behind the lodges, so that the troops could not get good shots at me. I jumped over the bank into the creek bed and found Big Head, Crow Neck, Cut-Lip-Bear, and Smoke standing there under the high bank. I joined these young men. The people were all running up the creek; the soldiers sat on their horses, lined up on both banks and firing into the camps, but they soon saw that the lodges were now nearly empty, so they began to advance up the creek, firing on the fleeing people. Our party was at the west end of the camps, not one hundred yards from the lodges. At this point the creek, made a bend, coming from the north and turning toward the southeast just at the upper end of the village. As the soldiers began to advance, we ran across to the west side of the creek to get under another high bank over there, but just as we reached this bank another body of cavalry came up and opened fire on us. We hardly knew what way to turn, but Big Head and the rest soon decided to go on. They ran on toward the west, but passing over a hill they ran into another body of troops just beyond and were surrounded and all killed.

After leaving the others, I started to run up the creek bed in the direction taken by most of the fleeing people, but I had not gone far when a party of about twenty cavalrymen got into the dry bed of the stream behind me. They chased me up the creek for about two miles, very close behind me and firing on me all the time. Nearly all the feathers were shot out of my war bonnet, and some balls passed through my shield; but I was not touched. I passed many women and children, dead and dying, lying in the creek bed. The soldiers had not scalped them yet, as they were busy chasing those that were yet alive. After the fight I came back down the creek and saw these dead bodies all cut up, and even the wounded scalped and slashed. I saw one old woman wandering about; her whole scalp had been taken off and the blood was running down into her eyes so that she could not see where to go.

I ran up the creek about two miles and came to the place where a large party of the people had taken refuge in holes dug in the sand up against the sides of the high banks. I stayed here until the soldiers withdrew. They were on both banks, firing down on us, but not many of us were killed. All who failed to reach these pits in the sand were shot down.

Source: Lottinville, Savoie, ed. *Life of George Bent, Written from His Letters by George E. Hyde.* Norman: University of Oklahoma Press, 1968, 153–154. Reprinted with permission.

Elsie Edwards, Interview, "Fort Gibson Civil War— Refugee Living Conditions"
(ca. 1864)

During the American Civil War, Elsie Edwards's family was forced to flee their home in Oklahoma for safety in the South, away from the threat of fighting. Edwards was a young girl when her family was forced to flee their home; however, like the forced removal of her people, the Creeks, from the southeastern United States during the 1830s, the trek into Texas was a traumatic

experience, as the following document illustrates. Reproduced here is an interview with Edwards done in 1937.

Somewhere upon the banks of the Grand River near Ft. Gibson lies an old grave of an old lady whose name was Sin-e-cha. I could lead you to that grave today. Sin-e-cha had come with her tribal town of Ke-cho-ba-da-gee during the removal to the new country. When the events with never no more to live in the east had taken place, she, too, remembered that she had left her home with shattered happiness, she carried a small bundle of her few belongings and reopening and retying her pitiful bundle, she began a sad song which was later taken up by the others on board the ship at the time of the wreck and the words of her song was: "I have no more land, I am driven away from home, driven up the red waters, let us all go, let us all die together and somewhere you on the banks will be there."

When the war of the south was in progress, it has been told that those of us that live along the Wod-ko Hu-chee (Coon Creek), which is between McAlester and Crowder City, went to the south to escape the war. The neighboring people were so excited that they were just running around getting ready to go somewhere. Men folks were fixing up the wagons while the women folks were busy getting the quilts ready, gathering up pots and other cooking utensils, and loading up the wagons. Ropes were made of cow hides cut in long strips and these were used to tie small bundles. They loaded up the light articles, such as mattresses and quilts, upon the horses and securely tied with the cow hide ropes.

At that time Jackson Barnett, who has been considered the richest Indian of recent time, but is now dead, was my playmate. He was in the same group that I was in when we went south and we stayed in the same group all the four years that we were away in the South. Swatt Grayson was the main leader of the group on the trip with the aid of Tustanuggie Jimboy (Jim Topler who had been named after his father, Jim Topler). Jimboy was my father.

I traveled to the south on a horse and a mattress which had been placed on the horse and tied with the cowhide ropes. Most of the trip I rode with Jackson Barnett, as both of us were small then.

I remember that we made our camp across the Red River near a high hill. The people made shelter in any way and out of anything that could be used, but most of the people made their crude houses out of bark which was usually of hickory bark. Some covered their shelter with twigs and covered it over with cowhides. The children never did anything but eat, play and sleep, and the men would usually go hunting. They never would let us small ones out of the camp.

The bark houses were arranged along a street like clearing with the houses opposite each one and in the center of the street was dug a long ditch, running the length of the street, and this was used to build a fire in it and cooking was done over the fire in the ditch. Stout sticks would be stuck into the ground on each side of the ditch and a long pole fastened or laid between the forks of each stick and the pots could be hung from the pole directly over the fire and slow cooking done.

At one time during our stay in Texas, there was fighting right near our camp and we had gone to a high hill to hide while some of our men stayed in camp to protect the camp but a good many of them were killed, but General Cooper in command of the Confederate Soldiers was forced to retreat when enforcements reached the place.

The Jim Crow law had not yet been made so that the whites, Indians, negroes and half-breeds just mixed with one another and there was no law against the number of wives that man wished to have. My father had four wives, two being Indians and two negro women.

After we had returned to Ft. Gibson upon government orders, before we returned to our homes after the war ended, we were given rations, but were finally permitted to go to our homes.

Oxen teams made long and slow trips from Texarkanna, Texas, to Ft. Smith and also, they came across from Tishomingo going to Ft. Smith.

Source: Elsie Edwards interviewed by Billie Byrd. "Fort Gibson Living Conditions." September 17, 1937. Indian Pioneer Papers, Volume 27. Western History Collections, University of Oklahoma, Norman. http://digital.libraries.ou.edu/whc/pioneer/papers/7571%20Edwards.pdf.

Bear Head, Account of the Massacre on the Marias
(1870)

The powerful Blackfeet Indians inhabited the northwestern plains during the turn of the 19th century. However, like almost all other Indians, they were under constant pressure from whites as Americans tried to satiate their hunger for land. In addition, the Blackfeet suffered several smallpox epidemics that left their numbers decimated. Still trying to solve the Indian problem, General Philip Sheridan decided to once again attack Indians during the winter. In January 1870, he caught a gathering of Blackfeet by surprise; these Blackfeet were also trying to recover from the latest smallpox outbreak. In this narrative, recorded in 1935, Bear Head recounts the Massacre on the Marias—named for the river the Indians were gathered at.

In Falling-Leaves Moon (September) we moved back across Big River, and were camped on Two Medicine Lodges River when winter came. All the other bands of our tribe were east of us, here and there along Bear (Marias) River. A white man called "Big Nose" (Hiram Baker), who had come with a wagonload of cartridges and other things to trade for our buffalo robes and furs, told that the whites were more and more angry about the killing of Four Bears, and were trying to get their seizers (soldiers) to make a big killing of our tribe and so avenge his death. However, the seizer chiefs (army officers) seemed not to listen to their demand. Our chiefs talked over that news and thought little of it. As Heavy Runner said, the killing of Four Bears did not concern us. If the whites wanted to get revenge for it, they should kill Owl Child.

As the winter wore on the buffalo herds drifted farther and farther away from the mountains, and we had to follow them or starve. We moved down to the mouth of Two Medicine Lodges River; then in Middle-Winter Moon (January), moved down on Bear River and camped in a bottom that Mountain Chief's band had just left, they going a little way farther down the river. It was an unhappy time: the whites had given us of their terrible white-scabs disease (smallpox), and some of our band were dying. And the buffalo herds remained so far out from the river that we had to go for a two or three days' hunt in order to get meat for our helpless ones. One evening I arranged to go on a hunt with a number of our band. We were to travel light, take only two lodges to accommodate us all; my mother and one of my sisters were to go with me to help with my kills. Came morning and I set out for my horses; could not find them on the plain. Sought them in the timbered bottoms of the valley; did not come upon them until late in the day. The hunting party had long since gone. I told my mother that we would join the next party of hunters to go out. We still had dried meat to last us for some days.

On the following morning I found my horses in the timber well above camp and was nearing it with them when, suddenly, I ran into a multitude of white men: seizers. I was so astonished, so frightened, that I could not move. One of the seizers came and grasped my arm; spoke; tapped his lips with his fingers: I was not to speak, shout. He was a chief, this seizer, had strips of yellow metal on his shoulders, had a big knife, a five-shots pistol. He made me advance with him; all of the seizers were advancing.

We came to the edge of the camp; close before us were the lodges. Off to our right were many more seizers looking down upon them. It was a cold day. The people were all in their lodges, many still in their beds. None knew that the seizers had come.

A seizer chief up on the bank shouted something, and at once all of the seizers began shooting into the lodges. Chief Heavy Runner ran from his lodge toward the seizers on the bank. He was shouting to them and waving a paper writing that our agent had given him, a writing saying that he was a good and peaceful man, a friend of the whites. He had run but a few steps when he fell, his body pierced with bullets. Inside the lodges men were yelling; terribly frightened women and children, screaming—screaming from wounds, from pain as they died.

I saw a few men and women, escaping from their lodges, shot down as they ran. Most terrible to hear of all was the crying of little babies at their mothers' breasts. The seizers all advanced upon the lodges, my seizer still firmly holding my arm. They shot at the tops of the lodges; cut the binding of the poles so the whole lodge would collapse upon the fire and begin to burn—burn and smother those within. I saw my lodge so go down and burn. Within it my mother, my almost-mothers, my almost-sisters. Oh, how pitiful were their screamings as they died, and I there, powerless to help them!

Soon all was silent in the camp, and the seizers advanced, began tearing down the lodges that still stood, shooting those within them who were still alive, and then trying to burn all that they tore down, burnt the dead under the heaps of poles, lodge-skins and lodge furnishings; but they did not burn well.

At last my seizer released my arm and went about with his men looking at the smoking piles, talking, pointing, laughing, all of them. And finally the seizers rounded up all of our horses, drove them up the valley a little way, and made camp.

I sat before the ruin of my lodge and felt sick. I wished that the seizers had killed me, too. In the center of the fallen lodge, where the poles had fallen upon the fire, it had burned a little, then died out. I could not pull up the lodge-skin and look under it. I could not bear to see my mother, my almost-mothers, my almost-sisters lying there, shot or smothered to death. When I went for my horses, I had not carried my many-shots gun. It was there in the ruin of the lodge. Well, there it would remain.

From the timber, from the brush around about, a few old men, a few women and children came stealing out and joined me. Sadly we stared at our ruined camps; spoke but little; wept. Wailed wrinkled old Black Antelope: "Why, oh, why had it to be that all of our warriors, our hunters, had to go out for buffalo at this time. But for that, some of the white seizers would also be lying here in death."

"One was killed. I saw him fall," I said.

"*Ah.* Only one seizer. And how many of us. Mostly women and children; newborn babies. Oh, how cruel, how terribly cruel are the white men," old Curlew Woman wailed.

"Killed us off without reason for it; who have done nothing against the whites," said old Three Bears, and again we wept.

As we sat there, three men arrived from Mountain Chief's camp below. They stared and stared at our fallen, half-burned lodges, at our dead, lying here and there, and could hardly believe what they saw. They rode over to us, asked what had happened, and when we had told then of the white seizers' sudden attack upon us, it was long before they could speak, and they said that we were to live with them; they would take good care of us poor, bereaved ones.

Source: Schultz, James Willard (Apikuni). *Blackfeet and Buffalo: Memories of Life among the Indians.* Norman: University of Oklahoma Press, 1962, 300–302. Reprinted with permission.

Chief Red Cloud, Speech on Indian Rights
(1870)

Red Cloud, a leader of the Oglala Lakota, achieved fame as a warrior during the two-year conflict waged by the Lakota and their Cheyenne allies to close the Bozeman Trail in northern Wyoming. After Red Cloud's victory in 1868, he urged his people to live at peace with the United States. Red Cloud tried to help his people adapt to a new way of life on the reservation. In 1870, he visited Washington, D.C., where he met with President Ulysses Grant and Commissioner of Indian Affairs Ely Parker, a Seneca Indian. His visit to the East led Red Cloud to believe that resistance to the United States was futile, and he sought to help his people adapt to the changes that he knew would inevitably be thrust upon them. Red Cloud gave the following speech in July 1870 during his trip East. The speech reflects his desire not to accommodate the United States, but to ensure the survival of his people.

My brethren and my friends who are here before me this day, God Almighty has made us all, and He is here to bless what I have to say to you today. The Good Spirit made us both. He gave you lands and He gave us lands; He gave us these lands; you came in here, and we respected you as brothers. God Almighty made you but made you all white and clothed you; when He made us He made us with red skins and poor; now you have come.

When you first came we were very many, and you were few; now you are many, and we are getting very few, and we are poor. You do not know who appears before you today to speak. I am a representative of the original American race, the first people of this continent. We are good and not bad. The reports that you hear concerning us are all on one side. We are always well-disposed to them. You are here told that we are traders and thieves, and it is not so. We have given you nearly all our lands, and if we had any more land to give we would be very glad to give it. We have nothing more. We are driven into a very little land, and we want you now, as our dear friends, to help us with the government of the United States.

The Great Father made us poor and ignorant—made you rich and wise and more skillful in these things that we know nothing about. The Great Father, the Good Father in Heaven, made you all to eat tame food—made us to eat wild food—gives us the wild food. You ask anybody who has gone through our country to California; ask those who have settled there and in Utah, and you will find that we have treated them always well. You have children; we have children. You want to raise your children and make them happy and prosperous; we want to raise and make them happy and prosperous. We ask you to help us to do it.

At the mouth of the Horse Creek, in 1852, the Great Father made a treaty with us by which we agreed to let all that country open for fifty-five years for the transit of those who were going through. We kept this treaty; we never treated any man wrong; we never committed any murder or depredation until afterward the troops were sent into that country, and the troops killed our people and ill-treated them, and thus war and trouble arose; but before the troops were sent there we were quiet and peaceable, and there was no disturbance. Since that time there have been various goods sent from time to time to us, the only ones that ever reached us, and then after they reached us (very soon after) the government took them away. You, as good men, ought to help us to these goods.

Colonel Fitzpatrick of the government said we must all go to farm, and some of the people went to Fort Laramie and were badly treated. I only want to do that which is peaceful, and the Great Fathers know it, and also the Great Father who made us both. I came to Washington to see the Great Father in order to have peace and in order to have peace continue. That is all we want, and that is the reason why we are here now.

In 1868 men came out and brought papers. We are ignorant and do not read papers, and they did not tell us right what was in these papers. We wanted them to take away their forts, leave our country, would not make war, and give our traders something. They said we had bound ourselves to trade on the Missouri, and we said, no, we did not want that. The interpreters deceived us. When I went to Washington I saw the Great Father. The Great Father showed me what the treaties were; he showed me all these points and showed me that the interpreters had deceived me and did not let me know what the right side of the treaty was. All I want is right and justice. . . . I represent the Sioux Nation; they will be governed by what I say and what I represent. . . .

Look at me. I am poor and naked, but I am the Chief of the Nation. We do not want riches, we do not ask for riches, but we want our children properly trained and brought up. We look to you for your sympathy. Our riches will . . . do us no good; we cannot take away into the other world anything we have—we want to have love and peace. . . . We would like to know why commissioners are sent out there to do nothing but rob [us] and get the riches of this world away from us?

I was brought up among the traders and those who came out there in those early times. I had a good time for they treated us nicely and well. They taught me how to wear clothes and use tobacco,

and to use firearms and ammunition, and all went on very well until the Great Father sent out another kind of men—men who drank whisky. He sent out whisky-men, men who drank and quarreled, men who were so bad that he could not keep them at home, and so he sent them out there. I have sent a great many words to the Great Father, but I don't know that they ever reach the Great Father. They were drowned on the way, therefore I was a little offended with it. The words I told the Great Father lately would never come to him, so I thought I would come and tell you myself.

And I am going to leave you today, and I am going back to my home. I want to tell the people that we cannot trust his agents and superintendents. I don't want strange people that we know nothing about. I am very glad that you belong to us. I am very glad that we have come here and found you and that we can understand one another. I don't want any more such men sent out there, who are so poor that when they come out there their first thoughts are how they can fill their own pockets.

We want preserves in our reserves. We want honest men, and we want you to help to keep us in the lands that belong to us so that we may not be a prey to those who are viciously disposed. I am going back home. I am very glad that you have listened to me, and I wish you good-bye and give you an affectionate farewell.

Source: The Latter-Day Saints' Millennial Star. Vol. 32. Liverpool: H. S. Eldredge, 1870, 470–471.

Strikes Two and Bear's Belly, Story of an Expedition under General George Custer to the Black Hills

(1874)

Gold was discovered during George Armstrong Custer's 1874 Black Hills Expedition. The Black Hills were part of the Great Sioux Reservation, *set aside for the tribe as per the terms of the Fort Laramie Treaty of 1868. The Black Hills represent the sacred center of the world to both the Lakota and Cheyenne peoples, who have each controlled the region historically. In the following document, Strikes Two and Bear's Belly provide a Native account of the discovery of gold during Custer's expedition. After the discovery of gold in the Black Hills, telegraph operators and newspapers spread news of the discovery from one coast to the other. By 1875, Custer City and Deadwood were established and more than 20,000 Americans made their way to the gold diggings. The Lakota refused to sell the Black Hills to the United States, setting off a year of bloody fighting known as the Great Sioux War of 1876.*

The scouts on the expedition were as follows: Bloody Knife and Lean Bear, as leaders; Bear's Arm, Strikes Two, Bear's Belly, Enemy Heart, Young Hawk, Red Bear, Little Sioux, Bear's Eyes, Left Hand (different in his discharge papers), Goose, Angry Bear (Mandan name, He-ra-ta-ke), Red Angry Bear, Crooked Horn (Arikara), Elk Face, Angry Bull (half Dakota and half Arikara), Left Hand (Dakota), Spotted Horse Eagle (Dakota), Shoots the Bear (Dakota), two Blackfoot, and twenty-five Santee scouts.

They started from their camp at the bottom of a hill on the present site of Mandan and joined Custer at his fort [Abraham Lincoln]. They went south on the hill, crossing the Cannon Ball at the sacred stone or the stone with the holy writing on it. After two or three nights [July 11, 1874], they camped at a place they called the cave or den. The Arikara were told by the Dakota scouts that they were near big den or cave, so that they camped and went to look for it. The walls were covered with painted designs, and toward the interior were carved figures on the walls. On the ceiling, a flash of lightning was figured. The dung of deer covered all the floor to the opening into the interior. Here the ceiling was out of reach, and it was wholly dark. At the opening of the interior were offering of beads in a heap and bracelets. From here they picked up a flintlock and took it to Custer. Beyond the cave were two piles of stones put up by the Dakota, and still farther on from the opening was a large flat

rock. When they first found this cave, they saw on the flat rock a woman taking the hair off a deer hide with an old-fashioned scraper. She ran away, and they could not find her. They thought she hid in the cave, far in.

Beyond the flat rock was a spring. Here was a large hollow rock full of water like a trough in a pasture, and the tracks of the deer were all about like cow tracks at a watering place. The soldiers came after this to explore the cave. They had three candles and a pick and shovel. The Arikara scouts went in till the cave floor slanted steeply down, and then they went back. The Mandan scout was with the soldiers and stayed after the other scouts left. But he turned back too after he was about halfway down.

The next morning, their interpreter for the Dakotas, Baker, told them that the soldiers found it wet and muddy and had to turn back after going knee-deep without reaching the end. The next morning they broke camp and came to a butte shining with selenite, and large pieces at the bottom.

The next place was Black Butte; heavy cedar timber was all over it. Here Custer sent two scouts back with mail, Bull Neck and Skunk Head. They now entered the timber; it looked like a prairie that had been burned, it was so black. They camped at a river, shallow like the Little Missouri. They called it the Big River, and the Dakotas call it Beautiful River. There was pine timber on both sides of the river. Across the river was the Cut Butte, with two high points, and they camped here. The scouts were on a hill, and the soldiers were in a valley [Prospect Valley, July 14]. Their interpreter told them that two soldiers were quarreling, and one of them asked Custer for permission to finish the fight. Custer said, "I don't care," and one of the soldiers got his gun out. The scouts heard someone call, "Hold on, hold on," and then a shot, and then another. The soldier shot his comrade through the arm and then through the heart. The dead body was carried on in a wagon. Custer came to the scouts and told them that the doctor was planning to cut up the body to see why he was so quarrelsome. The scouts saw the doctor cut the body open, put salt in the body, put all the parts back, and then the body was buried. The soldiers fired a salute over the grave.

The next morning, they set out through the timber, and they tried to keep track of the number of days they were in the woods. When they came to a butte, they went up and saw only timber, no earth at all. They found an old Dakota camp [July 26] where they had been preparing tepee poles, peeling bark and leaning the poles up on trees nearby. The camp was old, but presently they struck a fresh Dakota trail. Custer told them to go on duty, and a few scouts went ahead to scout. A fresh Dakota camp was reported by the scouts, and they all went on to the places and found coals of fire not yet out, deer bones freshly gnawed, dried meat still hanging here and there.

All the scouts lined up under Custer's orders, and he picked out the best of them to scout ahead to look for the Dakota camp. Strikes Two was one of these and two white men—soldiers, not officers. At a place where there was a junction of two ravines, they saw at their right up the ravine the Dakota camp. There were five tepees, and it was as far as from Bear's Belly's house to Red Bear's house. They sent the two white soldiers back to Custer to notify him. They stood together at the top of the hill and looked across the ravine. They could hear scattered shots from the Dakota hunters. The soldiers came up, and Custer sent one party of scouts to surround the camp and the others were to charge straight in. Strikes Two was with the first party, and Bear's Belly was with the second. The first party surrounded the camp and waited for the others to charge. Then they heard the horses charging in, and they ran out of the woods. They saw two boys with a yellow blanket on, and they were afraid and cried and ran up where there was a creek. They threw away their blanket, and the scouts saw the fish they had. Then a naked warrior ran out with a gun, which he held up against the charging scouts. Red Angry Bear reached him first and struck him with his whip, and the others did the same. The women ran out and tried to get away into the woods, but the scouts

told them to go to their tent. They found out the warrior's gun had no hammer, and he [Slow Bull] was the only man there. Then he went inside and came out with a pipe, which he held towards the scouts as a peace sign.

Custer then came up with his men and called up the Dakota scouts, and they told Custer that the camp would follow, as they were prisoners. He left one white man in the camp to see that they came on and one white man on a hill to watch them. When three Dakota hunters came back, they told the man in camp they were going to buy a gun of the soldiers, so he went with them to the other white soldier, and they all came on to Custer's camp. One Dakota came to where the scouts were and by signs told them that he wanted to get a gun in exchange for a horse. He said he would go and get his horse, and Custer said all right but told the other two to stay behind. The other Dakota scouts went along with the Dakota captives, but one lagged back and ran away to a creek. Then they saw the other Dakota [Long Bear] wrestling on horseback with his captor. The Dakota scout drew his revolver and fired, but the two Dakotas got away. The Arikara scouts fired one shot apiece, and the Dakota scouts held one of the Dakota captive, the old man [One Stab]. They all rode on to the old camp, but all the Dakotas were gone. They follow[ed] hard on the trail till dark then gave it up.

They returned and found the old Dakota tied outside to an iron picket pin. His feet were hobbled, he had a string around his waist, and his leg was bandaged, but his hands were not tied. Custer came to the Arikaras and made signs that he at first planned to have them kill this Dakota captive, but that now he was to be guide. The captive tried to tell them that they were coming to more Dakotas than their whole number and all would be killed.

At last [July 30] they came to the Shell River [Ruby Creek]. Here the Dakota guide pointed out distant smoke on the prairie and said it was a train and a town. Custer said he was to stop and give up and return on the back trail. The officer the Arikaras called the Lucky Man (Charley Reynolds) was given papers by Custer and he went on alone. He was a good hunter and a dead shot. He was to go to the town in the direction of the smoke. The Dakota captive cried in the night and by signs said that his children would cut their hair as for his death, since he was as good as dead. At one place, Custer signed to the scouts that he proposed to let the Dakota captive go. He gave the Dakota a good suit, hat, and other things, and thought the Arikaras planned to kill him, Custer got him off in the night, and they never saw him again.

From this they camped at a broken place [Golden Park, August 1]. Red Angry Bear found some gold in a spring, and word was sent in the Arikara language that they were all to come and get some of the pretty yellow stuff to trim their bridles with. They all got some, and their arms were sparkling with the golden dust. Custer asked them where they got the gold, and they showed him. He sounded a bugle and called the soldiers and put pickets out to keep all others away. Then Custer came with some gold in a cloth and opened it before the Arikaras saying, "You scouts have found this, which is money, and you shall have your share"; as he said this, he picked up and then threw down gold by handfuls. "You shall

have it like this," he said. The soldiers had gotten this gold from the spring, digging where the Indians had first found it. He said this land would be marked, and it was marked so they could find it again. Piles of stones were put up, and the soldiers went about putting up marks or signs.

They marched to the Bear Butte [August 15], and six scouts were sent with mail to Fort Lincoln. Three of these were Arikara scouts, Strikes Two, Angry Bear, and Left Hand. The other three were Dakota scouts, one of them was called Goose. Strikes Two had a horse with mailbags, and Custer gave him a flask of whiskey. They rode off at sunset and rode all night, and after a rest they rode on all day and reached the Beautiful River. After crossing the river, they traveled one-half the night and all day. They took six days to get to Fort Lincoln. They were here a day when the Lucky Man got in. He had delivered his papers and had come on to Fort Lincoln by rail. After twelve days, Custer's party came in.

Source: Bear, Alfred. *Collections of the State Historical Society of North Dakota* 6 (1920): 163–170.

Wooden Leg, Account of the Battle of the Little Bighorn (1876)

Cheyenne warrior Wooden Leg's account of the Battle of the Little Bighorn is one of the fullest of those provided by American Indians. He vividly illustrates, for example, some of the confusion of the battle. Before the Little Bighorn, Wooden Leg fought U.S. troops during the Battle of Fort Kearny in 1866, and the Battle of Powder River in the months prior to the Little Bighorn in June 1876.

In my sleep I dreamed that a great crowd of people were making lots of noise. Something in the noise startled me. I found myself wide awake, sitting up

and listening. My brother too awakened, and we both jumped to our feet. A great commotion was going on among the camps. We heard shooting. We hurried out from the trees so we might see as well as hear. The shooting was somewhere at the upper part of the camp circles. It looked as if all of the Indians there were running away towards the hills to the westward or down toward our end of the village. Women were screaming and men were letting out war cries. Through it all we could hear old men calling:

"Soldiers are here! Young men, go out and fight them."

We ran to our camp and to our home lodge. Everybody there was excited. Women were hurriedly making up little packs for flight. Some were going off northward or across the river without any packs. Children were hunting for their mothers. Mothers were anxiously trying to find their children. I got my lariat and my six shooter. I hastened on down toward where had been our horse herd. I came across three of our herder boys. One of them was catching grasshoppers. The other two were cooking fish in the blaze of a little fire. I told them what was going on and asked them where were the horses. They jumped on their picketed ponies and dashed for the camp, without answering me. Just then I heard Bald Eagle calling out to hurry with the horses. Two other boys were driving them toward the camp circle. I was utterly winded from the running. I never was much for running. I could walk all day, but I could not run fast nor far. I walked on back to the home lodge.

My father had caught my favorite horse from the herd brought in by the boys and Bald Eagle. I quickly emptied out my war bag and set myself at getting ready to go into battle. I jerked off my ordinary clothing. I jerked on a pair of new breeches that had been given to me by an Uncpapa Sioux. I had a good cloth shirt, and I put it on. My old moccasins were kicked off and a pair of beaded moccasins substituted for them. My father strapped a blanket upon my horse and arranged the rawhide lariat into a bridle. He stood holding my mount.

"Hurry," he urged me.

I was hurrying, but I was not yet ready. I got my paints and my little mirror. The blue-black circles soon appeared around my face. The red and yellow colorings were applied on all of the skin inside the circle. I combed my hair. It properly should have been oiled and braided neatly, but my father again was saying, "Hurry," so I just looped a buckskin thong about it and tied it close up against the back of my head, to float loose from there. My bullets, caps, and powder horn put me into full readiness. In a moment afterward I was on my horse and was going as fast as it could run toward where all of the rest of the young men were going. My brother

already had gone. He got his horse before I got mine, and his dressing was only a long buckskin shirt fringed with crow Indian hair. The hair had been taken from a Crow at a past battle with them.

The air was so full of dust I could not see where to go. But it was not needful that I see that far. I kept my horse headed in the direction of movement by the crowd of Indians on horseback. I was led out around and far beyond the Uncpapa camp circle. Many hundreds of Indians on horseback were dashing to and fro in front of a body of soldiers. The soldiers were on the level valley ground and were shooting with rifles. Not many bullets were being sent back at them, but thousands of arrows were falling among them. I went on with a throng of Sioux until we got beyond and behind the white men. By this time, though, they had mounted their horses and were hiding themselves in the timber. A band of Indians were with the soldiers. It appeared they were Crows or Shoshones. Most of these Indians had fled back up the valley. Some were across east of the river and were riding away over the hills beyond.

Suddenly the hidden soldiers came tearing out on horseback, from the woods. I was around on that side where they came out. I whirled my horse and lashed it into a dash to escape from them. All others of my companions did the same. But soon we discovered they were not following us. They were running away from us. They were going as fast as their tired horses could carry them across an open valley space and toward the river. We stopped, looked a moment, and then we whipped our ponies into swift pursuit. A great throng of Sioux also were coming after them. My distant position put me among the leaders in the chase. The soldier horses moved slowly, as if they were very tired. Ours were lively. We gained rapidly on them.

I fired four shots with my six shooter. I do not know whether or not any of my bullets did harm. I saw a Sioux put an arrow into the back of a soldier's head. Another arrow went into his shoulder. He tumbled from his horse to the ground. Others fell dead either from arrows or from stabbings or jabbings or from blows by the stone war clubs of the Sioux. Horses limped or staggered or sprawled out dead or dying. Our war cries and war songs were mingled with many jeering calls, such as: "You are only boys. You ought not to be fighting. We whipped you on the Rosebud. You should have brought more Crows or Shoshones with you to do your fighting."

Little Bird and I were after one certain soldier. Little Bird was wearing a trailing warbonnet. He was at the right and I was at the left of the fleeing man. We were lashing him and his horse with our pony whips. It seemed not brave to shoot him. Besides, I did not want to waste my bullets. He pointed back his revolver, though, and sent a bullet into Little Bird's thigh. Immediately I whacked the white man fighter on his head with the heavy elk-horn handle of my pony whip. The blow dazed him. I seized the rifle strapped on his back. I wrenched it and dragged the looping strap over his head. As I was getting possession of this weapon he fell to the ground. I did not harm him further. I do not know what became of him. The jam of oncoming Indians swept me on. But I had now a good soldier rifle.

Source: Marquis, Thomas B. *Wooden Leg: A Warrior Who Fought Custer.* Minneapolis: Midwest Co., 1931, 217–221.

Crazy Horse, "We Preferred Our Own Way of Living"
(1877)

Crazy Horse, an Oglala Lakota, is perhaps one of the most celebrated Native American leaders of the 19th century. He fought against American encroachment of Lakota land by participating in Red Cloud's War, the Great Sioux War of 1876, and other engagements. Today, Crazy Horse is a powerful symbol of resistance from which strength and motivation are drawn. In the following document, Crazy Horse speaks to his parents on his deathbed. He discusses some of the experiences of his life leading up to his being bayoneted by a soldier in a guardhouse on the Great Sioux Reservation in 1877.

My friend, I do not blame you for this. Had I listened to you this trouble would not have happened to me. I was not hostile to the white men. Sometimes my young men would attack the Indians who were their enemies and took their ponies. They did it in return.

We had buffalo for food, and their hides for clothing and for our teepees. We preferred hunting to a life of idleness on the reservation, where we were driven against our will. At times we did not get enough to eat, and we were not allowed to leave the reservation to hunt.

We preferred our own way of living. We were no expense to the government. All we wanted was peace and to be left alone. Soldiers were sent out in the winter, who destroyed our villages.

Then Long Hair (Custer) came in the same way. They say we massacred him, but he would have done the same thing to us had we not defended ourselves and fought to the last. Our first impulse was to escape without squaws and papooses, but we were so hemmed in we had to fight.

After that I went up on the Tongue River with a few of my people and lived in peace. But the government would not let me alone. Finally, I came back to the Red Cloud Agency. Yet I was not allowed to remain quiet.

I was tired of fighting. I went to the Spotted Tail Agency and asked that chief and his agent to let me live there in peace. I came here with the agent (Lee) to talk with the Big White Chief but was not given a chance. They tried to confine me. I tried to escape, and a soldier ran his bayonet into me.

I have spoken.

Source: Wheeler, Homer W. *Buffalo Days.* Indianapolis: Bobbs-Merrill Co., 1905, 199–200.

Chief Joseph, an Indian's View of Indian Affairs
(1879)

Chief Joseph was a famous chief of the Nez Percé tribe of the northwestern United States. Rather than submit to the U.S. military, he led his people across the border into Canada in 1877 as they chased freedom. After a betrayal, Chief Joseph decided to surrender, rather than submit his people to a bloody battle. This document, created after his capture, illustrates Joseph's intelligence and insights into the interactions between whites and Indians.

My friends, I have been asked to show you my heart. I am glad to have a chance to do so. I want the white people to understand my people. Some of you think an Indian is like a wild animal. This is a great mistake. I will tell you all about our people, and then you can judge whether an Indian is a man or not. I believe much trouble and blood would be saved if we opened our hearts more. I will tell you in my way how the Indian sees things. The white man has more words to tell you how they look to him, but it does not require many words to speak the truth. What I have to say will come from my heart, and I will speak with a straight tongue. *Ah-cum-kin-i-ma-me-hut* (the Great Spirit) is looking at me, and will hear me.

My name is *In-mut-too-yah-lat-lat* (Thunder traveling over the Mountains). I am chief of the *Wal-lam-wat-kin* band of *Chute-pa-lu*, or Nez Percés (nose-pierced Indians). I was born in eastern Oregon, thirty-eight winters ago. My father was chief before me. When a young man, he was called Joseph by Mr. Spaulding, a missionary. He died a few years ago. He left a good name on earth. He advised me well for my people.

Our fathers gave us many laws, which they had learned from their fathers. These laws were good. They told us to treat all men as they treated us; that we should never be the first to break a bargain; that it was a disgrace to tell a lie; that we should speak only the truth; that it was a shame for one man to take from another his wife, or his property without paying for it. We were taught to believe that the Great Spirit sees and hears everything, and that he never forgets; that hereafter he will give every man a spirit-home according to his desserts: if he has been a good man, he will have a good home; if he has been a bad man, he will have a bad home. This I believe, and all my people believe the same.

We did not know there were other people besides the Indian until about one hundred winters ago, when some men with white faces came to our country. They brought many things with them to trade for furs and skins. They brought tobacco, which was new to us. They brought guns with flint stones on them, which frightened our women and children. Our people could not talk with these white-faced men, but they used signs which all people understand. These men were Frenchmen, and they called our people "Nez Percés," because they wore rings in their noses for ornaments. Although very few of our people wear them now, we are still called by the same name. These French trappers said a great many things to our fathers, which have been planted in our hearts. Some were good for us, but some were bad. Our people were divided in opinion about these men. Some thought they taught more bad than good. An Indian respects a brave man, but he despises a coward. He loves a straight tongue, but he hates a forked tongue. The French trappers told us some truths and some lies.

The first white men of your people who came to our country were named Lewis and Clarke. They also brought many things that our people had never seen. They talked straight, and our people gave them a great feast, as a proof that their hearts were friendly. These men were very kind. They made presents to our chiefs and our people made presents to them. We had a great many horses, of which we gave them what they needed, and they gave us guns and tobacco in return. All the Nez Percés made friends with Lewis and Clarke, and agreed to let them pass through their country, and never to make war on white men. This promise the Nez Percés have never broken. No white man can accuse them of bad faith, and speak with a straight tongue. It has always been the pride of the Nez Percés that they were the friends of the white men. When my father was a young man there came to our country a white man (Rev. Mr. Spaulding) who talked spirit law. He won the affections of our

people because he spoke good things to them. At first he did not say anything about white men wanting to settle on our lands. Nothing was said about that until about twenty winters ago, when a number of white people came into our country and built houses and made farms. At first our people made no complaint. They thought there was room enough for all to live in peace, and they were learning many things from the white men that seemed to be good. But we soon found that the white men were growing rich very fast, and were greedy to possess everything the Indian had. My father was the first to see through the schemes of the white men, and he warned his tribe to be careful about trading with them. He had suspicion of men who seemed anxious to make money. I was a boy then, but I remember well my father's caution. He had sharper eyes than the rest of our people.

Next there came a white officer (Governor Stevens), who invited all the Nez Percés to a treaty council. After the council was opened he made known his heart. He said there were a great many white people in our country, and many more would come; that he wanted the land marked out so that the Indians and white men could be separated. If they were to live in peace it was necessary, he said, that the Indians should have a country set apart for them, and in that country they must stay. My father, who represented his band, refused to have anything to do with the council, because he wished to be a free man. He claimed that no man owned any part of the earth, and a man could not sell what he did not own.

Mr. Spaulding took hold of my father's arm and said, "Come and sign the treaty." My father pushed him away, and said: "Why do you ask me to sign away my country? It is your business to talk to us about spirit matters and not to talk to us about parting with our land." Governor Stevens urged my father to sign his treaty, but he refused. "I will not sign your paper," he said; "you go where you please, so do I; you are not a child, I am no child; I can think for myself. No man can think for me. I have no other home than this. I will not give it up to any man. My people would have no home. Take away your paper. I will not touch it with my hand."

My father left the council. Some of the chiefs of the other bands of the Nez Percés signed the treaty, and then Governor Stevens gave them presents of blankets. My father cautioned his people to take no presents, for "after a while," he said, "they will claim that you have accepted pay for your country." Since that time four bands of the Nez Percés have received annuities from the United States. My father was invited to many councils, and they tried hard to make him sign the treaty, but he was firm as the rock, and would not sign away his home. His refusal caused a difference among the Nez Percés.

Eight years later (1863) was the next treaty council. A chief called Lawyer, because he was a great talker, took the lead in this council, and sold nearly all the Nez Percés country. My father was not there. He said to me: "When you go into council with the white man, always remember your country. Do not give it away. The white man will cheat you out of your home. I have taken no pay from the United States. I have never sold our land." In this treaty Lawyer acted without authority from our band. He had no right to sell the Wallowa (winding water) country. That had always belonged to my father's own people, and the other bands had never disputed our right to it. No other Indians ever claimed Wallowa.

In order to have all people understand how much land we owned, my father planted poles around it and said:

"Inside is the home of my people—the white man may take the land outside. Inside this boundary all our people were born. It circles around the graves of our fathers, and we will never give up these graves to any man."

The United States claimed they had bought all the Nez Percés country outside the Lapwai Reservation, from Lawyer and other chiefs, but we continued to live on this land in peace until eight years ago, when white men began to come inside the bounds my father had set. We warned them against this great wrong, but they would not leave our land, and some bad blood was raised. The white men represented that we were going upon the warpath. They reported many things that were false.

The United States Government again asked for a treaty council. My father had become blind and feeble. He could no longer speak for his people. It was then that I took my father's place as chief. In this council I made my first speech to white men. I said to the agent who held the council:

"I did not want to come to this council, but I came hoping that we could save blood. The white man has no right to come here and take our country. We have never accepted any presents from the Government. Neither Lawyer nor any other chief had authority to sell this land. It has always belonged to my people. It came unclouded to them from our fathers, and we will defend this land as long as a drop of Indian blood warms the hearts of our men."

The agent said he had orders, from the Great White Chief at Washington, for us to go upon the Lapwai Reservation, and that if we obeyed he would help us in many ways. "You must move to the agency," he said. I answered him: "I will not. I do not need your help; we have plenty, and we are contented and happy if the white man will let us alone. The reservation is too small for so many people with all their stock. You can keep your presents; we can go to your towns and pay for all we need; we have plenty of horses and cattle to sell, and we won't have any help from you; we are free now; we can go where we please. Our fathers were born here. Here they lived, here they died, here are their graves. We will never leave them." The agent went away, and we had peace for a little while.

Soon after this my father sent for me. I saw he was dying. I took his hand in mine. He said: "My son, my body is returning to my mother earth, and my spirit is going very soon to see the Great Spirit Chief. When I am gone, think of your country. You are the chief of these people. They look to you to guide them. Always remember that your father never sold this country. You must stop your ears whenever you are asked to sign a treaty selling your home. A few years more, and white men will be all around you. They have their eyes on this land. My son, never forget my dying words. This country holds your father's body. Never sell the bones of your father and your mother." I pressed my father's hand and told him I would protect his grave with my life. My father smiled and passed away to the spirit land.

I buried him in that beautiful valley of winding waters. I love that land more than all the rest of the world. A man who would not love his father's grave is worse than a wild animal.

For a short time we lived quietly. But this could not last. White men had found gold in the mountains around the land of winding water. They stole many horses from us, and we could not get them back because we were Indians. The white men told lies for each other. They drove off a great many of our cattle. Some white men branded our young cattle so they could claim them. We had no friend who would plead our cause before the law councils. It seemed to me that some of the white men in Wallowa were doing these things on purpose to get up a war. They knew that we were not strong enough to fight them. I labored hard to avoid trouble and bloodshed. We gave up some of our country to the white men, thinking that then we could have peace. We were mistaken. The white man would not let us alone. We could have avenged our wrongs many times, but we did not. Whenever the Government has asked us to help them against other Indians, we have never refused. When the white men were few and we were strong we could have killed them all off, but the Nez Percés wished to live at peace.

If we have not done so, we have not been to blame. I believe that the old treaty has never been correctly reported. If we ever owned the land we own it still, for we never sold it. In the treaty councils the commissioners have claimed that our country had been sold to the Government. Suppose a white man should come to me and say, "Joseph, I like your horses, and I want to buy them." I say to him, "No, my horses suit me, I will not sell them." Then he goes to my neighbor, and says to him: "Joseph has some good horses. I want to buy them, but he refuses to sell." My neighbor answers, "Pay me the money, and I will sell you Joseph's horses." The white man returns to me, and says, "Joseph, I have bought your horses, and you must let me have them." If we sold our lands to the Government, this is the way they were bought.

On account of the treaty made by the other bands of the Nez Percés, the white men claimed my lands. We were troubled greatly by white men crowding over the line. Some of these were good men, and we lived on peaceful terms with them, but they were not all good.

Nearly every year the agent came over from Lapwai and ordered us on to the reservation. We always replied that we were satisfied to live in Wallowa. We were careful to refuse presents or annuities which he offered.

Through all the years since the white men came to Wallowa we have been threatened and taunted by them and the treaty Nez Percés. They have given us no rest. We have had a few good friends among white men, and they have always advised my people to bear these taunts without fighting. Our young men were quick-tempered, and I have had great trouble in keeping them from doing rash things. I have carried a heavy load on my back ever since I was a boy. I learned then that we were but few, while the white men were many, and that we could not hold our own with them. We were like deer. They were like grizzly bears. We had a small country. Their country was large. We were contented to let things remain as the Great Spirit Chief made them. They were not; and would change the rivers and mountains if they did not suit them.

Year after year we have been threatened, but no war was made upon my people until General Howard came to our country two years ago and told us he was the white war-chief of all that country. He said: "I have a great many soldiers at my back. I am going to bring them up here, and then I will talk to you again. I will not let white men laugh at me the next time I come. The country belongs to the Government, and I intend to make you go upon the reservation."

I remonstrated with him against bringing more soldiers to the Nez Percés country. He had one house full of troops all the time at Fort Lapwai.

The next spring the agent at Umatilla agency sent an Indian runner to tell me to meet General Howard at Walla Walla. I could not go myself, but I sent my brother and five other head men to meet him, and they had a long talk.

General Howard said: "You have talked straight, and it is all right. You can stay in Wallowa." He insisted that my brother should go with him to Fort Lapwai. When the party arrived there General Howard sent out runners and called all the Indians in to a grand council. I was in that council. I said to General Howard, "We are ready to listen." He answered that he would not talk then, but would hold a council next day, when he would talk plainly. I said to General Howard: "I am ready to talk today. I have been in a great many councils, but I am no wiser. We are all sprung from a woman, although we are unlike in many things. We can not be made over again. You are as you were made, and as you were made you can remain. We are just as we were made by the Great Spirit, and you can not change us; then why should children of one mother and one father quarrel—why should one try to cheat the other? I do not believe that the Great Spirit Chief gave one kind of men the right to tell another kind of men what they must do."

General Howard replied: "You deny my authority, do you? You want to dictate to me, do you?"

Then one of my chiefs—Too-hool-hool-suit—rose in the council and said to General Howard: "The Great Spirit Chief made the world as it is, and as he wanted it, and he made a part of it for us to live upon. I do not see where you get authority to say that we shall not live where he placed us."

General Howard lost his temper and said: "Shut up! I don't want to hear any more of such talk. The law says you shall go upon the reservation to live, and I want you to do so, but you persist in disobeying the law" (meaning the treaty). "If you do not move, I will take the matter into my own hand, and make you suffer for your disobedience."

Too-hool-hool-suit answered: "Who are you, that you ask us to talk, and then tell me I sha'n't talk? Are you the Great Spirit? Did you make the world? Did you make the sun? Did you make the rivers to run for us to drink? Did you make the grass to grow? Did you make all these things, that you talk to us as though we were boys? If you did, then you have the right to talk as you do."

General Howard replied, "You are an impudent fellow, and I will put you in the guard house," and then ordered a soldier to arrest him.

Too-hool-hool-suit made no resistance. He asked General Howard: "Is that your order? I don't care. I have expressed my heart to you. I have nothing to take back. I have spoken for my country. You can arrest me, but you can not change me or make me take back what I have said."

The soldiers came forward and seized my friend and took him to the guard house. My men whispered among themselves whether they should let this thing be done. I counseled them to submit. I knew if we resisted that all the white men present, including General Howard, would be killed in a moment, and we would be blamed. If I had said nothing, General Howard would never have given another unjust order against my men. I saw the danger, and, while they dragged Too-hool-hool-suit to prison, I arose and said: "I am going to talk now. I don't care whether you arrest me or not." I turned to my people and said: "The arrest of Too-hool-hool-suit was wrong, but we will not resent the insult. We were invited to this council to express our hearts, and we have done so." Too-hool-hool-suit was prisoner for five days before he was released.

The council broke up for that day. On the next morning General Howard came to my lodge, and invited me to go with him and White-Bird and Looking-Glass, to look for land for my people. As we rode along we came to some good land that was already occupied by Indians and white people. General Howard, pointing to this land, said: "If you will come on to the reservation, I will give you these lands and move these people off."

I replied: "No. It would be wrong to disturb these people. I have no right to take their homes. I have never taken what did not belong to me. I will not now."

We rode all day upon the reservation, and found no good land unoccupied. I have been informed by men who do not lie that General Howard sent a letter that night, telling the soldiers at Walla Walla to go to Wallowa Valley, and drive us out upon our return home.

In the council, next day, General Howard informed me, in a haughty spirit, that he would give my people thirty days to go back home, collect all their stock, and move on to the reservation, saying, "If you are not here in that time, I shall consider that you want to fight, and will send my soldiers to drive you on."

I said: "War can be avoided, and it ought to be avoided. I want no war. My people have always been the friends of the white man. Why are you in such a hurry? I can not get ready to move in thirty days. Our stock is scattered, and Snake River is very high. Let us wait until fall, then the river will be low. We want time to hunt up our stock and gather supplies for winter."

General Howard replied: "If you let the time run over one day, the soldiers will be there to drive you on to the reservation, and all your cattle and horses outside of the reservation at that time will fall into the hands of the white men."

I knew I had never sold my country, and that I had no land in Lapwai; but I did not want bloodshed. I did not want my people killed. I did not want anybody killed. Some of my people had been murdered by white men, and the white murderers were never punished for it. I told General Howard about this, and again said I wanted no war. I wanted the people who lived upon the lands I was to occupy at Lapwai to have time to gather their harvest.

I said in my heart that, rather than have war, I would give up my country. I would give up my father's grave. I would give up everything rather than have the blood of white men upon the hands of my people.

General Howard refused to allow me more than thirty days to move my people and their stock. I am sure that he began to prepare for war at once.

When I returned to Wallowa I found my people very much excited upon discovering that the soldiers were already in the Wallowa Valley. We held a council and decided to move immediately, to avoid bloodshed.

Too-hool-hool-suit, who felt outraged by his imprisonment, talked for war, and made many of my young men willing to fight rather than be driven like dogs from the land where they were born. He declared that blood alone would wash out the disgrace General Howard had put upon him. It required a strong heart to stand up against such talk, but I urged my people to be quiet, and not to begin a war.

We gathered all the stock we could find, and made an attempt to move. We left many of our horses and cattle in Wallowa, and we lost several hundred in crossing the river. All of my people succeeded in getting across in safety. Many of the Nez Percés came together in Rocky Cañon to hold a grand council. I went with all my people. This council lasted ten days. There was a great deal of war talk, and a great deal of excitement. There was one young brave present whose father had been killed by a white man five years before. This man's blood was bad against white men, and he left the council calling for revenge.

Again I counseled peace, and I thought the danger was past. We had not complied with General Howard's order because we could not, but we intended to do so as soon as possible. I was leaving the council to kill beef for my family, when news came that the young man whose father has been killed had gone out with several other hot-blooded young braves and killed four white men. He rode up to the council and shouted: "Why do you sit here like women? The war has begun already." I was deeply grieved. All the lodges were moved except my brother's and my own. I saw clearly that the war was upon us when I learned that my young men had been secretly buying ammunition. I heard then that Too-hool-hool-suit, who had been imprisoned by General Howard, had succeeded in organizing a war party. I knew that their acts would involve all my people. I saw that the war could not be prevented. The time had passed. I counseled peace from the beginning. I knew that we were too weak to fight the United States. We had many grievances, but I knew that war would bring more. We had good white friends, who advised us against taking the war path. My friend and brother, Mr. Chapman, who has been with us since the surrender, told us just how the war would end. Mr. Chapman took sides against us, and helped General Howard. I do not blame him for doing so. He tried hard to prevent bloodshed. We hoped the white settlers would not join the soldiers. Before the war commenced we had discussed this matter all over, and many of my people were in favor of warning them that if they took no part against us they should not be molested in the event of war being begun by General Howard. This plan was voted down in the war council.

There were bad men among my people who had quarreled with white men, and they talked of their wrongs until they roused all the bad hearts in the council. Still I could not believe that they would begin the war. I know that my young men did a great wrong, but I ask, Who was first to blame? They had been insulted a thousand times; their fathers and brothers had been killed; their mothers and wives had been disgraced; they had been driven to madness by whisky sold to them by white men; they had been told by General Howard that all their horses and cattle which they had been unable to drive out of Wallowa were to fall into the hands of white men; and, added to all this, they were homeless and desperate.

I would have given my own life if I could have undone the killing of white men by my people. I blame my young men and I blame the white men. I blame General Howard for not giving my people time to get their stock away from Wallowa. I do not acknowledge that he had the right to order me to leave Wallowa at any time. I deny that either my father or myself ever sold that land. It is still our land. It may never again be our home, but my father sleeps there, and I love it as I love my mother. I left there, hoping to avoid bloodshed.

If General Howard had given me plenty of time to gather up my stock, and treated Too-hool-hool-suit as a man should be treated, there would have been no war.

My friends among white men have blamed me for the war. I am not to blame. When my young men began the killing, my heart was hurt. Although I did not justify them, I remembered all the insults I had endured, and my blood was on fire. Still I would have taken my people to the buffalo country without fighting, if possible.

I could see no other way to avoid a war. We moved over to White Bird Creek, sixteen miles away, and there encamped, intending to collect our stock before leaving; but the soldiers attacked us, and the first battle was fought. We numbered in that battle sixty men, and the soldiers a hundred. The fight lasted but a few minutes, when the soldiers retreated before us for twelve miles. They lost thirty-three killed, and had seven wounded. When an Indian fights, he only shoots to kill; but soldiers shoot at random. None of the soldiers were scalped. We do not believe in scalping, nor in killing wounded men. Soldiers do not kill many Indians unless they are wounded and left upon the battle field. Then they kill Indians.

Seven days after the first battle, General Howard arrived in the Nez Percés country, bringing seven hundred more soldiers. It was now war in earnest. We crossed the Salmon River, hoping General Howard would follow. We were not disappointed. He did follow us, and we got back between him and his supplies, and cut him off for three days. He sent out two companies to open the way. We attacked them, killing one officer, two guides, and ten men.

We withdrew, hoping the soldiers would follow, but they had got fighting enough for that day. They entrenched themselves, and next day we attacked them again. The battle lasted all day, and was renewed next morning. We killed four and wounded seven or eight.

About this time General Howard found out that we were in his rear. Five days later he attacked us with three hundred and fifty soldiers and settlers. We had two hundred and fifty warriors. The fight lasted twenty-seven hours. We lost four killed and several wounded. General Howard's loss was twenty-nine men killed and sixty wounded.

The following day the soldiers charged upon us, and we retreated with our families and stock a few miles, leaving eighty lodges to fall into General Howard's hands.

Finding that we were outnumbered, we retreated to Bitter Root Valley. Here another body of soldiers came upon us and demanded our surrender. We refused. They said, "You can not get by us." We answered, "We are going by you without fighting if you will let us, but we are going by you anyhow." We then made a treaty with these soldiers. We agreed not to molest any one, and they agreed that we might pass through the Bitter Root country in peace. We bought provisions and traded stock with white men there.

We understood that there was to be no more war. We intended to go peaceably to the buffalo country, and leave the question of returning to our country to be settled afterward.

With this understanding we traveled on for four days, and, thinking that the trouble was all over, we stopped and prepared tent poles to take with us. We started again, and at the end of two days we saw three white men passing our camp. Thinking that peace had been made, we did not molest them. We could have killed them or taken them prisoners, but we did not suspect them of being spies, which they were.

That night the soldiers surrounded our camp. About daybreak one of my men went out to look after his horses. The soldiers saw him and shot him down like a coyote. I have since learned that these soldiers were not those we had left behind. They had come upon us from another direction. The new white war chief's name was Gibbon. He charged upon us while some of my people were still asleep. We had a hard fight. Some of my men crept around and attacked the soldiers from the rear. In this battle we lost nearly all our lodges, but we finally drove General Gibbon back.

Finding that he was not able to capture us, he sent to his camp a few miles away for his big guns (cannons), but my men had captured them and all the ammunition. We damaged the big guns all we could, and carried away the powder and lead. In

the fight with General Gibbon we lost fifty women and children and thirty fighting men. We remained long enough to bury our dead. The Nez Percés never make war on women and children; we could have killed a great many women and children while the war lasted, but we would feel ashamed to do so cowardly an act.

We never scalp our enemies, but when General Howard came up and joined General Gibbon, their Indian scouts dug up our dead and scalped them. I have been told that General Howard did not order this great shame to be done.

We retreated as rapidly as we could toward the buffalo country. After six days General Howard came close to us, and we went out and attacked him, and captured nearly all his horses and mules (about two hundred and fifty head). We then marched on to the Yellowstone Basin.

On the way we captured one white man and two white women. We released them at the end of three days. They were treated kindly. The women were not insulted. Can the white soldiers tell me of one time when Indian women were taken prisoners, and held three days and then released without being insulted? Were the Nez Percés women who fell into the hands of General Howard's soldiers treated with as much respect? I deny that a Nez Percé was ever guilty of such a crime.

A few days later we captured two more white men. One of them stole a horse and escaped. We gave the other a poor horse and told him he was free.

Nine days' march brought us to the mouth of Clarke's Fork of the Yellowstone. We did not know what had become of General Howard, but we supposed that he had sent for more horses and mules. He did not come up, but another new war chief (General Sturgis) attacked us. We held him in check while we moved all our women and children and stock out of danger, leaving a few men to cover our retreat.

Several days passed, and we heard nothing of General Howard, or Gibbon, or Sturgis. We had repulsed each in turn, and began to feel secure, when another army, under General Miles, struck us. This was the fourth army, each of which outnumbered our fighting force, that we had encountered within sixty days.

We had no knowledge of General Miles' army until a short time before he made a charge upon us, cutting our camp in two, and capturing nearly all of our horses. About seventy men, myself among them, were cut off. My little daughter, twelve years old, was with me. I gave her a rope, and told her to catch a horse and join the others who were cut off from the camp. I have not seen her since, but I have learned that she is alive and well.

I thought of my wife and children, who were now surrounded by soldiers, and I resolved to go to them or die. With a prayer in my mouth to the Great Spirit Chief who rules above, I dashed unarmed through the line of soldiers. It seemed to me that there were guns on every side, before and behind me. My clothes were cut to pieces and my horse was wounded, but I was unhurt. As I reached the door of my lodge, my wife handed me my rifle, saying: "Here's your gun. Fight!"

The soldiers kept up a continuous fire. Six of my men were killed in one spot near me. Ten or twelve soldiers charged into our camp and got possession of two lodges, killing three Nez Percés and losing three of their men, who fell inside our lines. I called my men to drive them back. We fought at close range, not more than twenty steps apart, and drove the soldiers back upon their main line, leaving their dead in our hands. We secured their arms and ammunition. We lost, the first day and night, eighteen men and three women. General Miles lost twenty-six killed and forty wounded. The following day General Miles sent a messenger into my camp under protection of a white flag. I sent my friend Yellow Bull to meet him.

Yellow Bull understood the messenger to say that General Miles wished me to consider the situation; that he did not want to kill my people unnecessarily. Yellow Bull understood this to be a demand for me to surrender and save blood. Upon reporting this message to me, Yellow Bull said he wondered whether General Miles was in earnest. I sent him back with my answer, that I had made up my mind, but would think about it and send word soon. A little later he sent some Cheyenne scouts with another message. I went out to meet them. They said they believed that General Miles was sincere and really wanted peace. I walked on to General Miles' tent. He met me and we shook hands. He said, "Come, let us sit down by the fire and talk this matter over." I remained with him all night; next morning Yellow Bull came over to see if I was alive, and why I did not return.

General Miles would not let me leave the tent to see my friend alone.

Yellow Bull said to me: "They have got you in their power, and I am afraid they will never let you go again. I have an officer in our camp, and I will hold him until they let you go free."

I said: "I do not know what they mean to do with me, but if they kill me you must not kill the officer. It will do no good to avenge my death by killing him."

Yellow Bull returned to my camp. I did not make any agreement that day with General Miles. The battle was renewed while I was with him. I was very anxious about my people. I knew that we were near Sitting Bull's camp in King George's land, and I thought maybe the Nez Percés who had escaped would return with assistance. No great damage was done to either party during the night.

On the following morning I returned to my camp by agreement, meeting the officer who had been held a prisoner in my camp at the flag of truce. My people were divided about surrendering. We could have escaped from Bear Paw Mountain if we had left our wounded, old women, and children behind. We were unwilling to do this. We had never heard of a wounded Indian recovering while in the hands of white men.

On the evening of the fourth day General Howard came in with a small escort, together with my friend Chapman. We could now talk understandingly. General Miles said to me in plain words, "If you will come out and give up your arms, I will spare your lives and send you to your reservation." I do not know what passed between General Miles and General Howard.

I could not bear to see my wounded men and women suffer any longer; we had lost enough already. General Miles had promised that we might return to our own country with what stock we had left. I thought we could start again. I believed General Miles, or I never would have surrendered. I have heard that he has been censured for making the promise to return us to Lapwai. He could not have made any other terms with me at that time. I would have held him in check until my friends came to my assistance, and then neither of the generals nor their soldiers would have ever left Bear Paw Mountain alive.

On the fifth day I went to General Miles and gave up my gun, and said, "From where the sun now stands I will fight no more." My people needed rest—we wanted peace.

I was told we could go with General Miles to Tongue River and stay there until spring, when we would be sent back to our country. Finally it was decided that we were to be taken to Tongue River. We had nothing to say about it. After our arrival at Tongue River, General Miles received orders to take us to Bismarck. The reason given was, that subsistence would be cheaper there.

General Miles was opposed to this order. He said: "You must not blame me. I have endeavored to keep my word, but the chief who is over me has given the order, and I must obey it or resign. That would do you no good. Some other officer would carry out the order."

I believe General Miles would have kept his word if he could have done so. I do not blame him for what we have suffered since the surrender. I do not know who is to blame. We gave up all our horses—over eleven hundred—and all our saddles—over one hundred—and we have not heard from them since. Somebody has got our horses.

General Miles turned my people over to another soldier, and we were taken to Bismarck. Captain Johnson, who now had charge of us, received an order to take us to Fort Leavenworth. At Leavenworth we were placed on a low river bottom, with no water except river water to drink and cook with. We had always lived in a healthy country, where the mountains were high and the water was cold and clear. Many of my people sickened and died, and we buried them in this strange land. I can not tell how much my heart suffered for my people while at Leavenworth. The Great Spirit Chief who rules above seemed to be looking some other way, and did not see what was being done to my people.

During the hot days (July, 1878) we received notice that we were to be moved farther away from our own country. We were not asked if we were willing to go. We were ordered to get into railroad cars. Three of my people died on the way to Baxter Springs. It was worse to die there than to die fighting in the mountains.

We were moved from Baxter Springs (Kansas) to the Indian Territory, and set down without our lodges. We had but little medicine, and we were nearly all sick. Seventy of my people have died since we moved there.

We have had a great many visitors who have talked many ways. Some of the chiefs (General Fish and Colonel Stickney) from Washington came to see us, and selected land for us to live upon. We have not moved to that land, for it is not a good place to live.

The Commissioner Chief (E.A. Hayt) came to see us. I told him, as I told every one, that I expected General Miles' word would be carried out. He said it "could not be done; that white men now lived in my country and all the land was taken up; that, if I returned to Wallowa, I could not live in peace; that law-papers were out against my young men who began the war, and that the Government could not protect my people." This talk fell like a heavy stone upon my heart. I saw that I could not gain anything by talking to him. Other law chiefs (Congressional Committee) came to see me and said they would help me to get a healthy country.

I did not know who to believe. The white people have too many chiefs. They do not understand each other. They do not all talk alike.

The Commissioner Chief (Mr. Hayt) invited me to go with him and hunt for a better home than we have now. I like the land we found (west of the

Osage Reservation) better than any place I have seen in that country; but it is not a healthy land. There are no mountains and rivers. The water is warm. It is not a good country for stock. I do not believe my people can live there. I am afraid they will all die. The Indians who occupy that country are dying off. I promised Chief Hayt to go there, and do the best I could until the Government got ready to make good General Miles' word. I was not satisfied, but I could not help myself.

Then the Inspector Chief (General McNiel) came to my camp and we had a long talk. He said I ought to have a home in the mountain country north, and that he would write a letter to the Great Chief at Washington. Again the hope of seeing the mountains of Idaho and Oregon grew up in my heart.

At last I was granted permission to come to Washington and bring my friend Yellow Bull and our interpreter with me. I am glad we came. I have shaken hands with a great many friends, but there are some things I want to know which no one seems able to explain. I can not understand how the Government sends a man out to fight us, as it did General Miles, and then breaks his word. Such a government has something wrong about it. I can not understand why so many chiefs are allowed to talk so many different ways, and promise so many different things. I have seen the Great Father Chief (the President), the next Great Chief (Secretary of the Interior), the Commissioner Chief (Hayt), the Law Chief (General Butler), and many other law chiefs (Congressmen), and they all say they are my friends, and that I shall have justice, but while their mouths all talk right I do not understand why nothing is done for my people. I have heard talk and talk, but nothing is done. Good words do not last long unless they amount to something. Words do not pay for my dead people. They do not pay for my country, now overrun by white men. They do not protect my father's grave. They do not pay for all my horses and cattle. Good words will not give me back my children. Good words will not make good the promise of your War Chief General Miles. Good words will not give my people good health

and stop them from dying. Good words will not get my people a home where they can live in peace and take care of themselves. I am tired of talk that comes to nothing. It makes my heart sick when I remember all the good words and all the broken promises. There has been too much talking by men who had no right to talk. Too many misrepresentations have been made, too many misunderstandings have come up between the white men about the Indians. If the white man wants to live in peace with the Indian he can live in peace. There need be no trouble. Treat all men alike. Give them the same law. Give them all an even chance to live and grow. All men were made by the same Great Spirit Chief. They are all brothers. The earth is the mother of all people, and all people should have equal rights upon it. You might as well expect the rivers to run backward as that any man who was born a free man should be contented when penned up and denied liberty to go where he pleases. If you tie a horse to a stake, do you expect he will grow fat? If you pen an Indian up on a small spot of earth, and compel him to stay there, he will not be contented, nor will he grow and prosper. I have asked some of the great white chiefs where they get their authority to say to the Indian that he shall stay in one place, while he sees white men going where they please. They can not tell me.

I only ask of the Government to be treated as all other men are treated. If I can not go to my own home, let me have a home in some country where my people will not die so fast. I would like to go to Bitter Root Valley. There my people would be healthy; where they are now they are dying. Three have died since I left my camp to come to Washington.

When I think of our condition my heart is heavy. I see men of my race treated as outlaws and driven from country to country, or shot down like animals.

I know that my race must change. We can not hold our own with the white men as we are. We only ask an even chance to live as other men live. We ask to be recognized as men. We ask that the same law shall work alike on all men. If the Indian breaks the law, punish him by the law. If the white man breaks the law, punish him also.

Let me be a free man—free to travel, free to stop, free to work, free to trade where I choose, free to choose my own teachers, free to follow the religion of my fathers, free to think and talk and act for myself—and I will obey every law, or submit to the penalty.

Whenever the white man treats an Indian as they treat each other, then we will have no more wars. We shall all be alike—brothers of one father and one mother, with one sky above us and one country around us, and one government for all. Then the Great Spirit Chief who rules above will smile upon this land, and send rain to wash out the bloody spots made by brothers' hands from the face of the earth. For this time the Indian race are waiting and praying. I hope that no more groans of wounded men and women will ever go to the ear of the Great Spirit Chief above, and that all people may be one people.

In-mut-too-yah-lat-lat has spoken for his people.

Source: Chief Joseph. "An Indian's View of Indian Affairs." *North American Review* 127 (April 1879): 412–433.

Chief Joseph, "We Ask to Be Recognized as Men"

(1879)

Chief Joseph's words were recorded for the following document, which appeared in the North American Review *in April 1879. In this document, Joseph presents an account of the wrongs suffered by his people after their surrender in 1877. As he states in the text, his major desire was to see his people treated equally; as such, this document represents an early call for civil rights as the basis for Native American success in terms of economics, society, and culture.*

I only ask of the Government to be treated as all other men are treated. If I can not go to my own home, let me have a home in some country where my people will not die so fast. I would like to go to the Bitter Root Valley. There my people would be healthy; where they are now they are dying. Three have died since I left my camp to come to Washington.

When I think of our condition my heart is heavy. I see men of my race treated as outlaws and driven from country to country, or shot down like animals.

I know that my race must change. We can not hold our own with the white men as we are. We only ask an even chance to live as other men live.

We ask to be recognized as men. If the Indian breaks the law, punish him by the law. If the white man breaks the law, punish him also.

Let me be a free man—free to travel, free to stop, free to work, free to trade where I choose, free to choose my own teachers, free to follow the religion of my fathers, free to think and talk and act for myself—and I will obey every law, or submit to the penalty.

Whenever the white man treats the Indian as they treat each other, then we will have no more wars. We shall all be alike—brothers of one father and one mother, with one sky above us and one country around us, and one government for all. Then the Great Spirit Chief who rules above will smile upon this land, and send rain to wash out the bloody spots made by brothers' hands from the face of the earth. For this time the Indian race are waiting and praying. I hope that no more groans of wounded men and women will ever go to the ear of the Great Spirit Chief above, and that all people may be one people.

In-mut-too-yah-lat-lat has spoken for his people.

Source: Chief Joseph. "An Indian's View of Indian Affairs." *North American Review* 127 (April 1879): 412–433.

White Eagle, Statement Regarding the Removal of the Ponca Indians to Indian Territory

(1879)

In 1879, Lorrie Montiero and her father were sent to the Ponca Reserve to gather information about the people living there and to assess their condition. One of the people Montiero spoke with was White Eagle, who asked her to write a statement for him and translate it into English so all white people could read it. Montiero agreed. In the following document, White Eagle describes the tribe's consternation upon learning that they were to be moved to Indian Territory without their consent and their futile struggle to control their fate.

In the spring of 1877 we were all living quietly on our farms and at work. We have been working on our farms for the last three years, and we had laid plans to work harder than ever during the year of 1877, when suddenly there came to our reserve a white man who professed to have come from the President. His name was Kimble. He called us all to the church, and we went. We had seen this man before, and he had appeared to be a good friend of ours. He said to us: "The President has sent me with a message to you. He has sent me to tell you that you must pack up and move to Indian Territory." I answered him by saying, "Friend, I thought that when the President desired to transact business with people he usually consulted with them first, and then transacted his business with them afterward. This is the first that I have heard of his desire to remove us. Here are some men from the Yankton, Santee, and Omaha tribes, and here are also some soldiers who are friends of ours; I ask them if they have heard of this before. They have not. This has come on us suddenly. Give us time to think about it. Although I am an Indian, I want to tell God all about this before I do anything more. I want to know and see for myself what I had better do. I want to ask God to help me to decide."

I continued, "Now friends, if what you have told us from the President is true, raise your hands." Kemble, the leading man, refused to raise his hands. Hinman, who was with him, raised his hand, not up towards God, but low down toward the ground. Kemble then jumped to his feet and said, "The President told me to take you to the Indian Territory, and I have both hands full of the money which it will require to move you down there. When the President says anything it must be done. Everything is settled, and it is just the same as though you were there already." I answered, "I have never broken any of my treaties with the government. What does the President want to take my land away from me for? The President told me to work, and I have done it. He told me to not go on the warpath, even if the white men took away my horses and cattle, or killed my people. I promised I would not, and I have performed my promise. Although other people often move from place to place, yet I have always staid on our land. It is ours. My people have lived and died on this land as far back as we can remember. I have sown wheat and planted corn and have performed all my promises to the President. I have raised enough on my farm to support myself, and now it seems just as though the government were trying to drown me when he takes my land away from me. We have always been peaceful. The land is our own. We do not want to part with it. I have broken no treaties, and the President has no right to take it from me."

Kemble arose and said, "Stop your talking; don't say any more. The President told me to remove you as soon as I got here. The President is going to send all the Indians to the Indian Territory. He intends you to move first, so that you can have your choice of the best lands there. You can do nothing. What the President has said will be done. I do not want to say any more on this subject. The

President says you must move; get ready." I answered, "When people want to do anything, they think about it first, talk about it with others, and then, after deliberation, they decide. I want to think about it. I want to see the President and talk the whole matter over with him, and then I will do what I think best. I know it will not be to give up our land. You have no right to move us in this way without our consent or will." Kemble then said, "You must go right away. The President intends to the Santees and Yanktons also, and I shall start tomorrow to tell them so."

The next day he started for the Sioux and returned. I again talked with him. I said, "It will cost a great deal of money to remove us. Let the President keep his money. We do not want it. It might hurt him to part with it. Take the money, which you said you brought, back to him. We do not want to use it, and we do not want to part with our land."

Kemble said, "The President has plenty of money and he will not miss it." I said, "God made me and He also made you. Perhaps He made you long before He did me, and that may be the reason that you, as a nation, are more enterprising and powerful than we are. But God made me. I was born here. He gave me this land, and it is mine. When your people first came here and asked for our land our forefathers sold you some. When our fathers sold you this land they made a treaty with your government, which I now hold in my hand, and it is stated here how much was sold to you and how much remained to us; and it is also stated here that the land that we did not sell was ours. It belongs to none but us until we choose to sell it. The government has no right to it. It is ours and we do not wish to part with it."

Kemble answered by saying, "The President says that the treaty is worthless. It will not do you any good. The President does not count it as anything. When you get to the new country the President will give you a new treaty, and you shall have a good title to your land there. As you do not believe the President's message I will send a telegram to him." The next day he brought the return

telegram, and said, "I will read it to you. You will see for yourselves whether what I have told you is true or not. The President says in this telegram that he wants ten of your chiefs to go to Washington, but he wants me first to take you to the Indian Territory and see for yourselves, so that you may select a piece of land there, and then go on to Washington afterwards to talk it over." I answered, "We will go with you. If we are satisfied with the land we will tell the President so, but if we are not satisfied we will say so also."

He then took us ten chiefs down there, and left us in Indian Territory without money, pass, or interpreter, in a strange country, among a strange people, because we would not select a piece of land. He wished us to sign a paper saying that we would take that piece of land, and because we would not, and asked to be taken to Washington as he had promised, he left us to find our way back alone on foot. We could not believe that he had been authorized to treat us with such indignity, and we could not believe that the white people of the country would let such a wrong done in their name pass unnoticed; so, on our return to the Omaha Reserve, after enduring great hardship on the way, we made a statement of all the facts, requesting a friend to see that it was published in a paper. We also sent a telegram to the President, asking him if he has authorized these men to treat us in this manner; but we never received any answer.

After we had left the Omaha Reserve and had nearly reached home, we found Kemble and some soldiers already there. They had frightened our people and forced them to move in our absence, and they were just starting from the reserve. When we met our people we said to them, "Stop. Do not go on. When a man owns anything it is his until he gives it or sells it. This land is ours. We have not given or sold it to the President. He has no right to it. When we were left in the Indian Territory we believed that the government had left us alone for good; and now we find that this man has come back here, bringing the soldiers, and forcing you to move in our absence. Do not go any further." They obeyed us.

Two days after our return home Kemble sent for us again. When we reached the place we found the soldiers there, all armed, and Kemble sitting by the side of an officer. I gave the treaty to the officer to examine. I said to him, "I have never done anything wrong against the white people. I have never broken any treaties. Now what have I done that your soldiers stand here all armed against me? I have been working on my land. I have done that which I thought my duty. I believed that your soldiers were stationed here to protect me against all wrong and injury. Now show me what I have done that you stand here with your soldiers in arms against me? I have helped your soldiers. I have helped the white people who live around here. I have always been peaceful. When the Sioux carried off your cattle and horses and property, I have had it returned to you when in my power. I thought that you, at least, would help me in my time of trouble. Why do I find you here now armed against me? We had always believed that your government had ordered your soldiers to protect those who were peaceful and doing their duty, and to punish and bear arms only against those who had committed crimes. A short time ago I was here at work on my land. I was taken and left in the Indian Territory to find my way back alone. I thought that after being treated in the manner we were by this man, that when I came home I would find a protection from my enemy in you. And now, instead, I find you armed against me." I then turned to Kemble and said, "You profess to be a Christian, and to love God; and yet you would love to see blood shed. Have you no pity on the tears of these helpless women and children? We would rather die here on our land than be forced to go. Kill us all here on our land now, so that in the future when men will ask, 'Why have these died?' it shall be answered, 'They died rather than be forced to leave their land. They died to maintain their rights.' And perhaps there will be found some who will pity us and say, 'They only did what was right.'"

Kemble answered, "If blood is shed you only will be in fault. You only will be the cause. You have exceeded the time in which the President gave you to move by a good many days."

White Swan, or Frank La Flesche, then spoke to Kemble, and said, "You have been here several times before. You professed to be a great Christian and one of the chief ministers among your people. You preached to us and told us about God. You told me to give myself to him and join his people. I was willing and you baptized my family and myself. You held me by the hand and said you were my friend, and I looked on you as such. I never thought that you would ever try to lead me into the great fire, the hell of your people. You told me that God loved us all; that he had made laws which he wanted us to keep, and I promised that I would try to keep them. When you asked me to keep these laws, I said to myself, "He is a good friend; he tells me good things, and wants me to do right and to walk the good road." I did not think then that you would ever try to lead me into a bad road. You told me that God saw everything we did. If so, He has seen the wrong and wickedness in this matter. When I was baptized, and promised God that I would do as He wanted me to, I meant it, and now (raising his hand to heaven) I call on God to witness that I have tried to keep my promise; but you have lied to him. He is the judge that I speak the truth. When you left us in Indian Territory I thought that you had gone to tell the President that we refused to give up our land; and now I come home to find that you have not. You said you wanted to save my soul from hell when I should die; but now I find that you wish to send my soul to hell while I am yet living, and I wish to keep out of it. You professed to be our friend. Could you not so much as have said to the President, 'These people do not want to part with their land. You are powerful and they are weak. Have mercy on them and do not make them go.' Could you not have done this much after all your professions of friendship? I would like to see you go to a white man yonder, who is living on his farm, and say to him, "Get off from here, the President wants this land and you must move on and go somewhere else." What do you suppose he would answer? The President has no more right to take our land from us than he has that of the white man."

Kemble answered, "What you have said about God is all right; but this business I have come to tend to has nothing to do with God or anything of the kind. It is another subject altogether. You had better not say that I want to lead you into hell. I want to lead you into the good road. It is you who want to take the bad road. You ought to be on the road to the Indian Territory by this time. The President will get out of patience; so I want you to start tomorrow. The President wanted me to do this errand as soon as I got here, but you have kept me waiting this long. The President has sent me word that if you refuse to go I must push you out. Your head-chief, White Eagle, has talked of the shedding of blood rather than go. I did not want you to let God hear you say such a thing, but he has heard you. This is all I have to say, and now I give you in charge of this officer and his soldiers."

Then the Indian chief of the police arose and said: "Our chiefs here have appointed me captain of our police, but they did not appoint me to bear arms against the weak and innocent, but that I might help and protect them. Your officer has brought his soldiers armed against my tribe. I shall not resist him. If he chooses to kill us, unarmed as we are, he can do it. You say your President has sent the money by you which is to take us to the Indian Territory. Take it back to your President. We will not leave our land, and we are afraid of the land in the Indian Territory. Take your money home. When you took our chiefs to the Indian Territory, you took some money to pay for their fare there. If the money belonged to the President, we want you to give it back to him from our own fund. This fund is the money which we received in payment for our land which we sold." The man who made this speech was one of the first to die when we reached the Indian Territory.

The next morning after this council the soldiers, some on horses and some in wagons, went around to the houses, and where they found the doors locked (for some of the people had shut up their houses and fled to the woods), kicked or broke them open, and put their household goods, such as could be carried with ease, into the wagons. In this way Kemble started off with a party composed of about ten families, while the soldiers remained behind with the rest of us. After this first party had been carried off, I took an interpreter with me to Niobrara City, and there found a lawyer, to whom I stated all these facts, and telling him that I thought the whole thing had been done unlawfully; asked him to help us maintain our rights. I wanted him to send a telegram to the President, asking him whether he knew of what had been done in his name. The lawyer said, "I will do so if you give me the money to pay for it." I answered that I had no money, but that I had a horse which I could sell to pay for the telegram. The lawyer sent a telegram, but he never received an answer.

Meanwhile the first party, which Kemble had taken, had been left by him on the other side of Niobrara, while he himself went to Washington. I then collected those of us who were yet on the reserve together and, gathering thirty-four of our horses, we sold them to pay the lawyer's expenses to Washington. When the lawyer got to Washington and went to see the President, he found Kemble sitting and talking with him. While we were awaiting the lawyer's return, we almost starved, as Campbell had taken the provisions which belonged to us and carried them away with the first party. After some time, the lawyer sent a telegram saying that he had been unable to do anything for us, except to keep them from fulfilling the threat of starving and treating us with indignity on the way down because of our refusal to go.

Before the lawyer had time to return, a new agent by the name of Howard was sent to take us down. He remained on the other side of the river and sent for us to come down, but we refused to go. He sent again, and went to him. The place where we met him was in a wild place by the river side. He spoke kindly to us, and was the first and only who did so of those who had been sent from Washington. He said: "Friends, although I am white and you are Indians, I am a man just as you are, and have a heart just the same as yours. I know you have been treated unjustly, and I feel sorry for you; but I cannot help you. The President has sent me to take you down. I will do all in my power to make the journey comfortable for you so that you may not suffer." I said to him, "Friend, it is good when men meet as friends and talk kindly to each other. You have spoken the first kind word we have heard for a long time. We had made up our minds to resist and die on our own land rather than go to a strange one to die; but, now you have come, we do not know what we will do."

We then separated, and calling all the men of our tribe together, I said to them, "My people, we, your chiefs, have worked hard to save you from this. We have resisted until we are worn out, and now we know not what more we can do. We leave the matter into your hands to decide. If you say that we fight and die on our lands, so be it." There was utter silence. Not a word was spoken. We all arose and started for our homes, and there we found that in our absence the soldiers had collected all our women and children together, and were standing guard over them. The soldiers got on their horses, went to all the houses, broke open the doors, took our household utensils, put them in their wagons, and pointing their bayonets at our people, ordered them to move. They took all our plows, mowers, hay-forks, grindstones, farming implements of all kind, and everything too heavy to be taken on a journey, and locked them up in a large house. We never knew what became of them afterwards. Many of these things of which we were robbed we had bought with money earned by the work of our hands. They promised us

more when we should get down here, but we have never received anything in place of them.

We left in our land two hundred and thirty-six houses, which we had built with our own hands. We cut the logs, hauled them, and built them ourselves. We have now in place of them six little shanties, built for us by the government. They are one story high, with two doors and two windows. They are full of holes and cracks, and let in the wind and rain. We hear that our houses which we left in Dakota have all been pulled down. To show how much the tribe had been robbed of, we will count the household possessions of a single one of our families in Dakota before we came down. Two stoves, one a kitchen-stove and the other a parlor-stove, with all the accompanying utensils; two bedsteads, two plows, and one double-plow; one harrow, one spade, two hay-forks, one hand-saw, and one large two-handed saw; one grindstone, one hay-rake, a cupboard, and four chairs. We have now no stoves, chairs, or bedsteads. We have nothing but our tents and their contents, composed mostly of clothing. The tribe owned two reapers, eight mowers, a flour and saw mill. They are gone from us also. We brought with us thirty-five yoke of oxen. They all died when we got here, partly from the effects of the toilsome journey, and partly by disease. We have not.

Source: White Eagle's statement regarding the removal of the Ponca Indians to Indian Territory. American Native Press Archives and Sequoyah Research Center. http://anpa .ualr.edu/digital_library/Ponca%20Account.htm. Reprinted with permission.

Sarah Winnemucca, Narrative (1883)

Like many Native American women of her time, Sarah Winnemucca straddled two worlds. She was born in western Nevada in the mid-19th century, the daughter of the chief of a small band of the

Northern Paiute. In the early part of her life, Winnemucca's people had limited contact with white people. However, she received her first introduction to white society via her grandfather, who had guided John C. Frémont's mapmaking expedition and fought in the Mexican–American War, when he took her on a trip to Sacramento. Sarah Winnemucca eventually learned to read and write in English when her grandfather placed her in a European American household in Carson City, Nevada.

As a result of her exposure to white culture, Winnemucca became an important liaison between European Americans and Native Americans. She held a number of jobs that reflected this dual role, including interpreting for the Paiutes Indian agent, Samuel Parrish, and as a translator for the U.S. Army during the Bannock War, in which the Paiutes allegedly fought against the United States. She went with her tribe when they were force-marched to Washington State, and as a result of their mistreatment she went on a lecture circuit to draw attention to the plight of her people. While lecturing in San Francisco, she met and married Lewis Hopkins, an Indian Department employee. Soon after, they traveled east so Winnemucca could continue to lecture. This experience helped Winnemucca develop the materials for her book, Life among the Paiutes, *which is excerpted in the following text.*

Although many narratives about Native women emphasize either their dependency or the violence enacted against them, Winnemucca's life and writing reveal the important role that Indian women could play in mediating tensions between European Americans and Natives. Winnemucca's education and her early introduction to white culture gave her the skills to bridge the two cultures, a role that mirrors the actions of Native women who came before her, including Sacagawea.

Our children are very carefully taught to be good. Their parents tell them stories, traditions of old times, even of the first mother of the human race; and love stories, stories of giants, and fables; and when they ask if these last stories are true, they answer, "Oh, it is only coyote," which means that they are make-believe stories. Coyote is the name

of a mean, crafty little animal, half wolf, half dog, and stands for everything low. It is the greatest term of reproach one Indian has for another. Indians do not swear,—they have no words for swearing till they learn them of white men. The worst they call each is bad or coyote; but they are very sincere with one another, and if they think each other in the wrong they say so.

We are taught to love everybody. We don't need to be taught to love our fathers and mothers. We love them without being told to. Our tenth cousin is as near to us as our first cousin; and we don't marry into our relations. Our young women are not allowed to talk to any young man that is not their cousin, except at the festive dances, when both are dressed in their best clothes, adorned with beads, feathers or shells, and stand alternately in the ring and take hold of hands. These are very pleasant occasions to all the young people.

Many years ago, when my people were happier than they are now, they used to celebrate the Festival of Flowers in the spring. I have been to three of them only in the course of my life.

Oh, with what eagerness we girls used to watch every spring for the time when we could meet with our hearts' delight, the young men, whom in civilized life you call beaux. We would all go in company to see if the flowers we were named for were yet in bloom, for almost all the girls are named for flowers. We talked about them in our wigwams, as if we were the flowers, saying, "Oh, I saw myself today in full bloom!" We would talk all the evening in this way in our families with such delight, and such beautiful thoughts of the happy day when we should meet with those who admired us and would help us to sing our flower-songs which we made up as we sang. But we were always sorry for those that were not named after some flower, because we knew they could not join in the flower-songs like ourselves, who were named for flowers of all kinds.

At last one evening came a beautiful voice, which made every girl's heart throb with happiness. It was the chief, and every one hushed to hear what he said to-day.

"My dear daughters, we are told that you have seen yourselves in the hills and in the valleys, in full bloom. Five days from to-day your festival day will come. I know every young man's heart stops beating while I am talking. I know how it was with me many years ago. I used to wish the Flower Festival would come every day. Dear young men and young women, you are saying, 'Why put it off five days?' But you all know that is our rule. It gives you time to think, and to show your sweetheart your flower."

All the girls who have flower-names dance along together, and those who have not go together also. Our fathers and mothers and grandfathers and grandmothers make a place for us where we can dance. Each one gathers the flower she is named for, and then all weave them into wreaths and crowns and scarfs, and dress up in them.

Some girls are named for rocks and are called rock-girls, and they find some pretty rocks which they carry; each one such a rock as she is named for, or whatever she is named for. If she cannot, she can take a branch of sage-brush, or a bunch of rye-grass, which have no flower.

They all go marching along, each girl in turn singing of herself; but she is not a girl any more,— she is a flower singing. She sings of herself, and her sweetheart, dancing along by her side, helps her sing the song she makes.

I will repeat what we say of ourselves. "I, Sarah Winnemucca, am a shell-flower, such as I wear on my dress. My name is Thocmetony. I am so beautiful! Who will come and dance with me while I am so beautiful? Oh, come and be happy with me! I shall be beautiful while the earth lasts. Somebody will always admire me; and who will come and be happy with me in the Spirit-land? I shall be beautiful forever there. Yes, I shall be more beautiful than my shell-flower, my Thocmetony! Then, come, oh come, and dance and be happy with me!" The young men sing with us as they dance beside us.

Our parents are waiting for us somewhere to welcome us home. And then we praise the sage-brush and the rye-grass that have no flower, and the pretty rocks that some are named for; and then we present our beautiful flowers to these companions who could carry none. And so all are happy; and that closes the beautiful day.

My people have been so unhappy for a long time they wish now to *disincrease,* instead of multiply. The mothers are afraid to have more children, for fear they shall have daughters, who are not safe even in their mother's presence.

Source: Winnemucca, Sarah. *Life Among the Piutes: Their Wrongs and Claims.* New York: G. P. Putnam's Sons, 1883, 45–48.

Sitting Bull, Report to a Senate Committee
(1883)

In 1883, the U.S. Senate sent a committee to investigate the conditions of American Indians in Montana and the Dakota Territory. Chairing the committee was Henry Dawes, who later sponsored the Dawes Act. The committee met with the Sioux and with Sitting Bull. What follows is Sitting Bull's comments to the five-man committee.

If a man loses anything, and goes back and looks carefully for it he will find it, and that is what the Indians are doing now when they ask you to give them the things they were promised them in the past. And I do not consider that they should be treated like a beast, and that is the reason I have grown up with the feelings I have.

Whatever you wanted of me I have obeyed, and I have come when you called me. The Great Father sent me word that what ever he had against me in the past had been forgiven and thrown aside, and he would have nothing against me in the future, and I accepted his promises and came in. And he told me not to step aside from the white man's path, and I told him I would not, and I am doing my best to travel that path.

I feel that my country has gotten a bad name, and I want it to have a good name. It used to have a good name, and I sit sometimes and wonder who it is that has given it a bad name. You are the only people now who can give it a good name, and I want you to take care of my country and respect it.

When we sold the Black Hills we got a very small price for it, and not what we ought to have received. I used to think that the size of the payments would remain the same all the time, but they are growing smaller all the time.

I want you to tell the Great Father everything I have said, and that we want some benefits from the promises he has made to us. And I don't think I should be tormented with anything about giving up any part of my land until those promises are fulfilled. I would rather wait until that time, when I will be ready to transact any business he may desire.

I consider that my country takes in the Black Hills, and runs from the Powder River to the Missouri, and that all of this land belongs to me. Our reservation is not as large as we want it to be, and I suppose the Great Father owes us money now for land he has taken from us in the past.

You white men advise us to follow your ways, and therefore I talk as I do. When you have a piece of land, and anything trespasses on it, you catch it and keep it until you get damages, and I am doing the same thing now. And I want you to tell this to the Great Father for me. I am looking into the future for the benefit of my children, and that is what I mean, when I say I want my country taken care of for me.

My children will grow up here, and I am looking ahead for their benefit and for the benefit of my children's children, too; and even beyond that again. I sit here and look around me now, and I see my people starving, and I want the Great Father to make an increase in the amount of food that is allowed us now, so that they may be able to live. We want cattle to butcher—I want you to kill 300 head of cattle at a time. That is the way you live and we want to live the same way. This is what I want you to tell the Great Father when you go back home.

If we get the things we want, our children will be raised like the white children. When the Great Father told me to live like his people I told him to send me six teams of mules, because that is the way white people make a living, and I wanted my children to have these things to help them to make a living. I also told him to send me two spans of horses with wagons, and everything else my children would need. I also asked for a horse and buggy for my children. I was advised to follow the ways of the white man, and that is why I asked for those things.

I never ask for anything that is not needed. I also asked for a cow and a bull for each family, so that they can raise cattle of their own. I asked for four yokes of oxen and wagons with them. Also a yoke of oxen and a wagon for each of my children to haul wood with.

It is your own doing that I am here. You sent me here, and advised me to live as you do, and it is not right for me to live in poverty. I asked the Great Father for hogs, male and female, and for male and female sheep for my children to raise from. I did not leave out anything in the way of animals that the white men have; I asked for every one of them. I want you to tell the Great Father to send me some agricultural implements, so that I will not be obliged to work bare-handed.

Whatever he sends to this agency our agent will take care of for us, and we will be satisfied because we know he will keep everything right. Whatever is sent here for us he will be pleased to take care of for us. I want to tell you that our rations have been reduced to almost nothing, and many of the people have starved to death.

Now I beg of you to have the amount of rations increased so that our children will not starve, but will live better than they do now. I want clothing, too, and I will ask for that, too. We want all kinds of clothing for our people. Look at the men around here, and see how poorly dressed they are. We want some clothing this month, and when it gets cold we want more to protect us from the weather.

That is all I have to say.

Source: Sitting Bull's Report to a Senate Committee, 1883. 48th Congress, 1st Session, Senate Rep. No 283, Serial 2164, 80–81.

Zitkala-Sa, "Impressions of an Indian Childhood: My Mother" (ca. 1883)

Zitkala-Sa, born Gertrude Simmons on the Pine Ridge reservation, traveled east to Indiana to attend Earlham College and to teach at the Carlisle Indian School. Later, she became a writer and an activist for Native American rights, founding the National Council for American Indians in 1926. The following excerpt describes a conversation she had with her mother when she was seven years old.

A wigwam of weather-stained canvas stood at the base of some irregularly ascending hills. A footpath wound its way gently down the sloping land till it reached the broad river bottom; creeping through the lone swamp grasses that bent over it on either side, it came out on the edge of the Missouri.

Here, morning, noon, and evening, my mother came to draw water from the muddy stream for our household use. Always, when my mother started for the river, I stopped my play to run along with her. She was only of medium height. Often she was sad and silent, at which times her full arched lips were compressed into hard and bitter lines, and shadows fell under her black eyes. Then I clung to her hand and begged to know what made the tears fall.

"Hush; my little daughter must never talk about my tears"; and smiling through them, she patted my head and said, "Now let me see how fast you can run today." Whereupon I tore away at my highest possible speed with my long black hair blowing in the breeze.

I was a wild little girl of seven. Loosely clad in a slip of brown buckskin, and lightfooted with a pair of soft moccasins on my feet, I was as free as the wind that blew my hair, and no less spirited than a bounding deer. These were my mother's pride—my wild freedom and overflowing spirits. She taught me no fear save that of intruding myself upon others.

Having gone many paces ahead I stopped, panting for breath, and laughing with glee as my mother watched my every movement. I was not wholly conscious of myself, but was more keenly alive to the fire within. It was as if I were the activity, and my hands and feet were only experiments for my spirit to work upon.

Returning from the river, I tugged beside my mother, with my hand upon the bucket I believed I was carrying. One time, on such a return, I remember a bit of conversation we had. My grown-up cousin, Warca-Ziwin (Sunflower), who was then seventeen, always went to the river alone for water for her mother. Their wigwam was not far from ours; and I saw her daily going to and from the river. I admired my cousin greatly. So I said, "Mother, when I am tall as my cousin Warca-Ziwin, you shall not have to come for water. I will do it for you."

With a strange tremor in her voice which I could not understand, she answered, "If the paleface does not take away from us the river we drink."

"Mother, who is this bad paleface?" I asked.

"My little daughter, he is a sham—a sickly sham! The bronzed Dakota is the only real man."

I looked up into my mother's face while she spoke; and seeing her bite her lips, I knew she was unhappy. This aroused revenge in my small soul. Stamping my foot on the earth, I cried aloud, "I hate the paleface that makes my mother cry!"

Setting the pail of water on the ground, my mother stooped, and stretching her left hand out on the level of my eyes, she placed her other arm about me; she pointed to the hill where my uncle and my only sister lay buried.

"There is what the paleface has done! Since then your father too has been buried in a hill nearer the rising sun. We were once very happy. But the paleface has stolen our lands and driven us hither. Having defrauded us of our land, the paleface forced us away.

"Well, it happened on the day we moved camp that your sister and uncle were both very sick. Many others were ailing, but there seemed to be no help. We traveled many days and nights; not in the grand, happy way that we moved camp when I was a little girl, but we were driven, my child, driven like a herd of buffalo. With every step, your sister, who was not as large as you are now, shrieked with the painful jar until she was hoarse with crying. She grew more and more feverish. Her little hands and cheek were burning hot. Her little lips were parched and dry, but she would not drink the water I gave her. Then I discovered that her throat was swollen and red. My poor child, how I cried with her because the Great Spirit had forgotten us!

"At last, when we reached this western country, on the first weary night your sister died. And soon your uncle died also, leaving a widow and an orphan daughter, your cousin Warca-Ziwin. Both your sister and uncle might have been happy with us today, had it not been for the heartless paleface."

My mother was silent the rest of the way to our wigwam. Though I saw no tears in her eyes, I knew that was because I was with her. She seldom wept before me.

Lone Man, Account of the Death of Sitting Bull
(1890)

After Sitting Bull surrendered to U.S. authorities, he lived at the Standing Rock Agency in the Dakotas. He also participated in Buffalo Bill's Wild West Show. However, the U.S. Indian agent at Standing Rock, James McLaughlin, feared Sitting Bull was going to run away to join the Ghost Dancers. As such, he ordered his arrest. Early one December morning in 1890, authorities sent a body of about 39 men to approach the cabin that Sitting Bull was in. Exactly what happened is controversial, and there are differing accounts of what happened. Regardless of how it happened, Sitting Bull was shot dead. The following is one witness's account of what happened. Lone Man knew Sitting Bull and had fought Custer at the Battle of the Little Bighorn in 1876. Many scholars regard Lone Man's account of Sitting Bull's death as one of the best.

Daybreak was drawing near and Lieut. Bullhead asked that we offer up a prayer before starting out and without waiting or calling upon anyone else, led us in prayer. After this, order was issued to saddle up our horses. When everyone was ready we took our places by two and at the command "hopo" we started.

We had to go through rough places and the roads were slippery. As we went through the Grand River bottoms it seemed as if the owls were hooting at us and the coyotes were howling all around us that one of the police remarked that the owls and the coyotes were giving us a warning—"so beware" he said.

Before we started, Bullhead assigned Red Bear and White Bird to have the favorite white horse of Sitting Bull's (which was always kept in the shed or in the coral at nights) caught and saddled up and be in readiness for the Chief to ride to the Agency upon his arrest. The rest of the force were ordered to station themselves all around Sitting Bull's cabin for the purpose of keeping order while the officers went into the cabin and caused the arrest. Bullhead said to me "now you used to belong to this outfit and was always on the good side of the Chief. I wish you would use your influence to keep order among the leaders who are going to become hostile."

We rode in a dogtrot gait till we got about a mile from the camp, then we galloped along and when we were about a mile from the camp, then we galloped along and when we were about a quarter of a mile, we rode up as if we attacked the camp. Upon our arrival at Sitting Bull's cabin, we quickly dismounted and while the officers went inside we all scattered round the cabin. I followed the police officers and as per orders, I took my place at the door. It was still dark and everybody was asleep and only dogs which were quite numerous, greeted us upon our arrival and no doubt by their greetings had aroused and awaken the ghost dancers.

Bullhead, followed by Red Tomahawk and Shavehead, knocked at the door and the Chief answered "how, timalhel hiy wo," "all right come in." The door was opened and Bullhead said "I come after you to take you to the Agency. You are under arrest." Sitting Bull said, "How," "Let me put on my clothes and go with you." He told one of his wives to get his clothes which was complied with. After he was dressed, arose to go and ordered

his son to saddle up his horse. The police told him that it was already outside waiting for him. When Sitting Bull started to go with the police instead of bidding him good bye, the way it was done by the civilized people, one of Sitting Bull's wives burst into a loud cry which drew attention. No sooner had this started, when several leaders were rapidly making their way toward Sitting Bull's cabin making all sorts of complaints about the actions of the Indian police. Mato wawoyuspa, the Bear that Catches, particularly came up close saying "Now, here are the 'ceska maza'—'metal breasts' (meaning police badges) just as we had expected all the time. You think you are going to take him. You shall not do it." Addressing the leaders, "Come on now, let us protect our Chief." Just about this time, Crow Foot got up, moved by the wailing of his mother and the complaining remarks of Bear that Catches, said to Sitting Bull: "Well—you always called yourself a brave chief. Now you are allowing yourself to be taken by the Ceska maza." Sitting Bull then changed his mind and in response to Crow Foot's remark said, "Ho ca mni kte sni yelo." "Then I will not go." By this time the ghost dancers were trying to get close to the Chief in every possible manner, trying to protect him and the police did their best, begging in their way, not to cause any trouble but they would not listen, instead they said "You shall not take away our Chief."

Lieut. Bullhead said to the Chief: "Come, now, do not listen to any one." I said to Sitting Bull in an imploring way: "Uncle, nobody is going to harm you. The Agent wants to see you and then you are to come back,—so please do not let others lead you into any trouble." But the Chief's mind was made up not to go so the three head officers laid their hands on him. Lieut. Bullhead got a hold on the Chief's right arm, Shavehead on the left arm, and Red Tomahawk back of the Chief—pulling him outside. By this time the whole camp was in commotion—women and children crying while the men gathered all round us—said everything mean imaginable but had not done anything to hurt us. The police tried to keep order but was useless—it was like trying to extinguish a treacherous prairie fire. Bear that Catches in the heat of the excitement, pulled out a gun, from under his blanket, and fired into Lieut. Bullhead and wounded him. Seeing that one of my dearest relatives and my superior, shot, I ran up toward where they were holding the Chief, when Bear that Catches raised his gun—pointed and fired at me, but it snapped. Being so close to him I scuffled with him and without any great effort overcame him, jerked the gun away from his hands and with the butt of the gun, I struck him somewhere and laid him out. It was about this moment that Lieut. Bullhead fired into Sitting Bull while still holding him and Red Tomahawk follows with another shot which finished the Chief.

The rest of the police now seeing nothing else for them to do but to defend themselves became engaged in a bitter encounter with the ghost dancers. It was day-break and the ghost dancers fled to the timber and some already started running away into the breaks south of the Grand River. The police took refuge behind the sheds and corrals adjoining the Chief's residence, knocked the chinks out, firing in the direction of the fleeing ghost dancers. One of our police was lying on the ground behind a shed when some ghost dancer shot him in the head and killed him instantly. This was my brother-in-law John Strong Arms, who came with me from our camp.

Finally, there was no more firing and we proceeded gathering up our dead and the wounded.

Hawkman, another relative of mine, a cousin, who hailed from same camp I came from, was sent to carry the news of the fight to the Military Forces. We brought them to the cabin and cared for them. While we were doing this, my friend, Running Hawk, said to the police: "Say, my friends, it seems there is something moving behind the curtain in the corner of the cabin." The cabin, instead of being plastered, the walls were, covered with strips of sheeting, sewed together and tacked on the walls making quite a bright appearance within. All eyes were directed to the corner mentioned and without

waiting for any orders I raised the curtain. There stood Crow Foot and as soon as he was exposed to view, he cried out, "My uncles, do not kill me. I do not wish to die." The police asked the officer what to do. Lieut. Bullhead, seeing what was up, said, "Do what you like with him. He is one of them that has caused this trouble." I do not remember who really fired the shot that killed Crow Foot—several fired at once.

It was about this time that the soldiers appeared on the top of high hills toward the Agency. According to the instructions received we were expecting them but they did not show up in our critical moment. Maybe it was just as well they did not for they would have made things worse as heretofore they generally did this. Immediately they fired a cannon toward where we were. Being ordered to display a "flag of truce" I tore off a piece of the white curtain, tied it on a long pole, ran out where they could see me, thinking they would cease firing but all was of no avail. They continued firing and the cannon balls came very close to where I was that at times I dodged. Finally, they stopped firing and made a bee-line toward us. They arrived and upon learning what had happened the officer ranking highest proceeded to where Sitting Bull's corpse was and with a (branch/brush) took the third coup and said: "Sitting Bull—big chief, you brought this disaster upon yourself and your people." Louis Primeau was interpreting.

The soldiers having dismounted rushed to the camp—ransacking anything worth keeping. Red Tomahawk took charge of the police force and after everything was prepared to take the dead and the wounded Indian police as well as Sitting Bull's corpse, discharged us from this campaign, and having complimented us for doing our duty as we did, asked us to attend the funeral of our comrades, killed in the fight. Strong Arm, Hawkman, Little Eagle, and Akicita were killed. Bullhead, Shavehead, and Middle were wounded seriously. Seven ghost-dancers besides Sitting Bull were killed on the Sitting Bull's side.

About this time, some of the relatives of the police killed arrived and such lamenting over the dead was seldom known in the history of my race. Taking a last look on my dead friends and relatives, I, in company with Charles Afraid of Hawk, started for home. On the way, we passed several deserted homes of the ghost dancers and felt sorry that such a big mistake was made by listening to outsiders who generally cause us nothing but trouble.

I reached home and before our reunion I asked my wife, brothers, sisters, and mother to prepare a sweat bath for me, that I may cleanse myself for participating in a bloody fight with my fellow men. After doing this, new or clean clothes were brought to me and the clothes I wore at the fight were burned up. I then, was reunited with my family. God spared my life for their sake.

The next day I took my family into the Agency. I reported to Major McLaughlin. He laid his hand on my shoulders, shook hands with me and said: "He alone is a Man, I feel proud of you for the very brave way you have carried out your part in the fight with the Ghost Dancers." I was not very brave right at that moment. His comment nearly set me a crying.

Source: Vestal, Stanley, ed. *New Sources of Indian History, 1850–1891.* Norman: University of Oklahoma Press, 1934, 49–55.

Wovoka, Message to the Cheyennes and the Arapahos
(ca. 1890)

Wovoka was a Paiute Indian. Known to whites as Jack Wilson, he experienced a vision around 1889. His vision developed into the Ghost Dance. The Ghost Dance was a way for Indians, especially the Lakota, to renew their world and to see their departed relatives. The dance was fast-paced and frightened white observers, who worked to suppress it. The suppression of the Ghost Dance led to the Wounded Knee massacre in 1890. In the following message, Wovoka attempts to tell both whites and Indians that his message is pure and true, and there is nothing to fear from it.

When you get home you must make a dance to continue five days. Dance four successive nights, and the last night keep up the dance until the morning of the fifth day, when all must bathe in the river and then disperse to their homes. You must all do in the same way.

I, Jack Wilson, love you all, and my heart is full of gladness for the gifts you have brought me. When you get home I shall give you a good cloud which will make you feel good. I give you a good spirit and give you all good paint. I want you to come again in three months, some from each tribe there.

There will be a good deal of snow this year and some rain. In the fall there will be such a rain as I have never given you before.

Grandfather says, when your friends die you must not cry. You must not hurt anybody or do harm to anyone. You must not fight. Do right always. It will give you satisfaction in life. This young man has a good father and mother. [Possibly this refers to Casper Edison, the man who transcribed this message.]

Do not tell the white people about this. Jesus is now upon the earth. He appears like a cloud. The dead are all alive again. I do not know when they will be here; may be this fall or in the spring. When the time comes there will be no more sickness and everyone will be young again.

Do not refuse to work for the whites and do not make any trouble with them until you leave them. When the earth shakes do not be afraid. It will not hurt you.

I want you to dance every six weeks. Make a feast at the dance and have food that everybody may eat. Then bathe in the water. That is all. You will receive good words again from me some time. Do not tell lies.

Source: Mooney, James. "The Ghost-Dance Religion and the Sioux Outbreak of 1890," Fourteenth Annual Report of the Bureau of American Ethnology, 1892–93, Part 2. Washington, DC: Government Printing Office, 1896, 781.

Ghost Dance Songs

(1890s)

The Ghost Dance created a number of songs. The songs that follow are from various Plains Indians.

GHOST DANCE SONGS OF THE ARAPAHO

My children, when at first I liked the Whites,
My children, when at first I liked the Whites,
I gave them fruits,
I gave them fruits.
Father, have pity on me,
Father, have pity on me;
I am crying for thirst,
I am crying for thirst;
All is gone—I have nothing to eat,
All is gone—I have nothing to eat.

GHOST DANCE SONGS OF THE SIOUX

The whole world is coming,
A nation is coming, a nation is coming,
The Eagle has brought the message to the tribe.
The father says so, the father says so.
Over the whole earth they are coming.
The buffalo are coming, the buffalo are coming,
The Crow has brought the message to the tribe,
The father says so, the father says so.

GHOST DANCE SONGS OF THE PAIUTE

A slender antelope, a slender antelope,
A slender antelope, a slender antelope,
He is wallowing upon the ground,
He is wallowing upon the ground,
He is wallowing upon the ground,
He is wallowing upon the ground.
The black rock, the black rock,
The black rock, the black rock,
The rock is broken, the rock is broken,
The rock is broken, the rock is broken.
The wind stirs the willows,
The wind stirs the willows,
The wind stirs the willows,
The wind stirs the grasses,
The wind stirs the grasses,
The wind stirs the grasses.
Fog! Fog!
Lightning! Lightning!
Whirlwind! Whirlwind!
The whirlwind! The whirlwind!
The whirlwind! The whirlwind!
The snowy earth comes gliding, the snowy earth comes gliding;
The snowy earth comes gliding, the snowy earth comes gliding.
There is dust from the whirlwind,
There is dust from the whirlwind,

There is dust from the whirlwind.
The whirlwind on the mountain,
The whirlwind on the mountain,
The whirlwind on the mountain.
The rocks are ringing,
The rocks are ringing,
The rocks are ringing.
They are ringing in the mountains,
They are ringing in the mountains,
They are ringing in the mountains.
The cottonwoods are growing tall,
The cottonwoods are growing tall,
The cottonwoods are growing tall.
They are growing tall and verdant.
They are growing tall and verdant,
They are growing tall and verdant.

GHOST DANCE SONGS OF THE KIOWA

The Father will descend,
The Father will descend.

The earth will tremble.
The earth will tremble.
Everybody will arise,
Everybody will arise.
Stretch out your hands,
Stretch out your hands.
The spirit host is advancing, they say,
The spirit host is advancing, they say.
They are coming with the buffalo, they say,
They are coming with the buffalo, they say.
They are coming with the (new) earth, they say,
They are coming with the (new) earth, they say.
That wind, that wind,
Shakes my tipi, shakes my tipi,
And sings a song for me,
And sings a song for me.

Source: Mooney, James. "The Ghost Dance Religion and the Sioux Outbreak of 1890," Fourteenth Annual Report of the Bureau of American Ethnology 1892–1893, Part 2. Washington, DC: Government Printing Office, 1896, 961–977, 1072, 1053–1055, 1082–1087.

Black Elk, Account of the Wounded Knee Massacre
(1890)

In the following account, Black Elk, an Oglala Lakota, describes the events of December 29, 1890, the Wounded Knee massacre. As an elder, Black Elk was an influential spiritual leader among his people. While still a boy of 12, Black Elk fought in the Battle of the Little Bighorn in 1876 and took his first scalp on the first day of fighting against Custer's Seventh Cavalry. In 1887, Black Elk traveled to Europe as part of Buffalo Bill's Wild West Show, an experience he discussed in his book, Black Elk Speaks. *In 1890, Black Elk and the Lakota people were eking out an existence on their reservations in South Dakota when they received the Ghost Dance from*

Wovoka, a Paiute spiritual leader. The Ghost Dance ceremony provided many Lakota with a sense of hope; however, as the following account illustrates, the fear held by many local white settlers regarding the Ghost Dance religion led to a bitter clash between the Lakota and the U.S. military in which approximately 200 Native Americans were massacred.

It was about this time that bad news came to us from the north. We heard that some policemen from Standing Rock had gone to arrest Sitting Bull on Grand River, and that he would not let them take him; so there was a fight, and they killed him.

It was now near the end of the Moon of Popping Trees, and I was twenty-seven years old [December 1890]. We heard that Big Foot was coming down from the Badlands with nearly four hundred people. Some of these were from Sitting Bull's band. They had run away when Sitting Bull was killed, and joined Big Foot on Good River. There were only about a hundred warriors in this band, and all the others were women and children and some old men. They were all starving and freezing, and Big Foot was so sick that they had to bring him along in a pony drag. They had all run away to hide in the Badlands, and they were coming in now because they were starving and freezing. Soldiers were over there looking for them. The soldiers had everything and were not freezing and starving. Near Porcupine Butte the soldiers came up to the Big Foots, and they surrendered and went along with the soldiers to Wounded Knee Creek.

It was in the evening when we heard that the Big Foots were camped over there with the soldiers, about fifteen miles by the old road from where we were. It was the next morning [December 29, 1890] that something terrible happened.

That evening before it happened, I went in to Pine Ridge and heard these things, and while I was there, soldiers started for where the Big Foots were. These made about five hundred soldiers that were there next morning. When I saw them starting I felt that something terrible was going to happen. That night I could hardly sleep at all. I walked around most of the night.

In the morning I went out after my horses, and while I was out I heard shooting off toward the east, and I knew from the sound that it must be wagon-guns [cannon] going off. The sounds went right through my body, and I felt that something terrible would happen. . . . [He donned his ghost shirt, and armed only with a bow, mounted his pony and rode in the direction of the shooting, and was joined on the way by others.]

In a little while we had come to the top of the ridge where, looking to the east, you can see for the first time the monument and the burying ground on the little hill where the church is. That is where the terrible thing started. Just south of the burying ground on the little hill a deep dry gulch runs about east and west, very crooked, and it rises westward to nearly the top of the ridge where we were. It had no name, but the Wasichus [white men] sometimes called Battle Creek now. We stopped on the ridge not far from the head of the dry gulch. Wagon guns were still going off over there on the little hill, and they were going off again where they hit among the gulch. There was much shooting down yonder, and there were many cries, and we could see cavalrymen scattered over the hills ahead of us. Cavalrymen were riding along the gulch and shooting into it, where the women and children were running away and trying to hide in the gullies and the stunted pines . . .

We followed down along the dry gulch, and what we saw was terrible. Dead and wounded women and children and little babies were scattered all along there where they had been trying to run away. The soldiers had followed along the gulch, as they ran, and murdered them in there. Sometimes they were in heaps because they had huddled together, and some were scattering all along. Sometimes bunches of them had been killed and torn to pieces where the wagon guns hit them. I saw a little baby trying to suck its mother, but she was bloody and dead.

There were two little boys at one place in this gulch. They had guns and they had been killing soldiers all by themselves. We could see the soldiers they had killed. The boys were all alone there, and they were not hurt. These were very brave little boys.

When we drove the soldiers back, they dug themselves in, and we were not enough people to drive them out from there. In the evening they marched off up Wounded Knee Creek, and then we saw all that they had done there.

Men and women and children were heaped and scattered all over the flat at the bottom of the little hill where the soldiers had their wagon-guns, and westward up the dry gulch all the way to the high ridge, the dead women and children and babies were scattered.

When I saw this I wished that I had died too, but I was not sorry for the women and children. It was better for them to be happy in the other world, and I wanted to be there too. But before I went there I wanted to have revenge. I thought there might be a day, and we should have revenge.

In the morning the soldiers began to take all the guns away from the Big Foots, who were camped in the flat below the little hill where the monument and burying ground are now. The people had stacked most of their guns, and even their knives, by the teepee where Big Foot was lying sick. Soldiers were on the little hill and all around, and there were soldiers across the dry gulch to the south and over east along Wounded Knee Creek too. The people were nearly surrounded, and the wagon-guns were pointed at them.

It was a good winter day when all this happened. The sun was shining. But after the soldiers marched away from their dirty work, a heavy snow began to fall. The wind came up in the night. There was a big blizzard, and it grew very cold. The snow drifted deep in the crooked gulch, and it was one long grave of butchered women and children and babies, who had never done any harm and were only trying to run away.

Red Cloud, Speech on the Massacre at Wounded Knee (1891)

In the following speech, Red Cloud, a Lakota leader and brilliant military strategist, discusses what he believes to be the causes of the massacre at Wounded Knee. Red Cloud emphasizes the culpability of the United States in the massacre by arguing that the Americans placed the Lakota in a desperate situation by meddling with their culture, society, and economy. The seizure of horses and cuts in rations were especially difficult for the Lakota to suffer; the Ghost Dance provided hope during a period of great difficulty and deprivation.

I will tell you the reason for the trouble. When we first made treaties with the Government, our old life and our old customs were about to end; the game on which we lived was disappearing; the whites were closing around us, and nothing remained for us but to adopt their ways,—the Government promised us all the means necessary to make our living out of the land, and to instruct us how to do it, and with abundant food to support us until we could take care of ourselves. We looked forward with hope to the time we could be as independent as the whites, and have a voice in the Government.

The army officers could have helped better than anyone else but we were not left to them. An Indian Department was made with a large number of agents and other officials drawing large salaries— then came the beginning of trouble; these men took care of themselves but not of us. It was very hard to deal with the government through them— they could make more for themselves by keeping us back than by helping us forward.

We did not get the means for working our lands; the few things they gave us did little good. Our rations began to be reduced; they said we were lazy. That is false. How does any man of sense suppose that so great a number of people could get work at once unless they were at once supplied with the means to work and instructors enough to teach them?

Our ponies were taken away from us under the promise that they would be replaced by oxen and large horses; it was long before we saw any, and then we got very few. We tried with the means we had, but on one pretext or another, we were shifted from one place to another, or were told that such a transfer was coming. Great efforts were made to break up our customs, but nothing was done to introduce us to customs of the whites. Everything was done to break up the power of the real chiefs. Those old men really wished their people to improve, but little men, so-called chiefs, were made to act as disturbers and agitators. Spotted Tail wanted the ways of the whites, but an assassin was found to remove him. This was charged to the Indians because an Indian did it, but who set on the Indian? I was abused and slandered, to weaken my influence for good. This was done by men paid by the government to teach us the ways of the whites. I have visited many other tribes and found that the same things were done amongst them; all was done to discourage us and nothing to encourage us. I saw men paid by the government to help us, all very busy making money for themselves, but doing nothing for us . . .

The men who counted (census) told all around that we were feasting and wasting food. Where did he see it? How could we waste what we did not have? We felt we were mocked in our misery; we had no newspaper and no one to speak for us. Our rations were again reduced. You who eat three times a day and see your children well and happy around you cannot understand what a starving Indian feels! We were faint with hunger and maddened by despair. We held our dying children and felt their little bodies tremble as their soul went out and left only a dead weight in our hands. They were not very heavy but we were faint and the dead weighed us down. There was no hope on earth. God seemed to have forgotten. Some one had been talking of the Son of God and said He had come. The people did not know; they did not care; they snatched at hope; they screamed like crazy people to Him for mercy they caught at the promise they heard He had made.

The white men were frightened and called for soldiers. We begged for life and the white men thought we wanted theirs; we heard the soldiers were coming. We did not fear. We hoped we could tell them our suffering and could get help. The white men told us the soldiers meant to kill us; we did not believe it but some were frightened and ran away to the Bad Lands. The soldiers came. They said: "don't be afraid—we come to make peace, not war." It was true; they brought us food. But the hunger-crazed who had taken fright at the soldiers' coming and went to the Bad Lands could not be induced to return to the horrors of reservation life. They were called Hostiles and the Government sent the army to force them back to their reservation prison.

Source: Johnson, W. Fletcher. *Life of Sitting Bull.* Edgewood Press, 1891, 461–467. http://dev.prenhall.com/divisions/hss/app/historyresourcecenter/TextualDocuments/trage.htm.

Simon Pokagon Offers the Red Man's Greeting

(1893)

Simon Pokagon was a Potawatomi from southwestern Michigan. Although his lifetime witnessed the forced removal of many of his fellow American Indians, this group of Potawatomi was never forced to leave. He was invited to address the World's Fair in Chicago during 1893. He provides a critical assessment of American society and civilization, much of which came from, in his eyes, American Indians.

Shall not one line lament our forest race,
For you struck out from wild creation's face,
Freedom—the selfsame freedom you adore,
Bade us defend our violated shore.

In behalf of my people, the American Indians, I hereby declare to you, the pale-faced race that has usurped our lands and homes, that we have no spirit to celebrate with you the great Columbian Fair now being held in this Chicago city, the wonder of the world.

No sooner would we hold the high joy day over the graves of our departed than to celebrate our own funeral, the discovery of America. And while you who are strangers, and you who live here, bring the offerings of the handiwork of your own lands and your hearts in admiration rejoice over the beauty and grandeur of this young republic and you say, "Behold the wonders wrought by our children in this foreign land," do not forget that this success has been at the sacrifice of *our* homes and a once happy race.

Where these great Columbian show-buildings stretch skyward, and where stands this "Queen City of the West" *once* stood the red man's wigwams; here met their old men, young men, and maidens; here blazed their council fires. But now the eagle's eye can find no trace of them. Here was the center of their wide-spread hunting grounds; stretching far eastward, and to the great salt Gulf southward, and to the lofty Rocky Mountain chain westward; and all about and beyond the Great Lakes northward roamed vast herds of buffalo that no man could number, while moose, deer, and elk were found from ocean to ocean; pigeons, ducks, and geese in a near bow shot moved in great clouds through the air, while fish swarmed our streams, lakes and seas close to shore. All were provided by the Great Spirit for our use; we destroyed none except for food and dress; had plenty and were contented and happy.

But alas! The pale faces came by chance to our shores, many times very needy and hungry. We nursed and fed them, fed the ravens that were soon to pluck out our eyes and the eyes of our children; or no sooner had the news reached the Old World that a new continent had been found, peopled with another race of men, that, locust-like, they swarmed on all our coast; and, like the carrion crows in spring, that they find and feast upon the dead, so these strangers from the East long circuits made, and turkey-like they gobbled in our ears, "Give us gold, give us gold." "Where find you gold? Where find you gold?"

We gave for promises and "geegaws" all the gold we had and showed them where to dig for more; to repay us, they robbed our homes of fathers, mothers, sons, and daughters; some were forced across the sea for slaves in Spain, while multitudes were dragged into the mines to dig for gold, and held in slavery there until all who escaped not, died under the lash of the cruel task-master. It finally passed into their history that, "the red man of the West, unlike the black man of the East, will die before he'll be a slave." Our hearts were crushed by such base ingratitude; and, as the United States has now decreed, "No Chinaman shall land upon our shores," so we then felt that no such barbarians as they, should land on *ours*.

In those days that tried our fathers' souls, tradition says, "A crippled, grey-haired sire told his tribe that in the visions of the night he was lifted high above the earth, and in great wonder beheld a vast spider web spread out over the land from the Atlantic Ocean toward the setting sun. Its net-work was made of rods of iron; along its lines in all directions rushed monstrous spiders, greater in strength, and larger far than any beast of earth, clad in brass and stripping in their course the flight of birds that fled before them. Hissing from their nostrils came forth fire and smoke, striking terror to both fowl and beast. The red men hid themselves in fear, or fled away, while the white men trained these monsters for the war path, as warriors for battle."

The old man who saw the vision claimed it meant that the Indian race would surely pass away before the pale-faced strangers. He died a martyr to his belief. Centuries have passed since that time, and we now behold in the vision as in a mirror, the present net-work of railroads, and the monstrous engines with their fire, smoke, and hissing steam, with cars attached, as they go sweeping through the land.

The cyclone of civilization rolled westward; the forests of untold centuries were swept away; streams dried up; lakes fell back from their ancient bounds; and all our fathers once loved to gaze upon was destroyed, defaced, or marred, except the sun, moon, and starry skies above, which the Great Spirit in his wisdom hung beyond their reach.

Still on the storm-cloud rolled, while before its lightening and thunder the beasts of the field and the fowls of the air withered like grass before the flame—were shot for love of power to kill alone, and left to spoil upon the plains. Their bleaching bones now scattered far and near, in shame declare the wanton cruelty of pale-faced men. The storm unsatisfied on land swept our lakes and streams, while before its clouds of hooks, nets, and glistening spears the fish vanished from our waters like the morning dew before the rising sun. Thus our inheritance was cut off, and we were driven and scattered as sheep before the wolves.

Nor was this all. They brought among us fatal disease our fathers knew not of; our medicine-men tried in vain to check the deadly plague; but they themselves died, and our people fell as fall the leaves before the autumn's blast. To be just, we must acknowledge there were some good men with these strangers who gave their lives for ours, and in great kindness taught us the revealed will of the Great Spirit through his Son Jesus, the mediator between God and man. But while we were being taught to love the Lord our God with all our heart, mind, and strength, and our neighbors as ourselves, and our children were taught to lisp "Our Father who art in heaven, hallowed be thy name," bad men of the same race, whom we thought of the same belief, shocked our faith in the revealed will of the Father, as they came among us with bitter oaths upon their lips, something we had never heard before, and cups of "fire-water" in their hand, something we had never seen before. They pressed the sparkling glasses to our lips and

said, "Drink, and you will be happy." We drank thereof, we and our children, but alas! Like the serpent that charms to kill, the drink habit coiled about the heart-strings of its victims, shocking unto death love, honor, manhood—all that makes men good and noble; crushing out all ambition, and leaving naught but a culprit vagabond in the place of a man.

Now as we have been taught to believe that our first parents ate of the forbidden fruit, and fell, so we fully believe that this fire-water is the hard-cider of the white man's devil, made from the fruit of that tree that brought death into the world, and all our woes. The arrow, the scalping-knife, and the tomahawk used on the war-path were *merciful* compared with it; *they* were used in our defense, but the accursed drink came like a serpent in the form of a dove. . . .

You say of us that we are treacherous, vindictive, and cruel; in answer to the charge, we declare to all the world with our hands uplifted before high Heaven, that before the white man came among us, we were kind, outspoken, and forgiving. Our real character has been misunderstood because we have resented the breaking of treaties made with the United States, as we honestly understood them. The few of our children who were permitted to attend your schools, in great pride tell us that they read in our own histories, how William Penn, a Quaker, and a good man, made treaties with nineteen tribes of Indians, and that neither he nor they ever broke them; and further, that during seventy years while Pennsylvania was controlled by the Quakers, not a drop of blood was shed nor a war-whoop sounded by our people. Your own historians, and our traditions, show that for nearly two hundred years, different Eastern powers were striving for the mastery in the new world, and that our people were persuaded by the different factions to take the war path, being generally led by white men who had been discharged from prisons for crimes committed in the Old World. . . .

It is clear that for years after the discovery of this country, we stood before the coming strangers as a block of marble before the sculptor, ready to be shaped into a statue of grace and beauty; but in their greed for gold, the block was hacked to pieces and destroyed. Child-like we trusted in them with all our hearts; and as the young nestling while yet blind swallows each morsel given by the parent bird, so we drank in all they said. They showed us the compass that guided them across the trackless deep, and as its needle swung to and fro only resting to the north, we looked upon it as a thing of life from the eternal world. We could not understand the lightning and thunder of their guns, believing they were weapons of the gods; nor could we fathom their wisdom in knowing and telling us the exact time in which the sun or moon should be darkened; hence we looked upon them as divine; we revered them—yes, we trusted in them, as infants trust in the arms of their mothers.

But again and again was our confidence betrayed, until we were compelled to know that greed for gold was all the balance-wheel they had. The remnant of the beasts are now wild and keep beyond the arrow's reach, the fowls fly high in air, the fish hide themselves in deep waters. We have been driven from the homes of our childhood and from the burial places of our kindred and friends, and scattered far westward into desert places, where multitudes have died from homesickness, cold, and hunger, and are suffering and dying still for want of food and blankets.

As the hunted deer close chased all day long, when night comes on, weary and tired, lies down to rest, mourning for companions of the morning herd, all scattered, dead, and gone, so we through weary years have tried to find some place to safely rest. But all in vain! Our throbbing hearts unceasing say, "The hounds are howling on our tracks." Our sad history has been told by weeping parents to their children from generation to generation; and as the fur of the fox in the duckling is hatched, so the wrongs we have suffered are transmitted to our children, and they look upon the white man with distrust as soon as they are born. Hence our worst acts of cruelty should be viewed by all the world with Christian charity, as being but the echo of bad treatment dealt out to us. . . .

We never shall be happy here any more; we gaze into the faces of our little ones, for smiles of infancy to please, and into the faces of our young men and maidens, for joys of youth to cheer advancing age, but alas! Instead of smiles of joy we find but looks of sadness there. Then we fully realize in the anguish of our souls that their young and tender hearts, in keenest sympathy with ours, have drunk in the sorrows we have felt, and their sad faces reflect it back to us again. No rainbow of promise spans the dark cloud of our afflictions; no cheering hopes are painted on our midnight sky. We only stand with folded arms and watch and wait to see the future deal with us no better than the past. No cheer of sympathy is given us; but in answer to our complaints we are told the triumphal march of the Eastern race westward is by the unalterable decree of nature, termed by them "the survival of the fittest." And so we stand as upon the seashore, chained hand and foot, while the incoming tide of the great ocean of civilization rises slowly but surely to overwhelm us.

Source: Pokagon, Simon. *The Red Man's Greeting.* Hartford, MI: C. H. Engle, 1893.

Charles Eastman, "The Laughing Philosopher"
(1902)

Charles Eastman, known as Ohíye S'a among the Dakota, wrote Indian Boyhood *in 1902. The following is an excerpt from that work. Eastman* *was a prolific author, lecturer, and activist. Among his many contributions to American culture include the Boy Scouts of America, a*

group he helped found in 1910. Eastman
disagreed with many Friends of the Indian
organizations that argued for the complete
assimilation of Native Americans. Eastman
believed American Indians could retain their
traditional cultural and spiritual beliefs while still
contributing to the betterment and advancement
of the United States. His life and contributions to
this country are proof that Eastman was correct.
The following document illustrates Eastman's
remarkable talent as a storyteller and his ability
to educate white U.S. populations regarding
indigenous culture and society, providing his
audience with a more realistic perspective of
American Indians.

There is scarcely anything so exasperating to me as the idea that the natives of this country have no sense of humor and no faculty for mirth. This phase of their character is well understood by those whose fortune or misfortune it has been to live among them day in and day out at their homes. I don't believe I ever heard a real hearty laugh away from the Indians' fireside. I have often spent an entire evening in laughing with them until I could laugh no more. There are evenings when the recognized wit or story-teller of the village gives a free entertainment which keeps the rest of the community in a convulsive state until he leaves them. However, Indian humor consists as much in the gestures and inflections of the voice as in words, and is really untranslatable.

Matogee (Yellow Bear) was a natural humorous speaker, and a very diffident man at other times. He usually said little, but when he was in the mood he could keep a large company in a roar. This was especially the case whenever he met his brother-in-law, Tamedokah.

It was a custom with us Indians to joke more particularly with our brothers- and sisters-in-law. But no one ever complained, or resented any of these jokes, however personal they might be. That would be an unpardonable breach of etiquette.

"Tamedokah, I heard that you tried to capture a buck by holding on to his tail," said Matogee,

laughing. "I believe that feat cannot be performed any more; at least, it never has been since the pale-face brought us the knife, the 'mysterious iron,' and the pulverized coal that makes bullets fly. Since our ancestors hunted with stone knives and hatchets, I say, that has never been done."

The fact was that Tamedokah had stunned a buck that day while hunting, and as he was about to dress him the animal got up and attempted to run, whereupon the Indian launched forth to secure his game. He only succeeded in grasping the tail of the deer, and was pulled about all over the meadows and the adjacent woods until the tail came off in his hands. Matogee thought this too good a joke to be lost.

I sat near the door of the tent, and thoroughly enjoyed the story of the comical accident.

"Yes," Tamedokah quietly replied, "I thought I would do something to beat the story of the man who rode a young elk, and yelled frantically for help, crying like a woman."

"Ugh! That was only a legend," retorted Matogee, for it was he who was the hero of this tale in his younger days. "But this is a fresh feat of to-day. Chankpayuhah said he could not tell which was the most scared, the buck or you," he continued. "He said the deer's eyes were bulging out of their sockets, while Tamedokah's mouth was constantly enlarging toward his ears, and his hair floated on the wind, shaking among the branches of the trees. That will go down with the traditions of our fathers," he concluded with an air of satisfaction.

"It was a singular mishap," admitted Tamedokah.

The pipe had been filled by Matogee and passed to Tamedokah good-naturedly, still with a broad smile on his face. "It must be acknowledged," he resumed, "that you have the strongest kind of a grip, for no one else could hold on as long as you did, and secure such a trophy besides. That tail will do for an eagle feather holder."

By this time the teepee was packed to overflowing. Loud laughter had been heard issuing from the lodge of Matogee, and everybody suspected that he had something good, so many had come to listen.

"I think we should hear the whole matter," said one of the late comers.

The teepee was brightly lit by the burning embers, and all the men were sitting with their knees up against their chests, held in that position by wrapping their robes tightly around loins and knees. This fixed them something in the fashion of a rocking-chair.

"Well, no one saw him except Chankpayuhah," Matogee remarked.

"Yes, yes, he must tell us about it," exclaimed a chorus of voices.

"This is what I saw," the witness began. "I was tracking a buck and a doe. As I approached a small opening at the creek side 'boom!' came a report of a mysterious iron. I remained in a stooping position, hoping to see a deer cross the opening. In this I was not disappointed, for immediately after the report a fine buck dashed forth with Tamedokah close behind him. The latter was holding on to the deer's tail with both hands and his knife was in his mouth, but it soon dropped out. 'Tamedokah,' I shouted, 'haven't you got hold of the wrong animal?' but as I spoke they disappeared into the woods.

"In a minute they both appeared again, and then it was that I began to laugh. I could not stop. It almost killed me. The deer jumped the longest jumps I ever saw. Tamedokah walked the longest paces and was very swift. His hair was whipping the trees as they went by. Water poured down his face. I stood bent forward because I could not straighten my back-bone, and was ready to fall when they again disappeared.

"When they came out for the third time it seemed as if the woods and the meadow were moving too. Tamedokah skipped across the opening as if he were a grasshopper learning to hop. I fell down.

"When I came to him he was putting water on my face and head, but when I looked at him I fell again, and did not know anything until the sun had passed the mid-sky."

The company was kept roaring all the way through this account, while Tamedokah himself heartily joined in the mirth.

"Ho, ho, ho!" they said; "he has made his name famous in our annals. This will be told of him henceforth."

"It reminds me of Chadozee's bear story," said one.

"His was more thrilling, because it was really dangerous," interposed another.

"You can tell it to us, Bobdoo," remarked a third.

The man thus addressed made no immediate reply. He was smoking contentedly. At last he silently returned the pipe to Matogee, with whom it has begun its rounds. Deliberately he tightened his robe around him, saying as he did so:

"Ho (Yes). I was with him. It was by a very little that he saved his life. I will tell you how it happened.

"I was hunting with these two men, Nageedah and Chadozee. We came to some wild cherry bushes. I began to eat of the fruit when I saw a large silver-tip crawling towards us. 'Look out! there is a grizzly here,' I shouted, and I ran my pony out on to the prairie; but the others had already dismounted.

"Nageedah had just time to jump upon his pony and get out of the way, but the bear seized hold of his robe and pulled it off. Chadozee stood upon the verge of a steep bank, below which there ran a deep and swift-flowing stream. The bear rushed upon him so suddenly that when he took a step backward, they both fell into the creek together. It was a fall of about twice the height of a man."

"Did they go out of sight?" some one inquired.

"Yes, both fell headlong. In his excitement Chadozee laid hold of the bear in the water, and I never saw a bear try so hard to get away from a man as this one did."

"Ha, ha, ha! Ha, ha, ha!" they all laughed.

"When they came to the surface again they were both so eager to get to the shore that each let go, and they swam as quickly as they could to opposite sides. Chadozee could not get any further, so he clung to a stray root, still keeping a close watch of the bear, who was forced to do the same. There they both hung, regarding each other with looks of contempt and defiance."

"Ha, ha, ha! Ha, ha, ha!" they all laughed again.

"At last the bear swam along the edge to a lower place, and we pulled Chadozee up by means of our lariats. All this time he had been groaning so loud that we supposed he was badly torn; but when I looked for his wounds I found a mere scratch."

Again the chorus of appreciation from his hearers.

"The strangest thing about this affair of mine," spoke up Tamedokah, "is that I dreamed the whole thing the night before."

"There are some dreams come true, and I am a believer in dreams," one remarked.

"Yes, certainly, so are we all. You know Hachah almost lost his life by believing in dreams," commented Matogee.

"Let us hear that story," was the general request.

"You have all heard of Hachah, the great medicine man, who did many wonderful things. He once dreamed four nights in succession of flying from a high cliff over the Minnesota river. He recollected every particular of the scene, and it made a great impression upon his mind.

"The next day after he had dreamed it for the fourth time, he proposed to his wife that they go down to the river to swim, but his real purpose was to see the place of his dream.

"He did find the place, and it seemed to Hachah exactly like. A crooked tree grew out of the top of the cliff, and the water below was very deep."

"Did he really fly?" I called impatiently from the doorway, where I had been listening and laughing with the rest.

"Ugh, that is what I shall tell you. He was swimming about with his wife, who was a fine swimmer; but all at once Hachah disappeared. Presently he stood up the very tree that he had seen in his dream, and gazed out over the water. The tree was very springy, and Hachah felt sure that he could fly; so before long he launched bravely forth from the cliff. He kicked out vigorously and swung both arms as he did so, but nevertheless he came down to the bottom of the water like a crow that had been shot on the wing."

"Ho, ho, ho! Ho, ho, ho!" and the whole company laughed unreservedly.

"His wife screamed loudly as Hachah whirled downward and went out of sight like a blue heron after a fish. Then she feared he might be stunned, so she swam to him and dragged him to the shore. He could not speak, but the woman overwhelmed him with reproaches."

"What are you trying to do, you old idiot? Do you want to kill yourself?" she screamed again and again.

"'Woman, be silent,' he replied, and he said nothing more. He did not tell his dream for many years afterward. Not until he was a very old man and about to die, did Hachah tell any one how he thought he could fly."

And at this they all laughed louder than ever.

Source: Eastman, Charles A. *Indian Boyhood.* New York: McClure, Phillips, & Co., 1902, 267–272.

Zitkala-Sa, "Why I Am a Pagan"

(1902)

Zitkala-Sa wrote the following article for the Atlantic Monthly *in 1902. In "Why I Am a Pagan," Zitkala-Sa explains her resistance to accepting Christianity. During her lifetime,*

Zitkala-Sa witnessed the erosion of the traditional spiritual beliefs of many of her friends and family, and the Lakota people more generally. Zitkala-Sa explains her own powerful spiritual beliefs, which she experiences while communing with nature, walking among the green hills of her people. Her refusal to be bullied into accepting Christianity by either missionaries or her relatives makes her narrative a powerful example of resistance and persistence.

WHEN the spirit swells my breast I love to roam leisurely among the green hills; or sometimes, sitting on the brink of the murmuring Missouri, I marvel at the great blue overhead. With half closed eyes I watch the huge cloud shadows in their noiseless play upon the high bluffs opposite me, while into my ear ripple the sweet, soft cadences of the river's song. Folded hands lie in my lap, for the time forgot. My heart and I lie small upon the earth like a grain of throbbing sand. Drifting clouds and tinkling waters, together with the warmth of a genial summer day, bespeak with eloquence the loving Mystery round about us. During the idle while I sat upon the sunny river bank, I grew somewhat, though my response be not so clearly manifest as in the green grass fringing the edge of the high bluff back of me.

At length retracing the uncertain footpath scaling the precipitous embankment, I seek the level lands where grow the wild prairie flowers. And they, the lovely little folk, soothe my soul with their perfumed breath.

Their quaint round faces of varied hue convince the heart which leaps with glad surprise that they, too, are living symbols of omnipotent thought. With a child's eager eye I drink in the myriad star shapes wrought in luxuriant color upon the green. Beautiful is the spiritual essence they embody.

I leave them nodding in the breeze but take along with me their impress upon my heart. I pause to rest me upon a rock embedded on the side of a foothill facing the low river bottom. Here the Stone-Boy, of whom the American aborigine tells, frolics about, shooting his baby arrows and shouting aloud with glee at the tiny shafts of lightning that flash from the flying arrow-beaks. What an

ideal warrior he became, baffling the siege of the pests of all the land till he triumphed over their united attack. And here he lay,—Invan, our great-great-grandfather, older than the hill he rested on, older than the race of men who love to tell of his wonderful career.

Interwoven with the thread of this Indian legend of the rock, I fain would trace a subtle knowledge of the native folk which enabled them to recognize a kinship to any and all parts of this vast universe. By the leading of an ancient trail, I move toward the Indian village.

With the strong, happy sense that both great and small are so surely enfolded in His magnitude that, without a miss, each has his allotted individual ground of opportunities, I am buoyant with good nature.

Yellow Breast, swaying upon the slender stem of a wild sunflower, warbles a sweet assurance of this as I pass near by. Breaking off the clear crystal song, he turns his wee head from side to side eyeing me wisely as slowly I plod with moccasined feet. Then again he yields himself to his song of joy. Flit, flit hither and yon, he fills the summer sky with his swift, sweet melody. And truly does it seem his vigorous freedom lies more in his little spirit than in his wing.

With these thoughts I reach the log cabin whither I am strongly drawn by the tie of a child to an aged mother. Out bounds my four-footed friend to meet me, frisking about my path with unmistakable delight. Chan is a black shaggy dog, "a thorough bred little mongrel," of whom I am very fond. Chan seems to understand many words in Sioux, and will go to her mat even when I whisper the word, though generally I think she is guided by the tone of the voice. Often she tries to imitate the sliding inflection and long drawn out voice to the amusement of our guests, but her articulation is quite beyond my ear. In both my hands I hold her shaggy head and gaze into her large brown eyes. At once the dilated pupils contract into tiny black dots, as if the roguish spirit within would evade my questioning.

Finally resuming the chair at my desk I feel in keen sympathy with my fellow creatures, for I seem to see clearly again that all are akin.

The racial lines, which once were bitterly real, now serve nothing more than marking out a living mosaic of human beings. And even here men of the same color are like the ivory keys of one instrument where each represents all the rest, yet varies from them in pitch and quality of voice. And those creatures who are for a time mere echoes of another's note are not unlike the fable of the thin sick man whose distorted shadow, dressed like a real creature, came to the old master to make him follow as a shadow. Thus with a compassion for all echoes in human guise, I greet the solemn-faced "native preacher" whom I find awaiting me. I listen with respect for God's creature, though he mouths most strangely the jangling phrases of a bigoted creed.

As our tribe is one large family, where every person is related to all the others, he addressed me:—

"Cousin, I came from the morning church service to talk with you."

"Yes," I said interrogatively, as he paused for some word from me.

Shifting uneasily about in the straight-backed chair he sat upon, he began: "Every holy day (Sunday) I look about our little God's house, and not seeing you there, I am disappointed. This is why I come to-day. Cousin, as I watch you from afar, I see no unbecoming behavior and hear only good reports of you, which all the more burns me with the wish that you were a church member. Cousin, I was taught long years ago by kind missionaries to read the holy book. These godly men taught me also the folly of our old beliefs.

"There is one God who gives reward or punishment to the race of dead men. In the upper region the Christian dead are gathered in unceasing song and prayer. In the deep pit below, the sinful ones dance in torturing flames."

"Think upon these things, my cousin, and choose now to avoid the after-doom of hell fire!" Then followed a long silence in which he clasped tighter and unclasped again his interlocked fingers.

Like instantaneous lightning flashes came pictures of my own mother's making, for she, too, is now a follower of the new superstition.

"Knocking out the chinking of our log cabin, some evil hand thrust in a burning taper of braided dry grass, but failed of his intent, for the fire died out and the half burned brand fell inward to the floor. Directly above it, on a shelf, lay the holy book. This is what we found after our return from a several days' visit. Surely some great power is hid in the sacred book!"

Brushing away from my eyes many like pictures, I offered midday meal to the converted Indian sitting wordless and with downcast face. No sooner had he risen from the table with "Cousin, I have relished it," than the church bell rang.

Thither he hurried forth with his afternoon sermon. I watched him as he hastened along, his eyes bent fast upon the dusty road till he disappeared at the end of a quarter of a mile.

The little incident recalled to mind the copy of a missionary paper brought to my notice a few days ago, in which a "Christian" pugilist commented upon a recent article of mine, grossly perverting the spirit of my pen. Still I would not forget that the pale-faced missionary and the hoodooed aborigine are both God's creatures, though small indeed their own conceptions of Infinite Love. A wee child toddling in a wonder world, I prefer to their dogma my excursions into the natural gardens where the voice of the Great Spirit is heard in the twittering of birds, the rippling of mighty waters, and the sweet breathing of flowers. If this is Paganism, then at present, at least, I am a Pagan.

Source: Zitkala-Sa. "Why I Am a Pagan." *Atlantic Monthly* 90 (1902): 801–803.

Geronimo, Narrative
(1906)

Geronimo was a member of the Chiricahua Apache and a skilled resistance leader who for decades fought against the encroachments of Mexico and the United States into his people's territory in Arizona and New Mexico. By 1886, after relentless pursuit by General Nelson Miles and the army, Geronimo finally surrendered. He was held as a prisoner of war for many years by the U.S. military and was never allowed to return to his homeland. In 1904, late in his life, Geronimo agreed to share his life story with S. M. Barrett, the superintendent of education in Lawton, Oklahoma, close to where Geronimo was being held at Fort Sill. In the excerpt from his autobiography that follows, Geronimo discusses family relationships among the Chiricahua Apache and some of the interactions he had with white culture while he was held as a prisoner of war, including a trip to the 1904 St. Louis World's Fair.

My grandfather, Maco, had been our chief. I never saw him, but my father often told me of the great size, strength, and sagacity of this old warrior. Their principal wars had been with the Mexicans. They had some wars with other tribes of Indians also, but were seldom at peace for any great length of time with the Mexican towns.

Maco died when my father was but a young warrior, and Mangas-Colorado became chief of the Bedonkohe Apaches. When I was but a small boy my father died, after having been sick for some time. When he passed away, carefully the watchers closed his eyes, then they arrayed him in his best clothes, painted his face afresh, wrapped a rich blanket around him, saddled his favorite horse, bore his arms in front of him, and led his horse behind, repeating in wailing tones his deeds of valor as they carried his body to a cave in the mountain. Then they slew his horses, and we gave away all of his other property, as was customary in our tribe, after which his body was deposited in the cave, his arms beside him. His grave is hidden by piles of stone. Wrapped in splendor he lies in seclusion, and the winds in the pines sing a low requiem over the dead warrior.

After my father's death I assumed the care of my mother. She never married again, although according to the customs of our tribe she might have done so immediately after his death. Usually, however, the widow who has children remains single after her husband's death for two or three years; but the widow without children marries again immediately. After a warrior's death his widow returns to her people and may be given away or sold by her father or brothers. My mother chose to live with me, and she never desired to marry again. We lived near our old home and I supported her.

In 1846, being seventeen years of age, I was admitted to the council of the warriors. Then I was very happy, for I could go wherever I wanted and do whatever I liked. I had not been under the control of any individual, but the customs of our tribe prohibited me from sharing the glories of the war path until the council admitted me. When opportunity offered, after this, I could go on the war path with my tribe. This would be glorious. I hoped soon to serve my people in battle. I had long desired to fight with our warriors.

Perhaps the greatest joy to me was that now I could marry the fair Alope, daughter of No-po-so. She was a slender, delicate girl, but we had been lovers for a long time. So, as soon as the council granted me these privileges I went to see her father concerning our marriage. Perhaps our love was of no interest to him; perhaps he wanted to keep Alope with him, for she was a dutiful daughter; at any rate he asked many ponies for her. I made no reply, but in a few days appeared before his wigwam with the herd of ponies and took with me Alope. This was all the marriage ceremony necessary in our tribe.

Not far from my mother's tepee I had made for us a new home. The tepee was made of buffalo hides and in it were many bear robes, lion hides, and other trophies of the chase, as well as my spears, bows, and arrows. Alope had made many little decorations of beads and drawn work on buckskin, which she placed in our tepee. She also drew many pictures on the walls of our home. She was a good wife, but she was never strong. We followed the traditions of our fathers and were happy. Three children came to us—children that played, loitered, and worked as I had done.

When I was at first asked to attend the St. Louis World's Fair I did not wish to go. Later, when I was told that I would receive good attention and protection, and that the President of the United States said that it would be all right, I consented. I was kept by parties in charge of the Indian Department, who had obtained permission from the President. I stayed in this place for six months. I sold my photographs for twenty-five cents, and was allowed to keep ten cents of this for myself. I also wrote my name for ten, fifteen, or twenty-five cents, as the case might be, and kept all of that money. I often made as much as two dollars a day, and when I returned I had plenty of money—more than I had ever owned before.

Many people in St. Louis invited me to come to their homes, but my keeper always refused. Every Sunday the President of the Fair sent for me to go to a Wild West show. I took part in the roping contests before the audience. There were many other Indian tribes there, and strange people of whom I had never heard.

When people first came to the World's Fair they did nothing but parade up and down the streets. When they got tired of this they would visit the shows. There were many strange things in these shows. The Government sent guards with me when I went, and I was not allowed to go anywhere without them.

In one of the shows some strange men with red caps had some peculiar swords, and they seemed to want to fight. Finally their manager told them they might fight each other. They tried to hit each other over the head with these swords, and I expected both to be wounded or perhaps killed, but neither one was harmed. They would be hard people to kill in a hand-to-hand fight.

In another show there was a strange-looking negro. The manager tied his hands fast, then tied him to a chair. He was securely tied, for I looked myself, and I did not think it was possible for him to get away. Then the manager told him to get loose.

He twisted in his chair for a moment, and then stood up; the ropes were still tied but he was free. I do not understand how this was done. It was certainly a miraculous power, because no man could have released himself by his own efforts.

In another place a man was on a platform speaking to the audience; they set a basket by the side of the platform and covered it with red calico; then a woman came and got into the basket, and a man covered the basket again with the calico; then the man who was speaking to the audience took a long sword and ran it through the basket, each way, and then down through the cloth cover. I heard the sword cut through the woman's body, and the manager himself said she was dead; but when the cloth was lifted from the basket she stepped out, smiled, and walked off the stage. I would like to know how she was so quickly healed, and why the wounds did not kill her.

I have never considered bears very intelligent, except in their wild habits, but I had never before seen a white bear. In one of the shows a man had a white bear that was as intelligent as a man. He would do whatever he was told—carry a log on his shoulder, just as a man would; then, when he was told, would put it down again. He did many other things, and seemed to know exactly what his keeper said to him. I am sure that no grizzly bear could be trained to do these things.

One time the guards took me into a little house that had four windows. When we were seated the little house started to move along the ground. Then the guards called my attention to some curious things they had in their pockets. Finally they told me to look out, and when I did so I was scared, for our little house had gone high up in the air, and the people down in the Fair Grounds looked no larger than ants. The men laughed at me for being scared;

then they gave me a glass to look through (I often had such glasses which I took from dead officers after battles in Mexico and elsewhere), and I could see rivers, lakes and mountains. But I had never been so high in the air, and I tried to look into the sky. There were no stars, and I could not look at the sun through this glass because the brightness hurt my eyes. Finally I put the glass down, and as they were all laughing at me, I, too, began to laugh. Then they said, "Get out!" and when I looked we were on the street again. After we were safe on the land I watched many of these little houses going up and coming down, but I cannot understand how they travel. They are very curious little houses.

One day we went into another show, and as soon as we were in it, it changed into night. It was real night, for I could feel the damp air; soon it began to thunder, and the lightnings flashed; it was real lightning, too, for it struck just above our heads. I dodged and wanted to run away but I could not tell which way to go in order to get out. The guards motioned me to keep still and so I stayed. In front of us were some strange little people who came out on the platform; then I looked up again and the clouds were all gone, and I could see stars shining. The little people on the platform did not seem in earnest about anything they did; so I only laughed at them. All the people around where we sat seemed to be laughing at me.

We went into another place and the manager took us into a little room that was made like a cage; then everything around us seemed to be moving; soon the air looked blue, then there were black clouds moving with the wind. Pretty soon it was clear outside; then we saw a few thin white clouds; then the clouds grew thicker, and it rained and hailed with thunder and lightning. Then the thunder retreated and a rainbow appeared in the distance; then it became dark, the moon rose and thousands of stars came out. Soon the sun came up, and we got out of the little room. This was a good show, but it was so strange and unnatural that I was glad to be on the streets again.

We went into one place where they made glassware. I had always thought that these things were made by hand, but they are not. The man had a curious little instrument, and whenever he would blow through this into a little blaze the glass would take any shape he wanted it to. I am not sure, but I think that if I had this kind of an instrument I could make whatever I wished. There seems to be a charm about it. But I suppose it is very difficult to get these little instruments, or people would have them. The people in this show were so anxious to buy the things the man made that they kept him so busy he could not sit down all day long. I bought many curious things in there and brought them home with me.

At the end of one of the streets some people were getting into a clumsy canoe, upon a kind of shelf, and sliding down into the water. They seemed to enjoy it, but it looked too fierce for me. If one of these canoes had gone out of its path the people would have been sure to get hurt or killed.

There were some little brown people at the Fair that United States troops captured recently on some islands far away from here.

They did not wear much clothing, and I think that they should not have been allowed to come to the Fair. But they themselves did not seem to know any better. They had some little brass plates, and they tried to play music with these, but I did not think it was music it was only a rattle. However, they danced to this noise and seemed to think they were giving a fine show.

I do not know how true the report was, but I heard that the President sent them to the Fair so that they could learn some manners, and when they went home teach their people how to dress and how to behave.

I am glad I went to the Fair. I saw many interesting things and learned much of the white people. They are a very kind and peaceful people. During all the time I was at the Fair no one tried to harm me in any way. Had this been among the Mexicans I am sure I should have been compelled to defend myself often.

I wish all my people could have attended the Fair.

Source: Geronimo, Stephen Melvil Barrett. *Geronimo's Story of His Life.* New York: Duffield & Company, 1906, 35–39, 197–206.

Henry Roe Cloud, Education of the American Indian
(1914)

Henry Roe Cloud was born in Nebraska in 1884. A Winnebago, his vocation was teaching, and he earned both a bachelor's and a master's degree from Yale University. Furthermore, under the influence of missionaries, he was ordained a Presbyterian minister. The following document is his address to the Lake Mohonk Conference in 1914.

Education is for life,—life in the workaday world with all its toil, successes, discouragements and heartaches. Education unrelated to life is of no use. "Educare"—education is the leading-out process of the young until they know themselves what they are best fitted for in life. Education is for complete living; that is, the educational process must involve the heart, head, and hand. The unity of man is coming to the forefront in the thought of the day. We cannot pay exclusive attention to the education of one part and afford to let the other part or parts suffer. Education is for service; that is, the youth is led to see the responsibilities as well as the privileges of his education so that he lends a helping hand to those who are in need. Indian is no exception to these general principles.

The educational needs of the Indian can be seen in the light of his problem,—he has before him a twofold problem, the white man's problem and his own peculiar racial problem. The problem confronting the white child is the Indian's problem for, if the goal for the Indian is citizenship, it means sharing the responsibilities, as well as the opportunities, of this great Republic.

The task of educating the American young is a stupendous one. The future welfare of the American nation depends upon it. Children everywhere must be brought into an appreciation of the great fundamental principles of the Republic as well as the full realization of its dangers. It required a long, toilsome march of peoples beyond the sea to give us our present-day civilization. Trial by jury came by William the Conqueror. America's freedom was at the cost of centuries of struggle. America's democracy is the direct and indirect contribution of every civilized nation. The wide, open door of opportunity was paid for by untold sacrifice of life and labors. It involves the story of the sturdy and brave frontiersmen, the gradual extension of transportation facilities westward, the rise of cities on the plains. So great and rapid has been this progress that already the cry of the conservation of our natural resources is ringing in our ears.

To lead the white youth of the land into an appreciation of the history of American institutions, into their meaning for this generation and the generation to come, so that somewhere in the course of his education he feels possessed of some permanent interest which commands all his ambitions and devotion, is no small task.

Along with these great blessings there are the national dangers stalking through the land. I need but mention them.

The stupendous economic development has meant the amassing of great and unwieldy wealth into few hands. It has meant the creation of a wide gap between the rich and the poor. The industrial order has been revolutionized by the introduction of machinery. There has now grown up the problem of the relation of labor and capital. Our railroad strikes and mine wars are but symptoms of this gigantic problem. Immigration and the consequent congested districts in our cities has put the controlling political power in the hands of the "boss." There is the tenement problem—physical degeneracy and disease. It requires no prophet to foresee the increase of these problems and dangers owing to the war now raging across the sea. The desolation of those countries, the inevitable tax burdens, will mean an even greater influx of immigration into this country.

There is the problem of "fire water" that has burned out the souls of hundreds of thousands, to say nothing of the greater suffering of wives, mothers, and children. There is the big national problem of race prejudice. Is America truly to be the "melting pot" of the nations?

These are the problems confronting the white youth, and, I repeat, they are the Indian's problems, also. Besides this, the Indian has his own peculiar race problem to meet.

There is the problem of home education. Education in the home is almost universally lacking. The vast amount of education which the white child receives in the home—a great many of them cultured and Christian homes, where between the age of ten and fourteen the child reads book after book on travel, biography, and current events—goes to make up for the deficiencies of the public schools. The Indian youth goes back into homes that have dominant interests altogether different from what has been taught at school. I have seen many a young man and young woman bravely struggle to change home conditions in order to bring them into keeping with their training, and they have at last gone down. The father and the mother have never been accustomed, in the modern sense, to a competitive form of existence. The father has no trade or vocation. The value of a dollar, of time, of labor, is unknown in that home. The parents have not the insight into educational values to appreciate the boy's achievements and to inspire him further. What is to be done under such circumstances? In many cases he finds himself face to face with a shattered home. The marriage problem, the very core of his social problem, stares him in the face. Many a young man and woman, realizing these home conditions, have gone away to establish a home of their own. As soon as the thrifty Indian accumulates a little property his relatives and tribesmen, in keeping with the old custom of communal ownership of property, come and live at his expense. There was virtual communal ownership of property in the old days under the unwritten laws of hospitality, but the omission in these days, of that corresponding equal distribution of labor plays havoc with the young Indian home.

What is the Indian youth to do under such circumstances?

The Indian has his own labor problem. He has here a race inertia to overcome. The sort of labor he is called upon to do these days is devoid of exploit. It is a change from the sporadic effort to that of routine labor calling for the qualities of self-control, patience, steady application, and a long look ahead. Shall he seek labor outside the reservation? Shall he work his own allotment? What bearing has his annuity money and his lease money on his labor problem? Does it stifle effort on his part? Does it make him content to eke out a living from year to year without labor? If he works, how is he to meet the ubiquitous grafter with his insistence upon chattel mortgages? How is he to avoid the maelstrom of credit into which so many have fallen?

The health problems of the Indian race may well engage the entire attention and life-work of many young Indian men and women. What about the seventy to eighty thousand Indians suffering now from trachoma? What about thirty thousand tubercular Indians? Is this due to housing conditions?

There is the legal problem to which special attention was just called. Is the Indian a ward of the government or a citizen? What are his rights and duties? His legal problem involves his land problem? Ought he to pay taxes? Will he ever secure his rights to be respected in the local courts unless he pays taxes? Will he ever secure his rights and be respected in the local courts unless he pays taxes? Is not this question most fundamental?

Shall the Indian youth ignore the problem of religion? Of the many religions on the reservation, which one shall energize his life? Shall it be the sun dance, the medicine lodge, the mescal, or the Christian religion? Shall he take in all religions, as so many do? What do these different religions stand for?

There is finally the whole problem of self-support. If he is to pursue the lines of agriculture, he must study the physical environment and topography of his particular reservation, for these in a large measure control the fortunes of his people. If the reservation is mountainous, covered with timber, he must relate his study to it. If it is a fertile plain, it means certain other studies. It involves the study of soils, of dry farming, irrigation, of stock-farming, of stock and sheep raising. The Indian must conquer nature if he is to achieve his race adoption.

My friends, here are problems of unusual difficulty. In the face of these larger problems—city, State, and National, as well as the Indian's own peculiar race problem, and the two are inextricably interwoven,—what shall be the Indian's preparation to successfully meet them? What sort of education must he have? Miss Kate Barnard told us something of the problem as it exists in Oklahoma. Into this maelstrom of political chicanery, of intrigue and corrupting influences of great vested interests shall we send Indian youth with only an eighth grade education? In vast sections of that Oklahoma country ninety per cent of the farms of white men were under mortgage last year. It means that even they with their education and inheritance were failing. Well might one rise up like Jeremiah of old and cry out, "My people perish for lack of knowledge,"—knowledge of the truth as it exists in every department of life,—this can truly make us free.

The first effort, it seems to me, should be to give as many Indians as are able all the education that the problem he faces clearly indicates he should have. This means all the education the grammar schools, secondary schools, and colleges of the land can give him. This is not any too much for the final equipment for the leaders of the race. If we are to have leaders that will supply the disciplined mental power in our race development, they cannot be merely grammar school men. They must be trained to grapple with these economic, educational, political, religious and social problems. They must be men who will take up the righteous cause among their people, interpret civilization to their people, and restore race confidence, race virility. Only by such leaders can race segregation be overcome. Real segregation of the Indian consists in segregation of thought and inequality of education.

We would not be so foolish as to demand a college education for every Indian child in the land irrespective of mental powers and dominant vocational interests, but on the other hand we do not want to make the mistake of advocating a system of education adapted only to the average Indian child. If every person in the United States had only an eighth grade education with which to wrestle with the problems of life and the nation, this country would be in a bad way. We would accelerate the pace in the Government grammar schools of such Indian youth as to show a capacity for more rapid progress. For the Indian of exceptional ability, who wishes to lay his hand upon the more serious problems of our race, the industrial work however valuable in itself, necessarily retards him in the grammar school until his is man-grown. He cannot afford to wait until he is twenty-four or twenty-five to enter the high school. This system is resulting in an absolute block upon the entrance of our ablest young people into the schools and colleges of the land which stand open to them. There are hundreds of the youth of the Oriental [and] other native races in our colleges. As an Indian it is impossible for me to believe that the fact that there are almost no Indians under such training today is due to the failure of my race in mental ability. The difficulty lies in the system rather than in the race. According to the census of the last decade, there were three hundred thousand college men and women to ninety millions of people in the United States, or one to every three hundred. In the same proportion there should be one thousand college Indian men and women in the United States, taking as a total population three hundred thousand Indians. Allowing for racial handicaps, let us say there should be at least five hundred instead of one thousand Indian college men and women.

Actually there is not one in thirty thousand, and most of these in early life escaped the retarding process in the Government schools.

This is not in any way disparaging to the so-called industrial education in the Government Indian grammar schools, such as Carlisle, Haskell, Chilocco. Education—as education that seeks to lead the Indians into outdoor vocational pursuits, is most necessary. Our Government Indian Bureau feels the need for vocational training among the

Indians, and I am very glad that it does. Productive skill we must have if we are to live on in this competitive age. However, in this policy of industrial training for the Indian youth, the Government should not use the labor of the students to reduce the running expenses of the different schools, but only where the aim is educational, to develop the Indian's efficiency, and mastery of the trade. Recent Congressional charges of shifting students from one trade to another so that they master no trade have been made and the charges sustained. I worked two years in turning a washing machine in a Government school to reduce the running expenses of the school. It did not take me long to learn how to run a washing machine. The rest of the work is not educative. It begets a hatred for work, especially where there is no pay for such labor. The Indian will work under such conditions because he is under authority, but the moment he becomes free he is going to get as far as he can from it. I, personally, would hail the day with joy when the Government Indian schools can redeem the moral discipline of even drudgery work connected with the schools by some system of compensation of value received for work expended. Others before me, such as Dr. Walter C. Roe, have dreamed of founding a Christian, educational institution for developing a strong native, Christian leadership for the Indians of the United States. I, too, have dreamed. For, after all, it is Christian education that is going to solve these great problems confronting the Indian. Such an institution is to recognize the principle that man shall not live by bread alone and yet at the same time to show the dignity and divineness of toil by the sweat of one's brow. The school is to teach self-support. The Indian himself must rise up and do for himself by the help of Almighty God. It is to be Christian education, because every problem that confronts us in the last analysis is a moral problem. In the words of Sumner, "Capital is another word for self-denial." The gift of millions for Indian education is the people's self-denial. In whatever activity we may enter for life work, we must pay the price of self-control if we are to achieve any degree of success. The moral qualities, therefore, are so necessary for our successful advance. Where shall we look for our final authority in these moral questions? We must look to nothing this side of the Great Spirit for our final authority. Having then brought into the forefront of the Indian race men of sound morality, intellectual grasp, and productive skill, we shall have leaders who are like the great oak tree on the hill. Storm after storm may break upon them, but they will stand because they are deeply rooted and the texture of their soul is strong.

Source: Cloud, Henry Roe. "Education of the American Indian." *Quarterly Journal* 2 (1914): 203–209.

Chauncey Yellow Robe, "The Menace of the Wild West Show" (1914)

Chauncey Yellow Robe, a Lakota, was a graduate of Carlisle Indian School in Pennsylvania. In the document that follows, he discusses what he believes to be the root of the Indian problem, the Wild West shows of men like Buffalo Bill. According to Yellow Robe, Wild West shows played a major part in the commercialization of the Indian and, along with participation in the film and art industries, Native Americans who left the reservation for work in these occupations were exposed to a host of negative vices, especially alcohol. Additionally, the stereotype of the savage Indian was spread with the help of Wild West shows and then consumed by the public, ultimately leading to the reification of a host of negative images in American popular culture for decades to come.

Some time ago, Judge Sells, the United States Commissioner on Indian Affairs, said: "Let us save the American Indian from the curse of whiskey." I believe these words hold the key to the Indian problem of today, but how can we save the American Indian if the Indian Bureau is permitting special privileges in favor of the wild-west Indian shows, moving-picture concerns, and fair associations for commercializing the Indian? This is the greatest hindrance, injustice, and detriment to the present progress of the American Indian toward civilization. The Indians should be protected from the curse of the wild-west show schemes, wherein the Indians have been led to the white man's poison cup and have become drunkards.

In some of the celebrations, conventions, and county fairs in Rapid City and other reservation border towns, in order to make the attraction a success, they think they cannot do without wild-west Indian shows, [and] consequently certain citizens have the Indian show craze. In fact, the South Dakota State Fairs always have largely consisted of these shows. We can see how this state of affairs that the white man is persistently perpetuating the tribal habits and customs. We see that the showman is manufacturing the Indian plays intended to amuse and instruct young children, and is teaching them that the Indian is only a savage being. We hear now and then of a boy or girl who is hurt or killed by playing savage. These are the direct consequences of the wild-west Indian shows and moving pictures that depict lawlessness and hatred.

Before the closing of the nineteenth century an awful crime was committed in this great Christian nation. It was only a few days after the civilized nations of the world had celebrated the message of the heavenly host [at Christmas] saying, "Fear not for behold I bring you good tidings of great joy which shall be to all people" and "Glory to God in the highest and on earth, peace, good will toward men." A band of Sioux Indians, including women and children, unarmed, were massacred. The wounded were left on the field to die without care at Wounded Knee by the United States troops just because they had founded a new religion called "The Indian Messiah." This was a cowardly and criminal act without diplomacy. Twenty-three years afterward, on the same field of Wounded Knee, the tragedy was reproduced for "historical preservation" in moving-picture films and called *The Last Great Battle of the Sioux*. The whole production of the field was misrepresented and yet approved by the Government. This is a disgrace and injustice to the Indian race.

I am not speaking here from selfish and sensitive motives, but from my own point of view, for cleaner civilization, education, and citizenship for my race. We have arrived at the point where the great demands must be met. "To the American Indian let there be given equal opportunities, equal responsibilities, equal education."

Source: Yellow Robe, Chauncey. "The Menace of the Wild West Show." *The Quarterly Journal of the Society of American Indians* (July–September 1914): 224–225.

Alice Becenti, A Navajo Writes Home from Boarding School
(1914–1916)

Alice Becenti was a student at the Sherman Institute in California. While she was there, she wrote several letters home. They are not addressed to her parents, however; rather, they are addressed to Samuel Stacher, head of the Crowpoint Indian Agency in New Mexico. She may have sent them to him because that was where all mail was sent, or, more likely, her parents were illiterate, and she depended on Stacher to deliver and read the letters to her parents. The letters provide a glimpse into the struggles many American Indian children experienced when they were sent away to boarding schools.

August 24, 1914

Dear Friend Mr. Stacher,

This morning I am going a few lines to let you know how I am getting along here at this place. Well, I am trying to make myself happy all time. But I can not do. I always have to be sick. I have been very sick again. I am here at the hospital now, in bed. I haven't been here for a long time. Last time I had to stay here for a month. Most of the time I stay at the hospital I can get along fine because I am sick. I can eat nothing.

I eat but it comes right out. Can[']t stay. I am very weak so no use to eat again after this: last year I was sick all summer too. This year again. That's why they wont let me go out working because I was weak to work that's what they told me once. Last year they were going to send me home but they didn't. Because I did want to go home that time. I don't know where Grace Padilla is. She was here with me last week. She came to see me. Well how are all my folks getting along now. Well, you told me why don't I ask Mr. Consor to go out working. Because they told me that I was too weak to go out working and it is too hot for me too; that's what they told me once. Ever since I been here I never did feel well. I always sick.

Well, Mr. Stacher I want to go home. I am sure Mr. Consor will let me go because he let the boys and girls go home when they sick like me. I don't want to stay here. I want to go home and get well. Will you think abut that Mr Stacher and tell my folks abut it too. I am sure they have money enough to take me home.

Say where is E.B. and D.B. are they working over there yet or not. Also I got faint last night. I didn't know what I was doing all night. Before that I got like that too that time I was down the Farm.

This will be all so I must close now. Hope to hear from you soon if you please.

To Mr. Stacher
From Alice Becenti
Give my best love to Mrs. Stacher
Also to Earl B.

November 3, 1915

Dear Friends:
Mr. Stacher and the family
Mr. Stacher, I received you letter alright but the package you spoke of hasn't reach me yet.

I have no idea what had delay on the way I am also still looking every day.

Well Mr. Stacher if you only knew how tickle I was when I got you letter saying enclosing a letter with Navajo bread.

I was so tickle to death, I couldn't help but read my letter up to my room mate. Now I am quite disappointed.

The girls always ask me if my bread has come yet.

Indeed I get often cheap.

Oh well, I supposed it was sended or it's lost.

Tell my mother or brother, I'm much rather have them send my Navajo blankets that I wonder about two months ago, than to have them take trouble sending bread.

Indeed that was very nice of you to think of taking lot of trouble sending what I never expected.

But I haven't got yet.

But I wish you cold please kindly see about my blankets, see if they are planning to sended.

Excuse me for bothering you Mr. Stacher, as you know very well, I have no one to depended on.

I am always glad to hear everything in its perfectly condition at home, its surely dose make me feel or look more brighter with my school work.

About a hundred or more of the children have had the measles, but most are well and back to their school.

But it has not reach us Grace and I. I hope it would.

Last Saturday night we had a nice masqueraded party, everyone seem to enjoyed very much, some of the girls and boys dressed up in odd fashion. Will close with many regards to you all.

Your friend,
Alice Becenti
Write soon.
But please send telegraph that's the quickest way I can hear about my people.

May 1916

Dear Mr. Stacher,

This afternoon I am going to write a few lines to you to let you know how I am getting along at Sherman. I am getting along very fine indeed with all the school children but now there are only few children here. Because some of them are gone out working. Tomorrow some girls are going home. I would like to know how my mother getting along. I am very sorry to hear that my mother sick and beside that my brother died. Which my brother is that? But I hope my mother will be better soon. Supt. is not here and I not tell him if I could go and see my mother. Well Mr. Stacher I wish you could tell her to not to worry about. We having to died someday. I guess that's what made her sick. Dear mother don't worry.

This will be all.

Be sure and tell me weather its so or not. I am just sick about it.

From Alice Becenti

Why don't they tell me along ago when was sick

P.S. Please Mr. Stacher; if you will send for me as soon as possible for its quite a long while for me to sit around with tease and worrying. Especially to think that my mother is sick and worrying. I am sure it wouldn't do me any good for me to sit around crying day after day, to waite for 20 days to be up. I don't see while I can't go as some children are already going home from east. Mr. Conser is not here just now, but please Mr. Stacher, I am asking this with my tears. For you to send a word or telegraph to Mr. Conser as soon as you get this letter.

Source: Alice Becenti to Superintendent Samuel Stacher. "A Navajo Writes Home from Boarding School." Eastern Navajo Agency. Crown Point, New Mexico. General Correspondence, 1910–1916; General Correspondence, 1912–1916 "B"; Box 5; Record Group 75, Records of the Bureau of Indian Affairs, The National Archives at Riverside.

Helen Sekaquaptewa, "Phoenix Indian School"
(1915)

The U.S. government saw education as a key part of assimilating Indians to white values and lifestyles. A number of boarding schools appeared all over the country, designed specifically to train Native American children to become white. Helen Sekaquaptewa, a young girl from a traditional Hopi family, was one child who ended up at a government-run boarding school, first in Keams Canyon, then later in Phoenix. The following document describes Helen's experiences at the Phoenix Indian School and offers an Indian perspective on the process of assimilation.

Time passed by, and I grew older, and it was better for me at school. I was weaned away from home. The girls from the other mesas gradually became more friendly. The twenty or so of us who stayed at school all summer became close friends. The teachers and everyone treated us pretty well.

At the end of the school year in 1915 I had finished sixth grade, which was as far as one could go at Keams Canyon. I wanted to go somewhere else and continue my schooling. I could not go without the consent of my parents, which they would not give. I was joined by a few others of like mind, and we begged the Superintendent, Mr. Leo Crane, to let us go to Phoenix Indian School. We even suggested, "You could say we are a little older than we are." He finally agreed to let us go on our own responsibility.

That summer, another girl and I were trusted to go home on our promise not to do what our parents told us, and to come back in two weeks. We said to each other, "We will humor our parents. We will do what they want; dress in Hopi traditional clothes; let them fix our hair in whorls while we are here, anything to please them." I had lived at the school so long that it seemed like my home. I stayed with my parents in Hotevilla only ten days and went back to the dormitory at Keams Canyon.

[Dr. Breid] came to Keams Canyon to make the arrangements and supervise the trip of the Indian boys and girls to Phoenix in the fall of 1915. It took two days by team and wagon to Holbrook, with boys and girls in separate wagons. From there we went by train—about seventy of us, all in one car—to Flagstaff, Ash Fork, Prescott, and finally Phoenix. A matron traveled with us.

I was one of the four girls whom Dr. Breid invited to ride with him in his buggy out to the Indian School. As they came to the administration building the new students were met by the school band, a military type of welcome. The students were formed into lines and marched to their assigned dormitories to the music of the band.

It was a military school. We marched to the dining room three times a day to band music. We arose to a bell and had a given time for making our beds, cleaning our rooms, and being ready for breakfast. Everything was done on schedule, and there was no room for idleness.

Our clothing was furnished by the government. We had long black stockings and heavy black shoes, but the dresses were of good material made in the sewing room to fit individually. Some of the bigger girls worked about the town doing housework on Saturday and bought their own dress shoes when they could. We went to school half a day and worked half a day.

The home economics department had a big production room where all girls' clothing and shirts for the boys were made, and we did a lot of sewing there. Besides this sewing the girls were assigned to laundry and home-cleaning details. The boys were put on janitor work, caring for the premises and learning shop skills. The school had a dairy. The boys took care of the cows and did the milking, and the girls learned to care for the milk.

Sunday morning all pupils had to be in their uniforms and stand for inspection at 7:30. All lined up outside their buildings and stood at attention while being inspected by the principal, head matron, head disciplinarian, and the doctor. The boys gave a military salute as the officers passed, and the girls held out their hands to be inspected. The officers noted every detail and would say, "Your shoe string is not tied right," "Your hands are dirty," or "Your shoes do not shine." Following inspection we marched to the auditorium for church services.

At first I was homesick for Keams Canyon, but it soon wore off. During the very first week Superintendent Brown came looking for two girls to work in his home. I was one chosen, I was paid five dollars a month. The Brown family consisted of a grown son, away at school, and daughters aged thirteen, eleven, and seven. I was sixteen. I was required to sleep at the dormitory. Sometimes after I had eaten in the dining room Mrs. Brown would want me to come back and help in the kitchen in the evening and I would get to eat twice. Sometimes she would save a piece of pie or cake for me.

Clara, the other girl in the Brown home, had always been given the shirts to iron while I did the plain pieces, but then Clara was sick for a week Mrs. Brown found out that I could do the fancy ironing too. She let me run the whole house when she saw that I could do it. It was the policy to have the girls change assignments every few months, but Mrs. Brown always wanted me back. They treated me like one of the family and took me with them when they went for a ride in their Ford car. I enjoyed riding out to orchards for fruit and to farms for vegetables. They even took me a few times on weekend camping trips. I worked for them during the summer the first year. After two years with the Browns, the matron decided it would be good for me to have other experience so she put me in the sewing room where the older girls made the school clothing.

School life was obnoxious to many students, and discipline was military style. Corporal punishment was given as a matter of course; whipping with a harness strap was administered in an upstairs room to the most unruly. One held the culprit while another administered the strap. Girls were not often whipped, but one big Yuma girl grabbed the strap and chased both the matron and the disciplinarian from the room. Sometimes boys and even girls would run away, even though they were locked in at night, they managed to get out somehow. Often a boy and a girl would have it planned and go at the same time. They would usually start to go home. Older boys with records of

dependability would be sent to find and bring them back. Emory was often sent. He would go to town on the streetcar and look around the streets, but sometimes they would get as far away as Glendale or Peoria. Then Emory would have to go by train, and when he found them bring them back and deliver the boys to their disciplinarian and the girls to the matron. Punishment for the girls might be cleaning the yards, even cutting grass with scissors, while wearing a card that said, "I ran away." Boys were put in the school jail, a small adobe house with high windows. Repeaters had their heads shaved and had to wear a dress to school. Some of them forgot how to wear pants.

Source: From *Me and Mine: The Life Story of Helen Sekaquaptewa as Told to Louise Udall by Louise Udall.* Tucson: University of Arizona Press, 1969. © 1969 The Arizona Board of Regents. Reprinted by permission of the University of Arizona Press.

Arthur C. Parker, "Social Elements of the Indian Problem"
(1916)

Arthur C. Parker was a Seneca who served as editor of the Society of American Indians' Quarterly Journal. *He spoke on many topics, most notably education. The following article appeared in the* American Journal of Sociology. *It is a fascinating, cogent, and thorough critique of the issues facing American Indians in the early 20th century. Furthermore, not only does he cite other experts to provide evidence for his conclusions but Parker also suggests excellent solutions to the problems he lists.*

The problem of what to do with the native American Indians has been the cause of much effort and discussion for three centuries. The white race in its endeavor to take possession of the continent has experimented with three great plans of

dealing with the aborigines and none of them has so far entirely succeeded. In the beginning there was an endeavor to occupy the land forcibly and by various means to exterminate its barbaric owners. These things could not be at once successfully done. With the establishment of the United States as a government another plan came into vogue. The idea of extermination persisted for a long time, to be sure, but there was enough sentiment to bring about a new course—that of segregation. The Indian up to 1850, let us say, refused to be exterminated, and his fight for life and territory has no parallel in history. Segregation, however, did more to exterminate the Indian than did bullets. Rigorously guarded reservations became a place of debasement. The "noble red men" could not exist upon them. As wards, ruled over, guarded, fed, clothed, thought for, and done for, they lost much of their ancient spirit. With the Dawes Act of 1887 another experiment was launched. Its purpose was absorption. The Indian under certain restrictions was to be made a citizen. But how could men who believed themselves robbed and without a court of justice, who were confused, blind, and broken in spirit, become citizens? What could citizenship mean to them? What manner of man is the reservation Indian today? One needs only to look to see that there has been a calamity. But who is responsible? One may ask. Every man who by neglect and indifference has permitted the soul of a race of men to sink beneath the evils of civilization into misery, ignorance, disease, and despondency. Today because of these things there is an Indian problem. But what is this problem?

There is little real understanding of the blight that has fallen upon the red race within the United States. Notwithstanding the immense effort that is put forth by missionary bodies and by the federal government to remedy the unhappy situation of the Indian, neither of these forces acts as if it surely knew the elements with which it was dealing. But as between the church and the state, if a comparison were drawn, the church understands better and responds more intelligently to the vital necessities of the race. Even so, there is no clearly defined philosophy that reveals causes and points out remedies.

The Indian Bureau of the Department of the Interior is charged by Congress with the administration of Indian affairs. Its avowed purpose is the protection of Indian property and the transformation of race, to the end that the Indians may become good citizens. Yet the Bureau is not achieving as great a measure of success as its commissioner and other earnest officials might wish.

The church has a similar but broader object, expressed in its own words, "to save the souls of the Indians"—in other words, to build manhood and character. But even the church has its trials, and its missionaries pray for greater and more permanent influence over the morals of the red men whom they have set out to redeem.

Neither the church nor the state with all its powers of organization, however, proceeds as if it had discovered why its task is so greatly hampered or why it must apply so much unproductive effort. It appears that the Indians are perverse, are naturally inclined to degradation, are inferior and heedless as a race, or that they are an accursed people as some of the early colonists thought. Yet both church and state labor on, for they feel that Providence has intrusted a benighted people to their keeping. Each factor is an instrument of American civilization, the one of civic power, the other of moral force. Each sees the Indian problem in the light of its own standards. Each translates its conception of the needs of the Indian in terms of its own liking. Each understands through its own system of thinking and bases its acts upon a confident line the plan of its action and to explain why it thinks thus and so, and to submit such a plan to a psychologist, a sociologist, or an ethnologist for criticism or suggestion. Each has more or less definitely expressed the idea of "the white man's burden," of the obligation of American civilization and Anglo-Saxon blood to lead mankind to higher goals. Each body resents any aspersion upon the integrity or the inherent moral qualities of the race it represents, for is not the Anglo-American the most charitable, the most conscientious of all races?

Nevertheless is there not a fundamental blindness, caused shall we say by a moral blind spot? Is there not a lack of feeling due, shall we say, to local anesthesia? Is there not a certain cerebral center in the cortices of the social brain that seems insensible to certain impressions? The people of the country who do have the welfare of an unhappy race at heart must both recognize and come to understand the true nature of the injury the red man has sustained through his contact with civilization.

For the sake of definiteness and to stimulate constructive thought we wish to lay down seven charges, out of perhaps many more, that the Indian makes at the bar of American justice. Whether the white man believes them just or not, true or not, he cannot discharge his obligation to the red man until he considers them and understands that the Indian makes them because he at least feels that they are just. There will be white Americans who will see the charges as rightfully made and there will no doubt be some Indians who, trained in the philosophies of the narrow school of the conqueror, will not admit them. But notwithstanding such objections we desire to submit the charges. The Indian's present view must be known if his sight is to be directed to broader visions.

THE SEVEN STOLEN RIGHTS

The people of the United States through their governmental agencies, and through the aggression of their citizens have: (1) robbed the American Indian of freedom of action; (2) robbed the American Indian of economic independence; (3) robbed the American Indian of social organization; (4) robbed a race of men—the American Indian—of intellectual life; (5) robbed the American Indian of moral standards and of racial ideals; (6) robbed the American Indian of a good name among the peoples of the earth; (7) robbed the American Indian of a definite civic status.

Each of the factors we have named is essential to the life of a man or a nation. Picture a citizen of this republic without freedom, intellectual or social life, with limited ability to provide his own food and clothing, having no sure belief in an Almighty Being, no hero to admire, and no ideals to foster, with no legal status, and without a reputable name among men. Picture a nation or a people so unhappy. Yet civilization has conspired to produce in varying degrees all these conditions for the American Indians.

So much for the seven great robberies of the race. We have not even cared to mention the minor loss of territory and of resources—these are small things indeed, compared with the greater losses that we have named.

But though the robbery has been committed, the government and great citizens will exclaim, "We have given much to atone for your loss, brother red men!"

Let us examine then the nature of these gifts. The federal government and the kind hearts of friends have (1) given reserved tracts of land where the Indians may live unmolested (but are they unmolested?); (2) given agents and superintendents as guardians, and constituted a division of the Department of the Interior as a special bureau for the protection of the red race (but is the Indian protected?); (3) given schools with splendid mechanical equipment (but is the Indian educated in any adequate degree?); (4) given the ignorant and poor clerks who will think and act for them, and handle their money (does this develop manhood, ability, and good citizenship?); (5) given food, clothing, and peace (has the ration system been honest and adequate?); (6) given a new civilization (and with it a host of alluring evils); (7) given a great religion (but in the light of hypocrisy and a commercial conscience how could the Indian absorb it or be absorbed by it?).

So great and good gifts must have a price, the conqueror thought, for men cannot have these boons without suffering some disability. Measures are necessary to protect the givers and even government itself from the results of its own charity and leniency to a people but lately regarded as enemies. The government therefore as a price has denied the Indians the real benefits of civilization and placed them in a position where they have become the prey of every moral, social, and commercial evil. The Indians have been made the material for exploitation.

The Indians were not at once denied the fundamental rights of human beings, living in an organized civilized community. It was only as the seven great robberies became more or less complete and the reservation system grew that the great denials took effect. The robberies and the denials are of a subtle psychological character and many there are who will ingeniously argue that the Indians still have all the things we have mentioned, or may have them if they will to, and that the seven gifts are but the gratuities of a charitable government.

But the men who so argue are devoid of finer spiritual perceptions or, perchance, they are unable to see from another man's viewpoint when they have one of their own. There are not wanting men and women who are unable to realize that another man can be hungry when their own stomachs are full. There are men having considerable mental endowments and a knowledge of the world who say, "If I were in his place, I would do thus and so. I would seize opportunity and soon all would be well." Men of this character are still mentally blind and spiritually dull and are the first to deny that any great wrong has been done after all. They are insensible to the fact that the red man has felt his debasement and that his soul and his children's souls are bitter with a grief they cannot express and which they cannot cast out.

The result of such denials of basic human rights to proud men and women is definite and deep. Whether he can express his thoughts in words or not, whether the turmoil in his heart finds voice or not, every American Indian who has suffered the oppression that is worse than death feels that civilization has (1) made him a man without a country; (2) usurped his responsibility; (3) demeaned his manhood; (4) destroyed his ideals; (5) broken faith with him; (6) humiliated his spirit; (7) refused to listen to his petitions.

The old reservation Indian feels all these things and they burn his very soul, leaving him a wretched, dispirited man. Only those who have escaped from the bondage of their race and have, as rare exceptions, entered into the freedom, the education, and the religion of the conquering race, have been able to keep up hope for the ultimate salvation of their people, and these often feel their bitterness the more.

If these statements seem to tinge of satire and of bitter invective to the civilized man, they are nevertheless very real things to the Indian who knows wherein he is wounded. To him this analysis will seem mild indeed, for it says nothing of a thousand deeds that made the four centuries of contact years of cruel misunderstanding. Yet to him these earlier years were better years than now, for he was then a free man who could boast a nation, who could speak his thought, and who bowed to no being save

God, his superior and guardian. Nor will we here mention the awful wars against women and children, the treacherous onslaughts on sleeping Indian villages, the murders of the old and helpless, the broken promises, the stolen lands, the robbed orphans and widows—for all of which men professing civilization and religion are responsible—for this is aside from our argument. We mention what is more awful than the robbery of lands, more hideous than the scalping and burning of Indian women and babies, more harrowing than tortures at the stake—we mean the crushing of a noble people's spirit and the usurpation of its right to be responsible and self-supporting.

Let it be affirmed as a deep conviction that until the American Indian is given back the right of assuming responsibility for his own acts and until his spirit is roused to action that awakened ideals will give him, all effort, all governmental protection, all gifts are of small value to him.

The Indian must be given back the things of which he has been robbed, with the natural accumulation of interest that the world's progress has earned. American civilization and Christianity must return the seven stolen rights without which no race or community of men can live. The people of the United States through the Congress, through the Indian Bureau, and through the activities of its conscientious citizenship must return to the Indian:

1. An intellectual life: In his native state the Indian had things to think about, things and forces vital to his existence. Unless he thought, he could not live. These things in their several subjects were a part of his organized mental and external activities. Using the thoughts that came, Indians could plan, organize, invent, and promote. Their thoughts clustered about concepts with which they were familiar. All men must have a thought nucleus. Rationally associated concepts become the basis of intellectual activity. When thought springs from activity and leaps to action, interest and desire are created, and the man finds thoughts things that keep him alert. He knows that his friends and associates are thinking along similar lines

because they are familiar with similar things. Human beings have a primary right to an intellectual life, but civilization has swept down upon groups of Indians and, by destroying their relationship to nature, blighted or banished their intellectual life, and left a group of people mentally confused. From thinking out of themselves they began to contemplate their own inward misery and to act under the depressing impulses that sprang from it. Yet nothing that could be easily or effectively understood was given to replace this mental life, primitive though it was. The Indians must have a thought-world given back. Their intellectual world must have direct relation to their world of responsible acts and spontaneous experiences.

2. The social organization: The Indians were always fond of mingling together. They had many councils and conferences. They had associations, societies, fraternities, and pastimes. These things grew out of their social needs, and each organization, game dance, feast, or custom filled some social need. They understood what they wanted and strove to meet the want. Civilization swept down upon them and with an iron hand broke up dances, forbade councils and ceremonies, and refused to sanction customs, because they were "barbarous." Yet nothing was given that ever effectually replaced these customs, speaking broadly and considering the social setting of the individual. Civilization will not have done its part until every Indian again finds a definite setting and an active part in the organized activities of communities of men. Every man must have the right to be an exponent of a certain ideal or group of ideals. In these he finds himself and takes his keenest pleasure.

3. Economic independence: In his native state the Indian needed no government warehouses wherein to contain his food and clothing, he needed no mills in New York to make his blankets, no plantations in Brazil to furnish his breakfast drink, no laboratory in Detroit to decant his medical extracts. Each Indian tribe and to a large extent each individual was a master of his own resources. The Indians could produce, cultivate, or make their life necessities.

They could make what they used, hunt or grow the food they ate. Civilization gave the Indians garments, and utensils they could not make. To get them they had to trade skins or lands. When the hunting-grounds were diminished and the Indians driven upon small barren tracts they became dependent for food, dishes, tools, and clothing upon an external source. They were issued rations. Deep indeed was their humiliation. From a self-supporting people they had become abject paupers. Thousands died from eating decayed food, thousands froze because the clothing issued was stolen before it reached them, thousands without doubt died from broken hearts. Then disease swept over them and reaped a full harvest, for the fields were ripe for the grim gleaner. Today the reservation Indian has neither the freedom, the capacity, nor oftentimes the desire to create or control his own economic life.

4. The right of freedom: The first and greatest love of the American Indian was his freedom. Freedom had been his heritage from time immemorial. The red man by nature cannot endure enforced servitude or imprisonment. By nature he is independent, proud, and sensitive. Freedom to the red man is no less sweet, no less the condition of life itself, than to other men. With Dryden the red man may exclaim, "The love of liberty with life is given, and life itself the inferior gift of heaven!" The fathers of the American Republic had suffered the hand of oppression. They could not endure the torment of being governed by a hand that wrote its laws across the sea. The will of the mother-country was not the will of her children and there was a revolt. Patrick Henry expressed the feeling in the hearts of his compatriots when he shouted: "Give me liberty or give me death." Benjamin Franklin wrote: "Where liberty dwells, there is my country," and Thomas Jefferson in his Summary View of the Rights of British America laid down the principle, "The God who gave us life gave us liberty at the same time." In how many instances do all these thoughts paraphrase the expression and the actions of the freedom-loving red men, who are now governed, not by their own kindred, but by a hand

that reaches out far across the country. The voice of great men rang out many times in the council halls of the nations of red men. The words of King Philip, Garangula, Dekanissora, Red Jacket, Tecumseh, Pontiac, Black Hawk, Osceola, Red Cloud, and others, sound even yet, in eulogy of native freedom. The time was when red men were not afraid to speak, for back of them was power. How masterful was the speech of Garangula in reply to the governor of Canada, who came to intimidate the Five Nations and force them to trade with France alone, when he answered: "Hear, Yonondio, I do not sleep. I have my eyes open and the sun enlightens me. . . . We are born free, we neither depend on Yonondio nor Corlear; we may go when we please and carry with us whom we please, buy and sell what we please. If your allies be your slaves, use them as such. . . ." Imagine a reservation chief talking that way today to so small an official as a politically appointed agent set over his tribe! The chief would be sent to the agency jail. This very year two Indians were put in jail for circulating copies of a congressional investigation of their reservation—so despotic still some Indian agents conceive their power to be.

5. The God of nations: The American Indian must have restored to him moral standards that he can trust. A weak and hypocritical Christianity will make the red man of today what his ancestors never were—an atheist. It has been difficult for some to realize what the disruption of an ancient faith can mean to the moral nature of a man. The old way is abandoned; its precepts and superstitions are cast to the scrap heap. Yet no wrath of the spirits comes as punishment. The new way is more or less not understood. Perhaps the convert may find that the magic and the taboos of the new religion have far less potency than he imagined, for no horrible calamity befalls him when he violates the laws of his newfound religion. The convert may then become morally worse than before. All restraint has been eliminated and every sea seems safe to sail, for there are no monsters there, as superstition said. His moral anchor is torn from its moorings and he is free and adrift. Thousands

of Indians who have not understood Christianity, who have been unable to distinguish between the ethics of Christ and the immorality of some individual who was presumably a Christian, have become moral wrecks, just as thousands of others who have seen the light have gone their way rejoicing, singing, "God's in his heaven, All's right with the world!" The red man as he is today, more than even he himself realizes, needs to know God. The basis of all his ancient faith was God. To him God was the beginning and the end of all human experience. Though he could not comprehend the Deity, he could revere him as the Great Mystery, whose all-seeing eye looked upon his every act. Civilization through its churches and mission agencies must restore the Indian to a knowledge of his Maker. Civilization through its schools and social institutions must give back to the red man great ideals over which he may map his life and by which he may rebuild his character.

6. A good name among nations: No race of men has been more unjustly misrepresented by popular historians than the American Indian. Branded as an ignorant savage, treacherous, cruel, and immoral in his inmost nature, the Indian has received little justice from the ordinary historian whose writings influence the minds of school children. None of these popular writers tell of the white man's savagery, once he held the power over the red man's soul and body. The churchman would bid us be silent when we tell of the wars of Pilgrim Fathers on Indians. Some would not have us know that when the Pequot men, women, and children had been murdered, the Puritan preacher rose in his pulpit to thank God that the militia had "sent six hundred heathen souls to hell!" It is not considered good form to mention that Christian Indians were hunted and murdered like dogs in Pennsylvania and Ohio, and even shot in church as they knelt to pray for God's blessing on their persecutors. We are not allowed to know that Indians were hunted as wolves and that the states of Virginia, Ohio, Pennsylvania, North Carolina, New Jersey, and even New York offered bounties for Indian

scalps. The Pennsylvania schedule was as follows: "For every male above ten years captured, $150; for every male above ten years scalped, being killed, $134; for every female or male under ten years captured, $130; for every female above ten years scalped, being killed $50." Historians tell the white youth that Indians scalped their enemies and killed defenseless women, yet no mention is made that white men plundered, murdered, raped, and tortured Indians. Nor are all these atrocities of an ancient day—Wounded Knee is not yet forgotten, and scores of local raids and unprovoked attacks are remembered. President Sherman Coolidge as a boy was saved as if by Providence from a machine-gun attack on a peaceful Arapahoe village.

It may safely be said that most Indian raids or wars were provoked by a long series of contributing causes which the patient Indians could no longer ignore. Proud people may not be forever goaded by abuse and broken promises.

A great nation like the United States needs not to vilify the history of its aborigines. They were men and brave men. Their cruelty and treachery were no more than those of the white men they fought, and each deed of violence they committed—as "ignorant savages"—can be matched by more revolting deeds committed by "educated, civilized men." . . .

The Indians have a right to know that their name as a people is not hidden forever from its place among the nations of the earth. They have a right to ask that the false statements and the prejudice that obstructs historic justice be cast aside. They have a right to ask that their children know the history of their fathers and to know that the sins and savagery of their race were no worse than those of other races called great for bravery and conquest. Yet the Indian youth in government schools are denied a true knowledge of their ancestors, as may be judged from merely reading the essays of Indian students on the past history of their people. The reservation Indian of today is not the noble red man of yesterday, though all elements of that nobility have not departed. The world is entitled to know why the change has come; the United States must know the facts we have pointed out and respond to the obligation that knowledge entails. The Indian must again be given a name that may be honored, else what sort of men and women will these future citizens be, who are to look to their ancestral blood as that of an accursed and inferior race?

7. The right of an assured status: With the whole of his social, economic, and political life and organization taken from him, with his relations to things, persons, and groups completely broken, who today, we may well inquire, is the Indian? What is he in the eyes of the law? The legal status of the Indian has never been defined. He is not an alien, he is not a foreigner, he is not a citizen. There is urgent need for a new code of law defining the status of Indians and regulating Indian matters so that a definite program replaces chaos. A commission such as the Society of American Indians has petitioned for in its memorial to the President should be empowered to draft a code of law and submit it to Congress. If a new day of friendship and co-operation has come, a new law should govern the red man in his relations with the federal government. The present laws in many instances are barriers to progress and conspire to produce conditions of life that make the assimilation of the Indians well nigh impossible. As I have elsewhere stated:

Definite legal status in an organized community has an important psychological value. It is for want of this subtle psychological asset that the Indian suffers most grievously. It is the tap root of most of his material evils. Witness the change that has come over the red man of the plains in the last fifty years. The old initiative has been crushed out and in spirit the poor Indian is low indeed. . . .

There can be nothing but bewilderment and anarchy when a man knows not what his status in his country is. This is especially true when the individual has property interests and matters at hazard in the courts handled at the initiative of others. A group of people whose civic status is insecure becomes demoralized and the panic spirit spreads to the individual. This fact is understood by the thoughtful student of human progress. Hon. Franklin E. Lane, the present Secretary of the Interior, summarizes this view in his annual report for 1914. He makes no attempt to excuse his country for its errors or lack of policy nor does he say that in spite of this " . . . any Indian who desires can step through any day and stand clothed immediately with any legal right that is enjoyed by a citizen," as did an Indian school authority recently.

The Secretary understands the psychic equation and candidly states:

That the Indian is confused in mind as to his status and very much at sea as to our ultimate purpose toward him is not surprising. For a hundred years he has been spun around like a blindfolded child in a game of blindman's buff. Treated as an enemy at first, overcome, driven from his lands, negotiated with most formally as an independent nation, given by treaty a distinct boundary which was never to be changed "while water runs and grass grows," he later found himself pushed beyond that boundary line, negotiated with again, and then set down upon a reservation, half captive, half protégé. What could an Indian, simple thinking and direct of mind, make of all this? To us it might give rise to a deprecatory smile. To him it must have seemed the systematized malevolence of a cynical civilization. And if this perplexed individual sought solace in a bottle of whiskey or followed after some daring and visionary medicine man who promised a way out of this hopeless maze, can we wonder?

Manifestly the Indian has been confused in his thought because we have been confused in ours. It has been difficult for Uncle Sam to regard the Indian as enemy, national menace, prisoner of war, and babe in arms all at the same time. The United States may be open to the charge of having treated the Indian with injustice, of having broken promises, and sometimes neglected an unfortunate people, but we may plead by way of confession and avoidance that we did not mark ourselves a clear course, and so, "like bats that fly at noon," we have "spelled out our paths in syllables of pain."

Professor F. A. McKenzie points out a number of pertinent facts entirely in harmony with this argument when he states:

I maintain that the Indian has not been incorporated into our national life, and cannot be until we radically change a number of fundamental things. We must give him a defined status, early citizenship and control of his property, adequate education, efficient government and schools, broad and deep religious training, and genuine social recognition. We must give him full rights in our society and demand from him complete responsibility.

The Indians today, the great mass of them, are still a broken and beaten people, scattered, isolated, cowed and disheartened, confined and restricted, pauperized and tending to degeneracy. They are a people without a country, strangers at home, and with no place to which to flee. I know there are thousands of exceptions to these statements, but yet they remain true for the great majority. The greatest injustice we do them is to consider them inferior and incapable. The greatest barrier to their restoration to normality and efficiency lies in their passivity and discouragement. We have broken the spring of hope and ambition.

To a people so hampered and dispirited, civilization and religion have been offered, as if their very environment were not adverse to these agencies. It should not require our argument or the statement of the Secretary of the Interior to make apparent the fact that the government through Congress should at once determine the legal status of the Indians. The whole situation brought about by this fundamental neglect of the country is summed up in the memorial of the Society of American Indians to President Wilson, which was presented on December 10, 1914. This memorial was the result of a special conference convened in the city of Washington by order of the University of Wisconsin Conference of the Society in 1914. In drafting it many of the most distinguished Indians in the United States took part. These included an Indian Congressman, the Registrar of the Treasury, lawyers, scientists, business and financial experts, clergymen, teachers, and newspaper men. Indorsing this memorial of these Indians were many distinguished friends of the race, including a university president, United States army officers, representatives of all the principal religious denominations and of various philanthropic bodies interested in Indian welfare. The memorial in part reads:

As a race, the Indian under the jurisdiction of the United States has no standing in court or nation. No man can tell what its status is, either civic or legal. Confusion and chaos are the only words descriptive of the situation. This condition is a barrier to the progress of our people, who aspire to higher things and greater success.

We hold it incontrovertible that federal authority should define our status in this nation. We request, therefore, that as the first essential to a proper solution of the Indian problem, and even for the benefit of the nation itself, this matter be placed in the hands of a commission of three men—the best, the most competent and the kindliest men to be found—and that they be authorized to study this question, and recommend to you and to the Congress the passage of a code of Indian law which shall open the door of hope and progress to our people. . . .

We plead, sir, that you give us the cheer of your word, that you consider our request—to grant the American Indians those fundamental rights and privileges, which are essential to release them from enforced hardship, dependence, and consequent degeneracy; and that you will advocate measures that will, according to the recognized principles of civic and economic development, speedily secure their admission to the field of even chance for individual efficiency and competency. . . . For the weak and helpless, for the discouraged and hopeless of our race scattered over this broad land we make this plea and petition.

If the church and the state are sincere in their desire to bring moral and civic salvation to the American Indian, each must man-fully face the conditions that have made the red man a problem. The psychological character of the problem must be recognized, for most of the red man's woes are diseases of mental attitude. The miseries of his external life are the results of a bewildered, dispirited, and darkened mind. The work of the agencies of good is to give order and hope, incentive and ambition, education and ideals. Every effort of the federal government should be directed to these ends, and men must be made to feel the thrill of manhood, the joy of having a part in the making of their country, and a sure faith in ultimate justice.

It is our belief that if we would atone for our injury to a suffering race we must see its trouble as it is. If need be, let it prick our conscience and so cause us to stir ourselves to renewed effort along more logical lines. Let this effort be to refuse longer to deny the Indian his first and greatest right. Let us acknowledge our present substantial failure. Let us remember that until we do the basic things first our failures will continue to go from bad to worse. When the government has done its primary duty, and when the good citizen has broken with his infidelity of opinion toward the Indian, then the school and the church may hope for large and splendid progress. Then shall a race of men—the red race—know its redemption.

Source: Parker, Arthur C. "The Social Elements of the Indian Problem." *The American Journal of Sociology* 22, no. 2 (1916): 252–267.

Carlos Montezuma, M.D., "Let My People Go"
(1916)

Carlos Montezuma, a Yavapai Apache, was a founding member of the Society of American Indians in 1911. Montezuma's work as a doctor enabled him to travel to various reservations throughout the United States and to witness firsthand the deplorable conditions in which many

Indians lived. These experiences led Montezuma to become a staunch opponent of the Bureau of Indian Affairs (BIA). In the article that follows, Montezuma borrows from Moses in pleading that the BIA stop holding back his people from realizing their roles as self-sufficient workers and producers.

The iron hand of the Indian Bureau has us in charge. The slimy clutches of horrid greed and selfish interests are gripping the Indian's property. Little by little the Indian's land and everything else is fading into a dim and unknown realm.

The Indian's prognosis is bad—unfavorable, no hope. The foreboding prodromic signs are visible here and there now—and when all the Indian's money in the United States Treasure is disposed of—when the Indian's property is all taken from him—when the Indians have nothing in this wide, wide world—when the Indians will have no rights, no place to lay their heads—and when the Indians will be permitted to exist only in the outskirts of the towns—when they must go to the garbage boxes in alleys, to keep them from starving—when the Indians will be driven into the streets, and finally the streets will be no place for them—what then will the Indian Bureau do for them? Nothing, but drop them. The Indian Department will go out of business.

In other words, when the Indians will need the most help in this world that philanthropic department of the government that we call the Indian Bureau, will cease to exist; bankrupt with liabilities—billions and billions—no assets, O Lord, my God, what a fate has the Indian Bureau for my people.

If we depend on the employees of the Indian Bureau for our life, liberty and pursuit of happiness, we wait a long while. They are too busy looking after the machinery of Indian Affairs; they have no time to look ahead; they have no time to feel the pulse of the Indian; they have no time to think of outside matters; they have no time to adjust matters. "Well, what time have they?" you may ask. All of their time is devoted to the pleasure and will of their master at Washington, that we called the Indian Bureau.

Blindly they think they are helping and uplifting, when in reality they are a hindrance, a drawback and a blockade on the road that would lead the Indian to freedom, that he may find his true place in the realms of mortal beings.

The reservation Indians are prisoners; they cannot do anything for themselves. We are on the outside, and it is the outsiders that must work to free the Indians from Bureauism. There is no fear of the general public. They are our friends. When they find out we are not free, they will free us. We have a running chance with the public, but no chance with the Indian Bureau.

The abolishment of the Indian Bureau will not only benefit the Indians, but the country will derive more money annually from the Indians than the government has appropriated to them. Why? Because by doing away with the Indian Bureau, you stop making paupers and useless beings, and start the making of producers and workers.

Does this seem like a dream to you? Is your position a foreign attitude? From aloft, do you look down? Have you gone so far as to forget your race? Have you quenched the spirit of our fathers? As their children, dare we stay back, hide ourselves and be dumb at this hour, when we see our race abused, misused, and driven to its doom? If this not be so, then let whatever loyalty and racial pride be in you awaken and manifest itself in this greatest movement of "Let My People Go!"

The highest duty and greatest object of the Society of American Indians, is to have a bill introduced in our next Congress to have the Indian Bureau abolished and to let the Indians go. We cannot be disinterested in this matter, we cannot be jealous or hate one another, we cannot quibble or be personal in this matter. There must be no suspicion.

We must act as one. Our hearts must throb with love—our souls must reach to God to guide us—and our bodies and souls must be used to gain our people's freedom.

In behalf of our people, with the spirit of Moses, I ask this—The United States of America—"Let My People Go."

Source: The American Indian Magazine published as the *Quarterly Journal of the Society of American Indians* IV, no. 1 (Jan.–Mar. 1916): 32–33.

Delos Lone Wolf, "How to Solve the Problem"
(1916)

Delos Lone Wolf was the nephew of the well-known Kiowa leader Lone Wolf. Delos served as an interpreter for his uncle during the Supreme Court case Lone Wolf v. Hitchcock *(1903). Delos was a star football player for Carlisle in the late 19th century, but in the 20th century, he became active in the Native American Church, which blended Christian and Indian beliefs, especially the use of peyote.*

In the excerpt that follows, Delos discusses his thoughts on the benefits of blending Christianity with Peyotism to introduce Indians to Christian churches. Delos also discusses his opinions regarding the Bureau of Indian Affairs and whether the institution should be dissolved and what function it should play within Indian communities.

I have been listening here to these speeches. I have been thinking of the Indians that are talking. From their talk I can make out they were raised among the white people: that is, the principle [sic] speakers; and then I heard a white man, (R.D. Hall), talk about these Indians and he was raised among the Indians! The man said something about the students. Of course these other speakers were raised among the white people and some of them live there yet. I am one of the returned students; a graduate of the Carlisle Indian School. I have been among the Indians, among my people, ever since I graduated at Carlisle in 1896. What I want to say is not what Indians tell me or what I learned from the Quakers. I am going to tell what I know from personal experience. I listened to the speeches about peyote yesterday. I had a word to say about it but I thought it was not best at the time. Now you Christian people who are trying to civilize the Indians, why don't you take your civilization and your Christianity to the lost Indians who are using peyote. Right there is where the fault comes in. This thing of talking about peyote killing the

Indians, there is no such thing. I used peyote for fifteen years. I have been right in with these "lost Indians" as a Christian Indian. There is a certain time when the Indians reach out, a certain time about three o'clock when the influence comes on them, they naturally reach out to get hold of something, their worship, right then I have been brave enough to go there, not what the Christian people or missionary or anybody else say [sic], but I talk Jesus Christ to them and through my influence and through the instrument of peyote some of the hardest cases that the missionary or anybody else could not reach they gave been converted and introduced into Christian churches.

Now as to abolishing the Indian Bureau and things like that; the position I have taken is on record. The Secretary of the Interior wrote several personal letters to me. One asked me several questions and one of them was, "Do you think the Government ought to turn Indians loose, and state in full why you think so?" He said in the beginning he wanted this information because he wanted to help the Indians in the best way and the best way possible, and here is the answer I wrote him. I feel just like Montezuma about freedom but because *of the conditions I could not recommend turning the Indians loose today,* but there is the recommendation I wrote to him. I said, "If you want to help us, leave our land and our restrictions just like they are until trust period runs out which is about nine or ten years from now, but give us more liberal use of our funds." I was talking about the younger people, say people about fifty years and down. But over that, of course, the Government will have to take care of them. I was speaking for the young people. I said, Give us our money, and if we are good enough to work, and let us have the privilege to handle our own money. Give us our money and if we use it all and blow it just like you been saying we would do, then we got no place to look to for

[sic] any more. Then we will have to go to work, and that is only salvation. *Work is the only salvation for Indians.* I spoke about handling our own allotments. If you will let us lease them, practical experience will teach us better and quicker than any of the best teachers and instructors you can send out among us. I said if an Indian makes a bad deal in leasing his land, next time he will see and he will make better trade and at the end of his trust period he will know just how to handle his allotment and he will get on well just like everybody else. Here is another statement I made; *as long as we have undivided money in the United States Treasury we will not do much work.* That is the trouble with anybody, I don't care who it is. You white people have got your living coming from somebody somewhere you will not exert yourself at all. Let us have what is ours and give us a chance to work.

Source: The American Indian Magazine published as the *Quarterly Journal of the Society of American Indians* IV, no. 1 (Jan.–Mar. 1916): 257–259.

Elsie Clews Parsons, Recording of a Nativity Myth at Laguna (1918)

Most Christians are familiar with the traditional nativity story. An angel appeared to Mary and told her she would bear a child who was the Son of God. As the baby was about to be born, she and her betrothed, Joseph, found that there was no room for them to stay at any inn in the town. As a result, Jesus was born in a manger, where he was soon visited by three wise men had who followed a bright star. American Indians who were exposed to Christianity sometimes developed their own versions of the nativity story. In the following document, anthropologist Elsie Clews Parsons records a nativity story related to her by a Laguna Catholic Indian.

During a visit to Laguna in February, 1918, I had noticed in the church a model in miniature of the Nativity group. Jesus, Mary, and Joseph, the ox and the mule, were represented, and there was a large flock of sheep. José or Tsiwema or Tsipehus, the "sextana," was one of my Laguna informants, and, on asking him the meaning of the crib, he narrated as follows:

The baby (*uwak*) was José Crito, god's child (*hus ka iach,* "god his child") was brought from a far country by his father José and his mother Mari. They took the journey about the time he was going to be born. He was born in a stable. A big fire, a big star, came down from the sky. There was an ox in the stable. When he was born, the ox came there. He blew on the baby. A little after a shepherd (*shtura*) came. That is the reason the priest put the sheep there. That was the way he was born. He went from there to another town, to the king's house (*re gama*), his mother and father and himself, on a horse. He grew up at the king's house. After he had grown up, the Jews (*Uriu*), were not satisfied with him. They were going to kill him. There were three brothers, three children of god; but this one born in the stable was the leader. They were hunting everywhere for him to kill him. One of the Jews asked the middle (*tsunatseiche*) brother which was Jesus. The Jew said, "Which one is it?" He said, "I am not going to tell you." They said, "Yes, you must tell us." So they bribed him. So another party of Jews came into his house. They were all sitting at the table, and still they kept asking which one was it. He was sitting in the north direction. "That's he." So they took him. "Wait a little," he said. "Wait a little, my brothers [*tiumu temishe*]! Which one of you has been given some money?"—"None of us." The one sitting at the east end of the table was the one that had been bribed. "You are the one, you have been paid some money. Now I am going away. I am going up to Konamats ['place of being thankful']." So they took him out of the room. They stood up a cross (*shukasetse*). He was a spirit (*kokimun*). So it took some time for them to get ready. When god's child made everything ready, they nailed him to the cross through the middle of his hands. There was one who could not see. There was another who was lame, so his brother carried him on his back. They pierced him through the heart. "Now all is ready," said the Jews. They made the blind man and the lame man pierce his heart. When they pierced him, the blood spurted everywhere. In this way (that is the reason why) from the spattered blood all living things came, horses and mules and all creatures. The man that was lame got up and walked, and the blind man could see, because they had been spattered with the blood. So at last they dug a hole and stood up the cross. They dug the hole so deep, that the cross could never be taken up. They buried him in this deep hole; they threw dirt and rocks on him, some of the rocks so big that they could hardly lift them; still they threw them in. They buried him. The first day, the second day, he was still buried; the third day he was to leave his grave. He went up to Konamats, back to his father, God. The Jews kept shooting upwards. His father was glad he came back up, so they would live there together in Konamats. The season when he was treated so mean is coming back again. Tomorrow is the first day of mass (*misa*). For seven weeks (*domik*) I have to ring the bell. On the sixth (seventh?) Sunday (*domiku*) it will be *kuitishi*. On the seventh Sunday it is coming back to the same time he went up to heaven. On the Wednesday before *kuitishi* will be the covering (*kaitamishe*). All the people come in to take a turn watching. It is covered Wednesday (*tsuna kaiich*), Thursday (*shuwewise*), Friday (*hienis*). On Saturday (*sauwawu*) it is uncovered. He goes back to his father. It will be *kucheachsi* [end or breaking of taboo]. That is all (*hemetsa*).

Source: Parsons, Elsie Clews. "Nativity Myth at Laguna and Zuñi." *Journal of American Folklore* 31, no. 120 (April–June 1918): 256–257.

"Hunting Song" (Navajo)
(1918)

Like poetry, songs are a significant part of a culture's collective memory. They can document famous stories, important people, dramatic events, or cultural procedures. They are also vital aspects of religious beliefs and rituals. The following is a Navajo hunting song, translated by an anthropologist. It is meant to be sung in such a way that the deer would be brought closer and closer to the hunter so he would have an easy time making his kill.

Comes the deer to my singing,
Comes the deer to my song,
Comes the deer to my singing.
He, the blackbird, he am I,
Bird beloved of the wild deer.
Comes the deer to my singing.
From the Mountain Black,
From the summit,
Down the trail, coming, coming now,
Comes the deer to my singing.
Through the blossoms,
Through the flowers, coming, coming now,
Comes the deer to my singing.
Through the flower dew-drops,
Coming, coming now,

Comes the deer to my singing.
Through the pollen, flower pollen,
Coming, coming now,
Comes the deer to my singing.
Starting with his left fore-foot,
Stamping, turns the frightened deer,
Comes the deer to my singing.
Quarry mine, blessed am I

In the luck of the chase.
Comes the deer to my singing.
Comes the deer to my singing,
Comes the deer to my song,
Comes the deer to my singing.

Source: Cronyn. George W., ed. *The Path on the Rainbow: An Anthology of Songs and Chants From the Indians of North America.* New York: Boni and Liveright, 1918, 142–143.

Robert Yellowtail, Call for Self-Determination
(1919)

Robert Yellowtail was a Crow Indian from Montana. He attended Indian boarding schools in Montana and California. He studied law after high school before returning home to Montana to be a cattle rancher. Not long after, he entered local politics and led opposition to the opening, to non-Indians, of tribal lands not yet allotted to Indians. The following excerpts are from an address he gave to the U.S. Senate Committee on Indian Affairs in defense of maintaining the existing boundaries of the Crow reservation.

Mr. Chairman and gentlemen of the committee, the American Indian, also a creature of God, claims, as you yourselves do, to be endowed with certain inalienable rights, among which are life, liberty, and the pursuit of happiness. He further maintains as his inherent right the right to choose the manner in which he shall seek his own happiness. . . .

Now then, Mr. Chairman, if you look through these sacred covenants you will not find in any of them any reservations or prior agreements to take or sell any portion of our lands so set aside against our wishes for schools or any other purposes to any State or to anybody else, but, on the other hand, it was solemnly agreed that no portion of it shall be disposed of until our consent thereto had been duly given. This was the condition of our agreement then.

Mr. Chairman, the fact of the matter has been that from the day that we treated with your commissioners for presumably a new birth of freedom equal to at least the one which we gave up at your bidding, and in many respects you assured us that it would be better, and taking you at your word and right then and there turning right about face, we followed you as a child follows its father, believing, because of your presence and the faith we reposed in you, that there would be no cause for any alarm, we followed you into what was then a perfect dark. Mr. Chairman, how well you have fulfilled this trust that we unhesitatingly reposed in you we leave to the world at large to judge.

Mr. Chairman, it is peculiar and strange to me, however, that after such elaborate and distinct understandings it should develop that today, after over half a century since our agreement, you have not upon your statute books nor in your archives of law, so far as I know, one law that permits us to think free, act free, expand free, and to decide free without first having to go and ask a total stranger that you call the Secretary of the Interior, in all humbleness and humiliation, "How about this, Mr. Secretary, can I have permission to do this"? and "Can I have permission to do that'? etc. Ah, Mr. Chairman, if you had given us an inkling then of what has since transpired. I am sure that our fathers would have then held their ground until every last one of them were dead or until you saw fit to guarantee to us in more explicit assurances something more humane, something more of that blessing of civil life, peculiar to this country alone that you call "Americanism."

Mr. Chairman, your President but yesterday assured the people of this great country, and also the people of the whole world, that the right of self-determination shall not be denied to any people, no matter where they live, nor how small or weak they may be, nor what their previous conditions of servitude may have been. He has stood before the whole world for the past three years at least as the champion of the rights of humanity and the cause of the weak and dependent nations was conceived for the express purpose of lifting from the shoulders of burdened humanity this unnecessary load of care. If that be the case, Mr. Chairman, I shall deem it my most immediate duty to see that every Indian in the United States shall do what he can for the speedy passage of that measure, but, on the other hand, Mr. Chairman, this thought has often occurred to me, that perhaps the case of the North American Indian may never have entered the mind of our great President when he uttered those solemn words; that, perhaps, in the final draft of this league of nations document a proviso might be inserted to read something like this: "That in no case shall this be construed to mean that the Indians of the United States shall be entitled to the rights and privileges expressed herein, but that their freedom and future shall be left subject to such rules and regulations as the Secretary of the Interior may, in his discretion, prescribe." I and the rest of my people sincerely hope and pray that the President, in his great scheme of enforcing upon all the nations of the earth the adoption of this

great principle of the brotherhood of man and nations, and that I hope, Mr. Chairman, that he will not forget that within the boundaries of his own nation are the American Indians, who have no rights whatsoever—not even the right to think for themselves. . . .

Mr. Chairman, I hold that the Crow Indian Reservation is a separate semisovereign nation in itself, not belonging to any State, nor confined within the boundary lines of any State of the Union, and that until such proper cessions, as has been agreed to and as expressed in our covenant, have been duly complied with no Senator, or anybody else, so far as that is concerned introduction of bills here without our consent and simply because of our geographical proximity to his State or his home, or because his constituents prevail upon him so to act; neither has he the right to dictate to us what we shall hold as our final homesteads in this our last stand against the ever-encroaching hand, nor continue to disturb our peace of mind by a constant agitation to deprive us of our lands, that were, to begin with, ours not his, and not given to us by anybody. This nation should be only too ready, as an atonement for our treatment in the past, to willingly grant to the Indian people of this country their unquestionable and undeniable right to determine how much of their own lands they shall retain as their homes and how much they shall dispose of to outsiders. . . .

Now, in conclusion, Mr. Chairman, permit me to say that the Indians of this country will grow better and become better and more intelligent useful citizens, just in proportion as you make it possible for them to be freer and happier; just in proportion as you permit fewer thrusts and snatches at their lands; just in proportion as you allow them to exercise more intellectual liberty; just in proportion as you permit them personal liberty, free thought, and the freest expression thereof, for free thought never gave us anything else but the truth; just exactly the same as your own race has grown better, just in proportion to their exercise of freedom of body, and mind, and thought, plus the freest expression thereof; the history of all nations tell us that they have grown only better just in proportion as they have grown free, and I am here, gentlemen, to advocate that proposition for the American Indian, who still is held in bondage as a political slave; by this great Government as intellectual slaves, and as intellectual serfs; and now, gentlemen, I ask of you, that has not the time arrived when we ought to begin at least to think of giving to these people more of the essence of that happier life as you live it, and to permit them to enjoy a little civil life that you call "Americanism"?

Source: "Address by Robert Yellowtail in Defense of the Rights of the Crow Indians, and the Indians Generally, Before the Senate Committee on Indian Affairs, September 9, 1919." U.S. Senate Report 219, 66th Cong., 1st Session, serial 7590. Washington, DC: Government Printing Office, 1919.

Zitkala-Sa, Discussion of the Paris Peace Conference
(1919)

The Treaty of Versailles ended World War I. Although many American Indians served in the war, they were not yet citizens of the country they served. In this document, Gertrude Simmons Bonnin, who was serving as the secretary of the Society of American Indians, used the ideals of Wilsonianism and the end of the "War to End All Wars" to call attention to the issues facing American Indians.

The eyes of the world are upon the Peace Conference sitting at Paris.

Under the sun a new epoch is being staged!

Little peoples are to be granted the right of self determination!

Small nations and remnants of nations are to sit beside their great allies at the Peace Table; and their just claims are to be duly incorporated in the terms of a righteous peace.

Paris, for the moment, has become the center of the world's thought, Divers[e] human petitions daily ascend to its Peace Table through foreign emissaries, people's representatives and the interest's lobbyist. From all parts of the earth, claims for adjustments equitable and otherwise are cabled and wirelessed. What patience and wisdom is needed now to render final decisions upon these highly involved and delicate enigmas reeking with inhumanities! The task may be difficult and the exposures of wrongs innumerable, still we believe,—yes, we know; the world is to be made better as a result of these stirring times.

Immortal justice is the vortex around which swing the whirl of human events!

We are seeking to know justice, not as a fable but as a living, active, practical force in all that concerns our welfare!

Actions of the wise leaders assembled in Paris may be guided ostensibly by temporary man-made laws and aims, dividing human interests into domestic and international affairs, but even so those leaders cannot forget the eternal fact that humanity is essentially one undivided, closely intertwined, fabric through which spiritual truth will shine with increasing brightness until it is fully understood and its requirements fulfilled. The universal cry for freedom from injustice is the voice of a multitude united by afflictions. To appease this human cry the application of democratic principles must be flexible enough to be universal.

Belgium is leading a historic procession of little peoples seeking freedom!

From the very folds of the great allied nations are many classes of men and women clamoring for a hearing. Their fathers, sons, brothers and husbands fought and died for democracy. Each is eager to receive the reward for which supreme sacrifice was made. Surely will the blood-soaked fields of No-Man's Land unceasingly cry out until the high principles for which blood spilled itself, are established in the governments of men.

Thus in vast procession to Paris, we recognize and read their flying banners.

Labor organizations are seeking representation at the Peace Conference. Women of the world, mothers of the human race, are pressing forward for recognition. The Japanese are taking up the perplexing problem of race discrimination.

The Black man of America is offering his urgent petition for representation at the Conference; and already President Wilson has taken some action in his behalf by sending to Paris, Dr. Moton, of Tuskeegee Institute accompanied by Mr. DuBois.

A large New York assembly of American men and women wirelessed, it is reported, to President Wilson while he was in mid-ocean, enroute to Paris, requesting his aid in behalf of self-government for the Irish people.

The Red man asks for a very simple thing—citizenship in the land that was once his own,—America. Who shall represent his cause at the World's Peace Conference? The American Indian, too, made the supreme sacrifice for liberty's sake. He loves democratic ideals. What shall world democracy mean to his race?

There never was a time more opportune than now for America to enfranchise the Red man!

Source: Bonnin, Gertrude. "Editorial Comment." *American Indian Magazine* 6, no. 4 (Winter 1919): 161–162.

"How Aua Became a Shaman"
(1920s)

In the 1920s, the Greenlander explorer Knud Rasmussen first met and interviewed the Inuit shaman Aua. At the time, Christian missionaries were increasingly visiting Aua's people, representing a threat to the continued existence of and belief in Inuit religious practices. The following is Aua's account of how he acquired his shamanic power.

I was yet but a tiny unborn infant in mother's womb when anxious folk began to enquire sympathetically about me; all the children my mother had had before had lain crosswise and been stillborn. As soon as my mother now perceived that she was with child, the child that one day was to be me, she spoke thus to her house fellows:

Now I have again that within me which will turn out no real human being.

All were very sorry for her and a woman named Ardjauq, who was a shaman herself, called up her spirits that same evening to help my mother. And the very next morning it could be felt that I had grown, but it did me no good at the time, for Ardjuaq had forgotten that she must do no work the day after a spirit-calling, and had mended a hole in a mitten. This breach of taboo at once had its effect upon me; my mother felt the birth-pangs coming on before the time, and I kicked and struggled as if trying to work my way out through her side. A new spirit-calling then took place, and as all precepts were duly observed this time, it helped both my mother and myself.

But then one day it happened that my father, who was going out on a journey to hunt, was angry and impatient, and in order to calm him, my mother went to help him harness the dogs to the sledge. She forgot that in her condition, all work was taboo. And so, hardly had she picked up the traces and lifted one dog's paw before I began again kicking and struggling and trying to get out through her naval; and again we had to have a shaman to help us.

Old people now assured my mother that my great sensitiveness to any breach of taboo was a sign that I should live to become a great shaman; but at the same time, many dangers and misfortunes would pursue me before I was born.

My father had got a walrus with its unborn young one, and when he began cutting it out, without reflection that my mother was with child, I again fell to struggling within the womb, and this time in earnest. But the moment I was born, all life left me, and I lay there dead as a stone. Ardjuaq, who lived in another village, was at once sent for, and a special hut was built for my mother. When Ardjuaq came and saw me with my eyes sticking right out of my head, she wiped my mother's blood from my body with the skin of a raven, and made a little jacket for me of the same skin.

He is born to die, but he shall live, she said.

And so Ardjuaq stayed with my mother, until I showed signs of life. Mother was put on very strict diet, and had to observe difficult rules of taboo. If she had eaten part of a walrus, for instance, then that walrus was taboo to all others; the same with seal and caribou. She had to have special pots, from which no one else was allowed to eat. No woman was allowed to visit her, but men might do so. My clothes were made after a particular fashion; the hair of the skins must never lie pointing upwards or down, but fall athwart the body. Thus I lived in the birth-hut, unconscious of all the care that was being taken with me.

For a whole year my mother and I had to live entirely alone, only visited now and again by my father. He was a great hunter, and always out after game, but in spite of this he was never allowed to sharpen his own knives; as soon as he did so, his hand began to swell and I fell ill. A year after my birth, we were allowed to have another person in the house with us; it was a woman, and she had to be very careful herself; whenever she went out she must throw her hood over her head, wear boots without stockings, and hold the tail of her fur coat lifted high in one hand.

I was already a big boy when my mother was first allowed to go visiting; all were anxious to be kind, and she was invited to all the other families. But she stayed out too long; the spirits do not like women with little children to stay too long away from their house, and they took vengeance in this wise; the skin of her head peeled off, and I, who had no understanding of anything at that time, beat her about the body with my little fists as she went home, and made water down her back.

No one who is to become a skilful hunter or a good shaman must remain out too long when visiting strange houses; and the same holds good for a woman with a child in her amaut.

At last I was big enough to go out with the grown-up men to the blowholes after seal. The day I harpooned my first seal, my father had to lie down on the ice with upper part of his body naked, and the seal I had caught was dragged across his back while it was still alive. Only men were allowed to eat of my first catch, and nothing must be left. The skin and the head were set on the ice, in order that I might be able later on to catch the same seal again. For three days and nights, none of the men who had eaten of it might go out hunting or do any kind of work.

The next animal I killed was a caribou. I was strictly forbidden to use a gun, and had to kill it with bow and arrows; this animal also only men were allowed to eat; no women might touch it.

Some time passed, and I grew up and was strong enough to go out hunting walrus. The day I harpooned my first walrus my father shouted at the top of his voice the names of all the villages he knew, and cried: Now there is food for all!

The walrus was towed in to land, while it was still alive, and not until we reached the shore was it finally killed. My mother, who was to cut it up, had the harpoon line made fast to her body before the harpoon head was withdrawn. After having killed this walrus, I was allowed to eat all those delicacies which had formerly been forbidden, yes, even entrails, and women were now allowed to eat of my catch, as long as they were not with child or recently delivered. Only my own mother had still to observe great caution, and whenever she had any sewing to do, a special hut had to be built for her. I had been named after a little spirit, Aua, and it was said that it was in order to avoid offending this spirit that my mother had to be so particular about everything she did. It was my guardian spirit, and took great care that I should not do anything that was forbidden. I was never allowed, for instance, to remain in a snow hut where young women were undressing for the night; nor might any woman comb her hair while I was present.

Even after I had been married a long time, my catch was still subject to strict taboo. If there but lived women with infants near us, my own wife was only allowed to eat meat of my killing, and no other woman was allowed to satisfy her hunger with the meat of any animal of which my wife had eaten. Any walrus I killed was further subject to the rule that no woman might eat of its entrails, which are reckoned a great delicacy, and this prohibition was maintained until I had four children of my own. And it was really only since I had grown old that the obligations laid on me by Ardjuaq in order that I might live have ceased to be needful.

Everything was thus made ready for me beforehand, even from the time I was yet unborn; nevertheless, I endeavored to become a shaman by the help of others; but in this I did not succeed. I visited many famous shamans, and gave them great gifts, which they at once gave away to others; for if they had kept the things for themselves, they and their children would have died. This they believed because my own life had been threatened from birth. Then I sought solitude, and there I soon became very melancholy. I would sometimes fall to weeping, and feel unhappy without knowing why. Then, for no reason, all would suddenly be changed, and I felt a great, inexplicable joy, a joy so powerful that I could not restrain it, but had to break into song, a mighty song, with only room for

the one word: joy, joy! And I had to use the full strength of my voice. And then in the midst of such a fit of mysterious and overwhelming delight I became a shaman, not knowing myself how it came about. But I was a shaman. I could see and hear in a totally different way. I had gained my qaumaneq, my enlightenment, the shaman-light of brain and body, and this in such a manner that it was not only I who could see through the darkness of life, but the same light also shone out from me, imperceptible to human beings, but visible to all the spirits of earth and sky and sea, and these now came to me and became my helping spirits.

My first helping spirit was my namesake, a little Aua. When it came to me, it was as if the passage and roof of the house were lifted up, and I felt such a power of vision, that I could see right through the house, in through the earth and up into the sky; it was the little Aua that brought me all this inward light, hovering over me as long as I was singing. Then it placed itself in a corner of the passage, invisible to others, but always ready if I should call it.

An Aua is a little spirit, a woman, that lives down by the sea shore. There are many of these shore spirits, who run about with a pointed skin hood on their heads; their breeches are queerly short, and made of bearskin; they wear long boots with a black pattern, and coast of sealskin. Their feet are twisted upward, and they seem to walk only on their heels. They hold their hands in such a fashion that the thumb is always bent in over the palm; their arms are held raised up on high with the hands together, and incessantly stroking the head. They are bright and cheerful when one calls them, and resemble most of all sweet little live dolls; they are no taller than the length of a man's arm.

My second helping spirit was a shark. One day when I was out in my kayak, it came swimming up to me, lay alongside quite silently and whispered my name. I was greatly astonished, for I had never seen a shark before; they are very rare in these waters. Afterwards it helped me with my hunting, and was always near me when I had need of it. These two, the shore spirit and the shark, were my principal helpers, and they could aid me in everything I wished. The song I generally sang when calling them was of few words, as follows:

Joy, joy,
Joy, joy!
I see a little shore spirit,
A little aua,
I myself am also aua,
The shore spirit's namesake,
Joy, joy!

These words I would keep on repeating, until I burst into tears, overwhelmed by a great dread; than I would tremble all over, crying only: "Ah-a-a-a-a, joy, joy! Now I will go home, joy, joy!"

Once I lost a son, and felt that I could never again leave the spot where I had laid his body. I was like a mountain spirit, afraid of human kind. We stayed for a long time up inland, and my helping spirits forsook me, for they do not like live human beings to dwell upon any sorrow. But one day the song about joy came to me all of itself and quite unexpectedly. I felt once more a longing for my fellow men, my helping spirits returned to me, and I was myself once more.

Source: "Knud Rasmussen." In *Native American Autobiography*, edited by Arnold Krupat. © 1994 by the Board of Regents of the University of Wisconsin System. Reprinted by permission of The University of Wisconsin Press.

The Indian New Deal and a Turn to the Militant

(1921–1973)

Joseph Medicine Crow, "What Has Happened to the Crow Indian Horses" (1922)

Beginning in the 1920s, the U.S. government implemented a policy of forced livestock reduction on the Crow Reservation. Many white ranchers purchased Crow lands for the purpose of establishing ranches and many were successful; however, the presence of large numbers of Crow horses meant competition for scarce grass resources. Pressure from white ranchers to eradicate what they considered nuisance animals was an important factor in initiating the reduction campaign. The result of livestock reduction for the Crow people was catastrophic. Horses were and still are integral to Crow cultural identity, and the loss of so many thousands of these animals represented an attack on this tribe's cultural foundations. In the following document by Joseph Medicine Crow, the author describes the tempestuous events of the 1920s in which more than 40,000 Crow horses were slaughtered for white economic gain. According to the author and other authorities on this subject, the actual number of horses killed may have been as high as 100,000.

In 1882 the Crow tribe ceded the western portion of the vast Crow Indian Reservation to the United States and moved to the eastern sector. The Indian agents' new headquarters or agency was established in the Little Bighorn Valley about thirteen miles south of what is now Hardin, Montana, in 1884. The Crow families scattered to various areas of the diminished reservation, generally under the leadership of a chief or several chiefs. The main occupation of the Crow men was the traditional raising of and caring for horses, which was all they knew and enjoyed doing. During the Spanish-American War, the conflicts of the 1890s, and World War I, the Crow horse ranchers began to farm, raising garden produce, small grains, and hay for the horses. Family herds increased rapidly.

By the turn of the century, the number of horses the Crows owned was increasing rapidly, and by the end of World War I, the ranges were teeming with horses, which were becoming unmanageable and quite wild. By this time many non-Indian cattlemen and sheepmen had acquired grazing permits to large blocks of reservation land, and they were doing very well. They started complaining that wild Indian ponies were eating off their ranges, and some refused to pay their grazing fees. Before long these permittees and lessees, aided by Montana senators and congressmen, began pressuring the government to get rid of the Indian horses.

About 1919 the secretary of the interior issued orders that the Crows must get rid of their horses. This was like ordering a people to relinquish the traditions, customs, and values of their culture, their way of life! Naturally, no Crow could abide by the secretary's orders. The ultimatum came about 1923, that the government would get rid of the horses. Local non-Indian cattle outfits were contracted to kill the horses on a bounty basis. The killer would be paid four dollars per animal when he produced the tip of a horse's ear. Some killers would bring in big sacks of ears. One large outfit had to import Texas gunmen to do the shooting as local cowboys were soon disgusted with the slaughter. Of course, the Crows would not kill the horses.

In a matter of three years nearly all the so-called wild mustangs were killed off. About one hundred heads of the wildest ones were found in the rough Rotten Grass Breaks after World War II, and the same stockman who hired the Texas gunmen hired planes and helicopters and ran the poor horses to death. In the first slaughter the government said that about forty thousand heads were exterminated, but the Crows said it was many more, including many tame ranch horses which the gunmen preyed on when it got difficult to find wild ones. Thus by 1930 the great and proud horse people, the Absarokee, were bereft of horses. When the horse was gone, the Crow culture was severely damaged. To say the least, this was a traumatic and tragic experience for a proud horse-oriented tribe; it was worse than actual military defeat, which some Plains tribes sustained.

The Northern Cheyenne tribe, whose reservation adjoined the Crow Reservation on the east, also suffered the same fate. A Cheyenne historian used to recall that a new Indian agent arrived for duty just before the onset of the horse slaughter. After surveying conditions on the reservation, he announced that the Cheyenne were in a sad state and that he would put them back on their feet as soon as possible. The agent did not speak with a forked tongue, the Cheyenne historian would add. Within a short time, all the Cheyenne horses were killed off and the Cheyenne were set on foot.

In 1934 John Collier was appointed Commissioner of Indian Affairs under the new Roosevelt Administration. When the Indian Reorganization Act was passed, Collier immediately launched his program to restructure the Indian Service, giving the tribes wide and generous latitude in managing their own reservation affairs. Corporate charters were issued to tribes accepting the new policy.

The commissioner appointed Robert Yellowtail, then forty-three years old, as the new superintendent of his own Crow Indian Reservation. Yellowtail was well educated and had taken a law course in California. He served as counsel and interpreter for Crow chiefs such as Plenty Coups and Medicine Crow in their many negotiations with the government over attempts by Montana senators and congressmen to open the Crow Reservation for homesteading by whites. Yellowtail knew how to deal with the whites.

The new superintendent immediately launched an ambitious program to rehabilitate his Crow people from the horse disaster, the ongoing drought, and the national Depression. The Crow people had to be economically and culturally invigorated! While taking advantage of the National Recovery Act programs, the superintendent also pursued long-range economic rehabilitation plans. His main goals were to restock the reservation with horses, as well as buffalo and elk. The buffalo program was quickly accomplished, as several hundred heads of bison were donated by Yellowstone Park, by the National Bison Range of Western Montana, and by some private individuals. To start the horse program, Yellowtail purchased and begged for registered stallions of various breeds and launched a full-scale breeding program. He named a Morgan stallion Roosevelt. This stallion sired many top calf-roping horses for Crow rodeo cowboys.

The Crow had lost his horses but not his love and ability to handle horses nor the importance he attached to horses in his culture. Former Crow horsemen enthusiastically joined the horse crusade, and before too long the horses were back. Lost concepts and values in Crow culture were revived.

With the resumption of the annual Crow Fair and Celebration after World War II, a steady demand grew for race horses, rodeo horses, parade horses, and just kid horses. With the easy availability of fine registered sires and mares in the country now, the Crow Indians have been increasing their herds with fine stock.

Today during the annual August tribal celebration, billed as the Tepee Capital of the World, attended by thousands of tribal people from throughout the United States and Canada, these fine modern Crow horses are to be seen by the hundreds in the daily parades through the camp, on the race track in the afternoon meets, and in the rodeo arena.

This is a sight to behold, truly a rare privilege to see, when hundreds of people, from tiny tots to octogenarians, pass in parade riding beautifully decorated mounts—a horse culture in action.

Thanks to Columbus for bringing the horse back to America!

Source: Reprinted from *The Crow Indians' Own Stories* by Joseph Medicine Crow by permission of the University of Nebraska Press. Copyright 1992 by Joseph Medicine Crow.

A Klamath Story
(1922)

The Klamath live in the Pacific Northwest. The following story is meant to provide stories and lessons in Klamath history and life. It relates the origins of a disagreement between the storyteller and an old woman, which has been ongoing for an incredibly long time. In the process, readers learn a wealth of information about these people.

(Mrs. Oregon Jim, from the house Erkigér-i or "Hair-ties" in the town of Pékwan, speaking): You want to know why old Louisa and I never notice each other? Well, I'll tell you why. I wouldn't speak to that old woman to save her life. There is a quarrel between her and me, and between her people and my people.

The thing started, so far as I know, with the bastard son of a woman from that big old house in Wáhsek that stands crossways—the one they call Wáhsek-héthlqau. They call it that, of course,

because it is behind the others. It kind of sets back from the river. This woman lived with several different men; first with a young fellow from the house next door, and then, when she left him, with a strolling fellow from Smith River. When she left him for a Húpa, they all began to call her kimolin, "dirty." Not one of these men had paid a cent for her, although she came of good people. She lived around in different places. Two of her children died, but a third one grew up at the Presbyterian Mission.

He had even less sense than the Presbyterians have. He came down to Kepél one time, when the people there were making the Fish Dam. It was the last day of the work on the dam. The dam was being finished, that day. That's the time nobody can get mad. Nobody can take offense at anything. This boy heard people calling each other bad names. They were having a dance. The time of that dance is different from all other times. People say the worst things! It sounds funny to hear the people say, for example, to old Kimorets, "Well, old One-Eye! you are the best dancer." They think of the worst things to say! A fellow even said to Mrs. Poker Bob, "How is your grandmother?"; when Mrs. Poker Bob's grandmother was already dead. It makes your blood run cold to hear such things, even though you know it's in fun.

This young fellow I am telling you about, whom they called Fred Williams, and whose Indian name was Sär, came down from the Mission school to see the Fish Dam Dance at Kepel. He was dressed up. He went around showing off. He wore a straw hat with a ribbon around it. He stood around watching the dance. Between the songs, he heard what people were saying to each other. He heard them saying all sorts of improper things. He thought that was smart talk. He thought he would try it when he got a chance. The next day, he went down by the river and saw Tuley-Creek Jim getting ready his nets. "Get your other hand cut off," he said. "Then you can fish with your feet!" Two or three people who were standing by, heard him. Tuley-Creek Jim is pretty mean. They call him "Coyote." He looked funny. He stood there. He didn't know what to say.

Young Andrew, who was there, whose mother was from the house called "Down-river House" in Qovtep, was afraid for his life. He was just pushing off his boat. He let go of the rope. The boat drifted off. He was afraid to pull it back. He went up to the house. "Something happened," he told the people there. "I wish I was somewhere else. There is going to be trouble along this Klamath River."

The talk soon went around that Coyote-Jim was claiming some money. It was told us that he was going to make the boy's mother's father pay fifteen dollars. "That's my price," he said. "I won't do anything to the boy, for he isn't worth it. Nobody paid for his mother. Also, I won't charge him much. But his mother's people are well-to-do, and they will have to pay this amount that I name. Otherwise, I will be mad." As a matter of fact, he was afraid to do anything, for he, himself, was afraid of the soldiers at Húpa. He just made big

talk. Besides, what he wanted was a headband ornamented with whole woodpecker heads, that the boy's grandfather owned. He thought he could make the old man give it up, on account of what his grandson had said.

The boy went around, hollering to everybody. "I don't have to pay," he said. "I heard everybody saying things like that! How did I know that they only did it during that one day? Besides, look at me! Look at my shirt. Look at my pants." He showed them his straw hat. "Look at my hat! I am just like a white man. I can say anything I please. I don't have to care what I say."

Every day somebody came along the river, telling us the news. There was a big quarrel going on. I was camped at that time, with my daughter, above Meta, picking acorns. All the acorns were bad that year—little, and twisted, and wormy. Even the worms were little and kind of shriveled that year. That place above Meta was the only place where the acorns were good. Lots of people were camped there. Some paid for gathering acorns there. My aunt had married into a house at Meta, the house they call Wóogi, "In the-middle-House," so I didn't have to pay anything. People used to come up from the river to where we acorn pickers were camped, to talk about the news. They told us the boy's mother's people were trying to make some people at Smith River pay. "He's the son of one of their men," the old grandfather said. "They've got to pay for the words he spoke. I don't have to pay." The thing dragged on. Three weeks later they told us the old man wouldn't pay yet.

Somebody died at the old man's house that fall. The people were getting ready to have a funeral. The graveyard for that house called Héthlqau, in Wáhsek, is just outside the house door. They went into that kämethl, in that corpse-place, what you whites call a cemetery. They dug a hole and had it ready. They were singing "crying-songs" in that house where the person had died.

Tuley-Creek Jim's brother-in-law was traveling down the river in a canoe. When he got to Wáhsek he heard "crying songs." "Somebody has died up there," they told him. "We better stop! No use trying to go by. We better go ashore till the burial is over." Tuley-Creek Jim's brother-in-law did not want to stop. "They owe some money to my wife's brother," he said. "One of their people said something to Jim. They don't pay up. Why should I go ashore?" So they all paddled down to the landing-place. They started to go past, going down-river. A young fellow at the landingplace grabbed their canoe. "You got to land here," he said. "My aunt's people are having a funeral. It ain't right for anybody to go by in a canoe." The people in the canoe began to get mad. They pushed on the bottom with their paddles. The canoe swung around. Coyote-Jim's brother-in-law stood up. He was pretty mad. They had got his shirt wet. He waved his paddle around. He hollered. He got excited.

One of the men on the bank was Billy Brooks, from the mouth of the river. "Hey! You fellow-living-with-a-woman-you-haven't-paid-for!" he said to Billy Brooks, "make these fellows let go of my canoe."

Billy was surprised. He hadn't been holding the canoe. And anyway, he did not expect to be addressed that way. "Las-son" is what he had heard addressed to him. That means "half-married, or improperly married, to a woman in the house by the trail." Brooks had no money to pay for a wife, so he went to live with his woman instead of taking her home to him. That is what we call being half-married. Everybody called Billy that way, behind his back. "Half-married-into-the-house-by-the-trail" was his name.

When Billy got over being surprised at this form of address, he got mad. He pointed at the fellow in the canoe. He swore the worst way a person can swear. What he said was awful. He pointed at him. He was mad clear through. He didn't care what he said. "Your deceased relatives," is what he said to Coyote-Jim's brother-in-law, in the canoe. He said it right out loud. He pointed at the canoe. That's the time he said "Your deceased relatives." "All your deceased relatives," he said to those in the canoe.

Coyote-Jim's brother-in-law sat down in the canoe. Nobody tried to stop the canoe after that.

The canoe went down-river. Billy Brooks went up to the house.

He waited. After a while the people there buried that person who was dead, and the funeral was over. "I've got to pay money," Billy Brooks said to them then. "I got mad and swore something terrible at Coyote-Jim's brother-in-law. That was on account of you people. If you had paid what you owed to Coyote-Jim, Coyote-Jim's brother-in-law wouldn't have gone past your house while you were crying, and you wouldn't have held his canoe, and he wouldn't have addressed me as he did, and I wouldn't have said what I did. Moreover, Wóhkel Dave was in the canoe, and when I said that which I said, it applied to him, too. I feel terrible mean about what I said. I've got to have trouble with both those men. There were others in the canoe, too, but they are poor people, and don't amount to anything. But Dave is a rich man. Now all this trouble is on your account, and you've got to pay me two dollars and a half."

The old man at Wáhsek was in trouble. "First my mouse says to Coyote-Jim what should not in any case have been said," the old man complained. (We call illegitimate children "mice," because they eat, and stay around, and nobody has paid for them.) "Now on account of what my mouse said, all this other trouble has happened."

Everybody was talking about the quarrel now. That is the time. They left off talking about the old man's troubles, and began talking about what Billy Brooks said to the Coyote's brother-in-law in the canoe, and to Wóhkel Dave. It finally came out that the fellow who was steering the canoe, and who called Billy Brooks "Las-son," was out of the quarrel. His deceased relatives had been referred to, but, on the other hand, his father had only paid twenty-five dollars for his mother, so nobody cared much about him. He talked around but nobody paid any attention, so he decided that he had better keep still about it, and maybe people would forget that he had been insulted.

Wóhkel Dave, however, was a man of importance. His people were married into all the best houses up and down the river. Everybody was wondering what he and Brooks would do. Billy Brooks was kind of a mean man himself. He had a bad reputation. One time he even made a white man pay up for something he did. The white man took a woman from Brooks' people to live with him. Brooks looked him up, and made him pay for her. Everybody was afraid of Brooks. Some people said, "Brooks won't pay. He's too mean. He's not afraid. He'd rather fight it out." Other people said, "That's all right, as far as ordinary people are concerned. Wóhkel Dave, though, is not ordinary. His father paid a big price for his mother. She had one of the most stylish weddings along the river. Dave won't let anybody get the best of him." People used to argue that way. Some said one thing, and some said another. They used to almost quarrel about it.

Suddenly news came down the river that Billy Brooks was going to pay up for what he said. Someone came along and told us that Billy was going to pay. "He offered twenty-five dollars," this fellow said. The next day we heard that Dave wouldn't take it. He wanted forty dollars. They argued back and forth. It was February before they got it settled. Billy had to pay twenty dollars in money, a shot-gun made out of an army musket, bored out, and a string of shell money, not a very good one. The shells were pretty small, but the string was long-reaching from the chest bone to the end of the fingers.

The next thing that happened is what involved me and old Louisa. It came about because Billy didn't have twenty dollars in cash. He had to get hold of the twenty dollars. About that time, certain Indians stole some horses. They were not people from our tribe. They were Chilula from Bald Hills, or people from over in that direction somewhere. Those people were awful poor. They couldn't pay for a woman. They couldn't pay for anything. They had to marry each other. In the springtime they got pretty wild. They were likely to do things. This time they took some horses from a white man. This white man complained to the agent at Húpa. So some soldiers from Húpa went out to chase these Indians. Billy Brooks was a great hunter. He has

been all over everywhere, hunting and trapping. The soldiers needed a guide. They offered Billy twenty-five dollars to serve as a "scout" for the Government, to chase these Indians. So Billy, because he had to have twenty dollars, went as a scout, that time. The soldiers went to Redwood Creek. Billy Brooks went along. There was a sergeant and six men, they say. Two of the men went that Indian town six miles above the mouth of Redwood Creek, the name of which is Otlép. That town belongs to the Chilula. These two soldiers went there, looking for the men who stole the horses. There was trouble after a while at that place. The soldiers got into a quarrel with the Indians.

The trouble was about a woman. One of the soldiers wanted her, but the woman would not go with him. She did not feel like it. I don't know exactly what happened, but the soldier insisted, and the woman insisted, and finally her relatives told the soldier that if the woman didn't want to, she didn't have to. There was a fight that time. There was a tussel about the soldier's revolver. Somebody got hit over the head with it. The front sight was sharp. That soldier had filed down the sight on his revolver, to make it fine. That sight dug into a man's face, and cut it open, from his jaw bone up to his eye.

There was big trouble there that time, they say. Everybody got to hollering. That woman had a bad temper. She hit a soldier with a rock. She broke his head open. The man whose face was cut open went for his gun. He couldn't see very well. He didn't get the percussion cap on properly. He tried to shoot the soldier, but the gun wouldn't go off. The cap had dropped off the nipple. The soldier saw the Indian aiming the gun at him, so he fired at the Indian. There was blood in the soldier's eyes, for the woman had cut his head open with a rock. So he missed the Indian who was aiming at him, but he hit old Louisa's nephew, Jim Williams. The bullet went through his thigh. Two years passed before Jim Williams could walk straight after that.

Now that is the trouble between old Louisa and me. Her nephew was hurt, and she blames Billy

Brooks, because Billy Brooks was with the soldiers, helping them, the time this happened. Billy would never "pay up" for this. One time it was reported that he was going to pay, but he never did.

Now Billy is a relative of mine by marriage. His sister married my father's brother's oldest boy. That old woman, whose nephew was shot, doesn't like me, because I am a relative of Billy who guided the soldiers.

One time she played me a dirty trick. My nephew was fishing with a gill-net on the river here. The game warden made a complaint and had him arrested, for he had one end of his net fast to the bank. That old woman, that old Louisa, went to Eureka and told the judge there, that one end of the net was fast to the bank. They say she got money for doing that. Somebody said she got two dollars a day. My nephew was put in jail for sixty days. I am not saying anything to that old woman, but I am keeping a watch on her. If anybody talks to her, then I have nothing to do with them.

One time a white man from down below came along this river, asking about baskets. He wanted to know the name of everything. He was kind of crazy, that fellow. They used to call him "Hapo'o," or "Basket-designs." He was always asking, "What does that mean?" or "What is the name of that?"

He wanted to know all about baskets. He talked to old Louisa for a day and a half about her baskets. Then he came through the fence to my house. I wouldn't say a word to him, and he went away. My friends won't talk to Louisa, or her friends. It will be that way forever.

It all goes back to that boy Sir. If he had not talked about Tuley-Creek Jim having only one hand, Jim's brother-in-law would not have paddled past a house where there was a person lying dead, and his canoe would not have been seized, and there would have been no quarrel about the canoe, and Billy Brooks would not have sworn at anybody, so he would not have had to pay money, and he would not have hired out as a scout to the Government, and the fellow in Redwood Creek would not have been shot, and old Louisa would not have testified about my nephew. To make people pay is all right. That is what always happens when there is a quarrel.

But to put my nephew in jail is not right.

I'll never speak to that old lady again, and neither will any of my people.

Source: Waterman, T. T. "All is Trouble Along the Klamath." In *American Indian Life, by Several of its Students*, edited by Elsie Clews Parsons, 289–298. New York: B. W. Huebsch, Inc., 1922.

Luther Standing Bear Recalls His First Buffalo Hunt
(1928)

Luther Standing Bear is one of the most famous American Indians who attended the Carlisle Indian School in Pennsylvania. Upon his graduation, he wrote an autobiography and other works on American Indian culture and history. He grew up a traditional Lakota and was known as Plenty Kill. In the following excerpt from his work My People the Sioux, *he describes his first buffalo hunt and how white hunters affected the buffalo.*

Our scouts, who had gone out to locate the buffalo, came back and reported that the plains were covered with dead bison. These had been shot by the white people. The Indians never were such wasteful, wanton killers of this noble game animal. We kept moving, fully expecting soon to run across plenty of live buffalo; but we were disappointed. I saw the bodies of hundreds of dead buffalo lying about, just wasting, and the odor was terrible.

Now we began to see white people living in dugouts, just like wild bears, but without the long snout. These people were dirty. They had hair all over their faces, heads, arms and hands. This was the first time many of us had ever seen white people, and they were very repulsive to us. None of us had ever seen a gorilla, else we might have thought that Darwin was right concerning these people.

Outside these dugouts we saw bale after bale of buffalo skins, all packed, ready for market. These people were taking away the source of the clothing and lodges that had been provided for us by our Creator, and they were letting our food lie on the plains to rot. They were to receive money for all this, while the Indians were to receive only abuse. We thought these people must be devils, for they had no sympathy. Do you think such treatment was fair to the Indian?

But some of you may say, "Oh, the plains had to be cleared of the buffalo, and that was the only way." That may all be very true; but did you ever stop to think of the thousands of Indians who had to go hungry in consequence of this wholesale slaughter?

Why not look at it this way: Suppose a man had a farm with lots of cattle, and it was thought a good idea to build a town on his farm. Should you consider it right if other people had gone in and shot and killed all the farm's cattle without paying him for the slaughter? No, you would not consider such a proposition fair or just. They would first have to pay the farmer for destroying his herds, so he could buy clothing and food for his family.

When we camped at this place where the dugouts were built, I remember that our mothers told us to hurry and go to sleep, or the hairy men would "get us." We knew they carried long sticks which made a great noise, with which they killed our buffalo. These "sticks" we called "mazawaken," or "holy iron." These people cared nothing for us, and it meant nothing to them to take our lives, even through starvation and cold. This was the beginning of our hatred for the white people. But still we did not kill them.

Source: Standing Bear, Luther. *My People the Sioux.* Boston: Houghton Mifflin, 1928, 67–68.

Wooden Leg, "A Tamed Old Man"

(1930)

Wooden Leg, a northern Cheyenne Indian, told his life story to Dr. Thomas Marquis, who published a biography of the warrior and judge in 1930. In the excerpt that follows, Wooden Leg discusses his life as a tamed old man and the role he played in implementing U.S. assimilation policies through his position as a tribal judge. The policy Wooden Leg discusses is the prohibition against multiple wives. Forcing the northern Cheyenne men to choose which one of their wives they would keep and which they would send away caused a great deal of animosity, and it is unlikely that without the acquiescence of respected men like Wooden

Leg the government would have achieved compliance. As this document illustrates, many Native Americans feared the potential consequences that resistance to assimilation policy could bring. Rather than risk the lives of their loved ones, most northern Cheyenne men agreed to send away one or more of their wives.

We had good medicine men in the old times. It may be they did not know as much about sickness as the white men doctors know, but our doctors knew more about Indians and how to talk to them. Our people then did not die young so much as they do now. In present times our Indian doctors are put into jail if they make medicine for our sick people. Whoever of us may become sick or injured must have the agency white man doctor or none at all. But he can not always come, and there are some who do not like him. I think it is best and right if each sick one be allowed to choose which doctor he wants. When Eddy was agent he let us keep our own old ways in all these matters. Our people liked him the best of all the agents we have had.

A policeman came to my place, one time, and told me that Eddy wanted to see me at the agency office. He did not say what was wanted. I thought: "What have I done?" I went right away. I never had been much about the agency, and I did not know Eddy very well. But the people all the time were saying he was a good man, so I was not afraid. When I got there, a strange white man was at the office. The interpreter told me this man was from Washington. Eddy and the other man talked to me a little while, about nothing of importance. Then Eddy said:

"We want you to be judge."

The Indian court was held at the agency. My home place was where it now is, over a divide from the agency and on the Tongue river side of the reservation. I accepted the appointment. I was paid ten dollars each month for going to the agency and attending to the court business one or two times each month. Not long after I had been serving as judge, Eddy called me into his office. He said:

"A letter from Washington tells me that Indians having two or more wives must send away all but one. You, as judge, must do your part toward seeing that the Cheyennes do this."

My heart jumped around in my breast when he told me this. He went on talking further about the matter, but I could not pay close attention to him. My thoughts were racing and whirling. When I could get them steady enough for speech, I said to him:

"I have two wives. You must get some other man to serve as judge."

He sat there and looked straight at me, saying nothing for a little while. Then he began talking again:

"Somebody else as judge would make you send away one of your wives. It would be better if you yourself managed it. All of the Indians in the United States are going to be compelled to put aside their extra wives. Washington has sent the order."

I decided to keep the office of judge. It appeared there was no getting around the order, so I made up my mind to be the first one to send away my extra wife, then I should talk to the other Cheyennes about the matter. I took plenty of time to think about how I should let my wives know about what was coming. Then I allowed the released one some further time to make arrangements as to where she should go. The first wife, the older one, had two daughters. The younger wife has no children. It seemed this younger one ought to leave me. I was in very low spirits. When a wagon came to get her and her personal packs, I went out and sat on a knoll about a hundred yards away. I could not speak to her. It seemed I could not move. All I could do was just sit there and look at the ground. She went back to her own people, on another reservation. A few years later I heard she was married to a good husband. Oh, how glad it made my heart to hear that!

I sent a policeman to tell all Cheyennes having more than one wife to come and see me. One of them came that same afternoon. After we had smoked together, I said:

"The agent tells me that I as the judge must order all Cheyennes to have only one wife. You must send away one of yours."

"I shall not obey that order," he answered me.

"Yes, it will have to be that way," I insisted.

"But who will be the father to the children?" he asked.

"I do not know, but I suppose that will be arranged."

"Wooden Leg, you are crazy. Eddy is crazy."

"No. If anybody is crazy, it is somebody in Washington. All of the Indians in the United States have this order. If we resist it, our policemen will put us into jail. If much trouble is made about it, soldiers may come to fight us. Whatever man does not put aside his extra wife may be the cause of the whole tribe being killed."

Many of our men were angered by the order. My heart sympathized with them, so I never became offended at the strong words they sometimes used. Finally, though, all of them sent away their extra wives. Afterward, from time to time, somebody would tell me about some man living a part of the time at one place with one wife and a part of the time at another place with another wife. I just listened, said nothing, and did nothing. These were old men, and I considered it enough of a change for

them that they be prevented from having two wives at the same place. At this present time I know of only one old Cheyenne who has two wives. They are extremely old, are sisters, and they have been his two wives for sixty or more years. He stays a part of the time with one of them and a part of the time with the other. The sister-wives visit each other, but they have different homes, several miles apart.

Source: Wooden Leg. *Wooden Leg: A Warrior Who Fought Custer.* Lincoln: University of Nebraska Press, 1931, 365–369.

Kay Bennett (Kaibah), "The White Man's Depression of 1930"

Kay Bennett, Kaibah, was a Navajo author, artist, and entrepreneur. In 1964, Bennett published her autobiography, from which the following narrative is excerpted. This passage describes the encounter of Kaibah, her family, and a white man in the early years of the Great Depression. It is an interesting encounter, one in which a poor white man seeks help from Native Americans to ease his hunger and the pain in his feet. The events described in this account were probably repeated many times on Indian reservations across the Southwest, as white inhabitants of the Great Plains made their way to California, hoping to find work. This document provides an interesting addendum to the story of westward migrations during the Great Depression—the role of Native Americans in helping people survive the difficult journey across the Southwest.

One day while Tesbah and Kaibah were playing in the sun with the baby, and Mother Chischillie was planning a stick game with the Yellow Hill woman for the following Sunday, Kaibah looked toward the highway and saw a man turn off and shuffle up the path toward them. He was a wretched

looking creature; dressed in rags. His toes stuck out of his shoes, which were held together with pieces of rope. His light brown hair hung below his battered hat, almost to his shoulders, and his face was half hidden by a curly brown beard matted with sweat and the dust of the road. As he approached Kaibah, she moved over behind her mother.

"Oh my!" said Mother Chischillie. "Who is that?"

"He looks worse than our old scarecrow," whispered Kaibah.

"That's a tramp," said Tesbah. "He looks sick."

They sat still, and waited to see what the tramp would do. Sensing their fright, the man stopped about ten yards away, and sat down on a rock. Mother Chischillie asked, "What do you want?"

The man, unable to understand Navajo spoke in English, but they could not understand a word he said.

Mother Chischillie waved her arm in the direction of the road, and said, "Go on your way!"

The tramp pointed to a bucket of water, and made motions at his mouth to show he wanted to drink.

Mother Chischillie said, "Kaibah, the man is thirsty. Get him a drink." Kaibah couldn't move.

Her mother shook her and repeated, "Give the man some water!"

Kaibah rose, walked slowly to the bucket, and filled a cup, then turned and approached him. Halfway she stopped, but was urged on by her mother and Tesbah. The man smiled, and held out his hand. Kaibah stretched her arm as far as possible, and when his fingers touched the cup she dropped it and ran. The tramp picked up the cup, drank the few drops that were left, and held it out for more.

Tesbah said, "He is very thirsty. Get him another cup." This time Kaibah gave him the cup without spilling the water. He drank quickly, and motioned for more. When he had finished drinking, he pointed at some meat hung to dry outside the Hogan, and pointed to his mouth as he pretended to chew. Mother Chischillie said, "He is hungry, Kaibah. Build a fire, and we will fix him food to eat, so he will not steal from us."

When the fire was going, Mother Chischillie started mixing dough for fried bread. "We will eat now, too," she said. "Give the man a watermelon to eat, while I make some fried bread and stew."

Kaibah walked over to a pile of melons and took one to the tramp. She was getting used to him sitting there. The tramp had taken off his shoes and was rubbing his feet. He smiled at her, as he tried to convince her that he was friendly.

"Give him this knife to cut the melon," said Tesbah, smiling, as she put the baby down to go chop some more wood for the fire. She walked over to the wood pile and started chopping.

The tramp, seeing what she was doing, walked over to her and motioned for her to give him the ax. Tesbah held it out to him, and he took it and started chopping. He chopped until Kaibah laid a bowl of stew and some fried bread on the rock for him to eat, then breathing heavily, he walked over and started eating fast.

Kaibah watched him, fascinated at the way he parted his beard and stuffed food into his mouth.

"Don't stare at him," scolded Mother Chischillie. "It is not polite to watch people when they are eating. Get a bag out of the storehouse, and we will give him some food to take with him." She put some bread, corn, boiled meat, raw meat, flour, and coffee in the sack while he ate. Tesbah went to her hogan, and took down an old pair of shoes, which were hanging from the wall. "I don't know who left these old shoes," she said, "but they are better than the ones he has. Maybe they will fit him." The tramp put the shoes on and hung the old ones over his shoulder. Mother Chischillie handed him the sack of food and motioned for him to go. The tramp, with tears in his eyes, bobbed his head and tried to thank them. He walked down the path to the highway, turned and waved, then trudged southward, and was soon lost to sight beyond the cross hills.

This was just one of many single tramps and wandering families who passed Mother Chischillie's hogan that winter and during the next year. People from the middle west were moving into California and the southwest where they believed they could find jobs. They walked, or drove broken down cars, loaded with all their possessions. Those who stopped at the hogan were fed and given a little food to carry away with them.

Kaisheen started work along the highway. He fashioned a drag from logs and pulled it with two wagon horses along the shoulders of the road until he had a pile of weeds; then set fire to them. From the top of the hills Kaibah could see the fires, and could tell Tesbah where her husband was working. Mother Chischillie warned Kaibah to keep the herd away from the highway, as there were many tramps on the road, and some of them might hurt her. "Always keep your pinto near you," she advised. "If anyone comes close to you, get on your horse's back and ride home for me."

The weather became colder, and some days Mother Chischillie would wrap rags around Kaibah's shoes to keep her feet warm. When the snow was heavy, Kaisheen took the sheep to graze, and Kaibah stayed at home, helping her mother with the wool, mending clothes, and learning to cook. Often her mother would stop to tell her of the old days, when the world was young, or of the days when the Spaniards were fighting the Navajo nation, or of the black days when the American soldiers and all the surrounding Indian tribes chased the Navajos through the mountains and killed nearly all of them. She told of the days when her own parents fled from the soldiers, and how they were captured, and made to walk with the remnants of the once powerful tribe to the prison camp at Fort Sumner. Sometimes she and Kaibah would play games, and she would tell her daughter the legends behind the games, and how they had been given to their ancestors by the gods.

This was the first time since her marriage as a young girl that Mother Chischillie had not had a hogan full of children to take care of. Now she could give her undivided attention to this child of her late years, and she talked on and on, as if she felt that this was her last chance to pass on all the knowledge acquired from her husband and her elders during her full life, and to make sure it would not be lost to her family when she died.

Source: Bennett, Kay. *Kaibah: Recollection of a Navajo Girlhood.* Los Angeles: Westernlore Press, 1964, 179–183.

Black Elk, "Across the Big Water"
(1932)

Black Elk was a famous medicine man of the Oglala Sioux. Born around 1864, he lived a highly adventurous life. He participated in two major events of the Indian Wars—the Battle of the Little Bighorn (1876) and the massacre at Wounded Knee (1890). During the 1880s, he traveled to Europe with Buffalo Bill's Wild West Show. The following excerpt from John G. Neihardt's Black Elk Speaks, *which is based on conversations between Black Elk and the author, describes the events surrounding Black Elk's decision to travel with Buffalo Bill, as well as his experiences meeting "Grandmother England," Queen Victoria, during her jubilee year.*

As I told you, it was in the summer of my twentieth year [1883] that I performed the ceremony of the elk. That fall, they say, the last of the bison herds was slaughtered by the Wasichus. I can remember when the bison were so many that they could not be counted, but more and more Wasichus came to kill them until there were only heaps of bones scattered where they used to be. The Wasichus did not

kill them to eat; they killed them for the metal that makes them crazy, and they took only the hides to sell. Sometimes they did not even take the hides, only the tongues; and I have heard that fire-boats came down the Missouri River loaded with dried bison tongues. You can see that the men who did this were crazy. Sometimes they did not even take the tongues; they just killed and killed because they liked to do that. When we hunted bison, we killed only what we needed. And when there was nothing left but heaps of bones, the Wasichus came and gathered up even the bones and sold them.

All our people now were settling down in square gray houses, scattered here and there across this hungry land, and around them the Wasichus had drawn a line to keep them in. The nation's hoop was broken, and there was no center any longer for the flowering tree. The people were in despair. They seemed heavy to me, heavy and dark; so heavy that it seemed they could not be lifted; so dark that they could not be made to see any more. Hunger was among us often now, for much of what the Great Father in Washington sent us must have been stolen by Wasichus who were crazy to get money. There were many lies, but we could not eat them. The forked tongue made promises.

I kept on curing the sick for three years more, and many came to me and were made over; but when I thought of my great vision, which was to save the nation's hoop and make the holy tree to bloom in the center of it, I felt like crying, for the sacred hoop was broken and scattered. The life of the people was in the hoop, and what are many little lives if the life of those lives be gone?

But late in my twenty-third summer [1886], it seemed that there was a little hope. There came to us some Wasichus who wanted a band of Ogalalas for a big show that the other Pahuska had. They told us this show would go across the big water to strange lands, and I thought I ought to go, because I might learn some secret of the Wasichu that would help my people somehow. In my great vision, when I stood at the center of the world, the two men from the east had brought me the daybreak-star herb and they had told me to drop it on the earth; and where it touched the ground it took root and bloomed four-rayed. It was the herb of understanding. Also, where the red man of my vision changed into a bison that rolled, the same herb grew and bloomed when the bison had vanished, and after that the people in my vision found the good red road again. Maybe if I could see the great world of the Wasichu, I could understand how to bring the sacred hoop together and make the tree to bloom again at the center of it.

I looked back on the past and recalled my people's old ways, but they were not living that way any more. They were traveling the black road, everybody for himself and with little rules of his own, as in my vision. I was in despair, and I even thought that if the Wasichus had a better way, then maybe my people should live that way. I know now that this was foolish, but I was young and in despair.

My relatives told me I should stay at home and go on curing people, but I would not listen to them.

The show people sent wagons from Rushville on the iron road to get us, and we were about a hundred men and women. Many of our people followed us half way to the iron road and there we camped and ate together. Afterward we left our people crying there, for we were going very far across the big water.

That evening where the big wagons were waiting for us on the iron road, we had a dance. Then we got into the wagons. When we started, it was dark, and thinking of my home and my people made me very sad. I wanted to get off and run back. But we went roaring all night long, and in the morning we ate at Long Pine. Then we started again and went roaring all day and came to a very big town in the evening.

Then we roared along all night again and came to a much bigger town. There we stayed all day and all night; and right there I could compare my people's ways with Wasichu ways, and this made me sadder than before. I wished and wished that I had not gone away from home.

Then we went roaring on again, and afterwhile we came to a still bigger town—a very big town. We walked through this town to the place where the show was. Some Pawnees and Omahas were there, and when they saw us they made war-cries and charged, couping us. They were doing this for fun and because they felt glad to see us. I was surprised at the big houses and so many people, and there were bright lights at night, so that you could not see the stars, and some of these lights, I heard, were made with the power of thunder.

We stayed there and made shows for many, many Wasichus all that winter. I liked the part of the show we made, but not the part the Wasichus made. Afterwhile I got used to being there, but I was like a man who had never had a vision. I felt dead and my people seemed lost and I thought I might never find them again. I did not see anything to help my people. I could see that the Wasichus did not care for each other the way our people did before the nation's hoop was broken. They would take everything from each other if they could, and so there were some who had more of everything than they could use, while crowds of people had nothing at all and maybe were starving. They had forgotten that the earth was their mother. This could not be better than the old ways of my people.

There was a prisoner's house on an island where the big water came up to the town, and we saw that one day. Men pointed guns at the prisoners and made them move around like animals in a cage. This made me feel very sad, because my people too were penned up in islands, and maybe that was the way the Wasichus were going to treat them.

In the spring it got warmer, but the Wasichus had even the grass penned up. We heard then that we were going to cross the big water to strange lands. Some of our people went home and wanted me to go with them, but I had not seen anything good for my people yet; maybe across the big water there was something to see, so I did not go home, although I was sick and in despair.

They put us all on a very big fire-boat, so big that when I first saw, I could hardly believe it; and when it sent forth a voice, I was frightened. There were other big fire-boats sending voices, and little ones too.

Afterwhile I could see nothing but water, water, water, and we did not seem to be going anywhere, just up and down; but we were told that we were going fast. If we were, I thought that we must drop off where the water ended; or maybe we might have to stop where the sky came down to the water. There was nothing but mist where the big town used to be and nothing but water all around.

We were all in despair now and many were feeling so sick that they began to sing their death songs.

When evening came, a big wind was roaring and the water thundered. We had things that were meant to be hung up while we slept in them. This I learned afterward. We did not know what to do with these, so we spread them out on the floor and lay down on them. The floor tipped in every direction, and this got worse and worse, so that we rolled from one side to the other and could not sleep. We were frightened, and now we were all very sick too. At first the Wasichus laughed at us; but very soon we could see that they were frightened too, because they were running around and were very much excited. Our women were crying and even some of the men cried, because it was

terrible and they could do nothing. Afterwhile the Wasichus came and gave us things to tie around us so that we could float. I did not put on the one they gave me. I did not want to float. Instead, I dressed for death, putting on my best clothes that I wore in the show, and then I sang my death song. Others dressed for death too, and sang, because if it was the end of our lives and we could do nothing, we wanted to die brave. We could not fight this that was going to kill us, but we could die so that our spirit relatives would not be ashamed of us. Everything we had eaten came right up, and then it kept on trying to come up when there was nothing there.

We did not sleep at all, and in the morning the water looked like mountains, but the wind was not so strong. Some of the bison and elk that we had with us for the show died that day, and the Wasichus threw them in the water. When I saw the poor bison thrown over, I felt like crying, because I thought right there they were throwing part of the power of my people away.

After we had been on the fire-boat a long while, we could see many houses and then many other fire-boats tied close together along the bank. We thought now we could get off very soon, but we could not. There was a little fire-boat that had come through the gate of waters and it stopped beside us, and the people on it looked at everything on our fire-boat before we could get off. We went very slowly nearly all day, I think, and afterwhile we came to where there were many, many houses close together, and more fire-boats than could be counted. These houses were different from what we had seen before. The Wasichus kept us on the fire-boat all night and then they unloaded us, and took us to a place where the show was going to be. The name of this very big town was London. We were on land now, but we still felt dizzy as though we were still on water, and at first it was hard to walk.

We stayed in this place six moons; and many, many people came to see the show.

One day we were told that Majesty was coming. I did not know what that was at first, but I learned afterward. It was Grandmother England [Queen Victoria], who owned Grandmother's Land where we lived awhile after the Wasichus murdered Crazy Horse.

She came to the show in a big shining wagon, and there were soldiers on both sides of her, and many other shining wagons came too. That day other people could not come to the show—just Grandmother England and some people who came with her.

Sometimes we had to shoot in the show, but this time we did not shoot at all. We danced and sang, and I was one of the dancers chosen to do this for the Grandmother, because I was young and limber then and could dance many ways. We stood right in front of Grandmother England. She was little but fat and we liked her, because she was good to us. After we had danced, she spoke to us. She said something like this: "I am sixty-seven years old. All over the world I have seen all kinds of people; but to-day I have seen the best-looking people I know. If you belonged to me, I would not let them take you around in a show like this." She said other good things too, and then she said we must come to see her, because she had come to see us. She shook hands with all of us. Her hand was very little and soft. We gave a big cheer for her, and then the shining wagons came in and she got into one of them and they all went away.

In about a half-moon after that we went to see the Grandmother. They put us in some of those shining wagons and took us to a very beautiful place where there was a very big house with sharp, pointed towers on it. There were many seats built high in a circle, and these were just full of Wasichus who were all pounding their heels and yelling: "Jubilee! Jubilee! Jubilee!" I never heard what this meant.

They put us together in a certain place at the bottom of the seats. First there appeared a beautiful black wagon with two black horses, and it went all around the show place. I heard that the Grandmother's grandson, a little boy, was in that wagon. Next came a beautiful black wagon with four gray horses. On each of the two right-hand horses there was a rider, and a man walked, holding the front left-hand horse. I heard that some of Grandmother's relatives were in this wagon. Next came eight buckskin horses, two by two, pulling a shining black wagon. There was a rider on each right-hand horse and a man walked, holding the front left-hand horse. There were soldiers, with bayonets, facing outward all around this wagon. Now all the people in the seats were roaring and yelling "Jubilee!" and "Victoria!" Then we saw Grandmother England again. She was sitting in the back of the wagon and two women sat in the front, facing her. Her dress was all shining and her hat was all shining and her wagon was all shining and so were the horses. She looked like a fire coming.

Afterward I heard that there was yellow and white metal all over the horses and the wagon.

When she came to where we were, her wagon stopped and she stood up. Then all those people stood up and roared and bowed to her; but she bowed to us. We sent up a great cry and our women made the tremolo. The people in the crowd were so excited that we heard some of them got sick and fell over. Then when it was quiet, we sang a song to the Grandmother.

That was a very happy time.

We liked Grandmother England, because we could see that she was a fine woman, and she was good to us. Maybe if she had been our Grandmother, it would have been better for our people.

Source: Reprinted by permission from *Black Elk Speaks: Being the Life Story of a Holy Man of the Oglala Sioux, The Premier Edition* by John G. Neihardt, the State University of New York Press © 2008, State University of New York. All rights reserved.

Luther Standing Bear, "What the Indian Means to America"
(1933)

Luther Standing Bear was a businessman, performer, actor, and Native American rights activist during a lifetime in which his people, the Lakota Nation, experienced many changes to their way of life. Standing Bear was educated at the Carlisle Indian School in Pennsylvania, toured with Buffalo Bill Cody and the Wild West Show, and later moved to Hollywood and starred in many motion pictures; however, he also wrote books that called attention to the experiences of his people living on reservations in North and South Dakota. In the following excerpt from his book, Land of the Spotted Eagle, *Standing Bear discusses the significance of Native Americans, including what he perceived to be their value and cultural contributions to the larger American society.*

The feathered and blanketed figure of the American Indian has come to symbolize the American continent. He is the man who through centuries has been moulded and sculpted by the same hand that shaped its mountains, forests, and plains, and marked the course of its rivers.

The American Indian is of the soil, whether it be the region of forests, plains, pueblos, or mesas. He fits into the landscape, for the hand that fashioned the continent also fashioned the man for his surroundings. He once grew as naturally as the wild sunflowers; he belongs just as the buffalo belonged.

With a physique that fitted, the man developed fitting skills—crafts which today are called American. And the body had a soul, also formed and moulded by the same master hand of harmony. Out of the Indian approach to existence there came a great freedom—an intense and absorbing love for nature; a respect for life; enriching faith in a Supreme Power; and principles of truth, honesty, generosity, equity, and brotherhood as a guide to mundane relations.

Becoming possessed of a fitting philosophy and art, it was by them that native man perpetuated his identity; stamped it into the history and soul of this country—made land and man one.

By living—struggling, losing, meditating, imbibing, aspiring, achieving—he wrote himself into inerasable evidence—an evidence that can be and often has been ignored, but never totally destroyed. Living—and all the intangible forces that constitute that phenomenon—are brought into being by Spirit, that which no man can alter. Only the hand of the Supreme Power can transform man; only Wakan Tanka can transform the Indian. But of such deep and infinite graces finite man has little comprehension. He has, therefore, no weapons with which to slay the unassailable. He can only foolishly trample.

The white man does not understand the Indian for the reason that he does not understand America. He is too far removed from its formative processes. The roots of the tree of his life have not yet grasped the rock and soil. The white man is still troubled with primitive fears; he still has in his consciousness the perils of this frontier continent, some of its vastnesses not yet having yielded to his questing footsteps and inquiring eyes. He shudders still with the memory of the loss of his forefathers upon its scorching deserts and forbidding mountain-tops. The man from Europe is still a foreigner and an alien. And he still hates the man who questioned his path across the continent.

But in the Indian the spirit of the land is still vested; it will be until other men are able to divine and meet its rhythm. Men must be born and reborn to belong. Their bodies must be formed of the dust of their forefathers' bones.

The attempted transformation of the Indian by the white man and the chaos that has resulted are but the fruits of the white man's disobedience of a fundamental and spiritual law. The pressure that has been brought to bear upon the native people, since the cessation of armed conflict, in the attempt to force conformity of custom and habit has caused a reaction more destructive than war, and the injury has not only affected the Indian, but has extended to the white population as well. Tyranny, stupidity, and lack of vision have brought about the situation now alluded to as the "Indian Problem."

There is, I insist, no Indian problem as created by the Indian himself. Every problem that exists today in regard to the native population is due to the white man's cast of mind, which is unable, at least reluctant, to seek understanding and achieve adjustment in a new and a significant environment into which it has so recently come.

The white man excused his presence here by saying that he had been guided by the will of his God; and in so saying absolved himself of all responsibility for his appearance in a land occupied by other men.

Then, too, his law was a written law; his divine decalogue reposed in a book. And what better proof that his advent into this country and his subsequent acts were the result of divine will! He brought the Word! There ensued a blind worship of written history, of books, of the written word, that has denuded the spoken word of its power and sacredness. The written word became established as a criterion of the superior man—a symbol of emotional fineness. The man who could write his name on a piece of paper, whether or not he possessed the spiritual fineness to honor those words in speech, was by some miraculous formula a more highly developed and sensitized person than the one who had never had a pen in hand, but whose spoken word was inviolable and whose sense of honor and truth was paramount. With false reasoning was the quality of human character measured by man's ability to make with an implement a mark upon paper. But granting this mode of reasoning be correct and just, then where are to be placed the thousands of illiterate whites who are unable to read and write? Are they, too, "savages"? Is not humanness a matter of heart and mind, and is it not evident in the form of relationship with men? Is not kindness more powerful than arrogance; and truth more powerful than the sword?

True, the white man brought great change. But the varied fruits of his civilization, though highly colored and inviting, are sickening and deadening. And if it be the part of civilization to maim, rob, and thwart, then what is progress?

I am going to venture that the man who sat on the ground in his tipi meditating on life and its meaning, accepting the kinship of all creatures, and acknowledging unity with the universe of things was infusing into his being the true essence of civilization. And when native man left off this form of development, his humanization was retarded in growth.

Another most powerful agent that gave native man promise of developing into a true human was the responsibility accepted by parenthood. Mating among Lakotas was motivated, of course, by the same laws of attraction that motivate all beings; however, considerable thought was given by parents of both boy and girl to the choosing of mates. And a still greater advantage accrued to the race by the law of self-mastery which the young couple voluntarily placed upon themselves as soon as they discovered they were to become parents. Immediately, and for some time after, the sole thought of the parents was in preparing the child for life. And true civilization lies in the dominance of self and not in the dominance of other men.

How far this idea would have gone in carrying my people upward and toward a better plane of existence, or how much of an influence it was in the development of their spiritual being, it is not possible to say. But it had its promises. And it cannot be gainsaid that the man who is rising to a higher estate is the man who is putting into his being the essence of humanism. It is self-effort that develops, and by this token the greatest factor today in dehumanizing races is the manner in which the machine is used—the product of one man's brain doing the work for another. The hand is the tool that has built man's mind; it, too, can refine it.

THE SAVAGE

After subjugation, after dispossession, there was cast the last abuse upon the people who so entirely resented their wrongs and punishments, and that was the stamping and the labeling of them as savages. To make this label stick has been the task of the white race and the greatest salve that it has been able to apply to its sore and troubled conscience now hardened through the habitual practice of injustice.

But all the years of calling the Indian a savage have never made him one; all the denial of his virtues has never taken them from him; and the very resistance he has made to save the things inalienably his has been his saving strength—that which will stand him in need when justice does make its belated appearance and he undertakes rehabilitation.

All sorts of feeble excuses are heard for the continued subjection of the Indian. One of the most common is that he is not yet ready to accept the society of the white man—that he is not yet ready to mingle as a social entity.

This, I maintain, is beside the question. The matter is not one of making over the external Indian into the likeness of the white race—a process detrimental to both races. Who can say that the white man's way is better for the Indian? Where resides the human judgment with the competence to weigh and value Indian ideals and spiritual concepts; or substitute for them other values?

Then, has the white man's social order been so harmonious and ideal as to merit the respect of the Indian, and for that matter the thinking class of the white race? Is it wise to urge upon the Indian a foreign social form? Let none but the Indian answer!

Rather, let the white brother face about and cast his mental eye upon a new angle of vision. Let him look upon the Indian world as a human world; then let him see to it that human rights be accorded to the Indians.

And this for the purpose of retaining for his own order of society a measure of humanity.

THE INDIAN SCHOOL OF THOUGHT

I say again that Indians should teach Indians; that Indians should serve Indians, especially on reservations where the older people remain. There is a definite need of the old for the care and sympathy of the young and they are today perishing for the joys that naturally belong to old Indian people. Old Indians are very close to their progeny. It was their delightful duty to care for and instruct the very young, while in turn they looked forward to being cared for by sons and daughters. These were the privileges and blessings of old age.

Many of the grievances of the old Indian, and his disagreements with the young, find root in the far-removed boarding school which sometimes takes the little ones at a very tender age. More than one tragedy has resulted when a young boy or girl has returned home again almost an utter stranger. I have seen these happenings with my own eyes and I know they can cause naught but suffering. The old Indian cannot, even if he wished, reconcile himself to an institution that alienates his young. And there is something evil in a system that brings about an unnatural reaction to life; when it makes young hearts callous and unheedful of the needs and joys of the old.

The old people do not speak English and they never will be English-speaking. To place upon such people the burden of understanding and functioning through an office bound up with the routine and red tape of the usual Government office is silly and futile, and every week or so I receive letters from the reservation evidencing this fact. The Indian's natural method of settling questions is by council and conference. From time immemorial, for every project affecting their material, social, and spiritual lives, the people have met together to "talk things over."

To the end that young Indians will be able to appreciate both their traditional life and modern life they should be doubly educated. Without forsaking reverence for their ancestral teachings, they can be trained to take up modern duties that relate to tribal and reservation life. And there is no problem of reservation importance but can be solved by the joint efforts of the old and the young Indians.

There certainly can be no doubt in the public mind today as to the capacity of the younger Indians in taking on white modes and manners. For many years, and particularly since the days of

General Pratt, the young Indian has been proving his efficiency when entering the fields of white man's endeavor and has done well in copying and acquiring the ways of the white man.

The Indian liked the white man's horse and straightway became an expert horseman; he threw away his age-old weapons, the bow and arrow, and matched the white man's skill with gun and pistol; in the field of sports—games of strength and skill—the Indian enters with no shame in comparison; the white man's beads the Indian woman took, developed a technique and an art distinctly her own with no competitor in design; and in the white man's technique of song and dance the Indian has made himself a creditable exponent.

However, despite the fact that Indian schools have been established over several generations, there is a dearth of Indians in the professions. It is most noticeable on the reservations where the numerous positions of consequence are held by white employees instead of trained Indians. For instance, why are not the stores, post-offices, and Government office jobs on the Sioux Reservation held by trained Indians? Why cannot Sioux be reservation nurses and doctors; and road-builders too? Much road work goes on every summer, but the complaint is constant that it is always done by white workmen, and in such manner as to necessitate its being done again in a short time. Were these numerous positions turned over to trained Indians, the white population would soon find reservation life less attractive and less lucrative.

With school facilities already fairly well established and the capability of the Indian unquestioned, every reservation could well be supplied with Indian doctors, nurses, engineers, road- and bridge-builders, draughtsmen, architects, dentists, lawyers, teachers, and instructors in tribal lore, legends, orations, song, dance, and ceremonial ritual. The Indian, by the very sense of duty, should become his own historian, giving his account of the race—fairer and fewer accounts of the wars and more of state-craft, legends, languages, oratory, and philosophical conceptions. No longer should the Indian be dehumanized in order to make material for lurid and cheap fiction to embellish street stands. Rather, a fair and correct history of the native American should be incorporated in the curriculum of the public school.

Caucasian youth is fed, and rightly so, on the feats and exploits of their old-world heroes, their revolutionary forefathers, their adventurous pioneer trailblazers, and in our Southwest through pageants, fiestas, and holidays the days of the Spanish *conquistador* is kept alive.

But Indian youth! They, too, have fine pages in their past history; they, too, have patriots and heroes. And it is not fair to rob Indian youth of their history, the stories of their patriots, which, if impartially written, would fill them with pride and dignity. Therefore, give back to Indian youth all, everything in their heritage that belongs to them and augment it with the best in the modern schools. I repeat, doubly educate the Indian boy and girl.

What a contrast this would make in comparison with the present unhealthy, demoralized place the reservation is today, where the old are poorly fed, shabbily clothed, divested of pride and incentive; and where the young are unfitted for tribal life and untrained for the world of white man's affairs except to hold an occasional job!

Why not a school of Indian thought, built on the Indian pattern and conducted by Indian instructors? Why not a school of tribal art?

Why should not America be cognizant of itself; aware of its identity? In short, why should not America be preserved?

There were ideals and practices in the life of my ancestors that have not been improved upon by the present-day civilization; there were in our culture elements of benefit; and there were influences that would broaden any life. But that almost an entire public needs to be enlightened as to this fact need not be discouraging. For many centuries the human mind labored under the delusion that the world was flat; and thousands of men have believed that the heavens were supported by the strength of an Atlas. The human mind is not yet free from fallacious reasoning; it is not yet an open mind and its deepest recesses are not yet swept free of errors.

But it is now time for a destructive order to be reversed, and it is well to inform other races that the aboriginal culture of America was not devoid of beauty. Furthermore, in denying the Indian his ancestral rights and heritages the white race is but robbing itself. But America can be revived, rejuvenated, by recognizing a native school of thought. The Indian can save America.

THE LIVING SPIRIT OF THE INDIAN—HIS ART

The spiritual health and existence of the Indian was maintained by song, magic, ritual, dance, symbolism, oratory (or council), design, handicraft, and folk-story.

Manifestly, to check or thwart this expression is to bring about spiritual decline. And it is in this condition of decline that the Indian people are today. There is but a feeble effort among the Sioux to keep alive their traditional songs and dances, while among other tribes there is but a half-hearted attempt to offset the influence of the Government school and at the same time recover from the crushing and stifling regime of the Indian Bureau.

One has but to speak of Indian verse to receive uncomprehending and unbelieving glances. Yet the Indian loved verse and into this mode of expression went his deepest feelings. Only a few ardent and advanced students seem interested; nevertheless, they have given in book form enough Indian translations to set forth the character and quality of Indian verse.

Oratory receives a little better understanding on the part of the white public, owing to the fact that oratorical compilations include those of Indian orators.

Hard as it seemingly is for the white man's ear to sense the differences, Indian songs are as varied as the many emotions which inspire them, for no two of them are alike. For instance, the Song of Victory is spirited and the notes high and remindful of an unrestrained hunter or warrior riding exultantly over the prairies. On the other hand, the song of the *Cano unye* is solemn and full of urge, for it is meant to inspire the young men to deeds of valor. Then there are the songs of death and the spiritual songs which are connected with the ceremony of initiation. These are full of the spirit of praise and worship, and so strong are some of these invocations that the very air seems as if surcharged with the presence of the Big Holy.

The Indian loved to worship. From birth to death he revered his surroundings. He considered himself born in the luxurious lap of Mother Earth and no place was to him humble. There was nothing between him and the Big Holy. The contact was immediate and personal, and the blessings of Wakan Tanka flowed over the Indian like rain showered from the sky. Wakan Tanka was not aloof, apart, and ever seeking to quell evil forces. He did not punish the animals and the birds, and likewise he did not punish man. He was not a punishing God. For there was never a question as to the supremacy of an evil power over and above the power of Good. There was but one ruling power, and that was *Good*.

Of course, none but an adoring one could dance for days with his face to the sacred sun, and that time is all but done. We cannot have back the days of the buffalo and beaver; we cannot win back our clean blood-stream and superb health, and we can never again expect that beautiful *rapport* we once had with Nature. The springs and lakes have dried and the mountains are bare of forests. The plow has changed the face of the world. Wiwila is dead! No more may we heal our sick and comfort our dying with a strength founded on faith, for even the animals now fear us, and fear supplants faith.

And the Indian wants to dance! It is his way of expressing devotion, of communing with unseen power, and in keeping his tribal identity. When the Lakota heart was filled with high emotion, he danced. When he felt the benediction of the warming rays of the sun, he danced. When his blood ran hot with success of the hunt or chase, he danced. When his heart was filled with pity for the orphan, the lonely father, or bereaved mother, he danced. All the joys and exaltations of life, all his gratefulness and thankfulness, all his acknowledgments of the mysterious power that guided life, and all his aspirations for a better life, culminated in one great dance—the Sun Dance.

Today we see our young people dancing together the silly jazz—dances that add nothing to the beauty and fineness of our lives and certainly nothing to our history, while the dances that record the life annals of a people die. It is the American Indian who contributes to this country its true folk-dancing, growing, as we did, out of the soil. The dance is far older than his legends, songs, or philosophy.

Did dancing mean much to the white people they would better understand ours? Yet at the same time there is no attraction that brings people from such distances as a certain tribal dance, for the reason that the white mind senses its mystery, for even the white man's inmost feelings are unconsciously stirred by the beat of the tomtom. They are heartbeats, and once all men danced to its rhythm.

When the Indian has forgotten the music of his forefathers, when the sound of the tomtom is no more, when noisy jazz has drowned the melody of the flute, he will be a dead Indian. When the memory of his heroes are no longer told in story, and he forsakes the beautiful white buckskin for factory shoddy, he will be dead. When from him has been taken all that is his, all that he has visioned in nature, all that has come to him from infinite sources, he then, truly, will be a dead Indian. His spirit will be gone, and though he walk crowded streets, he will, in truth, be—*dead!*

But all this must not perish; it must live, to the end that America shall be educated no longer to regard native production of whatever tribe—folk-story, basketry, pottery, dance, song, poetry—as curios, and native artists as curiosities. For who but the man indigenous to the soil could produce its song, story, and folk-tale; who but the man who loved the dust beneath his feet could shape it and put it into undying, ceramic form; who but he who loved the reeds that grew beside still waters, and the damp roots of shrub and tree, could save it from seasonal death, and with almost superhuman patience weave it into enduring objects of beauty—into timeless art!

Regarding the "civilization" that has been thrust upon me since the days of reservation, it has not added one whit to my sense of justice; to my reverence for the rights of life; to my love for truth, honesty, and generosity; nor to my faith in Wakan Tanka—God of the Lakotas. For after all the great religions have been preached and expounded, or have been revealed by brilliant scholars, or have been written in books and embellished in fine language with finer covers, man—all man—is still confronted with the Great Mystery.

So if today I had a young mind to direct, to start on the journey of life, and I was faced with the duty of choosing between the natural way of my forefathers and that of the white man's present way of civilization, I would, for its welfare, unhesitatingly set that child's feet in the path of my forefathers. I would raise him to be an Indian!

Source: Reprinted from *Land of the Spotted Eagle* by Luther Standing Bear by permission of the University of Nebraska Press. Copyright 1933 by Luther Standing Bear. Copyright 1960 by May Jones.

Petition from Pine Ridge Sioux to Eleanor Roosevelt
(1934)

President Franklin Delano Roosevelt's wife, Eleanor, was a first lady unlike any other the United States had seen up to that time. Her husband was stricken by polio and used a wheelchair, a fact unknown to many Americans. As such, he relied on his wife to travel the country and report back to him on the issues facing Americans from all across the country.

Part of the Indian New Deal of the 1930s was a restructuring of American Indian education on reservations, proposed by John Collier, Roosevelt's commissioner of Indian Affairs. The Pine Ridge Sioux sent the following petition to Eleanor Roosevelt, asking her to intervene on their behalf regarding Collier's education plans.

Dear Mrs. Roosevelt,

We, the undersigned Indians of the Pine Ridge Reservation, write to you as one parent to another. We know you [are] a good mother who has raise[d] your children as good Christian men and women and we want to do the same with our children.

Mr. Collier, the Commissioner of Indian Affairs has started a program that he calls the FIVE POINT educational plan, which means the end of our mission boarding schools. The missionaries have been our friends for years and have helped us in every way and now Mr. Collier who doesn't know the good the Mission schools have done like we do, is going to stop them from taking our children. It is our money that has helped to pay for these Mission Schools and they have not [cost] the Government a cent.

The United States Supreme Court in the Quick Bear case said that we had a right to use our money to have our children receive religious education at our own cost, and that to prevent us from doing so would prohibit the free exercise of religion, which is one of the most precious rights of the American citizen.

We know that you would not want some man who does not know your family affairs like you do to stop you from sending your children to a religious school at your own expense if you wanted to do so.

We Indians have read and heard about you and we hope our cry to you will be heard. We know how busy your husband is and how little time he can give to us poor Indians but won't you please see him and help us. As a mother you know that our children are more precious to us than anything else. Please help us, Mrs. Roosevelt.

[Attached to the letter were hundreds of Indian names.]

Source: Red Cloud Indian School Records. Department of Special Collections and University Archives, Marquette University Libraries.

Eva Spicer Whitetree Nichols Interview
(April 21, 1937)

Eva Spicer Whitetree Nichols, a Seneca Indian, was born in Missouri in 1869. Her parents migrated to Indian Territory (Oklahoma) at an unknown date. In the following excerpt from an interview conducted with Nichols under the auspices of the Federal Writer's Project in 1937, she describes significant events and activities from her life, including annual rituals and everyday activities, such as entertainment and home economy.

Eva Spicer Whitetree Nichols (Seneca Indian) was born in 1869 when the papaws were ripe near Tiff

City, Missouri. Her parents were Dan and Melinda Spicer (Senecas). I do not know where or when they were born or when or how they came to Indian Territory and the only clue I have is a remark made by my grandmother who said one day that they traveled many days in a bark canoe which had a top or cover supported by poles.

MEMORIES OF CHILDHOOD

I remember going with my parents to Council Hollow in the month of December when the snow was thick on the ground to attend the White Dog Dance and also the Shuck Dance. We camped in tents with great fires built in front of the tents and in the long log house where the dance was held. This building was roofed and had holes through the roof for the smoke to go through. The best white dog that could be found was killed and fastened to a pole or tree on a high spot and for three days, day and night, dances were held in the long house, both men and women taking part in the dance. The fourth day the Shuck Dance was held. At this the men, I remember, wore braids of shucks around their heads and carried a branch with many shucks fastened to it, which they used in some gestures. This ceremony, I think, was giving thanks.

Medicine Men

Our medicine was herbs and barks prepared for the various ills. Wild cherry bark was boiled and the syrup was taken and maple syrup from the maple tree added; this was boiled together down and used for colds. The wild plum bark was used the same way and also used for colds. Each spring and fall the medicine Man would come to each home and go from room to room of the house shaking his turtle rattle and repeating cantations (*sic*) to drive out sickness and disease from that home. You could hear him coming for a mile through the woods as he wore sleigh bells fastened around his lower leg. I was afraid of him, and I remember him called Wooden Face and that his face was ugly.

Clothes

Many of the men wore, at my earliest recollection, the breech cloth and leggings, some fringed and some trimmed with a sort of ribbon fringe. Some wore buckskin suits and some of the women's dresses were of buckskin, mostly made one piece.

Wild Game

Wild game was plentiful. For meat we had the deer, wild hog, coon, wild turkey, and prairie chicken. Squirrels and quails were plentiful, but seldom used for food. The hunter who killed the wild hog had to be careful to kill the animal for if only wounded he would attack and fight. The men used a rifle that carried a round bullet and used a rod to place it some way. When a mess of fish was wanted, the men cut a long grape vine, and men, taking hold of each end, waded down the stream with it and this held the fish and when they reached the end of pool or body of water, they chose the fish that they wanted and threw the rest back into the stream. So we only took what we wanted for food and did not destroy.

Crops

My father raised much Indian corn, which is different from the corn of today, as the grain is softer and flatter at the end. This was white, some little red, some spotted and some blue. The blue was used to make hominy. The white was carried to the mill and made into meal. These mills were located on some stream and run by the flowing water. Buckwheat was raised and this insured that the bees would make us plenty of honey for the winter. The wheat was cut by hand and heaped on an open clean spot and flailed by hand with long sticks. These crops together with what other things we raised in smaller quantities, and the wild fruits and berries and so forth went far toward supplying our winter supply. We did not can things in those days but dried most things that we put away.

Twice a year my father would take the team of ponies and go to Neosho, Missouri, and bring home a supply of sugar, coffee, and the things that we could not prepare, together with what clothing, ammunition, and things needed. Money for these supplies came mostly through payments which, as I remember were about $30.00 twice a year.

Oxen

We had four yoke of oxen which were used to farm but seldom used for driving any distance as they traveled so slow and were harder than the ponies to drive. However, I remember once, my father did drive them and was returning from Fort Scott, and, when they neared Spring River near Baxter Springs, they smelled the water so they had to unhitch them and let them go to the river to drink; for when they were thirsty and smelled water, they would go straight to it regardless of ditches or anything and would possibly turn the wagon over, so they just unhitched and let them go and after they drank brought them back and rehitched them and came on home.

Plaster

Once my father, needing plaster for the home, built a big fire with a heap of logs and on this he piled large limestone rocks and kept this fire going till the rocks cracked and became soft and after they had been beaten to a pulp, he added sand that had been brought from the river, mixed with water and added some hog hair and the plaster was ready for use.

Pocket Books

Have you ever noticed that the pocket books that the ladies carry have a fringe and sometimes the end of the fringe is tipped with jingly things. Why this, you say. If anyone picks up your pocket book, it makes noise, and you hear it.

Amusements

Besides our various dances, Games of Cross Stick Ball were played. Each player had a certain mark or color so in the playing they could be distinguished and the object of the game was to put the ball through the goal at the opposite end from where they started. The players were divided into two sides facing their goal. Nine players on each side. Indian football was played by both the men and women, the men playing against the women.

But much of our amusement came from horse racing. We had a track at the old stomp ground on the Cowskin (Elk) River. The peach-seed game was always looked forward to each summer and often lasted a week. The tribe is divided into two clans. My father belonged to the Wolf Clan and

took the boys with him on the south side. My mother was a Turtle and the girls went with her on the north side. The seeds were filed smooth and one side is left the light natural color and the other side is stained brown and in the game these seeds are thrown like dice. (Here Mrs. Nichols requested that I let another member of her tribe describe the game to me.) I attended school at the Wyandotte Mission.

Marriage

In May 1883, I married Frank Whitetree, a Shawnee (he was called an Expense Shawnee). We were married by Dr. Cook, Superintendent at the Wyandotte Mission, and went to live near the mouth of Cowskin River. He was a musician and taught the Splitlog Band. These players had the same instruments that are used today. We had three children, Susie, Scott, and Frank Jr. My husband died January 16, 1902, and I left the place and went to live at my father's. We had always chilled on the River. One June 17, 1907, I married Alex Nichols, who lived just [south] of Turkeyford, and had one child, Nettie, by him. His chief interest was horse racing and threshing machines. He was often away from home with his horses at different places and I helped him, and I think today I could order any part of a threshing machine from a catalogue. He passed on a few years ago and today I live with my daughter, Nettie, who is a student at the Business College here.

Old Landmarks

The old log long house was destroyed when some white people bought the place. There is nothing left to mark the site; also the old race track and stomp ground are now in cultivation. About old cemeteries, there was one on Cowskin on the Old Snow Young, later John Snow, place and this I think contains no markers. However, I would ask Mrs. Logan as her husband is buried there. My parents are buried at the mouth of Sycamore on the George Spicer place. I haven't been there for a long time. The old Wyandotte Cemetery was west of the present town and near the site of the old Agency and Mission. I am told that a man by the name of Hollis bought this land and had all the markers and stones piled up, and ploughed it up, saying he didn't have any use for it.

Source: Eva Spicer Whitetree Nichols interviewed by Nannie Lee Burns. "Story of Eva Spicer Whitetree Nichols." April 21, 1937. Indian Pioneer Papers, Vol. 67. Western History Collections, University of Oklahoma, Norman. http://digital.libraries.ou.edu/whc/pioneer/paper.asp?pID=4476&vID=67.

Esther Naktewa, Letter to Santa Claus
(1937)

American Indian boarding schools had enduring effects on their pupils. Although there are many stories about the lengths teachers went to rid their pupils of any vestiges of their traditional culture and heritage, less is known about pupils who were able to adjust. Esther Naktewa was a Zuni student, and the following letter illustrates the effects of the education and Christianity she received.

I am a Zuni Indian girl and go to St. Anthony Indian School; my name is Esther. I thought it would please you if I would tell you about our Merry Christmas at the Mission. The celebration in church is very solemn and a large crowd of Indians come for midnight Mass. The church is decorated very beautifully. The altar is surrounded by stately cedar trees and the lights shining thru the branches looks like glittering stars. The crib is very pretty and many people pray devoutly before the Holy Infant. The boys and girls who have gone to St. Anthony's School receive Holy Communion with us children. The pupils of our class are the choir members and are all happy to sing the "Guardian Angel Mass" which we have practiced for this occasion. We children and all the Zuni people like the Christmas celebration in church very much.

Then, dear Santa Claus, Christmas in school is certainly a surprise for us children. We often wonder when you come to our school. Of course, when we see the shades pulled down then we surmise that you must have been there. We are always very anxious to find out what you have brought to us. Some of the boys try to peep thru the transom before we are allowed to enter the classroom. Sister opens the door [everybody] looks with big eyes at the desk and begins to smile and joyously shouts, "Santa has been here," seeing a pretty handkerchief or a toy, an apple and an orange you so kindly have brought to each one of us. Yes, dear Santa, we are always very happy on Christmas. But, you should see the little ones. They think themselves little queens and kings with their presents from you.

Dear Santa Claus, I would like to have a merry Christmas for my father and mother, my brothers and sisters. My brother Walter will get a Christmas tree from the woods; and when at night everybody is asleep I shall put the tree in the room. Sister will let us make Christmas decorations from tinfoil during our industrial period at school. But I would like to have some presents to put on the table. May I kindly ask you for a handkerchief for my parents? My brother Willie sings in the choir and Sister says that he has a sweet voice. He will be happy with a mouth harp. Aggie has big black eyes and I think she would like a pink dress. Emilia is the baby girl and she would sing a Zuni lullabye to a little doll. Harold is my baby brother and he likes to play with a little dog.

Dear Santa, I know that you are very busy right now reading the letters from boys and girls the world over. But I assure you that I very gratefully shall appreciate your kindness in helping me to make a "Merry Christmas" to my dear ones.

Your Indian friend,
Esther Naktewa

Source: Bureau of Catholic Indian Mission Records. Department of Special Collections and University Archives, Marquette University Libraries.

Mary Free, "Life of a Cherokee Woman"
(1937)

In the 1930s, researchers undertook the Indian-Pioneer History Project for Oklahoma as part of the Works Progress Administration. At this time, a number of Native Americans were interviewed for information about their history and culture. John Daugherty interviewed Mary Free of Sulphur, Oklahoma, in May 1937. The following excerpt from that interview describes what it was like growing up in Indian Territory during the Civil War. Her father and brother were both active in the Union Army.

My father was Jim Gunter and my mother was Margaret Banister Gunter. They were born in North Carolina (dates unknown). They came to the territory in 1838 with the Indians. Many of the Indians became so weary and their supplies and goods became such a burden to them that they threw them into the Mississippi river as they crossed it.

Father was a stockman, until mother became ill, then they traveled all over the northeastern part of Indian Territory and parts of Arkansas and Missouri. I was born on the Verdigris River near Verdigris Hill, December 28, 1847. I had six brothers and sisters. I didn't go to school, because father moved so many times for mother's health, that I didn't have a chance.

We had no needles nor pins in those days. We sewed with a buffalo needle which was made from a buffalo horn. It was sharpened and a hole punched in one end for the eye. During the war one of the soldiers dropped a needle while at our house, and I found it after they were gone. I prized that above everything and guarded it carefully so that it should not be lost. We made our fires on a skillet lid by pouring a small amount of gunpowder on the lid. A piece of cotton was placed near the powder and we would strike a flint rock with steel, and the spark from this would ignite the powder, and the cotton would be set from this. We moved from Grand Prairie to a farm east of Ft. Smith, about the time the Civil War began. Mother died here, and when the war began, father was a scout and was gone from home much of the time. My oldest brother was captain in the Federal Army and I was the oldest child at home. We had plenty of food. We killed a hog and dressed it one day. We had plenty of honey, and our cellar was full of canned fruit. The Rebels came many times to our house to eat and they were so rude. They climbed on our beds with their boots on and in the middle of the bed and ate what [food] we brought them. They robbed our beehive . . . cellar and took what they wanted.

My brother got sick and came home. We had a hard time trying to hide him from the Rebels. We hid him in the smoke house. One day when he was well he wanted to get back to his army and we had to smuggle him out for the Rebels watched our home day and night. I saw a bunch of them coming and we were washing, so I said to my sister, "Louisa, Mrs. Allen doesn't feel like washing any longer. She has the toothache, and I'm going to take her home." We dressed him up in mother's hoops and a dress of hers. Then we put a bonnet on him and I fixed some hot ashes in a cotton cloth for him to hold to his jaw. I went with him across the creek and when we were out of sight of the Rebels, he tore his disguise from him and away he ran. During these days my youngest brother who was at home with us became ill and died. There was nobody to care for him but my sisters and me, so we took him and buried him by mother in Oak Bend on the Arkansas River. The first Yankee Regiment to come to our house was the negro infantry. I was so frightened I could hardly stand up but they didn't even come in the house. We fed them and they went on.

When the Federal Army captured Ft. Smith, the Rebels fled past our place. They had the wheels of their wagons and cannons wrapped with burlap to prevent their rattling sound as they passed along the road. They stopped and took food from our place. They threatened to hang my sister. I had grown rather brave by this time, and I told them they had better not put a rope around her neck, but they could hang me instead of her. This amused them and they told me they were not going to hang either of us. My brother was hanged during this time. Father found him just as he was pulling the rope from around his neck. The Rebels had left him supposing him to be dead. His escape was a miracle. My sister lived in Ft. Smith and she decided to come to see us. Her husband wanted her to bring some army equipment to our house. She bought a team and wagon, and before she got there her team gave out. So she came on one of the mules. When she started back she took me with her. The Rebels were burning houses and killing cattle and horses. One didn't dare start out with a horse, for it would be stolen from under its rider and perhaps its rider would be killed. That is why we had the mule. We drove up to a woman's house about dark and her son had been shot. We helped her get him in the house. He asked if I could sing. I sang the following song for him:

"Brother Green, do come to me
For I am shot and bleeding

I must die, no more to see
My wife and my dear children."

He died before morning. The poor mother gave us a good meal and we went on our way.

Finally, we were moved to Ft. Smith in government wagons. There were about fifteen wagons in the train, loaded with women and children who needed protection.

My sister and I got tired of riding and we got out and walked part of the way. We were far behind in the Cash Mountains, when we met Buck Brown and his bushwhackers. They asked who we were and I told him we were some starved people trying to get where we could get something to eat, and if he would leave us alone we might get there. He threatened to burn the wagons, and I told him if he treated a bunch of orphans and widows that way, he would surely be punished in some manner. He patted me on the head, and said I was a brave girl. He took a box from his pocket, wrote his name on it and gave it to me for good luck. I kept that box for many years.

One thing which I shall never forget was three wagons loaded with negroes which my cousin was taking south to sell. Only their heads could be seen above the sides of the wagons. It was indeed a sight never to be forgotten. They were packed in these wagons like cattle.

I was married to John Free at Mount Vernon, Missouri, March 13, 1865, just after the war was ended. He was an ex-soldier, and a jockey and race horse man. We moved six miles north of McAlester. We had a nice ranch there on which we raised horses and some cattle and hogs. My husband made a road around and over Coal Mountain and we had a ferry boat which I operated across Coal Creek, between McAlester and Crowder City. We had a toll gate. We charged $1.00 for a four-horse wagon, 50 cents for a two-horse wagon, and 25 cents for a rider. As this was the only way to get across the Creek near there, we had much travel through our gate. The ferry ran on a wire cable stretched from one bank to the other. I would push it with poles until we got to the deep water and then I had paddles to drive it across.

I attended the Greenleaf District Payment in 1894 when the Government paid the Cherokee Indians for the Cherokee Strip. I told fortunes for those full blood Indians for which I received large sums of money, moccasins, and blankets. I had the blankets and moccasins for many years. There were thousands of people there, all trying to get some of the Indians' money. There was every kind of a gambling device, shows, eating places and stores.

I have lived in Murray County since 1917. My husband is buried north of McAlester, west of Reams Switch, in a family graveyard.

Source: Mary Free interviewed by John F. Daugherty. "Life of a Cherokee Woman." May 13, 1937. Indian Pioneer Papers, Volume 32. Western History Collections, University of Oklahoma, Norman. http://digital.libraries. ou.edu/whc/pioneer/paper.asp?pID=2207&vID=32.

Kate Shaw Ahrens Interview
(1937)

During the 1930s, employees of the federal government interviewed thousands of Oklahoma's Native Americans. The following is one of those interviews. Kate Shaw Ahrens, a Creek Indian woman born in 1864, discusses her experiences with education and her job as a teacher. Without the work of the federal government, many of these unique voices might have been lost forever.

LIFE AND EXPERIENCES OF A PIONEER CREEK INDIAN WOMAN: MRS. KATE SHAW AHRENS (WAGONER, OKLAHOMA)

I was born at Boggy Depot, in 1864. My mother, Kizzie Lewis, was a full-blood Creek Indian and my father, William Shaw, a white man. He was a native of Maryland and came to Indian Territory before the Civil War. I was their only child.

As many of the Indians did, my parents immigrated to Texas to escape the ravages of war. At the close of the war they returned to the Choctaw Nation and lived for a time at Boggy Depot, where I was born. During that time, exact date not known, my father made a trip to Fort Smith to attend to

some property he owned. He was taken suddenly ill and died and was buried there. As travel was difficult and conditions so unsettled in the Territory at that time, my mother was unable to go and we never knew the exact location of his grave.

Being left alone, my mother returned to the Creek Nation to live among her own tribe and relatives. We settled at Old Town, near the present site of Eufaula. As we lived near Asbury Mission, a Methodist school, I attended school there and also Sunday school. I lived in that vicinity until I was sixteen years old, when I went north to school.

In 1879, Reverend Dwight L. Moody of Northfield, Massachusetts, who had gained worldwide fame, saw the need of a school where young people of small means could secure a sound education; such as he had been deprived of in his youth. His contact with people in every walk of life, not only emphasized the need of such an institution but gave him the opportunity to lay the idea before those who could help him formulate his plan and carry out his hopes.

In the fall of 1879, about a year after the first purchase of property in Northfield was made, a class of twenty-five girls arrived to live in Mr. Moody's own home until the first dormitory could be completed. The dormitory that housed the students was a large brick building, the dining room and kitchen being some distance away. Nearly 100 students were enrolled the following year, 1880. Today, with 11,250 alumnae, 543 students, 79 buildings on a 12,000 acre campus, Northfield Seminary continues to offer a sound Christian education at about half the annual cost, to girls, who, lacking this opportunity, would be seriously handicapped.

There were three underlying principles governing the school; first, that the Bible should be taught, a part of the regular curriculum, during every year the student was in attendance; second, that each girl should participate in the manual work; third, that the cost should be so low that practically any girl could afford to attend and that scholarships for girls, unable to pay, should be available. These principles have remained unchanged and the graduates from this school girdled the globe.

Encouraged and inspired by the phenomenal growth and marvelous success for girls, Mr. Moody opened a similar school for boys in 1881. This school, which was located across the Connecticut River and known as Mount Hermon, has enjoyed the same measure of success as Northfield Seminary.

In 1880, Mr. Moody sent his principal teacher, Miss Tucker, to the Indian Territory to secure students for the school, offering the same advantages to Indian girls as was offered to others. Miss Tucker came to Eufaula, Creek Nation, and conducted examinations for entrance credit. They were given in reading, writing, mathematics, and history. As I was fortunate enough to make the grade, I was among the sixteen Indian girls selected to go from the Indian Territory. Only a partial list who went at that time is available. They were: Jennie Ironsides, Cherokee; Kate Timberlake, Cherokee (now Mrs. James E. Wolf of Los Angeles, California); Jennie and Rose Yargee, Creek; Mary Colbert, Creek; Lydia Keys, Cherokee (now Mrs. Charles Taylor, Fremont, Nebraska); Hattie Ward, Choctaw; Lonie Stidham, Creek; Ida Stephens, Cherokee; Annie Rogers, Cherokee; Ida Beatty, Cherokee; Mamie Ross, Cherokee; and myself, Kate Shaw, Creek. Fannie Keys, sister of Lydia Keys, came a year later.

As we had to have a starting point, the girls from the southern part of the Territory met at Muskogee. A special coach was furnished for our accommodation by Jay Gould, Head of the MK&T Railroad System at that time. The girls from the northern part of the Territory boarded the train at Vinita. As no meals were furnished on the train, each girl was supplied with a lunch basket, generously filled at home with home-cooking. That was the last home-cooking I enjoyed for four years.

We left Muskogee on Monday evening at nine o'clock and arrived at Northfield Thursday noon. As travel was not as rapid in those days as it is now, that was considered good time. Our coach was attached to an outgoing train whenever it was necessary to change routes.

As I had never been among northern people before, many things were very queer to me. Especially, the way they talked; and I am sure we were just as queer to them. The cooking was another thing that was quite different. I had never seen sugar put in corn-bread before and we Indian Girls didn't like it. Rice was served with sugar and cream as a dessert, where we had always eaten it as a vegetable. The school maintained a fine dairy herd and there was an abundance of milk, cream and butter. We also had plenty of fresh vegetables during the season.

I well remember the fine chestnut hunts we had on Saturdays. Mr. Moody would announce that morning that we were going and to get the lunch baskets filled. He and Mrs. Moody often went along and always the teachers.

Mr. Moody was absent a great deal of the time during 1880 and 1881, for it was during those years that he conducted his evangelistic campaign in England that gave him worldwide fame. He returned in the fall of 1881 and that was when he opened the school for boys at Mount Hermon.

We were taught all of the home arts and spent one hour a day in the performance of our duties. We assisted in the housekeeping, cooking, serving meals, and laundry work, for which we were given credit in our school course.

As we were so far from home and railway travel quite expensive, I did not come home during vacations. One summer I visited one of the girls in Montreal, Canada, and another summer I went to Ontario, Canada. Those were very enjoyable times.

Many distinguished ministers visited our school from time to time. A large convocation was held there and ministers from all over the world were in attendance. We waited on the tables and I was amazed when they seated the negro delegates with the white delegates. Those in charge of the dining room service could not understand any reason why they should be discriminated against in a matter of that kind.

Once the Jubilee Singers were there and we enjoyed them immensely.

As we had students enrolled from all parts of the United States and Canada, they were an interesting group and we learned a great deal from each other. One day a girl asked me to go with her to the meat market and I asked, "Where is that, I never heard of such a place." And she said, "Where do you get your meat at home?" I told her that we killed and cured our own hog meat in the winter and when we wanted fresh beef, we had one butchered and divided it among the neighbors. The neighbors, in turn, did likewise. We always had baked beans, brown bread and coffee for Sunday morning breakfast. The beans were baked in our own oven but there was a public oven in the town where people took their beans, prepared and in the pot, on Saturday evening and went for them on Sunday morning.

While I was in school (1882), my mother married to Motey Tiger, a prominent Creek Indian, who afterward became Chief of the Creeks.

At the end of the four years, I returned to my home in the Indian Territory. I went by boat to New York City where I visited some of the girls who had attended school there. Lydia Keys, Kate Timberlake, and myself stayed the entire four years. On getting home, I at once set about to secure a school for I felt that I must get to work. I attended the Teachers Institute held each year at Okmulgee and was assigned a school west of Eufaula, which I taught for one year. I then entered colleges at Lexington, Missouri, where I graduated. On returning home, I secured a position in the Boarding School for Creek

Girls, at Muskogee, which at that time was under the supervision of Miss Alice Robertson, afterward a Congresswoman from Oklahoma. Miss Carlotta Archer and Miss Addie Willey, both Cherokees, taught there at the same time. Miss Alice's mother, Miss A.E.W. Robertson, was with her then and they lived in the building known as Minerva Home. At the close of the first year, a call had come to Colonel D.M. Wisdom, Indian Agent at Muskogee, for a teacher in the Government School at Ponca Agency and he offered me the position, which I accepted. The Agency was located among what was termed the wild tribes, to which the Poncas belonged. The Otoe Agency was near, as the Otoe Reservation joined that of the Poncas. They, too, belonged to the wild tribe. We had large brick building, comfortable and substantial. There were one hundred students enrolled. In the summer, the Indians lived in little houses built for them by the Government, but went down on Salt Fork River and camped during the winter.

The food for the school was secured at the Government Commissary and cooked in large vats. That was not very appetizing to the teachers. No attempt was made to teach the students table manners and the food was served with no regard to style. It seemed to us teachers a very poor way, if their intentions were to civilize the Indians. The teachers combined and employed a cook and we had our meals served separately, each paying their pro rata of the expenses.

We were employed the twelve months of the year at a salary of $50.00 per month and we paid our own expenses. We were on duty all summer unless a leave of absence was granted.

It was against the rule for the children to be taken home often, and then, only with the consent of the superintendent. One day the mother of Dell Yellowbird, a little boy, came for him and on being refused permission to take him, drew a long knife from the folds of her blanket and threw it at the superintendent, barely missing him.

We visited often at the Otoe Agency as there were a number of white government employees there.

I taught at Ponca Agency from 1888 to 1891, when I resigned to be married to Mr. A.J.W. Ahrens, of St. Louis, Missouri. Mr. Ahrens was employed at that time by the Simmons-Gregory Wholesale Dry Goods House of St. Louis. We went immediately to that city and lived there for three years. We then came back to the Territory and located at Eufaula, where my husband engaged in the mercantile business, operating his own store until a big fire occurred and burned the building as well as the stock. In 1899, thirty-eight years ago, we moved to our present home, a farm adjoining the town of Wagoner.

We have two children, a daughter, Mrs. George Harrison of Sand Springs and a son, Henry, of Tulsa; and two grandchildren, the children of Mr. and Mrs. Harrison.

I have seen many changes in this country since my childhood, but with the majority of the Indians, I think, it lacks a great deal of being an improvement.

Source: Kate Shaw Ahrens interviewed by Ella M. Robinson. "Life and Experiences of a Pioneer Creek Indian Woman." September 1, 1937. Indian Pioneer Papers, Volume 67. Western History Collections, University of Oklahoma, Norman. http://digital.libraries .ou.edu/whc/pioneer/papers/7374%20Ahrens.pdf.

Joe Medicine Crow, "Counting Coup and Capturing Horses" (1944)

In the document that follows, Joe Medicine Crow, the last war chief of the Crow Nation, recounts exploits from his service in Europe during World War II. To become a war chief, it is necessary for a Crow warrior to complete four tasks. The four tasks that Joe Medicine Crow completed while serving in Europe included touching a living enemy during battle, taking an enemy's weapon, leading a successful war party, and, finally, stealing an enemy's horse. In the following excerpt, Medicine Crow relates how he was able to accomplish these tasks while fighting German soldiers.

I had many adventures while in France in the Second World War. The first one happened when we started to push across this little creek, about like Lodge Grass Creek, that separated France and Germany, the Siegfried Line. That was the first time any American units reached the German line, and the Stars and Stripes photographers were there for the historic moment.

I was a platoon runner, carrying messages back and forth, and the CO (Commanding Officer) said, "All right, Chief, let's see you jump over the creek here to Germany." We got into Germany and before long we ran into foxholes loaded with Germans. We got to the top of this hill that was a network of trenches every which way, and the top was kinda steep and muddy and by the time about thirty guys were there it was just slippery. A guy in front of me, fat and heavy, kept falling back on top of me and when the German opened fire I think that was the only reason I didn't get killed that day—the guys on top were all wiped out. We stayed in the side trenches all night and threw hand grenades.

Come daylight the message came to send some men to get dynamite to blow up the big guns and the CO says, "Well, Chief, if anybody can get through, you can get through. Get six men and go up there." Boy, it was a high hill, loaded with mines. So the guns from the American side started throwing these smoke screen shells. Pretty soon that whole hillside's just one white mass of smoke. We didn't know where the mines were, we just took off. The Germans knew something was happening and began throwing in mortar shells and sometimes they'd get awfully close.

We finally reached our platoon center and they gave us the boxes of dynamite and fuses and we threw them on our shoulders and started down through that smoke again. I tell you, that was a terrible thing, but we came back without a scratch and they went ahead and dynamited two or three big guns. That earned me the war honor of being assigned to lead a war party and come back safely.

The next one came in March 1944 when the big push was on and we came to a little German town about the size of Hardin, Montana. We came from behind while the other outfits made a straight attack. There was still snow and we came through this slough with it up to our chests. I was a corporal then and took about five or six guys up a back alley. There was a lot of fighting in the main street but it was kind of quiet in the alley. There was a stone fence about ten feet high and a gate and I was heading for that gate to look around. A German had the same idea and he was running and here he came around and by golly I somehow knocked him down, knocked his rifle down. He landed on his back and I was on top of him. And he was reaching for his rifle, but I kicked that out of the way and sat on his chest and grabbed his throat and started choking him.

The rest of the guys showed up ready to blow his brains out but I had my hands there. This German guy had tears running down and hollered, "Hitler kaputt, Hitler kaputt, Hitler nicht gut." I felt sorry for him and let him go.

The story I particularly wanted to tell Jack was about the captured horses. This happened in March 1944. One late afternoon I was on scout duty ahead of my company (Co. K, 411th Inf. Reg.). We were on the road along the top of low mountains, close to the Siegfried Line which separated France from Germany. Going around a corner I caught up with a column of horseback riders. They were German soldiers! I followed them closely and carefully. Then the riders left the road and headed for some buildings below us. It was getting quite late in the evening. Upon reaching the buildings, apparently some kind of ranch, the riders dismounted and turned the horses inside a small pasture on a large corral. They went inside a large house.

When my company arrived I reported to the Company Commander all about what I had been watching. By the time we reached the "ranch" it was already dark. We quickly surrounded the place and planned to attack at daybreak.

Towards morning I suggested to the Commander that I could easily remove the horses preventing the enemy from escaping. The Commander approved the idea. I asked him to give me about 5 minutes before the jump off.

The time came! I took a private and had him help me chase the horses out of the open gate. I jumped on a horse and easily chased the herd and headed for the hills. The horses were hungry and stopped to nibble on what grass they could find. For about 15 minutes I enjoyed riding a horse and looking at about 50 head of horses. These were beautiful animals, not ordinary horses, ridden by no ordinary soldiers. These were the parade horses of SS officers.

After the war I came home to my reservation town of Lodge Grass, Montana. Elders gathered in a circle, according to tradition, and listened to my recital of war deeds. Afterwards I was given a "coup" for capturing 50 head of enemy horses. They also gave me three other coups for other brave performances. Then I was given a full chieftain's rank, perhaps the last Plains Indian war chief.

Source: Medicine Crow, Joe. *The People of the Buffalo.* Volume I, Military Art Warfare and Change: Essays in Honor of John C. Ewers, vol. 1, edited by Colin F. Taylor and Hugh A. Dempsey. Wyk, Germany: Tatanka Press, 2003, 168 and 172.

House Concurrent Resolution 108 (August 1, 1953)

This resolution, passed by Congress on August 1, 1953, established the United States' policy of termination by abolishing federal supervision over Native American tribes. Henceforth, tribes would be subjected to the same laws, responsibilities, and privileges as other American citizens. As a result of this resolution, the federal government ceased to provide protection to the culture of the Native American territory. The federal government also stopped providing health care, fire and police protection, and a host of other services that, once termination went into effect, many tribes were unable to provide on their own. Termination had long-lasting effects for many Native Americans.

Whereas it is the policy of Congress, as rapidly as possible, to make the Indians within the territorial limits of the United States subject to the same laws and entitled to the same privileges and responsibilities as are applicable to other citizens of the United States, to end their status as wards of the United States, and to grant them all of the rights and prerogatives pertaining to American citizenship; and

Whereas the Indians within the territorial limits of the United States should assume their full responsibilities as American citizens: Now, therefore, be it

Resolved by the House of Representatives (the Senate concurring), That it is declared to be the sense of Congress that, at the earliest possible time, all of the Indian tribes and the individual members thereof located within the States of California, Florida, New York, and Texas, and all of the following named Indian tribes and individual members thereof, should be freed from Federal supervision and control and from all disabilities and limitations specially applicable to Indians: The Flathead Tribe of Montana, the Klamath Tribe of Oregon, the Menominee Tribe of Wisconsin, the Potowatamie Tribe of Kansas and Nebraska, and those members of the Chippewa Tribe who are on the Turtle Mountain Reservation, North Dakota. It is further declared to be the sense of Congress that, upon the release of such tribes and individual members thereof from such disabilities and limitations, all offices of the Bureau of Indian Affairs in the States of California, Florida, New York, and Texas and all other offices of the Bureau of Indian Affairs whose primary purpose was to serve any Indian tribe or individual Indian freed from Federal supervision should be abolished. It is further declared to be the sense of Congress that the Secretary of the Interior should examine all existing legislation dealing with such Indians, and treaties between the Government of the United States and each such tribe, and report to Congress at the earliest practicable date, but not later than January 1, 1954, his recommendations for such legislation as, in his judgment, may be necessary to accomplish the purposes of this resolution.

Passed August 1, 1953.

Source: House Concurrent Resolution 108. U.S. Statutes at Large 67 (1953): B132.

George Webb, "Progress"
(1959)

The Pima, or Akimel O'odham, live along the Gila River and other regions of south-central Arizona. In 1959, George Webb, a member of the Pima Indian Nation, published his autobiography in which he describes the rich culture and history of his people. Much of Webb's autobiography centers on his childhood; in the excerpt that follows, the idea of progress is discussed.

Webb describes boarding school experiences and the fear of losing one's language and culture.

"PROGRESS"

The government agency established at Sacaton served all the Indians along the Gila River as well as along the Salt River. A little later, these Indian villages were set aside as a Reservation.

Up to that time most of the Pimas and Maricopas wore long hair. One of the first steps towards their "civilization" was to get them to cut their hair. Finding this a difficult problem, the agency offered a hat to anyone who cut his hair.

Also at that time the Pimas and Maricopas were still using the *olas-ki* (round house) although a few built square houses from cactus ribs, plastered over with mud.

The agency tried to get them to build adobe houses. But they soon found out that all these improvements could not be made unless the Indian was educated. A number of Pimas were sent east to school. Some went to Santa Fe, Albuquerque, Grand Junction, and Carlisle. Some stayed a few months, some a few years before they managed to get back home. It is said that some Pimas who went to an eastern school for two months came home thinking they had forgotten their own language.

They would stammer: "Wha-wa-wa-sha" for *huas-ha'a* which means "plate" in Pima. But they remembered the words for what went on a plate. Pretty soon they were speaking the language as good as any other Pima.

The agency had a hard time getting those Pimas to give up their *olas-ki* to build and live in adobe houses. Adobe houses were supposed to be more civilized than the old arrow-weed shelters. But the Pimas did not want to change. So the agency issued a wagon to any Pima family who wanted to build and live in an adobe house. The only thing was, they forgot to issue plans, so a Pima who wanted a free wagon built an adobe house according to his old ideas of a house, with a small door and no windows. These were warm on the few cold nights, but there was no ventilation.

Some older people in my family did what the agency told them to do. They built and lived in an adobe house. When they died they all died of tuberculosis.

Our people now build good houses with plenty of windows. All those early ones were abandoned many years ago. You can still see the ruined walls of some of them on the Reservation.

Near the foothills of the Estrella Mountains, Eaglefeathers made his final home. He was now along in years and no more able to carry on the affairs of his village. Keli'hi was selected to take his place.

Across the Santa Cruz River from where Eaglefeathers lived were the farms of Grayhorse, Swift Arrow, and Keli'hi. This settlement is still called Hya-thob meaning that the people who live there are Pimas who come from east of Pima Butte.

Keli'hi often went to Sacaton to consult chief Azul about tribal matters. Chief Azul was the head chief and the village chiefs were subject to his orders. All sub-chiefs made trips to Sacaton to get their orders.

The ruins of Chief Azul's house can still be seen to the right as you enter the town of Sacaton from the north—a two-story structure with the roof fallen in. In front, across the road to the south is a monument which was put up in memory of the first Indian killed in World War One who was a Pima Indian from our tribe.

As time went on, a missionary came to preach to the Pimas. Charles H. Cook was the first missionary and made his headquarters at Sacaton. The Pimas were slow to grasp the white man's religion. But once they understood it they became faithful believers.

Pimas who were converted at Gila Crossing would journey forty-five miles to Sacaton every weekend to attend church. It took almost two days each way to make the trip on foot.

Today the name Dr. Cook is still respected throughout the Pima villages. At Sacaton there is a large church built in his memorial.

When the Railroad had just been built along the south side of the Gila River, connecting California to the east, it was a great sight to the Pimas to see the engine coming along the tracks. Some of them would run around the corner of a house for fear the engine would swallow them.

After a while they got used to it, and the train-crew men would ask the Pimas to get on and go for a ride, and they would get on and go down to Yuma or up to Tucson. They did this for a while but the trains got into a wreck so often, killing some of the Pimas riding on them, that the government put a stop to it.

Grayhorse, Swift Arrow, and Keli'hi were now busy on their new farms at Gila Crossing, or Santa Cruz Village as it is now called.

The people of this village had dug a canal from the river to their farms. When a brush-dam would wash out, they would build another.

In those days there was always a good stream flowing in the Gila River. They were never out of irrigating water and the crops were always good.

About this time there was born of Keli'hi and Rainbow's Ends a son. They named him Buzzing Feather.

At the time Buzzing Feather was born, Keli'hi and Rainbow's Ends had five other children.

Eaglefeathers was my grandfather, Juana Losso my grandmother. Grayhorse and Swift Arrow were my uncles.

Keli'hi was my father, and Rainbow's Ends was my mother.

So Buzzing Feather, just now coming into the story, is myself!

Source: From *A Pima Remembers* by George Webb. © 1959 The Arizona Board of Regents. Reprinted by permission of the University of Arizona Press.

Martin Thom, "A Statement Made for the Young People"
(1964)

During the administration of President Lyndon Johnson (1963–1969), Congress passed the Economic Opportunity Act, which was an important part of the War on Poverty. The act was notable for its inclusion of Native Americans, who were primarily granted aid through the appropriations of the Bureau of Indian Affairs. This inclusion did not come easily. To convince officials to include Indians in the proposed legislation, the American Indian Capital Conference on Poverty was convened in Washington, DC, in 1964.

The conference was made up of a large number of Native Americans, as well as whites. During the conference, a number of young Native activists, members of the Red Power movement, were asked to speak before the other delegates. One of them was Martin Thom, a Paiute from Nevada, whose speech is excerpted here. In it, he calls for Native youths to become more involved in the economic development of the reservations and the protection of Indian culture.

The conference was successful, and Native Americans were included in the final version of the act. Afterward, Indians were asked to design and present proposals for economic development programs that would directly benefit their reservations. If the proposals were approved, Natives would be given money and allowed to run the programs themselves.

We are gathered here today to present the findings and recommendations of the poverty conditions which exist in our Indian homes. Poverty is nothing new to us. Many of us grew up in such conditions. We are joining in a concerted effort to remove the causes of poverty that destroys life among our people; this condition continues to eat away at our existence.

I would like to point out a little more about the basic Indian feeling toward the way he is being treated in regard to poverty. It is not easy to just sit down and make out a plan of action to remove poverty. It is not easy to even admit that we are poor. It is especially difficult for young people to say "We are poor—please help us." It is not easy to follow somebody always asking for help. The image of the American Indian is that of always asking. But the Indian youth fears this poverty and we have got to take a good look at what approach we are going to use to be rid of poverty.

The young people of the Indian tribes are going to be the ones to live with this, and sometime the Indian people are going to have to make a great effort—a concerted effort to remove poverty and the other conditions that have held the Indian people back from enjoying the comforts of life which we should be entitled to.

We as Indian youths know we cannot get away from the life which brought us here. To be an Indian is a very life to us and the conditions under which we live and the lives of our parents and relatives are affected. We cannot relax until this condition is removed; our conscience will never be clear until we have put forth effort to improve our conditions and the conditions of those at home.

We must recognize and point out to others that we do want to live under better conditions, but we want to remember that we are Indians. We want to remain Indian people. We want this country to know that our Indian lands and homes are precious to us. We never want to see them taken away from us.

As Indian youths we say to you today that the Indian cannot be pushed into the mainstream of American life. Our recognition as Indian people and Indian tribes is very dear to us. We cannot work to destroy our lives as Indian people. This will never serve the needs of the Indian people or this country.

Many of our friends feel that the Indian's greatest dream is to be free from second-class citizenship. We as youths have been taught that this freedom from second-class citizenship should be our goal. Let it be heard from Indian youth today that we do not want to be freed from our special relationship with the Federal Government. We only want our relationship between Indian Tribes and the Government to be one of good working relationship. We do not want to destroy our culture, our life that brought us through the period in which the Indians were almost annihilated.

We do not want to be pushed into the mainstream of American life. The Indian youth fears this, and this fear should be investigated and removed. We want it to be understood by all those concerned with Indian welfare that no people can ever develop when there is fear and anxiety. There is fear among our Indian people today that our tribal relationship with the Federal Government will be terminated soon. This fear must be removed and life allowed to develop by free choices. The policy to push Indians into the mainstream of American life must be reevaluated. We must have hope. We must have a goal. But that is not what the

Indian people want. We will never be able to fully join in on that effort.

For any program or policy to work we must be involved at the grassroots level. The responsibility to make decisions for ourselves must be placed in Indian hands. Any real help for Indian people must take cultural values into consideration. Programs set up to help people must fit into the cultural framework. . . .

We need to take a careful look at special programs. We need help for immediate plans and we also need to take into consideration the long-range policies and programs and where they are leading. What is needed at this time is a large national picture. The attitude that non-Indians, and some Indians, have is that someday the Indians are just going to disappear and that we should be working to make the Indians disappear is very wrong. We are not going to disappear. We have got to educate the American public and also our leaders that we are here to stay and that in staying here we have got to find a place for resolving our problem that will give us a life that has meaning for us and our Indian children and that there is a real hope that a complete life can be realized.

Indian tribes need greater political power to act. This country respects power and is based on the power system. If Indian communities and Indian tribes do not have political power we will never be able to hang on to what we have now. At the present time we have a right to own land—to exist as federal corporations—we have the self-building means to control this. There is a matter of putting that to work. We have a lot of communication to do. This communication has to come from the Indians themselves. We have got to get the message across. In the past our friends have taken it upon themselves to bring the message to the public and to the helping agencies. We have got to take a greater part in this role.

This conference is a good example of how we can work toward bringing our needs to the attention of the public and the helping agencies. The Indian youth should have an important role for he will be the one to be dealing with the benefits of the program also. We must make an effort to achieve the goals of Indian people to act completely for themselves and a lot rests with the younger people. We have to stir up an interest among Indian youth that they have got to get together to make a concerted effort with our leading tribes and with the older Indian leadership.

We have to cooperate and learn to work together. The Indian youth have got to take this upon themselves because in many cases our older people do not have the means to communicate this message and too many of our young people have drifted off and gone to American cities and not served the Indians where they are needed. There is a great amount of work ahead for the Indians and their friends.

If the findings and recommendations of this conference can be realized we will have taken a big step in the way toward a better life for the Indian people. Maybe someday we will look back and realize that at this conference the first big step was taken and how our future efforts were built on this work.

Clyde Warrior, "We Are Not Free"
(1967)

In February 1967, Clyde Warrior, a Ponca Indian, delivered the following speech. Warrior was an Indian activist who in 1961 co-founded the National Indian Youth Council. Warrior witnessed prejudice and discrimination against Native people, severe poverty in Indian communities, and ineptitude in the Bureau of Indian Affairs, all of which drove him to fight injustice and promote Native pride. Warrior's legacy was to pave the way for a new generation of Indian activists during the 1960s and 1970s, through his use of confrontational Indian activism. Warrior did not live to see the Native American civil rights movement expand and flourish as he had hoped. His frustrations with the conditions of Native Americans led to years of alcohol abuse. He died of liver failure in July 1968 at the age of 28. The following is one of his most famous speeches.

Most members of the National Indian Youth Council can remember when we were children and spent many hours at the feet of our grandfathers listening to stories of the time when Indians were a great people, when we were free, when we were rich, when we lived the good life. At the same time we heard stories of droughts, famines, and pestilence. It was only recently that we realized that there was surely great material deprivation in those days, but that our old people felt rich because they were free. They were rich in things of the spirit, but if there is one thing that characterizes Indian life today it is poverty of the spirit. We still have human passions and depth of feeling (which may be something rare in these days), but we are poor in spirit because we are not free—free in the most basic sense of the word. We are not allowed to make those basic human choices and decisions about our personal life and about the destiny of our communities which is the mark of free mature people. We sit on our front porches or in our yards, and the world and our lives in it pass us by without our desires or aspirations having any effect.

We are not free. We do not make choices. Our choices are made for us; we are the poor. For those of us who live on reservations these choices and decisions are made by federal administrators, bureaucrats, and their "yes men," euphemistically called tribal governments. Those of us who live in non-reservation areas have our lives controlled by local white power elites. We have many rulers. They are called social workers, "cops," school teachers, churches, etc., and now OEO employees. They call us into meetings to tell us what is good for us and how they've programmed us, or they come into our homes to instruct us and their manners are not always what one would call polite by Indian standards or perhaps by any standards. We are rarely accorded respect as fellow human beings. Our children come home from school to us with shame in their hearts and a sneer on their lips for their home and parents. We are the "poverty problem" and that is true; and perhaps it is also true that our lack of reasonable choices, our lack of freedoms, and our poverty of the spirit is not unconnected with our material poverty.

The National Indian Youth Council realizes there is a great struggle going on in America between those who want more "local" control of programs and those who would keep the power and the purse strings in the hands of the federal government. We are unconcerned with that struggle because we know that no one is arguing that the dispossessed, the poor, be given any control over their own destiny. The local white power elites who protest the loudest against federal control are the very ones who would keep us poor in spirit and worldly goods in order to enhance their own personal and economic station in the world.

Nor have those of us on reservations fared any better under the paternalistic control of federal administrations. In fact, we shudder at the specter of what seems to be the forming alliances in Indian areas between federal administrations and local elites. Some of us fear this is the shape of things to come in the War on Poverty effort. Certainly, it is in those areas where such an alliance is taking place that the poverty program seems to be "working well." That is to say, it is in those areas of the country where the federal government is getting the least "static" and where federal money is being used to bolster the local power structure and local institutions. By "everybody being satisfied," I mean the people who count and the Indian or poor does not count.

Let us take the Head Start Program as an instance. We are told in the not-so-subtle racist vocabulary of the modern middle class that our children are "deprived." Exactly what they are deprived of seems to be unstated. We give our children love, warmth and respect in our homes and the qualities necessary to be a warm human being. Perhaps many of them get into trouble in their teens because we have given them too much warmth, love, passion, and respect. Perhaps they have a hard time reconciling themselves to being a number on an IBM card. Nevertheless, many educators and politicians seem to assume that we, the poor, the Indians, are not capable of handling our own affairs and even raising our own children and that state institutions must do the job for us and take them away from us as soon as they can. My grandmother said last week, "Train your child well now for soon she will belong to her teacher and the schools."

Many of our fears about the Head Start Program which we had from listening to the vocabulary of educators and their intentions were not justified, however. In our rural areas the program seems to have turned out to be just a federally subsidized kindergarten which no one seems to take too seriously. It has not turned out to be, as we feared, an attempt to "re-thread" the "twisted head" of the child from a poor home. Head Start, as a program, may not have fulfilled the expectations of elitist educators in our educational colleges, and the poor may not be ecstatic over the results, but the local

powers are overjoyed. This is the one program which has not upset any one's apple cart and which has strengthened local institutions in an acceptable manner, acceptable at least to our local "patrons."

Fifty years ago the federal government came into our communities and by force carried most of our children away to distant boarding schools. My father and many of my generation lived their childhoods in an almost prison-like atmosphere. Many returned unable even to speak their own language. Some returned to become drunks. Most of them had become white haters or that most pathetic of all modern Indians—Indian haters. Very few ever became more than very confused, ambivalent and immobilized individuals—never able to reconcile the tensions and contradictions built inside themselves by outside institutions. As you can imagine, we have little faith in such kinds of federal programs devised for our betterment nor do we see education as a panacea for all ills. In recent days, however, some of us have been thinking that perhaps the damage done to our communities by forced assimilation and directed acculturative programs was minor compared to the situation in which our children now find themselves. There is a whole generation of Indian children who are growing up in the American school system. They still look to their relatives, my generation, and my father's to see if they are worthy people. But their judgment and definition of what is worthy is now the judgment most Americans make. They judge worthiness as competence and competence as worthiness. And I am afraid me and my fathers do not fare well in the light of this situation and that they individually are not worthy. Even if by some stroke of good fortune prosperity was handed to us "on a platter" that still would not soften the negative judgment our youngsters have of their people and themselves. As you know, people who feel themselves to be unworthy and feel they cannot escape this unworthiness turn to drink and crime and self-destructive acts. Unless there is some way that we as Indian individuals and communities can prove ourselves competent and worthy in the eyes of our youngsters there will be a generation of Indians grow to adulthood whose reaction to their situation will make previous social ills seem like a Sunday School picnic.

For the sake of our children, for the sake of the spiritual and material well-being of our total community we must be able to demonstrate competence to ourselves. For the sake of our psychic stability as well as our physical well-being we must be free men and exercise free choices. We must make decisions about our own destinies. We must be able to learn and profit from our own mistakes. Only then can we become competent and prosperous communities. We must be free in the most literal sense of the word—not sold or coerced into accepting programs for our own good, not of our own making or choice. Too much of what passes for "grassroots democracy" on the American scene is really a slick job of salesmanship. It is not hard for sophisticated administrators to sell tinsel and glitter programs to simple people—programs which are not theirs, which they do not understand and which cannot but ultimately fail and contribute to already strong feelings of inadequacy. Community development must be just what the word implies, Community Development. It cannot be packaged programs wheeled into Indian communities by outsiders which Indians can "buy" or once again brand themselves as unprogressive if they do not "cooperate." Even the best of outside programs suffer from one very large defect—if the program falters helpful outsiders too often step in to smooth over the rough spots. At that point any program ceases to belong to the people involved and ceases to be a learning experience for them. Programs must be Indian experiences because only then will Indians understand why a program failed and not blame themselves for some personal inadequacy. A better program built upon the failure of an old program is the path of progress. But to achieve this experience, competence, worthiness, sense of achievement and the resultant material prosperity Indians must have the responsibility in the ultimate sense of the word. Indians must be free in the sense that other more prosperous Americans are free. Freedom and prosperity are different sides of the same coin and there can be no freedom without complete responsibility. And I do not mean the fictional responsibility and democracy of passive consumers of programs; programs which emanate from and whose responsibility for success rests in the hands of outsiders—be they federal administrators or local white elitist groups.

Many of our young people are captivated by the lure of the American city with its excitement and promise of unlimited opportunity. But even if educated they come from powerless and inexperienced communities and many times carry with them a strong sense of unworthiness. For many of them the promise of opportunity ends in the gutter on the skid rows of Los Angeles and Chicago. They should and must be given a better chance to take advantage of the opportunities they have. They must grow up in a decent community with a strong sense of personal adequacy and competence.

America cannot afford to have whole areas and communities of people in such dire social and economic circumstances. Not only for her economic well-being but for her moral well-being as well. America has given a great social and moral message to the world and demonstrated (perhaps not forcefully enough) that freedom and responsibility as an ethic is inseparable from and, in fact, the "cause" of the fabulous American standard of living. America has not however been diligent enough in promulgating this philosophy within her own borders. American Indians need to be given this freedom and responsibility which most Americans assume as their birthright. Only then will poverty and powerlessness cease to hang like the sword of Damocles over our heads stifling us. Only then can we enjoy the fruits of the American system and become participating citizens—Indian Americans rather than American Indians.

Perhaps, the National Indian Youth Council's real criticism is against a structure created by bureaucratic administrators who are caught in this American myth that all people assimilate into American society, that economics dictates assimilation and integration. From the experience of the National Indian Youth Council, and in reality, we cannot emphasize and recommend strongly enough the fact that no one integrates and disappears into American society. What ethnic groups do is not integrate into American society and economy individually, but enter into the mainstream of American society as a people, and in particular as communities of people. The solution to Indian poverty is not "government programs" but the competence of the person and his people. The real solution to poverty is encouraging the competence of the community as a whole.

The National Indian Youth Council recommends for "openers" that to really give these people "the poor, the dispossessed, the Indians," complete freedom and responsibility is to let it become a reality not a much-heard-about dream and let the poor decide for once, what is best for themselves.

Source: Rural Poverty. Hearings before the National Advisory Committee on Rural Poverty. Memphis, Tennessee. Washington, DC, 1967, 143–147.

Indian Civil Rights Act of 1968

The passage of this act in 1968 was a direct response to revelations concerning the mistreatment of many Native Americans by abusive, corrupt, and incompetent tribal officials over many years. Congressional testimony both documented and provided an awareness of the extent of abuses. The Indian Civil Rights Act provided Native Americans with many of the same protections as the American Bill of Rights, including the right to free speech, protection against unreasonable search and seizure, the right to trial by jury, and equal protection under the law.

For purposes of this subchapter, the term—

1. "Indian tribe" means any tribe, band, or other group of Indians subject to the jurisdiction of the United States and recognized as possessing powers of self-government;

2. "powers of self-government" means and includes all governmental powers possessed by an Indian tribe, executive, legislative, and judicial, and all offices, bodies, and tribunals by and through which they are executed, including courts of Indian offenses; and means the inherent power of Indian tribes, hereby recognized and affirmed, to exercise criminal jurisdiction over all Indians;

3. "Indian court" means any Indian tribal court or court of Indian offense.

No Indian tribe in exercising powers of self-government shall—

1. make or enforce any law prohibiting the free exercise of religion, or abridging the freedom of speech, or of the press, or the right of the people peaceably to assemble and to petition for a redress of grievances;

2. violate the right of the people to be secure in their persons, houses, papers, and effects against unreasonable search and seizures, nor issue warrants, but upon probable cause, supported by oath or affirmation, and particularly describing the place to be searched and the person or thing to be seized;

3. subject any person for the same offense to be twice put in jeopardy;

4. compel any person in any criminal case to be a witness against himself;

5. take any private property for a public use without just compensation;

6. deny to any person in a criminal proceeding the right to a speedy and public trial, to be informed

of the nature and cause of the accusation, to be confronted with the witnesses against him, to have compulsory process for obtaining witnesses in his favor, and at his own expense to have the assistance of counsel for his defense;

7. require excessive bail, impose excessive fines, inflict cruel and unusual punishments, . . . impose for conviction of any one offense any penalty or punishment greater than imprisonment for a term of one year and [1] a fine of $5,000, or both; . . .

8. deny to any person within its jurisdiction the equal protection of its laws or deprive any person of liberty or property without due process of law;

9. pass any bill of attainder or ex post facto law; or

10. deny to any person accused of an offense punishable by imprisonment the right, upon request, to a trial by jury of not less than six persons.

. . . The privilege of the writ of habeas corpus shall be available to any person, in a court of the United States, to test the legality of his detention by order of an Indian tribe.

Source: Indian Civil Rights Act. U.S. Statutes at Large 82 (1968): 77–81.

Sohappy v. Smith

(1969)

In the landmark court case Sohappy v. Smith, *the U.S. District Court for the District of Oregon acknowledged the right of several tribes of Native Americans to fish the Columbia River with minimal regulation by the federal and state governments. David Sohappy, one of the plaintiffs in this case, was a Yakama Indian who fought to preserve the hunting and fishing rights of his people.*

In 1969, Judge Robert Belloni decided in favor of the tribes, ruling that the states could control Indian fishing only when deemed essential for conservation purposes and that they must ensure that the treaty tribes would have a fair and equitable share of the salmon runs. In addition, Belloni mandated that the tribes must be permitted meaningful participation in the rule-making process.

Sohappy continued to fight for his people and the rights of Native Americans throughout the 1970s and 1980s. As he resisted encroachment of indigenous rights, Sohappy became a martyr, eventually locked up in federal prison in Minnesota for selling salmon to undercover federal agents.

While in prison, Sohappy's health quickly deteriorated. He was finally released from prison in 1988 and he died in 1991, fighting until the end.

Opinion
BELLONI, District Judge

Fourteen individual members of the Confederated Tribes and Bands of the Yakima Indian Nation filed case No. 68–409 against the members and director of the Fish Commission of the State of Oregon and the Oregon State Game Commission. They seek a decree of this court defining their treaty right "of taking fish at all usual and accustomed places" on the Columbia River and its tributaries and the manner and extent of the State of Oregon may regulate Indian fishing.

Shortly thereafter the United States on its own behalf and on behalf of the Confederated Tribes and Bands of the Yakima Reservation, the Confederated Tribes and Bands of the Umatilla Reservation composed of the Walla Walla, Cayuse and Umatilla Bands or Tribes, the Nez Perce Indian

Tribe and "all other tribes similarly situated" filed case No. 68–513. Upon their individual motions the Warm Springs Tribe, the Yakimas, the Umatillas and the Nez Perce Tribe were permitted to intervene in their own behalf. Following the intervention of the Warm Springs Tribe and upon the inability of government counsel to identify any other tribes who were "similarly situated", the State's motion to strike the reference to such other tribes was granted.

In both actions the defendants moved that the cases be heard by a three-judge court pursuant to 28 U.S.C. § 2281 and that the actions be dismissed for failure to join the State of Washington as an indispensable party pursuant to Rule 19. Defendants also moved to dismiss No. 68–409 as being a suit against the state in contravention of the Eleventh Amendment of the United States Constitution, and for lack of plaintiffs' standing to sue as individuals. All of the foregoing motions were denied. These cases challenge the validity of certain Oregon Statutes and regulations under the Supremacy Clause of the Constitution of the United States as being contrary to certain treaties of the United States.

In 1855 the United States negotiated separate treaties with each of the above named Indian tribes. These treaties were ratified and proclaimed by the United States in 1859. Treaty of June 9, 1855, with the Yakima Tribe (12 Stat. 951); Treaty of June 25, 1855, with the Tribes of Middle Oregon (12 Stat. 963); Treaty of June 9, 1855, with the Umatilla Tribe (12 Stat. 945); Treaty of June 11, 1855, with the Nez Perce Tribe (12 Stat. 957). Each of these treaties contained a substantially identical provision securing to the tribes "the right of taking fish at all usual and accustomed places in common with citizens of the Territory."

Most of the argument has centered around the state's interpretation of that provision. It believes that it gives the treaty Indians only the same rights as given to all other citizens. Such a reading would not seem unreasonable if all history, anthropology, biology, prior case law and the intention of the parties to the treaty were to be ignored.

I will review some of these factors and declare the rights of the parties.

Subsequent to the execution of the treaties and in reliance thereon the members of said four tribes have continued to fish for subsistence and commercial purposes at their usual and accustomed fishing places. Such fishing provided and still provides an important part of their subsistence and livelihood. Both prior to and subsequent to the treaties, the Indians used a variety of means to take fish, including various types of nets, weirs and gaff hooks.

The policy of the United States to extinguish Indian rights in the Oregon Territory by negotiation rather than by conquest was firmly established in the Act of August 14, 1848 (9 Stat. 323) which established the Oregon Territory. That act declared that nothing in it "shall be construed to impair the rights of persons or property now pertaining to the Indians in said Territory, so long as such rights shall remain unextinguished by treaty between the United States and such Indians." The act also extended to the Oregon Territory the provisions of the Northwest Ordinance of 1787 which provided, among other things, that "good faith shall always be observed towards the Indians; their land and property shall never be taken from them without their consent."

The treaties with which we are here concerned are parts of the result of that policy. They are not treaties of conquest but were negotiated at arm's length. The word of the United States was pledged. Today, some 114 years later, all of the parties to those treaties are in essential agreement as to their meaning and they have joined in asking this court to confirm that construction. Only the State of Oregon, successor to many of the rights of the United States, disagrees with the interpretation which the parties to the treaties assert here.

It hardly needs restatement that Indian treaties, like international treaties, entered into by the United States are part of the supreme law of the land which the states and their officials are bound to observe. The Supreme Court has on numerous occasions noted that while the courts cannot vary the plain language of an Indian treaty, such treaties are to be construed:

> as "that unlettered people" understood it, and, "as justice and reason demand in all cases where power is exerted by the strong over those to whom they owe care and protection," and counterpoise the inequality "by the superior justice which looks only to the substance of the right, without regard to technical rules."

The Columbia River has long been one of the world's major producers of salmonid fish. Several species of salmon and steelhead trout inhabit the river and its tributaries. They are spawned in the tributaries, headwaters and mainstem, migrate to the Pacific Ocean where they spend the bulk of their adult life, return generally to the river or stream of their origin, spawn, and, in case of salmon, die. From aboriginal times these salmon and steelhead have been a highly prized source of food. They are also a major recreational attraction to sports fishermen.

From the earliest known times, up to and beyond the time of the treaties, the Indians comprising each of the intervenor tribes were primarily a fishing, hunting and gathering people dependent almost entirely upon the natural animal and vegetative resources of the region for their subsistence and culture. They were heavily dependent upon such fish for their subsistence and for trade with other tribes and later with the settlers. They cured and dried large quantities for year around use. With the advent of canning technology in the latter half of the 19th century the commercial exploitation of the salmonid resource by non-Indians increased tremendously. Indians, fishing under their treaty-secured rights, also participated in this expanded commercial fishery and sold many fish to non-Indian packers and dealers.

During the negotiations which led to the signing of the treaties the tribal leaders expressed great concern over their right to continue to resort to their fishing places and hunting grounds. They were reluctant to sign the treaties until given assurances that they could continue to go to such places and take fish and game there. The official records of the treaty negotiations prepared by the United States representatives reflect this concern and also the assurances given to the Indians on this point as inducement for their acceptance of the treaties.

The Supreme Court has recently restated the nature of the non-exclusive off-reservation fishing rights secured by these Indian treaties. In *Puyallup Tribe et al. v. Department of Game et al.,* it declared:

> The right to fish "at all usual and accustomed" places may, of course, not be qualified by the State, even though all Indians born in the United States are now citizens of the United States. But the manner of fishing, the size of the take, the restriction of commercial fishing, and the like may be regulated by the State in the interest of conservation, provided the regulation meets appropriate standards and does not discriminate against the Indians.

It will facilitate an understanding of the issues involved in these cases if we note briefly certain points that are not here in issue. None of the plaintiffs or intervenor tribes denies the jurisdiction of the State of Oregon to regulate Indian exercise of these off-reservation fishing rights. Nor do they deny the need for regulation of Indian commercial fishing on the Columbia River to protect fish stocks. As the issue is stated in the Government's brief, "The concept of necessary regulation we accept, and we accept the states as being one class of agents of the public to determine and administer such regulations—provided they act with due regard to their responsibilities under the laws of this land, including these treaties."

The issue in these cases concerns the limitation on the state's power to regulate the exercise of the Indians' federal treaty right. At least three such limitations are indicated by the Supreme Court in its *Puyallup* decision. First, the regulation must be "necessary for the conservation of the fish." Second, the state restrictions on Indian treaty fishing must "not discriminate against the Indians." And third, they must meet "appropriate standards."

The regulations and policies heretofore applied by the state's regulatory and enforcement agencies have been premised upon the belief that, except for a right of access over private lands and exemption from the payment of license fees, the treaties afforded the Indians no rights beyond those accorded under the Fourteenth Amendment of the United States Constitution and under Article 1, Section 20, of the Oregon Constitution. The state argues that its regulatory scheme complies with the treaty requirements so long as the specific regulations applicable at any particular time or place impose no greater restriction on Indians fishing at such time or place than are imposed upon others fishing there. The state contends that the Indians' right to take fish at their usual and accustomed places is not a right that must be given any separate recognition or protection or be separately dealt with in the state's regulatory scheme. It argues that it may, in the interest of conservation, impose any restriction on treaty Indians fishing at their usual and accustomed places which it may impose upon non-Indians fishing at those same locations, even to the point of completely closing certain such areas to all forms of commercial fishing. It further argues, on the basis of its reading of a number of federal court decisions, including *Puyallup Tribe et al. v. Department of Game,* supra, that it may not allow Indians to fish at their usual and accustomed places in any manner or at any time that it does not similarly allow non-Indians to fish at those same locations. There is no support in any of these federal cases for any such narrow interpretation of the state's authority to distinguish between the regulation of Indian treaty-protected fishing and that of fishing by others.

The plaintiffs and intervenor tribes contend that before Oregon may regulate the taking and disposition of fish by treaty Indians at their usual and accustomed fishing places:

"(a) It must establish preliminary to regulation that the specific proposed regulation is both reasonable and necessary for the conservation of the fish resource. In order to be necessary, such regulations must be the least restrictive which can be imposed consistent with assuring the necessary escapement of fish for conservation purposes; the burden of establishing such facts is on the state.

"(b) Its regulatory agencies must deal with the matter of the Indians' treaty fishing as a subject separate and distinct from that of fishing by others. As one method of accomplishing conservation objectives it may lawfully restrict or prohibit non-Indians fishing at the Indians' usual and accustomed fishing places without imposing similar restrictions on treaty Indians."

"(c) It must so regulate the taking of fish that the treaty tribes and their members will be accorded an opportunity to take, at their usual and accustomed fishing places, by reasonable means feasible to them, a fair and equitable share of all fish which it permits to be taken from any given run."

They also contend that ORS 511.106(1), 506.006(4), and certain orders of the Fish Commission establishing closed areas or seasons above Bonneville Dam may not be applied so as to prevent Indians from taking fish at their usual and accustomed places east of the confluence of the Columbia and Deschutes Rivers under their treaty rights because such application is not reasonable and necessary for conservation and constitutes an arbitrary and unreasonable total prohibition against the exercise of such treaty rights. In addition, they contend that such application of the regulations violates ORS 506.045.

As is discussed more fully below, I believe that these contentions of the plaintiffs and the tribes correctly state the law applicable to state regulation of the Indians' federal treaty right.

Under Oregon law responsibility for the management of the fish resources of the state is divided between the Fish Commission and the Game Commission, with the former having exclusive jurisdiction over all fish other than game fish. ORS 506.040. The Game Commission has jurisdiction over game fish. ORS 496.160. Salmon and steelhead are food fish except when taken by angling, in which case they are classified as game fish. Subject to certain statutory limitations, the Fish Commission and Game Commission are each given broad authority to regulate the times, places and manner of taking fish and the possession and disposition of fish in waters or areas under the state's jurisdiction. One such statutory limitation, dating back to 1901 and presently contained in ORS 511.106(1) permanently closes the area east of the confluence of the Columbia and Deschutes Rivers to any fishing by any means other than angling.

The defendants' narrow interpretation of the Indians' rights under the treaties has been consistently rejected by the higher federal courts. The question was most recently examined by the Supreme Court in *Puyallup Tribe et al. v. Department of Game et al.,* supra, where, as previously noted, certain limitations on the state's regulatory authority over this federal right were mentioned. We turn now to a discussion of those limitations.

The parties place differing interpretations on the limitations on state authority inherent in the requirement that the state restriction on treaty-referenced fishing must be "necessary for the conservation of the fish."

By this reference the Supreme Court was undoubtedly speaking of conservation in the sense of perpetuation or improvement of the size and reliability of the fish runs. It was not endorsing any particular state management program which is based not only upon that factor but also upon allocation of fish among particular user groups or harvest areas, or classification of fish to particular uses or modes of taking.

The state may regulate fishing by non-Indians to achieve a wide variety of management or "conservation" objectives. Its selection of regulations to achieve these objectives is limited only by its own organic law and the standards of reasonableness required by the Fourteenth Amendment. But when it is regulating the federal right of Indians to take fish at their usual and accustomed places it does not have the same latitude in prescribing the management objectives and the regulatory means of achieving them. The state may not qualify the federal right by subordinating it to some other state objective or policy. It may use its police power only to the extent necessary to prevent the exercise of that right in a manner that will imperil the continued existence of the fish resource. The measure of the legal propriety of a regulation concerning the time and manner of exercising this "federal right" is, therefore, "distinct from the federal constitutional standard concerning the scope of the police power of the State." To prove necessity, the state must show there is a need to limit the taking of fish and that the particular regulation sought to be imposed upon the exercise of the treaty right is necessary to the accomplishment of the needed limitation. This applies to regulations restricting the type of gear which Indians may use as much as it does to restrictions on the time at which Indians may fish.

Oregon's conservation policies are concerned with allocation and use of the state's fish resource as well as with their perpetuation. It has divided the regulatory and promotional control between two agencies—one concerned with the protection and promotion of fisheries for sportsmen and the other concerned with protection and promotion of commercial fisheries. The regulations of these agencies, as well as their extensive propagation efforts, are designed not just to preserve the fish but to perpetuate and enhance the supply for their respective user interests. This is shown not only in the documentary evidence in this case but in the deposition testimony of Fish Commission personnel.

The Director of the Fish Commission testified as follows:

Q: Now, isn't it true that in fixing seasons, establishing gear limitations and the like below the escapement goal point, wherever it is, what the Fish Commission is doing really is only deciding where the harvestable portion of the run is to be caught?

A: That is one of the things we are doing. We are also more accurately assuring that we might get the escapement.

Q: Paraphrasing from what you said a moment ago, would it not be best to have one regulatory agency regulate both the offshore landing, sports control and also the in-river landings, both commercial, gill and Indian and sports?

A: It's been our stated position that a single resource such as anadromous fish could best be managed by a single entity.

Q: Correct. Now, if a single entity has that authority and that responsibility, is it not true that that single entity must make some determination between the various user groups or taking groups as to what *percentage or what use or what landing of the resource* that this particular user group may make of it?

A: *In some way, deliberately or inadvertently,* this decision must be made. (Schoning Dep. Ex. 45 Vol. III, pp. 44, 90–91) (Emphasis supplied) The research biologist and project leader for the Commission's Columbia River investigations testified:

Q: Now, these people that fish in the lower river, if you open up an area above Bonneville Dam, and consequently have to reduce the fishing that is done below Bonneville Dam and still maintain the escapement goal, a run that will reach your escapement goal, by setting the length of season at various places along the river, in effect, you are determining who catches the fish, aren't you?

A: *To some extent, I am sure we are.* Every regulation we set for fishermen below Bonneville, someone objects to it; because they feel they are being discriminated against because there are more fish going out of Astoria, and they have to fish up at Portland. So, many fish up at Astoria and some fish up around Corbett.

Q: Isn't it your experience at these meetings with the Washington Department of Fisheries and the Oregon Fish Commission, that they try in some manner to come up with a regulation that is not unpopular?

A: I think as much as possible if you could still achieve the escapement goal. They try to accommodate *as many people as possible* just within the authority and within their responsibility as they see it and maintain the resource. They try to do it. I think it is a fair statement.

Q: You also have to take into consideration those compromises among those different people that are dissatisfied that you mentioned earlier?

A: I don't personally. The Commission does. (Oakley Dep., Ex. A-46, pp. 58–59, 60–61, 62) (Emphasis supplied)

There is no evidence in this case that the defendants have given any consideration to the treaty rights of Indians as an interest to be recognized or a fishery to be promoted in the state's regulatory and developmental program. This same discriminatory aspect of the state's conservation policy was recognized earlier by the court of appeals in *Maison v. Confederated Tribes of the Umatilla Indian Reservation.*

The parties also place widely differing interpretations upon the Supreme Court's criteria that the state's restriction on the time and manner of fishing by treaty Indians must not discriminate against the Indians. The state believes that this means only that each law or regulation must be equally applicable to Indian and non-Indian. The United States, on the other hand, contends that the state's over-all regulation of the fishery must not discriminate against the Indians' exercise of their treaty rights in favor of the taking of fish by others at other locations—that it is the treaty right which must be given equal protection with other interests in the state's regulatory scheme. It says that in the case of anadromous fish the total impact of the state's regulations on the entire run as it proceeds through the area of the state's jurisdiction must be considered; that a nondiscriminatory set of regulations requires that treaty Indians be given an opportunity to catch fish at their usual and accustomed places equal to that of other users to catch fish at locations preferred by them or by the state.

In considering the problem of salmon and steelhead conservation in the Columbia River and its tributaries, it is necessary to consider the entire Columbia River system. The off-shore fishery in the Pacific Ocean has some effect on the numbers of fish that enter the river. The salmon and steelhead that enter the Columbia River are anadromous fish and spend much of their adult life in the Pacific Ocean. Therefore, they must pass as fingerlings down the Columbia River to the sea; and as adults they must pass up the Columbia River into the particular tributary or area where they spawn.

One of the principal tools which the states of Oregon and Washington use for managing most runs of the anadromous fish resources of the Columbia River system is the "escapement goal." This goal is set by the Fish Commission, generally in conjunction with the Washington Department of Fisheries, as being the estimated numbers of fish which must escape above all commercial fishing in order that, considering all factors which influence the matter above that point, the greatest aggregate numbers of fish from such fish run will be produced and return down the Columbia to the Pacific Ocean. In establishing the escapement goal for a particular run the Fish Commission and its biological staff consider the losses which will occur above the escapement goal point from all causes, including natural causes, losses at dams and the sports catch on the upstream and tributaries in Oregon, Washington and Idaho. All the estimated numbers of fish in a given run in excess of the escapement goal are regarded by the Fish Commission as harvestable.

The state regulates fishing within its borders from the Continental Shelf to the upper limits of the river and its tributaries. It manages its resources to allow the harvest to be taken on whatever portions of the river it desires. It must manage the overall fish run in a way that does not discriminate against the treaty Indians as it has heretofore been doing. Oregon recognizes sports fishermen and commercial fishermen and seems to attempt to make an equitable division between the two. But the state seems to have ignored the rights of the Indians who acquired a treaty right to fish at their historic off-reservation fishing stations. If Oregon intends to maintain a separate status of commercial and sports fisheries, it is obvious a third must be added, the Indian fishery. The treaty Indians, having an absolute right to that fishery, are entitled to a fair share of the fish produced by the Columbia River system.

The Supreme Court has said that the right to fish at all usual and accustomed places may not be qualified by the state. I interpret this to mean that the state cannot so manage the fishery that little or no harvestable portion of the run remains to reach the upper portions of the stream where the historic Indian places are mostly located.

It is clear that the state has the full and complete power to regulate all kinds of fishing, including the Indian fishery, to the end that the resource is preserved. There is no reason to believe that a ruling which grants the Indians their full treaty rights will affect the necessary escapement of fish in the least. The only effect will be that some of the fish now taken by sportsmen and commercial fishermen must be shared with the treaty Indians, as our forefathers promised over a hundred years ago.

In prescribing restrictions upon the exercise of Indian treaty rights the state may adopt regulations permitting the treaty Indians to fish at their usual and accustomed places by means which it prohibits to non-Indians. While the treaties do not give the Indians the right to insist that the state restrict non-Indians to a greater degree than it restricts Indians, neither do they limit the state's authority to restrict non-Indian fishing.

In determining what is an "appropriate" regulation one must consider the interests to be protected or objective to be served. In the case of regulations affecting Indian treaty fishing rights the protection of the treaty right to take fish at the Indians' usual and accustomed places must be an objective of the state's regulatory policy co-equal with the conservation of fish runs for other users. The restrictions on the exercise of the treaty right must be expressed with such particularity that the Indian can know in advance of his actions precisely the extent of the restriction which the state has found to be necessary for conservation.

This court cannot prescribe in advance all of the details of appropriate and permissible regulation of the Indian fishery, nor do the plaintiffs ask it to. As the Government itself acknowledges, "proper anadromous fishery management in a changing environment is not susceptible of rigid pre-determination . . . the variables that must be weighed in each given instance make judicial *review* of state action, through retention of continuing jurisdiction, more appropriate than overly-detailed judicial predetermination." The requirements of fishery regulation are such that many of the specific restrictions, particularly as to timing and length of seasons, cannot be made until the fish are actually passing through the fishing areas or shortly before such time. Continuing the jurisdiction of this court in the present cases may, as a practical matter, be the only way of assuring the parties an opportunity for timely and effective judicial review of such restrictions should such review become necessary.

I also do not believe that this court should at this time and on this record attempt to prescribe the specific procedures which the state must follow in adopting regulations applicable to the Indian fishery. The state must recognize that the federal right which the Indians have is distinct from the fishing rights of others over which the state has a broader latitude of regulatory control and that the tribal entities are interested parties to any regulation affecting the treaty fishing right. They, as well as their members to whom the regulations will be directly applicable, are entitled to be heard on the subject and, consistent with the need for dealing with emergency or changing situations on short notice, to be given appropriate notice and opportunity to participate meaningfully in the rule-making process.

This does not mean that tribal consent is required for restrictions on the exercise of the treaty rights. As the Supreme Court has stated on several occasions, the state's police power gives it adequate authority to regulate the exercise of the treaty-secured Indian off-reservation fishing rights, provided its regulations meet the standards which that court has prescribed.

It is not necessary at this time, and it would be inappropriate on this record, to determine the extent, if any, of the authority of the Federal Government or of the intervenor tribes to prescribe regulations that would govern Indians in the exercise of the treaty-secured fishing rights. It is sufficient to say that the state's authority to prescribe restrictions within the limitations imposed by the treaties and directly binding upon the Indians is not dependent upon assent of the tribes or of the Secretary of the Interior. But certainly agreements with the tribes or deference to tribal preference or regulation on specific aspects pertaining to the exercise of treaty fishing rights are means which the state may adopt in the exercise of its jurisdiction over such fishing rights. Both the state and the tribes should be encouraged to pursue such a cooperative approach.

Two other contentions of defendant can be disposed of very briefly. Defendant urges that the treaty provisions were in some manner altered or affected by Oregon's admission to the Union on an "equal footing" basis subsequent to the time the treaties were negotiated and signed and prior to the time they were ratified and became effective as the law of the land. There is no merit in this contention. Statehood does not deprive the Federal Government of the power to enter into treaties affecting fish and game within a state, especially migratory species. Nor did subsequent statehood diminish the treaty-secured fishing right. Defendant also argues that the treaty provisions were modified or superseded by the subsequent congressional action approving the 1918 Columbia Interstate Compact.

At the time of presenting the treaty to the Cayuse, Walla Walla and Nez Perce for signing, Governor Stevens prompting a reluctant Nez Perce Chief stated: "Looking Glass knows that he can catch fish at any of the fishing stations." Record of Proceedings Walla Walla Valley Treaty Council June 9th, 1855, p. 145.

Source: Sohappy v. Smith, 302 F. Supp. 899. Dist. Court, D. Oregon (1969).

John Borbridge, Testimony on the Land Rights of Native Alaskans (1969)

For decades, John Borbridge, a member of the Tlingit people born in Juneau, Alaska, has been one of the leaders of the state's Native community. He has served as vice president of the Alaska Federation of Natives, president of the Central Council of the Tlingit and Haida Indians of Alaska, and president and chairman of the board of Sealaska Corporation. As chief lobbyist for southeast Alaska and for the Alaska Federation of Natives, Borbridge played a crucial role in the Alaska Native Land Claims Settlement of 1971. Following are excerpts from Borbridge's 1969 testimony to the U.S. government on the land rights of native Alaskans.

The natives of Alaska (Eskimos, Indians, and Aleuts), who are estimated to number approximately 54,000, today use and occupy extensive areas in Alaska for hunting, trapping, fishing, and other purposes. These are the same lands which they used and occupied for many centuries prior to the coming of the first Europeans.

Today, the descendants of these native groups still continue to hold, by "rights of aboriginal occupancy," the great bulk of the same territory.

Today, Alaska, the last great frontier and wilderness region of our nation, is the sole remaining part of the United States which includes extensive areas still used and claimed by the indigenous inhabitants, based on *rights of aboriginal occupancy.* Except for these large areas in Alaska, the Indian or native title to lands of our nation has, over the years, been acquired by the federal government.

As repeatedly held by the Supreme Court of the United States, aboriginal Indian title to lands embraces the *complete beneficial ownership based on the right of perpetual and exclusive use and occupancy.* Such title also carries with it the *right* of the tribe or native group *to be protected fully by the United States in such exclusive occupancy against any interference or conflicting use or taking by all others, including protection against the state governments.* In short, as declared by the Supreme Court, aboriginal Indian ownership is as sacred as the white man's ownership.

From some lips fall the familiar complaints that the native occupancy of lands is impeding the economic development and progress of the state of Alaska.

Our answer is that though we have the right of complete beneficial use of our aboriginally occupied lands and all the resources of such lands, we have been prevented and restrained from exercising our rights to deal with and develop such lands

and resources. We say that only after we have been permitted the reasonable opportunity to exercise such rights a judgment may fairly be made as to whether our occupancy is hampering the economic development and progress of Alaska.

We believe that we have sufficient leadership ability to direct the development of our lands and resources.

We believe that we have the capacity—at least equal to the federal and state bureaucracies—to make wise selection of experts and technicians to assist us, including engineers, geologists, foresters, managers, investment advisors, accountants, economists, and lawyers.

Some argue that since the discoveries of valuable oil and gas resources on the native lands have been recent and since the natives in their aboriginal way of life did not exploit their lands for oil and gas, the natives have no basis for complaint if the federal government permits the natives to continue to use the land solely for hunting, trapping, and fishing purposes, or if the federal government appropriates the lands and compensates the natives only for the value of the lands for such aboriginal uses without regard to the oil and gas values.

This is an argument which has been repeatedly rejected by the Supreme Court and the court of claims in cases involving Indian tribal lands.

By a parity of poor reasoning, it may be suggested that if Senator Jackson or Congressman Aspinall owned a 5,000-acre tract of mountain lands in his home state, which he used exclusively for hunting and for enjoying its beauty, and then valuable mineral deposits were discovered on the land, the federal government could, lawfully and in good conscience, appropriate the tract and pay Congressman Aspinall only for its value for hunting purposes and for its beauty.

Many have suggested that since the Alaska Statehood Act gave to the state of Alaska the right of selection of some 103,000,000 acres of land, a serious dilemma has been created in that the exercise of such right by the state would necessarily require the selection of much land presently held by the Alaska natives.

Our answer is that Congress was fully aware of this problem when the statehood act was passed. In accordance with the uniform federal policy to honor and protect lands held by aboriginal occupancy rights, Congress explicitly required the state of Alaska in the statehood act to "forever disclaim" all right or title to any lands held by Indian, Eskimo, and Aleut groups.

We say that any state selection of lands which are held by native aboriginal title is violative of the terms, intent, and spirit of the statehood act and contrary to other acts of Congress as well as federal policy.

Alaska natives have assumed a statesmanlike posture, reflective of a conscientious awareness of the welfare of all citizens by their expressed willingness to negotiate on a political or legislative solution through the United States Congress. We, who are the first Alaskans, desire the development of our home state. We only ask that justice and equity be done and that, in the future, Alaska's native people may become active participants in Alaska's development.

Although Alaska natives have agreed to negotiate politically and are, therefore, not making recourse to the courts, we must emphasize that we are negotiating from a position of right and strength. We stress the fact that while we eschew the litigatory route, we still choose to retain the right to define our substantive legal rights, for therein lies the strength of our bargaining position and the basis of our negotiating effectiveness. Nevertheless, *litigation is a viable alternative, which we have, thus far, chosen to avoid.*

We Alaska natives envision that provisions of an equitable settlement of the land claims will enable us to uplift the qualities of life for our people. Recognizing that frustrations may be derived from a minority status due to ethnic origin and economic powerlessness, we anticipate our ability to exercise the *prerogative of choice* within the context of our needs, our goals, and our desires. We will recognize that many of our people will choose life in the villages, because it is, for them, a fulfillment and a satisfaction, while others, desirous of projecting themselves into a competitive society, will have the means to do so.

Source: Alaska Native Land Claims Part II, Hearings before the Subcommittee on Indian Affairs of the Committee on Interior and Insular Affairs, House of Representatives, Ninety-first Congress First Session on H.R. 13142, H.R. 10193, and H.R. 14212, Bills to Provide for the Settlement of Certain Land Claims of Alaska Natives, and for Other Purposes. Washington, DC: U.S. Government Printing Office, 1970.

Taos Pueblo, New Mexico, Appeal to Congress for the Return of Blue Lake (1970)

In 1906, the U.S. government seized 48,000 acres of mountain land in Colfax County, New Mexico, that included Blue Lake, a site sacred to the Taos Pueblo people of the region. This land subsequently became a U.S. National Forest. In 1971, after many appeals from Pueblo leaders, including the one presented here, Congress passed legislation, signed by President Richard Nixon, that returned Blue Lake and the surrounding lands to the Pueblo. Today, only members of the tribe are allowed to visit Blue Lake.

Mr. Chairman, it has been many years and several congresses since we first came before this subcommittee to appeal for the return of our sacred Blue Lake lands. Our spirits were lifted yesterday as we heard the President of the United States endorse H.R. 471. Like Job in the Biblical story, our people have patiently endured great hardship and deprivation fighting to save the religious heritage embodied in this holy land. In this fight we are also struggling to preserve the identity of our people as a tribe, to preserve our Indian way of life, and to obtain restitution of land wrongfully taken from us.

We are poor village people, and it has been hard for us to bear the costs of this long struggle for justice over the years since 1906 when the federal government first took the land and put it in the national forest. Even the young children of our village have contributed their pennies to bring our representatives to Washington time and again.

Apart from the financial hardship, we have had to contend with the irreverent curiosity and even mockery that this distasteful prolonged public conflict has engendered among some white men such as the threat reported by one of our tribal members in 1968 of a stranger who had declared that he would force his way with a gun into our ceremonies at Blue Lake. That man did not carry out his threat; perhaps because we responded by posting guards to protect our people and the sanctity of their worship. But the incident typifies how difficult it is for everyone—non-Indians as well as Indians—to tolerate the present permit system under which the sacred land is treated on the one hand as an Indian special-use area, on the other as a public multiple-use area.

We ask you to resolve this inherent conflict once and for all by returning the sacred area to our stewardship for religious and traditional use, and by doing so to extend to our people the Constitutional right of all Americans to religious freedom and self-determination.

Of the two bills now pending before this committee, H.R. 471 and S. 750, the Senate bill, S. 750, makes a mockery in every important respect of the religious and cultural needs of our Indian people. What does it do? We testify in good faith that our religious needs require the entire watershed to be maintained intact as an ecological unit, as is provided by H.R. 471; in direct repudiation of our simple request, S. 750 breaks this natural unit into four separate and distinct pieces for the benefit

of others; one piece, a tiny island of 1,640 acres around Blue Lake, would be earmarked for our exclusive use; a second piece, about 3,000 acres surrounding that island, is added to the Wheeler Peak Wilderness and opened to the public without restriction; the third piece, 34,500 acres mainly in the existing Permit Area, is made available for logging and other Forest Service uses with minor Indian use; and the fourth piece of approximately 8,000 acres is opened for logging and multiple use by the Forest Service and the public, with no provision whatever for our Indian needs.

Then we plead for protection of our religious privacy—as it is guaranteed by H.R. 471—so that our religion and strength will not be destroyed as those of other tribes have been; the response to this plea under S. 750 is to take away 4,600 acres from the Special Permit Area and convert 3,000 of those acres into a corridor around Blue Lake for free and unimpeded public access through the Wheeler Peak Wilderness Area into the remaining areas of the watershed. Under those conditions it would be impossible to preserve our sacred area from public intrusions under S. 750.

Again, we assert the profound belief of our people that the trees and all life and the earth itself within the watershed are comparable to human life and must not be cut or injured, but must be protected by wilderness status as is provided by H.R. 471. What does S. 750 do about this? S. 750 gives the Secretary of Agriculture discretion to harvest timber in 34,500 acres (including most of the watershed), to "manipulate vegetation" and fence off pastures in the interest of "water yield," and entirely excludes the 8,000 acres of critical drainage only one-half mile from the Rio Pueblo de Taos from any protection whatever against such desecration.

We ask this committee to reject S. 750 as the very opposite of the principles of religious freedom and self-determination upon which this nation was founded.

H.R. 471, on the other hand, would uphold those principles by placing the sacred area under the jurisdiction of the Interior Department in trust for

Taos Pueblo—the normal arrangement for Indian lands—and by requiring that it be maintained forever in wilderness status in accordance with the most fundamental tenets of our religion. The wasteful conflicts and confusion as between the purposes of the Forest Service and the real needs of Taos Pueblo would be ended without harming any other interests. . . .

Religious Use and Interferences. The entire watershed is permeated with holy places and shrines used regularly by our Indian people; there is no place the does not have religious significance to us. Each of the peaks or valleys or lakes, springs, and streams has a time in our religious calendar when homage in one form or another must be given, or plants that we have studied and used for centuries gathered, or rituals performed. Our religious leaders and societies go regularly to perform these duties in accordance with this yearly calendar throughout the area. They also supervise, for a period of 18 months, the preparation of our sons for manhood at various places throughout the sacred area.

In addition to the actual and threatened interference with our religious practices by disruptions of the natural condition of the watershed cited above, there have been continued and repeated interferences with those practices by non-Indian Forest Service employees and sportsmen. These include Forest Service trail-builders or construction workers from adjacent areas, and pleasure-seekers who treat the land as a public part of the national forest. They have been found camping and fishing at Blue Lake and at other places in the sacred area; they have been encountered at places where rituals were to be performed, and on the route to such places. . . .

Conservation and Water Rights. Taos Pueblo has used and occupied the watersheds of the Rio Pueblo and Rio Lucero for 700 years or more. We have always practiced conservation of those watersheds; they yield clear water today because of our long-standing care. Today it is more important than ever that the natural condition of those watersheds be preserved as the source of pure water in those streams. Our life depends upon that water even more than does the welfare of the non-Indians

downstream because we obtain our drinking water directly from the Rio Pueblo. For these reasons we want the protections of H.R. 471, which require the Secretary of the Interior to "be responsible for the establishment and maintenance of conservation measures for these lands, including without limitation, protection of forests from fire, disease, insects or trespass, prevention or elimination of erosion, damaging land use, or stream pollution, and maintenance of stream flow and sanitary conditions."

We also want the protection of wilderness, status for the watershed, which will prevent destruction of the natural values of that area more effectively than the present system. The Wilderness Society has inspected the area and has reported that it is suitable for wilderness status. Indeed, the Forest Service itself has repeatedly testified that the watershed is presently a "wild" area. . . .

Precedent Issue. It has been asserted that justice cannot be done for Taos Pueblo because other tribes might then seek similar legislation. The Interior Department has pointed out, however, that this is the only instance in which land claimed by a tribe has been continuously used and occupied by the claimant, and that no other tribe has a claim pending solely for religious and traditional use. . . .

All Indians yearn for Congress' recognition of the right to preserve their cultures, their religion, their tribal governments, and pride in their heritage. We want to take our rightful place in American society as Indians. Enactment of H.R. 471 would signal a new policy that will henceforth support Indian efforts to sustain their culture, their religions, and their tribal governments. Thus, H.R. 471 poses issues that are national in scope and touch Indians everywhere. We urge you to proclaim such a policy by recommending enactment of H.R. 471.

The past and the future of our Indian heritage is in your hands.

Source: United States Congress and Senate. Committee on Interior and Insular Affairs. Subcommittee on Indian Affairs. Washington, DC: U.S. Government Printing Office, 1970.

Vine Deloria Jr., "This Country Was a Lot Better Off When the Indians Were Running It"

(1970)

Vine Deloria Jr., was born in Martin, South Dakota, near the Oglala Lakota Pine Ridge Indian Reservation. He was educated first on the reservation, then received his bachelor's degree in science at Iowa State University. After serving two years with the Marines, he earned a degree in theology from the Lutheran School of Theology in Illinois. He later earned a law degree from the University of Colorado at Boulder.

Deloria was a prolific author, a dedicated activist, and a well-known public speaker. He published more than 20 books dedicated to drawing attention to the Red Power movement and Indian issues in general. He served as executive director of the National Congress of American Indians from 1964 to 1967, growing the organization exponentially. He also worked on the 1974 Boldt decision, which validated Indian fishing rights. The following document is a mix of history, biography, and thoughtful commentary. It focuses on the Red Power movement and contains many references to Deloria's life.

On Nov. 9, 1969, a contingent of American Indians, led by Adam Nordwall, a Chippewa from Minnesota, and Richard Oakes, a Mohawk from New York, landed on Alcatraz Island in San Francisco Bay and claimed the 13-acre rock "by right of discovery." The island had been abandoned six and a half years ago, and although there had been various suggestions concerning its disposal nothing had been done to make use of the land. Since there are Federal treaties giving some tribes the right to abandoned Federal property within a tribe's original territory, the Indians of the Bay area felt that they could lay claim to the island.

For nearly a year the United Bay Area Council of American Indians, a confederation of urban Indian organizations, had been talking about submitting a bid for the island to use it as a West Coast Indian cultural center and vocational training headquarters. Then, on Nov. 1, the San Francisco American Indian Center burned down. The center had served an estimated 30,000 Indians in the immediate area and was the focus of activities of the urban Indian community. It became a matter of urgency after that and, as Adam Nordwall said, "it was GO." Another landing, on Nov. 20, by nearly 100 Indians in a swift midnight raid secured the island.

The new inhabitants have made "the Rock" a focal point symbolic of Indian people. Under extreme difficulty they have worked to begin repairing sanitary facilities and buildings. The population has been largely transient, many people have stopped by, looked the situation over for a few days, then gone home, unwilling to put in the tedious work necessary to make the island support a viable community.

The Alcatraz news stories are somewhat shocking to non-Indians. It is difficult for most Americans to comprehend that there still exists a living community of nearly one million Indians in this country. For many people, Indians have become a species of movie actor periodically dispatched to the Happy Hunting Grounds by John Wayne on the "Late, Late Show." Yet there are some 315 Indian tribal groups in 26 states still functioning as quasi-sovereign nations under treaty status; they range from the mammoth Navajo tribe of some 132,000 with 16 million acres of land to tiny Mission Creek of California with 15 people and a tiny parcel of property. There are over half a million Indians in the cities alone, with the largest concentrations in San Francisco, Los Angeles, Minneapolis and Chicago.

The takeover of Alcatraz is to many Indian people a demonstration of pride in being Indian and a dignified, yet humorous protest against current conditions existing on the reservations and in the cities. It is this special pride and dignity, the determination to judge life according to one's own values, and the unconquerable conviction that the tribes will not die that has always characterized Indian people as I have known them.

I was born in Martin, a border town of the Pine Ridge Indian Reservation in South Dakota, in the midst of the Depression. My father was an Indian missionary who served 18 chapels on the eastern half of the reservation. In 1934, when I was 1, the Indian Reorganization Act was passed, allowing Indian tribes full rights of self-government for the first time since the late eighteen-sixties. Ever since those days, when the Sioux had agreed to forsake the life of the hunter or that of the farmer, they had been systematically deprived of any voice in decisions affecting their lives and property. Tribal ceremonies and religious practices were forbidden. The reservation was fully controlled by men in Washington, most of whom had never visited a reservation and felt no urge to do so.

The first years on the reservations were extremely hard for the Sioux. Kept confined behind fences they were almost wholly dependent upon Government rations for their food supply. Many died of hunger and malnutrition. Game was scarce and few were allowed to have weapons for fear of another Indian war. In some years there was practically no food available. Other years rations were withheld until the men agreed to farm the tiny pieces of land each family had been given. In desperation many families were forced to eat stray dogs and cat to keep alive.

By World War I, however, many of the Sioux families had developed prosperous ranches. Then the Government stepped in, sold the Indians' cattle for wartime needs, and after the war leased the grazing land to whites, creating wealthy white ranchers and destitute Indian landlords.

With the passage of the Indian Reorganization Act, native ceremonies and practices were given full recognition by Federal authorities. My earliest memories are of trips along dusty roads to Kyle, a small settlement in the heart of the reservation, to attend the dances. Ancient men, veterans of battles even then considered footnotes to the settlement of the West, brought their costumes out of hiding and walked about the grounds gathering the honor they had earned half a century before. They danced as if the intervening 50 years had been a lost weekend from which they had fully recovered. I remember best Dewey Beard, then in his late 80's and a survivor of the Little Big Horn. Even at that late date Dewey was hesitant to speak of the battle for fear of reprisal. There was no doubt, as one watched the people's expressions, that the Sioux had survived their greatest ordeal and were ready to face whatever the future might bring.

In those days the reservation was isolated and unsettled. Dirt roads held the few mail routes together. One could easily get lost in the wild back country as roads turned into cowpaths without so much as a backward glance. Remote settlements such as Buzzard Basin and Cuny Table were nearly inaccessible. In the spring every bridge on the reservation would be washed out with the first rain and would remain out until late summer. But few people cared. Most of the reservation people, traveling by team and wagon, merely forded the creeks and continued their journey, almost contemptuous of the need for roads and bridges.

The most memorable event of my early childhood was visiting Wounded Knee where 200 Sioux, including women and children, were slaughtered in 1890 by troopers of the Seventh Cavalry in what is believed to have been a delayed act of vengeance for Custer's defeat. The people were simply lined up shot down much as was allegedly done, according to newspaper reports, at Songmy. The wounded were left to die in a three-day Dakota blizzard, and when the soldiers returned to the scene after the storm some were still alive and were saved. The massacre was vividly etched in the minds of many of the older reservation people, but it was difficult to find anyone who wanted to talk about it.

Many times, over the years, my father would point out survivors of the massacre, and people on the reservation always went out of their way to help them. For a long time there was a bill in Congress to pay indemnities to the survivors, but the War Department always insisted that it had been a "battle" to stamp out the Ghost Dance religion among the Sioux. This does not, however, explain bayoneted Indian women and children found miles from the scene of the incident.

Strangely enough, the Depression was good for Indian reservations, particularly for the people at Pine Ridge. Since their lands had been leased to non-Indians by the Bureau of Indian Affairs, they had only a small rent check and the contempt of those who leased their lands to show for their ownership. But the Federal programs devised to solve the national economic crisis were also made available to Indian people, and there was work available for the first time in the history of the reservations.

The Civilian Conservation Corps set up a camp on the reservation and many Indians were hired under the program. In the canyons north of Allen, S.D., a beautiful buffalo pasture was built by the C.C.C., and the whole area was transformed into a recreation wonderland. Indians would come from miles around to see the buffalo and leave with a strange look in their eyes. Many times I stood silently watching while old men talked to the buffalo about the old days. They would conclude by singing a song before respectfully departing, their eyes filled with tears and their minds occupied with the memories of other times and places. It was difficult to determine who was the captive—the buffalo fenced in or the Indian fenced out.

While the rest of America suffered from the temporary deprivation of its luxuries, Indian people had a period of prosperity, as it were. Paychecks were regular. Small cattle herds were started, cars were purchased, new clothes and necessities became available. To a people who had struggled along on $50 cash income per year, the C.C.C. was the greatest program ever to come along. The Sioux had climbed from absolute deprivation to mere poverty, and this was the best time the reservation ever had.

World War II ended this temporary prosperity. The C.C.C. camps were closed; reservation programs were cut to the bone and social services became virtually nonexistent; "Victory gardens" were suddenly the style, and people began to be aware that a great war was being waged over seas.

The war dispersed the reservation people as nothing ever had. Every day, it seemed, we would be bidding farewell to families as they headed west to work in the defense plants on the Coast.

A great number of Sioux people went west and many of the Sioux on Alcatraz today are their children and relatives. There may now be as many Sioux in California as there are on the reservations in South Dakota because of the great wartime migration.

Those who stayed on the reservation had the war brought directly to their doorstep when they were notified that their sons had to go across the seas and fight. Busloads of Sioux boys left the reservation for parts unknown. In many cases even the trip to nearby Martin was a new experience for them, let alone training in Texas, California or Colorado. There were always going-away ceremonies conducted by the older people who admonished the boys to uphold the old tribal traditions and not to fear death. It was not death they feared but living with an unknown people in a distant place.

I was always disappointed with the Government's way of handling Indian servicemen. Indians were simply lost in the shuffle of 3 million men in uniform. Many boys came home on furlough and feared to return. They were not cowards in any sense of the word but the loneliness and boredom of stateside duty was crushing their spirits. They spent months without seeing another Indian. If the Government had recruited all-Indian outfits it would have easily solved this problem and also had the best fighting units in the world at its disposal. I often wonder what an all-Sioux or Apache company, painted and singing its songs, would have done to the morale of elite German panzer units.

After the war Indian veterans straggled back to the reservations and tried to pick up their lives. It was very difficult for them to resume a life of poverty after having seen the affluent outside world. Some spent a few days with the old folks and then left again for the big cities. Over the years they have emerged as leaders of the urban Indian movement. Many of their children are the nationalists of today who are adamant about keeping the reservations they have visited only on vacations. Other veterans stayed on the reservations and entered tribal politics. The reservations radically changed after the war. During the Depression there were about five telephones in Martin. If there was a call for you, the man at the hardware store had to come down to your house and get you to answer it. A couple of years after the war a complete dial system was installed that extended to most of the smaller communities on the reservation. Families that had been hundreds of miles from any form of communication were now only minutes away from a telephone. Roads were built connecting the major communities of the Pine Ridge country. No longer did it take hours to go from one place to another. With these kinds of roads everyone had to have a car. The team and wagon vanished, except for those families who lived at various "camps" in inaccessible canyons pretty much as their ancestors had. (Today, even they have adopted the automobile for traveling long distances in search of work.)

I left the reservation in 1951 when my family moved to Iowa. I went back only once for an extended stay, in the summer of 1955, while on a furlough, and after that I visited only occasionally during summer vacations. In the meantime, I attended college, served a hitch in the Marines, and went to the seminary. After I graduated from the seminary, I took a job with the United Scholarship Service, a private organization devoted to the college and secondary-school education of American Indian and Mexican students. I had spent my last two years of high school in an Eastern preparatory school and so was probably the only Indian my age who knew what an independent Eastern school was like. As the program developed, we soon had some 30 students placed in Eastern schools.

I insisted that all the students who entered the program be able to qualify for scholarships as students and not simply as Indians. I was pretty sure we could beat the white man at his own educational game, which seemed to me the only way to gain his respect. I was soon to find that this was a dangerous attitude to have. The very people who were supporting the program—non-Indians in the national church establishments—accused me of trying to form a colonialist "élite" by insisting that only kids with strong test scores and academic patterns be sent east to school. They wanted to continue the ancient pattern of soft-hearted paternalism toward Indians. I didn't feel we should cry our way into the schools; that sympathy would destroy the students we were trying to help.

In 1964, while attending the annual convention of the National Congress of American Indians, I was elected its executive director. I learned more about life in the N.C.A.I., in three years than I had in the previous 30. Every conceivable problem that could occur in an Indian society was suddenly thrust at me from 315 different directions. I discovered that I was one of the people who were supposed to solve the problems. The only trouble was that Indian people locally and on the national level were being played off one against the other by clever whites who had either ego or income at stake. While there were many feasible solutions, few could be tried without whites with vested interests working day and night to destroy the unity we were seeking on a national basis.

In the mid-nineteen-sixties, the whole generation that had grown up after World War II and had left the reservations during the fifties to get an education was returning to Indian life as "educated Indians." But we soon knew better. Tribal societies had existed for centuries without going outside themselves for education and information. Yet many of us thought that we would be able to improve the traditional tribal methods. We were wrong.

For three years we ran around the conference circuit attending numerous meetings called to "solve" the Indian problems. We listened to and spoke with anthropologists, historians, sociologists, psychologists, economists, educators and missionaries. We worked with many Government agencies and with every conceivable doctrine, idea and program ever created. At the end of this happy round of consultations the reservation people were still plodding along on their own time schedule, doing the things they considered important. They continued to solve their problems their way in spite of the advice given them by "Indian experts."

By 1967 there was a radical change in thinking on the part of many of us. Conferences were proving unproductive. Where non-Indians had been pushed out to make room for Indian people, they had wormed their way back into power and again controlled the major programs serving Indians. The poverty programs, reservation and university technical assistance groups were dominated by whites who had pushed Indian administrators aside.

Reservation people, meanwhile, were making steady progress in spite of the numerous setbacks suffered by the national Indian community. So, in large part, younger Indian leaders who had been playing the national conference field began working at the local level to build community movements from the ground up. By consolidating local organizations into power they felt that they would be in a better position to influence national thinking.

Robert Hunter, director of the Nevada Intertribal Council, had already begun to build a strong state organization of tribes and communities. In South Dakota, Gerald One Feather, Frank LaPointe and Ray Briggs formed the American Indian Leadership Conference, which quickly welded the educated young Sioux in that state into a strong regional organization active in nearly every phase of Sioux life. Gerald is not running for the prestigious post of Chairman of the Oglala Sioux, the largest Sioux tribe, numbering some 15,000 members. Ernie Stevens, an Oneida from Wisconsin and Lee Cook, a Chippewa from Minnesota, developed a strong program for economic and community development in Arizona. Just recently Ernie has moved into the post of director of the California Intertribal Council, a statewide organization representing some 130,000 California Indians in cities and on the scattered reservations of that state.

By the fall of 1967, it was apparent that the national Indian scene was collapsing in favor of strong regional organizations, although the major national organizations such as the National Congress of American Indians and the National Indian Youth Council continued to grow. There was yet another factor emerging on the Indian scene: the old-timers of the Depression days had educated a group of younger Indians in the old ways and these people were now becoming a major force in Indian life. Led by Thomas Banyaca of the Hopi, Mad Bear Anderson of the Tuscaroras, Clifton Hill of the Creeks, and Rolling Thunder of the Shoshones, the traditional Indians were forcing the whole Indian community to rethink its understanding of Indian life.

The message of the traditionalists is simple. They demand a return to basic Indian philosophy, establishment of ancient methods of government by open council instead of elected officials, a revival of Indian religions and replacement of white laws with Indian customs; in short, a complete return to the ways of the old people. In an age dominated by tribalizing communications media, their message makes a great deal of sense.

But in some areas their thinking is opposed to that of the National Congress of American Indians, which represents officially elected tribal governments organized under the Indian Reorganization Act as Federal corporations. The contemporary problem is therefore one of defining the meaning of "tribe." Is it a traditionally organized band of Indians following customs with medicine men and chiefs dominating the policies of the tribe, or is it a modern corporate structure attempting to compromise at least in part with modern white culture?

The problem has been complicated by private foundations' and Government agencies' funding of Indian programs. In general this process, although it has brought a great amount of money into Indian country, has been one of cooptation. Government agencies must justify their appropriation requests every year and can only take chances on spectacular programs that will serve as showcases of progress. They are not willing to invest the capital funds necessary to build viable self-supporting communities on the reservation because these programs do not have an immediate publicity potential. Thus, the Government agencies are forever committed to conducting conferences to discover that one "key" to Indian life that will give them the edge over their rival agencies in the annual appropriations derby.

Churches and foundations have merely purchased an Indian leader or program that conforms with their ideas of what Indian people should be doing. The large foundations have bought up the well-dressed, handsome "new image" Indian who is comfortable in the big cities but virtually helpless at an Indian meeting. Churches have given money to Indians who are willing to copy black militant activist tactics, and the more violent and insulting the Indian can be, the more the churches seem to love it. They are wallowing in self-guilt and piety over the lot of the poor, yet funding demagogues of their own choosing to speak for the poor.

I did not run for reelection as executive director of the N.C.A.I. in the fall of 1967, but entered law school at the University of Colorado instead. It was apparent to me that the Indian revolution was well under way and that someone had better get a legal education so that we could have our own legal program for defense of Indian treaty rights. Thanks to a Ford Foundation program, nearly 50 Indians are now in law school, assuring the Indian community of legal talent in the years ahead. Within four years I foresee another radical shift in Indian leadership patterns as the growing local movements are affected by the new Indian lawyers.

There is an increasing scent of victory in the air in Indian country these days. The mood is comparable to the old days of the Depression when the men began to dance once again. As the Indian movement gathers momentum and individual Indians cast their lot with the tribe, it will become apparent that not only will Indians survive the electronic world of Marshall McLuhan, they will thrive in it. At the present time everyone is watching how mainstream America will handle the issues of pollution, poverty, crime, and racism when it does not fundamentally understand the issues. Knowing the importance of tribal survival, Indian people are speaking more and more of sovereignty, of the great political technique of the open council, and of the need for gaining the community's consensus on all programs before putting them into effect.

In 1965 I had a long conversation with an old Papago. I was trying to get the tribe to pay its dues to the National Congress of American Indians and I had asked him to speak to the tribal council for me. He said that he would but that the Papagos didn't really need the N.C.A.I. They were like, he told me, the old mountain in the distance. The Spanish had come and dominated them for 300 years and then left. The Mexicans had come and ruled them for a century, but they also left. "The Americans," he said, "have been here only about 80 years. They, too, will vanish but the Papagos and the mountain will always be here."

This attitude and understanding of life is what American society is searching for.

I wish the Government would give Alcatraz to the Indians now occupying it. They want to create five centers on the island. One center would be for a North American studies program; another would be a spiritual and medical center where Indian religions and medicines would be used and studied. A third center would concentrate on ecological studies based on an Indian view of nature—that man should live *with* the land and not simply *on* it. A job-training center and a museum would also be founded on the island. Certain of these programs would obviously require Federal assistance.

Some people may object to this approach, yet Health, Education and Welfare gave out $10 million last year to non-Indians to study Indians. Not one single dollar went to an Indian scholar or researcher to present the point of view of Indian people. And the studies done by non-Indians added nothing to what was already known about Indians.

Indian people have managed to maintain a viable and cohesive social order in spite of everything the non-Indian society has thrown at them in an effort to break the tribal structure. At the same time, non-Indian society has created a monstrosity of a culture where people starve while the granaries are filled and the sun can never break through the smog.

By making Alcatraz an experimental Indian center operated and planned by Indian people, we would be given a chance to see what we could do toward developing answers to modern social problems. Ancient tribalism can be incorporated with modern technology in an urban setting. Perhaps we would not succeed in the effort, but the Government is spending billions every year and still the situation is rapidly growing worse. It just seems to a lot of Indians that this continent was a lot better off when we were running it.

Source: Vine Deloria Jr. (1970) Reprinted from *Red Power: The American Indians' Fight for Freedom* (2nd ed.), edited by Alvin M. Josephy, Joane Nagel, and Troy Johnson, by permission of the University of Nebraska Press. Copyright 1971 by Alvin M. Josephy. Copyright renewed 1999 by the University of Nebraska Press.

Wamsutta James, Suppressed Speech for the 350th Anniversary Celebration of the Pilgrim's Arrival in the New World

(1970)

To mark the 350th anniversary of the Pilgrims' arrival in New England, a celebration was planned. Those who were instrumental in planning the event thought it would be great if an Indian would deliver a speech at the formal dinner they had planned. They asked Wamsutta James, a Wampanoag, if he would be interested in delivering the speech. He accepted. However, the event organizers asked to see an advance copy of his speech. They did not accept his speech, and it was never delivered. After reading the words that were suppressed in 1970, it is clear why those who planned a celebration of the Pilgrims' arrival would not want it delivered.

I speak to you as a man—a Wampanoag Man. I am a proud man, proud of my ancestry, my accomplishments won by a strict parental direction ("You must succeed—your face is a different color in this small Cape Cod community!"). I am a product of poverty and discrimination from these two social and economic diseases. I, and my brothers and sisters, have painfully overcome, and to some extent we have earned the respect of our community. We are Indians first—but we are termed "good citizens." Sometimes we are arrogant but only because society has pressured us to be so.

It is with mixed emotion that I stand here to share my thoughts. This is a time of celebration for you—celebrating an anniversary of a beginning for the white man in America. A time of looking back, of reflection. It is with a heavy heart that I look back upon what happened to my People.

Even before the Pilgrims landed it was common practice for explorers to capture Indians, take them to Europe and sell them as slaves for 220 shillings apiece. The Pilgrims had hardly explored the shores of Cape Cod for four days before they had robbed the graves of my ancestors and stolen their corn and beans. Mourt's Relation describes a searching party of sixteen men. Mourt goes on to say that this party took as much of the Indians' winter provisions as they were able to carry.

Massasoit, the great Sachem of the Wampanoag, knew these facts, yet he and his People welcomed and befriended the settlers of the Plymouth Plantation. Perhaps he did this because his Tribe had been depleted by an epidemic. Or his knowledge of the harsh oncoming winter was the reason for his peaceful acceptance of these acts. This action by Massasoit was perhaps our biggest mistake. We, the Wampanoag, welcomed you, the white man, with open arms, little knowing that it was the beginning of the end; that before 50 years were to pass, the Wampanoag would no longer be a free people.

What happened in those short 50 years? What has happened in the last 300 years? History gives us facts and there were atrocities; there were broken promises—and most of these centered around land ownership. Among ourselves we understood that there were boundaries, but never before had we had to deal with fences and stone walls. But the white man had a need to prove his worth by the amount of land that he owned. Only ten years later, when the Puritans came, they treated the Wampanoag with even less kindness in converting the souls of the so-called "savages." Although the Puritans were harsh to members of their own society, the Indian was pressed between stone slabs and hanged as quickly as any other "witch."

And so down through the years there is record after record of Indian lands taken and, in token, reservations set up for him upon which to live. The Indian, having been stripped of his power, could only stand by and watch while the white man took his land and used it for his personal gain. This the Indian could not understand; for to him, land was survival, to farm, to hunt, to be enjoyed. It was not to be abused. We see incident after incident, where the white man sought to tame the "savage" and convert him to the Christian ways of life. The early Pilgrim settlers led the Indian to believe that if he did not behave, they would dig up the ground and unleash the great epidemic again.

The white man used the Indian's nautical skills and abilities. They let him be only a seaman—but never a captain. Time and time again, in the white man's society, we Indians have been termed "low man on the totem pole."

Has the Wampanoag really disappeared? There is still an aura of mystery. We know there was an epidemic that took many Indian lives—some Wampanoags moved west and joined the Cherokee and Cheyenne. They were forced to move. Some even went north to Canada! Many Wampanoag put aside their Indian heritage and accepted the white man's way for their own survival. There are some Wampanoag who do not wish it known they are Indian for social or economic reasons.

What happened to those Wampanoags who chose to remain and live among the early settlers? What kind of existence did they live as "civilized" people? True, living was not as complex as life today, but they dealt with the confusion and the change. Honesty, trust, concern, pride, and politics wove themselves in and out of their [the Wampanoags'] daily living. Hence, he was termed crafty, cunning, rapacious, and dirty.

History wants us to believe that the Indian was a savage, illiterate, uncivilized animal. A history that was written by an organized, disciplined people, to expose us as an unorganized and undisciplined entity. Two distinctly different cultures met. One thought they must control life; the other believed life was to be enjoyed, because nature decreed it. Let us remember, the Indian is and was just as human as the white man. The Indian feels pain, gets hurt, and becomes defensive, has dreams, bears tragedy and failure, suffers from loneliness, needs to cry as well as laugh. He, too, is often misunderstood.

The white man in the presence of the Indian is still mystified by his uncanny ability to make him feel uncomfortable. This may be the image the white man has created of the Indian; his "savageness" has boomeranged and isn't a mystery; it is fear; fear of the Indian's temperament!

High on a hill, overlooking the famed Plymouth Rock, stands the statue of our great Sachem, Massasoit. Massasoit has stood there many years in silence. We the descendants of this great Sachem have been a silent people. The necessity of making a living in this materialistic society of the white man caused us to be silent. Today, I and many of my people are choosing to face the truth. We ARE Indians!

Although time has drained our culture, and our language is almost extinct, we the Wampanoags still walk the lands of Massachusetts. We may be fragmented, we may be confused. Many years have passed since we have been a people together.

Our lands were invaded. We fought as hard to keep our land as you the whites did to take our land away from us. We were conquered, we became the American prisoners of war in many cases, and wards of the United States Government, until only recently.

Our spirit refuses to die. Yesterday we walked the woodland paths and sandy trails. Today we must walk the macadam highways and roads. We are uniting. We're standing not in our wigwams but in your concrete tent. We stand tall and proud, and before too many moons pass we'll right the wrongs we have allowed to happen to us.

We forfeited our country. Our lands have fallen into the hands of the aggressor. We have allowed the white man to keep us on our knees. What has happened cannot be changed, but today we must work towards a more humane America, a more Indian America, where men and nature once again are important; where the Indian values of honor, truth, and brotherhood prevail.

You the white man are celebrating an anniversary. We the Wampanoags will help you celebrate in the concept of a beginning. It was the beginning of a new life for the Pilgrims. Now, 350 years later it is a beginning of a new determination for the original American: the American Indian.

There are some factors concerning the Wampanoags and other Indians across this vast nation. We now have 350 years of experience living amongst the white man. We can now speak his language. We can now think as a white man thinks. We can now compete with him for the top jobs. We're being heard; we are now being listened to. The important point is that along with these necessities of everyday living, we still have the spirit, we still have the unique culture, we still have the will and, most important of all, the determination to remain as Indians. We are determined, and our presence here this evening is living testimony that this is only the beginning of the American Indian, particularly the Wampanoag, to regain the position in this country that is rightfully ours.

Source: Suppressed speech of Wamsutta James, September 10, 1970. United American Indians of New England, Jamaica Plain, Massachusetts. http://www.uaine.org/wmsuta.htm. Reprinted with permission.

"We Hold the Rock!" The Alcatraz Proclamation to the Great White Father and His People

(1970)

Members of a wide array of Native American nations took control of Alcatraz Island in November 1969. The occupation of the island garnered a great deal of publicity for the Red Power movement, and subsequently, many young indigenous activists learned to use the power of the press to spread their message. In the document that follows, which was released shortly after the seizure of the island in late 1969, Adam Fortunate Eagle argued that the goal of the occupation was to create a cultural center, a training center, and other centers related to ecology and spirituality. In addition to these goals, many of the young activists wished to bring attention to the trail of broken treaties between the United States and tribal governments.

The occupation of Alcatraz ended in June 1971 without any of the tribal centers being built; however, the occupation did increase the visibility of Native Americans in this country and it also served as a training ground for activists within the Red Power movement.

Fellow citizens, we are asking you to join with us in our attempt to better the lives of all Indian people.

We are on Alcatraz Island to make known to the world that we have a right to use our land for our own benefit.

In a proclamation of November 20, 1969, we told the government of the United States that we are here "to create a meaningful use for our Great Spirit's Land."

We, the Native Americans, reclaim the land known as Alcatraz Island in the name of all American Indians by right of discovery.

We wish to be fair and honorable in our dealings with the Caucasian inhabitants of this land, and hereby offer the following treaty:

We will purchase said Alcatraz Island for twenty-four dollars in glass beads and red cloth, a precedent set by the white man's purchase of a similar island 300 years ago. We know that $24 in trade goods for these 16 acres is more than what was paid when Manhattan Island was sold, but we know that land values have risen over the years. Our offer of $1.24 per acre is greater than the $0.47 per acre the white men are now paying the California Indians for their lands.

We will give to the inhabitants of this island a portion of the land of their own to be held in trust . . . by the Bureau of Caucasian Affairs . . . in perpetuity—for as long as the sun shall rise and the rivers go down in the sea. We will further guide the inhabitants in the proper way of living. We will offer them our religion, our education, our way of life—ways in order to help them achieve our level of civilization and thus raise them and all their white brothers up from their savage and unhappy state. We offer this treaty in good faith and wish to be fair and honorable in our dealings with all white men.

We feel that this so-called Alcatraz Island is more than suitable for an Indian reservation, as determined by the white man's own standards. By this, we mean that this place resembles most Indian reservations in that:

1. It is isolated from modern facilities, and without adequate means of transportation.
2. It has no fresh running water.
3. It has inadequate sanitation facilities.
4. There are no oil or mineral rights.
5. There is no industry and so unemployment is very great.
6. There are no health-care facilities.
7. The soil is rocky and nonproductive, and the land does not support game.
8. There are no educational facilities.
9. The population has always exceeded the land base.
10. The population has always been held as prisoners and kept dependent upon others.

Further, it would be fitting and symbolic that ships from all over the world, entering the Golden Gate, would first see Indian land, and thus be reminded of the true history of this nation. This tiny island would be a symbol of the great lands once ruled by free and noble Indians.

What use will we make of this land?

Since the San Francisco Indian Center burned down, there is no place for Indians to assemble and carry on tribal life here in the white man's city. Therefore, we plan to develop on this island several Indian institutions:

1. A Center for Native American Studies will be developed which will educate them to the skills and knowledge relevant to improve the lives and spirits of all Indian peoples. Attached to this center will be travelling universities, managed by Indians, which will go to the Indian Reservations, learning this necessary and relevant materials now about.

2. An American Indian Spiritual Center, which will practice our ancient tribal religious and

sacred healing ceremonies. Our cultural arts will be featured and our young people trained in music, dance, and healing rituals.

3. An Indian Center of Ecology, which will train and support our young people in scientific research and practice to restore our lands and waters to their pure and natural state. We will work to de-pollute the air and waters of the Bay Area. We will seek to restore fish and animal life to the area and to revitalize sea life which has been threatened by the white man's way. We will set up facilities to desalt sea water for human benefit.

4. A Great Indian Training School will be developed to teach our people how to make a living in the world, improve our standard of living, and to end hunger and unemployment among all our people. This training school will include a center for Indian arts and crafts, and an Indian restaurant serving native foods, which will restore Indian culinary arts. This center will display Indian arts and offer Indian foods to the public, so that all may know of the beauty and spirit of the traditional Indian ways.

5. Some of the present buildings will be taken over to develop an American Indian museum which will depict our native food and other cultural contributions we have given to the world. Another part of the museum will present some of the things the white man has given to the Indians in return for the land and life he took: disease, alcohol, poverty and cultural decimation (as symbolized by old tin cans, barbed wire, rubber tires, plastic containers, etc.) Part of the museum will remain a dungeon to symbolize both those Indian captives who were incarcerated for challenging white authority and those who were imprisoned on reservations. The museum will show the noble and tragic events of Indian history, including the broken treaties, the documentary of the Trail of Tears, the Massacre of Wounded Knee, as well as the victory over Yellow-Hair Custer and his army.

In the name of all Indians, therefore, we reclaim this island for our Indian nations, for all these reasons. We feel this claim is just and proper, and that this land should rightfully be granted to us as long as the rivers run and the sun shall shine.

We hold the rock!

Source: Fortunate Eagle, Adam. *Alcatraz! Alcatraz!: The Indian Occupation of 1969–1971.* Berkeley, CA: Heyday Books, 1992, 44–47.

All-Indian University and Cultural Complex on Indian Land
(1970)

One of the more spectacular instances of Indian activism in the late 1960s was the seizing of Alcatraz Island in San Francisco Bay in late November 1969. San Francisco's Indian Center had burned down during the month, and there seemed little prospect of getting any help from the federal government for a new one as the Bureau of Indian Affairs expended very little of its resources on urban Indians. A group of Bay Area Indians, mostly university students, took over the island and proclaimed their intention to turn it into a cultural-educational center. The following statement was issued by the group, calling itself "Indians of All Tribes," in February 1970. Later that year, the federal government ousted the Indians from the island after several months of a precarious existence during which all supplies—even water—had to be brought over from the mainland.

Indians of All Tribes greet our brothers and sisters of all races and tongues upon our Earth Mother. We here on Indian land, Alcatraz, represent many tribes of Indians.

We are still holding the island of Alcatraz in the true names of freedom, justice, and equality, because our brothers and sisters of this earth have lent support to our just cause. We reach out our hands and hearts and send spirit messages to all Indians.

Our anger at the many injustices forced upon us since the first white men landed on these sacred shores has been transformed into a hope that we be allowed the long suppressed right of all men to plan and to live their own lives in harmony and cooperation with all fellow creatures and with nature. We have learned that violence breeds only more violence and we therefore have carried on our occupation of Alcatraz in a peaceful manner, hoping that the government will act accordingly.

Be it known, however, that we are quite serious in our demand to be given ownership of this island in the name of Indians of All Tribes. We are here to stay, men, women, and children. We feel that this request is but little to ask from a government which has systematically stolen our lands, destroyed a once beautiful landscape, killed off the creatures of nature, polluted air and water, ripped open the very bowels of our earth in senseless greed, and instituted a program to annihilate the many Indian tribes of this land by theft, suppression, prejudice, termination, and so-called relocation and assimilation.

We are a proud people! We are Indians! We have observed and rejected much of what so-called civilization offers. We are Indians! We will preserve our traditions and ways of life by educating our own children. We are Indians! We will join hands in a unity never before put into practice. Our Earth Mother awaits our voices. We are Indians of All Tribes!!!

We came to Alcatraz because we were sick and tired of being pushed around, exploited, and degraded everywhere we turned in our own country. We selected Alcatraz for many reasons but most importantly, we came to Alcatraz because it is a place of our own. Somewhere that is geographically unfeasible for everybody to come and interfere with what we would like to do with our lives. We can beat our drums all night long if we want to and not be bothered or harassed by non-Indians and police. We can worship, we can sing, and we can make plans for our lives and the future of our Indian people and Alcatraz.

After we landed on Alcatraz, we got a lot of attention and publicity. Support came in from the local areas and the nation, and even worldwide. People wanted to give us benefits, have us speak at schools, be in programs on television and radio, and even have movie premiers on the island. We were flooded with everything and everybody, from opportunists and vultures to sincere and dedicated people. Somehow, we survived all the glory and confusion even though we have never been the victims of attention before and the symbol of the American Indian shined out before the nation and the whole world.

Indians of All Tribes united on the Alcatraz issue and for the first time in the Bay area, Indian organizations representing over 40,000 Indian people, united and formed the Bay Area Native American Council, in order to push the government to deal with Alcatraz as the priority issue.

The Bay Area Native American Council is a support group for Alcatraz. They do not speak for Indians on Alcatraz, although we consult with them, and support them in their work to help Indians in the Bay area.

Our work on Alcatraz is different from BANAC. We are maintaining the island during the occupation, as a way of promoting the general welfare of all Indian people, which means that our occupation is not strictly Alcatraz but rather for all Indian people. We hope to concern and involve ourselves with national Indian problems as well as planning and building our own Indian university and cultural center.

We on Alcatraz formed a nonprofit corporation called Indians of All Tribes, Inc. We represent who we are, and we are Indians of All Tribes.

We don't speak for Indians all over the country. The Indians all over the country speak for themselves.

When Indian people come to see what Alcatraz is all about and to see what they can do for the Alcatraz movement, then they speak for themselves. We have a radio station that broadcasts live from the island where they speak about their reservations and it draws attention to their particular problems. We have a newsletter as well. Anyone is welcome to write what they have to say.

Before we took Alcatraz, people in San Francisco didn't even know that Indians were alive, and if that's a sample of what the local people knew, considering that this is the main relocation point for Indians through the Bureau of Indian Affairs, then there are people across the nation who never even knew that Indians were alive or ever even knew our problems. They never knew anything about our suicide rate that is ten times the national average, or our education level that is to the fifth grade. Alcatraz focused on the Indian people. Now the Indian people have a chance for the first time to say what they have to say and to make decisions about themselves, which has never happened before.

The decision we want to make is in governing ourselves and our own people, without interference from non-Indians. Naturally we don't have all the tools that we need in order to make decisions on the engineering or structural engineering on Alcatraz or the planning of the island, so we would need non-Indian advice as well. We need everyone's advice who has something to contribute.

Our main concern is with Indian people everywhere. One of the reasons we took Alcatraz was because the students were having problems in the universities and colleges they were attending. This was the first time that Indian people had ever had the chance to get into a university or college because relocation was all vocation-oriented and it was not until 1968 and 1969 that Indians started getting into the universities and colleges. So, when this happened, we all realized that we didn't want to go through the university machinery coming out

white-orientated like the few Indian people before us, or like the non-Indian people who were running our government, our Indian government, or our Indian Affairs. We didn't want to alienate ourselves from the non-Indian people because we were learning from everyone else as well, but we also wished to retain our own identity, with the whole conglomeration of everybody; We didn't want to melt with the melting pot, which was the object of federal relocation programs. We wanted to remain Indians. That's why native American studies became a prime issue, and when we had a big confrontation with the administration, we could see that we weren't going to fool ourselves about the university; we could see that we could never get everything through it. They would make small concessions, but still didn't give us what we needed. It was just a token of what we actually wanted and we didn't want to be used like that.

This was one of the reasons why we wanted our own Indian university, so that they would stop whitewashing Indians, which was happening, not only on the university level, but in the Indian boarding schools and summer home programs for Indians and just everything that the government had to do with Indians.

We were also concerned about our own lives and our children and what was happening on the reservations as well, because while we were physically away, we still had our families and people in our hearts and on our minds, the problems that they were facing, and the frustration of not being able to help them because we were trying to get the necessary tools so we could return to our reservations some day. In the meantime, there were all types of roadblocks. We needed attention brought to our people, and we needed a place to get together in the city so that we didn't become victims of assimilation. It finally all came to a point and we decided we would just go liberate our own land since all of our other lands had been taken away and the cities were so crowded and we had nowhere to go together for Indian dances or pow-wows or anything, or even to have our own religious ceremonies. We'd get arrested if we practised our own religion and had peyote in our home. In 1964 a Sioux landing party had taken Alcatraz which was federal surplus land that, according to the Sioux treaty, should revert back to the Indians after use. The Sioux wanted the government to live up to their treaty and they landed on Alcatraz and staked their claim. They were rejected and turned away, so we followed it through, when all of the proposals came out from Hunt, Treshman, and other millionaires.

What we want to do in the long-range view is to get some type of help for our people all across the nation. We must look at the problem back on the reservation, where it all begins, with the Bureau of Indian Affairs. There's going to have to be some changes made within our own government structure. We often thought of ourselves as a sovereign nation within a nation, but through the years, this has fallen apart, because the state has beaten us on jurisdiction rights on different reservations, and the termination of the Indian people is close in sight. We all can see those things that are coming on and we want to avoid having our life taken away from us. What few lands we do have left on the reservations, we want to keep. We have no government for our own people and we live under what is really a colonial system because we do not select the people who govern us, like the commissioner of Indian Affairs, who is appointed by the secretary of the interior, who is appointed by the President, and the superintendent on every reservation, who is appointed by the commissioner. We must somehow make up our own plan of government for ourselves and for our people, rather than have someone else decide or plan what is ahead for us. We must make up those plans and decisions for ourselves.

Alcatraz is a beginning, because we are doing that on Alcatraz now. We are making up our own plans. . . .

We'd like to change laws, which are not made for us. Even the Constitution of the United States, which says that all men are created equal, was made for white men at the time it was written, and didn't include any Third World people. The Constitution has not included us, as history will bear out. It's hard for us to look around and see all the destruction that has happened to our country and feel good about it. Every day that we go over on the boat, we can see all that garbage and junk that's in the water, and it makes us sad. The air that is being polluted around us covers the sun and the sun is our giver of life and without the sun there will be no life on this earth. Part of us is being taken away by this destruction of nature. If you destroy everything around us, then you are destroying us. Maybe other people who are living in this country will have more respect and pride for the home that they are living in if we bring this to their attention.

We want to establish a center on ecology, as part of our cultural complex. The cultural complex also involves the tradition of our religion. The base of anything we do is our religion. We must have a place for our spiritual leaders and our medicine men to come. We also plan to have our own library and archives to help us document the wrongs which have been done in this country and the wisdom that has been lost. Also, we plan to have a place where we can practise our dances and songs and music and drums, where we can teach our children and not let this die, as it's dying on the reservation today.

Our parents were forbidden to speak their own language, or dance their own dances, and they were pushed into government boarding schools that were trying to teach them how to be "civilized," which meant losing their own identity. We have been forced to fit into a pattern which had been thought out a long time ago, not by us, but by the government that was over us. When there's no employment on the reservation, the only jobs that you would get were with the Bureau of Indian Affairs or the government and in this way, they can continue to indoctrinate the Indian people on the reservation by holding money in front of their faces. Because the non-Indians live in another world where they have cars and clothes and food to eat, they can always use that as a lure to get our people to want the same things, and by doing this, then they can brainwash our people the way they want them to be so that they would eventually work against their own Indian people. This is what has been happening when the Bureau of Indian Affairs set up the mock tribal governments on reservations. Since the Civil Rights law has passed, it hasn't affected the Indian that much because they've only taken down the signs that say "No Dogs and Indians Allowed." The feeling is still there.

We feel that the island is the only bargaining power that we have with the federal government. It is the only way we have to get them to notice us or even want to deal with us. We are going to maintain our occupation, until the island which is rightfully ours is formally granted to us. Otherwise, they will forget us, the way they always have, but we will not be forgotten.

Source: Trudell, John, and LaNada Boyer. "Planning Grant Proposal to Develop an All Indian University and Cultural Complex on Indian Land, Alcatraz." February 1970. National Council on Indian Opportunity, Box 5, Folder 4. RG 220. National Archives and Records Administration, Washington, DC.

Native Alliance for Red Power (NARP) Eight-Point Program (ca. 1970)

The Native Alliance for Red Power (NARP) was formed in Vancouver in the late 1960s. Like other indigenous activist groups, such as the American Indian Movement (AIM), NARP focused on the themes of freedom and self-determination for the First Peoples of Canada. This document mirrors many of the demands outlined by AIM, and a comparison of the two programs offers a picture of transnational cooperation among Indian groups.

The NARP sought to change its relationship with the Canadian government in radical ways. The group demanded compensation for broken treaties and lost land as well as exemption from taxation. They also demanded a revision of the way Canadian history was taught, so as to present a more balanced account of the sufferings experienced by the tribes at the hands of colonial authorities. It is important to recognize that many of these ideas are the result of knowledge and experience shared with Native Americans. The Red Power movement was transnational in nature, affecting Native peoples worldwide.

1. We will not be free until we are able to determine our destiny. Therefore, we want power to determine the destiny of our reservations and communities. Gaining power in our reservations and communities, and power over our lives will entail the abolishment of the "Indian Act," and the destruction of the colonial office (Indian Affairs Branch).

2. This racist government has robbed, cheated and brutalized us, and is responsible for the deaths of untold numbers of our people. We feel under no obligation to support this government in the form of taxation. Therefore, we want an end to the collection of money from us in the form of taxes.

3. The history of Canada was written by oppressors, the invaders of this land. Their lies are perpetrated in the educational system of today. By failing to expose the true history of this decadent Canadian society, the schools facilitate our continued oppression. Therefore, we want an education that teaches us our true history and exposes the racist values of this society.

4. In this country, Indian and Métis represent 3% of the population, yet we constitute approximately 60% of the inmates in prisons and jails.

Therefore, we want an immediate end to unjust arrests and harassment of our people by the racist police.

5. When brought before the courts of this country, the redman cannot hope to get a fair hearing from white judges, jurors and court officials. Therefore, we want natives to be tried by a jury of people chosen from native communities or people of their racial heritage. Also, we want freedom for those of our brothers and sisters now being unjustly held in the prisons of this country.

6. The treaties pertaining to fishing, hunting, trapping and property rights and special privileges have been broken by this government. In some cases, our people did not engage in treaties with the government and have not been compensated for their loss of land. Therefore, for those of our people who have not made treaties, we want fair compensation. Also, we want the government to honour the statutes, as laid down in these treaties, as being supreme and not to be infringed upon by any legislation whatsoever.

7. The large industrial companies and corporations that have raped the natural resources of this country are responsible, along with their government, for the extermination of the resources upon which we depend for food, clothing and shelter. Therefore, we want an immediate end to this exploitation and compensation from these thieves. We want the government to give foreign aid to the areas comprising the Indian Nation, so that we can start desperately needed programs concerning housing, agriculture and industrial co-operatives. We want to develop our remaining resources in the interests of the redman, not in the interests of the white corporate-elite.

8. The white power structure has used every possible method to destroy our spirit, and the will to resist. They have divided us into status and non-status, American and Canadian, Métis and Indian. We are fully aware of their "divide and rule" tactic, and its effect on our people.

RED POWER IS THE SPIRIT TO RESIST

RED POWER IS PRIDE IN WHAT WE ARE

RED POWER IS LOVE FOR OUR PEOPLE

RED POWER IS OUR COMING TOGETHER TO FIGHT FOR LIBERATION

RED POWER IS NOW!

Source: NARP's Eight-Point Program. http://archive.lib.msu.edu/DMC/AmRad/americanindianmovement/ABW.pdf.

Sandra Osawa, "To Be Indian in Los Angeles"

(1971)

In the following essay, Sandra Osawa, a member of the Makah Nation of northwestern Washington, describes the difficulty of urban Native Americans in the 1970s. In terms of health care and housing, most of the indigenous inhabitants of Los Angeles were unable to secure government services. At the same time, this new phenomenon of large urban Indian populations, which arose in the postwar period, resulted in the loss of language, history, and culture. Many urban Indians were viewed with suspicion by their friends and family members who remained on the reservation. Osawa's essay represents an attempt to draw attention to the plight of urban Indians.

To be Indian in Los Angeles is to live in legal limbo, unseen, unheard and almost without a country. Urban-area Indians are terminated from federal services upon leaving the reservation even though half of the total Indian population was lured to the cities by the federal government's infamous "Relocation" craze.

In time, we began to understand that "relocation" was a nice word for displacement, deportation, alienation and finally termination of your existence as an Indian. The Bureau of Indian Affairs closes its eyes to any problem an "urban" Indian might have. In effect, the BIA acts like the teacher who promotes her failing student to the next grade. Urban Indians have been promoted and thus are no longer a problem to the BIA.

And so the split between urban and reservation Indians arises, created not by Indians, but by our colonial managers, the BIA. The Urban Indian is cut off from his only political and legal source, his own tribal government. Fearful that the small amount of services rendered to reservation Indians will have to be shared with his urban brother, tribal leaders are forced into seeing urban Indians as a potential enemy. Not without some historical validity, the reservation Indian fears that urban tribal members will terminate reservation and treaty rights in favor of a per capita payment if given too much voice.

Without federal or tribal protection, urban Indians thus fall *victim* to the state and local government. Victim because state and local governments have no mandate nor mechanism to deal with Indians. Los Angeles holds the largest urban-Indian population in the U.S. yet the city census keeps no vital social statistics for Indians as they do for Blacks and Chicanos. Indians are not numerically large enough in any one county to be statistically recorded and we must identify ourselves as "other" on the census.

Since not many Indians think of themselves as an "other" even a simple census fails to reflect the urban Indian. The problems magnify from there. With no statistics on income, housing and population factors, the Indian cannot successfully compete with the Blacks and Chicanos for a slice of the minority pie. Needless to say, the Indian does not get his slice.

INDIAN HOUSING IN L.A.

The problem with housing as with health and other urban Indian conditions is that no federal, state or local agency has jurisdiction to cope with the problem. Six months after you move into the city, for example, the BIA drops your records from its files. There is no further followup. It is as if after moving to the city, all your problems vanish.

Those not coming to the city on BIA relocation assistance, find no agency to help them upon arrival. All Indians must deal with landlord and housing problems on an individual basis. It is, therefore, not a coincidence that areas with a high Indian population are also those areas with the highest substandard housing.

What is most startling to discover is that local housing authorities, who are supposed to deal with low-income housing problems actually discriminate against large families.

One local Indian woman with 9 children, for example, was living in a dilapidated two-bedroom house. When she appealed for help to several housing authorities she was turned down! The reason they could not help her was that her family was too large. Housing authorities have only 3- or 4-bedroom homes and they could not legally move her out of her two-bedroom home because they would be sanctioning an overcrowded living situation!

Many Indians live in dilapidated or overcrowded apartments in which landlords are obviously negligent. Bad floors, roofs, walls, plumbing and heating problems exist along with roaches and other insects. Some have been thrown out of their apartments overnight for asking for small repairs. Fearful of being evicted, they accept unliveable conditions.

There are no accurate statistics available on Indian housing problems. From records kept by the Indian Center's departments, however, at least one-third of all clients are faced with a housing problem. And of course there is a vast majority of Indians—lost out there somewhere—without even a census count to identify them. These are the people in need who never request help.

HEALTH CARE? GO TO PHOENIX!

Indians in L.A. who check with their area Indian health office concerning hospital care, will find this startling response—you are eligible for care at your nearest Indian Health Service Hospital which happens to be in Phoenix, Arizona! Mr. Benny Atencio received a letter from Dr. Bedingfeld, of the Albuquerque Service Unit, explaining health services available to Pueblos in L.A. These services would apply to other tribes living in the city. The letter further stated that it was "unfortunate" that only Indians on relocation or in BIA school, or who were temporarily visiting L.A. would be eligible for assistance. Indians not in those categories could not obtain IHS payment for health care in Los Angeles.

In 1967, two Papagos living 15 miles off their reservation in Arizona, were denied welfare assistance. They took their case to the 9th U.S. Circuit Court of Appeals and in June of 1972 they won. The court ruled that the BIA may not deny welfare to needy Indians just because they live outside reservations. Judge Kilkenny ruled against "unauthorized residency restrictions." The Papago case (Ramon & Anita Ruiz) in Arizona, could lead to important results in terms of housing, health and other assistance being denied Indians in relocation cities such as Los Angeles.

Unfortunately, nobody speaks for the urban Indian. The Los Angeles Indian Center, now that it has received federal funds, is prohibited from any political activity. NCAI has a lobby for reservation Indians but excludes urban Indian representation. The newly formed NAIC, the urban organization, is also federally funded and therefore politically restricted.

With no federal assistance available, urban Indian housing and health problems will continue to be ignored. Until a political platform is built, Indians in L.A. and other cities will continue to live in legal limbo. We will continue to be estranged and suspected by tribal governments, unrecognized by the federal government and ignored by the state.

Source: Osawa, Sandra. "To Be Indian in Los Angeles." In *Indian Voice*. Albuquerque, NM: Southwestern Indian Polytechnic Institute, Native American Publishing Company, 1971, 16–17.

Alaska Native Claims Settlement Act
(December 18, 1971)

In 1968, oil was discovered at Prudhoe Bay, Alaska. The easiest method of moving the oil from its remote location along the Arctic coast was to build a pipeline, which would carry the oil to the port of Valdez, where it would be shipped by oil tankers south to the lower 48 states. However, the plan ran into difficulty because the U.S. government had not yet settled the land claims of Alaska Natives, which included Indians, Aleuts, and Eskimos, an issue that had been unresolved since the purchase of Alaska in 1867.

With the passage of the Alaska Native Claims Settlement Act on December 18, 1971, President Richard Nixon ultimately honored the claims asserted by Alaska Natives as the original owners of the land. The act first did a clean sweep by invalidating preexisting land claims by Alaska Natives. In return, 44 million acres of land and $963 million were paid out to 200 local villages and 13 newly created Native-owned corporations. This was the largest land claims settlement in U.S. history. It also created a system of land ownership *fundamentally different from the reservation system established for other Native Americans because the land was owned outright by the regional and village corporations, rather than in trust by the U.S. government, and as such can be used and sold at the discretion of the tribe.*

AN ACT TO PROVIDE FOR THE SETTLEMENT OF CERTAIN LAND CLAIMS OF ALASKA NATIVES, AND FOR OTHER PURPOSES

Be it enacted . . . , That this Act may be cited as the "Alaska Native Claims Settlement Act."

Declaration of Policy

Sec. 2. Congress finds and declares that—

a. there is an immediate need for a fair and just settlement of all claims by Natives and Native groups of Alaska, based on aboriginal land claims;

b. the settlement should be accomplished rapidly, with certainty, in conformity with the real economic and social needs of Natives, without litigation, with maximum participation by Natives in decisions affecting their rights and property, without establishing any permanent racially defined institutions, rights, privileges, or obligations, without creating a reservation system or lengthy wardship or trusteeship, and without adding to the categories of property and instructions enjoying special tax privileges or to the legislation establishing special relationships between the United States Government and the State of Alaska;

c. no provision of this Act shall replace or diminish any right, privilege, or obligation of Natives as citizens of the United States or of Alaska, or relieve, replace, or diminish any obligation of the United States or of the State of Alaska to protect and promote the rights or welfare of Natives as citizens of the United States or of Alaska; the Secretary is authorized and directed, together with other appropriate agencies of the United States Government, to make a study of all Federal programs primarily designed to benefit Native people and to report back to the Congress with his recommendations for the future management and operation of these programs within three years of the date of enactment of this Act;

d. no provision of this Act shall constitute a precedent for reopening, renegotiating, or legislating upon any past settlement involving land claims or other matters with any Native organization, or any tribe, band, or identifiable group of American Indians;

e. no provision of this Act shall effect a change or changes in the petroleum reserve policy reflected in sections 7421 through 7438 of title 10 of the United States Code except as specifically provided in this Act;

f. no provision of this Act shall be construed to constitute a jurisdictional act, to confer jurisdiction to sue, nor to grant implied consent to Natives to sue the United States or any of its officers with respect to the claims extinguished by the operation of this Act; and

g. no provision of this Act shall be construed to terminate or otherwise curtail the activities of the Economic Development Administration or other Federal agencies conducting loan or loan and grant programs in Alaska. For this purpose only, the terms "Indian reservation" and "trust or restricted Indian-owned land areas" in Public Law 89–136, the Public Works and Economic Development Act of 1965, as amended, shall be interpreted to include lands granted to Natives under this Act as long as such lands remain in the ownership of the Native villages or the Regional Corporations. . . .

Declaration of Settlement

Sec. 4. (a) All prior conveyances of public land and water areas in Alaska, or any interest therein, pursuant to Federal law, and all tentative approvals pursuant to section 6 (g) of the Alaska Statehood Act, shall be regarded as an extinguishment of the aboriginal title thereto, if any.

(b) All aboriginal titles, if any, and claims of aboriginal title in Alaska based on use and occupancy, including submerged land underneath all water areas, both inland and offshore, and including any aboriginal hunting or fishing rights that may exist, are hereby extinguished.

(c) All claims against the United States, the State, and all other persons that are based on claims of aboriginal right, title, use, or occupancy of land or water areas in Alaska, or that are based on any statute or treaty of the United States relating to Native use and occupancy, or that are based on the laws of any other nation, including any such claims that are pending before any Federal or state court or the Indian Claims Commission, are hereby extinguished.

Enrollment

Sec. 5. (a) The Secretary shall prepare within two years from the date of enactment of this Act a roll of all Natives who were born on or before, and who are living on, the date of enactment of this Act. Any decision of the Secretary regarding eligibility for enrollment shall be final.

(b) The roll prepared by the Secretary shall show for each Native, among other things, the region and the village or other place in which he resided on the date of the 1970 census enumeration, and he shall be enrolled according to such residence. Except as provided in subsection (c), a Native eligible for enrollment who is not, when the roll is prepared, a permanent resident of one of the twelve regions established pursuant to subsection 7(a) shall be enrolled by the Secretary in one of the twelve regions, giving priority in the following order to—

1. the region where the Native resided on the 1970 census date if he had resided there without substantial interruption for two or more years;
2. the region where the Native previously resided for an aggregate of ten years or more;
3. the region where the Native was born; and
4. the region from which an ancestor of the Native came.

The Secretary may enroll a Native in a different region when necessary to avoid enrolling members of the same family in different regions or otherwise avoid hardship.

(c) A Native eligible for enrollment who is eighteen years of age or older and is not a permanent resident of one of the twelve regions may, on the date he files an application for enrollment, elect to be enrolled in a thirteenth region for Natives who are nonresidents of Alaska, if such region is established pursuant to subsection 7(c). If such region is not established, he shall be enrolled as provided in subsection (b). His election shall apply to all dependent members of his household who are less than eighteen years of age, but shall not affect the enrollment of anyone else.

Alaska Native Fund

Sec. 6. (a) There is hereby established in the United States Treasury an Alaska Native Fund into which the following moneys shall be deposited:

1. $462,500,000 from the general fund of the Treasury, which are authorized to be appropriated according to the following schedule:

A. $12,500,000 during the fiscal year in which this Act becomes effective;

B. $50,000,000 during the second fiscal year;

C. $70,000,000 during each of the third, fourth, and fifth fiscal years;

D. $40,000,000 during the sixth fiscal year; and $30,000,000 during each of the next five fiscal years.

2. Four percent interest per annum, which is authorized to be appropriated, on any amount authorized to be appropriated by this paragraph that is not appropriated within six months after the fiscal year in which payable.

3. $500,000,000 pursuant to the revenue sharing provisions of section 9.

Regional Corporations

Sec. 7. (a) For purposes of this Act, the State of Alaska shall be divided by the Secretary within one year after the date of enactment of this Act into twelve geographic regions, with each region composed as far as practicable of Natives having a common heritage and sharing common interests. In the absence of good cause shown to the contrary, such regions shall approximate the areas covered by the operations of the following existing Native associations:

1. Arctic Slope Native Association (Barrow, Point Hope);

2. Bering Straits Association (Seward Peninsula, Unalakleet, Saint Lawrence Island);

3. Northwest Alaska Native Association (Kotzebue);

4. Association of Village Council Presidents (southwest coast, all villages in the Bethel area, including all villages on the Lower Yukon River and the Lower Kuskokwim River);

5. Tanana Chiefs' Conference (Koyukuk, Middle and Upper Yukon Rivers, Upper Kuskokwim, Tanana River);

6. Cook Inlet Association (Kenai, Tyonek, Eklutna, Iliamna);

7. Bristol Bay Native Association (Dillingham, Upper Alaska Peninsula);

8. Aleut League (Aleutian Islands, Pribilof Islands and that part of the Alaska Peninsula which is in the Aleut League);

9. Chugach Native Association (Cordova, Tatitlek, Port Graham, English Bay, Valdez, and Seward);

10. Tlingit-Haida Central Council (southeastern Alaska, including Metlakatla);

11. Kodiak Area Native Association (all villages on and around Kodiak Island); and

12. Copper River Native Association (Copper Center, Glennallen, Chitina, Mentasta).

Any dispute over the boundaries of a region or regions shall be resolved by a board of arbitrators consisting of one person selected by each of the Native associations involved, and an additional one or two persons, whichever is needed to make an odd number of arbitrators, such additional person or persons to be selected by the arbitrators selected by the Native associations involved.

(b) The Secretary may, on request made within one year of the date of enactment of this Act, by representative and responsible leaders of the Native associations listed in subsection (a), merge two or more of the twelve regions: Provided, That the twelve regions may not be reduced to less than seven, and there may be no fewer than seven Regional Corporations.

Conveyance of Lands

Sec. 14. (a) Immediately after selection by a Village Corporation for a Native village listed in section 11 which the Secretary finds is qualified for land benefits under this Act, the Secretary shall issue to the Village Corporation a patent to the surface estate in the number of acres shown in the following table:

Table 2   Alaska Native Claims Settlement Act

If the village had on the 1970 census enumeration date a Native population between—	It shall be entitled to a patent to an area of public lands equal to—
25 and 99	69,120 acres
100 and 199	92,160 acres
200 and 399	115,200 acres
400 and 599	138,240 acres
600 or more	161,280 acres

The lands patented shall be those selected by the Village Corporation pursuant to subsection 12(a). In addition, the Secretary shall issue to the Village Corporation a patent to the surface estate in the lands selected pursuant to subsection 12(b).

(b) Immediately after selection by any Village Corporation for a Native village listed in section 16 which the Secretary finds is qualified for land benefits under this Act, the Secretary shall issue to the Village Corporation a patent to the surface estate to 23,040 acres. The lands patented shall be the lands within the township or townships that enclose the Native village, and any additional lands selected by the Village Corporation from the surrounding townships withdrawn for the Native village by subsection 16(a) . . .

[U.S. Statutes at Large, 85:688–92, 702–3.]

Source: Alaska Native Claims Settlement Act, U.S. Statutes at Large 85 (1971): 688.

Menominee Restoration Act of 1973

As a result of the poor social and economic conditions that afflicted many Menominee after the Menominee Termination Act of 1954, this act was passed and signed in 1973. The act of 1954 terminated the Menominee tribe's status as a federally recognized Indian tribe. The termination policy was undertaken in hope that the tribes would be freed from the manipulation and interference of the government and thus become able to achieve personal and economic growth on their own. The Menominee were chosen for the termination program because they had forestry and lumbering industries that seemed capable of supporting the tribe economically. However, the lumber business could not supply sufficient jobs and fell; as a result, Menominee County soon lacked the tax base to provide basic services. It became clear by the late 1960s that termination was a failure. The 1973 act restored federally recognized sovereignty and federal services, including health care, to the Menominee tribe of Wisconsin. With federal responsibilities to the tribe reestablished, the Menominee were able to establish a police force, school district, and other vital services. The hunting and fishing rights (originally protected by treaty) that were taken away from the tribe in 1954 were also reestablished.

AN ACT TO REPEAL THE ACT TERMINATING FEDERAL SUPERVISION OVER THE PROPERTY AND MEMBERS OF THE MENOMINEE INDIAN TRIBE OF WISCONSIN; TO REINSTITUTE THE MENOMINEE INDIAN TRIBE OF WISCONSIN AS A FEDERALLY RECOGNIZED SOVEREIGN INDIAN TRIBE; AND TO RESTORE TO THE MENOMINEE TRIBE OF WISCONSIN THOSE FEDERAL SERVICES FURNISHED TO AMERICAN INDIANS BECAUSE OF THEIR STATUS AS AMERICAN INDIANS; AND FOR OTHER PURPOSES

Be it enacted by the Senate and House of Representatives of the United States of America in Congress assembled, That this Act may be cited as the "Menominee Restoration Act."

SEC. 2. For the purposes of this Act—

1. The term "tribe" means the Menominee Indian Tribe of Wisconsin.
2. The term "Secretary" means the Secretary of the Interior.

3. The term "Menominee Restoration Committee" means that committee of nine Menominee Indians who shall be elected pursuant to subsections 4(a) and 4(b) of this Act.

SEC. 3. (a) Notwithstanding the provisions of the Act of June 17, 1954 (68 Stat. 250; 25 U.S.C. 891–902), as amended, or any other law, Federal recognition is hereby extended to the Menominee Indian Tribe of Wisconsin and the provisions of the Act of June 18, 1934 (48 Stat. 984; 25 U.S.C. 461 et seq.), as amended, are made applicable to it.

(b) The Act of June 17, 1954 (68 Stat. 250; 25 U.S.C. 891–902), as amended, is hereby repealed and there are hereby reinstated all rights and privileges of the tribe or its members under Federal treaty, statute, or otherwise which may have been diminished or lost pursuant to such Act.

(c) Nothing contained in this Act shall diminish any rights or privileges enjoyed by the tribe or its members now or prior to June 17, 1954, under Federal treaty, statute, or otherwise, which are not inconsistent with the provisions of this Act.

(d) Except as specifically provided in this Act, nothing contained in this Act shall alter any property rights or obligations, any contractual rights or obligations, including existing fishing rights, or any obligations for taxes already levied.

Source: Menominee Restoration Act. U.S. Statutes at Large 87 (1973): 770–773.

United States v. Washington State (Boldt Decision)
(1974)

*Although the hunting and fishing rights of Native Americans residing in Washington State had precedent in the Supreme Court (*United States v. Winans, *1905), over the course of the 20th century the tribes continued to be displaced by European Americans who had more money, better technology, and important ties to the state government. As a result of the civil rights movement in the 1960s, Native Americans decided to reassert their rights to fish in their rivers via public demonstrations, such as fish-ins on the Puyallup River. One such fish-in took place in 1970, and 60 people were arrested.* United States v. Washington State *was filed in the U.S. District Court in the Western District of Washington. The trial began in 1973 and was presided over by Judge George Boldt.*

Over the course of the trial, Boldt heard from 49 experts and a large number of tribal members. Ultimately, he ruled that, according to the language of the treaty, the government had promised to secure the fisheries for the tribes— this granted the Native Americans the original right to the fish, and they had extended those rights to white settlers. As a result, the state had *an obligation to limit fishing by non-Indians. This ruling, which came to be called the "Boldt Decision," caused a number of skirmishes between state regulators, the tribes, and nontribal fishermen. However, it was reaffirmed by the U.S. Supreme Court in 1979 and now serves as precedent for native ownership of other resources, such as shellfish.*

In the present case a basic question is the amount of fish the plaintiff tribes may take in off reservation fishing under the express reservation of fishing rights recorded in their treaties. The evidence shows beyond doubt that at treaty time the opportunity to take fish for personal subsistence and religious ceremonies was the single matter of utmost concern to all treaty tribes and their members. The extent of taking fish by tribal members for these purposes is now less than in former times but for a substantial number of tribal members at or near poverty level their need in these particulars is little, if any, less than it was for their ancestors. For these reasons the court finds that the taking of fish for ceremonial and subsistence purposes has a special treaty significance distinct from and superior to the taking of fish for commercial purposes and therefore fish taken to serve ceremonial and subsistence needs shall not be counted in the share of fish that treaty right fishermen have the opportunity to take. Such needs shall be limited to the number of fish actually used for: (a) Traditional tribal ceremonies; and (b) Personal subsistence consumption by tribal members and their immediate families.

By dictionary definition and as intended and used in the Indian treaties and in this decision "in common with" means *sharing equally* the opportunity to take fish at "usual and accustomed grounds and stations"; therefore, non-treaty fishermen shall have the opportunity to take up to 50% of the harvestable number of fish that may be taken by all fishermen at usual and accustomed grounds and stations and treaty right fishermen shall have the opportunity to take up to the same percentage of harvestable fish, as stated above.

While emphasizing the basic principle of sharing equally in the opportunity to take fish at usual and accustomed grounds and stations, the court recognizes that innumerable difficulties will arise in the application of this principle to the fisheries resource. For the present time, at least, precise mathematical equality must give way to more practical means of determining and allocating the harvestable resource, with the methodology of allocation to be developed and modified in light of current data and future experience. However, it is necessary at the outset to establish the scope of the anadromous fish resource which is subject to being "shared equally." The amount of fish of a particular species, from which the harvestable portions allocable to treaty right fishermen and non-treaty right fishermen are to be determined, is not merely the number of harvestable fish of that species which pass through the usual and accustomed fishing places of the various treaty tribes.

It is uncontroverted in the evidence that substantial numbers of fish, many of which might otherwise reach the usual and accustomed fishing places of the treaty tribes, are caught in marine areas closely adjacent to and within the state of Washington, primarily by non-treaty right fishermen. These catches reduce to a significant but not specifically determinable extent the number of fish available for harvest by treaty right fishermen. A considerable amount of this harvest is beyond any jurisdiction or control of the State. Some of this harvest is subject to limited state control because the landings are made in areas of state jurisdiction. A considerable number of fish taken within the territorial waters of Washington are under the regulatory authority of the International Pacific Salmon Fisheries Commission, an international body established by treaty between the United States and Canada. While the defendants cannot determine or control the activities of that Commission, the Washington Department of Fisheries does have some input into development of the harvest program which is prescribed or permitted by that Commission, particularly as it pertains to harvest within Washington waters. The Commission is essentially concerned with assuring adequate spawning escapement from runs subject to its jurisdiction and equal division of the harvestable portion between the two countries. Its control over times, places and manner of harvest is designed to accomplish those results. Consequently, while it must be recognized that these large harvests by non-treaty fishermen cannot be regulated with any certainty or precision by the state defendants, it is incumbent upon such defendants to take all appropriate steps within their actual abilities to assure as nearly as possible an equal sharing of the opportunity for treaty and non-treaty fishermen to harvest every species of fish to which the treaty tribes had access at their usual and accustomed fishing places at treaty times. Some additional adjustments in the harvesting scheme under state jurisdiction may be necessary to approach more nearly an equal allocation of the opportunity to harvest fish at usual and accustomed grounds and stations.

Therefore, this court finds and holds that the amount of fish of each species from which the harvestable portions shall be determined for the purposes of allocation consistent with this opinion shall be:

1. The total number of fish within the regulatory jurisdiction of the State of Washington which, absent harvest en route, would be available for harvest at the treaty tribes' usual and accustomed fishing places; plus

2. An additional equitable adjustment, determined from time to time as circumstances may require, to compensate treaty tribes for the substantially disproportionate numbers of fish, many of which might otherwise be available to treaty right fishermen for harvest, caught by non-treaty fishermen in marine areas closely adjacent to but beyond the territorial waters of the State, or outside the jurisdiction of the State, although within Washington waters.

It is suggested in *Puyallup-II* that a distinction between native and propagated steelhead should be made in computing the allocation of fish to off reservation treaty right and to non-treaty right fishing. This appears to present many difficulties and problems which must be considered and determined with all deliberate speed, by agreement or by judicial decision. Discharge of that responsibility appears to be within the jurisdiction of this court by issues all parties have submitted to this court in the Final Pretrial Order in this case. However, under the *Puyallup-II* mandate to the State Supreme Court it appears appropriate to this court that the state courts hear and determine the matter referred to, at least in the first instance.

Certain issues in this case are specified in the Final Pretrial Order which involve reef net fisheries. The only parties in this case directly concerned with these issues are the defendant Reef Net Owners and the plaintiff Lummi Tribe, although it may be other parties and non-parties have the same or similar interests. In the Findings of Fact and Conclusions of Law filed herein, the court has found and held: (a) that there is evidence which the court finds reasonable, credible and sufficient to establish that plaintiff Lummi Tribe has treaty fishing rights in the reef net fishing areas involved; (b) that members of the Lummi Tribe are entitled to and shall have, as a matter of *right,* the opportunity to fish with reef nets in such areas; (c) that while non-treaty fishermen when licensed by the State to fish in reef net areas have the *privilege* of fishing in those areas "in common with" Lummi Tribal members, they do not have the *right* to do so.

The specific number and location of stations in the reef net areas at which Lummi Tribal members shall have the right and opportunity to fish and what, if any, conditions shall be applicable thereto, will be determined by or under direction of this court upon hearing of those matters at the earliest date reasonably convenient to counsel and the court.

Source: United States v. State of Washington, 384 F. Supp. 312–Dist. Court, WD Washington, Tacoma (1974).

Indian Self-Determination and Education Assistance Act
(1975)

Since the establishment of the reservation system, the U.S. government had struggled to enact policies that promoted Indian self-sufficiency. In 1919, for example, the Buy Indian Act encouraged the federal government to contract Indian workers for any project done on the reservation, and the

Indian Reorganization Act of 1934 created a legislative basis for modern tribal government. By the 1960s, however, it was clear that the government's earlier policies were failing. The civil rights movement had triggered a number of congressional studies on living conditions on the reservations, and Indian activists drew attention to Native American issues with headlining stunts such as the takeover of Alcatraz. As a result, President Lyndon Johnson made Indian self-determination a policy issue; however, it was President Richard Nixon who developed a blueprint for the Indian Self-Determination and Educational Assistance Act.

The act is process-oriented legislation, which means it outlines an approach to government policy rather than creating a funded program. The law gave official U.S. sanction to Indian self-governance by putting the tribes in charge of services previously controlled by the federal government, such as health care. So if a tribe wanted to build a new health clinic, for example, they could contract with federal agencies such as the Bureau of Indian Affairs and Indian Health Services for the construction and implementation of the project. This new process was ultimately more efficient as it allowed Natives to manage their affairs more directly, with less bureaucratic interference.

Be it enacted by the Senate and House of Representatives of the United States of America in Congress assembled, that this Act may be cited as the "Indian Self-Determination and Education Assistance Act."

SEC. 2. (a) The Congress, after careful review of the Federal Government's historical and special legal relationship with, and resulting responsibilities to, American Indian people, finds that—

(1) the prolonged Federal domination of Indian service programs has served to retard rather than enhance the progress of Indian people and their communities by depriving Indians of the full opportunity to develop leadership skills crucial to the realization of self-government, and has denied to the Indian people an effective voice in the planning and implementation of programs for the benefit of Indians which are responsive to the true needs of Indian communities; and

(2) the Indian people will never surrender their desire to control their relationships both among themselves and with non-Indian governments, organizations, and persons.

(b) The Congress further finds that—

(1) true self-determination in any society of people is dependent upon an educational process which will insure the development of qualified people to fulfill meaningful leadership roles;

(2) the Federal responsibility for and assistance to education of Indian children has not effected the desired level of educational achievement or created the diverse opportunities and personal satisfaction which education can and should provide; and

(3) parental and community control of the educational process is of crucial importance to the Indian people.

SEC. 3. (a) The Congress hereby recognizes the obligation of the United States to respond to the strong expression of the Indian people for self-determination by assuring maximum Indian participation in the direction of educational as well as other Federal services to Indian communities so as to render such services more responsive to the needs and desires of those communities.

(b) The Congress declares its commitment to the maintenance of the Federal Government's unique and continuing relationship with, and responsibility to, individual Indian tribes and to the Indian people as a whole through the establishment of a meaningful Indian self-determination policy which will permit an orderly transition from the Federal domination of programs for, and services to, Indians to effective and meaningful participation by the Indian people in the planning, conduct, and administration of those programs and services. In accordance with this policy, the United States is committed to supporting and assisting Indian tribes in the development of strong and stable tribal governments, capable of administering quality programs and developing the economies of their respective communities.

(c) The Congress declares that a major national goal of the United States is to provide the quantity and quality of educational services and opportunities which will permit Indian children to compete and excel in the life areas of their choice, and to achieve the measure of self-determination essential to their social and economic well-being.

SEC. 4. For purposes of this Act, the term—

(a) "construction programs" means programs for the planning, design, construction, repair, improvement, and expansion of buildings or facilities, including, but not limited to, housing, law enforcement and detention facilities, sanitation and water systems, roads, schools, administration and health facilities, irrigation and agricultural work, and water conservation, flood control, or port facilities;

(b) "contract funding base" means the base level from which contract funding needs are determined, including all contract costs;

(c) "direct program costs" means costs that can be identified specifically with a particular contract objective;

(d) "Indian" means a person who is a member of an Indian tribe;

(e) "Indian tribe" means any Indian tribe, band, nation, or other organized group or community, including any Alaska Native village or regional or village corporation as defined in or established pursuant to the Alaska Native Claims Settlement Act (85 Stat. 688), which is recognized as eligible for the special programs and services provided by the United States to Indians because of their status as Indians;

(f) "indirect costs" means costs incurred for a common or joint purpose benefiting more than one contract objective, or which are not readily assignable to the contract objectives specifically benefited without effort disproportionate to the results achieved;

(g) "indirect cost rate" means the rate arrived at through negotiation between an Indian tribe or tribal organization and the appropriate Federal agency;

(h) "mature contract" means a self-determination contract that has been continuously operated by a tribal organization for three or more years, and for which there are no significant and material audit exceptions in the annual financial audit of the tribal organization: Provided, That upon the request of a tribal organization or the tribal organization's Indian tribe for purposes of section 102(a) of this Act, a contract of the tribal organization

which meets this definition shall be considered to be a mature contract;

(i) "Secretary," unless otherwise designated, means either the Secretary of Health and Human Services or the Secretary of the Interior or both;

(j) "self-determination contract" means a contract (or grant or cooperative agreement utilized under section 9 of this Act) entered into under title I of this Act between a tribal organization and the appropriate Secretary for the planning, conduct and administration of programs or services which are otherwise provided to Indian tribes and their members pursuant to Federal law: Provided, That except as provided, 1 the last proviso in section 105(a) of this Act, no contract (or grant or cooperative agreement utilized under section 9 of this Act) entered into under title I of this Act shall be construed to be a procurement contract;

(k) "State education agency" means the State board of education or other agency or officer primarily responsible for supervision by the State of public elementary and secondary schools, or, if there is no such officer or agency, an officer or agency designated by the Governor or by State law;

(l) "tribal organization" means the recognized governing body of any Indian tribe; any legally established organization of Indians which is controlled, sanctioned, or chartered by such governing body or which is democratically elected by the adult members of the Indian community to be served by such organization and which includes the maximum participation of Indians in all phases of its activities: Provided, That in any case where a contract is let or grant made to an organization to perform services benefiting more than one Indian tribe, the approval of each such Indian tribe shall be a prerequisite to the letting or making of such contract or grant, and

(m) "construction contract" means a fixed-price or cost-reimbursement self-determination contract for a construction project, except that such term does not include any contract—

(1) that is limited to providing planning services and construction management services (or a combination of such services);

(2) for the Housing Improvement Program or roads maintenance program of the Bureau of Indian Affairs administered by the Secretary of the Interior; or

(3) for the health facility maintenance and improvement program administered by the Secretary of Health and Human Services.

SEC. 6. Whoever, being an officer, director, agent, or employee of, or connected in any capacity with, any recipient of a contract, subcontract, grant, or subgrant pursuant to this Act or the Act of April 16, 1934, as amended, embezzles, willfully misapplies, steals, or obtains by fraud any of the money, funds, assets, or property which are the subject of such grant, subgrant, contract, or subcontract, shall be fined not more than $10,000 or imprisoned for not more than two years, or both, but if the amount so embezzled, misapplied, stolen, or obtained by fraud does not exceed $100, he shall be fined not more than $1,000 or imprisoned not more than one year, or both.

SEC. 7. (a) All laborers and mechanics employed by contractors or subcontractors (excluding tribes and tribal organizations) in the construction, alteration, or repair, including painting or decorating of buildings or other facilities in connection with contracts or grants entered into pursuant to this Act, shall be paid wages at not less than those prevailing on similar construction in the locality, as determined by the Secretary of Labor in accordance with the Davis-Bacon Act of March 3, 1931 as amended. With respect to construction, alteration, or repair work to which the Act of March 3, 1921 is applicable under the terms of this section, the Secretary of Labor shall have the authority and functions set forth in Reorganization Plan Numbered 14 of 1950 and section 2 of the Act of June 13, 1934.

(b) Any contract, subcontract, grant, or subgrant pursuant to this Act, the Act of April 16, 1934, as amended, or any other Act authorizing Federal contracts with or grants to Indian organizations or for the benefit of Indians, shall require that to the greatest extent feasible—

(1) preferences and opportunities for training and employment in connection with the administration of such contracts or grants shall be given to Indians; and

(2) preference in the award of subcontracts and subgrants in connection with the administration of such contracts or grants shall be given to Indian organizations and to Indian-owned economic enterprises as defined in section 3 of the Indian Financing Act of 1974.

(c) Notwithstanding subsections (a) and (b), with respect to any self-determination contract, or portion of a self-determination contract, that is intended to benefit one tribe, the tribal employment or contract preference laws adopted by such tribe shall govern with respect to the administration of the contract or portion of the contract.

SEC. 8. Notwithstanding any other provision of law, any funds appropriated pursuant to the Act of November 2, 1921, for any fiscal year which are not obligated or expended prior to the beginning of the fiscal year succeeding the fiscal year for which such funds were appropriated shall remain available for obligation or expenditures during such succeeding fiscal year. In the case of amounts made available to a tribal organization under a self-determination contract, if the funds are to be expended in the succeeding fiscal year for the purpose for which they were originally appropriated, contracted or granted, or for which they are authorized to be used pursuant to the provisions of section 106(a)(3), no additional justification or documentation of such purposes need be provided by the tribal organization to the Secretary as a condition of receiving or expending such funds.

SEC. 9. The provisions of this Act shall not be subject to the requirements of chapter 63 of title 31, United States Code: Provided, That a grant agreement or a cooperative agreement may be utilized in lieu of a contract under sections 102 and 103(1) of this Act when mutually agreed to by the appropriate Secretary and the tribal organization involved.

Source: Indian Self-determination and Education Assistance Act. Public Law 93–638, U.S. Statutes at Large 88 (1975): 2203.

Leonard Peltier, Convicted of Being Chippewa and Sioux Blood
(1977)

On June 26, 1975, a gunfight occurred on the Pine Ridge Reservation in South Dakota. Two FBI agents, Jack Coler and Ronald Williams, were killed during the fighting. Leonard Peltier, a Dakota-Chippewa Indian who was present and participated in the gun battle, was later convicted of the execution-style murders of the federal agents in 1977. In the following narrative, read by Peltier before his sentence was delivered, he outlined the long series of injustices he believed himself to be a victim of at the hands of the federal government.

There is no doubt in my mind or my people's minds you are going to sentence me to two consecutive life terms. You are and have always been prejudiced against me and any Native Americans who have stood before you; you have openly favored the government all through this trial and you are happy to do whatever the FBI would want you to do in this case.

I did not always believe this to be so! When I first saw you in the courtroom in Sioux Falls, your dignified appearance misled me into thinking that you were a fair-minded person who knew something of the law and who would act in accordance with the law! Which meant that you would be impartial and not favor one side or the other in this lawsuit. That has not been the case and I now firmly believe that you will impose consecutive life terms solely because that way you think will avoid the displeasures of the FBI. Neither my people nor myself know why you would be so concerned about an organization that has brought so much shame to the American people. But you are! Your conduct during this trial leaves no doubt that you will do the bidding of the FBI without any hesitation!

You are about to perform an act which will close one more chapter in the history of the failure of the United States courts and the failure of the people of the United States to do justice in the case of a Native American. After centuries of murder . . . could I have been wise in thinking that you would break that tradition and commit an act of justice? Obviously not! Because I should have realized that what I detected was only a very thin layer of dignity and surely not of fine character. If you think my accusations have been harsh and unfounded, I will explain why I have reached these conclusions and why I think my criticism has not been harsh enough.

First, each time my defense team tried to expose FBI misconduct . . . and tried to present evidence of this, you claimed it was irrelevant to this trial. But the prosecution was allowed to present their case with evidence that was in no way relevant—for example, an automobile blowing up on a freeway in Wichita, Kansas; an attempted murder in Milwaukee, Wisconsin, for which I have not been found innocent or guilty; a van loaded with legally purchased firearms and a policeman who claims someone fired at him in Oregon state. The Supreme Court of the United States tried to prevent convictions of this sort by passing into law that only past convictions may be presented as evidence. . . . This court knows very well I have no prior convictions, nor am I even charged with some of these alleged crimes; therefore, they cannot be used as evidence in order to receive a conviction in this farce called a trial. This is why I strongly believe you will impose two life terms, running consecutively, on me.

Second, you could not make a reasonable decision about my sentence because you suffer from at least one of three defects that prevent a rational conclusion: you plainly demonstrated this in your decision about the Jimmy Eagle and Myrtle Poor Bear aspects of this case. In Jimmy's case, only a judge who consciously and openly ignores the law would call it irrelevant to my trial; in the mental torture of Myrtle Poor Bear you said her testimony would shock the conscience of the American people if believed! But YOU decided what was to be believed—not the jury! Your conduct shocks the conscience of what the American legal system stands for!—the search for the truth by a jury of citizens. What was it that made you so afraid to let that testimony in? Your own guilt of being part of a corrupted pre-planned trial to get a conviction no matter how your reputation would be tarnished? For these reasons, I strongly believe you will do the bidding of the FBI and give me two consecutive life terms.

Third, in my opinion, anyone who failed to see the relationship between the undisputed facts of these events surrounding the investigation used by the FBI in their interrogation of the Navajo youths—Wilford Draper, who was tied to a chair for three hours and denied access to his attorney; the outright threats to Norman Brown's life; the bodily harm threatened to Mike Anderson; and, finally, the murder of Anna Mae Aquash—must be blind, stupid, or without human feelings so there is no doubt and little chance that you have the ability to avoid doing today what the FBI wants you to do, which is to sentence me to two life terms running consecutively.

Fourth, you do not have the ability to see that the conviction of an A.I.M. activist helps to cover up what the government's own evidence showed: that large numbers of Indian people engaged in that fire fight on June 26, 1975. You do not have the ability to see that the government must suppress the fact that there is a growing anger amongst Indian people and that Native Americans will resist any further encroachments by the military forces of the capitalistic Americans, which is evidenced by the large number of Pine Ridge residents who took up arms on June 26, 1975, to defend themselves. Therefore, you do not have the ability to carry out your responsibility towards me in an impartial way and will run my two life terms consecutively.

Fifth, I stand before you as a proud man; I feel no guilt! I have done nothing to feel guilty about! I have no regrets of being a Native American activist—thousands of people in the United States, Canada, and around the world have and will continue to support me to expose the injustices which have occurred in this courtroom. I do feel pity for your people that they must live under such an ugly system. Under your system, you are taught greed, racism, and corruption—and most serious of all, the destruction of Mother Earth. Under the Native American system, we are taught all people are Brothers and Sisters; to share the wealth with the poor and needy. But the most important of all is to respect and preserve the Earth, who we consider to be our Mother. We feed from her breast; our Mother gives us life from birth and when it's time to leave this world, who again takes us back into her womb. But the main thing we are taught is to preserve her for our children and our grandchildren, because they are the next who will live upon her.

No, I'm not the guilty one here; I'm not the one who should be called a criminal—white racist America is the criminal for the destruction of our lands and my people; to hide your guilt from the decent human beings in America and around the world, you will sentence me to two consecutive life terms without any hesitation. . . .

Sixth, . . . If you were impartial, you would have had an open mind on all the factual disputes in this case. But you were unwilling to allow even the slightest possibility that a law enforcement officer would lie on the stand. Then how could you possibly be impartial enough to let my lawyers prove how important it is to the FBI to convict a Native American activist in this case? You do not have the ability to see that such conviction is an important part of the efforts to discredit those who are trying to alert their Brothers and Sisters to the new threat from the white man, and the attempt to destroy what little Indian land remains in the process of extracting our uranium, oil, and other minerals. Again, to cover up your part in this, you will call me a heartless, cold-blooded murderer who deserves two life sentences consecutively. . . .

Seventh, . . . No human being should be subjected to such treatment. . . . Again, the only conclusion that comes to mind is that you know and always knew you would sentence me to two consecutive life terms.

Finally, I honestly believe that you made up your mind long ago that I was guilty and that you were going to sentence me to the maximum sentence permitted under the law. But this does not surprise me, because you are a high-ranking member of the white racist American establishment which has consistently said, "In God We Trust," while they went about the business of murdering my people and attempting to destroy our culture.

Source: Leonard Peltier's Pre-Sentencing Statement. *United States v. Leonard Peltier*, CR NO. C77–3003 (Fargo, North Dakota, 1977).

American Indian Religious Freedom Act (AIRFA)
(1978)

In 1978, Congress passed a U.S. federal law and joint resolution titled the American Indian Religious Freedom Act (AIRFA). This act addressed the need to defend and preserve the traditional religious rights and cultural practices of American Indians, Aleuts, Eskimos, and Native Hawaiians. Among the various rights addressed by this law include access to sacred sites, the freedom to worship through ceremonial and traditional rights, and the possession of objects deemed to possess a sacred value.

Before this law was passed, Native American religious practices throughout the United States had been at odds with federal and state laws that prohibited their access to sacred sites or made illegal the possession of certain items used in religious ceremonies, including eagle feathers and bones and peyote. The AIRFA was a victory for Native Americans who, during the 1960s and 1970s, increasingly found themselves having to fight for the protection of their religious, economic, and treaty rights.

SECTION 1

On and after August 11, 1978, it shall be the policy of the United States to protect and preserve for the American Indians their inherent right of freedom to believe, express, and exercise the traditional religions of the American Indian, Eskimo, Aleut, and Native Hawaiians, including but not limited to access to sites, use and possession of sacred objects, and the freedom to worship through ceremonials and traditional rites.

SECTION 2

The President shall direct the various Federal departments, agencies, and other instrumentalities responsible for administering relevant laws to evaluate their policies and procedures in consultation with native traditional religious leaders in order to determine appropriate changes necessary to protect and preserve Native American religious cultural rights and practices. Twelve months after August 11, 1978, the President shall report back to Congress the results of his evaluation, including any changes which were made in administrative policies and procedures and any recommendations he may have for legislative action.

Source: American Indian Religious Freedom Act. Public Law 95–341, 42 U.S.C. (1996).

Indian Child Welfare Act (ICWA) (1978)

Up until the passage of the Indian Child Welfare Act (ICWA) of 1978, anywhere from 25 to 35 percent of Indian children were being removed from their families by state governments and placed with white foster families. Part of the reason for this high rate of removal was cultural misunderstanding; white social workers and religious groups did not recognize the value that tribal culture placed on the extended family, and as a result, children left with extended family members were considered abandoned. This widespread removal of Native children from their land and people threatened the long-term survival of Indian culture. The law, signed by President Jimmy Carter, was enacted to protect Indian culture and to protect the tribes from unnecessary state and federal intervention into family life.

The ICWA set up basic federal standards for dealing with Native American children. If the child lived on the reservation, then child custody proceedings such as adoption, voluntary and involuntary termination of parental rights, and foster care placement were placed under the exclusive jurisdiction of the tribe. If the child lived off the reservation, then the tribal court and the state court shared jurisdiction, but the tribe received preference.

An Act to establish standards for the placement of Indian children in foster or adoptive homes, to prevent the breakup of Indian families, and for other purposes.

. . . Sec. 2. Recognizing the special relationship between the United States and the Indian tribes and their members and the Federal responsibility to Indian people, the Congress finds—

1. that clause 3, section, 8, article I of the United States Constitution provides that "The Congress shall have Power to regulate Commerce with Indian tribes" and, through this and other constitutional authority, Congress has plenary power over Indian affairs;

2. that Congress, through statutes, treaties, and the general course of dealing with Indian tribes, has assumed the responsibility for the protection and preservation of Indian tribes and their resources;

3. that there is no resource that is more vital to the continued existence and integrity of Indian tribes than their children and that the United States has a direct interest, as trustee, in protecting Indian children who are members of or are eligible for membership in an Indian tribe;

4. that an alarmingly high percentage of Indian families are broken up by the removal, often unwarranted, of their children from them by nontribal public and private agencies and that an alarmingly high percentage of such children are placed in non-Indian foster and adoptive homes and institutions; and

5. that the States, exercising their recognized jurisdiction over Indian child custody proceedings through administrative and judicial bodies, have often failed to recognize the essential tribal relations of Indian people and the cultural and social standards prevailing in Indian communities and families.

Sec. 3. The Congress hereby declares that it is the policy of this Nation to protect the best interests of Indian children and to promote the stability and security of Indian tribes and families by the establishment of minimum Federal standards for the removal of Indian children from their families and the placement of such children in foster or adoptive homes which will reflect the unique values of Indian culture, and by providing for assistance to Indian tribes in the operation of child and family service programs.

TITLE I—CHILD CUSTODY PROCEEDINGS

Sec. 101. (a) An Indian tribe shall have jurisdiction exclusive as to any State over any child custody proceeding involving an Indian child who resides or is domiciled within the reservation of such tribe, except where such jurisdiction is otherwise vested in the State by existing Federal law. Where an Indian child is a ward of a tribal court, the Indian tribe shall retain exclusive jurisdiction, notwithstanding the residence or domicile of the child.

(b) In any State court proceeding for the foster care placement of, or termination of parental rights to, an Indian child not domiciled or residing within the reservation of the Indian child's tribe, the court, in the absence of good cause to the contrary, shall transfer such proceeding to the jurisdiction of the tribe, absent objection by either parent, upon the petition of either parent or the Indian custodian or the Indian child's tribe: Provided, That such transfer shall be subject to declination by the tribal court of such tribe. . . .

Sec. 103. (a) Where any parent or Indian custodian voluntarily consents to a foster care placement or to termination of parental rights, such consent shall not be valid unless executed in writing and recorded before a judge of a court of competent jurisdiction and accompanied by the presiding judge's certificate that the terms and consequences of the consent were fully explained in detail and were fully understood by the parent or Indian custodian. The court shall also certify that either the parent or Indian custodian fully understood the explanation in English or that it was interpreted into a language that the parent or Indian custodian understood. Any consent given prior to, or within ten days after, birth of the Indian child shall not be valid. . . .

Sec. 105. (a) In any adoptive placement of an Indian child under State law, a preference shall be given, in the absence of good cause to the contrary, to a placement with (1) a member of the child's extended family; (2) other members of the Indian child's tribe; or (3) other Indian families.

(b) Any child accepted for foster care or preadoptive placement shall be placed in the least restrictive setting which most approximates a family and in which his special needs, if any, may be met. The child shall also be placed within reasonable proximity to his or her home, taking into account any special needs of the child. In any foster care or preadoptive placement, a preference shall be given, in the absence of good cause to the contrary, to a placement with—

(i) a member of the Indian child's extended family;

(ii) a foster home licensed, approved, or specified by the Indian child's tribe;

(iii) an Indian foster home licensed or approved by an authorized non-Indian licensing authority; or

(iv) an institution for children approved by an Indian tribe or operated by an Indian organization which has a program suitable to meet the Indian child's needs.

TITLE II—INDIAN CHILD AND FAMILY PROGRAMS

Sec. 201. (a) The Secretary [of the Interior] is authorized to make grants to Indian tribes and organizations in the establishment and operation of Indian child and family service programs on or near reservations and in the preparation and implementation of child welfare codes. The objective of every Indian child and family service program shall be to prevent the breakup of Indian families and, in particular, to insure that the permanent removal of an Indian child from the custody of his parent or Indian custodian shall be a last resort. . . .

Sec. 202. The Secretary is also authorized to make grants to Indian organizations to establish and operate off-reservation Indian child and family service programs.

Source: Indian Child Welfare Act. Pub. L. 95–608. U.S. Statutes at Large 93 (1978): 3071.

United States v. Sioux Nation of Indians
(1980)

The Great Sioux Reservation was established for the Lakota people as part of the Fort Laramie Treaty of 1868. The reservation, fully half of the present-day state of South Dakota, stretched from the Missouri River in the east to the border with Wyoming in the west and included the Black Hills. Gold was discovered in the Black Hills during Lt. Colonel George Armstrong Custer's 1874 expedition, which led to a massive influx of white settlers beginning in 1875. Several communities, including Custer City and Deadwood, were quickly established in the Black Hills. Rather than kick out the miners, who were violating the terms of the 1868 treaty, President Ulysses Grant pursued a policy geared toward the acquisition of the region, first by attempting to purchase the Black Hills, and then through force in the Great Sioux War of 1876.

The following document is representative of the Lakota's fight to recover the lands that were illegally taken from them in the 19th century. Although the Lakota won the judgment in United States v. Sioux Nation of Indians, *they refused to take the money, which would end their legal attempts to reclaim the Black Hills. As the Lakota people have indicated time and again, nothing short of the return of their stolen lands will suffice.*

U.S. Supreme Court
UNITED STATES v. SIOUX NATION OF INDIANS
Argued March 24, 1980.
Decided June 30, 1980.

Under the Fort Laramie Treaty of 1868, the United States pledged that the Great Sioux Reservation, including the Black Hills, would be "set apart for the absolute and undisturbed use and occupation" of the Sioux Nation (Sioux), and that no treaty for the cession of any part of the reservation would be valid as against the Sioux unless executed and signed by at least three-fourths of the adult male Sioux population. The treaty also reserved the Sioux' right to hunt in certain unceded territories. Subsequently, in 1876, an "agreement" presented to the Sioux by a special Commission but signed by only 10% of the adult male Sioux population, provided that the Sioux would relinquish their rights to the Black Hills and to hunt in the unceded territories, in exchange for subsistence rations for as long as they would be needed. In 1877, Congress passed an Act (1877 Act) implementing this "agreement" and thus, in effect, abrogated the Fort Laramie Treaty. Throughout the ensuing years, the Sioux regarded the 1877 Act as a breach of that treaty, but Congress did not enact any mechanism by which they could litigate their claims against the United States until 1920, when a special jurisdictional Act was passed. Pursuant to this Act, the Sioux brought suit in the Court of Claims, alleging that the Government had taken the Black Hills without just compensation, in violation of the Fifth Amendment. In 1942, this claim was dismissed by the Court of Claims, which held that it was not authorized by the 1920 Act to question whether the compensation afforded the Sioux in the 1877 Act was an adequate price for the Black Hills and that the Sioux' claim was a moral one not protected by the Just Compensation Clause. Thereafter, upon enactment of the Indian Claims Commission Act in 1946, the Sioux resubmitted their claim to the Indian Claims Commission, which held that the 1877 Act effected a taking for which the Sioux were entitled to just compensation and that the 1942 Court of Claims decision did not bar the taking claim under res judicata. On appeal, the Court of Claims, affirming the Commission's holding that a want of fair and honorable dealings on the Government's part was evidenced, ultimately held that the Sioux were entitled to an award of at least $17.5 million, without interest, as damages under the Indian Claims Commission Act, for the lands surrendered and for gold taken by trespassing prospectors prior to passage of the 1877 Act. But the court further held that the merits of the Sioux' taking claim had been reached in its 1942 decision and that therefore such claim was barred by res judicata. The court noted that only if the acquisition of the Black Hills amounted to an unconstitutional taking would the Sioux be entitled to interest. Thereafter, in 1978, Congress passed an Act (1978 Act) providing for de novo review by the Court of Claims of the merits of the Indian Claims Commission's holding that the 1877 Act effected a taking of the Black Hills, without regard to res judicata, and authorizing the Court of Claims to take new evidence in the case. Pursuant to this Act, the Court of Claims affirmed the Commission's holding. In so affirming, the court, in order to decide whether the 1877 Act had effected a taking or whether it had been a noncompensable act of congressional guardianship over tribal property, applied the test of whether Congress had made a good-faith effort to give the Sioux the full value of their land. Under this test, the court characterized the 1877 Act as a taking in exercise of Congress' power of eminent domain over Indian property. Accordingly, the court held that the Sioux were entitled to an award of interest on the principal sum of $17.1 million (the fair market value of the Black Hills as of 1877), dating from 1877.

Held:

- Congress' enactment of the 1978 Act, as constituting a mere waiver of the res judicata effect of a prior judicial decision rejecting the validity of a legal claim against the United States, did not violate the doctrine of the separation of powers either on the ground that Congress impermissibly disturbed the finality of a judicial decree by rendering the Court of Claims' earlier judgments in the case mere advisory opinions, or on the ground that Congress overstepped its bounds by granting the Court of Claims jurisdiction to decide the merits of the Black Hills claim, while prescribing a rule for decision that left that court no adjudicatory function to perform. *Cherokee Nation v. United States.* Congress, under its

broad constitutional power to define and "to pay the Debts . . . of the United States," may recognize its obligation to pay a moral debt not only by direct appropriation, but also by waiving an otherwise valid defense to a legal claim against the United States. When the Sioux returned to the Court of Claims following passage of the 1978 Act, they were in pursuit of judicial enforcement of a new legal right. Congress in no way attempted to prescribe the outcome of the Court of Claims' new review of the merits.

- The Court of Claims' legal analysis and factual findings fully support its conclusion that the 1877 Act did not effect a "mere change in the form of investment of Indian tribal property," but, rather, effected a taking of tribal property which had been set aside by the Fort Laramie Treaty for the Sioux' exclusive occupation, which taking implied an obligation on the Government's part to make just compensation to the Sioux. That obligation, including an award of interest, must now be paid. The principles that it "must [be] presume[d] that Congress acted in perfect good faith in the dealings with the Indians of which complaint is made, and that [it] exercised its best judgment in the premises," *Lone Wolf v. Hitchcock,* are inapplicable in this case. The question whether a particular congressional measure was appropriate for protecting and advancing a tribe's interests, and therefore not subject to the Just Compensation Clause, is factual in nature, and the answer must be based on a consideration of all the evidence presented. While a reviewing court is not to second-guess a legislative judgment that a particular measure would serve the tribe's best interests, the court is required, in considering whether the measure was taken in pursuance of Congress' power to manage and control tribal lands for the Indians' welfare, to engage in a thorough and impartial examination of the historical record. A presumption of congressional good faith cannot serve to advance such an inquiry.

Source: United States v. Sioux Nation of Indians 448 U.S. 371 (1980).

Merrion v. Jicarilla Apache Tribe
(1982)

Merrion v. Jicarilla Apache Tribe *is an important U.S. Supreme Court case in which the court held that an Indian tribe had the authority to impose taxes on non-Indians conducting business on tribal lands and reservations as an inherent power under their tribal sovereignty. The case involved oil and gas leases that dated back to 1953 on the lands of the Jicarilla Apache tribe in New Mexico. Following standard practice, the plaintiffs negotiated the leases with the Bureau of Indian Affairs (BIA), which then presented them to the tribal council. Under the leases, the state of New Mexico received severance taxes, and the tribe was to receive a royalty that was to be collected by the BIA. However, the BIA was lax in its royalty collection and failed to pay the tribe its royalty earnings. The tribe then adopted an ordinance calling for the payment of a tribal severance tax. Unwilling to pay the tax, the plaintiffs filed the suit that launched the case in 1977.*

U.S. Supreme Court
Merrion v. Jicarilla Apache Tribe, 455 U.S. 130 (1982)
No. 80–11
Argued March 30, 1981
Reargued November 4, 1981
Decided January 25, 1982*
455 U.S. 130
CERTIORARI TO THE UNITED STATES COURT OF APPEALS FOR THE TENTH CIRCUIT
   Syllabus

Respondent Indian Tribe, pursuant to its Revised Constitution (which had been approved by the Secretary of the Interior (Secretary) as required by the Indian Reorganization Act of 1934), enacted an ordinance (also approved by the Secretary) imposing a severance tax on oil and gas production on the tribal reservation land. Oil and gas received by the Tribe as in-kind royalty payments from lessees of mineral leases on the reservation are exempted from the tax. Petitioners, lessees under Secretary-approved long-term leases with the Tribe to extract oil and natural gas deposits on reservation land, brought separate actions in Federal District Court to enjoin enforcement of the tax. The District Court, consolidating the actions, entered a permanent injunction, ruling that the Tribe had no authority to impose the tax, that only state and local authorities had the power to tax oil and gas production on Indian reservations, and that the tax violated the Commerce Clause. The Court of Appeals reversed, holding that the taxing power is an inherent attribute of tribal sovereignty that has not been divested by any treaty or Act of Congress, and that there was no Commerce Clause violation.

Held:

1. The Tribe has the inherent power to impose the severance tax on petitioners' mining activities as part of its power to govern and to pay for the costs of self-government. Pp. 455 U. S. 136-152.

   (a) The power to tax is an essential attribute of Indian sovereignty because it is a necessary instrument of self-government and territorial management. This power enables a tribal government to receive revenues for its essential services. The power does not derive solely from the Tribe's power to exclude non-Indians from tribal lands, but from the Tribe's general authority, as sovereign, to control economic activities within its jurisdiction, and to defray the cost of providing governmental services by requiring contributions from persons or enterprises engaged in such activities. Here, petitioners, who have availed themselves of Page 455 U. S. 131 the privilege of carrying on business on the reservation, benefit from police protection and other governmental services, as well as from the advantages of a civilized society assured by tribal government. Under these circumstances, there is nothing exceptional in requiring petitioners to contribute through taxes to the general cost of such government. The mere fact that the Tribe enjoys rents and royalties as the lessor of the mineral lands does not undermine its authority to impose the tax. Pp. 455 U. S. 137-144.

(b) Even if the Tribe's power to tax were derived solely from its power to exclude non-Indians from the reservation, the Tribe has the authority to impose the severance tax. Non-Indians who lawfully enter tribal lands remain subject to a tribe's power to exclude them, which power includes the lesser power to tax or place other conditions on the non-Indian's conduct or continued presence on the reservation. The Tribe's role as commercial partner with petitioners should not be confused with its role as sovereign. It is one thing to find that the Tribe has agreed to sell the right to use the land and take valuable minerals from it, and quite another to find that the Tribe has abandoned its sovereign powers simply because it has not expressly reserved them through a contract. To presume that a sovereign forever waives the right to exercise one of its powers unless it expressly reserves the right to exercise that power in a commercial agreement turns the concept of sovereignty on its head. Pp. 455 U. S. 144-148.

(c) The Federal Government did not deprive the Tribe of its authority to impose the severance tax by Congress' enactment of the 1938 Act establishing the procedures for leasing oil and gas interests on tribal lands. Such Act does not prohibit the Tribe from imposing the tax when both the tribal Constitution and the ordinance authoring the tax were approved by the Secretary. Nor did the 1927 Act permitting state taxation of mineral leases on Indian reservations divest the Tribe of its taxing power. The mere existence of state authority to tax does not deprive an Indian tribe of its power to tax. Moreover, the severance tax does not conflict with national energy policies. To the contrary, the fact that the Natural Gas Policy Act of 1978 includes taxes imposed by an Indian tribe in its definition of costs that may be recovered under federal energy pricing regulations indicates that such taxes would not contravene such policies, and that the tribal authority to do so is not implicitly divested by that Act. Pp. 455 U. S. 149-152.

2. The severance tax does not violate the "negative implications" of the Commerce Clause. Pp. 455 U. S. 152-158.

(a) Courts are final arbiters under the Commerce Clause only when Congress has not acted. Here, Congress has affirmatively acted by providing a series of federal checkpoints that must be cleared before a tribal tax can take effect, and, in this case, the severance tax was enacted in accordance with this congressional scheme. Pp. 455 U. S. 154-156.

(b) Even if judicial scrutiny under the Commerce Clause were necessary, the challenged tax would survive such scrutiny. The tax does not discriminate against interstate commerce, since it is imposed on minerals either sold on the reservation or transported off the reservation before sale. And the exemption for minerals received by the Tribe as in-kind payments on the leases and used for tribal purposes merely avoids the administrative make-work that would ensue if the Tribe taxed the minerals that it, as a commercial partner, received in royalty payments, and thus cannot be deemed a discriminatory preference for local commerce. Pp. 156–158.

617 F.2d 537, affirmed.

MARSHALL, J., delivered the opinion of the Court, in which BRENNAN, WHITE, BLACKMUN, POWELL, and O'CONNOR, JJ., joined. STEVENS, J., filed a dissenting opinion, in which BURGER, C.J., and REHNQUIST, J., joined, *post,* p. 455 U. S. 159. Page 455 U. S. 133.

JUSTICE MARSHALL delivered the opinion of the Court.

Pursuant to long-term leases with the Jicarilla Apache Tribe, petitioners, 21 lessees, extract and produce oil and gas from the Tribe's reservation lands. In these two consolidated cases, petitioners challenge an ordinance enacted by the Tribe imposing a severance tax on "any oil and natural gas severed, saved and removed from Tribal lands." *See* Oil and Gas Severance Tax No. 77-0-02, App. 38. We granted certiorari to determine whether the Tribe has the authority to impose this tax, and, if so, whether the tax imposed by the Tribe violates the Commerce Clause.

I

The Jicarilla Apache Tribe resides on a reservation in northwestern New Mexico. Established by Executive Order in 1887, [Footnote 1] the reservation contains 742,315 acres, all of which are held as tribal trust property. The 1887 Executive

Page 455 U. S. 134 Order set aside public lands in the Territory of New Mexico for the use and occupation of the Jicarilla Apache Indians, and contained no special restrictions except for a provision protecting preexisting rights of bona fide settlers. [Footnote 2] Approximately 2,100 individuals live on the reservation, with the majority residing in the town of Dulce, N.M., near the Colorado border.

The Tribe is organized under the Indian Reorganization Act of 1934, ch. 576, 48 Stat. 984, 2 U.S.C. § 461 *et seq.,* which authorizes any tribe residing on a reservation to adopt a constitution and bylaws, subject to the approval of the Secretary of the Interior (Secretary). [Footnote 3] The Tribe's first Constitution, approved by the Secretary on August 4, 1937, preserved all powers conferred by § 16 of the Indian Reorganization Act of 1934, ch. 576, 48 Stat. 987, 25 U.S.C. § 476. In 1968, the Tribe revised its Constitution to specify:

"The inherent powers of the Jicarilla Apache Tribe, including those conferred by Section 16 of the Act of June 18, 1934 (48 Stat. 984), as amended, shall vest in the tribal council and shall be exercised thereby subject only to limitations imposed by the Constitution of the United States, applicable Federal statutes and regulations of the Department of the Interior, and the restrictions established by this revised constitution."

Revised Constitution of the Jicarilla Apache Tribe, Art. XI, § 1. The Revised Constitution provides that "[t]he tribal council may enact ordinances to govern the development of tribal lands and other resources," Art. XI, § 1(a)(3). It further provides that

> "[t]he tribal council may levy and collect taxes and fees on tribal members, and may enact ordinances, subject to approval by the Secretary of the Interior, to impose taxes and fees on non-members of the tribe doing business on the reservation."

Art. XI, § 1(e). The Revised Constitution was approved by the Secretary on February 13, 1969.

To develop tribal lands, the Tribe has executed mineral leases encompassing some 69% of the reservation land. Beginning in 1953, the petitioners entered into leases with the Tribe. The Commissioner of Indian Affairs, on behalf of the Secretary, approved these leases, as required by the Act of May 11, 1938, ch.198, 52 Stat. 347, 25 U.S.C. §§ 396a-396g (1938 Act). In exchange for a cash bonus, royalties, and rents, the typical lease grants the lessee "the exclusive right and privilege to drill for, mine, extract, remove, and dispose of all the oil and natural gas deposits in or under" the leased land for as long as the minerals are produced in paying quantities. App. 22. Petitioners may use oil and gas in developing the lease without incurring the royalty. *Id.* at 24. In addition, the Tribe reserves the rights to use gas without charge for any of its buildings on the leased land, and to take its royalties in kind. *Id.* at 27–28. Petitioners' activities on the leased land have been subject to taxes imposed by the State of New Mexico on oil and gas severance and on oil and gas production equipment. *Id.* at 129. *See* Act of Mar. 3, 1927, ch. 299, § 3, 44 Stat. 1347, 25 U.S.C. § 398c (permitting state taxation of mineral production on Indian reservations) (1927 Act).

Pursuant to its Revised Constitution, the Tribal Council adopted an ordinance imposing a severance tax on oil and gas production on tribal land. *See* App. 38. The ordinance was approved by the

Secretary, through the Acting Director of the Bureau of Indian Affairs, on December 23, 1976. The tax applies to "any oil and natural gas severed, saved and removed from Tribal lands. . . . " *Ibid.* The tax is assessed at the wellhead at $0.05 per million Btu's of gas produced and $0.29 per barrel of crude oil or condensate produced on the reservation, and it is due at the time of severance. *Id.* at 38–39. Oil and gas consumed by the lessees to develop their leases or received by the Tribe as in-kind royalty payments are exempted from the tax. *Ibid.;* Brief for Respondent Jicarilla Apache Tribe 59, n. 42.

In two separate actions, petitioners sought to enjoin enforcement of the tax by either the tribal authorities or the Secretary. The United States District Court for the District of New Mexico consolidated the cases, granted other lessees leave to intervene, and permanently enjoined enforcement of the tax. The District Court ruled that the Tribe lacked the authority to impose the tax, that only state and local authorities had the power to tax oil and gas production on Indian reservations, and that the tax violated the Commerce Clause.

The United States Court of Appeals for the Tenth Circuit, sitting en banc, reversed. 617 F.2d 537 (1980). [Footnote 4] The Court of Appeals reasoned that the taxing power is an inherent attribute of tribal sovereignty that has not been divested by any treaty or Act of Congress, including the 1927 Act, 25 U.S.C. § 398c. The court also found no Commerce Clause violation. We granted certiorari, 449 U.S. 820 (1980), and we now affirm the decision of the Court of Appeals.

II

Petitioners argue, and the dissent agrees, that an Indian tribe's authority to tax non-Indians who do business on the reservation stems exclusively from its power to exclude such persons from tribal lands. Because the Tribe did not initially condition the leases upon the payment of a severance tax, petitioners assert that the Tribe is without authority to impose such a tax at a later time. We disagree with the premise that the power to tax derives only from the power to exclude. Even if that premise is accepted, however, we disagree with the conclusion that the Tribe lacks the power to impose the severance tax.

A

In *Washington v. Confederated Tribes of Colville Indian Reservation,* 447 U. S. 134 (1980) (*Colville*), we addressed the Indian tribes' authority to impose taxes on non-Indians doing business on the reservation. We held that

> "[t]he power to tax transactions occurring on trust lands and significantly involving a tribe or its members is a fundamental attribute of sovereignty which the tribes retain unless divested of it by federal law or necessary implication of their dependent status."

Id. at 1 447 U. S. 152. The power to tax is an essential attribute of Indian sovereignty, because it is a necessary instrument of self-government and territorial management. This power enables a tribal government to raise revenues for its essential services. The power does not derive solely from the Indian tribe's power to exclude non-Indians from tribal lands. Instead, it derives from the tribe's general authority, as sovereign, to control economic activity within its jurisdiction, and to defray the cost of providing governmental services by requiring contributions from persons or enterprises engaged in economic activities within that jurisdiction. *See, e.g., 22 U. S. Ogden,* 9 Wheat. 1, 22 U. S. 199 (1824).

The petitioners avail themselves of the "substantial privilege of carrying on business" on the reservation. *Mobil Oil Corp. v. Commissioner of Taxes,* 445 U. S. 425, 445 U. S. 437 (1980); *Wisconsin v. J. C. Penney Co.,* 311 U. S. 435, 311 U. S. 444-445 (1940). They benefit from the provision of police protection and other governmental services, as well as from "*the advantages of a civilized society*'" that are assured by the existence of tribal government. *Exxon Corp. v. Wisconsin Dept. of Revenue,* 447 U. S. 207, 447 U. S. 228 *(1980) (quoting Japan Line, Ltd. v. County of Los Angeles, 441 U. S. 434, 441 U. S. 445 (1979)). Numerous other governmental entities levy a general revenue tax similar to that imposed by the Jicarilla Tribe when they provide comparable services. Under these circumstances, there is nothing exceptional in requiring petitioners to contribute through taxes to the general cost of tribal government. [Footnote 5] Cf. Commonwealth Edison Co. v. Montana, 453 U. S. 609, 453 U. S. 624-629 (1981); id. at 453 U. S. 647 (BLACKMUN, J., dissenting); Mobil Oil Corp. v. Commissioner of Taxes, supra, at 445 U. S. 436-437.*

As we observed in *Colville, supra,* the tribe's interest in levying taxes on nonmembers to raise "revenues for essential governmental programs . . . is strongest when the revenues are derived from value generated on the reservation by activities involving the Tribes and when the taxpayer is the recipient of tribal services."

447 U.S. at 447 U. S. 156–157. This surely is the case here. The mere fact that the government imposing the tax also enjoys rents and royalties as the lessor of the mineral lands does not undermine the government's authority to impose the tax. *See infra* at 455 U. S. 145–148. The royalty payments from the mineral leases are paid to the Tribe in its role as partner in petitioners' commercial venture. The severance tax, in contrast, is petitioners' contribution "to the general cost of providing governmental services." *Commonwealth Edison Co. v. Montana, supra,* at 453 U. S. 623. State governments commonly receive both royalty payments and severance taxes from lessees of mineral lands within their borders.

Viewing the taxing power of Indian tribes as an essential instrument of self-government and territorial management has been a shared assumption of all three branches of the Federal Government. *Cf. Colville, supra,* at 447 U. S. 153. In *Colville,* the Court relied in part on a 1934 opinion of the Solicitor for the Department of the Interior. In this opinion, the Solicitor recognized that, in the absence of congressional action to the contrary, the tribes' sovereign power to tax "'may be exercised over members of the tribe and over nonmembers, so far as such nonmembers may accept privileges of trade, residence, etc., to which taxes may be attached as conditions.'"

447 U.S. at 447 U. S. 153 (quoting *Powers of Indian Tribes,* 55 I.D. 14, 46 (1934)). *Colville* further noted that official executive pronouncements have repeatedly recognized that "Indian tribes possess a broad measure of civil jurisdiction over the activities of non-Indians on Indian reservation lands in which the tribes have a significant interest, . . . including jurisdiction to tax." 447 U.S. at 447 U. S. 152-153 (citing 23 Op.Atty.Gen. 214 (1900); 17 Op.Atty.Gen. 134 (1881); 7 Op.Atty. Gen. 174 (1855)). [Footnote 6]

Similarly, Congress has acknowledged that the tribal power to tax is one of the tools necessary to self-government and territorial control. As early as 1879, the Senate Judiciary Committee acknowledged the validity of a tax imposed by the Chickasaw Nation on non-Indians legitimately within its territory:

> "We have considered [Indian tribes] as invested with the right of self-government and jurisdiction over the persons and property within the limits of the territory they occupy, except so far as that jurisdiction has been restrained and abridged by treaty or act of Congress. Subject to the supervisory control of the Federal Government, they may enact the requisite legislation to maintain peace and good order, improve their condition, establish school systems, and aid their people in their efforts to acquire the arts of civilized life; and *they undoubtedly possess the inherent right to resort to taxation to raise the necessary revenue for the accomplishment of these vitally important objects* — a right not in any sense derived from the Government of the United States." S.Rep. No. 698, 45th Cong., 3d Sess., 1–2 (1879) (emphasis added).

Thus, the views of the three federal branches of government, as well as general principles of taxation, confirm that Indian tribes enjoy authority to finance their governmental services through taxation of non-Indians who benefit from those services. Indeed, the conception of Indian sovereignty that this Court has consistently reaffirmed permits no other conclusion. As we observed in *United States v. Mazurie,* 419 U. S. 544, 419 U. S. 557 (1975), "'Indian tribes within Indian country' are a good deal more than *private, voluntary organizations.*" They "*are unique aggregations possessing attributes of sovereignty over both their members and their territory.*" *Ibid. See, e.g., 31 U. S. Georgia, 6 Pet. 515, 31 U. S. 557 (1832); Iron Crow v. Oglala Sioux Tribe of Pine Ridge Reservation, 231 F.2d 89, 92, 99 (CA8 1956); Crabtree v. Madden, 54 F. 426, 428–429 (CA8 1893); Cohen, "The Spanish Origin of Indian Rights in the Law of the United States," in The Legal Conscience 230, 234 (L. Cohen ed. 1960). Page 455 U. S. 141*

Adhering to this understanding, we conclude that the Tribe's authority to tax non-Indians who conduct business on the reservation does not simply derive from the Tribe's power to exclude such persons, but is an inherent power necessary to tribal self-government and territorial management.

Of course, the Tribe's authority to tax nonmembers is subject to constraints not imposed on other governmental entities: the Federal Government can take away this power, and the Tribe must obtain the approval of the Secretary before any tax on nonmembers can take effect. These additional constraints minimize potential concern that Indian tribes will exercise the power to tax in an unfair or unprincipled manner, and ensure that any exercise of the tribal power to tax will be consistent with national policies.

We are not persuaded by the dissent's attempt to limit an Indian tribe's authority to tax non-Indians by asserting that its only source is the tribe's power to exclude such persons from tribal lands. Limiting the tribes' authority to tax in this manner contradicts the conception that Indian tribes are domestic, dependent nations, as well as the common understanding that the sovereign taxing power is a tool for raising revenue necessary to cover the costs of government.

Nor are we persuaded by the dissent that three early decisions upholding tribal power to tax

nonmembers support this limitation. *Post* at 455 U. S. 175-183, discussing *Morris v. Hitchcock,* 194 U. S. 384 (1904); *Buster v. Wright,* 135 F. 947 (CA8 1905), *appeal dism'd,* 203 U.S. 599 (1906); *Maxey v. Wright,* 3 Ind.T. 243, 247–250, 54 S.W. 807, 809 (Ct.App.Ind.T.), *aff'd,* 105 F. 1003 (CA8 1900). In discussing these cases, the dissent correctly notes that a hallmark of Indian sovereignty is the power to exclude non-Indians from Indian lands, and that this power provides a basis for tribal authority to tax. None of these cases, however, establishes that the authority to tax derives *solely* from the power to exclude. Instead, these cases demonstrate that a tribe has the power to tax nonmembers only to the extent the nonmember enjoys the privilege of trade or other activity on the reservation to which the tribe can attach a tax. This limitation on tribal taxing authority exists not because the tribe has the power to exclude nonmembers, but because the limited authority that a tribe may exercise over nonmembers does not arise until the nonmember enters the tribal jurisdiction. We do not question that there is a significant territorial component to tribal power: a tribe has no authority over a nonmember until the nonmember enters tribal lands or conducts business with the tribe. However, we do not believe that this territorial component to Indian taxing power, which is discussed in these early cases, means that the tribal authority to tax derives solely from the tribe's power to exclude nonmembers from tribal lands.

Morris v. Hitchcock, for example, suggests that the taxing power is a legitimate instrument for raising revenue, and that a tribe may exercise this power over non-Indians who receive privileges from the tribe, such as the right to trade on Indian land. In *Morris,* the Court approved a tax on cattle grazing and relied in part on a Report to the Senate by the Committee on the Judiciary, which found no legal defect in previous tribal tax legislation having "a twofold object — to prevent the intrusion of unauthorized persons into the territory of the Chickasaw Nation, and *to raise revenue.*" 194 U.S. at 194 U. S. 389 (emphasis added). In *Maxey v. Wright,* the question of Indian sovereignty was not even raised: the decision turned on the construction of a treaty denying the Tribe any governing or jurisdictional authority over nonmembers. 3 Ind.T. at 247–248, 54 S.W. at 809. [Footnote 7]

Finally, the decision in *Buster v. Wright* actually undermines the theory that the tribes' taxing authority derives solely from the power to exclude non-Indians from tribal lands. Under this theory, a non-Indian who establishes lawful presence in Indian territory could avoid paying a tribal tax by claiming that no residual portion of the power to exclude supports the tax. This result was explicitly rejected in *Buster v. Wright*. In *Buster,* deeds to individual lots in Indian territory had been granted to non-Indian residents, and cities and towns had been incorporated. As a result, Congress had expressly prohibited the Tribe from removing these non-Indian residents. Even though the ownership of land and the creation of local governments by non-Indians established their legitimate presence on Indian land, the court held that the Tribe retained its power to tax. The court concluded that "[n]either the United States, nor a state, nor any other sovereignty loses the power to govern the people within its borders by the existence of towns and cities therein endowed with the usual powers of municipalities, *nor by the ownership nor occupancy of the land within its territorial jurisdiction by citizens or foreigners.*"

135 F. at 952 (emphasis Page 455 U. S. 144 added). [Footnote 8] This result confirms that the Tribe's authority to tax derives not from its power to exclude, but from its power to govern and to raise revenues to pay for the costs of government.

We choose not to embrace a new restriction on the extent of the tribal authority to tax, which is based on a questionable interpretation of three early cases. Instead, based on the views of each of the federal branches, general principles of taxation, and the conception of Indian tribes as domestic, dependent nations, we conclude that the Tribe has the authority to impose a severance tax on the mining activities of petitioners as part of its power to govern and to pay for the costs of self-government.

B

Alternatively, if we accept the argument, advanced by petitioners and the dissent, that the Tribe's authority to tax derives solely from its power to exclude non-Indians from the reservation, we conclude that the Tribe has the authority to impose the severance tax challenged here. Nonmembers who lawfully enter tribal lands remain subject to the tribe's power to exclude them. This power necessarily includes the lesser power to place conditions on entry, on continued presence, or on reservation conduct, such as a tax on business activities conducted on the reservation. When a tribe grants a non-Indian the right to be on Indian land, the tribe agrees not to exercise its *ultimate* power to oust the non-Indian as long as the non-Indian complies with the initial conditions of entry. However, it does not follow that the lawful property right to be on Indian land also immunizes the non-Indian from the tribe's exercise of its lesser-included power to tax or to place other conditions on the non-Indian's conduct or continued presence on the reservation. [Footnote 9] A nonmember who enters the jurisdiction of the tribe remains subject to the risk that the tribe will later exercise its sovereign power. The fact that the tribe chooses not to exercise its power to tax when it initially grants a non-Indian entry onto the reservation does not permanently divest the tribe of its authority to impose such a tax. [Footnote 10]

Petitioners argue that their leaseholds entitle them to enter the reservation and exempt them from further exercises of the Tribe's sovereign authority. Similarly, the dissent asserts that the Tribe has lost the power to tax petitioners' mining activities because it has leased to them the use of the mineral lands and such rights of access to the reservation as might be necessary to enjoy the leases. *Post* at 455 U. S. 186-190. [Footnote 11] However, this conclusion is not compelled by linking the taxing power to the power to exclude. Instead, it is based on additional assumptions and confusions about the consequences of the commercial arrangement between petitioners and the Tribe.

Most important, petitioners and the dissent confuse the Tribe's role as commercial partner with its role as sovereign. [Footnote 12]

This confusion relegates the powers of sovereignty to the bargaining process undertaken in each of the sovereign's commercial agreements. It is one thing to find that the Tribe has agreed to sell the right to use the land and take from it valuable minerals; it is quite another to find that the Tribe has abandoned its sovereign powers simply because it has not expressly reserved them through a contract.

Confusing these two results denigrates Indian sovereignty. Indeed, the dissent apparently views the tribal power to exclude, as well as the derivative authority to tax, as merely the power possessed by any individual landowner or any social group to attach conditions, including a "tax" or fee, to the entry by a stranger onto private land or into the social group, and not as a sovereign power. The dissent does pay lip service to the established views that Indian tribes retain those fundamental attributes of sovereignty, including the power to tax transactions that occur on tribal lands, which have not been divested by Congress or by necessary implication of the tribe's dependent status, *see Colville*, 447 U.S. at 447 U. S. 152, and that tribes "are a good deal more than *private, voluntary organizations.*'" *United States v. Mazurie, 419 U.S. at 419 U. S. 557. However, in arguing that the Tribe somehow "lost" its power to tax petitioners by not including* Page 455 U. S. 147 *a taxing provision in the original leases or otherwise notifying petitioners that the Tribe retained and might later exercise its sovereign right to tax them, the dissent attaches little significance to the sovereign nature of the tribal authority to tax, and it obviously views tribal authority as little more than a landowner's contractual right. This overly restrictive view of tribal sovereignty is further reflected in the dissent's refusal to apply established principles for determining whether other governmental bodies*

have waived a sovereign power through contract. See post at 455 U. S. 189, n. 50. See also infra at 455 U. S. 148.

Moreover, the dissent implies that the power to tax depends on the consent of the taxed, as well as on the Tribe's power to exclude non-Indians. Whatever place consent may have in contractual matters and in the creation of democratic governments, it has little if any role in measuring the validity of an exercise of legitimate sovereign authority. Requiring the consent of the entrant deposits in the hands of the excludable non-Indian the source of the tribe's power, when the power instead derives from sovereignty itself. Only the Federal Government may limit a tribe's exercise of its sovereign authority. *E.g., United States v. Wheeler,* 435 U. S. 313, 435 U. S. 322 (1978). [Footnote 13] Indian sovereignty is not conditioned on the assent of a nonmember; to the contrary, the nonmember's presence and conduct on Indian lands are conditioned by the limitations the tribe may choose to impose.

Viewed in this light, the absence of a reference to the tax in the leases themselves hardly impairs the Tribe's authority to impose the tax. Contractual arrangements remain subject to subsequent legislation by the presiding sovereign. *See, e.g., 310 U. S. Sixth Ward Building & Loan Assn. of Newark* 310 U. S. 32 (1940); *Home Building & Loan Assn. v. Blaisdell,* 290 U. S. 398 (1934). Even where the contract at issue requires payment of a royalty for a license or franchise issued by the governmental entity, the government's power to tax remains unless it "has been specifically surrendered in terms which admit of no other reasonable interpretation." *St. Louis v. United R. Co.,* 210 U. S. 266, 210 U. S. 280 (1908).

To state that Indian sovereignty is different than that of Federal, State or local Governments, *see post* at 455 U. S. 189, n. 50, does not justify ignoring the principles announced by this Court for determining whether a sovereign has waived its taxing authority in cases involving city, state, and federal taxes imposed under similar circumstances.

Each of these governments has different attributes of sovereignty, which also may derive from different sources. These differences, however, do not alter the principles for determining whether any of these governments has waived a sovereign power through contract, and we perceive no principled reason for holding that the different attributes of Indian sovereignty require different treatment in this regard. Without regard to its source, sovereign power, even when unexercised, is an enduring presence that governs all contracts subject to the sovereign's jurisdiction, and will remain intact unless surrendered in unmistakable terms.

No claim is asserted in this litigation, nor could one be, that petitioners' leases contain the clear and unmistakable surrender of taxing power required for its extinction. We could find a waiver of the Tribe's taxing power only if we inferred it from silence in the leases. To presume that a sovereign forever waives the right to exercise one of its sovereign powers unless it expressly reserves the right to exercise that power in a commercial agreement turns the concept of sovereignty on its head, and we do not adopt this analysis. [Footnote 14]

C

The Tribe has the inherent power to impose the severance tax on petitioners, whether this power derives from the Tribe's power of self-government or from its power to exclude. Because Congress may limit tribal sovereignty, we now review petitioners' argument that Congress, when it enacted two federal Acts governing Indians and various pieces of federal energy legislation, deprived the Tribe of its authority to impose the severance tax.

In *Colville,* we concluded that the "widely held understanding within the Federal Government has always been that *federal law to date has not worked a divestiture of Indian taxing power.*" 447 U.S. at 447 U. S. 152 (emphasis added). Moreover, we noted that "[n]o federal statute cited to us shows any congressional departure from this view." *Id.* at 447 U. S. 153. Likewise, petitioners can cite to no

statute that specifically divests the Tribe of its power to impose the severance tax on their mining activities. Instead, petitioners argue that Congress implicitly took away this power when it enacted the Acts and various pieces of legislation on which petitioners rely. Before reviewing this argument, we reiterate here our admonition in *Santa Clara Pueblo v. Martinez,* 436 U. S. 49, 436 U. S. 60 (1978): "a proper respect both for tribal sovereignty itself and for the plenary authority of Congress in this area cautions that we tread lightly in the absence of clear indications of legislative intent."

Petitioners argue that Congress preempted the Tribe's power to impose a severance tax when it enacted the 1938 Act, 25 U.S.C. §§ 396a–396g. In essence, petitioners argue that the tax constitutes an additional burden on lessees that is inconsistent with the Act's regulatory scheme for leasing and developing oil and gas reserves on Indian land. This Act, and the regulations promulgated by the Department of the Interior for its enforcement, establish the procedures to be followed for leasing oil and gas interests on tribal lands. However, the proviso to 25 U.S.C. 396b states that "the foregoing provisions *shall in no manner restrict the right of tribes . . .* to lease lands for mining purposes . . . *in accordance with the provisions of any constitution and charter adopted by any Indian tribe pursuant to sections 461, 462, 463, [464–475, 476–478], and 479 of this title.*" (Emphasis added.) [Footnote 15]

Therefore, this Act does not prohibit the Tribe from imposing a severance tax on petitioners' mining activities pursuant to its Revised Constitution, when both the Revised Constitution and the ordinance authorizing the tax are approved by the Secretary. [Footnote 16]

Petitioners also assert that the 1927 Act, 25 U.S.C. §§ 398a–398e, divested the Tribe's taxing power. We disagree. The 1927 Act permits state taxation of mineral lessees on Executive Order reservations, but it indicates no change in the taxing power of the affected tribes. *See* 25 U.S.C. § 398c. Without mentioning the tribal authority to tax, the

Act authorizes state taxation of royalties from mineral production on all Indian lands. Petitioners argue that the Act transferred the Indian power to tax mineral production to the States in exchange for the royalties assured the tribes. This claim not only lacks any supporting evidence in the legislative history, it also deviates from settled principles of taxation: different sovereigns can enjoy powers to tax the same transactions. Thus, the mere existence of state authority to tax does not deprive the Indian tribe of its power to tax. *Fort Mojave Tribe v. County of San Bernardino*, 543 F.2d 1253 (CA9 1976), *cert. denied*, 430 U.S. 983 (1977). *Cf. Colville*, 447 U.S. at 447 U. S. 158 ("There is no direct conflict between the state and tribal schemes, since each government is free to impose its taxes without ousting the other"). [Footnote 17]

Finally, petitioners contend that tribal taxation of oil and gas conflicts with national energy policies, and therefore the tribal tax is preempted by federal law. Again, petitioners cite no specific federal statute restricting Indian sovereignty. Nor do they explain why state taxation of the same type of activity escapes the asserted conflict with federal policy. *Cf. Commonwealth Edison Co. v. Montana*, 453 U. S. 609 (1981). Indeed, rather than forbidding tribal severance taxes, Congress has included taxes imposed by an Indian tribe in its definition of costs that may be recovered under federal energy pricing regulations. Natural Gas Policy Act of 1978, Pub.L. 95–621, §§ 110(a), (c)(1), 92 Stat. 3368, 15 U.S.C. §§ 3320(a), (c)(1) (1976 ed., Supp. IV). Although this inclusion may not reflect Congress' view with respect to the source of a tribe's power to impose a severance tax, [Footnote 18] it surely indicates that imposing such a tax would not contravene federal energy policy, and that the tribal authority to do so is not implicitly divested by that Act.

We find no "clear indications" that Congress has implicitly deprived the Tribe of its power to impose the severance tax. In any event, if there were ambiguity on this point, the doubt would benefit the Tribe, for "[a]mbiguities in federal law have been construed generously in order to comport with . . . traditional notions of sovereignty and with the federal policy of encouraging tribal independence."

White Mountain Apache Tribe v. Bracker, 448 U. S. 136, 448 U. S. 143-144 (1980). Accordingly, we find that the Federal Government has not divested the Tribe of its inherent authority to tax mining activities on its land, whether this authority derives from the Tribe's power of self-government or from its power to exclude.

III

Finding no defect in the Tribe's exercise of its taxing power, we now address petitioners' contention that the severance tax violates the "negative implications" of the Commerce Clause because it taxes an activity that is an integral part of the flow of commerce, discriminates against interstate commerce, and imposes a multiple burden on interstate commerce. At the outset, we note that reviewing tribal action under the Interstate Commerce Clause is not without conceptual difficulties. *E.g.,* nn. 21 and S. 130fn24, *infra.* Apparently recognizing these difficulties, the Solicitor General, on behalf of the Secretary, argues that the language, [Footnote 19] the structure, and the purposes of the Commerce Clause support the conclusion that the Commerce Clause does not, of its own force, limit Indian tribes in their dealings with non-Indians. Brief for Secretary of Interior 35–40. The Solicitor General reasons that the Framers did not intend "the courts, through the Commerce Clause, to impose their own views of the proper relationship between Indians and non-Indians and to strike down measures adopted by a tribe with which the political departments of government had not seen fit to disagree."

Id. at 39. Instead, where tribal legislation is inimical to the national welfare, the Solicitor asserts that the Framers contemplated that the remedies would be the negotiation or renegotiation of treaties, the enactment of legislation governing trade and other relations, or the exertion of superior force by the United States Government. *Id.* at 38–39. Using similar reasoning, the Solicitor suggests that, if the Commerce Clause does impose restrictions on tribal activity, those restrictions must arise from the Indian Commerce Clause, and not its interstate counterpart. *Id.* at 40–43.

To date, however, this Court has relied on the Indian Commerce Clause as a shield to protect Indian tribes from state and local interference, and has not relied on the Clause to authorize tribal regulation of commerce without any constitutional restraints. We see no need to break new ground in this area today: even if we assume that tribal action is subject to the limitations of the Interstate Commerce Clause, this tax does not violate the "negative implications" of that Clause.

A

A state tax may violate the "negative implications" of the Interstate Commerce Clause by unduly burdening or discriminating against interstate commerce. *See, e.g., Commonwealth Edison Co. v. Montana,* 453 U. S. 609 (1981); *Complete Auto Transit, Inc. v. Brady,* 430 U. S. 274 (1977). Judicial review of state taxes under the Interstate Commerce Clause is intended to ensure that States do not disrupt or burden interstate commerce when Congress' power remains unexercised: it protects the free flow of commerce, and thereby safeguards Congress' latent power from encroachment by the several States.

However, we only engage in this review when Congress has not acted or purported to act. *See, e.g., Prudential Insurance Co. v. Benjamin,* 328 U. S. 408, 328 U. S. 421-427 (1946). Once Congress acts, courts are not free to review state taxes or other regulations under the dormant Commerce Clause. When Congress has struck the balance it deems appropriate, the courts are no longer needed to prevent States from burdening commerce, and it matters not that the courts would invalidate the state tax or regulation under the Commerce Clause in the absence of congressional action. *See Prudential Insurance Co. v. Benjamin, supra,* at

328 U. S. 431. [Footnote 20] Courts are final arbiters under the Commerce Clause only when Congress has not acted. *See Japan Line, Ltd. v. County of Los Angeles,* 441 U.S. at 441 U. S. 454.

Here, Congress has affirmatively acted by providing a series of federal checkpoints that must be cleared before a tribal tax can take effect. [Footnote 21] Under the Indian Reorganization Act, 25 U.S.C. §§ 476, 477, a tribe must obtain approval from the Secretary before it adopts or revises its constitution to announce its intention to tax nonmembers. Further, before the ordinance imposing the severance tax challenged here could take effect, the Tribe was required again to obtain approval from the Secretary. *See* Revised Constitution of the Jicarilla Tribe, Art. XI, §§ 1(e), 2. *Cf.* 25 U.S.C. §§ 476, 477; 25 CFR § 171.29 (1980) (implementing the proviso to 25 U.S.C. § 396b, quoted in n 15, *supra*).

As we noted earlier, the severance tax challenged by petitioners was enacted in accordance with this congressional scheme. Both the Tribe's Revised Constitution and the challenged tax ordinance received the requisite approval from the Secretary. This course of events fulfilled the administrative process established by Congress to monitor such exercises of tribal authority. As a result, this tribal tax comes to us in a posture significantly different from a challenged state tax, which does not need specific federal approval to take effect, and which therefore requires, in the absence of congressional ratification, judicial review to ensure that it does not unduly burden or discriminate against interstate commerce. Judicial review of the Indian tax measure, in contrast, would duplicate the administrative review called for by the congressional scheme.

Finally, Congress is well aware that Indian tribes impose mineral severance taxes such as the one challenged by petitioners. *See* Natural Gas Policy Act of 1978, 15 U.S.C. §§ 3320(a), (c)(1) (1976 ed., Supp. IV). Congress, of course, retains plenary power to limit tribal taxing authority or to alter the current scheme under which the tribes may impose taxes. However, it is not our function nor our prerogative to strike down a tax that has traveled through the precise channels established by Congress, and has obtained the specific approval of the Secretary.

B

The tax challenged here would survive judicial scrutiny under the Interstate Commerce Clause, even if such scrutiny were necessary. In *Complete Auto Transit, Inc. v. Brady, supra,* at 430 U. S. 279, we held that a state tax on activities connected to interstate commerce is sustainable if it "is applied to an activity with a substantial nexus with the taxing State, is fairly apportioned, does not discriminate against interstate commerce, and is fairly related to the services provided by the State."

Petitioners do not question that the tax on the severance of minerals from the mines [Footnote 22] meets the first and the second tests: the mining activities taxed pursuant to the ordinance occur entirely on reservation land. Furthermore, petitioners do not challenge the tax on the ground that the amount of the tax is not fairly related to the services provided by the Tribe. *See* Supplemental Brief for Petitioners in No. 815, pp. 11, 17–20. [Footnote 23]

Instead, petitioners focus their attack on the third factor, and argue that the tax discriminates against interstate commerce. In essence, petitioners argue that the language "sold or transported off the reservation" exempts from taxation minerals sold on the reservation, kept on the reservation for use by individual members of the Tribe, and minerals taken by the Tribe on the reservation as in-kind royalty. Although petitioners admit that no sales have occurred on the reservation to date, they argue that the Tribe might induce private industry to locate on the reservation to take advantage of this allegedly discriminatory taxing policy. We do not accept petitioners' arguments; instead, we agree with the Tribe, the Solicitor General, and the Court of Appeals that the tax is imposed on minerals sold on the reservation or transported off the reservation before sale. *See* 617 F.2d at 546. *Cf.* n 22, *supra.* [Footnote 24] Under this interpretation, the tax does not treat minerals transported away from the reservation differently than it treats minerals that might be sold on the reservation. Nor does the Tribe's tax ordinance exempt minerals ultimately received by individual members of the Tribe. The ordinance does exempt minerals received by the Tribe as in-kind payments on the leases and used for tribal purposes, [Footnote 25] but this exemption merely avoids the administrative makework that would ensue if the Tribe, as local government, taxed the amount of minerals that the Tribe, as commercial partner, received in royalty payments. Therefore, this exemption cannot be deemed a discriminatory preference for local commerce. [Footnote 26]

IV

In *Worcester v. Georgia,* 6 Pet. at 31 U. S. 559, Chief Justice Marshall observed that Indian tribes had "always been considered as distinct, independent political communities, retaining their original natural rights." Although the tribes are subject to the authority of the Federal Government, the "weaker power does not surrender its independence — its right to self-government, by associating with a stronger, and taking its protection." *Id.* at 31 U. S. 661. Adhering to this understanding, we conclude that the Tribe did not surrender its authority to tax the mining activities of petitioners, whether this authority is deemed to arise from the Tribe's inherent power of self-government or from its inherent power to exclude nonmembers. Therefore, the Tribe may enforce its severance tax unless and until Congress divests this power, an action that Congress has not taken to date. Finally, the severance tax imposed by the Tribe cannot be invalidated on the ground that it violates the "negative implications" of the Commerce Clause.

Affirmed.

Together with No. 80–15, Amoco Production Co. et al. v. Jicarilla Apache Tribe, et al., also on certiorari to the same court.

[Footnote 1]

See 1 C. Kappler, Indian Affairs, Laws and Treaties 875 (1904) (Order of President Cleveland). Two earlier Orders setting aside land for the Tribe had been canceled. *See id.* at 874–875 (Orders of Presidents Hayes and Grant). The boundaries of the reservation were redefined or clarified by Executive Orders issued by President Theodore Roosevelt on November 11, 1907, and January 28, 1908, and by President Taft on February 17, 1912. *See* 3 C. Kappler, Indian Affairs, Laws and Treaties 681, 682, 684, 685 (1913).

The fact that the Jicarilla Apache Reservation was established by Executive Order, rather than by treaty or statute, does not affect our analysis; the Tribe's sovereign power is not affected by the manner in which its reservation was created. *E.g., Washington v. Confederated Tribes of Colville Reservation,* 447 U. S. 134 (1980).

[Footnote 2]

The proviso reads as follows:

"this order shall not be so construed as to deprive any bona fide settler of any valid rights he may have acquired under the law of the United States providing for the disposition of the public domain."

1 Kappler, *supra,* at 875.

[Footnote 3]

The Tribe is also chartered under the Indian Reorganization Act of 1934, ch. 576, 48 Stat. 988, 25 U.S.C. § 477, which permits the Secretary to issue to an Indian tribe a charter of incorporation that may give the tribe the power to purchase, manage, operate, and dispose of its property.

[Footnote 4]

Two judges dissented. Both argued that tribal sovereignty does not encompass the power to tax non-Indian lessees, 617 F.2d at 551–556 (Seth, C.J., dissenting); *id.* at 55565 (Barrett, J., dissenting) (also arguing the tax violates the Commerce Clause).

[Footnote 5]

Through various Acts governing Indian tribes, Congress has expressed the purpose of "fostering tribal self-government." *Colville,* 447 U.S. at 447 U. S. 155. We agree with Judge McKay's observation that

> "[i]t simply does not make sense to expect the tribes to carry out municipal functions approved and mandated by Congress without being able to exercise at least minimal taxing powers, whether they take the form of real estate taxes, leasehold taxes or severance taxes."

> 617 F.2d at 550 (McKay, J., concurring).

[Footnote 6]

Moreover, in its revision of the classic treatise on Indian Law, the Department of the Interior advances the view that the Indian tribes' power to tax is not limited by the power to exclude. *See* U.S. Solicitor for Dept. of Interior, Federal Indian Law 438 (1958) ("The power to tax does not depend upon the power to remove, and has been upheld where there was no power in the tribe to remove the taxpayer from the tribal jurisdiction") (footnote omitted). *See also* F. Cohen, Handbook of Federal Indian Law 142 (1942) ("One of the powers essential to the maintenance of any government is the power to levy taxes. That this power is an inherent attribute of tribal sovereignty which continues unless withdrawn or limited by treaty or by act of Congress is a proposition which has never been successfully disputed") (footnote omitted).

[Footnote 7]

The governing treaty in *Maxey v. Wright* restricted the tribal right of self-government and jurisdiction to members of the Creek or Seminole Tribes.

The court relied, at least in part, on opinions of the Attorney General interpreting this treaty. For example, one such opinion stated that, whatever the meaning of the clause limiting to tribal members the Tribes' unrestricted rights of self-government and jurisdiction, it did

> ""not limit the right of these tribes to pass upon the question, who . . . shall share their occupancy and upon what terms. That is a question which all private persons are allowed to decide for themselves; and even wild animals, not men, have a certain respect paid to the instinct which in his respect they share with man. The serious words *'jurisdiction' and 'self-government' are scarcely appropriate to the right of a hotel keeper to prescribe rules and charges for persons who become his fellow occupants.*""

3 Ind.T. at 250, 54 S.W. at 809 (quoting 18 Op.Atty. Gen. 4, 36, 37 (1884))

The court, as well as the opinion of the Attorney General, found that the Tribes' "natural instinct" to set terms on occupancy was unaltered by the treaty. Neither the court nor the Attorney General addressed the scope of Indian sovereignty when unlimited by treaty; instead, they identified a tribe's right, as a social group, to exclude intruders and place conditions on their occupancy. The court's dependence on this reasoning hardly bears on the more general question posed here: what is the source of the Indian tribes' sovereign power to tax absent a restriction by treaty or other federal law?

[Footnote 8]

Both the classic treatise on Indian law and its subsequent revision by the Department of the Interior, *see* n 6, *supra,* agree with this reading of *Buster v. Wright.* Federal Indian Law, *supra,* n. 6, at 438; Cohen, *supra,* n 6, at 142 (both citing *Buster v. Wright* for the proposition that the power to tax is an inherent sovereign power not dependent on the power to exclude).

[Footnote 9]

See also Barta v. Oglala Sioux Tribe of Pine Ridge Reservation, 259 F.2d 553 (CA8 1958) (lessees of tribal lands subject to Indian tax on use of land).

[Footnote 10]

Here, the leases extend for as long as minerals are produced in paying quantities, in other words, until the resources are depleted. Thus, under the dissent's approach, the Tribe would never have the power to tax petitioners regardless of the financial burden to the Tribe of providing and maintaining governmental services for the benefit of petitioners.

[Footnote 11]

But see Buster v. Wright, 135 F. at 958:

> "The ultimate conclusion of the whole matter is that purchasers of lots in town sites in towns or cities within the original limits of the Creek Nation, who are in lawful possession of their lots, are still subject to the laws of that nation prescribing permit taxes for the exercise by noncitizens of the privilege of conducting business in those towns. . . . "

[Footnote 12]

In contrast, the 1958 treatise on Indian law written by the United States Solicitor for the Department of the Interior recognized and distinguished the scope of these two roles when it embraced as the "present state of the law" the following summary:

> "'Over tribal lands, *the tribe has the rights of a landowner as well as the rights of a local government, dominion as well as sovereignty.* But over all the lands of the reservation, whether owned by the tribe, by members thereof, or by outsiders, the tribe has the sovereign power of determining the conditions upon which persons shall be permitted to enter its domain, to reside therein, and to do business, provided only such determination is consistent with applicable Federal laws and does not infringe any vested rights of persons now occupying reservation lands under lawful authority.'"

Federal Indian Law, *supra*, n 6, at 439 (quoting Solicitor's Opinion of Oct. 25, 1934) (emphasis added). *See* Cohen, *supra*, n 6, at 143.

[Footnote 13]

See also P. Maxfield, M. Dieterich, & F. Trelease, Natural Resources Law on American Indian Lands 4 (1977). Federal limitations on tribal sovereignty can also occur when the exercise of tribal sovereignty would be inconsistent with overriding national interests. *See Colville,* 447 U.S. at 447 U. S. 15. This concern is not presented here. *See ibid.*

[Footnote 14]

Petitioners and the dissent also argue that we should infer a waiver of the taxing power from silence in the Tribe's original Constitution. Although it is true that the Constitution in force when petitioners signed their leases did not include a provision specifically authorizing a severance tax, neither the Tribe's Constitution nor the Federal Constitution is the font of any sovereign power of the Indian tribes. *E.g., Iron Crow v. Oglala Sioux Tribe of Pine Ridge Reservation,* 231 F.2d 89, 94 (CA8 1956); *Buster v. Wright,* 135 F. at 950. Because the Tribe retains all inherent attributes of sovereignty that have not been divested by the Federal Government, the proper inference from silence on this point is that the sovereign power to tax remains intact. The Tribe's Constitution was amended to authorize the tax before the tax was imposed, and this is the critical event necessary to *effectuate* the tax. *See Barta v. Oglala Sioux Tribe of Pine Ridge Reservation,* 259 F.2d at 554, 556; *Iron Crow v. Oglala Sioux Tribe of Pine Ridge Reservation, supra,* at 99.

[Footnote 15]

The Secretary has implemented the substance of this proviso by the following regulation:

"The regulations in this part may be superseded by the provisions of any tribal constitution, bylaw or charter issued pursuant to the Indian Reorganization Act of June 18, 1934 (48 Stat. 984; 25 U.S.C. 461–479), . . . or by ordinance, resolution or other action authorized under such constitution, bylaw or charter. The regulations in this part, in so far as they are not so superseded, shall apply to leases made by organized tribes if the validity of the lease depends upon the approval of the Secretary of the Interior."

25 CFR 171.29 (1980).

[Footnote 16]

In arguing that the 1938 Act was intended to preempt the severance tax, petitioners attach great significance to the Secretary's approval of the leases. Curiously, they attach virtually no significance to the fact that the Secretary also approved the tax ordinance that they challenge here.

[Footnote 17]

The Tribe argues that the 1927 Act granting the States the power to tax mineral production on Indian land is inapplicable because the leases at issue here were signed pursuant to the 1938 Act. The 1938 Act, which makes uniform the laws applicable to leasing mineral rights on tribal lands, does not contain a grant of power to the States comparable to that found in the 1927 Act. As a result, the Tribe asserts that the State of New Mexico has no power to tax the production under petitioners' leases with the Tribe. Because the State of New Mexico is not a party to this suit, the Court of Appeals did not reach this issue. *See* 617 F.2d at 547 548, n. 5. For this reason, and because we conclude that the 1927 Act did not affect the Tribe's authority to tax, we likewise do not reach this issue.

[Footnote 18]

The statute provides that Indian severance taxes may be recovered through federal energy pricing. However, the legislative history indicates that Congress took no position on the source of the

Indian tribes' power to impose the tax in the first place:

> "While severance taxes which may be imposed by an Indian tribe are to be treated in the same manner as State imposed severance taxes, the conferees do not intend to prejudge the outcome of the cases on appeal before the Tenth Circuit Court of Appeals respecting the right of Indian tribes to impose taxes on persons or organizations other than Indians who are engaged in business activities on Indian reservations. The outcome of the cases on appeal will determine the legality of imposing such taxes."

S.Conf.Rep. No. 95–1126, p. 91 (1978); H.R.Conf. Rep. No. 96–1762, p. 91 (1978).

[Footnote 19]

The Commerce Clause empowers Congress "[t]o regulate Commerce with foreign Nations, and among the several States, and *with* the Indian Tribes." U.S.Const., Art. I, § 8, cl. 3 (emphasis added).

[Footnote 20]

In *Prudential Insurance Co. v. Benjamin,* this Court refused to invalidate a South Carolina tax on out-of-state insurance companies despite appellant's contention that the tax impermissibly burdened interstate commerce. The Court refused to entertain appellant's argument because Congress, in passing the McCarran-Ferguson Act, had provided that

"silence on the part of the Congress shall not be construed to impose any barrier to the regulation or taxation of [the business of insurance] by the several States."

59 Stat. 33, 15 U.S.C. § 1011.

[Footnote 21]

Although Congress has not expressly announced that Indian taxes do not threaten its latent power to regulate interstate commerce, it is unclear how Congress could articulate that intention any more convincingly than it has done here. In contrast to when Congress acts with respect to the States, when Congress acts with respect to the Indian tribes, it generally does so pursuant to its authority under the Indian Commerce Clause, or by virtue of its superior position over the tribes, not pursuant to its authority under the Interstate Commerce Clause. This is but one of the difficulties inherent in reviewing under the Interstate Commerce Clause both tribal action and congressional action regulating the tribes. Therefore, in determining whether Congress has "acted" to preclude judicial review, we do not find it significant that the congressional action here was not taken pursuant to the Interstate Commerce Clause.

[Footnote 22]

Petitioners initially contend that the ordinance taxes the transportation of the minerals from the reservation, not their severance from the mines. As a result, they argue that the ordinance impermissibly burdens interstate commerce by taxing the movement in commerce itself, which is not a local event. The tax, by its terms, applies to resources that are "produced on the Jicarilla Apache Tribe Reservation and sold or transported off the Reservation." App. 39. The Tribe explains that this language was used because no sale occurs prior to the transportation off the reservation. The Tribe's tax is due at the time of severance. *Id.* at 38. Therefore, we agree with the Court of Appeals that the taxable event defined by the ordinance is the removal of minerals from the soil, not their transportation from the reservation. *See* 617 F.2d at 546.

[Footnote 23]

The Court of Appeals noted that, because the lessees chose not to build a factual foundation to challenge the tax on this ground, there was no basis on which to find that the tax was not fairly related to the services provided by the Tribe. *See id.* at 545, n. 4. Indeed, when the Tribe attempted to introduce at trial evidence of the services it had provided to establish this relationship, the District Court rejected this evidence upon petitioners' objection that such evidence was irrelevant to their challenge. Brief for Respondent Jicarilla Apache Tribe 7–8; 6 Record 278–290, 294, 303–308.

[Footnote 24]

The ordinance does not distinguish between minerals remaining within New Mexico and those transported beyond the state boundary. As a result, petitioners' argument that the tax discriminates against interstate commerce by favoring local sales focuses on the boundary between the reservation and the State of New Mexico, and not on any interstate boundaries. We will assume for purposes of this argument only that this alleged reservation-state discrimination could give rise to a Commerce Clause violation.

[Footnote 25]

Paragraph 4 of the ordinance specifies that "[r]oyalty gas, oil or condensate taken by the Tribe in kind, and used by the Tribe shall be exempt from taxation." App. 39.

[Footnote 26]

Petitioners contend that, because New Mexico may tax the same mining activity at full value, the Indian tax imposes a multiple tax burden on interstate commerce in violation of the Commerce Clause. The multiple taxation issue arises where two or more taxing jurisdictions point to some contact with an enterprise to support a tax on the entire value of its multistate activities, which is more than the contact would justify. *E.g.,* Standard Oil Co. v. Peck, 342 U. S. 382, 342 U. S. 384-385 (1952). This Court has required an apportionment of the tax based on the portion of the activity properly viewed as occurring within each relevant State. See, e.g., *Exxon Corp. v. Wisconsin Dept. of Revenue,* 447 U. S. 207, 447 U. S. 219 (1980); *Washington Revenue Dept. v. Association of Washington Stevedoring Cos.,* 435 U. S. 734, 435 U. S. 746, and n. 16 (1978).

This rule has no bearing here, however, for there can be no claim that the Tribe seeks to tax any more of petitioners' mining activity than the portion occurring within tribal jurisdiction. Indeed, petitioners do not even argue that the Tribe is seeking to seize more tax revenues than would be fairly related to the services provided by the Tribe. *See supra* at 455 U. S. 157, and n. 23. In the absence of such an assertion, and when the activity taxed by the Tribe occurs entirely on tribal lands, the multiple taxation issue would arise only if a State attempted to levy a tax on the same activity, which is more than the state's contact with the activity would justify. In such a circumstance, any challenge asserting that tribal and state taxes create a multiple burden on interstate commerce should be directed at the state tax, which, in the absence of congressional ratification, might be invalidated under the Commerce Clause. These cases, of course, do not involve a challenge to state taxation, and we intimate no opinion on the possibility of such a challenge.

JUSTICE STEVENS, with whom THE CHIEF JUSTICE and JUSTICE REHNQUIST join, dissenting.

The Indian tribes that occupied North America before Europeans settled the continent were unquestionably sovereigns. They ruled themselves and they exercised dominion over the lands that nourished them. Many of those tribes, and some attributes of their sovereignty, survive today. This Court, since its earliest days, has had the task of identifying those inherent sovereign powers that survived the creation of a new Nation and the introduction of an entirely new system of laws applicable to both Indians and non-Indians.

In performing that task, this Court has guarded carefully the unique status of Indian tribes within this Nation. Over its own members, an Indian tribe's sovereign powers are virtually unlimited; the incorporation of the tribe into the United States has done little to change internal tribal relations. In becoming part of the United States, however, the tribes yielded their status as independent nations;

Indians and non-Indians alike answered to the authority of a new Nation, organized under a new Constitution based on democratic principles of representative government. In that new system of government, Indian tribes were afforded no general powers over citizens of the United States. Many tribes, however, were granted a power unknown to any other sovereignty in this Nation: a power to exclude nonmembers entirely from territory reserved for the tribe. Incident to this basic power to exclude, the tribes exercise limited powers of governance over nonmembers, though those nonmembers have no voice in tribal government. Since a tribe may exclude nonmembers entirely from tribal territory, the tribe necessarily may impose conditions on a right of entry granted to a nonmember to do business on the reservation.

The question presented in these cases is whether, after a tribe has granted nonmembers access to its reservation on specified terms and conditions to engage in an economic venture of mutual benefit, the tribe may impose a tax on the nonmembers' share of benefits derived from the venture. The Court today holds that it may do so. In my opinion this holding distorts the very concept of tribal sovereignty. Because I am convinced that the Court's treatment of these important cases gives inadequate attention to the critical difference between a tribe's powers over its own members and its powers over nonmembers, I set forth my views at greater length than is normally appropriate in a dissenting opinion.

I

The 2,100 members of the Jicarilla Apache Tribe live on a reservation in northern New Mexico. [Footnote 2/1] The area encompassed by the reservation became a part of the United States in 1848 when the Mexican War ended in the Treaty of Guadalupe Hidalgo. *See* 9 Stat. 922. Between 1848 and 1871, the United States did not enter into any treaty with the Jicarillas or enact any special legislation relating to them; in 1871, Congress outlawed any future treaties with Indian tribes.

[Footnote 2/2] In 1887, President Cleveland issued an Executive Order setting aside a tract of public lands in the Territory of New Mexico "as a reservation for the use and occupation of the Jicarilla Apache Indians." Except for a provision protecting bona fide settlers from deprivation of previously acquired rights, the Executive Order contained no special rules applicable to the reservation. [Footnote 2/3] The mineral leases at issue in this case were granted by the Jicarilla Apache Tribe on these reservation lands.

The record does not indicate whether any leasing activity occurred on the Jicarilla Reservation between 1887 and 1953. During that period, however, the authority of Indian tribes to enter into mineral leases was clarified. In 1891, Congress passed a statute permitting the mineral leasing of Indian lands. Act of Feb. 28, 1891, § 3, 26 Stat. 795, 25 U.S.C. § 397. Because the statute applied only to lands "occupied by Indians who have bought and paid for the same," the statute was interpreted to be inapplicable to reservations created by Executive Order. *See British-American Oil Producing Co. v. Board of Equalization,* 299 U. S. 159, 299 U. S. 161-162, 299 U. S. 164. In 1922, the Secretary of the Interior took the position that Indian reservations created by Executive Order were public lands, and that Indians residing on those reservations had no right to share in royalties derived from oil and gas leases. 49 I.D. 139. [Footnote 2/4]

In 1927, Congress enacted a statute expressly providing that unallotted lands on any Indian reservation created by Executive Order could be leased for oil and gas mining purposes with the approval of the Secretary of the Interior. [Footnote 2/5] The statute directed that all rentals, royalties, or bonuses for such leases should be paid to the Treasurer of the United States for the benefit of the tribe for which the reservation was created. [Footnote 2/6] The statute further provided that state taxes could be levied upon the output of such oil and gas leases, [Footnote 2/7] but made no mention of the possibility that the Indian tribes, in addition to receiving royalties, could impose taxes on the output. [Footnote 2/8]

In 1934, Congress enacted the Indian Reorganization Act, 48 Stat. 984, 25 U.S.C. § 461 *et seq.,* which authorized any Indian tribe residing on a reservation to adopt a constitution and bylaws, subject to the approval of the Secretary of the Interior. The Act provided that, "[i]n addition to all powers vested in any Indian tribe or tribal council by existing law," the constitution should vest certain specific powers, such as the power to employ legal counsel, in the tribe. [Footnote 2/9] The Act also authorized the Secretary of the Interior to issue a charter of incorporation to an Indian tribe, and provided that the charter could convey to the tribe the power to purchase, manage, and dispose of its property. [Footnote 2/10] The 1934 Act was silent concerning the right of an Indian tribe to levy taxes. [Footnote 2/11] The first Jicarilla Apache Constitution was approved by the Secretary of the Interior in 1937. [Footnote 2/12]

In 1953, the Tribe executed an oil and gas lease with the Phillips Petroleum Co. App. 220. The lease, prepared on a form provided by the Bureau of Indian Affairs of the Department of the Interior, presumably is typical of later leases executed between other companies and the Tribe. [Footnote 2/13] The lease provides that, in return for certain rents, royalties, and a cash bonus of $71,345.99, all to be paid to the treasurer of the Tribe, the Tribe, as lessor, granted to the lessee "the exclusive right and privilege to drill for, mine, extract, remove, and dispose of all the oil and natural gas deposits in or under" the described tracts of land, together with the right to construct and maintain buildings, plants, tanks, and other necessary structures on the surface. *Id.* at 22–23. The lease is for a term of 10 years following approval by the Secretary of the Interior "and as much longer thereafter as oil and/ or gas is produced in paying quantities from said land." *Ibid.* The lessee is obligated to use reasonable diligence in the development of the property, and to pay an annual rental of $1.25 per acre and a royalty of 12 1/2% "of the value or amount" of all oil and gas "produced and saved" from the leased land. *Id.* at 24, 26. Oil and gas used by the lessee for development and operation of the lease

is royalty-free. *Id.* at 24. The Tribe reserved the rights to use, free of charge, sufficient gas for any school or other building owned by the Tribe on the leased premises, and to take its royalty in kind. *Id.* at 27–28.

The lease contains no reference to the payment of taxes. The lessee does, however, agree to comply with all regulations of the Secretary of the Interior

> "now or hereafter in force relative to such leases: *Provided,* That no regulation hereafter approved shall effect a change in rate or royalty or annual rental herein specified without the written consent of the parties to this lease."

Id. at 27. The lease was approved by the Commissioner of Indian Affairs on behalf of the Secretary of the Interior. *Id.* at 32. Both of the 1953 leases described in the record are still producing.

In 1968, the Tribe adopted a Revised Constitution giving its Tribal Council authority, subject to approval by the Secretary of the Interior, "to impose taxes and fees on non-members of the tribe doing business on the reservation." [Footnote 2/14] Eight years later, the Tribal Council enacted an Oil and Gas Severance Tax Ordinance, which was approved by the Secretary of the Interior. The tribal ordinance provides that a severance tax "is imposed on any oil and natural gas severed, saved and removed from Tribal lands. . . . " *Id.* at 38. The rate of the tax is $0.05 per million Btu's of gas produced on the reservation and sold or transported off the reservation, and $0.29 per barrel of crude or condensate produced on the reservation and sold or transported off the reservation. *Id.* at 39. Royalty gas or oil taken by the Tribe, as well as gas or oil used by the Tribe, is exempt from the tax. *Ibid.* Thus, the entire burden of the tax apparently will fall on nonmembers of the Tribe. The tax, if sustained, will produce over $2 million in revenues annually. [Footnote 2/15]

II

The powers possessed by Indian tribes stem from three sources: federal statutes, treaties, and the tribe's inherent sovereignty. Neither the Tribe nor the Federal Government seeks to justify the Jicarilla Tribe's severance tax on the basis of any federal statute, [Footnote 2/16] and the Jicarilla Apaches, who reside on an Executive Order reservation, executed no treaty with the United States from which they derive sovereign powers. Therefore, if the severance tax is valid, it must be as an exercise of the Tribe's inherent sovereignty.

Tribal sovereignty is neither derived from nor protected by the Constitution. [Footnote 2/17] Indian tribes have, however, retained many of the powers of self-government that they possessed at the time of their incorporation into the United States. As stated by Justice M'Lean in *Worcester v. Georgia,* 6 Pet. 515, 31 U. S. 580 (concurring opinion):

> "At no time has the sovereignty of the country been recognised as existing in the Indians, but they have been always admitted to possess many of the attributes of sovereignty. All the rights which belong to self-government have been recognised as vested in them."

Similarly, the Court in *United States v. Kagama,* 118 U. S. 375, 118 U. S. 381-382, stated: "[The Indians] were, and always have been, regarded as having a semi-independent position when they preserved their tribal relations; not as States, not as nations, not as possessed of the full attributes of sovereignty, but as a separate people, with the power of regulating their internal and social relations, and thus far not brought under the laws of the Union or of the State within whose limits they resided."

Two distinct principles emerge from these early statements of tribal sovereignty: that Indian tribes possess broad powers of self-governance over tribal members, but that tribes do not possess the same attributes of sovereignty that the Federal Government and the several States enjoy. [Footnote 2/18] In determining the extent of the sovereign powers that the tribes retained in submitting to the authority of the United States, this Court has recognized a fundamental distinction between the right of the tribes to govern their own internal affairs and the right to exercise powers affecting nonmembers of the tribe.

The Court has been careful to protect the tribes from interference with tribal control over their own members. The Court has recognized that tribes have the power to prosecute members for violations of tribal criminal law, and that this power is an inherent attribute of tribal sovereignty. *United States v. Wheeler,* 435 U. S. 313. The tribes also retain the power to create substantive law governing internal tribal affairs. Tribes may define rules of membership, and thus determine who is entitled to the benefits of tribal citizenship, *Roff v. Burney,* 168 U. S. 218; establish rules of inheritance, which supersede applicable state law, *Jones v. Meehan,* 175 U. S. 1, 175 U. S. 29; and determine rights to custody of a child of divorced parents of the tribe, and thus preempt adoption proceedings brought in state court. *Fisher v. District Court,* 424 U. S. 382. This substantive tribal law may be enforced in tribal courts. *Williams v. Lee,* 358 U. S. 217; *Fisher v. District Court, supra.*

In many respects, the Indian tribes' sovereignty over their own members is significantly greater than the States' powers over their own citizens. Tribes may enforce discriminatory rules that would be intolerable in a non-Indian community. The equal protection components of the Fifth and Fourteenth Amendments, which limit federal or state authority, do not similarly limit tribal power. *See Santa Clara Pueblo v. Martinez,* 436 U. S. 49, 436 U. S. 56, and n. 7. [Footnote 2/19] The criminal jurisdiction of the tribes over their own members is similarly unconstrained by constitutional limitations applicable to the States and the Federal Government. [Footnote 2/20] Thus the use of the word "sovereign" to characterize tribal powers of self-government is surely appropriate.

In sharp contrast to the tribes' broad powers over their own members, tribal powers over nonmembers have always been narrowly confined. [Footnote 2/21] The Court has emphasized that "exercise of tribal power beyond what is necessary to protect tribal self-government or to control internal relations is inconsistent with the dependent status of the tribes, and so cannot survive without express congressional delegation."

Montana v. United States, 450 U. S. 544, 450 U. S. 564. In *Oliphant v. Suquamish Indian Tribe,* 435 U. S. 191, the Court held that tribes have no criminal jurisdiction over crimes committed by nonmembers within the reservations. [Footnote 2/22] In *Montana v. United States, supra,* the Court held that the Crow Tribe could not prohibit hunting and fishing by nonmembers on reservation land no longer owned by the Tribe, and indicated that the principle underlying *Oliphant* — that tribes possess limited power over nonmembers — was applicable in a civil, as well as a criminal, context. As stated by the Court, "[t]hough *Oliphant* only determined inherent tribal authority in criminal matters, the principles on which it relied support the general proposition that the inherent sovereign powers of an Indian tribe do not extend to the activities of nonmembers of the tribe." *Montana v. United States, supra,* at 450 U. S. 565 (footnote omitted). [Footnote 2/23]

The tribes' authority to enact legislation affecting nonmembers is therefore of a different character than their broad power to control internal tribal affairs. This difference is consistent with the fundamental principle that, "[i]n this Nation, each sovereign governs only with the consent of the governed." *Nevada v. Hall,* 440 U. S. 410, 440 U. S. 426. Since nonmembers are excluded from participation in tribal government, the powers that may be exercised over them are appropriately limited. Certainly, tribal authority over nonmembers — including the power to tax — is not unprecedented. An examination of cases that have upheld this power, however, demonstrates that the power to impose such a tax derives solely from the tribes' power to exclude nonmembers entirely from territory that has been reserved for the tribe. This "power to exclude" logically has been held to include the lesser power to attach conditions on a right of entry granted by the tribe to a nonmember to engage in particular activities within the reservation.

III

A study of the source of the tribes' power to tax nonmembers must focus on the extent of the tribal power to tax that existed in 1934, when the Indian Reorganization Act was enacted to prevent further erosion of Indian sovereign powers. [Footnote 2/24]

Shortly after the Act was passed, the Solicitor of the Department of the Interior issued a formal opinion setting forth his understanding of the powers that might be secured by an Indian tribe and incorporated in its constitution by virtue of the reference in the Reorganization Act to powers vested in an Indian tribe "by existing law." [Footnote 2/25] Solicitor Margold concluded that, among those powers, was a power of taxation; his opinion described the permissible exercise of that power:

"Except where Congress has provided otherwise, this power may be exercised over members of the tribe and over nonmembers, so far as such nonmembers may accept privileges of trade, residence, etc., to which taxes may be attached as conditions." 55 I.D. 14, 46 (1934).

Solicitor Margold cited three decisions in support of this opinion. These three cases, *Buster v. Wright,* 135 F. 947 (CA8 1905), *appeal dism'd,* 203 U.S. 599; *Morris v. Hitchcock,* 194 U. S. 384; and *Maxey v. Wright,* 3 Ind.T. 243, 54 S.W. 807 (Ct.App.Ind.T.), *aff'd,* 105 F. 1003 (CA8 1900), were decided shortly after the turn of the century, and are the three leading cases considering the power of an Indian tribe to assess taxes against nonmembers. [Footnote 2/26] The three cases are similar in result and in their reasoning. In each, the court upheld the tax; in each, the court relied on the Tribe's power to exclude non-Indians from its reservation, and concluded that the Tribe could condition entry or continued presence within the reservation on the payment of a license fee or tax; and in each, the court assumed that the ultimate remedy for nonpayment of the tax would be exclusion from the reservation.

In the first of these cases, *Maxey v. Wright,* the Court of Appeals of Indian Territory affirmed an order by a federal territorial court dismissing a complaint filed by non-Indian lawyers practicing in the Creek Nation. The complaint sought to enjoin the Indian agent for the Five Civilized Tribes from collecting an annual occupation tax of $25 assessed on each non-Indian lawyer residing and practicing his profession on the reservation. In rejecting the attorneys' claim, the Court of Appeals first analyzed the relevant treaties between the United States and the Creeks, and noted that the Indians had "carefully guarded their sovereignty, and their right to admit, and consequently to exclude, all white persons, except such as are named in the treaty."

3 Ind.T. at 247, 54 S.W. at 809. The court noted that the United States had agreed that all persons who were not expressly excepted and were present in the Creek Nation "without the consent of that Nation [were] deemed to be intruders," and that the Government had "pledge[d] itself to remove them." *Id.* at 248, 54 S.W. at 809. Because attorneys were not within any excepted class, [Footnote 2/27] the court concluded that the Tribe had the authority to require them either to pay the license fee or to be removed as "intruders." [Footnote 2/28] The court held:

> "[T]he Creek nation had the power to impose this condition or occupation tax, if it may be so called, upon attorneys at law (white men) residing and practicing their profession in the Indian Territory. And inasmuch as the government of the United States, in the treaty, had declared that all persons not authorized by its terms to reside in the Creek Nation should be deemed to be intruders, and had obligated itself to remove all such persons from the Creek Nation, the remedy to enforce this provision of the treaty was a removal by the United States from the Creek Nation of the delinquent as an intruder."*Id.* at 250, 54 S.W. at 809–810. [Footnote 2/29]

Morris v. Hitchcock, 194 U. S. 384, decided by this Court in 1904, also arose from a challenge to an enactment of one of the Five Civilized Tribes that required non-Indians to pay annual permit fees. The complainants owned cattle and horses that were grazing on land in the Chickasaw Nation pursuant to contracts with individual members of the Tribe. Complainants filed suit in the District of Columbia seeking an injunction preventing federal officials from removing their cattle and horses from the Indian Territory for failure to pay the permit fees assessed by the Tribe. An order dismissing the complaint was affirmed by the Court of Appeals for the District of Columbia, and by this Court.

This Court's opinion first noted that treaties between the United States and the Chickasaw Nation had granted the Tribe the right "to control the presence within the territory assigned to it of persons who might otherwise be regarded as intruders," [Footnote 2/30] and that the United States had assumed the obligation of protecting the Indians from aggression by persons not subject to their jurisdiction. *Id.* at 194 U. S. 389. The Court then reviewed similar legislation that had been adopted by the Chickasaw Nation in 1876, [Footnote 2/31] and noted that, in 1879, the Senate Committee on the Judiciary had specifically referred to the 1876 legislation and expressed an opinion that it was valid. *Id.* at 194 U. S. 389-390.

The Court also reviewed two opinions of the Attorney General that had concluded that the power of the Chickasaw to impose permit fees had not been withdrawn by Congress. [Footnote 2/32]

Although Congress subsequently had created an express exception in favor of owners of town lots, and thus protected them from eviction as intruders, the Court noted that no comparable protection had been given to owners of cattle and horses. *Id.* at 194 U. S. 392-393. On the basis of these authorities, the Court concluded that the Chickasaw legislation imposing grazing fees was valid.

In the third case, *Buster v. Wright,* 135 F. 947 (CA8 1905), nonmembers of the Creek Nation brought suit against federal inspectors to enjoin them from stopping the plaintiffs from doing business within the reservation; the nonmembers feared such action because they had refused to pay a permit tax assessed on traders by the Tribe. The Court of Appeals relied on *Morris v. Hitchcock* and *Maxey v. Wright* in upholding the tax. The opinion for the court by Judge Walter H. Sanborn emphasized that the tax was in the nature of a condition precedent to transacting business within the reservation, and that the plaintiffs had ample notice of the tax:

"The permit tax of the Creek Nation, which is the subject of this controversy, is the annual price fixed by the act of its national council, which was approved by the President of the United States in the year 1900, for the privilege which it offers to those who are not citizens of its nation of trading within its borders. The payment of this tax is a mere condition of the exercise of this privilege. No noncitizen is required to exercise the privilege or to pay the tax. He may refrain from the one, and he remains free from liability for the other. Thus, without entering upon an extended discussion or consideration of the question whether this charge is technically a license or a tax, the fact appears that it partakes far more of the nature of a license than of an ordinary tax, because it has the optional feature of the former, and lacks the compulsory attribute of the latter."

"Repeated decisions of the courts, numerous opinions of the Attorneys General, and the practice of years place beyond debate the propositions that, prior to March 1, 1901, the Creek Nation had lawful authority to require the payment of this tax as a condition precedent to the exercise of the privilege of trading within its borders, and that the executive department of the government of the United States had plenary power to enforce its payment through the Secretary of the Interior and his subordinates, the Indian inspector, Indian agent, and Indian police."

135 F. at 949–950. The court noted that the traders, who had purchased town lots of the Creek Nation pursuant to a 1901 agreement between the Creeks and the United States, could not rely on that agreement as an implied divestiture of a preexisting power to tax. [Footnote 2/33] The court held that, even though noncitizens of the Tribe had acquired lawful ownership of lots pursuant to the 1901 agreement, and could not be evicted from those lots, they had no right to conduct business within the reservation without paying the permit taxes. [Footnote 2/34]

Prior to the enactment of the Indian Reorganization Act in 1934, these three cases were the only judicial decisions considering the power of an Indian tribe to impose a tax on nonmembers. [Footnote 2/35] These cases demonstrate that the power of an Indian tribe to impose a tax solely on nonmembers doing business on the reservation derives from the tribe's power to exclude those persons entirely from tribal lands or, in the alternative, to impose lesser restrictions and conditions on a right of entry granted to conduct business on the reservation. [Footnote 2/36] This interpretation is supported by the fact that the remedy for the nonpayment of the tax in all three cases was exclusion from the reservation. [Footnote 2/37]

As I have noted, a limitation on the power of Indian tribes to tax nonmembers is not simply an archaic concept derived from three old cases that has no basis in logic or equity. Tribal powers over nonmembers are appropriately limited, because nonmembers are foreclosed from participation in tribal government. If the power to tax is limited to situations in which the tribe has the power to exclude, then the nonmember is subjected to the tribe's jurisdiction only if he accepts the conditions of entry imposed by the tribe. [Footnote 2/38] The limited source of the power to tax nonmembers — the power to exclude intruders — is thus consistent with this Court's recognition of the limited character of the power of Indian tribes over nonmembers in general. [Footnote 2/39] The proper source of the taxing authority asserted by the Jicarilla Apache Tribe in these cases, therefore, is not the Tribe's inherent power of self-government, but rather its power over the territory that has been set apart for its use and occupation. [Footnote 2/40]

This conclusion is consistent with our recent decision in *Washington v. Confederated Tribes of Colville Reservation,* 447 U. S. 134. In that case we held that a tribal tax on cigarettes sold on the reservations of the Colville, Makah, and Lummi Tribes to nonmembers of the Tribes was a permissible exercise of the Tribes' retained sovereign power to tax. [Footnote 2/41] We recognized that the power to tax non-Indians entering the reservation had not been divested by virtue of the Tribes' dependent status, and that no overriding federal interest would be frustrated by the tribal taxation. The Court quoted with approval, as an indication of the Executive Branch's understanding of the taxing power, Solicitor Margold's 1934 opinion. The Court noted further that "[f]ederal courts also have acknowledged tribal power to tax non-Indians entering the reservation to engage in economic activity," and cited *Buster v. Wright* and *Morris v. Hitchcock,* 447 U.S. at 447 U. S. 153. [Footnote 2/42] The tax in *Colville,* which was applied to nonmembers who entered the reservation and sought to purchase cigarettes, is clearly valid under the rationale that the tribes' power to tax derives from the right to exclude nonmembers from the reservation and the lesser right to attach conditions on the entry of such nonmembers seeking to do business there. [Footnote 2/43] *Colville* is consistent with the principles set forth above. The power of Indian tribes to tax nonmembers stems from the tribes' power to exclude those nonmembers; any exercise of this power must be consistent with its source. [Footnote 2/44]

IV

The power to exclude petitioners would have supported the imposition of a discriminatory tribal tax on petitioners when they sought to enter the Jicarilla Apache Reservation to explore for minerals. Moreover, even if no tax had been imposed at the time of initial entry, a discriminatory severance tax could have been imposed as a condition attached to the grant of the privilege of extracting minerals from the earth. [Footnote 2/45] But the Tribe did not impose any tax prior to petitioners' entry or as a condition attached to the privileges granted by the leases in 1953. As a result, the tax imposed in 1976 is not valid unless the Tribe retained its power either to exclude petitioners from the reservation or to prohibit them from continuing to extract oil and gas from reservation lands.

The leases executed by the Tribe and petitioners are clearly valid, and binding on both parties. The

Tribe does not contend that the leases were not the product of arm's length bargaining. Moreover, the leases were executed on a form prepared by the Department of the Interior, the Department gave specific approval to the terms of the leases, and they were executed pursuant to explicit congressional authority. [Footnote 2/46] Under the leases, petitioners clearly have the right to remain on the reservation to do business for the duration of the contracts. [Footnote 2/47]

There is no basis for a claim that exercise of the mining rights granted by the leases was subject to an additional unstated condition concerning the payment of severance taxes. [Footnote 2/48]

At the time the leases contained in the record were executed, the Jicarilla Apache Constitution contained no taxing authorization whatever; the severance tax ordinance was not enacted until many years after all lessees had been granted an unlimited right to extract oil and gas from the reservation. In addition, the written leases unambiguously stated:

"[N]o regulation hereafter approved shall effect a change in rate or royalty or annual rental herein specified without the written consent of the parties to this lease." App. 27.

Nor can it be said that notice of an inherent right to tax could have been gleaned from relevant statutory enactments. When Congress enacted legislation in 1927 granting the Indians the royalty income from oil and gas leases on reservations created by Executive Order, it neither authorized nor prohibited the imposition of any taxes by the tribes. Although the absence of such reference does not indicate that Congress preempted the right of the tribes to impose such a tax, [Footnote 2/49] the lack of any mention of tribal severance taxes defeats the argument that all parties were aware as a matter of law that a severance tax could be imposed at any time as a condition to the continued performance of a mineral lease.

Thus, nothing in the leases themselves or in any Act of Congress conveyed an indication that petitioners could accept the rights conferred by the leases only by accepting a condition that they pay any subsequently enacted severance tax. Nor could such a condition be presumed from prior taxing activity of the Tribe. In my opinion, it is clear that the parties negotiated the leases in question with absolutely no expectation that a severance tax could later be imposed; in the contemplation of the parties, the conditions governing petitioners' right to extract oil and gas were not subject to change during the terms of the agreements. There simply is no support for the proposition that the Tribe retained the power in the leases to impose an additional condition on petitioners' right to enter the reservation and extract oil and gas from reservation lands. Since that authority was not retained, the Tribe does not now have the power to alter unilaterally the terms of the agreement and impose an additional burden on petitioners' right to do business on the reservation. [Footnote 2/50]

In these cases, the Tribe seeks to impose a tax on the very activity that the leases granted petitioners the right to undertake. As Solicitor Margold wrote long ago:

"Over tribal lands, the tribe has the rights of a landowner as well as the rights of a local government, dominion as well as sovereignty. But on all the lands of the reservation, whether owned by the tribe, by members thereof, or by outsiders, the tribe has the sovereign power of determining the conditions upon which persons shall be permitted to enter its domain, to reside therein, and to do business, provided only such determination is consistent with applicable Federal laws and *does not infringe any vested rights of persons now occupying reservation land under lawful authority.*"

55 I.D. at 50 (emphasis added). Petitioners were granted authority by the Tribe to extract oil and gas from reservation lands. The Tribe now seeks to change retroactively the conditions of that authority. These petitioners happen to be prosperous oil companies. Moreover, it may be sound policy to find additional sources of revenue to better the economic conditions of many Indian tribes. If this retroactive imposition of a tax on oil companies is permissible, however, an Indian tribe may with equal legitimacy contract with outsiders for the construction of a school or a hospital, or for the rendition of medical or technical services, and then —after the contract is partially performed— change the terms of the bargain by imposing a gross receipts tax on the outsider. If the Court is willing to ignore the risk of such unfair treatment of a local contractor or a local doctor because the Secretary of the Interior has the power to veto a tribal tax, it must equate the unbridled discretion of a political appointee with the protection afforded by rules of law. That equation is unacceptable to me. Neither wealth, political opportunity, nor past transgressions can justify denying any person the protection of the law. [Footnote 2/1]

See Plaintiff's Exhibit E, p. 4.

[Footnote 2/2]

"[H]ereafter no Indian nation or tribe within the territory of the United States shall be acknowledged or recognized as an independent nation, tribe, or power with whom the United States may contract by treaty: *Provided, further,* That nothing herein contained shall be construed to invalidate or impair the obligation of any treaty heretofore lawfully made and ratified with any such Indian nation or tribe."

16 Stat. 566, current version at 25 U.S.C. § 71.

[Footnote 2/3]

The entire Executive Order reads as follows:
"*EXECUTIVE MANSION, FEBRUARY 11, 1887.*"

"It is hereby ordered that all that portion of the public domain in the Territory of New Mexico which, when surveyed, will be embraced in the following townships, viz:" "27, 28, 29, and 30 north, ranges 1 east, and 1, 2, and 3 west; 31 and 32 north, ranges 2 west and 3 west, and the south half of township 31 north, range 1 west," "be, and the same is hereby, set apart as a reservation for the use and occupation of the Jicarilla Apache Indians: *Provided,* That this order shall not be so construed as to deprive any bona fide settler of any valid rights he may have acquired under the law of the United States providing for the disposition of the public domain."

"Grover Cleveland"
1 C. Kappler, Indian Affairs, Laws and Treaties 875 (1904).

[Footnote 2/4]

The Secretary contended that the land on Executive Order reservations was subject to leasing, as "lands of the United States," under the Mineral Lands Leasing Act of February 25, 1920, 41 Stat. 437, 30 U.S.C. 181 *et seq.* In 1924, Attorney General Stone rendered an opinion stating that the Mineral Lands Leasing Act did not apply to Executive Order reservations. 34 Op.Atty. Gen. 181. In 1925, Stone instituted litigation in the District Court of Utah to cancel certain leases that had been authorized by the Secretary of the Interior pursuant to the Mineral Lands Leasing Act. *See* H.R.Rep. No. 1791, 69th Cong., 2d Sess., 5 (1927). The case was dismissed by stipulation after the enactment of the 1927 Act noted in the text. *See United States v. McMahon,* 273 U.S. 782.

A later decision by this Court suggests that the Secretary's position was correct. In *Sioux Tribe of Indians v. United States,* 316 U. S. 317, the Court held that an Indian tribe was not entitled to compensation from the United States when an Executive Order reservation was abolished. The Court said:

"Perhaps the most striking proof of the belief shared by Congress and the Executive that the Indians were not entitled to compensation upon the abolition of an executive order reservation is the very absence of compensatory payments in such situations. It was a common practice, during the period in which reservations were created by executive order, for the President simply to terminate the existence of a reservation by cancelling or revoking the order establishing it. That is to say, the procedure followed in the case before us was typical. No compensation was made, and neither the Government nor the Indians suggested that it was due."

"* * * *"

"We conclude therefore that there was no express constitutional or statutory authorization for the conveyance of a compensable interest to petitioner by the four executive orders of 1875 and 1876, and that no implied Congressional delegation of the power to do so can be spelled out from the evidence of Congressional and executive understanding. The orders were effective to withdraw from sale the lands affected and to grant the use of the lands to the petitioner. But the interest which the Indians received was subject to termination at the will of either the executive or Congress, and without obligation to the United States. The executive orders of 1879 and 1884 were simply an exercise of this power of termination, and the payment of compensation was not required."

Id. at 316 U. S. 330-331.

See also Tee-Hit-Ton Indians v. United States, 348 U. S. 272, 348 U. S. 279-282.

[Footnote 2/5]

Act of Mar. 3, 1927, 44 Stat. (part 2) 1347, current version at 25 U.S.C. § 398a. Section 1 of the Act provided:

"[U]nallotted lands within the limits of any reservation or withdrawal created by Executive order for Indian purposes or for the use or occupancy of any Indians or tribe may be leased for oil and gas mining purposes in accordance with the provisions contained in the Act of May 29, 1924 [26 U.S.C.§ 398]."

See also 25 U.S.C. 398. Unallotted land is land that had not been allotted in severalty to individual Indians pursuant to the General Allotment Act of 1887, 24 Stat. 388.

[Footnote 2/6]

Section 2 of the Act provided:

"[T]he proceeds from rentals, royalties, or bonuses of oil and gas leases upon lands within Executive order Indian reservations or withdrawals shall be deposited in the Treasury of the United States to the credit of the tribe of Indians for whose benefit the reservation or withdrawal was created or who are using and occupying the land, and shall draw interest at the rate of 4 per centum per annum and be available for appropriation by Congress for expenses in connection with the supervision of the development and operation of the oil and gas industry and for the use and benefit of such Indians: *Provided,* That said Indians, or their tribal council, shall be consulted in regard to the expenditure of such money, but no per capita payment shall be made except by Act of Congress."

44 Stat. (part 2) 1347, current version at 25 U.S.C. § 398b.

[Footnote 2/7]

Section 3 of the Act provided:

"[T]axes may be levied and collected by the State or local authority upon improvements, output of mines or oil and gas wells or other rights, property, or assets of any lessee upon lands within Executive order Indian reservations in the same manner as such taxes are otherwise levied and collected, and such taxes may be levied against the share obtained for the Indians as bonuses, rentals, and royalties, and the Secretary of the Interior is authorized and directed to cause such taxes to be paid out of the tribal funds in the Treasury: *Provided,* That such taxes shall not become a lien or charge of any kind against the land or other property of such Indians."

44 Stat. (part 2) 1347, current version at 25 U.S.C. § 398c.

[Footnote 2/8]

In 1938, Congress passed the Act of May 11, 1938, 52 Stat. 347, 25 U.S.C. §§ 396a-396g, which was designed in part to achieve uniformity for all mineral leases of Indian lands. Like the 1927 Act, the statute provided that the tribes were entitled to the royalties from such leases. The statute made no mention of taxes. *See* n. 45, *infra.*

[Footnote 2/9]

The statute provided, in part:

"Any Indian tribe, or tribes, residing on the same reservation, shall have the right to organize for its common welfare, and may adopt an appropriate constitution and bylaws, which shall become effective when ratified by a majority vote of the adult members of the tribe, or of the adult Indians residing on such reservation, as the case may be, at a special election authorized and called by the Secretary of the Interior under such rules and regulations as he may prescribe. . . . "

"In addition to all powers vested in any Indian tribe or tribal council by existing law, the constitution adopted by said tribe shall also vest in such tribe or its tribal council the following rights and powers: to employ legal counsel, the choice of counsel and fixing of fees to be subject to the approval of the Secretary of the Interior; to prevent the sale, disposition, lease, or encumbrance of tribal lands, interests in lands, or other tribal assets without the consent of the tribe; and to negotiate with the Federal, State, and local Governments."

25 U.S.C. § 476.

[Footnote 2/10]

The statute provided:

"The Secretary of the Interior may, upon petition by at least one-third of the adult Indians, issue a charter of incorporation to such tribe: *Provided,* That such charter shall not become operative until ratified at a special election by a majority vote of the adult Indians living on the reservation. Such charter may convey to the incorporated tribe the power to purchase, take by gift, or bequest, or otherwise, own, hold, manage, operate, and dispose of property of every description, real and personal, including the power to purchase restricted Indian lands and to issue in exchange therefor interests in corporate property, and such further powers as may be incidental to the conduct of corporate business, not inconsistent with law; but no authority shall be granted to sell, mortgage, or lease for a period exceeding ten years any of the land included in the limits of the reservation. Any charter so issued shall not be revoked or surrendered except by Act of Congress."

25 U.S.C. § 477.

[Footnote 2/11]

See F. Cohen, Handbook of Federal Indian Law 267 (1942) (hereinafter Cohen).

[Footnote 2/12]

The 1937 Constitution made no reference to any power to assess taxes against nonmembers. *See* 1937 Constitution and By-Laws of the Jicarilla Apache Tribe, Defendants' Exhibit G.

[Footnote 2/13]

This lease is attached to petitioners' complaint in No. 80–11. The lease attached to the complaint in No. 80–15 was also executed in 1953. *See* App. 62. The record does not disclose the date on which most of the leases with petitioners were executed, but the record does indicate that leases were executed as late as 1967. *See* Plaintiffs' Exhibit 1. Leases of Jicarilla tribal property cover in the aggregate over 500,000 acres of land, comprising almost 69% of the acreage within the Jicarilla Reservation. Brief for Respondent Jicarilla Apache Tribe 2.

[Footnote 2/14]

App. to Brief for Petitioners in No. 80–15, pp. 12a-13a. An earlier Constitution adopted in 1960 contained a similar provision permitting "taxes and fees on persons doing business on the reservation." *See* 1960 Constitution of the Jicarilla Apache Tribe, Art. VI, § 5, Defendant's Exhibit A.

[Footnote 2/15]

See District Court's Findings of Fact and Conclusions of Law, Finding No. 32, App. 130. The Tribe's answers to interrogatories indicate that, in 1976, the royalties on the leases received by the Tribe amounted to $3,995,469.69. *See* Plaintiff's Exhibit E, p. 7; Tr. 269.

[Footnote 2/16]

Congress may delegate "sovereign" powers to the tribes. *See United States v. Mazurie,* 419 U. S. 544.

As indicated, however, neither the 1927 statute permitting Indians to receive royalties from the lease of tribal lands nor the Indian Reorganization Act of 1934 conveys authority to the Indian tribes to tax. *See supra* at 455 U. S. 163-165.

[Footnote 2/17]

The only reference to Indian tribes in the Constitution is in Art. I, 8, Cl. 3, which provides that

> "[t]he Congress shall have Power . . . [t]o regulate Commerce with foreign Nations, and among the several States, and with the Indian Tribes."

More significant than this reference to Indian tribes is the absence of any mention of the tribes in the Tenth Amendment, which provides:

> "The powers not delegated to the United States by the Constitution, nor prohibited by it to the States, are reserved to the States respectively, or to the people."

[Footnote 2/18]

The Indian tribes often have been described as "domestic dependent nations." The term was first used in *Cherokee Nation v. Georgia,* 5 Pet. 1, where Chief Justice Marshall, writing for the Court, explained:

> "Though the Indians are acknowledged to have an unquestionable, and, heretofore, unquestioned right to the lands they occupy, until that right shall be extinguished by a voluntary cession to our government; yet it may well be doubted whether those tribes which reside within the acknowledged boundaries of the United States can, with strict accuracy, be denominated foreign nations. They may, more correctly, perhaps, be denominated domestic dependent nations. They occupy a territory to which we assert a title independent of their will, which must take effect in point of possession when their right of possession ceases. Meanwhile they are in a state of pupilage. Their relation to the United States resembles that of a ward to his guardian."

Id. at 30 U. S. 17.

The United States retains plenary authority to divest the tribes of any attributes of sovereignty. *See United States v. Wheeler,* 435 U. S. 313, 435 U. S. 319; *Winton v. Amos,* 255 U. S. 373, 255 U. S. 391-392; *Lone Wolf v. Hitchcock,* 187 U. S. 553, 187 U. S. 565; 1 American Indian Policy Review Commission, Final Report 106–107 (1977) (hereinafter AIPRC Final Report). Thus, for example, Congress can waive the tribes' sovereign immunity. *See United States v. United States Fidelity & Guaranty Co.,* 309 U. S. 506, 309 U. S. 512.

[Footnote 2/19]

The Indian Civil Rights Act of 1968, 82 Stat. 77, 25 U.S.C. §§ 1301–1303, prohibits Indian tribes from denying "to any person within its jurisdiction the equal protection of its laws." § 1302(8). In *Santa Clara Pueblo,* however, the Court held that sovereign immunity protected a tribe from suit under the Act, that the Act did not create a private cause of action cognizable in federal court, and that a tribal court was the appropriate forum for vindication of rights created by the Act.

[Footnote 2/20]

In *Talton v. Mayes,* 163 U. S. 376, the Court held that the Fifth Amendment right to indictment by grand jury does not apply to prosecutions in tribal courts. *See also United States v. Wheeler, supra,* at 435 U. S. 328-329.

[Footnote 2/21]

Certain treaties that specifically granted the right of self-government to the tribes also specifically excluded jurisdiction over nonmembers. *See, e.g.,* Treaty with the Cherokees, Art. 5, 7 Stat. 481 (1835); Treaty with the Choctaws and Chickasaws, Art. 7, 11 Stat. 612 (1855); Treaty with the Creeks and Seminoles, Art. 15, 11 Stat. 703 (1856).

[Footnote 2/22]

In support of that holding, the Court stated:

"Upon incorporation into the territory of the United States, the Indian tribes thereby come under the territorial sovereignty of the United States and their exercise of separate power is constrained so as not to conflict with the interests of this overriding sovereignty. '[T]heir rights to complete sovereignty, as independent nations, [are] necessarily diminished.' 8 Wheat. 21 U. S. 543, 21 U. S. 574 (1823)."

435 U.S. at 435 U. S. 209. *See also New York ex rel. Ray v. Martin,* 326 U. S. 498, 326 U. S. 499 (state court has jurisdiction to try a non-Indian for a crime committed against a non-Indian on a reservation).

[Footnote 2/23]

Preceding this statement, the Court noted that

"the Court [in *Oliphant*] quoted Justice Johnson's words in his concurrence in *Fletcher v. Peck,* 6 Cranch 87, 10 U. S. 147 — the first Indian case to reach this Court — that the Indian tribes have lost any 'right of governing every person within their limits except themselves.' 435 U.S. at 435 U. S. 209."

Montana v. United States, 450 U.S. at 450 U. S. 565. *See also Oneida Indian Nation v. County of Oneida,* 414 U. S. 661 (tribes cannot freely alienate to non-Indians the land they occupy); *Cherokee Nation v. Georgia,* 5 Pet. 1, 30 U. S. 17-18 (tribes cannot enter into direct commercial or foreign relations with other nations).

In *United States v. Wheeler, supra,* the Court held that the tribes' power to prosecute its members for tribal offenses was not "implicitly lost by virtue of their dependent status," but stated:

"The areas in which such implicit divestiture of sovereignty has been held to have occurred are those involving the relations between an Indian tribe and nonmembers of the tribe. . . . "

"These limitations rest on the fact that the dependent status of Indian tribes within our territorial jurisdiction is necessarily inconsistent with their freedom independently to determine their external relations. But the powers of self-government, including the power to prescribe and enforce internal criminal laws, are of a different type. They involve only the relations among members of a tribe. Thus, they are not such powers as would necessarily be lost by virtue of a tribe's dependent status."

"[T]he settled doctrine of the law of nations is that a weaker power does not surrender its independence — its right to self-government — by associating with a stronger, and taking its protection."

"*Worcester v. Georgia,* [6 Pet.] at 31 U. S. 560-561."

435 U.S. at 435 U. S. 326.

[Footnote 2/24]

The Indian Reorganization Act of 1934 confirmed, but did not enlarge, the inherent sovereign powers of the Indian tribes. Congress intended the Act to "stabilize the tribal organization of Indian tribes by vesting such tribal organizations with real, though limited, authority. . . . " S.Rep. No. 1080, 73d Cong., 2d Sess., 1 (1934). As one commentator interpreted § 16 of the Act:

> "[I]t would appear that powers originally held by tribes that were recognized and allowed to be retained by treaties or prior statutes, as well as any additional powers conferred in the same manner, would be retained by tribes that accepted the terms of the 1934 Act. . . . The provision is consistent with the act's purpose of enhancing tribal government, in that it recognized and reconfirmed those powers a tribe may already have had as a government."

Mettler, A Unified Theory of Indian Tribal Sovereignty, 30 Hastings L.Rev. 89, 97 (1978). Moreover, although the power given by the Reorganization Act to the Secretary of the Interior to approve or disapprove of the exercise of tribal powers places a limit on tribal sovereignty, that power does not enable the Secretary to add to the

inherent powers that a tribe possessed before the Act was passed.

On the other hand, the fact that an Indian tribe may never have had the occasion to exercise a particular power over nonmembers in its early history is not a sufficient reason to deny the existence of that power. Accordingly, the fact that there is no evidence that the Jicarilla Apache Tribe ever imposed a tax of any kind on a nonmember does not require the conclusion that it has no such taxing power. To the extent that the power to tax was an attribute of sovereignty possessed by Indian tribes when the Reorganization Act was passed, Congress intended the statute to preserve those powers for all Indian tribes that adopted a formal organization under the Act.

[Footnote 2/25]

55 I.D. 14 (1934). Solicitor Margold described the scope of this opinion as follows:

> "My opinion has been requested on the question of what powers may be secured to an Indian tribe and incorporated in its constitution and bylaws by virtue of the following phrase, contained in section 16 of the Wheeler-Howard Act (48 Stat. 984, 987) [the Reorganization Act of 1934]:"
>
> "In addition to *all powers vested in any Indian tribe or tribal council by existing law,* the constitution adopted by said tribe shall also vest. . . . "

"[Italics added.]"

"The question of what powers are vested in an Indian tribe or tribal council by existing law cannot be answered in detail for each Indian tribe without reference to hundreds of special treaties and special acts of Congress. It is possible, however, on the basis of the reported cases, the written opinions of the various executive departments, and those statutes of Congress which are of general import, to define the powers which have heretofore been recognized as lawfully within the jurisdiction of an Indian tribe. My answer to the propounded question, then, will be general, and subject to correction for particular tribes in the light of the treaties and statutes affecting such tribe wherever such treaties or statutes contain peculiar provisions restricting or enlarging the general authority of an Indian tribe."

Id. at 17–18.

[Footnote 2/26]

Felix Cohen, in his Handbook on Federal Indian Law published in 1942, also relies on these cases in his discussion of tribal taxation of nonmembers. Cohen 266–267. The Court, in *Washington v. Confederated Tribes of Colville Reservation,* 447 U. S. 134, cited both *Buster v. Wright* and *Morris v. Hitchcock* in upholding an exercise of the tribal power to tax. 447 U.S. at 447 U. S. 153. *See infra* at 455 U. S. 185.

[Footnote 2/27]

"Attorneys practicing in the United States courts are not persons who come within the exceptions, for they are not 'in the employment of the government of the United States,' or"

"persons peaceably traveling or temporarily sojourning in the country, or trading therein under license from the proper authority of the United States."

3 Ind.T. at 248–249, 54 S.W. at 809.

[Footnote 2/28]

In reaching this conclusion, the court relied heavily on two opinions of the Attorney General of the United States. In the first opinion, issued in 1881, Attorney General MacVeagh supported the validity of Indian permit laws that determined which persons would be permitted to reside on the Choctaw and Chickasaw Reservations. 17 Op.Atty.Gen. 134. In his discussion of the right of non-Indians to enter and remain on tribal lands, MacVeagh stated:

"Replying to your fourth question: it seems from what has been already said that, besides those persons or classes mentioned by you, only those who have been permitted by the Choctaws or Chickasaws to reside within their limits, or to be employed by their citizens as teachers, mechanics, or skilled agriculturists, have a right to enter and remain on the lands of these tribes; *and the right to remain is gone when the permit has expired.*"

Id. at 136 (emphasis added).

In a second opinion on the same subject, Attorney General Phillips stated in 1884 that, in the absence of a treaty or statute, the power of an Indian tribe "to regulate its own rights of occupancy, and to say who shall participate therein and upon what conditions, can not be doubted." 18 Op.Atty. Gen. 34, 36. Although the treaties applicable to the Choctaw and Chickasaw Tribes specifically excepted from the grant of self-government the power over nonmembers, the Attorney General did not construe this provision to limit the Tribes' power to exclude:

"I submit that, whatever this may mean, it does not limit the right of these tribes to pass upon the question, who (of persons *indifferent to the United States, i.e.,* neither employes, nor objectionable) shall share their *occupancy,* and upon what terms. That is a question which all private persons are allowed to decide for themselves. . . . "

Id. at 37.

[Footnote 2/29]

In other parts of its opinion, the court restated the propositions that the Tribe was "clothed with the power to admit white men, or not, at its option, which, as we hold, gave it the right to impose conditions," 3 Ind.T. at 253, 54 S.W. at 811, and that a lawyer who refused to pay for the privilege of remaining would become an "intruder":

"On the whole case, we therefore hold that a lawyer who is a white man, and not a citizen of the Creek Nation, is, pursuant to their statute, required to pay for the privilege of remaining and practicing his profession in that nation the sum of $25;

that, if he refuse the payment thereof, he becomes, by virtue of the treaty, an intruder, and that, in such a case, the government of the United States may remove him from the nation; and that this duty devolves upon the interior department. Whether the interior department or its Indian agents can be controlled by the courts by the writs of mandamus and injunction is not material in this case, because, as we hold, an attorney who refuses to pay the amount required by the statute by its very terms becomes an intruder, whom the United States promises by the terms of the treaty to remove, and therefore, in such cases, the officers and agents of the interior department would be acting clearly and properly within the scope of their powers."

Id. at 256–257, 54 S.W. at 812.

[Footnote 2/30]

The Court stated:

"And it is not disputed that, under the authority of these treaties, the Chickasaw Nation has exercised the power to attach conditions to the presence within its borders of persons who might otherwise not be entitled to remain within the tribal territory."

194 U.S. at 194 U. S. 389.

[Footnote 2/31]

The 1876 legislation required licensed merchants and traders to obtain a permit and pay a fee of $25.

[Footnote 2/32]

The Court relied on 23 Op.Atty.Gen. 214 (1900) and 23 Op.Atty.Gen. 528 (1901). In the first opinion, Attorney General John W. Griggs stated:

"The treaties and laws of the United States make all persons, with a few specified exceptions, who are not citizens of an Indian nation or members of an Indian tribe, and are found within an Indian nation without permission, intruders there, and require their removal by the United States. This closes the whole matter, absolutely excludes all

but the excepted classes, and fully authorizes these nations to absolutely exclude outsiders, or to permit their residence or business upon such terms as they may choose to impose, and it must be borne in mind that citizens of the United States, have, as such, no more right or business to be there than they have in any foreign nation, and can lawfully be there at all only by Indian permission; and that their right to be or remain or carry on business there depends solely upon whether they have such permission."

"As to the power or duty of your Department in the premises, there can hardly be a doubt. Under the treaties of the United States with these Indian nations, this Government is under the most solemn obligation, and for which it has received ample consideration, to remove and keep removed from the territory of these tribes all this class of intruders who are there without Indian permission. The performance of this obligation, as in other matters concerning the Indians and their affairs, has long been devolved upon the Department of the Interior."

23 Op.Atty.Gen. at 218.

[Footnote 2/33]

After citing the opinion of Attorney General Griggs quoted at length in *Morris v. Hitchcock,* Judge Sanborn wrote:

"Pursuant to this decision, the civilized tribes were charging, and the Indian agent was collecting, taxes from noncitizens engaged in business in these nations. It was under this state of facts that the United States and the Creek Nation made the agreement of 1901. Did they intend by that agreement that the Creek Nation should thereby renounce its conceded power to exact these permit taxes? Both parties knew that this power existed, and the United States, by the act of its President approving the law of the Creek national council, and the Secretary of the Interior, by enforcing it, had approved its exercise. The subject of these taxes was presented to the minds of the contracting parties, and was considered during the negotiation of the agreement, for that contract contains express stipulations that cattle grazed on rented allotments shall not be liable to any tribal tax (chapter 676, 31 Stat. 871, § 37), and that" "no noncitizen renting lands from a citizen for agricultural purposes as provided by law, whether such lands have been selected as an allotment or not, shall be required to pay any permit tax."

"(Chapter 676, 31 Stat. 871, § 39). But they made no provision that noncitizens who engaged in the mercantile business in the Creek Nation should be exempt from these taxes. As the law then in force required such noncitizens to pay such taxes, as both parties were then aware of that fact and considered the question, and as they made no stipulation to abolish these taxes, the conclusive presumption is that they intended to make no such contract, and that the power of the Creek Nation to exact these taxes, and the authority of the Secretary of the Interior and of his subordinates to collect them, were neither renounced, revoked, nor restricted, but that they remained in full force and effect after as before the agreement of 1901."

135 F. at 954.

[Footnote 2/34]

Ibid. The court stated:

"The legal effect . . . of the law prescribing the permit taxes is to prohibit noncitizens from conducting business within the Creek Nation without the payment of these taxes."

Id. at 955.

[Footnote 2/35]

Two decades after the Reorganization Act was passed, the problem was revisited by the Eighth Circuit. In *Iron Crow v. Oglala Sioux Tribe of Pine Ridge Reservation,* 231 F.2d 89 (1956), the court held that the Tribe had the power to assess a tax on a nonmember lessee of land within the reservation for the privilege of grazing stock on reservation land. And in *Barta v. Oglala Sioux Tribe of Pine Ridge Reservation,* 259 F.2d 553 (1958), the court held that the United States could bring an action on behalf of the Tribe to collect a license tax of 3 cents per acre per annum for grazing land and 15 cents per acre per annum for farm land levied on

nonmember lessees. The court in *Barta* held that the tax did not violate the constitutional rights of the nonmember lessees, stating in part:

"The tribe, by provisions of its treaty with the United States, has power to provide for the admission of nonmembers of the tribe onto the reservation. Having such power, it has the authority to impose restrictions on the presence of nonmembers within the reservation."

Id. at 556. Language in both *Iron Crow* and *Barta* suggests that the Court of Appeals, unlike the earlier courts, may not have rested the taxing power solely on the power to exclude. The Court of Appeals, of course, did not have the benefit of our decisions in *Oliphant v. Suquamish Indian Tribe,* 435 U. S. 191, *Wheeler,* and *Montana v. United States.*

[Footnote 2/36]

In the chapter of his treatise entitled "Taxation," Felix Cohen states:

"Though the scope of the power [to tax] as applied to nonmembers is not clear, it extends at least to property of nonmembers used in connection with Indian property, as well as to privileges enjoyed by nonmembers in trading with the Indians. The power to tax nonmembers is derived in the cases from the authority, founded on original sovereignty and guaranteed in some instances by treaties, to remove property of nonmembers from the territorial limits of the tribe. Since the tribal government has the power to exclude, it can extract a fee from nonmembers as a condition precedent to granting permission to remain or to operate within the tribal domain."

Cohen 266–267 (footnotes omitted).

In another chapter, entitled "The Scope of Tribal Self-Government," cited by the Secretary of the Interior and the Tribe here, Cohen describes the power of taxation as "an inherent attribute of tribal sovereignty which continues unless withdrawn or limited by treaty or by act of Congress. . . ." *Id.* at 142. After discussing *Buster v . Wright,* Cohen cites that case for the proposition that "[t]he power to tax does not depend upon the power to remove, and has been upheld where there was no power in the tribe to remove the taxpayer from the tribal jurisdiction."

Cohen 143. As demonstrated above, however, the license tax in *Buster* was predicated on the tribe's right to attach conditions on the right of nonmembers to conduct business on the reservation; the tribe could prevent such nonmembers from doing business regardless of whether it could physically remove them from the reservation. Moreover, in that same chapter on tribal self-government, Cohen recognizes that tribal taxes have been upheld on the basis of the tribe's power to remove nonmembers from the reservation, and that

"[i]t is therefore pertinent, in analyzing the scope of tribal taxing powers, to inquire how far an Indian tribe is empowered to remove nonmembers from its reservation."

Cohen 143.

The American Indian Policy Review Commission recognized that the court decisions upholding the tribes' taxing powers

"rely largely upon the power of tribes to remove persons from the reservation, and consequently, to prescribe the conditions upon which they shall enter,"

but argued for a broader source of the right to tax. AIPRC Final Report 178–179.

[Footnote 2/37]

In *Buster v. Wright,* the penalty for nonpayment of the tax was the closing of the nonmember's business, enforced by the Secretary of the Interior. 135 F. at 954. In *Morris v. Hitchcock,* the remedy was the removal of the nonmember's cattle from the reservation, again enforced by the United States. 194 U.S. at 194 U. S. 392. In *Maxey v. Wright,* an attorney refusing to pay the license fee to the Interior Department was subject to removal from the reservation. 3 Ind.T. at 250, 54 S.W. at 810.

[Footnote 2/38]

"No noncitizen is required to exercise a privilege or to pay the tax. He may refrain from the one, and he remains free from liability for the other." *Buster v. Wright,* 135 F. at 949.

[Footnote 2/39]

See supra at 455 U. S. 171-172. As I have indicated, *see* n. 21, *supra,* treaties recognizing the inherent power of tribal self-government have also deprived the tribes of jurisdiction over nonmembers. Nevertheless, those same treaties often specifically recognized the right of the tribe to exclude nonmembers from the reservation or to attach conditions on their entry. *See e.g.,* Treaty with the Choctaw and Chickasaw, Art. 7, 11 Stat. 612 (1855); Treaty with the Creeks and Seminoles, Art. 15, 11 Stat. 699 (1856). *See* 2 C. Kappler, Indian Affairs, Laws and Treaties 7, 9, 12, 15, 17, 20, 21, 27, 30, 42, 75, 418, 682, 699, 703, 719, 761, 774, 779, 790, 794, 800, 866, 886, 888, 929, 985, 990, 998, 1008, 1016, 1021 (1904).

[Footnote 2/40]

The various tribes may have taken a similar view of their power to tax at the time of the Indian Reorganization Act. Cohen's treatise notes:

"The power of an Indian tribe to levy taxes upon its own members and upon nonmembers doing business within the reservations has been affirmed in many tribal constitutions approved under the Wheeler-Howard Act [Indian Reorganization Act], as has the power to remove nonmembers from land over which the tribe exercises jurisdiction."

Cohen 143. The following clause from the 1935 Constitution of the Rosebud Sioux Tribe, which Cohen cites as a "typical" statement of such "tribal powers," indicates that the Tribe perceived the scope of its taxation powers over nonmembers to be narrower than the scope of that power over members. The Constitution conveys tribal power —

"(h) To levy taxes upon members of the tribe and to require the performance of reservation labor in lieu thereof, and to levy taxes or license fees, subject to review by the Secretary of the Interior, upon nonmembers doing business within the reservation."

"(i) To exclude from the restricted lands on the reservation persons not legally entitled to reside therein, under ordinances which shall be subject to review by the Secretary of the Interior."

Ibid.

[Footnote 2/41]

The Court stated:

"The power to tax transactions occurring on trust lands and significantly involving a tribe or its members is a fundamental attribute of sovereignty which the tribes retain unless divested of it by federal law or necessary implication of their dependent status."

447 U.S. at 447 U. S. 152.

[Footnote 2/42]

The Court also cited, without discussion, the Eighth Circuit's decision in *Iron Crow v. Oglala Sioux Tribe,* 231 F.2d 89 (1956). *See* n. 35, *supra.*

[Footnote 2/43]

A nonmember can avoid the tax by declining to do business on the reservation; the "sanction" imposed for refusal to pay the tax is denial of permission to buy cigarettes.

[Footnote 2/44]

In some respects, the tribal power to tax nonmembers may be greater than the taxing power of other sovereigns. States do not have any power to exclude nonresidents from their borders. Moreover, their taxing statutes, like their other laws, must comply with the Equal Protection Clause of the Fourteenth Amendment. They may not, therefore, impose discriminatory taxes as a condition attached to entry into the jurisdiction in order to engage in economic activity. But since an Indian tribe has exclusive control over the "use and occupancy" of land within its reservation, it arguably could attach special discriminatory conditions to any license to a nonmember to use or occupy a portion of that land. As stated earlier, at a minimum, the equal protection components of the Fifth and Fourteenth Amendments, which limit the sovereign powers of the Federal and State Governments, do not similarly restrict the sovereign powers of an Indian tribe. *See supra* at 455 U. S. 170.

[Footnote 2/45]

"[A]s the payment of a tax or license fee may be made a condition of entry upon tribal land, it may also be made a condition to the grant of other privileges, such as the acquisition of a tribal lease."

Cohen 143.

[Footnote 2/46]

Congress intended the Act of March 3, 1927 to make applicable to Executive Order reservations the leasing provisions already applicable to treaty reservations pursuant to the Act of May 29, 1924, ch. 210, 43 Stat. 244. S.Rep. No. 1240, 69th Cong., 2d Sess., 3 (1927). The 1927 Act thus permitted the leasing of unallotted Indian land for terms not to exceed 10 years and as much longer as oil and gas in paying quantities were found on the land. 44 Stat. (part 2) 1347. Among the purposes of the 1927 statute were to "[p]ermit the exploration for oil and gas on Executive order Indian Reservations," to "[g]ive the Indian tribes all the oil and gas royalties," and to "[p]lace with Congress the future determination of any changes of boundaries of Executive order reservations or withdrawals." S.Rep. No. 1240, *supra,* at 3. In light of these purposes, it is clear that Congress intended leases executed pursuant to the 1927 Act to be binding.

The Tribe contends that the leases in these cases were executed pursuant to the Act of May 11, 1938, 52 Stat. 347, and not the 1927 Act. The Tribe notes that the lease in No. 80–15 states that it was executed pursuant to the 1938 Act. *See* App. 64. In response, petitioners note that, although the Tribe argues that the 1938 Act — unlike the 1927 Act — does not require that royalties be paid to the Secretary of the Interior for the benefit of the Tribe, petitioners make their royalty payments to the United States Geological Survey for the benefit of the Jicarilla Apache. *See* Tr. 79–80. There is no need to resolve this question, because, for our purposes, the provisions of the 1938 Act do not vary significantly from the provisions of the 1927 Act. The 1938 Act, like the 1927 Act, permits the leasing of Indian lands for a period "not to exceed ten years and as long thereafter as minerals are produced in paying quantities." 25 U.S.C. § 396a. One of the purposes of the 1938 Act was to establish uniformity in the leasing of tribal lands by applying the law governing oil and gas leasing to all other mineral leasing as well. S.Rep. No. 985, 75th Cong., 1st Sess., 1–2 (1937). Other purposes were to "bring all mineral leasing matters in harmony with the Indian Reorganization Act," *id.* at 3, and to enact changes designed "to give the Indians the greatest return from their property." *Id.* at 2. There is no indication in the legislative history that the purposes of the 1938 Act are in any way inconsistent with the purposes of the 1927 Act and prior legislation. Presumably, the purposes of the earlier legislation were incorporated into the uniform scheme intended by the 1938 Act.

[Footnote 2/47]

As Attorney General MacVeagh stated in 1881, only those permitted by the tribe to remain on the reservation may do so, "and the right to remain is gone when the permit has expired." 17 Op.Atty. Gen. at 136.

[Footnote 2/48]

In *Colville,* the nonmember desiring to purchase cigarettes on the reservation knew that his right to

do so was conditioned on his consent to pay the tax. Attorney General Griggs, in his 1900 opinion on "Trespassers on Indian Lands," discussed in similar terms the effect on tribal laws of a federal statute providing for the sale of reservation lots to non-Indians:

> "[T]he legal right to purchase land within an Indian nation gives to the purchaser no right of exemption from the laws of such nation, nor does it authorize him to do any act in violation of the treaties with such nation. These laws requiring a permit to reside or carry on business in the Indian country existed long before and at the time this act was passed. And if any outsider saw proper to purchase a town lot under this act of Congress, he did so with full knowledge that he could occupy it for residence or business only by permission from the Indians."

23 Op.Atty.Gen., at 217.

In 1977, the American Indian Policy Review Commission noted that Indian tribes "do not both tax and receive royalties. Usually, they just receive royalties." AIPRC Final Report 344.

[Footnote 2/49]

The statute did authorize the collection of severance taxes by the States. Petitioners have argued that this authorization preempted any tribal power to impose a comparable tax. As recognized by the Court of Appeals, however, the legislative history indicates that Congress simply did not consider the question of tribal taxes on mineral output from reservation lands. 617 F.2d 537, 547 (CA10 1980).

[Footnote 2/50]

The Secretary of the Interior argues that a license or franchise issued by a governmental body does not prevent the later imposition of a tax unless the right to tax "*has been specifically surrendered in terms which admit of no other reasonable interpretation.*" *Brief for Secretary of Interior* 13, n. 7 (*quoting St. Louis v. United R. Co., 210 U. S. 266,*

210 U. S. 280). See also New Orleans City & Lake R. Co. v. New Orleans, 143 U. S. 192, 143 U. S. 195; New York Transit Corp. v. City of New York, 303 U. S. 573, 303 U. S. 590-593. The principal issue in these cases cited by the Secretary was whether the retroactive imposition of a franchise tax violated the Contract Clause of the Constitution or was so fundamentally unfair as to constitute a denial of due process in violation of the Fourteenth Amendment. Although this argument was by no means frivolous, *cf. Puerto Rico v. Russell & Co.,* 315 U. S. 610, no such issue is raised here. These cases are distinguishable from the instant cases because Indian tribes do not have the same attributes of sovereignty as do States and their subdivisions. *See supra at 455 U. S. 168-173.*

Source: Merrion v. Jicarilla Apache Tribe 455 U.S. 130 (1982)

Hodel v. Irving

(1987)

After Congress passed the Indian Land Consolidation Act in 1983, Mary Irving, Patrick Pumpkin Seed, and Eileen Bissonette filed suit against Donald Hodel, the secretary of the interior, for compensation of lost property. The act had been passed to deal with the long-term problem of fractionation of Indian lands. This problem had its origins in the late 19th century when Congress had allotted 320 acres to each male Sioux head of household. The government had hoped to assimilate the Indians by turning them into farmers, giving them land that could be passed on to their heirs. However, more often the Natives sold or leased their land to white settlers and lived off the revenues; worse, with each successive generation came multiple claimants to the parcels of land, until some parcels had hundreds of owners who collected as little as one cent off their fractional share.

Irving, Pumpkin Seed, and Bissonette were all heirs of deceased tribe members who stood to lose money from the loss of their fractional shares. They argued that the U.S. government's passage of the Indian Land Consolidation Act amounted to a takeover of property, and demanded compensation for their loss. The case made its way to the Supreme Court, which sided with the *Lakota. In the majority opinion, Justice Sandra Day O'Connor wrote that the right to will property to one's heirs was a cornerstone of common law in the United States, and the government's action was a violation of Native rights.*

HODEL v. IRVING

Argued October 6, 1986 Decided May 18, 1987

As a means of ameliorating the problem of extreme fractionation of Indian lands that, pursuant to federal statutes dating back to the end of the 19th century, were allotted to individual Indians and held in trust by the United States, and that, through successive generations, had been splintered into multiple undivided interests by descent or devise, Congress enacted 207 (later amended) of the Indian Land Consolidation Act of 1983. As originally enacted, 207 provided that no undivided fractional interest in such lands shall descend by intestacy or devise, but, instead, shall escheat to the tribe "if such interest represents 2 per centum or less of the total acreage in such tract and has earned to its owner less than $100 in the preceding year before it is due to escheat." No provision for the payment of compensation to the owners of the interests covered by 207 was made. Appellees are members of the Oglala Sioux Tribe and either are, or represent, heirs or devisees of Tribe members who died while the original terms of 207 were in effect and who owned fractional interests subject to 207. Appellees filed suit in Federal District Court, claiming that 207 resulted in a taking of property without just compensation in violation of the Fifth Amendment. The District Court held that the statute was constitutional, but the Court of Appeals reversed, concluding that appellees' decedents had a right, derived from the original Sioux allotment statute, to control disposition of their property at death, that appellees had standing to invoke such right, and that the taking of the right without compensation to decedents' estates violated the Fifth Amendment.

Held:

- Appellees have standing to challenge 207, which has deprived them of the fractional interests they otherwise would have inherited. This is sufficient injury-in-fact to satisfy the case-or-controversy requirement of Article III of the Constitution. Moreover, the concerns of the prudential standing doctrine are also satisfied, even though appellees do not assert that their own property rights have been taken unconstitutionally, but rather that their decedents' right to pass the property at death has been taken. For decedent Indians with trust property, federal statutes require the Secretary of the Interior to assume the general role of the executor or administrator of the estate in asserting the decedent's surviving claims. Here, however, the Secretary's responsibilities in that capacity include the administration of the statute that appellees claim is unconstitutional, so that he cannot be expected to assert decedents' rights to the extent that they turn on the statute's constitutionality. Under these circumstances, appellees can appropriately serve as their decedents' representatives for purposes of asserting the latters' Fifth Amendment rights.

- The original version of 207 effected a "taking" of appellees' decedents' property without just compensation. Determination of the question whether a governmental property regulation amounts to a "taking" requires ad hoc factual inquiries as to such factors as the impact of the regulation, its interference with reasonable investment-backed expectations, and the character of the governmental action. Here, the relative impact of 207 upon appellees' decedents can be substantial. Even assuming, arguendo, that the income generated by the parcels in question may be properly thought of as de minimis, their value may not be. Although appellees' decedents retain full beneficial use of the property during their lifetimes as well as the right to convey it inter vivos, the right to pass on valuable property to one's heirs is itself a valuable right. However, the extent to which any of appellees' decedents had investment-backed expectations in passing on the property is dubious. Also weighing weakly in favor of the statute is the fact that there is something of an "average reciprocity of advantage," to the extent that owners of escheatable interests maintain a nexus to the Tribe, and consolidation of lands in the Tribe benefits Tribe members since consolidated lands are more productive than fractionated lands. But the character of the Government regulation here is extraordinary since it amounts to virtually the abrogation of the right to pass on property to one's heirs, which right has been part of the Anglo-American legal system since feudal times. Moreover, 207 effectively abolishes both descent and devise of the property interest even when the passing of the property to the heir might result in consolidation of property—as, for instance, when the heir already owns another undivided interest in the property—which is the governmental purpose sought to be advanced.

JUSTICE O'CONNOR delivered the opinion of the Court.

I

Towards the end of the 19th century, Congress enacted a series of land Acts which divided the communal reservations of Indian tribes into individual allotments for Indians and unallotted lands for non-Indian settlement. This legislation seems to have been in part animated by a desire to force Indians to abandon their nomadic ways in order to "speed the Indians' assimilation into American society," and in part a result of pressure to free new lands for further white settlement. Ibid. Two years after the enactment of the General Allotment Act of 1887, Congress adopted a specific statute authorizing the division of the Great Reservation of the Sioux Nation into separate reservations and the allotment of specific tracts of reservation land to individual Indians, conditioned on the consent of three-fourths of the adult male Sioux. Under the Act, each male Sioux head of household took 320 acres of land and most other individuals 160 acres. In order to protect the allottees from the improvident disposition of their lands to white settlers, the Sioux allotment statute provided that the allotted lands were to be held in trust by the United States. Until 1910, the lands of deceased allottees passed to their heirs "according to the laws of the State or Territory" where the land was located, ibid., and after 1910, allottees were permitted to dispose of their interests by will in accordance with regulations promulgated by the Secretary of the Interior. Those regulations generally served to protect Indian ownership of the allotted lands.

The policy of allotment of Indian lands quickly proved disastrous for the Indians. Cash generated by land sales to whites was quickly dissipated, and the Indians, rather than farming the land themselves, evolved into petty landlords, leasing their allotted lands to white ranchers and farmers and living off the meager rentals. The failure of the allotment program became even clearer as successive generations came to hold the allotted lands. Thus 40-, 80-, and 160-acre parcels became splintered into multiple undivided interests in land, with some parcels having hundreds, and many parcels having dozens, of owners. Because the land was held in trust and often could not be alienated or partitioned, the fractionation problem grew and grew over time.

A 1928 report commissioned by the Congress found the situation administratively unworkable and economically wasteful. Good, potentially productive, land was allowed to lie fallow, amidst great poverty, because of the difficulties of managing property held in this manner. In discussing the Indian Reorganization Act of 1934, Representative Howard said:

It is in the case of the inherited allotments, however, that the administrative costs become incredible. . . . On allotted reservations, numerous cases exist where the shares of each individual heir from lease money may be 1 cent a month. Or one heir may own minute fractional shares in 30 or 40 different allotments. The cost of leasing, bookkeeping, and distributing the proceeds in many cases far exceeds the total income. The Indians and the Indian Service personnel are thus trapped in a meaningless system of minute partition in which all thought of the possible use of land to satisfy human needs is lost in a mathematical haze of bookkeeping.

But the end of future allotment by itself could not prevent the further compounding of the existing problem caused by the passage of time. Ownership continued to fragment as succeeding generations came to hold the property, since, in the order of things, each property owner was apt to have more than one heir. In 1960, both the House and the Senate undertook comprehensive studies of the problem. These studies indicated that one-half of the approximately 12 million acres of allotted trust lands were held in fractionated ownership, with over 3 million acres held by more than six heirs to a parcel.

Section 207 of the Indian Land Consolidation Act—the escheat provision at issue in this case—provided:

No undivided fractional interest in any tract of trust or restricted land within a tribe's reservation or otherwise subjected to a tribe's jurisdiction shall descedent [*sic*] by intestacy or devise but shall escheat to that tribe if such interest represents 2 per centum or less of the total acreage in such tract and has earned to its owner less than $100 in the preceding year before it is due to escheat.

Congress made no provision for the payment of compensation to the owners of the interests covered by 207. The statute was signed into law on January 12, 1983, and became effective immediately.

The three appellees—Mary Irving, Patrick Pumpkin Seed, and Eileen Bissonette—are enrolled members of the Oglala Sioux Tribe. They are, or represent, heirs or devisees of members of the Tribe who died in March, April, and June 1983. Eileen Bissonette's decedent, Mary Poor Bear-Little Hoop Cross, purported to will all her property, including property subject to 207, to her five minor children in whose name Bissonette claims the property. Chester Irving, Charles Leroy Pumpkin Seed, and Edgar Pumpkin Seed all died intestate. At the time of their deaths, the four decedents owned 41 fractional interests subject to the provisions of 207. The Irving estate lost two interests whose value together was approximately $100; the Bureau of Indian Affairs placed total values of approximately $2,700 on the 26 escheatable interests in the Cross estate and $1,816 on the 13 escheatable interests in the Pumpkin Seed estates. But for 207, this property would have passed, in the ordinary course, to appellees or those they represent.

Appellees filed suit in the United States District Court for the District of South Dakota, claiming that 207 resulted in a taking of property without just compensation in violation of the Fifth Amendment. The District Court concluded that the statute was constitutional. It held that appellees had no vested interest in the property of the decedents prior to their deaths and that Congress had plenary authority to abolish the power of testamentary disposition of Indian property and to alter the rules of intestate succession.

Although it agreed that appellees had no vested rights in the decedents' property, it concluded that their decedents had a right, derived from the original Sioux allotment statute, to control disposition of their property at death. The Court of Appeals held that appellees had standing to invoke that right and that the taking of that right without compensation to decedents' estates violated the Fifth Amendment.

II

The Court of Appeals concluded that appellees have standing to challenge 207. The Government does not contest this ruling. As the Court of Appeals recognized, however, the existence of a case or controversy is a jurisdictional prerequisite to a federal court's deliberations. We are satisfied that the necessary case or controversy exists in this case. Section 207 has deprived appellees of the fractional interests they otherwise would have inherited. This is sufficient injury-in-fact to satisfy Article III of the Constitution.

In addition to the constitutional standing requirements, we have recognized prudential standing limitations. As the court below recognized, one of these prudential principles is that the plaintiff generally must assert his own legal rights and interests. Appellees here do not assert that their own property rights have been taken unconstitutionally, but rather that their decedents' right to pass the property at death has been taken. Nevertheless, we have no difficulty in finding the concerns of the prudential standing doctrine met here.

For obvious reasons, it has long been recognized that the surviving claims of a decedent must be pursued by a third party. At common law, a decedent's surviving claims were prosecuted by the executor or administrator of the estate. For Indians with trust property, statutes require the Secretary of the Interior to assume that general role. Secretary's responsibilities in that capacity, however, include the administration of the statute that the appellees claim is unconstitutional, so that he can hardly be expected to assert appellees' decedents' rights to the extent that they turn on that point. Under these circumstances, appellees can appropriately serve as their decedents' representatives for purposes of asserting latters' Fifth Amendment rights. They are situated to pursue the claims vigorously, since their interest in receiving the property is indissolubly linked to the decedents' right to dispose of it by will or intestacy. A vindication of decedents' rights would ensure that the fractional interests pass to appellees; pressing these rights unsuccessfully would equally guarantee that appellees take nothing. In short, permitting appellees to raise their decedents' claims is merely an extension of the common law's provision for appointment of a decedent's representative. It is therefore a "settled practice of the courts" not open to objection on the ground that it permits a litigant to raise third parties' rights.

III

The Congress, acting pursuant to its broad authority to regulate the descent and devise of Indian trust lands, *Jefferson v. Fink*, enacted 207 as a means of ameliorating, over time, the problem of extreme fractionation of certain Indian lands. By forbidding the passing on at death of small, undivided interests in Indian lands, Congress hoped that future generations of Indians would be able to make more productive use of the Indians' ancestral lands. We agree with the Government that encouraging the consolidation of Indian lands is a public purpose of high order. The fractionation problem on Indian reservations is extraordinary and may call for dramatic action to encourage consolidation. The Sisseton-Wahpeton Sioux Tribe, appearing as amicus curiae in support of the Secretary of the Interior, is a quintessential victim of fractionation. Forty-acre tracts on the Sisseton-Wahpeton Lake Traverse Reservation, leasing for about $1,000 annually, are commonly subdivided into hundreds of undivided interests, many of which generate only pennies a year in rent. The average tract has 196 owners and the average owner undivided interests in 14 tracts.

There is no question that the relative economic impact of 207 upon the owners of these property rights can be substantial. Section 207 provides for the escheat of small undivided property interests that are unproductive during the year preceding the owner's death. Even if we accept the Government's assertion that the income generated by such parcels may be properly thought of as de minimis, their value may not be. While the Irving estate lost two interests whose value together was only approximately $100, the Bureau of Indian Affairs placed total values of approximately $2,700 and $1,816 on the escheatable interests in the Cross and Pumpkin Seed estates.

These are not trivial sums. There are suggestions in the legislative history regarding the 1984 amendments to 207 that the failure to "look back" more than one year at the income generated by the property had caused the escheat of potentially valuable timber and mineral interests. Of course, the whole of appellees' decedents' property interests were not taken by 207. Appellees' decedents retained full beneficial use of the property during their lifetimes as well as the right to convey it inter vivos. There is no question, however, that the right to pass on valuable property to one's heirs is itself a valuable right. Depending on the age of the owner, much or most of the value of the parcel may inhere in this "remainder" interest.

The extent to which any of appellees' decedents had "investment-backed expectations" in passing on the property is dubious. Though it is conceivable that some of these interests were purchased with the expectation that the owners might pass on the remainder to their heirs at death, the property has been held in trust for the Indians for 100 years and is overwhelmingly acquired by gift, descent, or devise. Because of the highly fractionated ownership, the property is generally held for lease rather than improved and used by the owners. None of the appellees here can point to any specific investment-backed expectations beyond the fact that their ancestors agreed to accept allotment only after ceding to the United States large parts of the original Great Sioux Reservation.

Also weighing weakly in favor of the statute is the fact that there is something of an "average reciprocity of advantage," to the extent that owners of escheatable interests maintain a nexus to the Tribe. Consolidation of Indian lands in the Tribe benefits the members of the Tribe. All members do not own escheatable interests, nor do all owners belong to the Tribe. Nevertheless, there is substantial overlap between the two groups. The owners of escheatable interests often benefit from the escheat of others' fractional interests. Moreover, the whole benefit gained is greater than the sum of the burdens imposed since consolidated lands are more productive than fractionated lands.

If we were to stop our analysis at this point, we might well find 207 constitutional. But the character of the Government regulation here is extraordinary. In *Kaiser Aetna v. United States,* we emphasized that the regulation destroyed "one of the most essential sticks in the bundle of rights that are commonly characterized as property—the right to exclude others." Similarly, the regulation here amounts to virtually the abrogation of the right to pass on a certain type of property—the small undivided interest—to one's heirs. In one form or another, the right to pass on property—to one's family in particular—has been part of the Anglo-American legal system since feudal times. The fact that it may be possible for the owners of these interests to effectively control disposition upon death through complex inter vivos transactions such as revocable trusts is simply not an adequate substitute for the rights taken, given the nature of the property. Even the United States concedes that total abrogation of the right to pass property is unprecedented and likely unconstitutional. Moreover, this statute effectively abolishes both descent and devise of these property interests even when the passing of the property to the heir might result in consolidation of property—as for instance when the heir already owns another undivided interest in the property. Since the escheatable interests are not, as the United States argues, necessarily de minimis, nor, as it also argues, does the availability of inter vivos transfer obviate the need for descent and devise, a total abrogation of these rights cannot be upheld.

In holding that complete abolition of both the descent and devise of a particular class of property may be a taking, we reaffirm the continuing vitality of the long line of cases recognizing the States', and where appropriate, the United States', broad authority to adjust the rules governing the descent and devise of property without implicating the guarantees of the Just Compensation Clause. The difference in this case is the fact that both descent and devise are completely abolished; indeed they are abolished even in circumstances when the governmental purpose sought to be advanced, consolidation of ownership of Indian lands, does not conflict with the further descent of the property.

There is little doubt that the extreme fractionation of Indian lands is a serious public problem. It may well be appropriate for the United States to ameliorate fractionation by means of regulating the descent and devise of Indian lands. Surely it is permissible for the United States to prevent the owners of such interests from further subdividing them among future heirs on pain of escheat. It may be appropriate to minimize further compounding of the problem by abolishing the descent of such interest by rules of intestacy, thereby forcing the owners to formally designate an heir to prevent escheat to the Tribe. What is certainly not appropriate is to take the extraordinary step of abolishing both descent and devise of these property interests even when the passing of the property to the heir might result in consolidation of property. Accordingly, we find that this regulation, in the words of Justice Holmes, "goes too far." The judgment of the Court of Appeals is Affirmed.

Source: Hodel v. Irving 481 U.S. 704 (1987).

House Concurrent Resolution 331
(1988)

In 1988, the U.S. Senate passed House Concurrent Resolution 331, which acknowledged the influence and contribution of the Iroquois Confederacy of Nations to the development of the U.S. Constitution.

H. Con. Res. 331
IN THE SENATE OF THE UNITED STATES
OCTOBER 5 (legislative day, SEPTEMBER 26), 1988
Received and referred to the Select Committee on Indian Affairs
OCTOBER 21 (legislative day, OCTOBER 18), 1988
Committee discharged

CONCURRENT RESOLUTION

To acknowledge the contribution of the Iroquois Confederacy of Nations to the development of the United States Constitution and to reaffirm the continuing government-to-government relationship between Indian tribes and the United States established in the Constitution.

Whereas the original framers of the Constitution, including, most notably, George Washington and Benjamin Franklin, are known to have greatly admired the concepts of the Six Nations of the Iroquois Confederacy;

Whereas the confederation of the original Thirteen Colonies into one republic was influenced by the political system developed by the Iroquois Confederacy as were many of the democratic principles which were incorporated into the Constitution itself; and

Whereas, since the formation of the United States, the Congress has recognized the sovereign status of Indian tribes and has, through the exercise of powers reserved to the Federal Government in the Commerce Clause of the Constitution (art. I, s.2, cl. 3), dealt with Indian tribes on a government-to-government basis and has, through the treaty clause (art. II, s.2, cl.2), entered into three hundred and seventy treaties with Indian tribal Nations;

Whereas, from the first treaty entered into with an Indian Nation, the treaty with the Delaware Indians of September 17, 1778, the Congress has assumed a trust responsibility and obligation to Indian tribes and their members;

Whereas this trust responsibility calls for Congress "to exercise the utmost good faith in dealings with Indians" as provided for in the Northwest Ordinance of 1787, (1 State. 50);

Whereas the judicial system of the United States has consistently recognized and reaffirmed this special relationship: Now, therefore, be it Resolved by the House of Representatives (the Senate concurring), That—

1. the Congress, on the occasion of the two hundredth anniversary of the signing of the United States Constitution, acknowledges the contribution made by The Iroquois Confederacy and other Indian Nations to The formation and development of the United States;

2. the Congress also hereby reaffirms the constitutionally recognized government-to-government relationship with Indian tribes which has been the cornerstone of this Nation's official Indian policy;

3. the Congress specifically acknowledges and reaffirms the trust responsibility and obligation of the United States Government to Indian tribes, including Alaska Natives, for their preservation, protection, and enhancement, including the provision of health, education, social

and economic assistance programs as necessary, and including the duty to assist tribes in their performance of governmental responsibility to provide for the social and economic well-being of their members and to preserve tribal cultural identity and heritage; and

4. the Congress also acknowledges the need to exercise the utmost good faith in upholding its treaties with the various tribes, as the tribes understood them to be, and the duty of a great Nation to uphold its legal and moral obligations for the benefit of all its citizens so that they and

their posterity may also continue to enjoy the rights they have enshrined in the United States Constitution for time immemorial.

Passed the House of Representatives October 4, 1988.
Attest: Donnald K. Anderson,
Clerk

Source: House Concurrent Resolution 331 (1988). 100th Congress, 2nd Session. http://www.senate.gov/reference/resources/pdf/hconres331.pdf.

Native American Grave Protection and Repatriation Act
(1990)

After centuries of losing Native American cultural items to looters, archaeologists, and tourists, Native American tribes successfully lobbied Congress into passing the Native American Graves Protection and Repatriation Act (NAGPRA) on November 16, 1990. Supporters of the act argued that existing laws for the protection of graves were insufficient for a number of reasons. For one thing, the existing law was based on the traditions of the colonizing population; this meant that states only protected marked graves, and Native American graves were often unmarked. For another, they argued that their First Amendment rights were being violated because Native burial practices were tied to their religious beliefs, which were being infringed upon when their dead were desecrated.

The NAGPRA contained several important aspects that helped protect the cultural rights of Native Americans. First, it established that items and remains excavated or found on tribal land after the enactment of the law belonged to the lineal descendents of the deceased, if any could be found. If a descendent could not be determined,

then the objects and/or persons belonged to the tribe in whose lands they rested. If a descendant or tribe requested the repatriation of certain remains found before November 1990, the law obligated the holder to return the requested items. Second, it required that anyone seeking to excavate on tribal land acquire permission before beginning the project. Third, it required any agency receiving federal money to catalog and summarize their existing inventories of Native American remains and funerary artifacts to allow tribes to identify any cultural items they wanted returned to the tribe or to specific individuals. Finally, NAGPRA criminalized trafficking in Native American remains and artifacts. Overall, the law delicately balances the tensions between respecting the rights of Native Americans to protect their dead and allowing for the continued advancement of knowledge about human history by promoting interactions between tribes, archaeologists, and museum officials.

101ST CONGRESS

HOUSE OF REPRESENTATIVES

REPORT, 2d Session, 101–877

PROVIDING FOR THE PROTECTION OF NATIVE AMERICAN GRAVES, AND FOR OTHER PURPOSES

OCTOBER 15, 1990. Committed to the Committee of the Whole House on the State of the Union and ordered to be printed.

Section 1. Short Title

This Act may be cited as the "Native American Grave Protection and Repatriation Act".

Sec. 2. Definitions

For purposes of this Act, the term

1. "burial site" means any natural or prepared physical location, whether originally below, on, or above the surface of the earth, into which as a part of the death rite or ceremony of a culture, individual human remains are deposited.

2. "cultural affiliation" means that there is a relationship of shared group identity which can be reasonably traced historically or prehistorically between a present day Indian tribe or Native Hawaiian organization and an identifiable earlier group.

3. "cultural items" means human remains and (A) "associated funerary objects" which shall mean objects that, as a part of the death rite or ceremony of a culture, are reasonably believed to have been placed with individual human remains either at the time of death or later, and both the human remains and associated funerary objects are presently in the possession or control of a federal agency or museum, except that other items exclusively made for burial purposes or to contain human remains shall be considered as associated funerary objects, (B) "unassociated funerary objects" which shall mean objects that, as a part of the death rite or ceremony of a culture, are reasonably believed to have been placed with individual human remains either at the time of death or later, where the remains are not in the possession or control of the Federal agency or

museum and the objects can be identified by a preponderance of the evidence as related to specific individuals or families or to known human remains or, by a preponderance of the evidence, as having been removed from a specific burial site of an individual culturally affiliated with a particular Indian tribe, (C) "sacred objects" which shall mean specific ceremonial objects which are needed by traditional Native American religious leaders for the practice of traditional Native American religions by their present day adherents, and (D) "cultural patrimony" which shall mean an object having ongoing historical, traditional, or cultural importance central to the Native American group or culture itself, rather than property owned by an individual Native American, and which, therefore, cannot be alienated, appropriated, or conveyed by any individual regardless of whether or not the individual is a member of the Indian tribe or Native Hawaiian organization and such object shall have been considered inalienable by such Native American group at the time the object was separated from such group.

4. "Federal agency" means any department, agency, or instrumentality of the United States and shall include, except as may be inconsistent with the provisions of P.L. 101–185, the Smithsonian Institution.

5. "Federal lands" means any land other than tribal lands which are controlled or owned by the United States.

6. "Hui Malama I Na Kupuna O Hawai'i Nei" means the nonprofit, Native Hawaiian organization incorporated under the laws of the State of Hawaii by that name on April 17, 1989, for the purpose of providing guidance and expertise in decisions dealing with Native Hawaiian cultural issues, particularly burial issues.

7. "Indian tribe" shall have the meaning given such term in section 4 of the Indian Self Determination and Education Assistance Act (25 U.S.C. 450b).

8. "museum" means any institution or State or local government agency (including any institution of higher learning) that receives Federal funds and has possession of, or control over,

Native American cultural items, but does not include any Federal agency.

9. "Native American" means of, or relating to, a tribe, people, or culture that is indigenous to the United States.

10. "Native Hawaiian" means any individual who is a descendant of the aboriginal people who, prior to 1778, occupied and exercised sovereignty in the area that now constitutes the State of Hawaii.

11. "Native Hawaiian organization" means any organization which (A) serves and represents the interests of Native Hawaiians, (B) has a primary and stated purpose the provision of services to Native Hawaiians, and (C) has expertise in Native Hawaiian Affairs, and shall include the Office of Hawaiian Affairs and Hui Malama I Na Kupuna O Hawai'i Nei.

12. "Office of Hawaiian Affairs" means the Office of Hawaiian Affairs established by the constitution of the State of Hawaii.

13. "right of possession" means possession obtained with the voluntary consent of an individual or group that had authority of alienation. The original acquisition of a Native American funerary object, sacred object, or object of cultural patrimony from an Indian tribe or Native Hawaiian organization with the voluntary consent of an individual or group with authority to alienate such object is deemed to give right of possession of that object. The original acquisition of Native American human remains which were excavated, exhumed, or otherwise obtained with full knowledge and consent of the next of kin or the official governing body of the appropriate culturally affiliated Indian tribe or Native Hawaiian organization is deemed to give right of possession to those remains. Nothing in this paragraph shall affect the application of relevant State law to the right of ownership of unassociated funerary objects, sacred objects, or objects of cultural patrimony.

14. "Secretary" means the Secretary of the Interior.

15. "tribal land" means (A) all lands within the exterior boundaries of any Indian reservation; (B) all dependent Indian communities; (C)

lands conveyed to, or subject to an interim conveyance of, Native Corporations pursuant to the Alaska Native Claims Settlement Act; and (D) any lands administered for the benefit of Native Hawaiians pursuant to the Hawaiian Homes Commission Act, 1920, and section 4 of Public Law 86–3.

Sec. 3. Ownership

(a) NATIVE AMERICAN HUMAN REMAINS AND OBJECTS. The ownership or control of Native American cultural items which are excavated or discovered on Federal or tribal lands after the date of enactment of this Act shall be (with priority given in the order listed)

1. in the case of Native American human remains and associated funerary objects, in the lineal descendants of the Native American; or

2. in any case in which such lineal descendants cannot be ascertained, and in the case of unassociated funerary objects, sacred objects, and objects of cultural patrimony;

(A) in the Indian tribe or Native Hawaiian organization on whose tribal land such objects or remains were discovered;

(B) in the Indian tribe or Native Hawaiian organization which has the closest cultural affiliation with such remains or objects and which, upon notice, states a claim for such remains or objects; or

(C) if the cultural affiliation of the objects cannot be reasonably ascertained and if the objects were discovered on Federal land that is recognized by a final judgement of the Indian Claims Commission as the aboriginal land of some Indian tribe

1. in the Indian tribe that is recognized as aboriginally occupying the area in which the objects were discovered, if upon notice, such tribe states a claim for such remains or objects, or

2. if it can be shown by a preponderance of the evidence that a different tribe has a stronger cultural relationship with the remains or objects than the tribe or organization specified in

paragraph (1), in the Indian tribe that has the strongest demonstrated relationship, if upon notice, such tribe states a claim for such remains or objects.

(b) UNCLAIMED NATIVE AMERICAN HUMAN REMAINS AND OBJECTS. Native American cultural items not claimed under subsection (a) shall be disposed of in accordance with regulations promulgated by the Secretary in consultation with the review committee established under section 8, Native American groups, representatives of museums and the scientific community.

(c) INTENTIONAL EXCAVATION AND REMOVAL OF NATIVE AMERICAN HUMAN REMAINS AND OBJECTS. The intentional removal from or excavation of Native American cultural items from Federal or tribal lands for purposes of discovery, study, or removal of such items is permitted only if

(1) such items are excavated or removed pursuant to a permit issued under section 4 of the Archaeological Resources Protection Act of 1979 (93 Stat. 721; 16 U.S.C. 470aa et seq.) which shall be consistent with this Act;

(2) such items are excavated or removed after consultation with or, in the case of tribal lands, consent of the appropriate (if any) Indian tribe or Native Hawaiian organization;

(3) the ownership and right of control of the disposition of such items shall be as provided in subsections (a) and (b); and

(4) proof of consultation or consent under paragraph (2) is shown.

(d) INADVERTENT DISCOVERY OF NATIVE AMERICAN REMAINS AND OBJECTS. (1) Any person who knows, or has reason to know, that such person has discovered Native American cultural items on Federal or tribal lands after the date of enactment of this Act shall notify,

in writing, the Secretary of the Department, or head of any other agency or instrumentality of the United States, having primary management authority with respect to Federal lands and the appropriate Indian tribe or Native Hawaiian organization with respect to tribal lands, if known or readily ascertainable. If the discovery occurred in connection with an activity, including (but not limited to) construction, mining, logging, and agriculture, the person shall cease the activity in the area of the discovery, make a reasonable effort to protect the items discovered before resuming such activity, and provide notice under this subsection. The activity may resume after a reasonable amount of time and following notification under this subsection.

(2) The disposition of and control over any cultural items excavated or removed under this subsection shall be determined as provided for in this section.

(3) If the Secretary of the Interior consents, the responsibilities (in whole or in part) under paragraphs (1) and (2) of the Secretary of any department (other than the Department of the Interior) or the head of any other agency or instrumentality may be delegated to the Secretary with respect to any land managed by such other Secretary or agency head.

(e) RELINQUISHMENT. Nothing in this section shall prevent the governing body of an Indian tribe or Native Hawaiian organization from expressly relinquishing control over any Native American human remains, or title to or control over any funerary object, or sacred object.

Sec. 4. Illegal Trafficking

ILLEGAL TRAFFICKING. Chapter 53 of title 18, United States Code, is amended by adding at the end thereof the following new section: SEC. 1170. ILLEGAL TRAFFICKING IN NATIVE AMERICAN HUMAN REMAINS AND CULTURAL ITEMS

1. "(a) Whoever knowingly sells, purchases, uses for profit, or transports for sale or profit, the

human remains of a Native American without the right of possession to those remains as provided in the Native American Graves Protection and Repatriation Act shall be fined in accordance with this title, or imprisoned not more than 12 months, or both, and in the case of a second or subsequent violation, be fined in accordance with this title, or imprisoned not more than 5 years, or both.

2. "(b) Whoever knowingly sells, purchases, uses for profit, or transports for sale or profit any Native American cultural items obtained in violation of the Native American Graves Protection and Repatriation Act shall be fined in accordance with this title, imprisoned not more than one year, or both, and in the case of a second or subsequent violation, be fined in accordance with this title, imprisoned not more than 5 years, or both."

Section. 5. Inventory for Human Remains and Associated Funerary Objects

IN GENERAL. Each Federal agency and each museum which has possession or control over holdings or collections of Native American human remains and associated funerary objects shall compile an inventory of such items and, to the extent possible based on information possessed by such museum or federal agency, identify the geographical and cultural affiliation of such item.

REQUIREMENTS. (1) The inventories and identifications required under subsection (a) shall be

(A) completed in consultation with tribal government and Native Hawaiian organization officials and traditional religious leaders;

(B) completed by not later than the date that is 5 years after the date of enactment of this Act, and

(C) made available both during the time they are being conducted and afterward to a review committee established under section 8.

(2) Upon request by an Indian tribe or Native Hawaiian organization which receives or should have received notice, a museum or federal agency shall supply additional available documentation to supplement the information required by subsection

(a) of this section. The term "documentation" means a summary of existing museum or Federal agency records, including inventories or catalogues, relevant studies, or other pertinent data for the limited purpose of determining the geographical origin, cultural affiliation, and basic facts surrounding acquisition and accession of Native American human remains and associated funerary objects subject to this section. Such term does not mean, and this Act shall not be construed to be an authorization for, the initiation of new scientific studies of such remains and associated funerary objects or other means of acquiring or preserving additional scientific information from such remains and objects.

(c) EXTENSION OF TIME FOR INVENTORY. Any museum which has made a good faith effort to carry out an inventory and identification under this section, but which has been unable to complete the process, may appeal to the Secretary for an extension of the time requirements set forth in subsection (b)(1)(B). The Secretary may extend such time requirements for any such museum upon a finding of good faith effort. An indication of good faith shall include the development of a plan to carry out the inventory and identification process.

(d) NOTIFICATION. (1) If the cultural affiliation of any particular Native American human remains or associated funerary objects is determined pursuant to this section, the Federal agency or museum concerned shall, not later than 6 months after the completion of the inventory, notify the affected Indian tribes or Native Hawaiian organizations.

(2) The notice required by paragraph (1) shall include information

(A) which identifies each Native American human remains or associated funerary objects and the circumstances surrounding its acquisition;

(B) which lists the human remains or associated funerary objects that are clearly identifiable as to tribal origin; and

(C) which lists the Native American human remains and associated funerary objects that are not clearly identifiable as being culturally affiliated with that Indian tribe or Native Hawaiian organization, but which, given the totality of circumstances surrounding acquisition of the remains or objects, are determined by a reasonable belief to be remains or objects culturally affiliated with the Indian tribe or Native Hawaiian organization.

(3) A copy of each notice provided under paragraph (1) shall be sent to the Secretary who shall publish each notice in the Federal Register.

Sec. 6. Summary for Unassociated Funerary Objects, Sacred Objects, and Cultural Patrimony

(a) IN GENERAL. Each Federal agency or museum which has possession or control over holdings or collections of Native American unassociated funerary objects, sacred objects, or objects of cultural patrimony shall provide a written summary of such objects based upon available information held by such agency or museum. The summary shall describe the scope of the collection, kinds of objects included, reference to geographical location, means and period of acquisition and cultural affiliation, where readily ascertainable.

(b) REQUIREMENTS. (1) The summary required under subsection (a) shall be

(A) in lieu of an object-by-object inventory;

(B) followed by consultation with tribal government and Native Hawaiian organization officials and traditional religious leaders; and

(C) completed by not later than the date that is 3 years after the date of enactment of this Act.

(2) Upon request, Indian tribes and Native Hawaiian organizations shall have access to records, catalogues, relevant studies or other pertinent data for the limited purposes of determining the geographic origin, cultural affiliation, and basic facts surrounding acquisition and accession of Native American objects subject to this section.

Such information shall be provided in a reasonable manner to be agreed upon by all parties.

Sec. 7. Repatriation

(a) REPATRIATION OF NATIVE AMERICAN HUMAN REMAINS AND OBJECTS POSSESSED OR CONTROLLED BY FEDERAL AGENCIES AND MUSEUMS. (1) If, pursuant to section 5, the cultural affiliation of Native American human remains and associated funerary objects with a particular Indian tribe or Native Hawaiian organization is established, then the Federal agency or museum, upon the request of a known lineal descendant of the Native American or of the tribe or organization and pursuant to subsections (b) and (e) of this section, shall expeditiously return such remains and associated funerary objects.

(2) If, pursuant to section 6, the cultural affiliation with a particular Indian tribe or Native Hawaiian organization is shown with respect to unassociated funerary objects, sacred objects or objects of cultural patrimony, then the Federal agency or museum, upon the request of the Indian tribe or Native Hawaiian organization and pursuant to subsections (b), (c) and (e) of this section, shall expeditiously return such objects.

(3) The return of cultural items covered by this Act shall be in consultation with the requesting lineal descendant or tribe or organization to determine the place and manner of delivery of such items.

(4) Where cultural affiliation of Native American human remains and funerary objects has not been established in an inventory prepared pursuant to section 5 or where Native American human remains and funerary objects are not included upon any such inventory, then, upon request and pursuant to subsections (b) and (e) and, in the case of unassociated funerary objects, subsection (c), such Native American human remains and funerary objects shall be expeditiously returned where the requesting Indian tribe or Native Hawaiian organization

can show cultural affiliation by a preponderance of the evidence based upon geographical, kinship, biological, archaeological, anthropological, linguistic, folkloric, oral traditional, historical, or other relevant information or expert opinion.

(5) Upon request and pursuant to subsections (b), (c) and (e), sacred objects and objects of cultural patrimony shall be expeditiously returned where

(A) the requesting party is the direct lineal descendant of an individual who owned the sacred object;

(B) the requesting Indian tribe or Native Hawaiian organization can show that the object was owned or controlled by the tribe or organization; or

(C) the requesting Indian tribe or Native Hawaiian organization can show that the sacred object was owned or controlled by a member thereof, provided that in the case where a sacred object was owned by a member thereof, there are no identifiable lineal descendants of said member or the lineal descendants, upon notice, have failed to make a claim for the object under this Act.

(b) SCIENTIFIC STUDY. If the lineal descendant, Indian tribe, or Native Hawaiian organization requests the return of culturally affiliated Native American cultural items, the Federal agency or museum shall expeditiously return such items unless such items are indispensable for completion of a specific scientific study, the outcome of which would be of major benefit to the United States. Such items shall be returned by no later than 90 days after the date on which the scientific study is completed.

(c) STANDARD OF REPATRIATION. If a known lineal descendant or an Indian tribe or Native Hawaiian organization requests the return of Native American unassociated funerary objects, sacred objects or objects of cultural patrimony pursuant to this Act and presents evidence which, if standing alone before the introduction of evidence to the contrary, would support a finding that the Federal agency or museum did not have the right

of possession, then such agency or museum shall return such objects unless it can overcome such inference and prove that it has a right of possession to the objects.

(d) SHARING OF INFORMATION BY FEDERAL AGENCIES AND MUSEUMS. Any Federal agency or museum shall share what information it does possess regarding the object in question with the known lineal descendant, Indian tribe, or Native Hawaiian organization to assist in making a claim under this section.

(e) COMPETING CLAIMS. Where there are multiple requests for repatriation of any cultural item and, after complying with the requirements of this Act, the Federal agency or museum cannot clearly determine which requesting party is the most appropriate claimant, the agency or museum may retain such item until the requesting parties agree upon its disposition or the dispute is otherwise resolved pursuant to the provisions of this Act or by a court of competent jurisdiction.

(f) MUSEUM OBLIGATION. Any museum which repatriates any item in good faith pursuant to this Act shall not be liable for claims by an aggrieved party or for claims of breach of fiduciary duty, public trust, or violations of state law that are inconsistent with the provisions of this Act.

Sec. 8 Review Committee

(a) ESTABLISHMENT. Within 120 days after the date of enactment of this Act, the Secretary shall establish a committee to monitor and review the implementation of the inventory and identification process and repatriation activities required under sections 5, 6 and 7.

(b) MEMBERSHIP. (1) The Committee established under subsection (a) shall be composed of 7 members,

(A) 3 of whom shall be appointed by the Secretary from nominations submitted by Indian tribes, Native

Hawaiian organizations, and traditional Native American religious leaders with at least 2 of such persons being traditional Indian religious leaders;

(B) 3 of whom shall be appointed by the Secretary from nominations submitted by national museum organizations and scientific organizations; and

(C) 1 who shall be appointed by the Secretary from a list of persons developed and consented to by all of the members appointed pursuant to subparagraphs (A) and (B).

(2) The Secretary may not appoint Federal officers or employees to the committee.

(3) In the event vacancies shall occur, such vacancies shall be filled by the Secretary in the same manner as the original appointment within 90 days of the occurrence of such vacancy.

(4) Members of the committee established under subsection (a) shall serve without pay but shall be reimbursed at a rate equal to the daily rate for GS-18 of the General Schedule for each day (including travel time) for which the member is actually engaged in committee business. Each member shall receive travel expenses, including per diem in lieu of subsistence, in accordance with sections 5702 and 5703 of title 5, United States Code.

Sec. 9. Penalty

(a) PENALTY. (1) Any museum that fails to comply with the requirements of this Act may be assessed a civil penalty by the secretary of Interior pursuant to procedures established by the Secretary through regulation. No penalty may be assessed under this subsection unless such museum is given notice and opportunity for a hearing with respect to such violation. Each violation shall be a separate offense.

(2) The amount of such penalty shall be determined under regulations promulgated pursuant to

this Act, taking into account, in addition to other factors

(A) the archeological, historical or commercial value of the item involved;

(B) the damages suffered, both economic and non-economic, by an aggrieved party;

(C) the number of violations that have occurred.

(3) Any museum aggrieved by an order assessing a civil penalty under this subsection may file a petition of judicial review of such order with the United States District Court for the District of Columbia or for any other district in which the museum is located. Such a petition may only be filed within the 30-day period beginning on the date the order making such assessment was issued. The court shall hear such action on the administrative record and sustain the imposition of the penalty if it is supported by substantial evidence on the record considered as a whole.

(4) If any museum fails to pay an assessment of a civil penalty after a final administrative order has been issued and not appealed or after a final judgement has been rendered, the Attorney General may institute a civil action in a district court of the United States for any district in which such museum is located to collect the penalty and such court shall have jurisdiction to hear and decide such action. In such action, the validity and amount of such penalty shall not be subject to review.

(5) Hearings held during proceedings for the assessment of civil penalties authorized by this subsection shall be conducted in accordance with section 554 of Title 5. Subpoenas may be issued for the attendance and testimony of witnesses and the production of relevant papers, books and documents. Witnesses summoned shall be paid the same fees and mileage that are paid to witnesses in the courts of the United States. In the case of contumacy or refusal to obey a subpoena served upon

any person pursuant to this paragraph, the district court of the United States for any district in which such person is located, resides or transacts business, upon application by the United States and after notice to such person shall have jurisdiction to issue an order requiring such person to appear and give testimony or produce documents, or both, and any failure to obey such order of the court may be punished by such court as a contempt thereof.

Sec. 10. Grants

(a) INDIAN TRIBES AND NATIVE HAWAIIAN ORGANIZATIONS. The Secretary is authorized to make grants to Indian tribes and Native Hawaiian organizations for the purpose of assisting such tribes and organizations in the repatriation of Native American cultural items.

(b) MUSEUMS. The Secretary is authorized to make grants to museums for the purpose of assisting the museums in conducting the inventories and identification required under sections 5 and 6.

Sec. 11. Savings Provisions

Nothing in this Act shall be construed to

(1) limit the authority of any Federal agency or museum to

(A) return or repatriate Native American cultural items to Indian tribes, Native Hawaiian organizations, or individuals, and

(B) enter into any other agreement with the consent of the culturally affiliated tribe or organization as to the disposition of control over items covered by this Act;

(2) delay actions on repatriation requests that are pending on the date of enactment of this Act;

(3) deny or otherwise affect access to any court;

(4) limit any procedural or substantive right which may otherwise be secured to individuals or Indian tribes or Native Hawaiian organizations; or

(5) limit the application of any State or Federal law pertaining to theft or stolen property.

Sec. 12. Special Relationship between the Federal Government and Indian Tribes

This Act reflects the unique relationship between the Federal government and Indian tribes and Native Hawaiian organizations and should not be construed to establish a precedent with respect to any other individual, organization or foreign government.

Sec. 13. Regulations

The Secretary shall promulgate regulations to carry out this Act within 12 months of enactment.

Sec. 14. Authorization of Appropriations

There is authorized to be appropriated such sums as may be necessary to carry out this Act.

Purpose

The purpose of H.R. 5237 is to protect Native American burial sites and the removal of human remains, funerary objects, sacred objects, and objects of cultural patrimony on Federal, Indian and Native Hawaiian lands. The Act also sets up a process by which Federal agencies and museums receiving federal funds will inventory holdings of such remains and objects and work with appropriate Indian tribes and Native Hawaiian organizations to reach agreement on repatriation or other disposition of these remains and objects.

Source: Native American Grave Protection and Repatriation Act. Public Law 101–601. U.S. Statutes at Large 104 (1990): 3048.

White House Conference on Indian Education
(1992)

A congressional report issued in November 1969, Indian Education: A National Tragedy—A National Challenge, made many recommendations for improving education for Native Americans in the United States, including the need for a White House conference. That report concluded that the failure of national educational policies and practices for Native Americans lay in the exclusion of American Indians from the planning process, and it was believed that a White House conference would reverse this trend. Senator Dennis DeConcini (D-AZ) introduced Senate Bill 1645, the Indian Education Amendments Act, in August 1987. The hearings on this bill led to the idea of the White House conference, which did live up to its expectations. Each state held a preconference, which involved Native American educators, and forwarded their findings and recommendations to the White House conference. The delegates to the White House conference were primarily Native American educators, and the results of that conference were a series of resolutions that can be found in the final report of the White House Conference on Indian Education. The following excerpt was taken from that document's executive summary.

EXECUTIVE SUMMARY ANALYSIS

Goals of Analysis

The goals of the Conference were categorized as education oriented. However the affected constituency and delegates did not confine their vision to the "traditional" construct of the definition of education.

Indian families and communities are very aware that the needs of their children are interwoven into all aspects of their lives. American Indian and Alaska Native communities have strong foundation of spiritual beliefs and philosophies most of which encompass the circular nature of life that upholds the interconnection between all beings and things. It was this outlook that provided the reenforcement to the White House Conference on Indian Education to address the educational needs in a holistic manner.

The task for collecting concerns which impacted the educational services of Indian communities, were drawn from a wide array of sources. It was the responsibility of the Task Force to attempt to portray these issues and concerns for the delegate's consideration in the most interrelated form possible.

The Task Force designed a matrix which appeared to embody the Indian community's identified issues of concern (see the full report). This circular matrix represented the all-encompassing nature of both issues and possible solutions. This "dream catcher's" universe of needs and opportunities is symbolic of the circumstances confronting Indian community. On one hand, the barriers and specific elements which comprise the present reality must be "caught" and addressed, but the goals and aspirations must also be sought and fostered.

This analysis will depict the issues by these goals and aspirations, as well as the means or mechanism proposed by the Delegates to resolve or eliminate barriers. The commonalities of concerns and recommendations, from topic area to topic area, will be identified for policy purposes. When differences in policy goals are proposed, for similar or overlapping issues and recommendations, these will also be summarized. This summary will portray these overlapping recommendations juxtaposed against those policies or issues they address to differentiate the instigating cause or intended outcome; such as local community control over actions which may be defined as a new effort and entity, or identified as tribally controlled.

The resultant blueprint for action will also convey future policy issues and implications. The many levels of involvement and action that are required to implement these recommendations will require comprehensive participation by all affected parties. When and how, such endeavors, from local Indian communities to national policy makers, should be undertaken are questions that this report should provoke.

Parameters of the Conference and Issues

The Conference was designed to be a "working" conference to develop long-term and short-term strategies from recommendations adopted by the Delegates. The 30 state and regional pre-conference activities, produced numerous recommendations for consideration by the Conference Delegates. The Delegates were mailed materials prior to the Conference which contained specific instructions to assist Delegates in their review and preparation. However, the range of issues and the number of issues, as well as other constraints, combined to place limitations on both the selection of issues chosen and the amount of specificity available for guidance.

These assumptions require a prior understanding of tribes and their relationship with the United States, to fully appreciate the Conference Delegates' concerns and their proposed solutions.

The Federal-Indian relationship is not one well understood by the general society. For many individuals, their sole exposure to "Indians" has been provided through movies and the print media from a non-Indian view and, usually, in the absence of accurate historical background. This deficiency in society's learning environment is at the root of some of the recommendations adopted by the Conference Delegates. A brief explanation is provided below to aid in understanding the Federal-Indian relationship. The Federal government has a government-to-government, political relationship with tribes that is rooted in the Constitution and further strengthened by congressionally ratified treaties, Executive Orders, case law, and specific and general statutes to assist American Indian and Alaska Native communities and individuals. This relationship even pre-dates the Declaration of Independence, when the colonial powers entered into formal agreements with tribes to exchange lands for peace, goods, and other purposes.

When the United States declared its independence and, eventually, adopted its constitution, there were three key clauses incorporated into this charter for the protection and benefit of tribes and their people. This provision, under Article I, Section 8, Clause 3 stated that only the United States (and not States) had the power to regulate and permit commerce with tribes. Article II, section 2, clause 2 grants Congress plenary power to regulate commerce with Indian tribes, as it does with foreign nations and the States. Section 14, Amendment XIV of the Constitution also exempts tribes from taxation. Subsequently, the courts, based on these authorities, recognized that tribes, as dependent nations, were beneficiaries of a trust responsibility on the part of the United States.

These principles of Federal-Indian law have been tested over the past two centuries. Yet, for the most part, the rights of tribes as sovereign nations whose relationship is with the United States first, and not those States or territories in which they reside, have been upheld.

As this relationship has been strengthened through successive laws and Executive Orders, and as tribes have continued their efforts to determine their own future, the nature of the relationship has also evolved. Where once Federal agencies decided what was appropriate and beneficial to tribes without tribal input, now there is recognition that tribal self-determination is one elemental aspect of their sovereignty. It is the principle of sovereignty and self-determination which underlies many of the issues raised and addressed by the delegates during the Conference. Each tribe has variations in its performance of its responsibilities to their people; based, in part, on the issue or region in which they are located. What may be true for one tribe, for

regulating the environment, health and other programs, may not be accurate for other tribes. The
reasons for this variation among tribal groups are
many and complex. That they exist and create
additional barriers, and sometimes opportunities,
is a critical element in the development of the
many adopted strategies by the Conference
Delegates to improve Indian education.

Additionally, during the past fifty years, as
Indian people relocated "off-reservation," either
under Federal actions and policies or for their own
purposes, there has grown a community of Indian
people outside the traditional bounds of "Indian
lands." These segments of the population, often
identified as rural or urban Indians, are now identified more as members of their home communities
rather than as displaced and unaffiliated individuals. The location of these rural and urban Indian
people has placed special needs and demands for
services to aid their growth and well-being.

The complexity of the Federal-Tribal relationship needs to be considered when reviewing the
adopted resolutions and plans of action. This complexity and the interdependency between American
Indian and Alaska Native people requires that
careful planning and action be undertaken to
implement strategies for improvements.

This analysis will identify concerns which
require a balancing of competing needs and a
means for transition from existing efforts to new
activities. The balancing and transition issues,
where not addressed by the Delegates in their resolution and plans of action, will especially require a
general understanding of the relationships and
roles between the United States and American
Indian/Alaska Native communities and people.

Analysis

The Conference Delegates endorsed several major
goals, which were designed to achieve improved
student outcomes and services. The resolutions
were designed to emphasize accountability to
improved standards, including culturally appropriate ones. However, the predominant underlying
principle was the premise that the Federal-Tribal

relationship entailed specific duties and responsibilities on the part of the United States, unlike
any other Federal-State-Local governmental
relationship.

The consistent call by the delegates for the
United States to recognize and reaffirm the Federal-
Tribal relationship indicates the serious concerns
that exist over whether Federal policy makers fully
appreciate and understand how their actions affect
this relationship. This repeated call expressed a
desire to require departments and agencies to
uphold this principle in daily operations and
reflects a desire to expand and strengthen tribal
participation on several fronts.

A strengthened U.S. policy is also expected to
provide the dictates necessary to accomplish the
more practical activities in realizing equitable
access to all relevant resources to produce the
desired achievements. There is a valid concern
expressed that all Federal agencies make an equal
effort to assist tribes and Indian communities.
Without a concerted outreach effort there will be a
continued lack of tribal participation and access to
available resources. The absence of participation
and access to opportunities can create limited outcomes which will diminish capabilities for elevat-
ing the quality of life for Indian people.

One major theme that was articulated was the
premise that tribal control and leadership in education was critical in the strengthening of services.
Local control and determination of needs is a
demand and goal of all segments of society. Indian
country is not different in this respect, but there is
additional weight behind this demand given the
inability of society to accurately perceive the cultural aspects integral to the values and goals of
Indian communities.

Both local control and determination of needs
must be viewed in conjunction with another major
theme of the inclusion, at every educational level,
of appropriate cultural values, language, beliefs,
accurate histories, and other expressions. Indian
and Alaska Native life is built on the foundation of
their tribal beliefs and identity. Yet, obtaining
respect for, and fostering such components in a

"traditional" education system, have not been very successful. A number of recommendations adopted addressed stronger tribal control over the incorporation of cultural facets in the reform and restructuring of these "traditional/formal" educational systems.

The Delegates did not overlook the need to instill or enhance governmental partnerships among affected entities, tribes, States, Federal, and other bodies. This major theme was an indication of the Indian community's need to interact more with other entities, as well as become involved in the larger issues confronting all communities.

This comprehensive approach should be viewed as an integral aspect of all the key principles and themes. In particular, when undertaking efforts to identify the scope of educational needs in Indian communities, there are concerns that education needs encompass all related issues and services for all ages and members of the community. Related issues and services were not so broadly interpreted that it could become a Herculean task. The parameters placed on education and related issues or services appeared to be whether there were direct correlations between a service and improved student outcomes, such areas as substance abuse prevention, family violence prevention, and career guidance.

The other key indicator in defining relevance was the correlation between the benefits derived by Indian communities and improved student outcomes. Two examples include the proposed requirement that economic enterprises provide employment in a manner planned by the tribe to coincide with graduating scholarship recipients, and requiring "pay back obligations" by students upon graduation for their scholarship assistance.

There are certain aspects that were not fully addressed or resolved by the Conference Delegates. The unresolved issues did not occur by premeditation or an unwillingness to tackle these issues.

The Delegates were required to work within the various topic areas in which they participated, plus review and approve those resolutions in the final day of the Conference from other topic groups.

Consequently, the Delegates were simply unable to fully reflect on the complete picture presented by their combined efforts. The Delegates began an effort to address and accurately present a comprehensive overview of education and related needs. These actions asserted that such needs should be locally determined since the affected Indian people and communities would be most able to recognize and ascertain these needs. While this is an important point, the ability to integrate this activity with the recommendation requiring that funds and services be provided on an equitable basis, becomes problematic.

The assumption to the first resolution is that there are, or will be, clearly understood and accepted criteria for determining true needs in all areas. The second recommendation's assumption is that the funds will be provided in sufficient amounts to ensure equitability, to provide "comparable" services in obtaining similar goals, such as eliminating illiteracy, substance abuse, and dropout rates.

To begin an administrative process for developing criteria for determining the "scope of need" requires several basic components. First, the data on eligible service population and present level of services available must be current. Second, a clearly defined goal of what is to be achieved through services to be provided must be understood and acceptable to the beneficiary population. Third, how growth will be achieved from the present status to the desired goals must be developed, approved and implemented. Each of these components will require an investment in manpower, resources, and time. When to apply this strategy to the targeted education or related program services must also be determined.

When the definition of need was raised, it was through the provision of services to "American Indian/Alaska Native" people. Yet, many available services are dependent on a variety of factors. Eligibility for services is not consistent from program to program, and agency to agency. One topic group addressed the abolition of the income eligibility requirement for the Head Start Program.

Another topic group recommended that eligibility for "Indian education services" should be in keeping with the respective tribal definitions and requirements for member enrollment. When tribes, tribal or Indian organizations provide services for their populations, a uniform definition for eligibility would eliminate multiple program requirements that must be fulfilled.

Overall, transitioning services into a means of accomplishing the identified education goals is not a process that can be precisely detailed. However, there are ground rules that should be considered on the difficulties confronting such transition. These ground rules include: where tribal input is needed; estimated time frames to accomplish identified tasks, level of risk involved and disclosure of advantages and disadvantages nationally and locally.

Recommendations and plans of action are not specific with respect to priority setting, other than needs and solutions should be tribally and locally determined. In order to have an effective process to implement the many education goals and tasks identified by the Conference Delegates, a means of ensuring fairness in priority setting and equitable allocation of resources must be planned and provided. For example, if certain actions throughout the country are expected to occur concurrently, assistance to Indian communities must follow common national criteria, yet be locally relevant. Specifically, preschool screening for exceptional and challenged Indian children has been recommended to be joined with efforts to expand early childhood services. This activity will require cooperative efforts in a multidisciplinary and multi-agency manner.

Potential Issues of Immediacy

There were common issues that Delegates expressed throughout the resolutions and plans of action. These issues were focused on providing resources to ensure a higher quality of standards and services.

Many recommendations have the potential for immediate implementation, utilizing existing authorities of the relevant agencies. There are recommendations which clearly require new authority, and a close scrutiny of agency's present authorities could determine which issues can be promoted absent such new authority. In some instances, new authority would be useful in preventing any action to transfer funds from one program into a new program diminishing available resources in the drained program.

Conclusion

The resolutions and plans of action adopted by the Conference Delegates are far reaching and, often, interdependent. It is a tremendous accolade to the Delegates that the Conference's work products are so comprehensive and thoughtful.

It will be this same spirit and commitment which will be required to undertake the actions needed to achieve these identified goals and tasks.

The issues that the Delegates addressed can be viewed as a map for the future of Indian education and other related needs. This future is perceived to be inclusive of benefits to both Indian and non-Indian people and communities.

These resolutions and plans of action require each person, community, and institution, to evaluate themselves for their strengths and capabilities. By contributing to each other to achieve better learning environments and student outcomes, the rewards increase exponentially throughout all spectrums of our society.

Source: The Final Report of the White House Conference on Indian Education: Executive Summary Analysis, May 22, 1992. Washington, DC: White House Conference on Indian Education, 1992.

Chief Oren Lyons Jr., Haudenosaunee Faithkeeper, Address to Delegates to the United Nations Organization to Open "The Year of the Indigenous Peoples" (1993) in the United Nations General Assembly Auditorium, United Nations Plaza, New York City

(December 10, 1992)

Oren Lyons Jr., a member of the Iroquois Nation, was born in 1930 and raised on the Seneca and Onondaga reservations in upstate New York. He served in the U.S. military and attended Syracuse University, where he was a highly acclaimed lacrosse player. After graduating, he joined the Red Power movement of the 1960s and participated in a number of important protest movements. He was a leader in the Trail of Broken Treaties (1972) and became a delegate to the first World Conference on Racism (1977).

Lyons's life is defined by his activism. He expanded his defense of Native Americans to include the defense of indigenous peoples all over the world. Because of this transnational identity and outlook, he was invited to speak at the General Assembly of the United Nations to open the International Year of the World's Indigenous People in 1993. Reproduced here is a transcript of his speech.

For all of us. I am Oren Lyons, Hau de no sau nee, and speaking on behalf of the Indigenous People of North America, this Great Turtle Island. Mr. President, distinguished delegates, Chiefs, Clan Mothers, Leaders and Members of the World's Indigenous Nations and Peoples, we thank you, The General Assembly, for the recognition and the proclamation of "1993, The International Year of the Indigenous Peoples," for the theme of, "Indigenous Peoples, a New Partnership." We thank Madam Chairman Repal Chur of the Working Group for Indigenous Populations for consistent, enthusiastic support, and Diaz. And at this time, we recognize the inspiration and spiritual force of Augusto Williamson Diaz, for his vision of such a day as this, and our gratitude to those leaders of Indigenous Peoples and people who also had the vision of this day for our people, who put their blood, their sweat and their tears into this moment. And to those who are no longer here, our profound gratitude and appreciation.

This proclamation brings home inspiration and renewed dedication to our quest for self-determination, justice, freedom and peace in our Homelands and our Territories. Indeed, the quest is a renewal of what we enjoyed before the coming of our White Brothers from across the sea. We lived contentedly under the Gai Eneshah Go' Nah, The Great Law of Peace. We were instructed to create societies based on the principles of Peace, Equity, Justice, and the Power of Good Minds.

Our societies are based upon great democratic principles of the authority of the people and equal responsibilities for the men and the women. This was a great way of life across this Great Turtle Island and freedom with respect was everywhere. Our leaders were instructed to be men of vision and to make every decision on behalf of the seventh generation to come; to have compassion and love for those generations yet unborn. We were instructed to give thanks for All That Sustains Us.

Thus, we created great ceremonies of thanksgiving for the life-giving forces of the Natural World, as long as we carried out our ceremonies, life would continue. We were told that "The Seed is the Law." Indeed, it is The Law of Life. It is The Law of Regeneration. Within the seed is the mysterious force of life and creation. Our mothers nurture and guard that seed and we respect and love them for that. Just as we love I hi do' hah, our Mother Earth, for the same spiritual work and mystery.

We were instructed to be generous and to share equally with our brothers and sisters so that all may be content. We were instructed to respect and love our Elders, to serve them in their declining years, to cherish one another. We were instructed to love our children, indeed, to love ALL children. We were told that there would come a time when parents would fail this obligation and we could judge the decline of humanity by how we treat our children.

We were told that there would come a time when the world would be covered with smoke, and that it would take our elders and our children. It was difficult to comprehend at the time, but now all we have to do is but to walk outside to experience that statement. We were told that there would come a time when we could not find clean water to wash ourselves, to cook our foods, to make our medicines, and to drink. And there would be disease and great suffering. Today we can see this and we peer into the future with great apprehension. We were told there would come a time when, tending our gardens, we would pull up our plants and the vines would be empty. Our precious seed would begin to disappear. We were instructed that we would see a time when young men would pace back and forth in front of their chiefs and leaders in defiance and confusion.

There are some specific issues I must bring forward on behalf of our Nations and Peoples.

North America. The issue of nuclear and toxic waste dumps on our precious lands; the policy of finding a place for the waste with the poorest and most defenseless of peoples today. This brings the issue of the degradation of our environment by these waste dumps, over-fishing, over-cutting of timber, and toxic chemicals from mining processes throughout our lands.

Treaty violations. We have with the United States and Canada 371 ratified Treaties and Agreements. The Ruby Valley Treaty of the Western Shoshone is a prime example of what the violation of treaties brings: human rights violations, forced removals, disenfranchisements of traditional people with confiscations of their property and livestock.

The refusal to recognize and support religious freedoms of our people and the decisions by the [U.S.] Supreme Court which incorporates this attitude into Federal Law. This translates into the violation of Sacred Sites. Mt. Graham in the Apache Country is now a project site for an observatory, causing great stress to the Apache People who have depended upon the spiritual forces of this mountain for survival. Ironically, a partner in this project is the Vatican. And even further, it has proposed to name this project "Columbus."

The appropriation of our intellectual properties is continuous and devastating. Land is the issue. Land has always been the issue with Indigenous Peoples. Original title is a problem for all of you. We must try to reach an agreement on a more level playing field that allows us to, at least, a chance for survival.

Out brother, Leonard Peltier, has been too long in prison, in 1993, to signal a new attitude—and what better than his release after 16 years—symbolic of the exercise of dominion over our Peoples.

All this has come from across the seas. The catastrophes that we have suffered at the hands of our brothers from across the seas have been unremitting and inexcusable. It has crushed our people, and our Nations down through the centuries. You brought us disease and death and the idea of Christian dominion over heathens, pagans, savages. Our lands were declared "vacant" by Papal Bulls, which created law to justify the pillaging of our land.

We were systematically stripped of our resources, religions and dignity. Indeed, we became resources of labor for goldmines and canefields. Life for us was unspeakable, cruel. Our black and dark-skinned brothers and sisters were brought here from distant lands to share our misery and suffering and death.

Yet we survived. I stand before you as a manifestation of the spirit of our people and our will to survive. The Wolf, our Spiritual Brother, stands beside us and we are alike in the Western mind: hated, admired, and still a mystery to you, and still undefeated.

So then, what is the message I bring to you today? Is it our common future? It seems to me that we are living in a time of prophecy, a time of definitions and decisions. We are the generation with the responsibilities and the option to choose the Path of Life for the future of our children. Or the life and path which defies the Laws of Regeneration.

Even though you and I are in different boats, you in your boat and we in our canoe, we share the same River of Life. What befalls me, befalls you. And downstream, downstream in this River of Life, our children will pay for our selfishness, for our greed, and for our lack of vision.

500 years ago, you came to our pristine lands of great forests, rolling plains, crystal clear lakes and streams and rivers. And we have suffered in your quest for God, for Glory, for Gold. But, we have survived. Can we survive another 500 years of "sustainable development?" I don't think so. Not

in the definitions that put "sustainable" in today. I don't think so.

So reality and the Natural Law will prevail; The Law of the Seed and Regeneration. We can still alter our course. It is NOT too late. We still have options. We need the courage to change our values to the regeneration of our families, the life that surrounds us. Given this opportunity, we can raise ourselves. We must join hands with the rest of Creation and speak of Common Sense, Responsibility, Brotherhood, and PEACE. We must understand that the law is the seed and only as true partners can we survive.

On behalf of the Indigenous People of the Great Turtle Island, I give my appreciation and thanks. Dah ney' to. Now I am finished.

Source: Chief Oren Lyons Jr. Address to Delegates to the United Nations Organization to Open "The Year of the Indigenous Peoples." UN General Assembly, 1992. http://www.ratical.org/many_worlds/6Nations/OLatUNin92.html.

Bonnie Ballard (Fort Hall Shoshone-Bannock), "No Matter What Happened to the Indians, We Will Always Have Our Spirit"

(1996)

In the document that follows, Bonnie Ballard, a 16-year-old Native American from American Falls, Idaho, discusses the major hurdles that she will be forced to overcome, including alcohol, pregnancy, and a lack of moral guidance, to realize her dreams. Although these hurdles and dangers exist for all American teens, regardless of race, the author exhibits the maturity and resolve to overcome any obstacle that would prevent her from reaching her goals.

I dream that I can improve the lives of my people someday by trying to help get our foster care system in order because I myself am in a foster home. I don't mind that I am, but there are some kids that

don't have what I have got and they need what I have. I feel a little sad for them because where I live there are kids that need a home right now but nobody wants them. This is a major thing I have thought about for a long time.

Because there are kids that grow up with nobody to love them and no one to tell them right from wrong, they grow up with many problems and then they don't have an education because nobody told them to go to school. This leads them to have no jobs so they go around stealing and just simply causing trouble so there begins a life of crime.

There are kids who have been taught to steal and all the things that go with it because their parents didn't have all they wanted, but that's because their parents didn't have a job and no money and plus they didn't go to school to get the learning they need.

My family, uncles, aunts, and my mother quit school in the 7th and 8th grade. I am going to finish school so I can get an education and get a job. My sister dropped out in the 11th grade, all she had to do was get up early and go to school for just one more year, but what stopped her was alcohol. I know that smoking and drinking is another major problem on a reservation but drinking is the important worry because when you drink you can't stop. Everybody drinks, even the little kids, their parents teach them.

When you drink you get to be a person nobody wants and so you commit suicide or run away. People who commit suicide are the ones who don't really care about themselves and life. Drinking can kill you because you can't focus on what you are doing. You can hurt someone when you are drunk and you wouldn't even know because your brain doesn't even work and you can't think clearly. You can do something and then you will forget. Parents who drink forget about their kids and abuse them because they don't even think about who they are hurting. So when the parents get drunk they go and take the kids and put them in foster homes because it protects them from the harm of their parents. I think when Indian kids get put in a foster home

they should be put in a foster home of their own kind. I'm not saying that white people can't take care of Indian kids but they will be taught a different way than they should be raised.

I think that things will change if we help each other and ourselves. One thing that would really help us would be if teenagers would not get pregnant. There would not be so many little children that people have to take care of. So there wouldn't be any need for foster care. If teens want to have sex they should do it safely because they bring a child into the world and they don't want it. When they get older they think they have something missing in their life. So, I would advise teens not to have sex or use a protection.

I think they should get more programs for alcoholics. So there won't be any more problems with people who drink. So that nobody else will get killed from people who are drunk. Drinking doesn't help anybody solve any problems. People who think will go a longer distance than people who don't use their brain cells.

No matter what happened to the Indians, we will always have our spirit.

Source: Ballard, Bonnie. "No Matter What Happened to the Indians, We Will Always Have Our Spirit." *Voices . . . Visions . . . : A Collection of Essays by Native American Youth.* Washington DC: Department of Housing and Urban Development Office of Public and Indian Housing, 1996, 77.

President Bill Clinton, Executive Order 13007, Indian Sacred Sites
(May 24, 1996)

On May 24, 1996, President Bill Clinton issued an executive order directing federal agencies to accommodate Native American religious practices at sites sacred to Indian tribes if they were located on federal land. The order stated that federally recognized tribes or authorized American Indian or Alaska Natives could identify these sacred sites to federal agencies, such as the Bureau of Land Management, the U.S. Forest Service, the National Park Service, and the U.S. Geological Survey. Once identified, these sites were to be left untouched and protected for the use of Natives in religious ceremonies. The order also forbids the dissemination of information about the sites, such as names or locations, in public literature. It was established as part of an ongoing policy to protect Indian religious practices.

By the authority vested in me as President by the Constitution and the laws of the United States, in furtherance of Federal treaties, and in order to protect and preserve Indian religious practices, it is hereby ordered:

Section 1. Accommodation of Sacred Sites. (a) In managing Federal lands, each executive branch agency with statutory or administrative responsibility for the management of Federal lands shall, to the extent practicable, permitted by law, and not clearly inconsistent with essential agency functions, (1) accommodate access to and ceremonial use of Indian sacred sites by Indian religious practitioners and (2) avoid adversely affecting the physical integrity of such sacred sites. Where appropriate, agencies shall maintain the confidentiality of sacred sites.

(b) For purposes of this order:

(i) "Federal lands" means any land or interests in land owned by the United States, including leasehold interests held by the United States, except Indian trust lands;

(ii) "Indian tribe" means an Indian or Alaska Native tribe, band, nation, pueblo, village, or community that the Secretary of the Interior acknowledges to exist as an Indian tribe pursuant to Public Law No. 103–454, 108 Stat. 4791, and "Indian" refers to a member of such an Indian tribe; and

(iii) "Sacred site" means any specific, discrete, narrowly delineated location on Federal land that is identified by an Indian tribe, or Indian individual determined to be an appropriately authoritative representative of an Indian religion, as sacred by virtue of its established religious significance to, or ceremonial use by, an Indian religion; provided that the tribe or appropriately authoritative representative of an Indian religion has informed the agency of the existence of such a site.

Sec.2. Procedures. (a) Each executive branch agency with statutory or administrative responsibility for the management of Federal lands shall, as appropriate, promptly implement procedures for the purposes of carrying out the provisions of section 1 of this order, including, where practicable and appropriate, procedures to ensure reasonable notice is provided of proposed actions or land management policies that may restrict future access to or ceremonial use of, or adversely affect the physical integrity of, sacred sites. In all actions pursuant to this section, agencies shall comply with the Executive memorandum of April 29, 1994, "Government-to-Government Relations with Native American Tribal Governments." . . .

Sec. 4. This order is intended only to improve the internal management of the executive branch and is not intended to, nor does it, create any right, benefit, or trust responsibility, substantive of procedural, enforceable at law or equity by any party against the United States, its agencies, officers, or any person.

Source: Executive Order 13007, May 24, 1996. *Federal Register,* vol. 61, no. 104, Presidential Documents, 1996, 26771–72.

Minnesota v. Mille Lacs Band of Chippewa Indians
(March 24, 1999)

This court case is the culmination of more than a century of changing U.S. government policy regarding Native American land located in the Great Lakes region. In the 1837 Treaty of St. Peters, land in present-day Minnesota and Wisconsin was ceded to the United States by several Chippewa bands in exchange for hunting, fishing, and gathering rights. President Zachary Taylor revoked these rights in 1850 and ordered the tribes to be removed from the territory. A few years later, another treaty set aside land for a Mille Lacs reservation but never addressed the issue of rights guaranteed by earlier treaties. In 1990, the Mille Lacs band sued the State of Minnesota, arguing that they retained their rights to use the land, and sought to prevent the state's interference with those rights. The U.S. Supreme Court ultimately upheld the Treaty of St. Peters, ruling that the Chippewa retained certain hunting, fishing, and gathering rights to the land they had ceded in 1837. The chief justice and three other justices vigorously dissented.

In 1837, the United States entered into a Treaty with several Bands of Chippewa Indians. Under the terms of this Treaty, the Indians ceded land in present-day Wisconsin and Minnesota to the United States, and the United States guaranteed to the Indians certain hunting, fishing, and gathering rights on the ceded land. We must decide whether the Chippewa Indians retain these usufructuary rights today. The State of Minnesota argues that the Indians lost these rights through an Executive Order in 1850, an 1855 Treaty, and the admission of Minnesota into the Union in 1858. After an examination of the historical record, we conclude that the Chippewa retain the usufructuary rights guaranteed to them under the 1837 Treaty.

We conclude that President Taylor's 1850 Executive Order was ineffective to terminate Chippewa usufructuary rights under the 1837 Treaty. The State has pointed to no statutory or constitutional authority for the President's removal order, and the Executive Order, embodying as it did one coherent policy, is inseverable. We do not mean to suggest that a President, now or in the future, cannot revoke the Chippewa usufructuary rights in accordance with the terms of the 1837 Treaty. All we conclude today is that the President's 1850 Executive Order was insufficient to accomplish this revocation because it was not severable from the invalid removal order.

To summarize, the historical record provides no support for the theory that the second sentence of Article 1 [of the Treaty of 1855] was designed to abrogate the usufructuary privileges guaranteed under the 1837 Treaty, but it does support the theory that the Treaty, and Article 1 in particular, was designed to transfer Chippewa land to the United States. At the very least, the historical record refutes the State's assertion that the 1855 Treaty "unambiguously" abrogated the 1837 hunting, fishing, and gathering privileges. Given this plausible ambiguity, we cannot agree with the State that the 1855 Treaty abrogated Chippewa usufructuary rights. We have held that Indian treaties are to be interpreted liberally in favor of the Indians.

Finally, the State argues that the Chippewa's usufructuary rights under the 1837 Treaty were extinguished when Minnesota was admitted to the Union in 1858. In making this argument, the State faces an uphill battle. Congress may abrogate Indian treaty rights, but it must clearly express its intent to do so. . . . . There must be "clear evidence that Congress actually considered the conflict between its intended action on the one hand and Indian treaty rights on the other, and chose to resolve that conflict by abrogating the treaty." . . . There is no such "clear evidence" of congressional intent to abrogate the Chippewa Treaty rights here.

The relevant statute—Minnesota's enabling Act—provides in relevant part:

[T]he State of Minnesota shall be one, and is hereby declared to be one, of the United States of America, and admitted into the Union on an equal footing with the original States in all respects whatever. . . .

This language, like the rest of the Act, makes no mention of Indian treaty rights; it provides no clue that Congress considered the reserved rights of the Chippewa and decided to abrogate those rights when it passed the Act. The State concedes that the Act is silent in this regard . . . and the State does not point to any legislative history describing the effect of the Act on Indian treaty rights. . . .

Accordingly, the judgment of the United States Court of Appeals for the Eighth Circuit is affirmed.

Source: Minnesota v. Mille Lacs Band of Chippewa Indians 526 U.S. 172 (1999).

Title IX, Safety for Indian Women, Violence Against Women Act (VAWA) (2005)

In 2005, the Violence Against Women Act (VAWA) was reauthorized with an added provision—Title IX, Safety for Indian Women. The VAWA was originally passed as Title IV of the Violent Crime Control and Law Enforcement Act (1994), and it was reauthorized in 2000 and in 2005. The Safety for Indian Women provision in the 2005 reauthorization brought the high rates of violence against indigenous women to the forefront, when Congress found that Native American women suffered the highest occurrences of domestic violence, sexual assault, and murder. The act proposes to decrease these rates and to increase the authority of tribal governments to protect women and to prosecute offenders. Following are excerpts from Title IX of the VAWA.

One Hundred Ninth Congress of the United States of America

AT THE FIRST SESSION

Begun and held at the City of Washington on Tuesday, the fourth day of January, two thousand and five

An Act to authorize appropriations for the Department of Justice for fiscal years 2006 through 2009, and for other purposes.

Be it enacted by the Senate and House of Representatives of the United States of America in Congress assembled,

SECTION 1. SHORT TITLE.

This Act may be cited as the "Violence Against Women and Department of Justice Reauthorization Act of 2005". . . .

TITLE IX—SAFETY FOR INDIAN WOMEN

SEC. 901. FINDINGS.

Congress finds that—

1. 1 out of every 3 Indian (including Alaska Native) women are raped in their lifetimes;

2. Indian women experience 7 sexual assaults per 1,000, compared with 4 per 1,000 among Black Americans, 3 per 1,000 among Caucasians, 2 per 1,000 among Hispanic women, and 1 per 1,000 among Asian women;

3. Indian women experience the violent crime of battering at a rate of 23.2 per 1,000, compared with 8 per 1,000 among Caucasian women;

4. during the period 1979 through 1992, homicide was the third leading cause of death of Indian females aged 15 to 34, and 75 percent were killed by family members or acquaintances;

5. Indian tribes require additional criminal justice and victim services resources to respond to violent assaults against women; and

6. the unique legal relationship of the United States to Indian tribes creates a Federal trust responsibility to assist tribal governments in safeguarding the lives of Indian women.

SEC. 902. PURPOSES.

The purposes of this title are—

1. to decrease the incidence of violent crimes against Indian women;

2. to strengthen the capacity of Indian tribes to exercise their sovereign authority to respond to violent crimes committed against Indian women; and

3. to ensure that perpetrators of violent crimes committed against Indian women are held accountable for their criminal behavior.

SEC. 903. CONSULTATION.

(a) IN GENERAL.—The Attorney General shall conduct annual consultations with Indian tribal governments concerning the Federal administration of tribal funds and programs established under this Act, the Violence Against Women Act of 1994 (title IV of Public Law 103–322; 108 Stat. 1902) and the Violence Against Women Act of 2000 (division B of Public Law 106–386; 114 Stat.1491).

(b) RECOMMENDATIONS.—During consultations under subsection (a), the Secretary of the Department of Health and Human Services and the Attorney General shall solicit recommendations from Indian tribes concerning—

1. administering tribal funds and programs;

2. enhancing the safety of Indian women from domestic violence, dating violence, sexual assault, and stalking; and

3. strengthening the Federal response to such violent crimes.

SEC. 904. ANALYSIS AND RESEARCH ON VIOLENCE AGAINST INDIAN WOMEN.

(a) NATIONAL BASELINE STUDY.—

(1) IN GENERAL.—The National Institute of Justice, in consultation with the Office on Violence Against Women, shall conduct a national baseline study to examine violence against Indian women in Indian country.

(2) SCOPE.—

(A) IN GENERAL.—The study shall examine violence committed against Indian women, including—

(i) domestic violence;
(ii) dating violence;
(iii) sexual assault;
(iv) stalking; and
(v) murder.

(B) EVALUATION.—The study shall evaluate the effectiveness of Federal, State, tribal, and local responses to the violations described in subparagraph (A) committed against Indian women.

(C) RECOMMENDATIONS.—The study shall propose recommendations to improve the effectiveness of Federal, State, tribal, and local responses to the violation described in subparagraph (A) committed against Indian women.

(3) TASK FORCE.—

(A) IN GENERAL.—The Attorney General, acting through the Director of the Office on Violence Against Women, shall establish a task force to assist in the development and implementation of the study under paragraph (1) and guide implementation of the recommendation in paragraph (2)(C).

(B) MEMBERS.—The Director shall appoint to the task force representatives from— (i) national tribal domestic violence and sexual assault nonprofit organizations; (ii) tribal governments; and (iii) the national tribal organizations.

(4) REPORT.—Not later than 2 years after the date of enactment of this Act, the Attorney General shall

submit to the Committee on Indian Affairs of the Senate, the Committee on the Judiciary of the Senate, and the Committee on the Judiciary of the House of Representatives a report that describes the study.

(5) AUTHORIZATION OF APPROPRIATIONS.—There is authorized to be appropriated to carry out this section $1,000,000 for each of fiscal years 2007 and 2008, to remain available until expended. (b) INJURY STUDY.—

(1) IN GENERAL.—The Secretary of Health and Human Services, acting through the Indian Health Service and the Centers for Disease Control and Prevention, shall conduct a study to obtain a national projection of—

(A) the incidence of injuries and homicides resulting from domestic violence, dating violence, sexual assault, or stalking committed against American Indian and Alaska Native women; and

(B) the cost of providing health care for the injuries described in subparagraph (A).

(2) REPORT.—Not later than 2 years after the date of enactment of this Act, the Secretary of Health and Human Services shall submit to the Committee on Indian Affairs of the Senate, the Committee on the Judiciary of the Senate, and the Committee on the Judiciary of the House of Representatives a report that describes the findings made in the study and recommends health care strategies for reducing the incidence and cost of the injuries described in paragraph (1).

(3) AUTHORIZATION OF APPROPRIATIONS.—There is authorized to be appropriated to carry out this section $500,000 for each of fiscal years 2007 and 2008, to remain available until expended.

SEC. 905. TRACKING OF VIOLENCE AGAINST INDIAN WOMEN.

(a) ACCESS TO FEDERAL CRIMINAL INFORMATION DATABASES.— Section 534 of title 28, United States Code, is amended—

1. by redesignating subsection (d) as subsection (e); and

2. by inserting after subsection (c) the following:

"(d) INDIAN LAW ENFORCEMENT AGENCIES.—The Attorney General shall permit Indian law enforcement agencies, in cases of domestic violence, dating violence, sexual assault, and stalking, to enter information into Federal criminal information databases and to obtain information from the databases."

(b) TRIBAL REGISTRY.—

(1) ESTABLISHMENT.—The Attorney General shall contract with any interested Indian tribe, tribal organization, or tribal nonprofit organization to develop and maintain—

(A) a national tribal sex offender registry; and

(B) a tribal protection order registry containing civil and criminal orders of protection issued by Indian tribes and participating jurisdictions.

(2) AUTHORIZATION OF APPROPRIATIONS.— There is authorized to be appropriated to carry out this section $1,000,000 for each of fiscal years 2007 through 2011, to remain available until expended.

SEC. 906. GRANTS TO INDIAN TRIBAL GOVERNMENTS.

(a) IN GENERAL.—Part T of title I of the Omnibus Crime Control and Safe Streets Act of 1968 (42 U.S.C. 3796gg et seq.) is amended by adding at the end the following:

"SEC. 2007. GRANTS TO INDIAN TRIBAL GOVERNMENTS.

"(a) GRANTS.—The Attorney General may make grants to Indian tribal governments and tribal organizations to—

"(1) develop and enhance effective governmental strategies to curtail violent crimes against and increase the safety of Indian women consistent with tribal law and custom;

"(2) increase tribal capacity to respond to domestic violence, dating violence, sexual assault, and stalking crimes against Indian women;

"(3) strengthen tribal justice interventions including tribal law enforcement, prosecution, courts, probation, correctional facilities;

"(4) enhance services to Indian women victimized by domestic violence, dating violence, sexual assault, and stalking;

"(5) work in cooperation with the community to develop education and prevention strategies directed toward issues of domestic violence, dating violence, and stalking programs and to address the needs of children exposed to domestic violence;

"(6) provide programs for supervised visitation and safe visitation exchange of children in situations involving domestic violence, sexual assault, or stalking committed by one parent against the other with appropriate security measures, policies, and procedures to protect the safety of victims and their children; and

"(7) provide transitional housing for victims of domestic violence, dating violence, sexual assault, or stalking, including rental or utilities payments assistance and assistance with related expenses such as security deposits and other costs incidental to relocation to transitional housing, and support services to enable a victim of domestic violence, dating violence, sexual assault, or stalking to locate and secure permanent housing and integrate into a community.

"(b) COLLABORATION.—All applicants under this section shall demonstrate their proposal was developed in consultation with a nonprofit, nongovernmental Indian victim services program, including sexual assault and domestic violence victim services providers in the tribal or local community, or a nonprofit tribal domestic violence and sexual assault coalition to the extent that they exist. In the absence of such a demonstration, the applicant may meet the requirement of this subsection through consultation with women in the community to be served.

"(c) NONEXCLUSIVITY.—The Federal share of a grant made under this section may not exceed 90 percent of the total costs of the project described in the application submitted, except that the Attorney General may grant a waiver of this match

requirement on the basis of demonstrated financial hardship. Funds appropriated for the activities of any agency of an Indian tribal government or of the Bureau of Indian Affairs performing law enforcement functions on any Indian lands may be used to provide the non-Federal share of the cost of programs or projects funded under this section."

"(b) AUTHORIZATION OF FUNDS FROM GRANTS TO COMBAT VIOLENT CRIMES AGAINST WOMEN.—Section 2007(b)(1) of the Omnibus Crime Control and Safe Streets Act of 1968 (42 U.S.C. 3796gg– 1(b)(1)) is amended to read as follows:

"(1) Ten percent shall be available for grants under the program authorized in section 2007. The requirements of this part shall not apply to funds allocated for such program."

"(c) AUTHORIZATION OF FUNDS FROM GRANTS TO ENCOURAGE STATE POLICIES AND ENFORCEMENT OF PROTECTION ORDERS PROGRAM.—Section 2101 of the Omnibus Crime Control and Safe Streets Act of 1968 (42 U.S.C. 3796hh) is amended by striking subsection (e) and inserting the following:

"(e) Not less than 10 percent of the total amount available under this section for each fiscal year shall be available for grants under the program authorized in section 2007. The requirements of this part shall not apply to funds allocated for such program."

"(d) AUTHORIZATION OF FUNDS FROM RURAL DOMESTIC VIOLENCE AND CHILD ABUSE ENFORCEMENT ASSISTANCE GRANTS.—Subsection 40295(c) of the Violence Against Women Act of 1994 (42 U.S.C. 13971(c)(3)) is amended by striking paragraph (3) and inserting the following:

"(3) Not less than 10 percent of the total amount available under this section for each fiscal year shall be available for grants under the program authorized in section 2007 of the Omnibus Crime Control and Safe Streets Act of 1968. The requirements of this paragraph shall not apply to funds allocated for such program."

"(e) AUTHORIZATION OF FUNDS FROM THE SAFE HAVENS FOR CHILDREN

PROGRAM.—Section 1301 of the Violence Against Women Act of 2000 (42 U.S.C. 10420) is amended by striking subsection (f) and inserting the following:

"(f) Not less than 10 percent of the total amount available under this section for each fiscal year shall be available for grants under the program authorized in section 2007 of the Omnibus Crime Control and Safe Streets Act of 1968. The requirements of this subsection shall not apply to funds allocated for such program."

(f) AUTHORIZATION OF FUNDS FROM THE TRANSITIONAL HOUSING ASSISTANCE GRANTS FOR CHILD VICTIMS OF DOMESTIC VIOLENCE, STALKING, OR SEXUAL ASSAULT PROGRAM.—Section 40299(g) of the Violence Against Women Act of 1994 (42 U.S.C. 13975(g)) is amended by adding at the end the following:

"(4) TRIBAL PROGRAM.—Not less than 10 percent of the total amount available under this section for each fiscal year shall be available for grants under the program authorized in section 2007 of the Omnibus Crime Control and Safe Streets Act of 1968. The requirements of this paragraph shall not apply to funds allocated for such program."

(g) AUTHORIZATION OF FUNDS FROM THE LEGAL ASSISTANCE FOR VICTIMS IMPROVEMENTS PROGRAM.—Section 1201(f) of the Violence Against Women Act of 2000 (42 U.S.C. 3796gg–6) is amended by adding at the end the following:

"(4) Not less than 10 percent of the total amount available under this section for each fiscal year shall be available for grants under the program authorized in section 2007 of the Omnibus Crime Control and Safe Streets Act of 1968. The requirements of this paragraph shall not apply to funds allocated for such program."

SEC. 907. TRIBAL DEPUTY IN THE OFFICE ON VIOLENCE AGAINST WOMEN.

Part T of title I of the Omnibus Crime Control and Safe Streets Act of 1968 (42 U.S.C. 3796gg

et seq.), as amended by section 906, is amended by adding at the end the following:

"SEC. 2008. TRIBAL DEPUTY.

"(a) ESTABLISHMENT.—There is established in the Office on Violence Against Women a Deputy Director for Tribal Affairs.

"(b) DUTIES.—

"(1) IN GENERAL.—The Deputy Director shall under the guidance and authority of the Director of the Office on Violence Against Women—

"(A) oversee and manage the administration of grants to and contracts with Indian tribes, tribal courts, tribal organizations, or tribal nonprofit organizations;

"(B) ensure that, if a grant under this Act or a contract pursuant to such a grant is made to an organization to perform services that benefit more than 1 Indian tribe, the approval of each Indian tribe to be benefitted shall be a prerequisite to the making of the grant or letting of the contract;

"(C) coordinate development of Federal policy, protocols, and guidelines on matters relating to violence against Indian women;

"(D) advise the Director of the Office on Violence Against Women concerning policies, legislation, implementation of laws, and other issues relating to violence against Indian women;

"(E) represent the Office on Violence Against Women In the annual consultations under section 903;

"(F) provide technical assistance, coordination, and support to other offices and bureaus in the Department of Justice to develop policy and to enforce Federal laws relating to violence against Indian women, including through litigation of civil and criminal actions relating to those laws;

"(G) maintain a liaison with the judicial branches of Federal, State, and tribal governments on matters relating to violence against Indian women;

"(H) support enforcement of tribal protection orders and implementation of full faith and credit educational projects and comity agreements between Indian tribes and States; and

"(I) ensure that adequate tribal technical assistance is made available to Indian tribes, tribal courts, tribal organizations, and tribal nonprofit organizations for all programs relating to violence against Indian women.

"(c) AUTHORITY.—

"(1) IN GENERAL.—The Deputy Director shall ensure that a portion of the tribal set-aside funds from any grant awarded under this Act, the Violence Against Women Act of 1994 (title IV of Public Law 103–322; 108 Stat. 1902), or the Violence Against Women Act of 2000 (division B of Public Law 106–386; 114 Stat. 1491) is used to enhance the capacity of Indian tribes to address the safety of Indian women.

"(2) ACCOUNTABILITY.—The Deputy Director shall ensure that some portion of the tribal set-aside funds from any grant made under this part is used to hold offenders accountable through—

"(A) enhancement of the response of Indian tribes to crimes of domestic violence, dating violence, sexual assault, and stalking against Indian women, including legal services for victims and Indian-specific offender programs;

"(B) development and maintenance of tribal domestic violence shelters or programs for battered Indian women, including sexual assault services, that are based upon the unique circumstances of the Indian women to be served;

"(C) development of tribal educational awareness programs and materials;

"(D) support for customary tribal activities to strengthen the intolerance of an Indian tribe to violence against Indian women; and

"(E) development, implementation, and maintenance of tribal electronic databases for tribal protection order registries."

SEC. 908. ENHANCED CRIMINAL LAW RESOURCES.

(a) FIREARMS POSSESSION PROHIBITIONS. —Section 921(33)(A)(i) of title 18, United States Code, is amended to read: "(i) is a misdemeanor under Federal, State, or Tribal law; and".

(b) LAW ENFORCEMENT AUTHORITY.— Section 4(3) of the Indian Law Enforcement Reform Act (25 U.S.C. 2803(3) is amended—

1. in subparagraph (A), by striking "or";
2. in subparagraph (B), by striking the semicolon and inserting ", or"; and
3. by adding at the end the following:

"(C) the offense is a misdemeanor crime of domestic violence, dating violence, stalking, or violation of a protection order and has, as an element, the use or attempted use of physical force, or the threatened use of a deadly weapon, committed by a current or former spouse, parent, or guardian of the victim, by a person with whom the victim shares a child in common, by a person who is cohabitating with or has cohabited with the victim as a spouse, parent, or guardian, or by a person similarly situated to a spouse, parent or guardian of the victim, and the employee has reasonable grounds to believe that the person to be arrested has committed, or is committing the crime."

SEC. 909. DOMESTIC ASSAULT BY AN HABITUAL OFFENDER.

Chapter 7 of title 18, United States Code, is amended by adding at the end the following:

"§ 117. DOMESTIC ASSAULT BY AN HABITUAL OFFENDER

"(a) IN GENERAL.—Any person who commits a domestic assault within the special maritime and territorial jurisdiction of the United States or Indian country and who has a final conviction on at least 2 separate prior occasions in Federal, State, or Indian tribal court proceedings for offenses that would be, if subject to Federal jurisdiction—

"(1) any assault, sexual abuse, or serious violent felony against a spouse or intimate partner; or

"(2) an offense under chapter 110A, shall be fined under this title, imprisoned for a term of not more than 5 years, or both, except that if substantial bodily injury results from violation under this section, the offender shall be imprisoned for a term of not more than 10 years.

"(b) DOMESTIC ASSAULT DEFINED.—In this section, the term 'domestic assault' means an assault committed by a current or former spouse, parent, child, or guardian of the victim, by a person with whom the victim shares a child in common, by a person who is cohabitating with or has cohabitated with the victim as a spouse, parent, child, or guardian, or by a person similarly situated to a spouse, parent, child, or guardian of the victim."

Source: Title IX, Safety for Indian Women, Violence Against Women Act (VAWA).

Declaration on the Rights of Indigenous Peoples
(2006)

The Declaration on the Rights of Indigenous Peoples sets out the individual and collective rights of indigenous peoples around the world. It establishes their rights to culture, employment, identity, language, education, health, and other important issues. The document also stresses the rights of indigenous peoples to preserve and even strengthen their own institutions, cultures, and traditions, and to pursue their development in keeping with their own wants and ambitions. One of the major aspects of this declaration is its stance on the discrimination of indigenous peoples. The declaration also promotes the complete and effective involvement of indigenous groups in all areas that concern them and their fundamental right to remain distinct and to pursue their economic and social development goals. On December 16, 2010, President Barack Obama held a press conference at which he stated that the United States agreed to sign this document.

The General Assembly,

Taking note of the recommendation of the Human Rights Council contained in its resolution 1/2 of 29 June 2006, by which the Council adopted the text of the United Nations Declaration on the Rights of Indigenous Peoples, Recalling its resolution 61/178 of 20 December 2006, by which it decided to defer consideration of and action on the Declaration to allow time for further consultations thereon, and also decided to conclude its consideration before the end of the sixty-first session of the General Assembly,

Adopts the United Nations Declaration on the Rights of Indigenous Peoples as contained in the annex to the present resolution.

Article 1

Indigenous peoples have the right to the full enjoyment, as a collective or as individuals, of all human rights and fundamental freedoms as recognized in the Charter of the United Nations, the Universal Declaration of Human Rights and international human rights law.

Article 2

Indigenous peoples and individuals are free and equal to all other peoples and individuals and have the right to be free from any kind of discrimination, in the exercise of their rights, in particular that based on their indigenous origin or identity.

Article 3

Indigenous peoples have the right to self-determination. By virtue of that right they freely determine their political status and freely pursue their economic, social and cultural development.

Article 4

Indigenous peoples, in exercising their right to self-determination, have the right to autonomy or self-government in matters relating to their internal and local affairs, as well as ways and means for financing their autonomous functions.

Article 5

Indigenous peoples have the right to maintain and strengthen their distinct political, legal, economic, social and cultural institutions, while retaining their right to participate fully, if they so choose, in the political, economic, social and cultural life of the State.

Article 6

Every indigenous individual has the right to a nationality.

Article 7

Indigenous individuals have the rights to life, physical and mental integrity, liberty and security of person.

Indigenous peoples have the collective right to live in freedom, peace and security as distinct peoples and shall not be subjected to any act of genocide or any other act of violence, including forcibly removing children of the group to another group.

Article 8

Indigenous peoples and individuals have the right not to be subjected to forced assimilation or destruction of their culture.

States shall provide effective mechanisms for prevention of, and redress for:

Any action which has the aim or effect of depriving them of their integrity as distinct peoples, or of their cultural values or ethnic identities;
Any action which has the aim or effect of dispossessing them of their lands, territories or resources;

Any form of forced population transfer which has the aim or effect of violating or undermining any of their rights;
Any form of forced assimilation or integration;
Any form of propaganda designed to promote or incite racial or ethnic discrimination directed against them.

Article 9

Indigenous peoples and individuals have the right to belong to an indigenous community or nation, in accordance with the traditions and customs of the community or nation concerned. No discrimination of any kind may arise from the exercise of such a right.

Article 10

Indigenous peoples shall not be forcibly removed from their lands or territories. No relocation shall take place without the free, prior and informed consent of the indigenous peoples concerned and after agreement on just and fair compensation and, where possible, with the option of return.

Article 11

Indigenous peoples have the right to practise and revitalize their cultural traditions and customs. This includes the right to maintain, protect and develop the past, present and future manifestations of their cultures, such as archaeological and historical sites, artefacts, designs, ceremonies, technologies and visual and performing arts and literature.

States shall provide redress through effective mechanisms, which may include restitution, developed in conjunction with indigenous peoples, with respect to their cultural, intellectual, religious and spiritual property taken without their free, prior and informed consent or in violation of their laws, traditions and customs.

Article 12

Indigenous peoples have the right to manifest, practice, develop and teach their spiritual and religious traditions, customs and ceremonies; the right to maintain, protect, and have access in privacy to their religious and cultural sites; the right to the use and control of their ceremonial objects; and the right to the repatriation of their human remains.

States shall seek to enable the access and/or repatriation of ceremonial objects and human remains in their possession through fair, transparent and effective mechanisms developed in conjunction with indigenous peoples concerned.

Article 13

Indigenous peoples have the right to revitalize, use, develop and transmit to future generations their histories, languages, oral traditions, philosophies, writing systems and literatures, and to designate and retain their own names for communities, places and persons.

States shall take effective measures to ensure that this right is protected and also to ensure that indigenous peoples can understand and be understood in political, legal and administrative proceedings, where necessary through the provision of interpretation or by other appropriate means.

Article 14

Indigenous peoples have the right to establish and control their educational systems and institutions providing education in their own languages, in a manner appropriate to their cultural methods of teaching and learning.

Indigenous individuals, particularly children, have the right to all levels and forms of education of the State without discrimination.

States shall, in conjunction with indigenous peoples, take effective measures, in order for indigenous individuals, particularly children, including those living outside their communities, to have access, when possible, to an education in their own culture and provided in their own language.

Article 15

Indigenous peoples have the right to the dignity and diversity of their cultures, traditions, histories and aspirations which shall be appropriately reflected in education and public information.

States shall take effective measures, in consultation and cooperation with the indigenous peoples concerned, to combat prejudice and eliminate discrimination and to promote tolerance, understanding and good relations among indigenous peoples and all other segments of society.

Article 16

Indigenous peoples have the right to establish their own media in their own languages and to have access to all forms of non-indigenous media without discrimination.

States shall take effective measures to ensure that State-owned media duly reflect indigenous cultural diversity. States, without prejudice to ensuring full freedom of expression, should encourage privately owned media to adequately reflect indigenous cultural diversity.

Article 17

Indigenous individuals and peoples have the right to enjoy fully all rights established under applicable international and domestic labour law.

States shall in consultation and cooperation with indigenous peoples take specific measures to protect indigenous children from economic exploitation and from performing any work that is likely to be hazardous or to interfere with the child's education, or to be harmful to the child's health or physical, mental, spiritual, moral or social development, taking into account their special vulnerability and the importance of education for their empowerment.

Indigenous individuals have the right not to be subjected to any discriminatory conditions of labour and, inter alia, employment or salary.

Article 18

Indigenous peoples have the right to participate in decision-making in matters which would affect their rights, through representatives chosen by themselves in accordance with their own procedures, as well as to maintain and develop their own indigenous decision-making institutions.

Article 19

States shall consult and cooperate in good faith with the indigenous peoples concerned through their own representative institutions in order to obtain their free, prior and informed consent before adopting and implementing legislative or administrative measures that may affect them.

Article 20

Indigenous peoples have the right to maintain and develop their political, economic and social systems or institutions, to be secure in the enjoyment of their own means of subsistence and development, and to engage freely in all their traditional and other economic activities.

Indigenous peoples deprived of their means of subsistence and development are entitled to just and fair redress.

Article 21

Indigenous peoples have the right, without discrimination, to the improvement of their economic and social conditions, including, inter alia, in the areas of education, employment, vocational training and retraining, housing, sanitation, health and social security.

States shall take effective measures and, where appropriate, special measures to ensure continuing improvement of their economic and social conditions.

Article 22

Particular attention shall be paid to the rights and special needs of indigenous elders, women, youth, children and persons with disabilities in the implementation of this Declaration.

States shall take measures, in conjunction with indigenous peoples, to ensure that indigenous women and children enjoy the full protection and guarantees against all forms of violence and discrimination.

Article 23

Indigenous peoples have the right to determine and develop priorities and strategies for exercising their right to development. In particular, indigenous peoples have the right to be actively involved in developing and determining health, housing and other economic and social programmes affecting them and, as far as possible, to administer such programmes through their own institutions.

Article 24

Indigenous peoples have the right to their traditional medicines and to maintain their health practices, including the conservation of their vital medicinal plants, animals and minerals. Indigenous individuals also have the right to access, without any discrimination, to all social and health services.

Indigenous individuals have an equal right to the enjoyment of the highest attainable standard of physical and mental health. States shall take the necessary steps with a view to achieving progressively the full realization of this right.

Article 25

Indigenous peoples have the right to maintain and strengthen their distinctive spiritual relationship with their traditionally owned or otherwise occupied and used lands, territories, waters and coastal seas and other resources and to uphold their responsibilities to future generations in this regard.

Article 26

Indigenous peoples have the right to the lands, territories and resources which they have traditionally owned, occupied or otherwise used or acquired.

Indigenous peoples have the right to own, use, develop and control the lands, territories and resources that they possess by reason of traditional ownership or other traditional occupation or use, as well as those which they have otherwise acquired.

States shall give legal recognition and protection to these lands, territories and resources. Such recognition shall be conducted with due respect to the customs, traditions and land tenure systems of the indigenous peoples concerned.

Article 27

States shall establish and implement, in conjunction with indigenous peoples concerned, a fair, independent, impartial, open and transparent process, giving due recognition to indigenous peoples' laws, traditions, customs and land tenure systems, to recognize and adjudicate the rights of indigenous peoples pertaining to their lands, territories and resources, including those which were traditionally owned or otherwise occupied or used. Indigenous peoples shall have the right to participate in this process.

Article 28

Indigenous peoples have the right to redress, by means that can include restitution or, when this is not possible, just, fair and equitable compensation, for the lands, territories and resources which they have traditionally owned or otherwise occupied or used, and which have been confiscated, taken, occupied, used or damaged without their free, prior and informed consent.

Unless otherwise freely agreed upon by the peoples concerned, compensation shall take the form of lands, territories and resources equal in quality, size and legal status or of monetary compensation or other appropriate redress.

Article 29

Indigenous peoples have the right to the conservation and protection of the environment and the productive capacity of their lands or territories and resources. States shall establish and implement assistance programmes for indigenous peoples for such conservation and protection, without discrimination.

States shall take effective measures to ensure that no storage or disposal of hazardous materials shall take place in the lands or territories of indigenous peoples without their free, prior and informed consent.

States shall also take effective measures to ensure, as needed, that programmes for monitoring, maintaining and restoring the health of indigenous peoples, as developed and implemented by the peoples affected by such materials, are duly implemented.

Article 30

Military activities shall not take place in the lands or territories of indigenous peoples, unless justified by a significant threat to relevant public interest or otherwise freely agreed with or requested by the indigenous peoples concerned.

States shall undertake effective consultations with the indigenous peoples concerned, through appropriate procedures and in particular through their representative institutions, prior to using their lands or territories for military activities.

Article 31

Indigenous peoples have the right to maintain, control, protect and develop their cultural heritage, traditional knowledge and traditional cultural expressions, as well as the manifestations of their sciences, technologies and cultures, including human and genetic resources, seeds, medicines, knowledge of the properties of fauna and flora, oral traditions, literatures, designs, sports and traditional games and visual and performing arts. They also have the right to maintain, control, protect and develop their intellectual property over such cultural heritage, traditional knowledge, and traditional cultural expressions.

In conjunction with indigenous peoples, States shall take effective measures to recognize and protect the exercise of these rights.

Article 32

Indigenous peoples have the right to determine and develop priorities and strategies for the development or use of their lands or territories and other resources.

States shall consult and cooperate in good faith with the indigenous peoples concerned through their own representative institutions in order to obtain their free and informed consent prior to the approval of any project affecting their lands or territories and other resources, particularly in connection with the development, utilization or exploitation of mineral, water or other resources.

States shall provide effective mechanisms for just and fair redress for any such activities, and appropriate measures shall be taken to mitigate adverse environmental, economic, social, cultural or spiritual impact.

Article 33

Indigenous peoples have the right to determine their own identity or membership in accordance with their customs and traditions. This does not impair the right of indigenous individuals to obtain citizenship of the States in which they live.

Indigenous peoples have the right to determine the structures and to select the membership of their institutions in accordance with their own procedures.

Article 34

Indigenous peoples have the right to promote, develop and maintain their institutional structures and their distinctive customs, spirituality, traditions, procedures, practices and, in the cases where they exist, juridical systems or customs, in accordance with international human rights standards.

Article 35

Indigenous peoples have the right to determine the responsibilities of individuals to their communities.

Article 36

Indigenous peoples, in particular those divided by international borders, have the right to maintain and develop contacts, relations and cooperation, including activities for spiritual, cultural, political, economic and social purposes, with their own members as well as other peoples across borders.

States, in consultation and cooperation with indigenous peoples, shall take effective measures to facilitate the exercise and ensure the implementation of this right.

Article 37

Indigenous peoples have the right to the recognition, observance and enforcement of treaties, agreements and other constructive arrangements concluded with States or their successors and to have States honour and respect such treaties, agreements and other constructive arrangements.

Nothing in this Declaration may be interpreted as diminishing or eliminating the rights of indigenous peoples contained in treaties, agreements and other constructive arrangements.

Article 38

States in consultation and cooperation with indigenous peoples, shall take the appropriate measures, including legislative measures, to achieve the ends of this Declaration.

Article 39

Indigenous peoples have the right to have access to financial and technical assistance from States and through international cooperation, for the enjoyment of the rights contained in this Declaration.

Article 40

Indigenous peoples have the right to access to and prompt decision through just and fair procedures for the resolution of conflicts and disputes with States or other parties, as well as to effective remedies for all infringements of their individual and collective rights. Such a decision shall give due consideration to the customs, traditions, rules and legal systems of the indigenous peoples concerned and international human rights.

Article 41

The organs and specialized agencies of the United Nations system and other intergovernmental organizations shall contribute to the full realization of the provisions of this Declaration through the mobilization, inter alia, of financial cooperation and technical assistance. Ways and means of ensuring participation of indigenous peoples on issues affecting them shall be established.

Article 42

The United Nations, its bodies, including the Permanent Forum on Indigenous Issues, and specialized agencies, including at the country level, and States shall promote respect for and full application of the provisions of this Declaration and follow up the effectiveness of this Declaration.

Article 43

The rights recognized herein constitute the minimum standards for the survival, dignity and well-being of the indigenous peoples of the world.

Article 44

All the rights and freedoms recognized herein are equally guaranteed to male and female indigenous individuals.

Article 45

Nothing in this Declaration may be construed as diminishing or extinguishing the rights indigenous peoples have now or may acquire in the future.

Article 46

Nothing in this Declaration may be interpreted as implying for any State, people, group or person any right to engage in any activity or to perform any act contrary to the Charter of the United Nations or construed as authorizing or encouraging any action which would dismember or impair, totally or in part, the territorial integrity or political unity of sovereign and independent States.

In the exercise of the rights enunciated in the present Declaration, human rights and fundamental freedoms of all shall be respected. The exercise of the rights set forth in this Declaration shall be subject only to such limitations as are determined by law, and in accordance with international human rights obligations. Any such limitations shall be non-discriminatory and strictly necessary solely for the purpose of securing due recognition and respect for the rights and freedoms of others and for meeting the just and most compelling requirements of a democratic society.

The provisions set forth in this Declaration shall be interpreted in accordance with the principles of justice, democracy, respect for human rights, equality, non-discrimination, good governance and good faith.

Source: Declaration on the Rights of Indigenous Peoples, 2006. http://www.un.org/esa/socdev/unpfii/en/drip.html.

Native American $1 Coin Act

(2007)

The Native American $1 Coin Act was passed on September 20, 2007. This law requires the U.S. Treasury to mint one $1 coin every year honoring Native Americans. Every coin will feature Sacagawea, the Shoshone woman who acted as a guide for the Lewis and Clark expedition, as a remaining figure. The obverse face will have a different design each year, "celebrating the important contributions made by Indian tribes and individual Native Americans to the development of the United States." The program went into effect in 2009.

PUBLIC LAW 110 82 SEPT. 20, 2007 121 STAT. 777 PUBLIC LAW 110–82 110TH CONGRESS

An Act to require the Secretary of the Treasury to mint and issue coins in commemoration of Native

Americans and the important contributions made by Indian tribes and individual Native Americans to the development of the United States and the history of the United States, and for other purposes. Sept. 20, 2007 [H.R. 2358]

Be it enacted by the Senate and House of Representatives of the United States of America in Congress assembled,

SECTION 1. SHORT TITLE.

This Act may be cited as the "Native American $1 Coin Act". Native American $1 Coin Act. 31 USC 5101 note.

SEC. 2. NATIVE AMERICAN $1 COIN PROGRAM.

Section 5112 of title 31, United States Code, is amended by adding at the end the following:

"(r) REDESIGN AND ISSUANCE OF CIRCULATING $1 COINS HONORING NATIVE AMERICANS AND THE IMPORTANT CONTRIBUTIONS MADE BY INDIAN TRIBES AND INDIVIDUAL NATIVE AMERICANS IN UNITED STATES HISTORY.—

"(1) REDESIGN BEGINNING IN 2008.—

"(A) IN GENERAL.—Effective beginning January 1, 2008, notwithstanding subsection (d), in addition to the coins to be issued pursuant to subsection (n), and in accordance with this subsection, the Secretary shall mint and issue $1 coins that—

"(i) have as the designs on the obverse the so called 'Sacagawea design'; and

"(ii) have a design on the reverse selected in accordance with paragraph (2)(A), subject to paragraph (3)(A).

"(B) DELAYED DATE.—If the date of the enactment of the Native American $1 Coin Act is after August 25, 2007, subparagraph (A) shall be applied by substituting '2009' for '2008'.

"(2) DESIGN REQUIREMENTS.—The $1 coins issued in accordance with paragraph (1) shall meet the following design requirements:

"(A) COIN REVERSE.—The design on the reverse shall bear—

"(i) images celebrating the important contributions made by Indian tribes and individual Native Americans to the development of the United States and the history of the United States;

"(ii) the inscription '$1'; and

"(iii) the inscription 'United States of America'.

"(B) COIN OBVERSE.—The design on the obverse shall—

"(i) be chosen by the Secretary, after consultation with the Commission of Fine Arts and review by the Citizens Coinage Advisory Committee; and

"(ii) contain the so-called 'Sacagawea design' and the inscription 'Liberty'.

"(C) EDGE-INCUSED INSCRIPTIONS.—

"(i) IN GENERAL.—The inscription of the year of minting and issuance of the coin and the inscriptions 'E Pluribus Unum' and 'In God We Trust' shall be edge-incused into the coin.

"(ii) PRESERVATION OF DISTINCTIVE EDGE.—The edge-incusing of the inscriptions under clause (i) on coins issued under this subsection shall be done in a manner that preserves the distinctive edge of the coin so that the denomination of the coin is readily discernible, including by individuals who are blind or visually impaired.

"(D) REVERSE DESIGN SELECTION.—The designs selected for the reverse of the coins described under this subsection—

"(i) shall be chosen by the Secretary after consultation with the Committee on Indian Affairs of the Senate, the Congressional Native

American Caucus of the House of Representatives, the Commission of Fine Arts, and the National Congress of American Indians;

"(ii) shall be reviewed by the Citizens Coinage Advisory Committee;

"(iii) may depict individuals and events such as—

"(I) the creation of Cherokee written language;

"(II) the Iroquois Confederacy;

"(III) Wampanoag Chief Massasoit;

"(IV) the 'Pueblo Revolt';

"(V) Olympian Jim Thorpe;

"(VI) Ely S. Parker, a general on the staff of General Ulysses S. Grant and later head of the Bureau of Indian Affairs; and

"(VII) code talkers who served the United States Armed Forces during World War I and World War II; and

"(iv) in the case of a design depicting the contribution of an individual Native American to the development of the United States and the history of the United States, shall not depict the individual in a size such that the coin could be considered to be a '2-headed' coin.

"(3) ISSUANCE OF COINS COMMEMORATING 1 NATIVE AMERICAN EVENT DURING EACH YEAR.—

"(A) IN GENERAL.—Each design for the reverse of the $1 coins issued during each year shall be emblematic of 1 important Native American or Native American contribution each year.

"(B) ISSUANCE PERIOD.—Each $1 coin minted with a design on the reverse in accordance with this subsection for any year shall be issued during the 1-year period beginning on January 1 of that year and shall be available throughout the entire 1-year period.

"(C) ORDER OF ISSUANCE OF DESIGNS.— Each coin issued under this subsection commemorating Native Americans and their contributions—

"(i) shall be issued, to the maximum extent practicable, in the chronological order in which the

Native Americans lived or the events occurred, until the termination of the coin program described in subsection (n); and

"(ii) thereafter shall be issued in any order determined to be appropriate by the Secretary, after consultation with the Committee on Indian Affairs of the Senate, the Congressional Native American Caucus of the House of Representatives, and the National Congress of American Indians.

"(4) ISSUANCE OF NUMISMATIC COINS.— The Secretary may mint and issue such number of $1 coins of each design selected under this subsection in uncirculated and proof qualities as the Secretary determines to be appropriate.

"(5) QUANTITY.—The number of $1 coins minted and issued in a year with the Sacagawea-design on the obverse shall be not less than 20 percent of the total number of $1 coins minted and issued in such year".

SEC. 3. TECHNICAL AND CONFORMING AMENDMENTS.

Section 5112(n)(1) of title 31, United States Code, is amended—

(1) by striking the paragraph designation and heading and all that follows through "Notwithstanding subsection (d)" and inserting the following:

"(1) REDESIGN BEGINNING IN 2007.— Notwithstanding subsection (d)";

(2) by striking subparagraph (B); and (3) by redesignating clauses (i) and (ii) as subparagraphs (A) and (B), respectively, and indenting the subparagraphs appropriately.

SEC. 4. REMOVAL OF BARRIERS TO CIRCULATION OF $1 COIN. 31 USC 5112 NOTE.

(a) IN GENERAL.—In order to remove barriers to circulation, the Secretary of the Treasury shall carry out an aggressive, cost effective, continuing campaign to encourage commercial enterprises to accept and dispense $1 coins that have as designs on the obverse the so-called "Sacagawea design".

(b) REPORT.—The Secretary of the Treasury shall submit to Congress an annual report on the success of the efforts described in subsection (a).

Approved September 20, 2007.

Source: H.R. 2358: *Congressional Record*, Vol. 153 (2007).

Lieutenant Bill Cody Ayon (Southern Cheyenne), New Mexico National Guard, Interviewed at Camp Cropper, Iraq
(September 16, 2007)

Native Americans have served in the U.S. military for more than two centuries and have made significant contributions to the defense of this nation. The wars in Iraq and Afghanistan are no exception, as many Native Americans continue to serve as members of America's armed forces. The following interview is with Lieutenant Bill Cody Ayon, a member of the Southern Cheyenne Nation who was serving in Iraq in 2007.

These ceremonies and returning ceremonies are to cleanse the person before they leave, so they know that they are supported at home, which makes their job a little bit easier when they leave. And also when they return home as a purification rite, showing that all the bad they've seen or all the hurt they have felt or all the evil that surrounded them in whatever portion of the world they may have been in, or what situation they may have been in, is left behind. Like one of my uncles used to say, "It follows them like a shadow cast off. It's behind them now."

By all the family coming together and helping send you off this way, and helping you come back in the same fashion, returning the same way, it reassures the service member he's not alone in this fight. Because when a warrior goes off, he goes off to defend his way of life, to defend what is our culture, what is deemed our way of being, our way of living. And when he returns, he needs to be brought back into that circle, into that light. By having all people around him support him in this manner, it's a cleansing aspect.

We sing Dog Soldier songs in the sweat lodge. Dog Soldier songs are very old. They were passed on to my father and his wife. And these songs are sung in times of great need, and great strength is needed to do something like this. My father and his wife sing these songs for me in the sweat lodge, so that I will have the courage to do what I have to do. Also, we sing many songs in the sweat for strength, for endurance that we'll need in the days to come.

When I stepped off to leave from our home and came over on this deployment, I was blessed with my father's eagle fan, and he said prayers over me with my family around me in a circle. And I feel that power that is created from their love and appreciation of what I'm doing, and from what other service members are doing.

I feel it is an honor to defend what is America now. Because it is where our people and where my family resides. Therefore, I am still carrying on the tradition that was passed on to us, which is to defend our homeland. That aspect hasn't changed. Whether it is an American flag or a camp circle of lodges. That unique representation has always been there inside me. To me there is no irony in that. There is only honor in defending what is yours, what is your way of life. The old ones did that because they felt they were being encroached upon and their lifestyle was threatened. The way they thought the world to be was threatened. So they fought for their very lives against overwhelming odds. And that is to be honored. As we see throughout history that people are subdued, or conquered if you will.

But their spirit never is. The spirit of that culture never is. I don't think there is a Cheyenne today that will tell you that we were conquered. I won't tell you that, and I don't expect any other Cheyenne to tell you that. Tricked, duped, maybe. That is a whole different ball of wax. But no, I feel no irony in defending my country and defending my way of life and my people and my family. I feel no irony in that. Like I said, I see only honor. And I'm glad to see my people still respect that. Whether it's a warrior for the United States flag or it's a warrior for the Cheyenne people. That is what it is to be honored. That is what it is to be a warrior.

We as Cheyenne people aren't going out to pick a fight. But when you come pick a fight, we bring a fight. And that is what I love about our culture. And whether you believe it or not, that is the same culture that America is built on. And I think that is why Native Americans hold close to that ideal.

I think that when you come from a society or a family like mine, where they raise you in this fashion, where they honor you to be in the military and serve your country, that's what you are supposed to do. To defend this country and defend your tribe and defend your people and your land, you are supposed to do that. You are supposed to give yourself for the betterment of the people and the betterment of man. I feel that when you go into something with that mind-set, you are light-years above a young man who might come into the service and say, "I did this for college money."

When you have eighteen years behind you, your family telling you every day, this is how a warrior is, these are the people you come from, look at the battles they fought, look at the trials they faced. You can stand up in front of a person like that and say, "This isn't that big of a deal." And when I return home, I'll be a stronger man because of it.

I would like to tell you the story of Two Twist. It was one of the first stories I was ever taught in my tribe. If you listen to the story, you will understand why I think the way I do.

It pretty much sums it up:

Long before the United States had conquered the western half of the United States, when our tribe was roaming free, there was a man and his name was Red Robe. Red Robe lost two sons in a conflict with our enemy the Crow. Because of this, he gave all that he had away. He was in mourning. He had a lot of horses, a lot of wealth for the time. He had a prominent family. He was an elder who was revered in the tribe. He gave everything away. He didn't want anything. He pretty much lived homeless.

The warrior societies in our tribe—the Bow String, the Fox, the Dog Soldiers, the Elk—they all came together and asked him to come back to the camp. Because he was living on the outskirts, away from the people. He didn't want to be a part of people's life.

They came together and honored this elder and asked him to come back. He still refused. He said that his sons had died and he was in mourning for them. The societies told him, "Your sons died in the best way that a Cheyenne ever could. And that is to die in battle. He didn't live to be an old man. He didn't live to die of sickness. Your sons died defending their people, their way of life, which is the warrior culture of our tribe."

There was a soldier, a leader of one of the societies, the Bow String Society. His name was Two Twist. Two Twist made a vow, a pledge that he would lead the tribe against the Crow. He would die in battle. This would be the last battle on earth. All the tribe at that time vowed to go with him when he made this pledge.

The tribe moved against the Crow in mass formation. Two Twist led the Cheyenne against the Crow. And the Crow scouts saw they were coming and dug in. They knew they were surrounded in this valley where they were at. The Cheyenne let up. Two Twist led the tribe. He sang his war songs. His Bow String war songs. Made his pledge that he would never walk on this earth again. And all he had was a weapon that he had captured from the enemy. He had a saber. And he led the tribe into battle on his pony with this saber, and nothing else. He charged into the Crow. And he made all the rest of the people stay back until he went first into the fight.

He jumped into the breastworks of the Crow and fought by himself. The people saw him go down in the dust. He was dragged down as he was fighting his way through the enemy. At that time, the Cheyenne moved forward, surrounded the Crow and scattered the Crow to the wind. And beat back their enemy and destroyed them.

Two Twist lived through this battle. They found him, and he was still alive. From that day on, he was revered as a great warrior and a tribal leader. Which he became later on in life. The people never let him fight again because he had made this vow for another man.

Red Robe took him as his son. Red Robe honored him. Red Robe told the rest of the people that in this way you honor those who go to combat for you, that go to war for you.

By telling you this story, I want to show you that we as native people, as Cheyenne, still do that to this day. People such as myself and my family and my loved ones and people I know have come forth to represent our country in times of need like this. When we come back home, our families carry on that tradition that Red Robe did. He was honored that Two Twist went to fight for him, to die for him. In this way, you give them honor, the support, the recognition they need. Just as in the old days. Two Twist was one of the greatest warriors our tribe has ever known. Because of this, our people move forward in that same fashion to this day.

Source: Clevenger, Steven. *America's First Warriors: Native Americans and Iraq.* Santa Fe: Museum of New Mexico Press, 2010. Reprinted with permission.

Cobell v. Salazar
(2009)

Cobell v. Salazar *(2009) is a court case concerning the U.S. government's management of more than 300,000 individual Native American trust accounts. In 1996, Elouise Cobell, along with three other persons, led a class-action lawsuit to recover millions of dollars of leases and royalties supposed to be held in trust by the Bureau of Indian Affairs (BIA) and paid out to individual and tribe owners. Under the Dawes Act (1887), her family, like many other Native American families, had been told that the government would lease a portion of their allotment to bring them income. When the BIA was unable to provide Cobell with a financial statement of income earned, Cobell filed a lawsuit that would last 14 years. On December 7, 2009,* Cobell *accepted a settlement of $1.4 billion. On December 8, 2010, President Barack Obama signed legislation approving funding for the settlement. Excerpted here from the* Cobell v. Salazar *(2010) Class Action Settlement Agreement are the "Background" and "Terms of Agreement" between the two parties.*

IN THE UNITED STATES DISTRICT COURT FOR THE DISTRICT OF COLUMBIA
ELOUISE PEPION COBELL, et al., Plaintiffs, vs. KEN SALAZAR, Secretary of the Interior, et al., Defendants.
Case No. 1:96CV01285-JR
December 7, 2009
US2000 11623208.1

CLASS ACTION SETTLEMENT AGREEMENT

This Class Action Settlement Agreement ("Agreement") is entered into by and between Elouise Pepion Cobell, Penny Cleghorn, Thomas Maulson and James Louis Larose (collectively, the "Named Plaintiffs"), on behalf of themselves and members of the Classes of individual Indians defined in this Agreement (collectively, "Plaintiffs"), on the one hand, and Ken Salazar, Secretary of the Interior, Larry Echohawk, Assistant Secretary of the Interior – Indian Affairs, and H. Timothy Geithner, Secretary of the Treasury and their successors in office, all in their official capacities (collectively, "Defendants"). Plaintiffs and Defendants are collectively referenced as the "Parties."

Subject to Court approval as required by Federal Rule of Civil Procedure ("FRCP") 23, the Parties hereby stipulate and agree that, in consideration of the promises and covenants set forth in this Agreement and upon entry by the Court of a Final Order and Judgment and resolution of any appeals from that Final Order and Judgment, this Action shall be settled and compromised in accordance with the terms of this Agreement.

The Parties agree that the Settlement is contingent on the enactment of legislation to authorize or confirm specific aspects of the Settlement as set forth below. If such legislation, which will expressly reference this Agreement, is not enacted on or before the Legislation Enactment Deadline as defined in this Agreement, unless such date is mutually agreed to be extended by the Parties, or is enacted with material changes, the Agreement shall automatically become null and void.

BACKGROUND

1. On June 10, 1996, a class action complaint (the "Complaint") was filed in the United States District Court for the District of Columbia (the "Court") entitled Elouise Pepion Cobell, et al. v. Bruce Babbitt, Secretary of Interior, et al., No. Civ. 96–1285 (RCL) (currently denominated as Elouise Pepion Cobell v. Ken Salazar, Secretary of Interior, et al., 96–1285 (JR)) (this "Action"), seeking to redress alleged breaches of trust by the United States, and its trustee delegates the Secretary of Interior, the Assistant Secretary of Interior-Indian Affairs, and the Secretary of the Treasury, regarding the management of Individual Indian Money ("IIM") Accounts held on behalf of individual Indians.

2. The Complaint sought, among other things, declaratory and injunctive relief construing the trust obligations of the Defendants to members of the Plaintiff class and declaring that Defendants have breached and are in continuing breach of their trust obligations to class members, an order compelling Defendants to perform these legally mandated obligations, and requesting an accounting by Interior Defendants (as hereinafter defined) of individual Indian trust assets. See Cobell v. Babbitt, 52 F.Supp. 2d 11, 19 (D.D.C. 1999) ("Cobell III").

3. On February 4, 1997, the Court granted Plaintiffs' Motion for Class Action Certification pursuant to FRCP 23(b)(1)(A) and (b)(2) "on behalf of a plaintiff class consisting of present and former beneficiaries of IIM Accounts (exclusive of those who prior to the filing of the Complaint herein had filed actions on their own behalf alleging claims included in the Complaint)" (the "February 4, 1997 Class Certification Order"), reserving the jurisdiction to modify the February 4, 1997 Class Certification Order as the interests of justice may require, id. at 2–3.

4. On December 21, 1999, the Court held, among other things, that Defendants were then in breach of certain of their respective trust duties, Cobell v. Babbitt, 91 F. Supp. 2d 1, 58 (D.D.C. 1999) ("Cobell V").

5. On February 23, 2001, the United States Court of Appeals for the District of Columbia Circuit (the "Court of Appeals") upheld the Court's determination that Defendants were in breach of their statutory trust duties, Cobell v. Norton, 240 F.3d 1081 (D.C. Cir. 2001) ("Cobell VI").

6. Subsequently, the Court made determinations that had the effect of modifying the February 4, 1997 Class Certification Order, determining on January 30, 2008, that the right to an accounting accrued on October 25, 1994, "for all then-living IIM beneficiaries: those who hold or at any point in their lives held IIM Accounts." Cobell v. Kempthorne, 532 F. Supp. 2d 37, 98 (D.D.C. 2008) ("Cobell XX").

7. The Court and the Court of Appeals have further clarified those individual Indians entitled to the relief requested in the Complaint in the following respects:

a.   Excluding income derived from individual Indian trust land that was received by an individual Indian beneficiary on a direct pay basis, Cobell XX, 532 F. Supp. 2d at 95–96;

b.   Excluding income derived from individual Indian trust land where such funds were managed by tribes, id.;

c.   Excluding IIM Accounts closed prior to October 25, 1994, date of passage of the American Indian Trust Fund Management Reform Act of 1994, Pub. L. No. 103–412, 108 Stat. 4239 codified as amended at 25 U.S.C. § 162a et. seq. (the "Trust Reform Act"), Cobell v. Salazar, 573 F.3d 808, 815 (D.C. Cir. 2009) (Cobell XXII); and

d.   Excluding heirs to money from closed accounts that were subject to final probate determinations, id.

8. On July 24, 2009, the Court of Appeals reaffirmed that "[t]he district court sitting in equity must do everything it can to ensure that [Interior Defendants] provide [plaintiffs] an equitable accounting," Id. at 813.

9. This Action has continued for over 13 years, there is no end anticipated in the foreseeable future, and the Parties are mindful of the admonition of the Court of Appeals that they work together "to resolve this case expeditiously and fairly," Cobell v. Kempthorne, 455 F.3d 317, 336 (D.C. Cir. 2006), and desire to do so.

10. Recognizing that individual Indian trust beneficiaries have potential additional claims arising from Defendants' management of trust funds and trust assets, Defendants have an interest in a broad resolution of past differences in order to establish a productive relationship in the future.

11. The Parties recognize that an integral part of trust reform includes accelerating correction of the fractionated ownership of trust or restricted land, which makes administration of the individual Indian trust more difficult.

12. The Parties also recognize that another part of trust reform includes correcting the problems created by the escheatment of certain individual Indians' ownership of trust or restricted land, which has been held to be unconstitutional (see Babbitt v. Youpee, 519 U.S. 234 (1997); Hodel v. Irving, 481 U.S. 704 (1987)) and which makes administration of the individual Indian trust difficult.

13. Plaintiffs believe that further actions are necessary to reform the individual Indian trust, but hope that such further reforms are made without the need for additional litigation. Plaintiffs are also hopeful that the Commission which Secretary Salazar is announcing contemporaneously with the execution of this Agreement will result in the further reform which Plaintiffs believe is needed.

14. The Parties have an interest in as complete a resolution as possible for individual Indian trust-related claims and agree that this necessarily includes establishing a sum certain as a balance for each IIM Account as of a date certain.

15. Defendants deny and continue to deny any and all liability and damages to any individual Indian trust beneficiary with respect to the claims or causes of action asserted in the Litigation or the facts found by the Court in this Litigation. Nonetheless, without admitting or conceding any liability or damages whatsoever and without admitting any wrongdoing, and without conceding the appropriateness of class treatment for claims asserted in

any future complaint, Defendants have agreed to settle the Litigation (as hereinafter defined) on the terms and conditions set forth in this Agreement, to avoid the burden, expense, and uncertainty of continuing the case.

16. Class Counsel have conducted appropriate investigations and analyzed and evaluated the merits of the claims made, and judgments rendered, against Defendants in the Litigation, the findings, conclusions and holdings of the Court and Court of Appeals in this Litigation, and the impact of this Settlement on Plaintiffs as well as the impact of no settlement, and based upon their analysis and their evaluation of a number of factors, and recognizing the substantial risks of continued litigation, including the possibility that the Litigation, if not settled now, might not result in any recovery, or might result in a recovery that is less favorable than that provided for in this Settlement, and that otherwise a fair judgment would not occur for several years, Class Counsel are satisfied that the terms and conditions of this Settlement are fair, reasonable and adequate and that this Settlement is in the best interests of all Class Members.

17. The Parties desire to settle the Litigation and resolve their differences based on the terms set forth in this Agreement.

TERMS OF AGREEMENT

NOW, THEREFORE, in consideration of this Background, the mutual covenants and promises set forth in this Agreement, as well as the good and valuable consideration provided for in this Agreement, the Parties agree to a full and complete settlement of the Litigation on the following terms.

A. DEFINITIONS

1. Accounting/Trust Administration Fund. "Accounting/Trust Administration Fund" shall mean the $1,412,000,000.00 that Defendants shall pay into a Settlement Account held in the trust department of a Qualified Bank (as hereinafter defined) selected by Plaintiffs and approved by the Court, as well as any interest or investment income earned before distribution. The $1,412,000,000.00 payment represents the maximum total amount that Defendants are required to pay to settle Historical Accounting Claims, Funds Administration Claims, and Land Administration Claims.

2. Amended Complaint. "Amended Complaint" shall mean the complaint amended by Plaintiffs solely as part of this Agreement, and for the sole purpose of settling this Litigation, to be filed with the Court concurrently with, and attached to, this Agreement.

3. Amount Payable for Each Valid Claim. "Amount Payable for Each Valid Claim" shall mean the amount prescribed in section E.3 and E.4 below.

4. Assigned Value. "Assigned Value" shall have the meaning set forth in subsection E(4)(b)(3) below.

5. Claims Administrator. "Claims Administrator" shall mean The Garden City Group, Inc., which shall provide services to the Parties to facilitate administrative matters and distribution of the Amount Payable for Each Valid Claim in accordance with the terms and conditions of this Agreement.

6. Classes. "Classes" shall mean the classes established for purposes of this Agreement: the Historical Accounting Class and the Trust Administration Class (both as hereinafter defined).

7. Class Counsel. "Class Counsel" shall mean Dennis Gingold, Thaddeus Holt and attorneys from Kilpatrick Stockton LLP, including Elliott H. Levitas, Keith Harper, William Dorris, David Smith, William Austin, Adam Charnes and Justin Guilder.

8. Class Members. "Class Members" shall mean members of the Classes.

9. Contact Information. "Contact Information" shall mean the best and most current information the Department of the Interior ("Interior") then has

available of a beneficiary's name, social security number, date of birth, and mailing address, and whether Interior's individual Indian trust records reflect that beneficiary to be a minor, non-compos mentis, an individual under legal disability, an adult in need of assistance or whereabouts unknown.

10. Day. "Day" shall mean a calendar day.

11. Defendants. "Defendants" shall mean Ken Salazar, Secretary of the Interior, Larry Echohawk, Assistant Secretary of the Interior – Indian Affairs, and H. Timothy Geithner, Secretary of the Treasury, and their successors in office, all in their official capacities.

12. Fairness Hearing. "Fairness Hearing" shall mean the hearing on the Joint Motion for Judgment and Final Approval referenced in Paragraph D(4) below.

13. Final Approval. "Final Approval" shall mean the occurrence of the following:

   a. Following the Fairness Hearing, the Court has entered Judgment; and

   b. The Judgment has become final. "Final" means the later of:

      1. The time for rehearing or reconsideration, appellate review, and review by petition for certiorari has expired, and no motion for rehearing or reconsideration and/or notice of appeal has been filed; or

      2. If rehearing, reconsideration, or appellate review, or review by petition for certiorari is sought, after any and all avenues of rehearing, reconsideration, appellate review, or review by petition for certiorari have been exhausted, and no further rehearing, reconsideration, appellate review, or review by petition for certiorari is permitted, or the time for seeking such review has expired, and the Judgment has not been modified, amended or reversed in any way.

14. Funds Administration Claims. "Funds Administration Claims" shall mean known and unknown claims that have been or could have been asserted through the Record Date for Defendants' alleged breach of trust and mismanagement of individual Indian trust funds, and consist of Defendants' alleged:

   a. Failure to collect or credit funds owed under a lease, sale, easement or other transaction, including without limitation, failure to collect or credit all money due, failure to audit royalties and failure to collect interest on late payments;

   b. Failure to invest;

   c. Underinvestment;

   d. Imprudent management and investment;

   e. Erroneous or improper distributions or disbursements, including to the wrong person or account;

   f. Excessive or improper administrative fees;

   g. Deposits into wrong accounts;

   h. Misappropriation;

   i. Funds withheld unlawfully and in breach of trust;

   j. Loss of funds held in failed depository institutions, including interest;

   k. Failure as trustee to control or investigate allegations of, and obtain compensation for, theft, embezzlement, misappropriation, fraud, trespass, or other misconduct regarding trust assets;

   l. Failure to pay or credit interest, including interest on Indian monies proceeds of labor (IMPL), special deposit accounts, and IIM Accounts;

   m. Loss of funds or investment securities, and the income or proceeds earned from such funds or securities;

   n. Accounting errors;

   o. Failure to deposit and/or disburse funds in a timely fashion; and

   p. Claims of like nature and kind arising out of allegations of Defendants' breach of trust and/or mismanagement of individual Indian trust funds through the Record Date, that have been or could have been asserted.

15. Historical Accounting Claims. "Historical Accounting Claims" shall mean common law or statutory claims, including claims arising under the Trust Reform Act, for a historical accounting through the Record Date of any and all IIM Accounts and any asset held in trust or restricted status, including but not limited to Land (as defined herein) and funds held in any account, and which now are, or have been, beneficially owned or held by an individual Indian trust beneficiary who is a member of the Historical Accounting Class. These claims include the historical accounting through the Record Date of all funds collected and held in trust by Defendants and their financial and fiscal agents in open or closed accounts, as well as interest earned on such funds, whether such funds are deposited in IIM Accounts, or in tribal, special deposit, or government administrative or operating accounts.

16. Historical Accounting Class. "Historical Accounting Class" means those individual Indian beneficiaries (exclusive of those who prior to the filing of the Complaint on June 10, 1996 had filed actions on their own behalf stating a claim for a historical accounting) alive on the Record Date and who had an IIM Account open during any period between October 25, 1994 and the Record Date, which IIM Account had at least one cash transaction credited to it at any time as long as such credits were not later reversed. Beneficiaries deceased as of the Record Date are included in the Historical Accounting Class only if they had an IIM Account that was open as of the Record Date. The estate of any Historical Accounting Class Member who dies after the Record Date but before distribution is in the Historical Accounting Class.

17. IIM Account. "IIM Account" means an IIM account as defined in title 25, Code of Federal Regulations, section 115.002.

18. Interior Defendants. "Interior Defendants" shall mean Ken Salazar, Secretary of the Interior, and Larry Echohawk, Assistant Secretary of the Interior – Indian Affairs, and their successors in office, all in their official capacities.

19. Land. "Land" shall mean land owned by individual Indians and held in trust or restricted status by Interior Defendants, including all resources on, and corresponding subsurface rights, if any, in the land, and water, unless otherwise indicated.

20. Land Consolidation Program. The fractional interest acquisition program authorized in 25 U.S.C. 2201 et seq., including any applicable legislation enacted pursuant to this Agreement.

21. Land Administration Claims. "Land Administration Claims" shall mean known and unknown claims that have been or could have been asserted through the Record Date for Interior Defendants' alleged breach of trust and fiduciary mismanagement of land, oil, natural gas, mineral, timber, grazing, water and other resources and rights (the "resources") situated on, in or under Land and consist of Interior Defendants' alleged:

a. Failure to lease Land, approve leases or otherwise productively use Lands or assets;

b. Failure to obtain fair market value for leases, easements, rights-of-way or sales;

c. Failure to prudently negotiate leases, easements, rights-of-way, sales or other transactions;

d. Failure to impose and collect penalties for late payments;

e. Failure to include or enforce terms requiring that Land be conserved, maintained, or improved;

f. Permitting loss, dissipation, waste, or ruin, including failure to preserve Land whether involving agriculture (including but not limited to failing to control agricultural pests), grazing, harvesting (including but not limited to permitting overly aggressive harvesting), timber lands (including but not limited to failing to plant and cull timber land for maximum yield), and oil, natural gas, mineral resources or other resources (including but not limited to failing to manage oil, natural gas, or mineral resources to maximize total production);

g. Misappropriation;

h. Failure to control, investigate allegations of, or obtain relief in equity and at law for, trespass, theft, misappropriation, fraud or misconduct regarding Land;

i. Failure to correct boundary errors, survey or title record errors, or failure to properly apportion and track allotments; and

j. Claims of like nature and kind arising out of allegations of Interior Defendants' breach of trust and/or mismanagement of Land through the Record Date, that have been or could have been asserted.

22. Legislation Enactment Deadline. "Legislation Enactment Deadline" shall mean December 31, 2009, 11:59 p.m. Eastern time.

23. Litigation. "Litigation" shall mean that which is stated in the Amended Complaint attached to this Agreement.

24. Named Plaintiffs; Class Representatives. "Named Plaintiffs" shall mean and include Elouise Pepion Cobell ("Lead Plaintiff"), Penny Cleghorn, Thomas Maulson, and James Louis Larose. The Named Plaintiffs are also referred to as the "Class Representatives."

25. Notice Contractor. "Notice Contractor" shall mean a mutually agreeable entity that shall provide services to the Parties needed to provide notice to the Classes.

26. Order Granting Preliminary Approval. "Order Granting Preliminary Approval" shall mean the Order entered by the Court preliminarily approving the terms set forth in this Agreement, including the manner and timing of providing notice to the Classes, the time period for objections and the date, time and location for a Fairness Hearing.

27. Parties. "Parties" shall mean the Named Plaintiffs, members of the Classes, and Defendants.

28. Preliminary Approval. "Preliminary Approval" shall mean that the Court has entered an Order Granting Preliminary Approval.

29. Qualifying Bank; Qualified Bank. "Qualifying Bank" or "Qualified Bank" shall mean a federally insured depository institution that is "well capitalized," as that term is defined in 12 CFR §325.103, and that is subject to regulation and supervision by the Board of Governors of the Federal Reserve System or the U.S. Comptroller of the Currency under 12 CFR §9.18.

30. Record Date. "Record Date" shall mean September 30, 2009, 11:59 p.m. Eastern time.

31. Settlement Account. "Settlement Account" shall mean the trust account(s) established by Class Counsel in a Qualified Bank approved by the Court for the purpose of effectuating the Settlement and into which the Accounting/Trust Administration Fund shall be deposited and from which Stage 1 and Stage 2 Distributions, among other things set forth in this Agreement, shall be paid.

32. Special Master. "Special Master" shall be the person appointed by the Court as provided in paragraph E.1.a.

33. Stage 1; Stage 1 Distribution. "Stage 1" and "Stage 1 Distribution" shall mean the distribution to the Historical Accounting Class as provided in paragraph E(3).

34. Stage 2; Stage 2 Distribution. "Stage 2" and "Stage 2 Distribution" shall mean the distribution to the Trust Administration Class as provided in paragraph E(4).

35. Trust Administration Class. "Trust Administration Class" shall mean those individual Indian beneficiaries (exclusive of persons who filed actions on their own behalf, or a group of individuals who were certified as a class in a class action, stating a Funds Administration Claim or a Land Administration Claim prior to the filing of the Amended Complaint) alive as of the Record Date and who have or had IIM Accounts in the "Electronic Ledger Era" (currently available electronic data in systems of the Department of the Interior dating from approximately 1985 to

the present), as well as individual Indians who, as of the Record Date, had a recorded or other demonstrable ownership interest in land held in trust or restricted status, regardless of the existence of an IIM Account and regardless of the proceeds, if any, generated from the Land. The Trust Administration Class does not include beneficiaries deceased as of the Record Date, but does include the estate of any deceased beneficiary whose IIM Accounts or other trust assets had been open in probate as of the Record Date. The estate of any Trust Administration Class Member who dies after the Record Date but before distribution is included in the Trust Administration Class.

36. Trust Land Consolidation Fund. "Trust Land Consolidation Fund" shall mean the $2,000,000,000.00 allocated to Interior Defendants and held in a separate account in Treasury for the purpose of acquiring fractional interests in trust or restricted land and such other purposes as permitted by this Agreement and applicable law.

Source: Cobell v. Salazar, 573 F. 3d 808 (2009).

Native American Heritage Day Act
(2009)

In July 2007, U.S. Senator Daniel Inouye of Hawaii introduced Senate Bill 1852 "to designate the Friday after Thanksgiving of each year as 'Native American Heritage Day' in honor of the achievements and contributions of Native Americans to the United States." Senators Daniel Akaka (D-HI), Samuel Brownback (R-KS), Byron Dorgan (D-ND), and Ted Stevens (R-AK) all cosponsored the bill. On June 26, 2009, the Native American Heritage Day Act was signed into law by President Barack Obama.

ONE HUNDRED ELEVENTH CONGRESS OF THE UNITED STATES OF AMERICA

AT THE FIRST SESSION

Begun and held at the City of Washington on Tuesday, the sixth day of January, two thousand and nine

Joint Resolution

To honor the achievements and contributions of Native Americans to the United States, and for other purposes.

Resolved by the Senate and House of Representatives of the United States of America in Congress assembled,

SECTION 1. SHORT TITLE.

This Act may be cited as the "Native American Heritage Day Act of 2009".

SEC. 2. FINDINGS.

Congress finds that—

1. Native Americans are the descendants of the aboriginal, indigenous, native people who were the original inhabitants of and who governed the lands that now constitute the United States;

2. Native Americans have volunteered to serve in the United States Armed Forces and have served with valor in all of the Nation's military actions from the Revolutionary War through the present day, and in most of those actions, more Native Americans per capita

served in the Armed Forces than any other group of Americans;

3. Native American tribal governments included the fundamental principles of freedom of speech and separation of governmental powers;

4. Native Americans have made distinct and significant contributions to the United States and the rest of the world in many fields, including agriculture, medicine, music, language, and art, and Native Americans have distinguished themselves as inventors, entrepreneurs, spiritual leaders, and scholars;

5. Native Americans should be recognized for their contributions to the United States as local and national leaders, artists, athletes, and scholars;

6. nationwide recognition of the contributions that Native Americans have made to the fabric of American society will afford an opportunity for all Americans to demonstrate their respect and admiration of Native Americans for their important contributions to the political, cultural, and economic life of the United States;

7. nationwide recognition of the contributions that Native Americans have made to the Nation will encourage self-esteem, pride, and self-awareness in Native Americans of all ages;

8. designation of the Friday following Thanksgiving of each year as Native American Heritage Day will underscore H. J. Res. 40–2 the government-to-government relationship between the United States and Native American governments;

9. designation of Native American Heritage Day will encourage public elementary and secondary schools in the United States to enhance understanding of Native Americans by providing curricula and classroom instruction focusing on the achievements and contributions of Native Americans to the Nation; and

10. the Friday immediately succeeding Thanksgiving Day of each year would be an appropriate day to designate as Native American Heritage Day.

SEC. 3. HONORING NATIVE AMERICAN HERITAGE IN THE UNITED STATES.

Congress encourages the people of the United States, as well as Federal, State, and local governments, and interested groups and organizations to honor Native Americans, with activities relating to—

1. appropriate programs, ceremonies, and activities to observe Native American Heritage Day;

2. the historical status of Native American tribal governments as well as the present-day status of Native Americans;

3. the cultures, traditions, and languages of Native Americans; and

4. the rich Native American cultural legacy that all Americans enjoy today.

Speaker of the House of Representatives.

Vice President of the United States and President of the Senate.

Source: Native American Heritage Day Act (2009). H.J.Res. 40 (111th).

Native American Apology Resolution

(2009)

On December 19, 2009, President Barack Obama signed into law the Native American Apology Resolution, which was included in the Department of Defense Appropriations Act (2010), Section 8113. The joint resolution was initially introduced into the Senate by Senator Sam Brownback (R-KS) in 2004.

The government was criticized for not doing more to publicize its "Apology to Native Peoples of the United States" through a press release or direct public address to the Native community. Here is the apology, excerpted from Title VIII of the Department of Defense Appropriations Act.

One Hundred Eleventh Congress of the United States of America

AT THE FIRST SESSION

Begun and held at the City of Washington on Tuesday, the sixth day of January, two thousand and nine

An Act Making appropriations for the Department of Defense for the fiscal year ending September 30, 2010, and for other purposes.

Be it enacted by the Senate and House of Representatives of the United States of America in Congress assembled,

SECTION 1. SHORT TITLE.

This Act may be cited as the "Department of Defense Appropriations Act, 2010"....

IN THE SENATE OF THE UNITED STATES

April 30, 2009

Mr. BROWNBACK (for himself, Mr. INOUYE, Mr. BAUCUS, Mrs. BOXER, Mr. CRAPO, Ms. CANTWELL, Mr. COBURN, Mr. HARKIN, Mr. LIEBERMAN, and Mr. TESTER) introduced the following joint resolution; which was read twice and referred to the Committee on Indian Affairs

JOINT RESOLUTION

To acknowledge a long history of official depredations and ill-conceived policies by the Federal Government regarding Indian tribes and offer an apology to all Native Peoples on behalf of the United States.

Whereas the ancestors of today's Native Peoples inhabited the land of the present-day United States since time immemorial and for thousands of years before the arrival of people of European descent;

Whereas for millennia, Native Peoples have honored, protected, and stewarded this land we cherish;

Whereas Native Peoples are spiritual people with a deep and abiding belief in the Creator, and for millennia Native Peoples have maintained a powerful spiritual connection to this land, as evidenced by their customs and legends;

Whereas the arrival of Europeans in North America opened a new chapter in the history of Native Peoples;

Whereas while establishment of permanent European settlements in North America did stir conflict with nearby Indian tribes, peaceful and mutually beneficial interactions also took place;

Whereas the foundational English settlements in Jamestown, Virginia, and Plymouth, Massachusetts, owed their survival in large measure to the compassion and aid of Native Peoples in the vicinities of the settlements;

Whereas in the infancy of the United States, the founders of the Republic expressed their desire for a just relationship with the Indian tribes, as evidenced by the Northwest Ordinance enacted by Congress in 1787, which begins with the phrase, 'The utmost good faith shall always be observed toward the Indians';

Whereas Indian tribes provided great assistance to the fledgling Republic as it strengthened and grew, including invaluable help to Meriwether Lewis and William Clark on their epic journey from St. Louis, Missouri, to the Pacific Coast;

Whereas Native Peoples and non-Native settlers engaged in numerous armed conflicts in which unfortunately, both took innocent lives, including those of women and children;

Whereas the Federal Government violated many of the treaties ratified by Congress and other diplomatic agreements with Indian tribes;

Whereas the United States forced Indian tribes and their citizens to move away from their traditional homelands and onto federally established and controlled reservations, in accordance with such Acts as the Act of May 28, 1830 (4 Stat. 411, chapter 148) (commonly known as the 'Indian Removal Act');

Whereas many Native Peoples suffered and perished—

1. during the execution of the official Federal Government policy of forced removal, including the infamous Trail of Tears and Long Walk;
2. during bloody armed confrontations and massacres, such as the Sand Creek Massacre in 1864 and the Wounded Knee Massacre in 1890; and
3. on numerous Indian reservations;

Whereas the Federal Government condemned the traditions, beliefs, and customs of Native Peoples and endeavored to assimilate them by such policies as the redistribution of land under the Act of February 8, 1887 (25 U.S.C. 331; 24 Stat. 388, chapter 119) (commonly known as the 'General Allotment Act'), and the forcible removal of Native children from their families to faraway boarding schools where their Native practices and languages were degraded and forbidden;

Whereas officials of the Federal Government and private United States citizens harmed Native Peoples by the unlawful acquisition of recognized tribal land and the theft of tribal resources and assets from recognized tribal land;

Whereas the policies of the Federal Government toward Indian tribes and the breaking of covenants with Indian tribes have contributed to the severe social ills and economic troubles in many Native communities today;

Whereas despite the wrongs committed against Native Peoples by the United States, Native Peoples have remained committed to the protection of this great land, as evidenced by the fact that, on a per capita basis, more Native Peoples have served in the United States Armed Forces and placed themselves in harm's way in defense of the United States in every major military conflict than any other ethnic group;

Whereas Indian tribes have actively influenced the public life of the United States by continued cooperation with Congress and the Department of the Interior, through the involvement of Native individuals in official Federal Government positions, and by leadership of their own sovereign Indian tribes;

Whereas Indian tribes are resilient and determined to preserve, develop, and transmit to future generations their unique cultural identities;

Whereas the National Museum of the American Indian was established within the Smithsonian Institution as a living memorial to Native Peoples and their traditions; and

Whereas Native Peoples are endowed by their Creator with certain unalienable rights, and among those are life, liberty, and the pursuit of happiness: Now, therefore, be it

Resolved by the Senate and House of Representatives of the United States of America in Congress assembled,

SECTION 1 RESOLUTION OF APOLOGY TO NATIVE PEOPLES OF THE UNITED STATES

SEC. 8113. (a) ACKNOWLEDGMENT AND APOLOGY.—The United States, acting through Congress—

1. recognizes the special legal and political relationship Indian tribes have with the United States and the solemn covenant with the land we share;
2. commends and honors Native Peoples for the thousands of years that they have stewarded and protected this land;
3. recognizes that there have been years of official depredations, ill-conceived policies, and the breaking of covenants by the Federal Government regarding Indian tribes;
4. apologizes on behalf of the people of the United States to all Native Peoples for the many instances of violence, maltreatment, and neglect inflicted on Native Peoples by citizens of the United States;

5. expresses its regret for the ramifications of former wrongs and its commitment to build on the positive relationships of the past and present to move toward a brighter future where all the people of this land live reconciled as brothers and sisters, and harmoniously steward and protect this land together;

6. urges the President to acknowledge the wrongs of the United States against Indian tribes in the history of the United States in order to bring healing to this land; and

7. commends the State governments that have begun reconciliation efforts with recognized Indian tribes located in their boundaries and encourages all State governments similarly to work toward reconciling relationships with Indian tribes within their boundaries. . . .

(b) DISCLAIMER.—Nothing in this section—

1. authorizes or supports any claim against the United States; or

2. serves as a settlement of any claim against the United States.

Source: Native American Apology Resolution (2009). 111th Congress, 1st Session, S. J. RES. 14. Library of Congress. http://thomas.loc.gov/cgi-bin/query/z?c111:S.J.RES.14.

Tribal Law and Order Act

(2010)

Signed by President Barack Obama on July 29, 2010, the Tribal Law and Order Act expands the abilities of Native American tribal courts to impose stiffer sentences in criminal cases. Before this measure, tribal courts were limited as to the punishment they could hand down, a restriction that gave defendants the impression that tribal courts were lower courts of limited jurisdiction and that their authority was of a less serious nature. In an effort to improve criminal law enforcement in Indian country, this act gives tribal courts throughout the United States the power to impose increased sentences to incarcerate defendants longer.

SEC. 202. FINDINGS; PURPOSES.

(a) Findings- Congress finds that—

1. the United States has distinct legal, treaty, and trust obligations to provide for the public safety of Indian country;

2. Congress and the President have acknowledged that—

A. tribal law enforcement officers are often the first responders to crimes on Indian reservations; and

B. tribal justice systems are often the most appropriate institutions for maintaining law and order in Indian country;

3. less than 3,000 tribal and Federal law enforcement officers patrol more than 56,000,000 acres of Indian country, which reflects less than 1/2 of the law enforcement presence in comparable rural communities nationwide;

4. the complicated jurisdictional scheme that exists in Indian country—

A. has a significant negative impact on the ability to provide public safety to Indian communities;

B. has been increasingly exploited by criminals; and

C. requires a high degree of commitment and cooperation among tribal, Federal, and State law enforcement officials;

5. (A) domestic and sexual violence against American Indian and Alaska Native women has reached epidemic proportions;

(B) 34 percent of American Indian and Alaska Native women will be raped in their lifetimes; and

(C) 39 percent of American Indian and Alaska Native women will be subject to domestic violence;

6. Indian tribes have faced significant increases in instances of domestic violence, burglary, assault, and child abuse as a direct result of increased methamphetamine use on Indian reservations; and

7. crime data is a fundamental tool of law enforcement, but for decades the Bureau of Indian Affairs and the Department of Justice have not been able to coordinate or consistently report crime and prosecution rates in tribal communities.

(b) Purposes- The purposes of this title are—

1. to clarify the responsibilities of Federal, State, tribal, and local governments with respect to crimes committed in Indian country;

2. to increase coordination and communication among Federal, State, tribal, and local law enforcement agencies;

3. to empower tribal governments with the authority, resources, and information necessary to safely and effectively provide public safety in Indian country;

4. to reduce the prevalence of violent crime in Indian country and to combat sexual and domestic violence against American Indian and Alaska Native women;

5. to prevent drug trafficking and reduce rates of alcohol and drug addiction in Indian country; and

6. to increase and standardize the collection of criminal data and the sharing of criminal history information among Federal, State, and tribal officials responsible for responding to and investigating crimes in Indian country.

SEC. 203. DEFINITIONS.

(a) In General- In this title:

1. INDIAN COUNTRY- The term 'Indian country' has the meaning given the term in section 1151 of title 18, United States Code.

2. INDIAN TRIBE- The term 'Indian tribe' has the meaning given the term in section 102 of the Federally Recognized Indian Tribe List Act of 1994 (25 U.S.C. 479a).

3. SECRETARY- The term 'Secretary' means the Secretary of the Interior.

4. TRIBAL GOVERNMENT- The term 'tribal government' means the governing body of a federally recognized Indian tribe.

(b) Indian Law Enforcement Reform Act- Section 2 of the Indian Law Enforcement Reform Act (25 U.S.C. 2801) is amended by adding at the end the following:

(10) The term 'tribal justice official' means—

A. a tribal prosecutor;
B. a tribal law enforcement officer; or
C. any other person responsible for investigating or prosecuting an alleged criminal offense in tribal court.'.

SEC. 204. SEVERABILITY.

If any provision of this title, an amendment made by this title, or the application of such a provision or amendment to any individual, entity, or circumstance, is determined by a court of competent jurisdiction to be invalid, the remaining provisions of this title, the remaining amendments made by this title, and the application of those provisions and amendments to individuals, entities, or circumstances other than the affected individual, entity, or circumstance shall not be affected.

SEC. 205. JURISDICTION OF THE STATE OF ALASKA.

Nothing in this Act limits, alters, expands, or diminishes the civil or criminal jurisdiction of the

State of Alaska, any subdivision of the State of Alaska, or any Indian tribe in that State.

SEC. 206. EFFECT.

Nothing in this Act confers on an Indian tribe criminal jurisdiction over non-Indians.

Subtitle A—Federal Accountability and Coordination

SEC. 211. OFFICE OF JUSTICE SERVICES RESPONSIBILITIES.

(a) Definitions- Section 2 of the Indian Law Enforcement Reform Act (25 U.S.C. 2801) is amended—

(1) by striking paragraph (8);

(2) by redesignating paragraphs (1) through (7) as paragraphs (2) through (8), respectively;

(3) by redesignating paragraph (9) as paragraph (1) and moving the paragraphs so as to appear in numerical order; and

(4) in paragraph (1) (as redesignated by paragraph (3)), by striking 'Division of Law Enforcement Services' and inserting 'Office of Justice Services'.

(b) Additional Responsibilities of Office- Section 3 of the Indian Law Enforcement Reform Act (25 U.S.C. 2802) is amended—

(1) in subsection (b), by striking '(b) There is hereby established within the Bureau a Division of Law Enforcement Services which' and inserting the following:

(b) Office of Justice Services- There is established in the Bureau an office, to be known as the 'Office of Justice Services', that';

(2) in subsection (c)—

(A) in the matter preceding paragraph (1), by striking 'Division of Law Enforcement Services' and inserting 'Office of Justice Services';

(B) in paragraph (8), by striking 'and' at the end;

(C) in paragraph (9), by striking the period at the end and inserting a semicolon; and

(D) by adding at the end the following:

(10) the development and provision of dispatch and emergency and E-911 services;

(11) communicating with tribal leaders, tribal community and victims' advocates, tribal justice officials, indigent defense representatives, and residents of Indian country on a regular basis regarding public safety and justice concerns facing tribal communities;

(12) conducting meaningful and timely consultation with tribal leaders and tribal justice officials in the development of regulatory policies and other actions that affect public safety and justice in Indian country;

(13) providing technical assistance and training to tribal law enforcement officials to gain access and input authority to utilize the National Criminal Information Center and other national crime information databases pursuant to section 534 of title 28, United States Code;

(14) in coordination with the Attorney General pursuant to subsection (g) of section 302 of the Omnibus Crime Control and Safe Streets Act of 1968 (42 U.S.C. 3732), collecting, analyzing, and reporting data regarding Indian country crimes on an annual basis;

(15) on an annual basis, sharing with the Department of Justice all relevant crime data, including Uniform Crime Reports, that the Office of Justice Services prepares and receives from tribal law enforcement agencies on a tribe-by-tribe basis to ensure that individual tribal governments providing data are eligible for programs offered by the Department of Justice;

(16) submitting to the appropriate committees of Congress, for each fiscal year, a detailed spending report regarding tribal public safety and justice programs that includes—

(A)(i) the number of full-time employees of the Bureau and tribal governments who serve as—

(I) criminal investigators;

(II) uniform police;

(III) police and emergency dispatchers;

(IV) detention officers;

(V) executive personnel, including special agents in charge, and directors and deputies of various offices in the Office of Justice Services; and

(VI) tribal court judges, prosecutors, public defenders, appointed defense counsel, or related staff; and

(i) the amount of appropriations obligated for each category described in clause (ii) for each fiscal year;

(B) a list of amounts dedicated to law enforcement and corrections, vehicles, related transportation costs, equipment, inmate transportation costs, inmate transfer costs, replacement, improvement, and repair of facilities, personnel transfers, detailees and costs related to their details, emergency events, public safety and justice communications and technology costs, and tribal court personnel, facilities, indigent defense, and related program costs;

(C) a list of the unmet staffing needs of law enforcement, corrections, and court personnel (including indigent defense and prosecution staff) at tribal and Bureau of Indian Affairs justice agencies, the replacement and repair needs of tribal and Bureau corrections facilities, needs for tribal police and court facilities, and public safety and emergency communications and technology needs; and

(D) the formula, priority list or other methodology used to determine the method of disbursement of funds for the public safety and justice programs administered by the Office of Justice Services;

(17) submitting to the appropriate committees of Congress, for each fiscal year, a report summarizing the technical assistance, training, and other support provided to tribal law enforcement and corrections agencies that operate relevant programs pursuant to self-determination contracts or self-governance compacts with the Secretary; and

(18) promulgating regulations to carry out this Act, and routinely reviewing and updating, as necessary, the regulations contained in subchapter B of title 25, Code of Federal Regulations (or successor regulations).;

(3) in subsection (d)—

(A) in paragraph (1), by striking 'Division of Law Enforcement Services' and inserting 'Office of Justice Services'; and

(B) in paragraph (4)(i), in the first sentence, by striking 'Division' and inserting 'Office of Justice Services';

(4) in subsection (e), by striking 'Division of Law Enforcement Services' each place it appears and inserting 'Office of Justice Services'; and

(5) by adding at the end the following:

(f) Long-term Plan for Tribal Detention Programs- Not later than 1 year after the date of enactment of this subsection, the Secretary, acting through the Bureau, in coordination with the Department of Justice and in consultation with tribal leaders, tribal courts, tribal law enforcement officers, and tribal corrections officials, shall submit to Congress a long-term plan to address incarceration in Indian country, including—

(1) a description of proposed activities for—

(A) the construction, operation, and maintenance of juvenile (in accordance with section 4220(a)(3) of the Indian Alcohol and Substance Abuse Prevention and Treatment Act of 1986 (25 U.S.C. 2453(a)(3)) and adult detention facilities (including regional facilities) in Indian country;

(B) contracting with State and local detention centers, upon approval of affected tribal governments; and

(C) alternatives to incarceration, developed in cooperation with tribal court systems;

(2) an assessment and consideration of the construction of Federal detention facilities in Indian country; and

(3) any other alternatives as the Secretary, in coordination with the Attorney General and in consultation with Indian tribes, determines to be necessary.'.

(c) Law Enforcement Authority- Section 4 of the Indian Law Enforcement Reform Act (25 U.S.C. 2803) is amended—

(1) in paragraph (2)(A), by striking '), or' and inserting 'or offenses processed by the Central Violations Bureau); or'; and

(2) in paragraph (3)—

(A) in subparagraph (B), by striking ', or' at the end and inserting a semicolon;

(B) in subparagraphs (B) and (C), by striking 'reasonable grounds' each place it appears and inserting 'probable cause';

(C) in subparagraph (C), by adding 'or' at the end; and

(D) by adding at the end the following:

(D) (i) the offense involves—

(I) a misdemeanor controlled substance offense in violation of—

(aa) the Controlled Substances Act (21 U.S.C. 801 et seq.);

(bb) title IX of the Personal Responsibility and Work Opportunity Reconciliation Act of 1996 (21 U.S.C. 862a et seq.); or

(cc) section 731 of the USA PATRIOT Improvement and Reauthorization Act of 2005 (21 U.S.C. 865);

(II) a misdemeanor firearms offense in violation of chapter 44 of title 18, United States Code;

(III) a misdemeanor assault in violation of chapter 7 of title 18, United States Code; or

(IV) a misdemeanor liquor trafficking offense in violation of chapter 59 of title 18, United States Code; and

(ii) the employee has probable cause to believe that the individual to be arrested has committed, or is committing, the crime;'.

SEC. 212. DISPOSITION REPORTS.

Section 10 of the Indian Law Enforcement Reform Act (25 U.S.C. 2809) is amended by striking subsections (a) through (d) and inserting the following:

(a) Coordination and Data Collection-

(1) INVESTIGATIVE COORDINATION- Subject to subsection (c), if a law enforcement officer or employee of any Federal department or agency terminates an investigation of an alleged violation of Federal criminal law in Indian country without referral for prosecution, the officer or employee shall coordinate with the appropriate tribal law enforcement officials regarding the status of the investigation and the use of evidence relevant to the case in a tribal court with authority over the crime alleged.

(2) INVESTIGATION DATA- The Federal Bureau of Investigation shall compile, on an annual basis and by Field Division, information regarding decisions not to refer to an appropriate prosecuting authority cases in which investigations had been opened into an alleged crime in Indian country, including—

(A) the types of crimes alleged;

(B) the statuses of the accused as Indians or non-Indians;

(C) the statuses of the victims as Indians or non-Indians; and

(D) the reasons for deciding against referring the investigation for prosecution.

(3) PROSECUTORIAL COORDINATION- Subject to subsection (c), if a United States Attorney declines to prosecute, or acts to terminate prosecution of, an alleged violation of Federal criminal law in Indian country, the United States Attorney shall coordinate with the appropriate tribal justice officials regarding the status of the investigation and the use of evidence relevant to the case in a tribal court with authority over the crime alleged.

(4) PROSECUTION DATA- The United States Attorney shall submit to the Native American Issues Coordinator to compile, on an annual basis and by Federal judicial district, information regarding all declinations of alleged violations of Federal criminal law that occurred in Indian country that were referred for prosecution by law enforcement agencies, including—

(A) the types of crimes alleged;

(B) the statuses of the accused as Indians or non-Indians;

(C) the statuses of the victims as Indians or non-Indians; and

(D) the reasons for deciding to decline or terminate the prosecutions.

(b) Annual Reports- The Attorney General shall submit to Congress annual reports containing, with respect to the applicable calendar year, the information compiled under paragraphs (2) and (4) of subsection (a)—

(1) organized—

(A) in the aggregate; and

(B)(i) for the Federal Bureau of Investigation, by Field Division; and

(ii) for United States Attorneys, by Federal judicial district; and

(2) including any relevant explanatory statements.

(c) Effect of Section-

(1) IN GENERAL- Nothing in this section requires any Federal agency or official to transfer or disclose any confidential, privileged, or statutorily protected communication, information, or source to an official of any Indian tribe.

(2) FEDERAL RULES OF CRIMINAL PROCEDURE- Nothing in this section affects or limits the requirements of Rule 6 of the Federal Rules of Criminal Procedure.

(3) REGULATIONS- The Attorney General shall establish, by regulation, standards for the protection of the confidential or privileged communications, information, and sources described in this section.

Source: Tribal Law and Order Act (2010). Public Law 111–211. Library of Congress. http://www.thomas.gov/cgi-bin/query/D?c111:5:./temp/~c111aOu3kP.

Claims Resolution Act, Title I

(2010)

On December 8, 2010, President Barack Obama signed into law the Claims Resolution Act of 2010. This legislation authorized various settlement agreements—the Pigford II *lawsuit brought by African American farmers, four separate water rights suits brought by Native American tribes, and the* Cobell v. Salazar *(2009) decision. In 1996, Elouise Cobell of the Blackfeet, along with three other persons, led a class action lawsuit to recover millions of dollars of leases and royalties supposed to be held in trust by the Bureau of Indian Affairs (BIA) and paid out to individuals. On December 7, 2009, Cobell accepted a settlement of $1.4 billion. Title I, excerpted below, authorizes the disbursement of monies awarded to Native groups in the 2009 settlement in the amount of $3.4 billion.*

One Hundred Eleventh Congress of the United States of America

AT THE SECOND SESSION

Begun and held at the City of Washington on Tuesday, the fifth day of January, two thousand and ten

An Act

This Act may be cited as "The Claims Resettlement Act of 2010."

Be it enacted by the Senate and House of Representatives of the United States of America in Congress assembled,

SECTION 1. SHORT TITLE; TABLE OF CONTENTS.

(a) SHORT TITLE.—This Act may be cited as the "Claims Resolution Act of 2010".

(b) TABLE OF CONTENTS.—The table of contents of this Act is as follows:

TITLE I—INDIVIDUAL INDIAN MONEY ACCOUNT LITIGATION SETTLEMENT

SEC. 101. INDIVIDUAL INDIAN MONEY ACCOUNT LITIGATION SETTLEMENT.

(a) DEFINITIONS.—In this section:

(1) AGREEMENT ON ATTORNEYS' FEES, EXPENSES, AND COSTS.—The term "Agreement on Attorneys' Fees, Expenses, and Costs" means the agreement dated December 7, 2009, between Class Counsel (as defined in the Settlement) and the Defendants (as defined in the Settlement) relating to attorneys' fees, expenses, and costs incurred by Class Counsel in connection with the Litigation and implementation of the Settlement, as modified by the parties to the Litigation.

(2) AMENDED COMPLAINT.—The term "Amended Complaint" means the Amended Complaint attached to the Settlement.

(3) FINAL APPROVAL.—The term "final approval" has the meaning given the term in the Settlement.

(4) LAND CONSOLIDATION PROGRAM.— The term "Land Consolidation Program" means a program conducted in accordance with the Settlement, the Indian Land Consolidation Act (25 U.S.C. 2201 et seq.), and subsection (e)(2) under which the Secretary may purchase fractional interests in trust or restricted land.

(5) LITIGATION.—The term "Litigation" means the case entitled Elouise Cobell et al. v. Ken Salazar et al., United States District Court, District of Columbia, Civil Action No. 96–1285 (TFH).

(6) PLAINTIFF.—The term "Plaintiff" means a member of any class certified in the Litigation.

(7) SECRETARY.—The term "Secretary" means the Secretary of the Interior.

(8) SETTLEMENT.—The term "Settlement" means the Class Action Settlement Agreement dated December 7, 2009, in the Litigation, as modified by the parties to the Litigation.

(9) TRUST ADMINISTRATION ADJUST-MENT FUND.—The term "Trust Administration Adjustment Fund" means the $100,000,000 deposited in the Settlement Account (as defined in the Settlement) pursuant to subsection (j)(1) for use in making the adjustments authorized by that subsection.

(10) TRUST ADMINISTRATION CLASS.— The term "Trust Administration Class" means the Trust Administration Class as defined in the Settlement.

(b) PURPOSE.—The purpose of this section is to authorize the Settlement.

(c) AUTHORIZATION.—

(1) IN GENERAL.—The Settlement is authorized, ratified, and confirmed.

(2) AMENDMENTS.—Any amendment to the Settlement is authorized, ratified, and confirmed, to the extent that such amendment is executed to make the Settlement consistent with this section.

(d) JURISDICTIONAL PROVISIONS.—

(1) IN GENERAL.—Notwithstanding the limitation on the jurisdiction of the district courts of the United States in section 1346(a)(2) of title 28, United States Code, the United States H. R. 4783—4 District Court for the District of Columbia shall have jurisdiction of the claims asserted in the Amended Complaint for purposes of the Settlement.

(2) CERTIFICATION OF TRUST ADMINISTRATION CLASS.—

(A) IN GENERAL.—Notwithstanding the requirements of the Federal Rules of Civil Procedure, the court in the Litigation may certify the Trust Administration Class.

(B) TREATMENT.—On certification under subparagraph (A), the Trust Administration Class shall be treated as a class certified under rule 23(b) (3) of the Federal Rules of Civil Procedure for purposes of the Settlement.

(e) TRUST LAND CONSOLIDATION.—

(1) TRUST LAND CONSOLIDATION FUND.—

(A) ESTABLISHMENT.—On final approval of the Settlement, there shall be established in the

Treasury of the United States a fund, to be known as the "Trust Land Consolidation Fund".

(B) AVAILABILITY OF AMOUNTS.— Amounts in the Trust Land Consolidation Fund shall be made available to the Secretary during the 10-year period beginning on the date of final approval of the Settlement— (i) to conduct the Land Consolidation Program; and

(ii) for other costs specified in the Settlement.

(C) DEPOSITS.—

(i) IN GENERAL.—On final approval of the Settlement, the Secretary of the Treasury shall deposit in the Trust Land Consolidation Fund $1,900,000,000 out of the amounts appropriated to pay final judgments, awards, and compromise settlements under section 1304 of title 31, United States Code.

(ii) CONDITIONS MET.—The conditions described in section 1304 of title 31, United States Code, shall be deemed to be met for purposes of clause (i).

(D) TRANSFERS.—In a manner designed to encourage participation in the Land Consolidation Program, the Secretary may transfer, at the discretion of the Secretary, not more than $60,000,000 of amounts in the Trust Land Consolidation Fund to the Indian Education Scholarship Holding Fund established under paragraph (3).

(2) OPERATION.—The Secretary shall consult with Indian tribes to identify fractional interests within the respective jurisdictions of the Indian tribes for purchase in a manner that is consistent with the priorities of the Secretary.

(3) INDIAN EDUCATION SCHOLARSHIP HOLDING FUND.—

(A) ESTABLISHMENT.—On final approval of the Settlement, there shall be established in the Treasury of the United States a fund, to be known as the "Indian Education Scholarship Holding Fund".

(B) AVAILABILITY.—Notwithstanding any other provision of law governing competition, public notification, or Federal procurement or assistance, amounts in the Indian Education Scholarship Holding Fund shall be made available, without further appropriation, to the Secretary to contribute to an Indian Education Scholarship Fund, as described in the Settlement, to provide scholarships for Native Americans. H. R. 4783—5

(4) ACQUISITION OF TRUST OR RESTRICTED LAND.—The Secretary may acquire, at the discretion of the Secretary and in accordance with the Land Consolidation Program, any fractional interest in trust or restricted land.

(5) TREATMENT OF UNLOCATABLE PLAINTIFFS.—A Plaintiff, the whereabouts of whom are unknown and who, after reasonable efforts by the Secretary, cannot be located during the 5-year period beginning on the date of final approval of the Settlement, shall be considered to have accepted an offer made pursuant to the Land Consolidation Program.

(f) TAXATION AND OTHER BENEFITS.—

(1) INTERNAL REVENUE CODE.—For purposes of the Internal Revenue Code of 1986, amounts received by an individual Indian as a lump sum or a periodic payment pursuant to the Settlement shall not be—

(A) included in gross income; or

(B) taken into consideration for purposes of applying any provision of the Internal Revenue Code that takes into account excludable income in computing adjusted gross income or modified adjusted gross income, including section 86 of that Code (relating to Social Security and tier 1 railroad retirement benefits).

(2) OTHER BENEFITS.—Notwithstanding any other provision of law, for purposes of determining initial eligibility, ongoing eligibility, or level of benefits under any Federal or federally assisted program, amounts received by an individual Indian as a lump sum or a periodic payment pursuant to the Settlement shall not be treated for any household member, during the 1-year period beginning on the date of receipt—

(A) as income for the month during which the amounts were received; or

(B) as a resource.

(g) INCENTIVE AWARDS AND AWARD OF ATTORNEYS' FEES, EXPENSES, AND COSTS UNDER SETTLEMENT AGREEMENT.—

(1) IN GENERAL.—Subject to paragraph (3), the court in the Litigation shall determine the amount to which the Plaintiffs in the Litigation may be entitled for incentive awards and for attorneys' fees, expenses, and costs— (A) in accordance with controlling law, including, with respect to attorneys' fees, expenses, and costs, any applicable rule of law requiring counsel to produce contemporaneous time, expense, and cost records in support of a motion for such fees, expenses, and costs; and (B) giving due consideration to the special status of Class Members (as defined in the Settlement) as beneficiaries of a federally created and administered trust. (2) NOTICE OF AGREEMENT ON ATTORNEYS' FEES, EXPENSES, AND COSTS.—The description of the request of Class Counsel for an amount of attorneys' fees, expenses, and costs required under paragraph C.1.d. of the Settlement shall include a description of all material provisions of the Agreement on Attorneys' Fees, Expenses, and Costs.

(3) EFFECT ON AGREEMENT.—Nothing in this subsection limits or otherwise affects the enforceability of the Agreement on Attorneys' Fees, Expenses, and Costs.

(h) SELECTION OF QUALIFYING BANK.— The United States District Court for the District of Columbia, in exercising the discretion H. R. 4783—6 of the Court to approve the selection of any proposed Qualifying Bank (as defined in the Settlement) under paragraph A.1. of the Settlement, may consider any factors or circumstances regarding the proposed Qualifying Bank that the Court determines to be appropriate to protect the rights and interests of Class Members (as defined in the Settlement) in the amounts to be deposited in the Settlement Account (as defined in the Settlement).

(i) APPOINTEES TO SPECIAL BOARD OF TRUSTEES.—The 2 members of the special board of trustees to be selected by the Secretary under paragraph G.3. of the Settlement shall be selected only after consultation with, and after considering the names of possible candidates timely offered by, federally recognized Indian tribes.

(j) TRUST ADMINISTRATION CLASS ADJUSTMENTS.—

(1) FUNDS.—

(A) IN GENERAL.—In addition to the amounts deposited pursuant to paragraph E.2. of the Settlement, on final approval, the Secretary of the Treasury shall deposit in the Trust Administration Adjustment Fund of the Settlement Account (as defined in the Settlement) $100,000,000 out of the amounts appropriated to pay final judgments, awards, and compromise settlements under section 1304 of title 31, United States Code, to be allocated and paid by the Claims Administrator (as defined in the Settlement and pursuant to paragraph E.1.e of the Settlement) in accordance with this subsection.

(B) CONDITIONS MET.—The conditions described in section 1304 of title 31, United States Code, shall be deemed to be met for purposes of subparagraph (A).

(2) ADJUSTMENT.—

(A) IN GENERAL.—After the calculation of the pro rata share in Section E.4.b of the Settlement, the Trust Administration Adjustment Fund shall be used to increase the minimum payment to each Trust Administration Class Member whose pro rata share is—

(i) zero; or

(ii) greater than zero, but who would, after adjustment under this subparagraph, otherwise receive a smaller Stage 2 payment than those Trust Administration Class Members described in clause (i).

(B) RESULT.—The amounts in the Trust Administration Adjustment Fund shall be applied in such a manner as to ensure, to the extent practicable (as determined by the court in the Litigation), that each Trust Administration Class Member receiving amounts from the Trust Administration Adjustment Fund receives the same total payment under Stage 2 of the Settlement after making the adjustments required by this subsection.

(3) TIMING OF PAYMENTS.—The payments authorized by this subsection shall be included with the Stage 2 payments under paragraph E.4. of the Settlement.

(k) EFFECT OF ADJUSTMENT PROVISIONS.—Notwithstanding any provision of this section, in the event that a court determines that the application of subsection (j) is unfair to the Trust Administration Class—

(1) subsection (j) shall not go into effect; and

(2) on final approval of the Settlement, in addition to the amounts deposited into the Trust Land Consolidation Fund H. R. 4783—7 pursuant to subsection (e), the Secretary of the Treasury shall deposit in that Fund $100,000,000 out of amounts appropriated to pay final judgments, awards, and compromise settlements under section 1304 of title 31, United States Code (the conditions of which section shall be deemed to be met for purposes of this paragraph) to be used by the Secretary in accordance with subsection (e).

Source: Claims Resolution Act, Title I (2010). Public Law 111–291. Washington DC: Government Printing Office, 2010. http://www.gpo.gov/fdsys/pkg/PLAW-111publ291/pdf/PLAW-111publ291.pdf.

Interview with John EchoHawk

(2012)

John EchoHawk graduated from the University of New Mexico's School of Law in 1970 and decided to put his education to use by assisting Native Americans who did not understand laws that could affect their lives. With the goal of providing aid to Native Americans, EchoHawk established the Native American Rights Fund in 1970. Over the past four decades he has worked tirelessly to provide legal representation and assistance to tribes. At times, EchoHawk works with other groups whose interests are closely aligned with those of Native Americans, including environmental groups. The following document discusses such a working relationship with the Natural Resources Defense Council.

Q: How did you come to join NRDC [Natural Resources Defense Council] as a Member of the Board of Trustees?

A: John Adams [Executive Director of NRDC] and I were brought together in 1986 by a mutual friend, Robert Redford [also a member of NRDC's Board.] He was concerned that Native Americans and environmentalists didn't know each other as well as they should. They were natural allies, but too often we had disagreements. One of the things that came out of that meeting was the fact that the environmental organizations had virtually no Native American people on their boards or their staffs. Two years later I was asked to join the board of NRDC.

Q: In what ways do you see Native Americans and environmentalists as natural allies?

A: They both have the same outlook toward the natural world. Environmentalists have an appreciation like most tribes do of the natural environment and the need to preserve it for future generations. They understand that these natural resources are not just there to be bought and sold and used for the gains of the present generation. We need to think long term, generations down the line. We need to understand that we have an obligation as individuals to take care of this earth and to live as part of it. In that sense there's an alliance there, a unity between tribes and environmentalists.

Q: But there are still problems between environmentalists and tribes?

A: Sometimes—mostly because environmentalists do not understand that tribal governments are sovereign governments like the states and like the federal government, and that they have jurisdiction over their lands to carry out the federal environmental laws. Environmental advocates are used to battling governments and all of a sudden they find out that here's another one. But they have to realize that tribal governments are different from the kinds of governmental officials they are used to.

Q: How are tribal governments different?

A: They have different world views, different perspectives. They're basically people who understand that their ancestors have been there from the beginning of time and they have an obligation to maintain those lands for future generations. They're greatly disturbed at the pollution that has occurred. And they are determined to change that, to control it and clean it up because they've got generations of tribal members to come.

Q: They have a lot to teach us about a sense of continuity.

A: Yes, and they've always had this perspective. Their land is truly home for them. They've always been there; they're always going to be there. They're not going anyplace; they're not moving. This is land they need to protect for their future generations just like it's been protected for them by their ancestors.

Q: What is the most pressing environmental issue facing Native Americans today?

A: I'm worried about the need to have environmental laws enforced on tribal lands. That has not happened as well as it should. In 1984 the EPA adopted a tribal environmental policy that recognized the primacy of tribal governments to administer the environmental laws on their lands pursuant to their status as sovereigns, but we've had difficulty implementing that policy since then.

Q: Why?

A: It's a funding problem. We have just barely started to get funding for tribal environmental programs that carry out the federal environmental laws like the states do. As a result, most of our tribes do not have environmental programs at all. In other words, nobody's minding the store on the Indian Reservations as far as the environment goes.

Q: Are the tribes making progress in this area?

A: With the support of the environmental organizations we're finally getting there. We've had a pretty good response from the Clinton administration on this. It took them a while, but they've established a tribal working group there at EPA and are starting to focus on this issue. But we still have a long way to go.

Q: Have you seen instances where the environment on tribal lands has been seriously degraded?

A: There are environmental problems out there. They've been surveyed. We've got mining pollution, water pollution, air pollution—basically, everything. Of course, we're talking about 50 million acres of land here in the lower 48, and then another 40 million acres of Native Lands in Alaska. That's about 3% of the country.

Q: I understand that many private and public interests now seek to negotiate with tribes over water, resources, and energy issues rather than fighting it out in court. Do you consider this a form of progress?

A: It is a form of progress and it's the result of people being educated about the sovereign status of tribes, and the recognition that there are different cultures and religions that are entitled to the same respect as other cultures and religions. I hope that we've been able to turn the corner here on the old myth of Native American people being the Vanishing Americans, and the whole Federal policy of terminating tribes and taking their lands and breaking the treaties.

Source: Interview with John EchoHawk. Natural Resources Defense Council. http://www.mixitproductions.com/prjsit/lookup/intecho.html.

'Twas the Night before Ojibwe Christmas

(2012)

Movies and other media have often portrayed Native Americans as other, as people being so culturally unique from other Americans that it is difficult to find common ground. The following document is an Ojibwe take on the traditional children's poem, "'Twas the Night before Christmas." The story is retold using the original format but substituting the Ojibwe language in key areas. This tactic allows the reader to instantly identify with the presentation of Ojibwe culture by associating it with the familiar tale of their childhood. In this sense, the poem acts as a cultural bridge, showing that Native Americans are not so other after all.

'Twas the night before Niibaa-anama'egiizhigad, when all through the wigwam

Not an awakaan was stirring, not even a waawaabiganoojiinh;

The moccasins were hung by the smoke hole with care,

In hopes that Miigiwe Miskwaa Gichi Inini soon would be there;

The abinoojiinhyag were nestled all snug in their nibaaganan,

While visions of ziinzibaakwad danced in their nishttigwaan;

And nimaama in her moshwens, and I in my makadewindibe,

Had just settled down for a long biiboon zhiibaangwashi,

When outside the wiigiwaam there arose such a clatter,

I sprang from the nibaagan to see what was the matter.

Away to the waasechigan I flew like inaabiwin,

Tore open the shutters and threw up the gibiiga'iganiigin.

The dibik-giizis on the breast of onaaband

Gave a shine like duct tape to objects zazagaamagad,

When, what to my wondering nishkiizhigoon should appear,

But a miniature toboggan, and eight tiny waawaaskeshi,

With a little old driver, so lively and wajepii,

I knew in a moment it must be Miigiwe Miskwaa Gichi Inini.

More rapid than migiziwag his coursers they came,

And he whistled, and biibaagi, and izhi-wiinde by name;

"Now, Bimibatoo! now, Niimi! now, Babaamishimo and Moozhikwe!

On, Anang! on Zaagi! on, Animikii and Wawaasese!

To the top of the porch! to the top of the wiigiwaam!

Now Bimibide! Ipide! Ombibidemagad!"

As dry leaves that before the wiindigoo fly,

When they meet with BIA, mount to the sky,

So up to the apakwaan the coursers they flew,

With the tobaggon full of toys, and Miigiwe Miskwaa Gichi Inini too.

And then, in a twinkling, I heard on the apakwaan

The prancing and pawing of each little inzid.

As I drew in my iniji, and was turning around,

Down the chimney Miigiwe Miskwaa Gichi Inini came with a bound.

He was dressed all in gipagawe, from his head to his foot,

And his clothes were all tarnished with bingwiand and soot;

A bundle of toys he mangiwane on his back,

And he looked like a adaawewinini just opening his pack.

His ishkiinzigoon—how they twinkled! his inowan how merry!

His miskwanowan were like roses,

his nose like a choke-cherry!

His droll little indoon was drawn up like a bow,

And the beard of his chin was as white as gichimookamaan;

The stump of a opwaagan he held tight in his wiibidaakaajiganan,

And the smoke it encircled his head like a miskwaanzigan;

He was full up on frybread with little round belly,

That shook, when he laughed like a wiigwaasinaagan of jelly.

He was chubby and wiinin, a right jolly old elf,

And I giimoodaapi when I saw him, in spite of myself;

A wink of his ishkiinzigoon and a twist of his mangindibe,

Soon gave me to know I had nothing to gotaaji;

He ojibwemo not a word, but went straight to his work,

And filled all the moccasins; then turned with a jerk,

And laying his ibinaakwaanininj aside of his nose,

And wewebikweni, up the smoke hole he rose;

He sprang to his toboggan, to his waawaaskeshi gave a whistle,

And away they all onjinizhimo like the down of a thistle.

But I heard him biibaagi, ere he drove out of sight,

"Happy Niibaa-anama'egiizhigad to all,

And to all baamaapii."

Adoptive Couple v. Baby Girl
(2013)

In Adoptive Couple v. Baby Girl *(2013), the U.S. Supreme Court, in a 5–4 decision, ruled to overturn a custody case decided in the South Carolina Supreme Court. The case involved the disputed custody of Baby Veronica, whose father, Dusten Brown, was a member of the Cherokee Nation. The South Carolina court had found Brown a fit parent and had denied the petition of a non-Native couple to adopt Veronica. The U.S. Supreme Court stated that the Indian Child Welfare Act (IWCA) of 1978, which was passed to protect the custodial rights of Native American parents, did not apply in this case because Brown did not have physical or legal custody of the child at the time of adoption. The U.S. Supreme Court sent the case back to the lower courts to determine Veronica's placement based on state law and the court's interpretation of the IWCA.*

Adoptive Couple v. Baby Girl, 133 S. Ct. 2552, 186 L. Ed. 2d 729 (2013)

Supreme Court of the United States

ADOPTIVE COUPLE, PETITIONERS v. BABY GIRL, A MINOR CHILD UNDER THE AGE OF FOURTEEN YEARS, ET AL.

No. 12–399

On Writ of Certiorari to the Supreme Court of South Carolina.

Argued April 16, 2013, Decided June 25, 2013 OCTOBER TERM, 2012 [**730] [*2554]

[**731] [**732] [**733] Syllabus

The Indian Child Welfare Act of 1978 (ICWA), which establishes federal standards for state-court child custody proceedings involving Indian children, was enacted to address "the consequences . . . of abusive child welfare practices that [separated] Indian children from their families and tribes through adoption or foster care placement, usually in non-Indian homes," Mississippi Band of Choctaw Indians v. Holyfield, 490 U. S. 30, 32. As relevant here, the ICWA bars involuntary termination of a parent's rights in the absence of a heightened showing that serious harm to the Indian child is likely to result from the parent's "[**734] continued custody" of the child, 25 U. S. C. § 1912(f); conditions involuntary termination of parental rights with respect to an Indian child on a showing that remedial efforts have been made to prevent the "breakup of the Indian family," § 1912(d); and provides placement preferences for the adoption of Indian children to members of the child's extended family, other members of the Indian child's tribe, and other Indian families, § 1915(a).

While Birth Mother was pregnant with Biological Father's child, their relationship ended and Biological Father (a member of the Cherokee Nation) agreed to relinquish his parental rights. Birth Mother put Baby Girl up for adoption through a private adoption agency and selected Adoptive Couple, non-Indians living in South Carolina. For the duration of the pregnancy and the first four months after Baby Girl's birth, Biological Father provided no financial assistance to Birth Mother or Baby Girl. About four months after Baby Girl's birth, Adoptive Couple served Biological Father with notice of the pending adoption. In the adoption proceedings, Biological Father sought custody and stated that he did not consent to the adoption. Following a trial, which took place [*2555] when Baby Girl was two years old, the South Carolina Family Court denied Adoptive Couple's adoption petition and awarded custody to Biological Father. At the age of 27 months, Baby Girl was handed over to Biological Father, whom she had never met. The State Supreme Court affirmed, concluding that the ICWA applied because the child custody proceeding related to an Indian child; that Biological Father was a "parent" under the ICWA; that §§ 1912(d) and (f) barred the termination of his parental rights; and that had his rights been terminated, § 1915(a)'s adoption-placement preferences would have applied.

Held:

1. Assuming for the sake of argument that Biological Father is a "parent" under the ICWA, neither § 1912(f) nor § 1912(d) bars the termination of his parental rights. Pp. 6–14.

(a) Section 1912(f) conditions the involuntary termination of parental rights on a heightened showing regarding the merits of the parent's "continued custody of the child." The adjective "continued" plainly refers to a pre-[***2] existing state under ordinary dictionary definitions. The phrase "continued custody" thus refers to custody that a parent already has (or at least had at some point in the past). As a result, § 1912(f) does not apply where the Indian parent never had custody of the Indian child. This reading comports with the statutory text, which demonstrates that the ICWA was designed primarily to counteract the unwarranted removal of Indian children from Indian families. See § 1901(4). But the ICWA's primary goal is not implicated when an Indian child's adoption is voluntarily and lawfully initiated by a non-Indian parent with sole custodial rights. Nonbinding guidelines issued by the Bureau of Indian Affairs (BIA) demonstrate that the BIA envisioned that § 1912(f)'s standard would apply only to termination of a custodial parent's rights. Under this reading, Biological Father should not have been able to invoke § 1912(f) in this case because he had never had legal or physical custody of Baby Girl as of the [**735] time of the adoption proceedings. Pp. 7–11.

(b) Section § 1912(d) conditions an involuntary termination of parental rights with respect to an Indian child on a showing "that active efforts have been made to provide remedial services . . . designed to prevent the breakup of the Indian family and that these efforts have proved unsuccessful." Consistent with this text, § 1912(d) applies only when an Indian family's "breakup" would be precipitated by terminating parental rights. The term "breakup" refers in this context to "[t]he discontinuance of a relationship," American Heritage Dictionary 235 (3d ed. 1992), or "an ending as an effective entity," Webster's Third New International Dictionary 273 (1961). But when an Indian parent abandons an Indian child prior to birth and that child has never been in the Indian parent's legal or physical custody, there is no "relationship" to be "discontinu[ed]" and no "effective entity" to be "end[ed]" by terminating the Indian parent's rights. In such a situation, the "breakup of the Indian family" has long since occurred, and § 1912(d) is inapplicable. This interpretation is consistent with the explicit congressional purpose of setting certain "standards for the removal of Indian children from their families," § 1902, and with BIA Guidelines. Section 1912(d)'s proximity to §§ 1912(e) and (f), which both condition the outcome of proceedings on the merits of an Indian child's "continued custody" with his parent, strongly suggests that the phrase "breakup of the Indian family" should be read in harmony with the "continued custody" requirement. Pp. 11–14. [*2556]

2. Section 1915(a)'s adoption-placement preferences are inapplicable in cases where no alternative party has formally sought to adopt the child. No party other than Adoptive Couple sought to adopt Baby Girl in the Family Court or the South Carolina Supreme Court. Biological Father is not covered by § 1915(a) because he did not seek to adopt Baby Girl; instead, he argued that his parental rights should not be terminated in the first place. And custody was never sought by Baby Girl's paternal grandparents, other members [***3] of the Cherokee Nation, or other Indian families. Pp. 14–16. 398 S. C. 625, 731 S. E. 2d 550, reversed and remanded.

ALITO, J., delivered the opinion of the Court, in which ROBERTS, C. J., and KENNEDY, THOMAS, and BREYER, JJ., joined. THOMAS, J., and BREYER, J., filed concurring opinions. SCALIA, J., filed a dissenting opinion. SOTOMAYOR, J., filed a dissenting opinion, in which GINSBURG and KAGAN, JJ., joined, and in which SCALIA, J., joined in part.

JUSTICE ALITO delivered the opinion of the Court.

This case is about a little girl (Baby Girl) who is classified as an Indian because she is 1.2% (3/256) Cherokee. Because Baby Girl is classified in this way, the South Carolina Supreme Court held that certain provisions of the federal Indian Child Welfare Act of 1978 required her to be taken, at the age of 27 months, from the only parents she had ever known and handed over to her biological father, who had attempted to relinquish his [**736] parental rights and who had no prior contact with the child. The provisions of the federal statute [*2557] at issue here do not demand this result.

Contrary to the State Supreme Court's ruling, we hold that 25 U. S. C. § 1912(f)—which bars involuntary termination of a parent's rights in the absence of a heightened showing that serious harm to the Indian child is likely to result from the parent's "continued custody" of the child—does not apply when, as here, the relevant parent never had custody of the child. We further hold that § 1912(d)—which conditions involuntary termination of parental rights with respect to an Indian child on a showing that remedial efforts have been made to prevent the "breakup of the Indian family" — is inapplicable when, as here, the parent abandoned the Indian child before birth and never had custody of the child. Finally, we clarify that § 1915(a), which provides placement preferences for the adoption of Indian children, does not bar a non-Indian family like Adoptive Couple from adopting an Indian child when no other eligible candidates have sought to adopt the child. We accordingly reverse the South Carolina Supreme Court's judgment and remand for further proceedings.

I

"The Indian Child Welfare Act of 1978 (ICWA), 92 Stat. 3069, 25 U. S. C. §§ 1901-1963, was the product of rising concern in the mid-1970's over the consequences to Indian children, Indian families, and Indian tribes of abusive child welfare practices that resulted in the separation of large numbers of Indian children from their families and tribes through adoption or foster care placement, usually in non-Indian homes." *Mississippi Band of Choctaw Indians v. Holyfield*, 490 U. S. 30, 32 (1989). Congress found that "an alarmingly high percentage of Indian families [were being] broken up by the removal, often unwarranted, of their children from them by nontribal public and private agencies." § 1901(4). This "wholesale removal of Indian children from their homes" prompted Congress to enact the ICWA, which establishes federal standards that govern state-court child custody proceedings involving Indian children. *Id.*, at 32, 36 (internal quotation marks omitted); see also § 1902 (declaring that the ICWA establishes "minimum Federal standards for the removal of Indian children from [***4] their families").[fn1]

Three provisions of the ICWA are especially relevant to this case. First, "[a]ny party seeking" an involuntary termination of parental rights to an Indian child under state law must demonstrate that "active efforts have been made to provide remedial services and rehabilitative programs designed to prevent the breakup of the Indian family and that these efforts have proved unsuccessful." § 1912(d). [**737] Second, a state court may not involuntarily terminate parental rights to an Indian child "in the absence of a determination, supported by evidence beyond a reasonable doubt, including testimony of qualified expert witnesses, that the continued custody of the child by the parent or Indian custodian is [*2558] likely to result in serious emotional or physical damage to the child." § 1912(f). Third, with respect to adoptive placements for an Indian child under state law, "a preference shall be given, in the absence of good cause to the contrary, to a placement with (1) a member of the child's extended family; (2) other members of the Indian child's tribe; or (3) other Indian families." § 1915(a).

II

In this case, Birth Mother (who is predominantly Hispanic) and Biological Father (who is a member of the Cherokee Nation) became engaged in

December 2008. One month later, Birth Mother informed Biological Father, who lived about four hours away, that she was pregnant. After learning of the pregnancy, Biological Father asked Birth Mother to move up the date of the wedding. He also refused to provide any financial support until after the two had married. The couple's relationship deteriorated, and Birth Mother broke off the engagement in May 2009. In June, Birth Mother sent Biological Father a text message asking if he would rather pay child support or relinquish his parental rights. Biological Father responded via text message that he relinquished his rights.

Birth Mother then decided to put Baby Girl up for adoption. Because Birth Mother believed that Biological Father had Cherokee Indian heritage, her attorney contacted the Cherokee Nation to determine whether Biological Father was formally enrolled. The inquiry letter misspelled Biological Father's first name and incorrectly stated his birthday, and the Cherokee Nation responded that, based on the information provided, it could not verify Biological Father's membership in the tribal records.

Working through a private adoption agency, Birth Mother selected Adoptive Couple, non-Indians living in South Carolina, to adopt Baby Girl. Adoptive Couple supported Birth Mother both emotionally and financially throughout her pregnancy. Adoptive Couple was present at Baby Girl's birth in Oklahoma on September 15, 2009, and Adoptive Father even cut the umbilical cord. The next morning, Birth Mother signed forms relinquishing her parental rights and consenting to the adoption. Adoptive Couple initiated adoption proceedings in South Carolina a few days later, and returned there with Baby Girl. After returning to South Carolina, Adoptive Couple allowed Birth Mother to visit and [***5] communicate with Baby Girl.

It is undisputed that, for the duration of the pregnancy and the first four months after Baby Girl's birth, Biological Father provided no financial assistance to Birth Mother or Baby Girl, even though he had the ability to do so. Indeed, Biological Father "made no meaningful attempts to assume his responsibility of parenthood" during this period. App. to Pet. for Cert. 122a (Sealed; internal quotation marks omitted).

Approximately four months after Baby Girl's birth, Adoptive Couple served Biological Father with notice of the pending adoption. (This was the first notification that they had provided [**738] to Biological Father regarding the adoption proceeding.) Biological Father signed papers stating that he accepted service and that he was "not contesting the adoption." App. 37. But Biological Father later testified that, at the time he signed the papers, he thought that he was relinquishing his rights to Birth Mother, not to Adoptive Couple.

Biological Father contacted a lawyer the day after signing the papers, and subsequently [*2559] requested a stay of the adoption proceedings.[fn2] In the adoption proceedings, Biological Father sought custody and stated that he did not consent to Baby Girl's adoption. Moreover, Biological Father took a paternity test, which verified that he was Baby Girl's biological father.

A trial took place in the South Carolina Family Court in September 2011, by which time Baby Girl was two years old. 398 S. C. 625, 634-635, 731 S. E. 2d 550, 555-556 (2012). The Family Court concluded that Adoptive Couple had not carried the heightened burden under § 1912(f) of proving that Baby Girl would suffer serious emotional or physical damage if Biological Father had custody. See id., at 648-651, 731 S. E. 2d, at 562-564. The Family Court therefore denied Adoptive Couple's petition for adoption and awarded custody to Biological Father. Id., at 629, 636, 731 S. E. 2d, at 552, 556. On December 31, 2011, at the age of 27 months, Baby Girl was handed over to Biological Father, whom she had never met.[fn3]

The South Carolina Supreme Court affirmed the Family Court's denial of the adoption and the award of custody to Biological Father. Id., at 629, 731 S. E. 2d, at 552. The State Supreme Court first determined that the ICWA applied because the case involved a child custody proceeding relating to an Indian child. Id., at 637, 643, n. 18, 731 S. E. 2d, at 556, 560, n. 18. It also concluded that Biological Father fell within the ICWA's definition of a "'parent.'" Id., at 644, 731 S. E. 2d, at 560. The court then held that two separate provisions of the ICWA barred the termination of Biological Father's parental rights. First, the court held that Adoptive Couple had not shown that "active efforts ha[d] been made to provide remedial services and rehabilitative programs designed to prevent the breakup of the Indian family." § 1912(d); see also id., at 647-648, 731 S. E. 2d, at 562. Second, the court concluded that Adoptive Couple had not shown that Biological Father's "custody of Baby Girl would result in serious emotional or physical harm to her beyond a reasonable doubt." Id., at 648-649, 731 S. E. 2d, at 562-563 (citing § 1912(f)). Finally, the court stated that, even if it had decided to terminate Biological Father's parental rights, § 1915(a)'s adoption-placement preferences [***6] would have applied. Id., at 655-657, 731 S. E. 2d, at 566-567. We granted certiorari. 568 U. S. ___ (2013). [**739]

III

It is undisputed that, had Baby Girl not been 3/256 Cherokee, Biological Father would have had no right to object to her adoption under South Carolina law. See Tr. of Oral Arg. 49; 398 S. C., at 644, n. 19, 731 S. E. 2d, at 560, n. 19 ("Under state law, [Biological] Father's consent to the adoption would not have been required"). The South Carolina Supreme Court held, however, that Biological Father is a "parent" under the ICWA and that two statutory provisions — namely, § 1912(f) and § 1912(d) — bar the termination of his parental rights. In this Court, Adoptive Couple contends that Biological Father is not a "parent" and that § 1912(f) and [*2560] § 1912(d) are inapplicable. We need not — and therefore do not — decide whether Biological Father is a "parent." See § 1903(9) (defining "parent").[fn4] Rather, assuming for the sake of argument that he is a "parent,"

we hold that neither § 1912(f) nor § 1912(d) bars the termination of his parental rights.

A

Section 1912(f) addresses the involuntary termination of parental rights with respect to an Indian child. Specifically, § 1912(f) provides that "[n]o termination of parental rights may be ordered in such proceeding in the absence of a determination, supported by evidence beyond a reasonable doubt, . . . that the continued custody of the child by the parent or Indian custodian is likely to result in serious emotional or physical damage to the child." The South Carolina Supreme Court held that Adoptive Couple failed to satisfy § 1912(f) because they did not make a heightened showing that Biological Father's "prospective legal and physical custody" would likely result in serious damage to the child. 398 S. C., at 651, 731 S. E. 2d, at 564. That holding was error.

Section 1912(f) conditions the involuntary termination of parental rights on a showing regarding the merits of "continued custody of the child by the parent." The adjective "continued" plainly refers to a preexisting state. As JUSTICE SOTOMAYOR concedes, post, at 11 (dissenting opinion) (hereinafter the dissent), "continued" means "[c]arried on or kept up without cessation" or "[e]xtended in space without interruption or breach of conne[ct]ion." Compact Edition of the Oxford English Dictionary 909 (1981 reprint of 1971 ed.) (Compact OED); see also American Heritage Dictionary 288 (1981) (defining "continue" in the following manner: "1. To go on with a particular action or in a particular condition; persist. . . . 3. To remain in the same state, capacity, or place"); Webster's Third New International Dictionary 493 (1961) (Webster's) (defining "continued" as "stretching out in time or space esp. without interruption"); Aguilar v. FDIC, 63 F. 3d 1059, 1062 (CA11 1995) (per curiam) (suggesting that the phrase "continue an action" means "go on with . . . an action" that is "preexisting"). The term "continued" also can mean "resumed after interruption." Webster's 493; see American Heritage Dictionary 288. The phrase "continued custody" therefore refers to custody that a parent [**740] already has (or at least had at some point in the past). As a result, § 1912(f) does not apply in cases where the Indian parent never had custody of the Indian child.[fn5]

Biological Father's contrary [***7] reading of § 1912(f) is nonsensical. Pointing to the provision's requirement that "[n]o termination of parental rights may be ordered . . . in the absence of a determination" relating to "the continued custody of the [*2561] child by the parent," Biological Father contends that if a determination relating to "continued custody" is inapposite in cases where there is no "custody," the statutory text prohibits termination. See Brief for Respondent Birth Father 39. But it would be absurd to think that Congress enacted a provision that permits termination of a custodial parent's rights, while simultaneously prohibiting termination of a noncustodial parent's rights. If the statute draws any distinction between custodial and noncustodial parents, that distinction surely does not provide greater protection for noncustodial parents.[fn6]

Our reading of § 1912(f) comports with the statutory text demonstrating that the primary mischief the ICWA was designed to counteract was the unwarranted removal of Indian children from Indian families due to the cultural insensitivity and biases of social workers and state courts. The statutory text expressly highlights the primary problem that the statute was intended to solve: "an alarmingly high percentage of Indian families [were being] broken up by the removal, often unwarranted, of their children from them by nontribal public and private agencies." § 1901(4); see also § 1902 (explaining that the ICWA establishes "minimum Federal standards for the removal of Indian children from their families"); Holyfield, 490 U. S., at 32-34. And if the legislative history of the ICWA is thought to be relevant, it further underscores that the Act was primarily intended to stem the unwarranted removal of Indian children from intact Indian families. See, e.g., H. R.

Rep. No. 95–1386, p. 8 (1978) (explaining that, as relevant here, "[t]he purpose of [the ICWA] is to protect the best interests of Indian children and to promote the stability and security of Indian tribes and families by establishing minimum Federal standards for the removal of Indian children from their families and the placement of such children in foster or adoptive homes"); id., at 9 (decrying the "wholesale separation of Indian children" from their Indian families); id., at 22 (discussing "the removal" of Indian children from their parents pursuant to §§ 1912(e) and (f) [**741]). In sum, when, as here, the adoption of an Indian child is voluntarily and lawfully initiated by a non-Indian parent with sole custodial rights, the ICWA's primary goal of preventing the unwarranted removal of Indian children and the dissolution of Indian families is not implicated.

The dissent fails to dispute that nonbinding guidelines issued by the Bureau of Indian Affairs (BIA) shortly after the ICWA's enactment demonstrate that the BIA envisioned that § 1912(f)'s standard would apply only to termination of a custodial parent's rights. Specifically, the BIA stated that, under § 1912(f), "[a] child may not be removed simply because there is someone else willing to raise the child who is [***8] likely to do a better job"; instead, "[i]t must be shown that . . . it is dangerous for the child to remain with his or her present custodians." Guidelines for State Courts; Indian Child Custody Proceedings, 44 Fed. Reg. 67593 (1979) (hereinafter Guidelines). Indeed, the Guidelines recognized that § 1912(f) applies only when there is pre-existing custody to evaluate. [*2562] See ibid. ("[T]he issue on which qualified expert testimony is required is the question of whether or not serious damage to the child is likely to occur if the child is not removed").

Under our reading of § 1912(f), Biological Father should not have been able to invoke § 1912(f) in this case, because he had never had legal or physical custody of Baby Girl as of the time of the adoption proceedings. As an initial matter, it is undisputed that Biological Father never had physical custody of Baby Girl. And as a matter of both South Carolina and Oklahoma law, Biological Father never had legal custody either. See S. C. Code Ann. § 63-17-20(B) (2010) ("Unless the court orders otherwise, the custody of an illegitimate child is solely in the natural mother unless the mother has relinquished her rights to the child"); Okla. Stat., Tit. 10, § 7800 (West Cum. Supp. 2013) ("Except as otherwise provided by law, the mother of a child born out of wedlock has custody of the child until determined otherwise by a court of competent jurisdiction").[fn7]

In sum, the South Carolina Supreme Court erred in finding that § 1912(f) barred termination of Biological Father's parental rights.

B

Section 1912(d) provides that "[a]ny party" seeking to terminate parental rights to an Indian child under state law "shall satisfy the court that active efforts have been made to provide remedial services and rehabilitative programs designed to prevent the breakup of the Indian family and that these efforts have proved unsuccessful." The South Carolina Supreme Court found that Biological Father's parental rights could not be terminated because Adoptive Couple had not demonstrated that Biological Father had [**742] been provided remedial services in accordance with § 1912(d). 398 S. C., at 647-648, 731 S. E. 2d, at 562. We disagree.

Consistent with the statutory text, we hold that § 1912(d) applies only in cases where an Indian family's "breakup" would be precipitated by the termination of the parent's rights. The term "breakup" refers in this context to "[t]he discontinuance of a relationship," American Heritage Dictionary 235 (3d ed. 1992), or "an ending as an effective entity," Webster's 273 (defining "breakup" as "a disruption or dissolution into component parts: an ending as an effective entity"). See also Compact OED 1076 (defining "break-up" as, inter alia, a "disruption, separation into parts, disintegration"). But when an Indian parent abandons an Indian child prior to birth and that child has never been in the Indian

parent's legal or physical custody, there is no "relationship" that would be "discontinu[ed]" — and no "effective entity" that would be "end[ed]" — by the termination of the Indian parent's rights. In such a situation, the "breakup of the Indian family" has long since occurred, and § 1912(d) is inapplicable. [*2563]

Our interpretation of § 1912(d) is, [***9] like our interpretation of § 1912(f), consistent with the explicit congressional purpose of providing certain "standards for the removal of Indian children from their families." § 1902; see also, e.g., § 1901(4); Holyfield, 490 U. S., at 32-34. In addition, the BIA's Guidelines confirm that remedial services under § 1912(d) are intended "to alleviate the need to remove the Indian child from his or her parents or Indian custodians," not to facilitate a transfer of the child to an Indian parent. See 44 Fed. Reg., at 67592.

Our interpretation of § 1912(d) is also confirmed by the provision's placement next to § 1912(e) and § 1912(f), both of which condition the outcome of proceedings on the merits of an Indian child's "continued custody" with his parent. That these three provisions appear adjacent to each other strongly suggests that the phrase "breakup of the Indian family" should be read in harmony with the "continued custody" requirement. See United Sav. Assn. of Tex. v. Timbers of Inwood Forest Associates, Ltd., 484 U. S. 365, 371 (1988) (explaining that statutory construction "is a holistic endeavor" and that "[a] provision that may seem ambiguous in isolation is often clarified by the remainder of the statutory scheme"). None of these three provisions creates parental rights for unwed fathers where no such rights would otherwise exist. Instead, Indian parents who are already part of an "Indian family" are provided with access to "remedial services and rehabilitative programs" under § 1912(d) so that their "custody" might be "continued" in a way that avoids foster-care placement under § 1912(e) or termination of parental rights under § 1912(f). In other words, the provision of "remedial services and rehabilitative programs" under § 1912(d) supports the "continued custody" that is protected by § 1912(e) and § 1912(f).[**743] [fn8]

Section 1912(d) is a sensible requirement when applied to state social workers who might otherwise be too quick to remove Indian children from their Indian families. It would, however, be unusual to apply § 1912(d) in the context of an Indian parent who abandoned a child prior to birth and who never had custody of the child. The decision below illustrates this point. The South Carolina Supreme Court held that § 1912(d) mandated measures such as "attempting to stimulate [Biological] Father's desire to be a parent." 398 S. C., at 647, 731 S. E. 2d, at 562. But if prospective adoptive parents were required to engage in the bizarre undertaking of "stimulat[ing]" a biological father's "desire to be a parent," it would surely dissuade some of them from seeking to [*2564] adopt Indian children.[fn9] And this would, in turn, unnecessarily place vulnerable Indian children at a unique disadvantage in finding a permanent and loving home, even in cases where neither an Indian parent nor the relevant tribe objects to the adoption.[fn10]

In sum, the South Carolina Supreme Court erred in finding that § 1912(d) barred termination of Biological Father's parental rights.

IV

In the decision below, the South Carolina Supreme Court suggested that if it had terminated Biological Father's rights, then § 1915(a)'s preferences for the adoptive placement of an Indian child would have been applicable. [***10] 398 S. C., at 655-657, 731 S. E. 2d, at 566-567. In so doing, however, the court failed to recognize a critical limitation on the scope of § 1915(a).

Section 1915(a) provides that "[i]n any adoptive placement of an Indian child under State law, a preference shall be given, in the absence of good cause to the contrary, to a placement with (1) a member of the child's extended family; (2) other members of the Indian child's tribe; or (3) other Indian families." Contrary to the South Carolina

Supreme Court's suggestion, § 1915(a)'s preferences are inapplicable in cases where no alternative party has formally sought to adopt the child. This is because there simply is no "preference" to apply if no alternative party that is eligible to be preferred under § 1915(a) has come forward. [**744]

In this case, Adoptive Couple was the only party that sought to adopt Baby Girl in the Family Court or the South Carolina Supreme Court. See Brief for Petitioners 19, 55; Brief for Respondent Birth Father 48; Reply Brief for Petitioners 13. Biological Father is not covered by § 1915(a) because he did not seek to adopt Baby Girl; instead, he argued that his parental rights should not be terminated in the first place.[fn11] Moreover, Baby Girl's paternal grandparents never sought custody of Baby Girl. See Brief for Petitioners 55; Reply Brief for Petitioners 13; 398 S. C., at 699, 731 S. E. 2d, at 590 (Kittredge, J., dissenting) (noting that the "paternal grandparents are not parties to this action"). Nor did other members of the Cherokee Nation or "other Indian families" seek to adopt Baby Girl, even though the Cherokee Nation had notice of — and intervened in — the adoption proceedings. See Brief [*2565] for Respondent Cherokee Nation 21–22; Reply Brief for Petitioners 13–14.[fn12]

* * *

The Indian Child Welfare Act was enacted to help preserve the cultural identity and heritage of Indian tribes, but under the State Supreme Court's reading, the Act would put certain vulnerable children at a great disadvantage solely because an ancestor — even a remote one — was an Indian. As the State Supreme Court read §§ 1912(d) and (f), a biological Indian father could abandon his child in utero and refuse any support for the birth mother — perhaps contributing to the mother's decision to put the child up for adoption — and then could play his ICWA trump card at the eleventh hour to override the mother's decision and the child's best interests. If this were possible, many prospective adoptive parents would surely pause before adopting any child who might possibly qualify as an Indian under the ICWA. Such an interpretation would raise equal protection concerns, but the plain text of §§ 1912(f) and (d) makes clear that neither provision applies in the present context. Nor do § 1915(a)'s rebuttable adoption preferences apply when no alternative party has formally sought to adopt the child. We therefore reverse the judgment of the South Carolina Supreme Court and remand the case for further proceedings not inconsistent with this opinion.

It is so ordered.

[Footnotes]

1. It is undisputed that Baby Girl is an "Indian child" as defined by the ICWA because she is an unmarried minor who "is eligible for membership in an Indian tribe and is the biological child of a member of an Indian tribe," § 1903(4)(b). See Brief for Respondent Birth Father 1, 51, n. 22; Brief for Respondent Cherokee Nation 1; Brief for Petitioners 44 ("Baby Girl's eligibility for membership in the Cherokee Nation depends solely upon a lineal blood relationship with a tribal ancestor"). It is also undisputed that the present case concerns a "child custody proceeding," which the ICWA defines to include proceedings that involve "termination of parental rights" and "adoptive placement," § 1903(1).

2. Around the same time, the Cherokee Nation identified Biological Father as a registered member and concluded that Baby Girl was an "Indian child" as defined in the ICWA. The Cherokee Nation intervened in the litigation approximately three months later.

3. According to the guardian ad litem, Biological Father allowed Baby Girl to speak with Adoptive Couple by telephone the following day, but then cut off all communication between them. Moreover, according to Birth Mother, Biological Father has made no attempt to contact her since the time he took custody of Baby Girl.

4. If Biological Father is not a "parent" under the ICWA, then § 1912(f) and § 1912(d) — which relate to proceedings involving possible termination of "parental" rights — are inapplicable. Because we conclude that these provisions are inapplicable for other reasons, however, we need not decide whether Biological Father is a "parent."

5. With a torrent of words, the dissent attempts to obscure the fact that its interpretation simply cannot be squared with the statutory text. A biological father's "continued custody" of a child cannot be assessed if the father never had custody at all, and the use of a different phrase — "termination of parental rights" — cannot change that. In addition, the dissent's reliance on subsection headings, post, at 9, overlooks the fact that those headings were not actually enacted by Congress. See 92 Stat. 3071–3072.

6. The dissent criticizes us for allegedly concluding that a biological father qualifies for "substantive" statutory protections "only when [he] has physical or state-recognized legal custody." Post, at 2, 6–7. But the dissent undercuts its own point when it states that "numerous" ICWA provisions not at issue here afford "meaningful" protections to biological fathers regardless of whether they ever had custody. Post, at 4–7, and nn. 1, 2.

7. In an effort to rebut our supposed conclusion that "Congress could not possibly have intended" to require legal termination of Biological Father's rights with respect to Baby Girl, the dissent asserts that a minority of States afford (or used to afford) protection to similarly situated biological fathers. See post, at 17–18, and n. 12. This is entirely beside the point, because we merely conclude that, based on the statute's text and structure, Congress did not extend the heightened protections of § 1912(d) and § 1912(f) to all biological fathers. The fact that state laws may provide certain protections to biological fathers who have abandoned their children and who have never had custody of their children in no way undermines our analysis of these two federal statutory provisions.

8. The dissent claims that our reasoning "necessarily extends to all Indian parents who have

never had custody of their children," even if those parents have visitation rights. Post, at 2–3, 13–14. As an initial matter, the dissent's concern about the effect of our decision on individuals with visitation rights will be implicated, at most, in a relatively small class of cases. For example, our interpretation of § 1912(d) would implicate the dissent's concern only in the case of a parent who abandoned his or her child prior to birth and never had physical or legal custody, but did have some sort of visitation rights. Moreover, in cases where this concern is implicated, such parents might receive "comparable" protections under state law. See post, at 15. And in any event, it is the dissent's interpretation that would have far-reaching consequences: Under the dissent's reading, any biological parent — even a sperm donor — would enjoy the heightened protections of § 1912(d) and § 1912(f), even if he abandoned the mother and the child immediately after conception. Post, at 14, n. 8.

9. Biological Father and the Solicitor General argue that a tribe or state agency could provide the requisite remedial services under § 1912(d). Brief for Respondent Birth Father 43; Brief for United States as Amicus Curiae 22. But what if they don't? And if they don't, would the adoptive parents have to undertake the task?

10. The dissent repeatedly mischaracterizes our opinion. As our detailed discussion of the terms of the ICWA makes clear, our decision is not based on a "[p]olicy disagreement with Congress' judgment." Post, at 2; see also post, at 8, 21.

11. Section 1915(c) also provides that, in the case of an adoptive placement under § 1915(a), "if the Indian child's tribe shall establish a different order of preference by resolution, the agency or court effecting the placement shall follow such order so long as the placement is the least restrictive setting appropriate to the particular needs of the child, as provided in [§ 1915(b)]." Although we need not decide the issue here, it may be the case that an Indian child's tribe could alter § 1915's preferences in a way that includes a biological father

whose rights were terminated, but who has now reformed. See § 1915(c). If a tribe were to take such an approach, however, the court would still have the power to determine whether "good cause" exists to disregard the tribe's order of preference. See §§ 1915(a), (c); In re Adoption of T. R. M., 525 N. E. 2d 298, 313 (Ind. 1988).

12. To be sure, an employee of the Cherokee Nation testified that the Cherokee Nation certifies families to be adoptive parents and that there are approximately 100 such families "that are ready to take children that want to be adopted." Record 446. However, this testimony was only a general statement regarding the Cherokee Nation's practices; it did not demonstrate that a specific Indian family was willing to adopt Baby Girl, let alone that such a family formally sought such adoption in the South Carolina courts. See Reply Brief for Petitioners 13–14; see also Brief for Respondent Cherokee Nation 21–22. [**745]

JUSTICE THOMAS, concurring.

I join the Court's opinion in full but write separately to explain why constitutional avoidance compels this outcome. Each party in this case has put forward a plausible interpretation [***11] of the relevant sections of the Indian Child Welfare Act (ICWA). However, the interpretations offered by respondent Birth Father and the United States raise significant constitutional problems as applied to this case. Because the Court's decision avoids those problems, I concur in its interpretation.

I

This case arises out of a contested state-court adoption proceeding. Adoption proceedings are adjudicated in state family courts across the country every day, and "domestic relations" is "an area that has long been regarded as a virtually exclusive province of the States." Sosna v. Iowa, 419 U. S. 393, 404 (1975). Indeed, "[t]he whole subject of the domestic relations of husband and wife, parent and child, belongs to the laws of the States and not to the laws of the United States." In re Burrus,

136 U. S. 586, 593-594 (1890). Nevertheless, when Adoptive Couple filed a petition in South Carolina Family Court to finalize their adoption of Baby Girl, Birth Father, who had relinquished his parental rights via a text message to Birth Mother, claimed a federal right under the ICWA to block the adoption and to obtain custody.

The ICWA establishes "federal standards that govern state-court child custody proceedings involving Indian children." Ante, at 2. The ICWA defines "Indian child" as "any unmarried person who is under age eighteen and is either (a) a [*2566] member of an Indian tribe or (b) is eligible for membership in an Indian tribe and is the biological child of a member of an Indian tribe." 25 U. S. C. § 1903(4). As relevant, the ICWA defines "child custody proceeding," § 1903(1), to include "adoptive placement," which means "the permanent placement of an Indian child for adoption, including any action resulting in a final decree of adoption," § 1903(1)(iv), and "termination of parental rights," which means "any action resulting in the termination of the parent-child relationship," § 1903(1)(ii).

The ICWA restricts a state court's ability to terminate the parental rights of an Indian parent in two relevant ways. Section 1912(f) prohibits a state court from involuntarily terminating parental rights "in the absence of a determination, supported by evidence beyond a reasonable doubt, including testimony of qualified expert witnesses, that the continued custody of the child by the parent or Indian custodian is likely to result in serious emotional or physical damage to the child." Section 1912(d) prohibits a state court from terminating parental rights until the court is satisfied "that active efforts have been made to provide remedial services and rehabilitative programs designed to prevent the breakup of the Indian family and that these efforts have proved unsuccessful." A third provision creates specific placement preferences for the adoption of Indian children, which favor placement with Indians over other adoptive families. § 1915(a). Operating together, these requirements often lead to different [**746] outcomes than would result under state law. That is precisely what happened

here. See ante, at 6 ("It is undisputed that, had Baby Girl not been 3/256 Cherokee, Biological Father would have had no right to object to her adoption [***12] under South Carolina law").

The ICWA recognizes States' inherent "jurisdiction over Indian child custody proceedings," § 1901(5), but asserts that federal regulation is necessary because States "have often failed to recognize the essential tribal relations of Indian people and the cultural and social standards prevailing in Indian communities and families," ibid. However, Congress may regulate areas of traditional state concern only if the Constitution grants it such power. Admt. 10 ("The powers not delegated to the United States by the Constitution, nor prohibited by it to the States, are reserved to the States respectively, or to the people"). The threshold question, then, is whether the Constitution grants Congress power to override state custody law whenever an Indian is involved.

II

The ICWA asserts that the Indian Commerce Clause, Art. I, § 8, cl. 3, and "other constitutional authority" provides Congress with "plenary power over Indian affairs." § 1901(1). The reference to "other constitutional authority" is not illuminating, and I am aware of no other enumerated power that could even arguably support Congress' intrusion into this area of traditional state authority. See Fletcher, The Supreme Court and Federal Indian Policy, 85 Neb. L. Rev. 121, 137 (2006) ("As a matter of federal constitutional law, the Indian Commerce Clause grants Congress the only explicit constitutional authority to deal with Indian tribes"); Natelson, The Original Understanding of the Indian Commerce Clause, 85 Denver U. L. Rev. 201, 210 (2007) (hereinafter Natelson) (evaluating, and rejecting, other potential sources of authority supporting congressional power over Indians). The assertion of plenary authority must, therefore, stand or fall on Congress' power under the Indian Commerce Clause. Although this Court has said that the "central function of [*2567] the Indian Commerce Clause is to provide Congress with plenary power to legislate in the field of Indian affairs," Cotton Petroleum Corp. v. New Mexico, 490 U. S. 163, 192 (1989), neither the text nor the original understanding of the Clause supports Congress' claim to such "plenary" power.

A

The Indian Commerce Clause gives Congress authority "[t]o regulate Commerce . . . with the Indian tribes." Art. I, § 8, cl. 3. "At the time the original Constitution was ratified, 'commerce' consisted of selling, buying, and bartering, as well as transporting for these purposes." United States v. Lopez, 514 U. S. 549, 585 (1995) (THOMAS, J., concurring). See also 1 S. Johnson, A Dictionary of the English Language 361 (4th rev. ed. 1773) (reprint 1978) (defining commerce as "Intercourse; exchange of one thing for another; interchange of any thing; trade; traffick"). "[W]hen Federalists and Anti-Federalists discussed the Commerce Clause during the ratification period, they often used trade (in its selling/bartering sense) and commerce interchangeably." Lopez, supra, at 586 ([**747] THOMAS, J., concurring). The term "commerce" did not include economic activity such as "manufacturing and agriculture," ibid., let alone noneconomic activity such as adoption of children.

Furthermore, the term "commerce with Indian [***13] tribes" was invariably used during the time of the founding to mean "'trade with Indians.'" See, e.g., Natelson, 215–216, and n. 97 (citing 18th-century sources); Report of Committee on Indian Affairs (Feb 20, 1787), in 32 Journals of the Continental Congress 1774–1789, pp. 66, 68 (R. Hill ed. 1936) (hereinafter J. Cont'l Cong.) (using the phrase "commerce with the Indians" to mean trade with the Indians). And regulation of Indian commerce generally referred to legal structures governing "the conduct of the merchants engaged in the Indian trade, the nature of the goods they sold, the prices charged, and similar matters." Natelson 216, and n. 99.

The Indian Commerce Clause contains an additional textual limitation relevant to this case: Congress is given the power to regulate Commerce "with the Indian tribes." The Clause does not give Congress the power to regulate commerce with all Indian persons any more than the Foreign Commerce Clause gives Congress the power to regulate commerce with all foreign nationals traveling within the United States. A straightforward reading of the text, thus, confirms that Congress may only regulate commercial interactions — "commerce" — taking place with established Indian communities — "tribes." That power is far from "plenary."

B

Congress' assertion of "plenary power" over Indian affairs is also inconsistent with the history of the Indian Commerce Clause. At the time of the founding, the Clause was understood to reserve to the States general police powers with respect to Indians who were citizens of the several States. The Clause instead conferred on Congress the much narrower power to regulate trade with Indian tribes — that is, Indians who had not been incorporated into the body-politic of any State.

1

Before the Revolution, most Colonies adopted their own regulations governing Indian trade. See Natelson 219, and n. 121 (citing colonial laws). Such regulations were necessary because colonial traders all too often abused their Indian trading partners, through fraud, exorbitant [*2568] prices, extortion, and physical invasion of Indian territory, among other things. See 1 F. Prucha, The Great Father 18–20 (1984) (hereinafter Prucha); Natelson 220, and n. 122. These abuses sometimes provoked violent Indian retaliation. See Prucha 20. To mitigate these conflicts, most Colonies extensively regulated traders engaged in commerce with Indian tribes. See e.g., Ordinance to Regulate Indian Affairs, Statutes of South Carolina (Aug. 31, 1751), in 16 Early American Indian Documents: Treaties and Laws, 1607–1789, pp. 331–334 (A.

Vaughan and D. Rosen eds. 1998).[fn1] Over time, commercial regulation at the colonial level proved largely ineffective, in part because "[t]here was [**748] no uniformity among the colonies, no two sets of like regulations." Prucha 21.

Recognizing the need for uniform regulation of trade with the Indians, Benjamin Franklin proposed his own "articles of confederation" to the Continental Congress on July 21, 1775, which reflected his view that central control over Indian affairs should predominate over local control. 2 J. Cont'l Cong. 195–199 (W. Ford [***14] ed. 1905). Franklin's proposal was not enacted, but in November 1775, Congress empowered a committee to draft regulations for the Indian trade. 3 id., at 364, 366. On July 12, 1776, the committee submitted a draft of the Articles of Confederation to Congress, which incorporated many of Franklin's proposals. 5 id., at 545, 546, n. 1. The draft prohibited States from waging offensive war against the Indians without congressional authorization and granted Congress the exclusive power to acquire land from the Indians outside state boundaries, once those boundaries had been established. Id., at 549. This version also gave Congress "the sole and exclusive Right and Power of . . . Regulating the Trade, and managing all Affairs with the Indians." Id. at 550.

On August 20, 1776, the Committee of the Whole presented to Congress a revised draft, which provided Congress with "the sole and exclusive right and power of . . . regulating the trade, and managing all affairs with the Indians." Id., at 672, 681–682. Some delegates feared that the Articles gave Congress excessive power to interfere with States' jurisdiction over affairs with Indians residing within state boundaries. After further deliberation, the final result was a clause that included a broad grant of congressional authority with two significant exceptions: "The United States in Congress assembled shall also have the sole and exclusive right and power of . . . regulating the trade and managing all affairs with the Indians, not members of any of the States, provided that the legislative right of any State within its own limits

be not infringed or violated." Articles of Confederation, Art. IX, cl. 4. As a result, Congress retained exclusive jurisdiction over Indian affairs outside the borders of the States; the States retained exclusive jurisdiction over relations with Member-Indians;[fn2] and Congress and [*2569] the States "exercise[d] concurrent jurisdiction over transactions with tribal Indians within state boundaries, but congressional decisions would have to be in compliance with local law." Natelson 230. The drafting of the Articles of Confederation reveals the delegates' concern with protecting the power of the States to regulate Indian persons who were politically incorporated into the States. This concern for state power reemerged during the drafting of the Constitution.

2

The drafting history of the Constitutional Convention also supports a limited construction of the Indian [**749] Commerce Clause. On July 24, 1787, the convention elected a drafting committee — the Committee of Detail — and charged it to "report a Constitution conformable to the Resolutions passed by the Convention." 2 Records of the Federal Convention of 1787, p.106 (M. Farrand rev. 1966) (J. Madison). During the Committee's deliberations, John Rutledge, the chairman, suggested incorporating an Indian affairs power into the Constitution. Id., at 137, n. 6, 143. The first draft reported back to the convention, however, provided Congress with authority "[t]o regulate commerce with foreign nations, and among the several States," id., at 181 (Madison) ([***15] Aug. 6, 1787), but did not include any specific Indian affairs clause. On August 18, James Madison proposed that the Federal Government be granted several additional powers, including the power "[t]o regulate affairs with the Indians as well within as without the limits of the U. States." Id., at 324 (J. Madison). On August 22, Rutledge delivered the Committee of Detail's second report, which modified Madison's proposed clause. The Committee proposed to add to Congress' power "[t]o regulate commerce with foreign nations, and among the several States" the words, "and with Indians, within the Limits of any State, not subject to the laws thereof." Id., at 366–367 (Journal). The Committee's version, which echoed the Articles of Confederation, was far narrower than Madison's proposal. On August 31, the revised draft was submitted to a Committee of Eleven for further action. Id., at 473 (Journal), 481 (J. Madison). That Committee recommended adding to the Commerce Clause the phrase, "and with the Indian tribes," id., at 493, which the Convention ultimately adopted.

It is, thus, clear that the Framers of the Constitution were alert to the difference between the power to regulate trade with the Indians and the power to regulate all Indian affairs. By limiting Congress' power to the former, the Framers declined to grant Congress the same broad powers over Indian affairs conferred by the Articles of Confederation. See Prakash, Against Tribal Fungibility, 89 Cornell L. Rev. 1069, 1090 (2004).

During the ratification debates, opposition to the Indian Commerce Clause was nearly nonexistent. See Natelson 248 (noting that Robert Yates, a New York Anti-Federalist was "almost the only writer who objected to any part [of] of the Commerce Clause — a clear indication that its scope was understood to be fairly narrow" (footnote omitted)). Given the Anti-Federalists' vehement opposition to the Constitution's other grants of power to the Federal Government, this silence is revealing. The ratifiers almost certainly understood the Clause to confer a relatively modest power on Congress — namely, the power to regulate trade with Indian tribes living beyond state borders. And this feature of the Constitution was welcomed by Federalists and Anti-Federalists alike due to the considerable interest in expanding trade with such Indian tribes. See, e.g., The Federalist No. 42, at 265 (J. Madison) ([*2570] praising the Constitution for removing the obstacles that had existed under the Articles of Confederation to federal control over "trade with Indians"); 3 J. Elliot, The Debates in the Several State Conventions on the Adoption of the Federal Constitution 580 (2d ed. 1863)

(Adam Stephens, at the Virginia ratifying [**750] convention, June 23, 1788, describing the Indian tribes residing near the Mississippi and "the variety of articles which might be obtained to advantage by trading with these people"); The Federalist No. 24, at 158 (A. Hamilton) (arguing that frontier garrisons would "be keys to the trade with the Indian nations"); Brutus, (Letter) X, N. Y. J., Jan. 24, 1788, in 15 The Documentary History of the [***16] Ratification of the Constitution 462, 465 (J. Kaminski & G. Saladino eds. 2012) (conceding that there must be a standing army for some purposes, including "trade with Indians"). There is little evidence that the ratifiers of the Constitution understood the Indian Commerce Clause to confer anything resembling plenary power over Indian affairs. See Natelson 247–250.

III

In light of the original understanding of the Indian Commerce Clause, the constitutional problems that would be created by application of the ICWA here are evident. First, the statute deals with "child custody proceedings," § 1903(1), not "commerce." It was enacted in response to concerns that "an alarmingly high percentage of Indian families [were] broken up by the removal, often unwarranted, of their children from them by nontribal public and private agencies." § 1901(4). The perceived problem was that many Indian children were "placed in non-Indian foster and adoptive homes and institutions." Ibid. This problem, however, had nothing to do with commerce.

Second, the portions of the ICWA at issue here do not regulate Indian tribes as tribes. Sections 1912(d) and (f), and § 1915(a) apply to all child custody proceedings involving an Indian child, regardless of whether an Indian tribe is involved. This case thus does not directly implicate Congress' power to "legislate in respect to Indian tribes." United States v. Lara, 541 U. S. 193, 200 (2004). Baby Girl was never domiciled on an Indian Reservation, and the Cherokee Nation had no jurisdiction over her. Cf. Mississippi Band of Choctaw

Indians v. Holyfield, 490 U. S. 30, 53-54 (1989) (holding that the Indian Tribe had exclusive jurisdiction over child custody proceedings, even though the children were born off the reservation, because the children were "domiciled" on the reservation for purposes of the ICWA). Although Birth Father is a registered member of The Cherokee Nation, he did not live on a reservation either. He was, thus, subject to the laws of the State in which he resided (Oklahoma) and of the State where his daughter resided during the custody proceedings (South Carolina). Nothing in the Indian Commerce Clause permits Congress to enact special laws applicable to Birth Father merely because of his status as an Indian.[*2571] [fn3]

Because adoption proceedings like this one involve neither "commerce" nor "Indian tribes," there is simply no constitutional basis for Congress' assertion of authority over such proceedings. Also, the notion that Congress [**751] can direct state courts to apply different rules of evidence and procedure merely because a person of Indian descent is involved raises absurd possibilities. Such plenary power would allow Congress to dictate specific rules of criminal procedure for state-court prosecutions against Indian defendants. Likewise, it would allow Congress to substitute federal law for state law when contract disputes involve Indians. But the Constitution does not grant Congress power to override state law whenever that law happens to be applied to Indians. Accordingly, application of the ICWA to these child custody proceedings [***17] would be unconstitutional.

* * *

Because the Court's plausible interpretation of the relevant sections of the ICWA avoids these constitutional problems, I concur.

[Footnotes]

1. South Carolina, for example, required traders to be licensed, to be of good moral character, and to post a bond. Ordinance to Regulate Indian Affairs, in 16 Early American Indian Documents, at 331–334. A potential applicant's name was posted publicly before issuing the license, so anyone with objections had an opportunity to raise them. Id., at 332. Restrictions were placed on employing agents, id., at 333–334, and names of potential agents had to be disclosed. Id., at 333. Traders who violated these rules were subject to substantial penalties. Id., at 331, 334.

2. Although Indians were generally considered "members" of a State if they paid taxes or were citizens, see Natelson 230, the precise definition of the term was "not yet settled" at the time of the founding and was "a question of frequent perplexity and contention in the federal councils," The Federalist No. 42, p. 265 (C. Rossiter ed. 1961) (J. Madison).

3. Petitioners and the guardian ad litem contend that applying the ICWA to child custody proceedings on the basis of race implicates equal protection concerns. See Brief for Petitioners 45 (arguing that the statute would be unconstitutional "if unwed fathers with no preexisting substantive parental rights receive a statutory preference based solely on the Indian child's race"); Brief for Respondent Guardian Ad Litem 48–49 (same). I need not address this argument because I am satisfied that Congress lacks authority to regulate the child custody proceedings in this case.

JUSTICE BREYER, concurring.

I join the Court's opinion with three observations. First, the statute does not directly explain how to treat an absentee Indian father who had next-to-no involvement with his child in the first few months of her life. That category of fathers may include some who would prove highly unsuitable parents, some who would be suitable, and a range of others in between. Most of those who fall within that category seem to fall outside the scope of the language of 25 U. S. C. §§ 1912(d) and (f). Thus, while I agree that the better reading of the statute is, as the majority concludes, to exclude most of those fathers, ante, at 8, 12, I also understand the risk that, from a policy perspective, the Court's interpretation could prove to exclude too many. See post, at 13, 22–23 (SOTOMAYOR, J., dissenting).

Second, we should decide here no more than is necessary. Thus, this case does not involve a father with visitation rights or a father who has paid "all of his child support obligations." See post, at 13. Neither does it involve special circumstances such as a father who was deceived about the existence of the child or a father who was prevented from supporting his child. See post, at 13 n. 8. The Court need not, and in my view does not, now decide whether or how §§ 1912(d) and (f) apply where those circumstances are present.

Third, other statutory provisions not now before us may nonetheless prove relevant in cases of this kind. Section 1915 (a) grants an adoptive "preference" to "(1) a member of the child's extended family; (2) other members of the Indian child's tribe; or (3) other Indian families. . . . in the absence of good cause to the contrary." Further, § 1915(c) allows the "Indian child's tribe" to "establish a different order of preference by resolution." Could these provisions allow an absentee father to re-enter the special statutory order of preference with support from the tribe, and subject to a court's consideration of "good cause?" I raise, but do not here try to answer, the question.

JUSTICE SCALIA, dissenting.

I join JUSTICE SOTOMAYOR's dissent except as to one detail. I reject the conclusion that the Court draws from the words "continued custody" in 25 U. S. C § 1912(f) not because "literalness may strangle meaning," see post, at 11, but because there is no reason that "continued" [**752] must refer to custody in the past rather than custody in the future. I read the provision as requiring the court to satisfy itself (beyond a reasonable doubt) [*2572] not merely that initial or temporary custody is not "likely to result in serious emotional or physical damage to the child," but that continued custody is not likely to do so. See Webster's New International Dictionary 577 (2d ed. 1950) (defining "continued" as "[p]rotracted in time or space, esp. without interruption; constant"). For the reasons set forth in JUSTICE SOTOMAYOR's dissent, that connotation is much more in accord with the rest of the statute.

While I am at it, I will add one thought. The Court's opinion, it seems to me, needlessly demeans the rights of parenthood. [***18] It has been the constant practice of the common law to respect the entitlement of those who bring a child into the world to raise that child. We do not inquire whether leaving a child with his parents is "in the best interest of the child." It sometimes is not; he would be better off raised by someone else. But parents have their rights, no less than children do. This father wants to raise his daughter, and the statute amply protects his right to do so. There is no reason in law or policy to dilute that protection.

JUSTICE SOTOMAYOR, with whom JUSTICE GINSBURG and JUSTICE KAGAN join, and with whom JUSTICE SCALIA joins in part, dissenting.

A casual reader of the Court's opinion could be forgiven for thinking this an easy case, one in which the text of the applicable statute clearly points the way to the only sensible result. In truth, however, the path from the text of the Indian Child Welfare Act of 1978 (ICWA) to the result the Court reaches is anything but clear, and its result anything but right.

The reader's first clue that the majority's supposedly straightforward reasoning is flawed is that not all Members who adopt its interpretation believe it is compelled by the text of the statute, see ante, at 1 (THOMAS, J., concurring); nor are they all willing to accept the consequences it will necessarily have beyond the specific factual scenario confronted here, see ante, at 1 (BREYER, J., concurring). The second clue is that the majority begins its analysis by plucking out of context a single phrase from the last clause of the last subsection of the relevant provision, and then builds its entire argument upon it. That is not how we ordinarily read statutes. The third clue is that the majority openly professes its aversion to Congress' explicitly stated purpose in enacting the statute. The majority expresses concern that reading the Act to mean what it says will make it more difficult to place Indian children in adoptive homes, see ante, at 14, 16, but the Congress that enacted the statute announced its intent to stop "an alarmingly high percentage of Indian families [from being] broken up" by, among other things, a trend of "plac[ing] [Indian children] in non-Indian . . . adoptive homes." 25 U. S. C. § 1901(4). Policy disagreement with Congress' judgment is not a valid reason for this Court to distort the provisions of the Act. Unlike the majority, I cannot adopt a reading of ICWA that is contrary to both its text and its stated purpose. I respectfully dissent.

I

Beginning its reading with the last clause of § 1912(f), the majority concludes [**753] that a single phrase appearing there—"continued custody" —means that the entirety of the subsection is inapplicable to any parent, however committed, who has not previously had physical or legal custody of his child. Working back to front, the majority then concludes that § 1912(d), tainted by its association with § 1912(f), is also inapplicable; in the majority's view, a family bond that does not take custodial form is not a family bond worth preserving [*2573] from "breakup." Because there are apparently no limits on the contaminating power of this single phrase, the majority [***19] does not stop there. Under its reading, § 1903(9), which makes biological fathers "parent[s]" under this federal statute (and where, again, the phrase "continued custody" does not appear), has substantive force only when a birth father has physical or state-recognized legal custody of his daughter.

When it excludes noncustodial biological fathers from the Act's substantive protections, this textually backward reading misapprehends ICWA's structure and scope. Moreover, notwithstanding the majority's focus on the perceived parental shortcomings of Birth Father, its reasoning necessarily extends to all Indian parents who have never had custody of their children, no matter how fully those parents have embraced the financial and emotional responsibilities of parenting. The

majority thereby transforms a statute that was intended to provide uniform federal standards for child custody proceedings involving Indian children and their biological parents into an illogical piecemeal scheme.

A

Better to start at the beginning and consider the operation of the statute as a whole. Cf. ante, at 13 ("[S]tatutory construction 'is a holistic endeavor[,]' and . . . '[a] provision that may seem ambiguous in isolation is often clarified by the remainder of the statutory scheme'" (quoting United Sav. Assn. of Tex. v. Timbers of Inwood Forest Associates, Ltd., 484 U. S. 365, 371 (1988))).

ICWA commences with express findings. Congress recognized that "there is no resource that is more vital to the continued existence and integrity of Indian tribes than their children," 25 U. S. C. § 1901(3), and it found that this resource was threatened. State authorities insufficiently sensitive to "the essential tribal relations of Indian people and the cultural and social standards prevailing in Indian communities and families" were breaking up Indian families and moving Indian children to non-Indian homes and institutions. See §§ 1901(4)-(5). As § 1901(4) makes clear, and as this Court recognized in Mississippi Band of Choctaw Indians v. Holyfield, 490 U. S. 30, 33 (1989), adoptive placements of Indian children with non-Indian families contributed significantly to the overall problem. See § 1901(4) (finding that "an alarmingly high percentage of [Indian] children are placed in non-Indian . . . adoptive homes").

Consistent with these findings, Congress declared its purpose "to protect the best interests of Indian children and to promote the stability and security of Indian tribes and families by the establishment of minimum Federal standards" applicable to child custody proceedings involving Indian children. § 1902. Section 1903 then goes on to establish the reach of these [**754] protections through its definitional provisions. For present purposes, two of these definitions are crucial to understanding the statute's full scope.

First, ICWA defines the term "parent" broadly to mean "any biological parent . . . of an Indian child or any Indian person who has lawfully adopted an Indian child." § 1903(9). It is undisputed that Baby Girl is an "Indian child" within the meaning of the statute, see § 1903(4); ante, at 2, n. 1, and Birth Father consequently qualifies [***20] as a "parent" under the Act. The statutory definition of parent "does not include the unwed father where paternity has not been acknowledged or established," § 1903(9), but Birth Father's biological paternity has never been questioned by any party and was confirmed by a DNA test during the [*2574] state court proceedings, App. to Pet. for Cert. 109a (Sealed).

Petitioners and Baby Girl's guardian ad litem devote many pages of briefing to arguing that the term "parent" should be defined with reference to the law of the State in which an ICWA child custody proceeding takes place. See Brief for Petitioners 19–29; Brief for Respondent Guardian Ad Litem 32–41. These arguments, however, are inconsistent with our recognition in Holyfield that Congress intended the critical terms of the statute to have uniform federal definitions. See 490 U. S., at 44-45. It is therefore unsurprising, although far from unimportant, that the majority assumes for the purposes of its analysis that Birth Father is an ICWA "parent." See ante, at 7.

Second, the Act's comprehensive definition of "child custody proceeding" includes not only "'adoptive placement[s],'" "'preadoptive placement[s],'" and "'foster care placement[s],'" but also "'termination of parental rights'" proceedings. § 1903(1). This last category encompasses "any action resulting in the termination of the parent-child relationship," § 1903(1)(ii). So far, then, it is clear that Birth Father has a federally recognized status as Baby Girl's "parent" and that his "parent-child relationship" with her is subject to the protections of the Act.

These protections are numerous. Had Birth Father petitioned to remove this proceeding to tribal court, for example, the state court would have been obligated to transfer it absent an objection from Birth Mother or good cause to the contrary. See § 1911(b). Any voluntary consent Birth Father gave to Baby Girl's adoption would have been invalid unless written and executed before a judge and would have been revocable up to the time a final decree of adoption was entered. [fn1] See §§ 1913(a), (c). And § 1912, the center of the dispute here, sets forth procedural and substantive standards applicable in "involuntary proceeding[s] in a State court," including foster care placements of Indian children and termination of parental rights proceedings. § 1912(a). I consider § 1912's provisions in order. [**755]

Section 1912(a) requires that any party seeking "termination of parental rights t[o] an Indian child" provide notice to both the child's "parent or Indian custodian" and the child's tribe "of the pending proceedings and of their right of intervention." Section 1912(b) mandates that counsel be provided for an indigent "parent or Indian custodian" in any "termination proceeding." Section 1912(c) also gives all "part[ies]" to a termination proceeding — which, thanks to §§ 1912(a) and (b), will always include a biological father if he desires to be present — the right to inspect all material "reports or other documents filed with the court." By providing notice, counsel, and access to relevant documents, the statute ensures a biological father's meaningful participation [***21] in an adoption proceeding where the termination of his parental rights is at issue.

These protections are consonant with the principle, recognized in our cases, that the biological bond between parent and child is meaningful. "[A] natural parent's desire for and right to the companionship, care, custody, and management of his or her children," we have explained, "is an interest far more precious than any property [*2575] right." Santosky v. Kramer, 455 U. S. 745, 758-759 (1982) (internal quotation marks omitted). See also infra, at 19–20. Although the Constitution does not compel the protection of a biological father's parent-child relationship until he has taken steps to cultivate it, this Court has nevertheless recognized that "the biological connection . . . offers the natural father an opportunity that no other male possesses to develop a relationship with his off-spring." Lehr v. Robertson, 463 U. S. 248, 262 (1983). Federal recognition of a parent-child relationship between a birth father and his child is consistent with ICWA's purpose of providing greater protection for the familial bonds between Indian parents and their children than state law may afford.

The majority does not and cannot reasonably dispute that ICWA grants biological fathers, as "parent[s]," the right to be present at a termination of parental rights proceeding and to have their views and claims heard there.[fn2] But the majority gives with one hand and takes away with the other. Having assumed a uniform federal definition of "parent" that confers certain procedural rights, the majority then illogically concludes that ICWA's substantive protections are available only to a subset of "parent[s]": those who have previously had physical or state-recognized legal custody of his or her child. The statute does not support this departure.

Section 1912(d) provides that

"Any party seeking to effect a foster care placement of, or termination of parental rights to, an Indian child under State law shall satisfy the court that active efforts have been made to provide remedial services and rehabilitative programs designed to prevent the breakup of the Indian family and that these efforts have proved unsuccessful."

In other words, subsection (d) requires that an attempt be made to cure familial deficiencies before the [**756] drastic measures of foster care placement or termination of parental rights can be taken.

The majority would hold that the use of the phrase "breakup of the Indian family" in this subsection means that it does not apply where a birth father has not previously had custody of his child. Ante, at 12. But there is nothing about this capacious phrase that licenses such a narrowing construction. As the majority notes, "breakup" means "'[t]he discontinuance of a relationship.'" Ante, at 12 (quoting American Heritage Dictionary 235

(3d ed. 1992)). So far, all of § 1912's provisions expressly apply in actions aimed at terminating the "parent-child relationship" that exists between a birth father and his child, and they extend to it meaningful protections. As a logical matter, that relationship is fully capable [***22] of being preserved via remedial services and rehabilitation programs. See infra, at 15–17. Nothing in the text of subsection (d) indicates that this blood relationship should be excluded from the category of familial "relationships" that the provision aims to save from "discontinuance."

The majority, reaching the contrary conclusion, asserts baldly that "when an Indian parent abandons an Indian child prior to birth and that child has never been in the Indian parent's legal or physical custody, there is no 'relationship' that would be 'discontinu[ed]' . . . by the termination of the Indian parent's rights." Ante, at 12. [*2576] Says who? Certainly not the statute. Section 1903 recognizes Birth Father as Baby Girl's "parent," and, in conjunction with ICWA's other provisions, it further establishes that their "parent-child relationship" is protected under federal law. In the face of these broad definitions, the majority has no warrant to substitute its own policy views for Congress' by saying that "no 'relationship'" exists between Birth Father and Baby Girl simply because, based on the hotly contested facts of this case, it views their family bond as insufficiently substantial to deserve protection.[fn3] Ibid.

The majority states that its "interpretation of § 1912(d) is . . . confirmed by the provision's placement next to § 1912(e) and § 1912(f)," both of which use the phrase "'continued custody.'" Ante, at 13. This is the only aspect of the majority's argument regarding § 1912(d) that is based on ICWA's actual text rather than layers of assertion superimposed on the text; but the conclusion the majority draws from the juxtaposition of these provisions is exactly backward. Section 1912(f) is paired with § 1912(e), and as the majority notes, both come on the heels of the requirement [**757] of rehabilitative efforts just reviewed. The language of the two provisions is nearly identical; subsection (e) is headed "Foster care placement orders," and subsection (f), the relevant provision here, is headed "Parental rights termination orders." Subsection (f) reads in its entirety,

"No termination of parental rights may be ordered in such proceeding in the absence of a determination, supported by evidence beyond a reasonable doubt, including testimony of qualified expert witnesses, that the continued custody of the child by the parent or Indian custodian is likely to result in serious emotional or physical damage to the child." § 1912(f).[fn4]

The immediate inference to be drawn from the statute's structure is that subsections (e) and (f) work in tandem with the rehabilitative efforts required by (d). Under subsection (d), state authorities must attempt to provide "remedial services and rehabilitative programs" aimed at avoiding foster care placement or termination of parental rights; (e) and (f), in turn, bar state authorities from ordering foster care or terminating parental rights until these curative efforts have failed and it is established that the child will suffer "serious emotional or physical damage" if his or her familial situation is not altered. Nothing in subsections (a) through (d) suggests a limitation [***23] on the types of parental relationships [*2577] that are protected by any of the provisions of § 1912, and there is nothing in the structure of § 1912 that would lead a reader to expect subsection (e) or (f) to introduce any such qualification. Indeed, both subsections, in their opening lines, refer back to the prior provisions of § 1912 with the phrase "in such proceeding." This language indicates, quite logically, that in actions where subsections (a), (b), (c), and (d) apply, (e) and (f) apply too.[fn5]

All this, and still the most telling textual evidence is yet to come: The text of the subsection begins by announcing, "[n]o termination of parental rights may be ordered" unless the specified evidentiary showing is made. To repeat, a "termination of parental rights" includes "any action resulting in the termination of the parent-child relationship," 25 U. S. C. § 1903(1)(ii) (emphasis added),

including the relationship Birth Father, as an ICWA "parent," has with Baby Girl. The majority's reading disregards the Act's sweeping definition of "termination of parental rights," which is not limited to terminations of custodial relationships.

The entire foundation of the majority's argument that subsection (f) does not apply is the lonely phrase "continued [**758] custody." It simply cannot bear the interpretive weight the majority would place on it.

Because a primary dictionary definition of "continued" is "'carried on or kept up without cessation,'" ante, at 8 (brackets omitted), the majority concludes that § 1912(f) "does not apply in cases where the Indian parent never had custody of the Indian child," ante, at 8. Emphasizing that Birth Father never had physical custody or, under state law, legal custody of Baby Girl, the majority finds the statute inapplicable here. Ante, at 10–11. But "literalness may strangle meaning." Utah Junk Co. v. Porter, 328 U. S. 39, 44 (1946). See also Robinson v. Shell Oil Co., 519 U. S. 337, 341-345 (1997) (noting that a term that may "[a]t first blush" seem unambiguous can prove otherwise when examined in the context of the statute as a whole).[fn6] In light of the structure of § 1912, which indicates that subsection (f) is applicable to the same actions to which subsections (a) through (d) are applicable; the use of the phrase "such proceeding[s]" at the start of subsection (f) to reinforce this structural inference; and finally, the provision's explicit statement that it applies to "termination of parental rights" proceedings, the necessary conclusion is that the word "custody" does not strictly denote a state-recognized custodial relationship. If one refers back to the Act's definitional section, this conclusion is not surprising. Section 1903(1) includes "any action resulting in the termination of the parent-child relationship" within the meaning of "child custody proceeding," thereby belying any congressional [*2578] intent to give the term "custody" a narrow and exclusive definition throughout the statute.

In keeping with § 1903(1) and the structure and language of § 1912 overall, the phrase "continued custody" is most sensibly read to refer generally to the continuation of the parent-child relationship that an ICWA "parent" has with his or her child. A court applying [***24] § 1912(f) where the parent does not have pre-existing custody should, as Birth Father argues, determine whether the party seeking termination of parental rights has established that the continuation of the parent-child relationship will result in "serious emotional or physical damage to the child."[fn7]

The majority is willing to assume, for the sake of argument, that Birth Father is a "parent" within the meaning of ICWA. But the majority fails to account for all that follows from that assumption. The majority repeatedly [**759] passes over the term "termination of parental rights" that, as defined by § 1903, clearly encompasses an action aimed at severing Birth Father's "parent-child relationship" with Baby Girl. The majority chooses instead to focus on phrases not statutorily defined that it then uses to exclude Birth Father from the benefits of his parental status. When one must disregard a statute's use of terms that have been explicitly defined by Congress, that should be a signal that one is distorting, rather than faithfully reading, the law in question.

B

The majority also does not acknowledge the full implications of its assumption that there are some ICWA "parent[s]" to whom §§ 1912(d) and (f) do not apply. Its discussion focuses on Birth Father's particular actions, but nothing in the majority's reasoning limits its manufactured class of semi-protected ICWA parents to biological fathers who failed to support their child's mother during pregnancy. Its logic would apply equally to noncustodial fathers who have actively participated in their child's upbringing.

Consider an Indian father who, though he has never had custody of his biological child, visits her and pays all of his child support obligations. [fn8] Suppose that, due to [*2579] deficiencies in the care the child received from her custodial parent, the State placed the child with a foster

family and proposed her ultimate adoption by them. Clearly, the father's parental rights would have to be terminated [**760] before the adoption could go forward.[fn9] On the majority's view, notwithstanding the fact that this father would be a "parent" under ICWA, he would not receive the benefit of either § 1912(d) or § 1912(f). Presumably the court considering the adoption petition would have to apply some standard to determine whether termination of his parental rights was appropriate. But from whence would that standard come?

Not from the statute Congress drafted, according to the majority. The majority suggests that it might come from state law. See ante, at 13, n. 8. But it is incongruous to suppose that Congress intended a patchwork of federal and state law to apply in termination of parental rights proceedings. Congress enacted a statute aimed at protecting the familial relationships between Indian parents and their children because it concluded that state authorities "often failed to recognize the essential tribal relations of Indian people and the cultural and social standards prevailing in Indian communities and families." 25 U. S. C. § 1901(5). It provided a "minimum Federal standar[d]," § 1902, for termination of parental [***25] rights that is more demanding than the showing of unfitness under a high "clear and convincing evidence" standard that is the norm in the States, see 1 J. Hollinger, Adoption Law and Practice § 2.10 (2012); Santosky, 455 U. S., at 767-768.

While some States might provide protections comparable to § 1912(d)'s required remedial efforts and § 1912(f)'s heightened standard for termination of parental rights, many will provide less. There is no reason to believe Congress wished to leave protection of the parental rights of a subset of ICWA "parent[s]" dependent on the happenstance of where a particular "child custody proceeding" takes place. I would apply, as the statute construed in its totality commands, the standards Congress provided in §§ 1912(d) and (f) to the termination [*2580] of all ICWA "parent[s']" parent-child relationships.

II

The majority's textually strained and illogical reading of the statute might be explicable, if not justified, if there were reason to believe that it avoided anomalous results or furthered a clear congressional policy. But neither of these conditions is present here.

A

With respect to § 1912(d), the majority states that it would be "unusual" to apply a rehabilitation requirement where a natural parent has never had custody of his child. Ante, at 14. The majority does not support this bare assertion, and in fact state child welfare authorities can and do provide reunification services for biological fathers who have not previously had custody of their children.[fn10] And notwithstanding the South Carolina [**761] Supreme Court's imprecise interpretation of the provision, see 398 S. C., at 647-648, 731 S. E. 2d, at 562, § 1912(d) does not require the prospective adoptive family to themselves undertake the mandated rehabilitative efforts. Rather, it requires the party seeking termination of parental rights to "satisfy the court that active efforts have been made" to provide appropriate remedial services.

In other words, the prospective adoptive couple have to make an evidentiary showing, not undertake person-to-person remedial outreach. The services themselves might be attempted by the Indian child's Tribe, a state agency, or a private adoption agency. Such remedial efforts are a familiar requirement of child welfare law, including federal child welfare policy. See 42 U. S. C. § 671(a)(15)(B) (requiring States receiving federal funds for foster care and adoption assistance to make "reasonable efforts . . . to preserve and reunify families" prior to foster care placement or removal of a child from its home).

There is nothing "bizarre," ante, at 14, about placing on the party seeking to terminate a fathers parental rights the burden of showing that the step is necessary as well as justified. "For . . . natural parents, . . . the consequence of an erroneous termination [of parental rights] is the un necessary destruction of their natural family." Santosky, 455 U. S., at 766. In any event, the question is a non issue in this case given the family court's finding that Birth Father is "a fit and proper person to have custody of his child" who "has demonstrated [his] ability to parent effectively" and who possesses "unwavering love for this child." App. to Pet. for [***26] Cert. 128a (Sealed). Petitioners cannot show that rehabilitative efforts have "proved unsuccessful," 25 U. S. C. § 1912(d), because Birth Father is not in need of rehabilitation.[*2581] [fn11]

B

On a more general level, the majority intimates that ICWA grants Birth Father an undeserved windfall: in the majority's words, an "ICWA trump card" he can "play . . . at the eleventh hour to override the mother's decision and the child's best interests." Ante, at 16. The implicit argument is that Congress could not possibly have intended to recognize a parent-child relationship between Birth Father and Baby Girl [**762] that would have to be legally terminated (either by valid consent or involuntary termination) before the adoption could proceed.

But this supposed anomaly is illusory. In fact, the law of at least 15 States did precisely that at the time ICWA was passed.[fn12] And the law of a number of States still does so. The State of Arizona, for example, requires that notice of an adoption petition be given to all "potential father[s]" and that they be informed of their "right to seek custody." Ariz. Rev. Stat. §§ 8-106(G)-(J) (West Supp. 2012). In Washington, an "alleged father['s]" consent to adoption is required absent the termination of his parental rights, Wash. Rev. Code §§ 26.33.020(1), 26.33.160(1)(b) (2012); and those rights may be terminated only "upon a showing by clear, cogent, and convincing evidence" not only that termination is in the best interest of the child and that the father is withholding his consent to adoption contrary to child's best interests, but also that the father "has failed to perform parental duties under circumstances showing a substantial lack of regard for his parental obligations," § 26.33.120(2).[*2582] [fn13]

Without doubt, laws protecting biological fathers' parental rights can lead — even outside the context of ICWA — to outcomes that are painful and distressing for both would-be adoptive families, who lose a much wanted child, and children who must make a difficult transition. See, e.g., In re Adoption of Tobias D., 2012 Me. 45, ¶ 27, 40 A. 3d 990, 999 (recognizing that award of custody of 2½-year-old child to biological father under applicable state law once paternity is established will result in the "difficult and painful" necessity of "removing the child from the only home he has ever known"). On the other hand, these rules recognize that biological fathers have a valid interest in a relationship with their child. See supra, at 6. And children have a reciprocal interest in knowing their biological parents. See Santosky, 455 U. S., at 760-761, n. 11 (describing the foreclosure of a newborn child's opportunity to "ever know his natural parents" as a "los[s] [[**763] that] cannot be measured"). These rules also reflect the understanding that the biological bond between a parent and a child is a strong foundation on which a stable and caring relationship may be built. Many jurisdictions apply a custodial preference for a fit natural parent over a party lacking this biological link. See, e.g., Ex parte Terry, 494 So. 2d 628, 632 (Ala. 1986); Appeal of H. R., 581 A. 2d 1141, 1177 (D. C. 1990) (opinion of Ferren, J.); Stuhr v. Stuhr, 240 Neb. 239, 245, 481 N. W. 2d 212, 216 (1992); In re Michael B., 80 N. Y. 2d 299, 309, 604 N. E. 2d 122, 127 (1992). Cf. Smith v. Organization of Foster Families For Equality & Reform, 431 U. S. 816, 845 (1977) (distinguishing a natural parent'[***27] s "liberty interest in family privacy," which has its source "in intrinsic human rights," with a foster parent's parallel interest in his or her relationship with a child, which has its "origins in an arrangement in which the State has been a partner from the outset"). This preference is founded in the "presumption that fit parents act in the best interests of their children." Troxel v. Granville, 530 U. S. 57, 68 (2000) (plurality opinion). "'[H]

istorically [the law] has recognized that natural bonds of affection [will] lead parents'" to promote their child's well-being. Ibid. (quoting Parham v. J. R., 442 U. S. 584, 602 (1979)).

Balancing the legitimate interests of unwed biological fathers against the need for stability in a child's family situation is difficult, to be sure, and States have, over the years, taken different approaches to the problem. Some States, like South Carolina, have opted to hew to the constitutional baseline established by this Court's precedents and do not require a biological father's consent to adoption unless he has provided financial support during pregnancy. See Quilloin v. Walcott, 434 U. S. 246, 254-256 (1978); Lehr, 463 U. S., at 261. Other States, however, have decided to give the rights of biological fathers more robust protection and to afford them consent rights on the basis of their biological link to the child. At the time that ICWA was passed, as noted, over one-fourth of States did so. See supra, at 17–18.

ICWA, on a straightforward reading of the statute, is consistent with the law of those States that protected, and protect, birth fathers' rights more vigorously. This reading can hardly be said to generate an anomaly. ICWA, as all acknowledge, was "the product of rising concern . . . [[*2583] about] abusive child welfare practices that resulted in the separation of large numbers of Indian children from their families." Holyfield, 490 U. S., at 32. It stands to reason that the Act would not render the legal status of an Indian father's relationship with his biological child fragile, but would instead grant it a degree of protection commensurate with the more robust state-law standards.[fn14]

C

The majority also protests that a [**764] contrary result to the one it reaches would interfere with the adoption of Indian children. Ante, at 14, 16. This claim is the most perplexing of all. A central purpose of ICWA is to "promote the stability and security of Indian . . . families," 25 U. S. C. § 1902, in part by countering the trend of placing "an alarmingly high percentage of [Indian] children . . . in non-Indian foster and adoptive homes and institutions." § 1901(4). The Act accomplishes this goal by, first, protecting the familial bonds of Indian parents and children, see supra, at 4–12; and, second, establishing placement preferences should an adoption take place, see § 1915(a). ICWA does not interfere with the adoption of Indian children except to the extent that it attempts to avert the necessity of adoptive placement and makes adoptions of Indian children by non-Indian families less likely.

The majority may consider this scheme unwise. But no principle of construction licenses a court to interpret a statute with a view to averting the very consequences Congress expressly stated [***28] it was trying to bring about. Instead, it is the "'judicial duty to give faithful meaning to the language Congress adopted in the light of the evident legislative purpose in enacting the law in question.'" Graham County Soil and Water Conservation Dist. v. United States ex rel. Wilson, 559 U. S. 280, 298 (2010) (quoting United States v. Bornstein, 423 U. S. 303, 310 (1976)).

The majority further claims that its reading is consistent with the "primary" purpose of the Act, which in the majority's view was to prevent the dissolution of "intact" Indian families. Ante, at 9–10. We may not, however, give effect only to congressional goals we designate "primary" while casting aside others classed as "secondary"; we must apply the entire statute Congress has written. While there are indications that central among Congress' concerns in enacting ICWA was the removal of Indian children from homes in which Indian parents or other guardians had custody of them, see, e.g., §§ 1901(4), 1902, Congress also recognized that "there is no resource that is more vital to the continued existence and integrity of Indian tribes than their children," § 1901(3). As we observed in Holyfield, ICWA protects not only Indian parents' interests but also those of Indian tribes. See 490 U. S., at 34, 52. A tribe's interest in its next generation of citizens is adversely [*2584] affected by the placement of Indian children in homes with no connection to the tribe, whether or not those children were initially in the custody of an Indian parent.[fn15]

Moreover, the majority's focus on "intact" families, ante, at 10, begs the question of what Congress set out to accomplish with ICWA. In an ideal world, perhaps [**765] all parents would be perfect. They would live up to their parental responsibilities by providing the fullest possible financial and emotional support to their children. They would never suffer mental health problems, lose their jobs, struggle with substance dependency, or encounter any of the other multitudinous personal crises that can make it difficult to meet these responsibilities. In an ideal world parents would never become estranged and leave their children caught in the middle. But we do not live in such a world. Even happy families do not always fit the custodial-parent mold for which the majority would reserve IWCA's substantive protections; unhappy families all too often do not. They are families nonetheless. Congress understood as much. ICWA's definitions of "parent" and "termination of parental rights" provided in § 1903 sweep broadly. They should be honored.

D

The majority does not rely on the theory pressed by petitioners and the guardian ad litem that the canon of constitutional avoidance compels the conclusion that ICWA is inapplicable here. See Brief for Petitioners 43–51; Brief for Respondent Guardian Ad Litem 48–58. It states instead that it finds the statute clear.[fn16]Ante, at 17. But the majority nevertheless offers the suggestion that a contrary result would create an equal protection problem. Ibid. Cf. Brief for Petitioners 44–47; Brief for Respondent Guardian Ad Litem 53–55.

It is difficult to make sense of this suggestion in light of [***29] our precedents, which squarely hold that classifications based on Indian tribal membership are not impermissible racial classifications. See United States v. Antelope, 430 U. S. 641, 645-647 (1977); Morton v. Mancari, 417 U. S. 535, 553-554 (1974). The majority's repeated, analytically unnecessary references to the fact that Baby Girl is 3/256 Cherokee by ancestry do nothing to elucidate its intimation that the statute may violate the Equal Protection Clause as applied here. See ante, at 1, 6; see also ante, at 16 (stating that ICWA "would put certain vulnerable children at a great disadvantage solely because an ancestor — even a remote one — was an Indian" (emphasis added)). I see no ground for this Court to second-guess the membership requirements of federally [*2585] recognized Indian tribes, which are independent political entities. See Santa Clara Pueblo v. Martinez, 436 U. S. 49, 72, n. 32 (1978). I am particularly averse to doing so when the Federal Government requires Indian tribes, as a prerequisite for official recognition, to make "descen[t] from a historical Indian tribe" a condition of membership. 25 CFR § 83.7(e) (2012). [**766]

The majority's treatment of this issue, in the end, does no more than create a lingering mood of disapprobation of the criteria for membership adopted by the Cherokee Nation that, in turn, make Baby Girl an "Indian child" under the statute. Its hints at lurking constitutional problems are, by its own account, irrelevant to its statutory analysis, and accordingly need not detain us any longer.

III

Because I would affirm the South Carolina Supreme Court on the ground that § 1912 bars the termination of Birth Father's parental rights, I would not reach the question of the applicability of the adoptive placement preferences of § 1915. I note, however, that the majority does not and cannot foreclose the possibility that on remand, Baby Girl's paternal grandparents or other members of the Cherokee Nation may formally petition for adoption of Baby Girl. If these parties do so, and if on remand Birth Father's parental rights are terminated so that an adoption becomes possible, they will then be entitled to consideration under the order of preference established in § 1915. The majority cannot rule prospectively that § 1915 would not apply to an adoption petition that has not yet been filed. Indeed, the statute applies "[i]n any adoptive placement of an Indian child under State law," 25

U. S. C. § 1915(a) (emphasis added), and contains no temporal qualifications. It would indeed be an odd result for this Court, in the name of the child's best interests, cf. ante, at 15, to purport to exclude from the proceedings possible custodians for Baby Girl, such as her paternal grandparents, who may have well-established relationships with her.

* * *

The majority opinion turns § 1912 upside down, reading it from bottom to top in order to reach a conclusion that is manifestly contrary to Congress' express purpose in enacting ICWA: preserving the familial bonds between Indian parents and their children and, more broadly, Indian tribes' relationships with the future citizens who are "vital to [their] continued existence and integrity." § 1901(3).

The majority [***30] casts Birth Father as responsible for the painful circumstances in this case, suggesting that he intervened "at the eleventh hour to override the mother's decision and the child's best interests," ante, at 16. I have no wish to minimize the trauma of removing a 27-month-old child from her adoptive family. It bears remembering, however, that Birth Father took action to assert his parental rights when Baby Girl was four months old, as soon as he learned of the impending adoption. As the South Carolina Supreme Court recognized, "'[h]ad the mandate of . . . ICWA been followed [in 2010], . . . much potential anguish might have been avoided[;] and in any case the law cannot be applied so as automatically to "reward those who obtain custody, whether lawfully or otherwise, and maintain it during any ensuing (and protracted) litigation."'" 398 S. C., at 652, 731 S. E. 2d, at 564 (quoting Holyfield, 490 U. S., at 53-54).

The majority's hollow literalism distorts the statute and ignores Congress' purpose in order to rectify a perceived wrong that, while heartbreaking at the time, was a [*2586] correct application of federal law and that in any case cannot be undone. Baby Girl [**767] has now resided with her father for 18 months. However difficult it must have been for her to leave Adoptive Couple's home when she was just over 2 years old, it will be equally devastating now if, at the age of 3½, she is again removed from her home and sent to live halfway across the country. Such a fate is not foreordained, of course. But it can be said with certainty that the anguish this case has caused will only be compounded by today's decision.

I believe that the South Carolina Supreme Court's judgment was correct, and I would affirm it. I respectfully dissent.

Source: Adoptive Couple v. Baby Girl, 133 S. Ct. 2552 (2013).

Selected Bibliography

Economics, Work, and Education

Adams, David Wallace. *Education for Extinction: American Indians and the Boarding School Experience, 1875–1928.* Lawrence: University of Kansas Press, 1995.

Ambler, Marjane. *Breaking the Iron Bonds: Indian Control of Energy Development.* Lawrence: University of Kansas Press, 1990.

Archuleta, Margaret L., Brenda J. Child, and K. Tsianina Lomawaima. *Away from Home: American Indian Boarding School Experiences, 1879–2000.* Santa Fe, NM: Distributed by the Museum of New Mexico Press/Heard Museum, 2000.

Bowker, Ardy. *Sisters in the Blood: The Education of Women in Native America.* Newton, MA: WEEA Publishing Center, 1993.

Champagne, Duane, and Jay Stauss, eds. *Native American Studies in Higher Education: Models for Collaboration between Universities and Indigenous Nations.* Walnut Creek, CA: AltaMira Press, 2002.

Coleman, Michael C. *American Indian Children at School, 1850–1930.* Jackson: University Press of Mississippi, 1993.

Dejong, David H. *Promises of the Past: A History of Indian Education.* Golden, CO: North American Press, 1993.

Deloria, Vine, Jr., and Daniel R. Wildcat. *Power and Place: Indian Education in America.* Golden, CO: Fulcrum Resources, 2001.

Hosmer, Brian, and Colleen O'Neill, eds. *Native Pathways: American Indian Culture and Economic Development in the Twentieth Century.* Boulder: University of Colorado Press, 2004.

Huff, Delores J. *To Live Heroically: Institutional Racism and American Indian Education.* Albany: State University of New York Press, 1997.

Kamp, Kathryn A., ed. *Children in the Prehistoric Puebloan Southwest.* Salt Lake City: University of Utah Press, 2002.

Kasari, Patricia. *The Impact of Occupational Dislocation: The American Indian Labor Force at the Close of the Twentieth Century.* New York: Garland Publishers, 1999.

Krupat, Arnold. *Red Matters: Native American Studies.* Philadelphia: University of Pennsylvania Press, 2002.

Littlefield, Alice, and Martha C. Knack, eds. *Native Americans and Wage Labor.* Norman: University of Oklahoma Press, 1996.

Lomawaima, Tsianina K. *"To Remain Indian": Lessons in Democracy from a Century of Native American Education.* New York: Teachers College Press, 2006.

Mann, Henrietta. *Cheyenne-Arapaho Education 1871–1982.* Niwot: University of Colorado Press, 1997.

O'Neill, Colleen M. *Working the Navajo Way: Labor and Culture in the Twentieth Century.* Lawrence: University Press of Kansas, 2005.

Shoemaker, Nancy, ed. *Clearing a Path: Theorizing the Past in Native American Studies.* New York: Routledge, 2002.

Thorne, Tanis C. *The World's Richest Indian: The Scandal over Jackson Barnett's Oil Fortune.* New York: Oxford University Press, 2003.

Trennert, Robert A., Jr. *The Phoenix Indian School: Forced Assimilation in Arizona, 1891–1935.* Norman: University of Oklahoma Press, 1988.

Weaver, Jace, ed. *Defending Mother Earth: Native American Perspectives on Environmental Justice.* New York: Orbis Books, 1996.

History

Algier, Keith. *The Crow and the Eagle: A Tribal History from Lewis and Clark to Custer.* Caldwell, ID: Caxton Printers, 1993.

Bailey, Garrick, and Roberta Glenn Bailey. *A History of the Navajos: The Reservation Years.* Santa Fe, NM: School of American Research Press, 1986.

Bayer, Laura, with Floyd Montoya and the Pueblo of Santa Ana. *Santa Ana: The People, the Pueblo, and the History of Tamaya.* Albuquerque: University of New Mexico Press, 1994.

Blackbird, Andrew J. *History of the Ottawa and Chippewa Indians of Michigan.* Ypsilanti, MI: Ypsilantian Job Printing House, 1887.

Bradley, James W. *Evolution of the Onondaga Iroquois: Accommodating Change, 1500–1655.* Syracuse, NY: Syracuse University Press, 1987.

Brown, Dee. *Bury My Heart at Wounded Knee: An Indian History of the American West.* New York: Bantam Books, 1971.

Cleland, Charles. *Rites of Conquest: The History and Culture of Michigan's Native Americans.* Ann Arbor: University of Michigan Press, 1992.

Conn, Steven. *History's Shadow: Native Americans and Historical Consciousness in the Nineteenth Century.* Chicago: University of Chicago Press, 2004.

Conser, Walter H., and Sumner B. Twiss, eds. *Religious Diversity and American Religious History: Studies in Traditions and Cultures.* Athens: University of Georgia Press, 1997.

Dale, Edward Everett, and Gaston Litton, eds. *Cherokee Cavaliers: Forty Years of Cherokee History as Told in the Correspondence of the Ridge-Watie-Boudinot Family.* Norman: University of Oklahoma Press, 1939.

Deloria, Philip J., and Neal Salisbury, eds. *A Companion to American Indian History.* Malden, MA: Blackwell Publishing, 2004.

Fenton, William N. *The Great Law and the Longhouse: A Political History of the Iroquois Confederacy.* Norman: University of Oklahoma Press, 1998.

Ferguson, T. J., and Chip Colwell-Chanthaphonh. *History Is in the Land: Multivocal Tribal Traditions in Arizona's San Pedro Valley.* Tucson: University of Arizona Press, 2006.

Hart, E. Richard. *Pedro Pino: Governor of Zuni Pueblo, 1830–1878.* Logan: Utah State University Press, 2003.

Hele, Karl, ed. *Lines Drawn upon the Water: First Nations and the Great Lakes Borders and Borderlands.* Waterloo, ON: Wilfrid Laurier Press, 2008.

Hoxie, Frederick E., ed. *Talking Back to Civilization: Indian Voices from the Progressive Era.* Boston, MA: Bedford/St. Matins, 2001.

Hoxie, Frederick E., Peter C. Mancall, and James H. Merrell. *American Nations: Encounters in Indian Country, 1850 to the Present.* New York: Routledge, 2001.

Jemison, G. Peter, and Anna M. Schein, eds. *Treaty of Canandaigua, 1794: 200 Years of Treaty Relations between the Iroquois Confederacy and the United States.* Santa Fe, NM: Clear Light, 2000.

Mann, Charles C. *1491: New Revelations of the Americas before Columbus.* New York: Alfred A. Knopf, 2005.

Martin, Calvin, ed. *The American Indian and the Problem of History.* New York: Oxford University Press, 1987.

McCoy, Isaac. *History of Baptist Indian Missions.* Washington, DC: W. M. Morrison, 1840.

Nabokov, Peter. *A Forest of Time: American Indian Ways of History.* New York: Cambridge University Press, 2002.

Richter, Daniel K. *Facing East from Indian Country: A Native History of Early America.* Cambridge, MA: Harvard University Press, 2001.

Rusco, Elmer. *A Fateful Time: The Background and Legislative History of the Indian Reorganization Act.* Reno: University of Nevada Press, 2000.

Schoolcraft, Henry R. *History of the Indian Tribes of the United States.* Philadelphia, PA: J. B. Lippincott & Co., 1857.

Speroff, Leon. *Carlos Montezuma, M.D.: A Yavapai American Hero, the Life and Times of an American Indian, 1866–1923.* Portland, OR: Arnica Publishers, 2003.

Terrell, John Upton. *The Navajos: The Past and Present of a Great People—The Story of the Largest Indian Tribe in America.* New York: Weybright and Talley, 1970.

Thomas, Davis, and Karin Ronnefeldt, eds. *People of the First Man: Life among the Plains in Their Final Days of Glory, the Firsthand Account of Prince Maximillian's Expedition Up the Missouri River, 1833–34.* 1843. Reprint, New York: Promontory Press, 1982.

Thorton, Russell. *American Indian Holocaust and Survival: A Population History since 1492.* Norman: University of Oklahoma Press, 1987.

Trachenberg, Alan. *Shades of Hiawatha: Staging Indians, Making Americans, 1880–1930.* New York: Hill and Wang, 2004.

Underhill, Ruth M. *Red Man's America: A History of Indians in the United States.* Chicago: University of Chicago Press, 1953.

Washburn, Wilcomb, ed. *The American Indian and the United States: A Documentary History.* 4 vols. New York: Random House, 1973.

Whalen, Michael E., and Paul E. Minnis. *Casas Grandes and Its Hinterland: Prehistoric Organization in Northeast Mexico.* Tucson: University of Arizona Press, 2001.

White, Richard. *The Middle Ground: Indians, Empires, and Republics in the Great Lakes Region, 1650–1815.* New York: Cambridge University Press, 1991.

Wilkinson, Charles. *Blood Struggle: The Rise of Modern Indian Nations.* New York: W. W. Norton and Company, 2005.

Wright, Ronald. *Stolen Continents: The "New World" through Indian Eyes since 1492.* New York: Viking, 1992.

Wunder, John R., ed. *Native American Sovereignty.* New York: Garland Publishing, 1999.

Young, Richard K. *The Ute Indians of Colorado in the Twentieth Century.* Norman: University of Oklahoma Press, 1997.

Identity, Culture, and Community

Ackerman, Lilian A. *A Necessary Place: Gender and Power among Indians on the Columbian Plateau.* Norman: University of Oklahoma Press, 2003.

Acoose, Janice (Misko-Kisikawihkwe). *Iskwewak Kah Ki Yaw Ni Wahkomakanak: Neither Indian Princesses nor Easy Squaws.* Ontario: Women's Press, 1995.

Allen, Paula Gunn. *The Sacred Hoop: Recovering the Feminine in American Indian Traditions.* Boston: Beacon Press, 1986.

Archambault, Marie Therese, Mark Thiel, and Christopher Vecsey, eds. *The Crossing of Two Roads: Being Catholic and Native in the United States.* Maryknoll, NY: Orbis Books, 2003.

Axtell, James. *Natives and Newcomers: The Cultural Origins of North America.* Oxford: Oxford University Press, 2001.

Basso, Keith H. *Wisdom Sits in Places: Landscape and Language among the Western Apache.* Albuquerque: University of New Mexico Press, 1996.

Bataille, Gretchen M., ed. *Native American Representations: First Encounters, Distorted Images, and Literary Appropriations.* Lincoln: University of Nebraska Press, 2001.

Blue Spruce, Duane, ed. *Spirit of a Native Place: Building the National Museum of the American Indian.* Washington, DC: Smithsonian Institution in association with National Geographic, 2004.

Bordewich, Fergus M. *Killing the White Man's Indian: Reinventing Native Americans at the End of the Twentieth Century.* New York: Doubleday, 1996.

Boyd, Loree. *Spirit Moves: The Story of Six Generations of Native Women.* Novato, CA: New World Library, 1996.

Boyer, Ruth McDonald, and Narcissus Duffy Gayton. *Apache Mothers and Daughters.* Norman: University of Oklahoma Press, 1992.

Brooks, James F., ed. *Confounding the Color Line: The Indian-Black Experience in North America.* Lincoln: University of Nebraska Press, 2002.

Champagne, Duane. *American Indian Societies: Strategies and Conditions of Political and Cultural Survival.* Cambridge, MA: Harvard University Press, 1989.

Clifton, James A. *The Invented Indian: Cultural Fictions and Government Policies.* New Brunswick, NJ: Transaction Publishers, 1994.

DeMallie, Raymond J., and Alphonso Ortiz, eds. *North American Indian Anthropology: Essays on Society and Culture.* Norman: University of Oklahoma Press, 1994.

Edmunds, R. David. *The New Warriors: Native American Leaders since 1900.* Lincoln: University of Nebraska Press, 2001.

Fixico, Donald L. *The American Indian Mind in a Linear World: American Indian Studies & Traditional Knowledge.* New York: Routledge, 2003.

Greymorning, Stephen, ed. *A Will to Survive: Indigenous Essays on the Politics of Culture, Language, and Identity.* Boston, MA: McGraw Hill, 2004.

Hertzberg, Hazel W. *The Search for an American Indian Identity: Modern Pan-Indian Movements.* Syracuse, NY: Syracuse University Press, 1971.

Higham, John. *Strangers in the Land: Patterns of American Nativism, 1860–1925.* Rutgers, NJ: Rutgers University Press, 2002.

Lobo, Susan, and Kurt Peters, eds. *American Indians and the Urban Experience.* Walnut Creek, CA: AltaMira Press, 2001.

Nagel, Joane. *American Indian Ethnic Renewal: Red Power and the Resurgence of Identity and Culture.* New York: Oxford University Press, 1996.

Peters, Virginia Bergman. *Women of the Earth Lodges: Tribal Life on the Plains.* Norman: University of Oklahoma Press, 2000.

Sando, Joe S. *Pueblo Profiles: Cultural Identity through Centuries of Change.* Santa Fe, NM: Clear Light Publishers, 1998.

Thomas, David Hurst. *Skull Wars: Kennewick Man, Archaeology, and the Battle for Native American Identity.* New York: Basic Books, 2000.

Thwaites, Reuben Gold, ed. *The Jesuit Relations and Allied Documents: Travel and Explorations of the Jesuit Missionaries in New France, 1610–1791.* 73 vols. New York: Pageant Books, 1959.

Tinker, George E. *Missionary Conquest: The Gospel and Native American Cultural Genocide.* Minneapolis, MN: Fortress Press, 1993.

Trafzer, Clifford E. *Medicine Ways: Disease, Health, and Survival among Native Americans.* Walnut Creek, CA: AltaMira Press, 2001.

Weibel-Orlando, Joan. *Indian Country, L.A.: Maintaining Ethnic Community in Complex Society.* Urbana: University of Illinois Press, 1999.

White, Robert H. *Tribal Assets: The Rebirth of Native America.* New York: Holt, 1991.

Wyss, Hilary E. *Writing Indians: Literacy, Christianity, and Native Community in Early America.* Amherst: University of Massachusetts Press, 2000.

Young, M. Jane. *Signs from the Ancestors: Zuni Cultural Symbolism and Perceptions of Rock Art.* Albuquerque: University of New Mexico Press, 1988.

Literature, Arts, and Media

Abbott, Lawrence, ed. *I Stand in the Center of the Good: Interviews with Contemporary Native American Artists.* Lincoln: University of Nebraska Press, 1994.

Allen, Paula Gunn, ed. *Spider Woman's Granddaughters: Traditional Tales and Contemporary Writing by Native American Women.* New York: Fawcett Columbine, 1989.

Angel, Michael. *Preserving the Sacred: Historical Perspectives on the Ojibwa Midewiwin.* Winnipeg: University of Manitoba Press, 2002.

Bataille, Gretchen M., and Charles L. Silet, eds. *The Pretend Indians: Images of Native Americans in the Movies.* Ames: Iowa State University Press, 1980.

Bellin, Joshua David. *The Demon of the Continent: Indians and the Shaping of American Literature.* Philadelphia: University of Pennsylvania Press, 2000.

Berkhofer, Robert F., Jr. *The White Man's Indian: Images of the American Indian from Columbus to the Present.* New York: Vintage Books, 1978.

Bird, Gloria, and Joy Harko, eds. *Reinventing the Enemy's Language: Contemporary Native Women's Writing of North America.* New York: W. W. Norton, 1997.

The Book of Elders: The Life Stories and Wisdom of Great American Indians. As told to Sandy
    Johnson and photographed by Dan Budnick. New York: Harper Collins, 1994.

Bruchac, Joseph, ed. *Survival This Way: Interviews with American Indian Poets.* Tucson:
    University of Arizona Press, 1987.

Caldwell, E. K., ed. *Dreaming the Dawn: Conversations with Native Artists and Activists.*
    Lincoln: University of Nebraska Press, 1999.

Carmack, W. C., ed. *Indian Oratory: Famous Speeches by Noted Indian Chieftains.* Norman:
    University of Oklahoma Press, 1971.

Cody, Iron Eyes. *My Life as a Hollywood Indian.* New York: Everest House, 1982.

Cook-Lynn, Elizabeth. *Why I Can't Read Wallace Stegner and Other Essays: A Tribal Voice.*
    Madison: University of Wisconsin Press, 1996.

Coward, John M. *The Newspaper Indian: Native American Identity in the Press, 1820–1890.*
    Urbana: University of Illinois Press, 1999.

de Ramirez, Susan Berry Brill. *Contemporary American Indian Literatures and the Oral
    Tradition.* Tucson: University of Arizona Press, 1999.

Harris, LaDonna, with Henrietta H. Stockel. *LaDonna Harris: A Comanche Life.* Lincoln:
    University of Nebraska Press, 2000.

Jacobs, Sue Ellen, and Josephine Binford with M. Ellien Carroll, Henrietta Smith, and Tilar
    Mazzeo, eds. *My Life in San Juan Pueblo: Stories of Esther Martinez.* Champaign:
    University of Illinois Press, 2004.

Katanski, Amelia V. *Learning to Write "Indian:" The Boarding School Experience and
    American Indian Literature.* Norman: University of Oklahoma Press, 2005.

Kilcup, Karen L., ed. *Native American Women's Writing, c. 1800–1924: An Anthology.*
    Oxford: Blackwell Publishers, 2000.

LaDuke, Winona. *The Winona LaDuke Reader: A Collection of Essential Writings.* Stillwater,
    MN: Voyaguer Press, 2002.

Larson, Sidner. *Captured in the Middle: Tradition and Experience in Contemporary Native
    American Writing.* Seattle, WA: University of Washington Press, 2000.

Liberty, Margot, ed. *American Indian Intellectuals of the Nineteenth and Twentieth Centuries.*
    Norman: University of Oklahoma Press, 2002.

Luthin, Herbert W. *Surviving through the Days: Translations of Native California Stories and
    Songs.* Berkeley, CA: University of California Press, 2002.

Maddox, Lucy. *Removals: Nineteenth Century American Literature and the Politics of Indian
    Affairs.* New York: Oxford University Press, 1991.

Moore, Marilyn, ed. *Genocide of the Mind: New Native American Writing.* New York:
    Thunder's Mouth Press, 2003.

Owens, Lois. *Mixed Blood Messages: Literature, Film, Family, Place.* Norman: University of
    Oklahoma Press, 1998.

Parker, Robert Dale. *The Invention of Native American Literature.* Ithaca, NY: Cornell
    University Press, 2003.

Schubell, Matthias. *N. Scott Momaday: The Cultural and Literary Background.* Norman:
    University of Oklahoma Press, 1985.

Tedlock, Barbara. *The Beautiful and the Dangerous: Dialogues with the Zuni Indians.* New
    York: Penguin Books, 1993.

Velie, Alan R., ed. *Native American Perspectives on Literature and History.* Norman:
    University of Oklahoma Press, 1995.

Walker, Cheryl. *Indian Nation: Native American Literature and Nineteenth Century Nationalisms.* Durham, NC: Duke University Press, 1997.

Walters, Anna Lee. *Talking Indian: Reflections on Survival and Writing.* Ithaca, NY: Firebrand, 1992.

Weaver, Jace. *Other Words: American Indian Literature, Law, and Culture.* Norman: University of Oklahoma Press, 2001.

Weaver, Jace. *That People Might Live: Native American Literatures and Native American Community.* New York: Oxford University Press, 1997.

Weaver, Jace, Craig S. Womack, and Robert Warrior. *American Indian Literary Nationalism.* Albuquerque: University of New Mexico Press, 2005.

Weston, Mary Ann. *Native America in the News: Images of Indians in the Twentieth Century Press.* Westport, CT: Greenwood, 1996.

Wiget, Andrew, ed. *Critical Essays on Native American Literature.* Boston, MA: G. K. Hall, 1985.

Witt, Shirley Hill, and Stan Steiner, eds. *The Way: An Anthology of American Indian Literature.* New York: Vintage Books, 1972.

Womack, Craig. *Red on Red: Native American Literary Separatism.* Minneapolis: University of Minnesota Press, 1999.

Politics, Law, and Activism

Banks, Dennis, with Richard Erdoes. *Ojibwa Warrior: Dennis Banks and the Rise of the American Indian Movement.* Norman: University of Oklahoma Press, 2004.

Blue Cloud, Peter, ed. *Alcatraz Is Not an Island.* Berkeley, CA: Wingbow Press, 1972.

Boldt, Menno. *Surviving as Indians: The Challenge of Self-Government.* Toronto: University of Toronto Press, 1993.

Bolt, Christine. *American Indian Policy and American Reform: Case Studies of the Campaign to Assimilate the American Indians.* Boston, MA: Allen and Unwin, 1987.

Bray, Tamara L., ed. *The Future of the Past: Archaeologists, Native Americans, and Repatriation.* New York: Garland Publishers, 2001.

Callicot, J. Baird, and Michael P. Nelson. *American Indian Environmental Ethics: An Ojibwa Case Study.* Upper Saddle River, NJ: Pearson/Prentice Hall, 2004.

Carr, Helen. *Inventing the American Primitive: Politics, Gender, and the Representation of Native American Literary Traditions, 1789–1936.* New York: New York University Press, 1996.

Castile, George Pierre. *Taking Charge: Native American Self-Determination and Federal Indian Policy, 1975–1993.* Tucson: University of Arizona Press, 2006.

Champagne, Duane. *Social Order and Political Change: Constitutional Governments among the Cherokee, the Choctaw, the Chickasaw, and the Creek.* Stanford, CA: Stanford University Press, 1992.

Cornell, Stephen. *The Return of the Native: American Indian Political Resurgence.* New York: Oxford University Press, 1988.

Darian-Smith, Eve. *New Capitalists: Law, Politics, and Identity Surrounding Casino Gaming on Native American Land.* Belmont, CA: Thomas/Wadsworth, 2004.

Grande, Sandy. *Red Pedagogy: Native American Social and Political Thought.* Lanham, MD: Rowman & Littlefield Publishers, 2004.

Green, Michael. *The Politics of Indian Removal: Creek Government and Society.* Lincoln: University of Nebraska Press, 1982.

Johnson, Troy, ed. *Contemporary Native American Political Issues.* Walnut Creek, CA: AltaMira Press, 1999.

Konkle, Maureen. *Writing Indian Nations: Native Intellectuals and the Politics of Historiography, 1827–1863.* Chapel Hill: University of North Carolina Press, 2004.

Mason, W. Dale. *Indian Gaming: Tribal Sovereignty and American Politics.* Norman: University of Oklahoma Press, 2000.

Meyer, John M., ed. *American Indians and U.S. Politics: A Companion Reader.* Westport, CT: Praeger, 2002.

Prucha, Francis Paul. *American Indian Treaties: The History of a Political Anomaly.* Berkeley: University of California Press, 1994.

Pulitano, Elvira. *Toward a Native American Critical Theory.* Lincoln: University of Nebraska Press, 2003.

Unser, Daniel H. *Indians, Settlers, and Slaves in a Frontier Exchange Economy: The Lower Mississippi Valley before 1783.* Chapel Hill: University of North Carolina Press, 1992.

Viola, Herman J. *Ben Nighthorse Campbell: An American Warrior.* Boulder, CO: Johnson Books, 2002.

Wilkins, David E. *American Indian Politics and the American Political System.* 2nd ed. New York: Rowan & Littlefield Publishers, 2007.

Wilkins, David E. *The Navajo Political Experience.* Tsaile, AZ: Dine College Press, 1999.

Wilkens, David E., and Tsianina Lomawaima. *Uneven Ground: American Indian Sovereignty and Federal Law.* Norman: University of Oklahoma Press, 2001.

Williams, Robert A. *The American Indian in Western Legal Thought: The Discourses of Conquest.* New York: Oxford University Press, 1990.

Young, Robert W. *A Political History of the Navajo Tribe.* Tsaile, AZ: Navajo Community College Press, 1978.

Spirituality and Religion

Boyd, Doug. *Mad Bear: Spirit, Healing, and the Sacred in the Life of a Native American Medicine Man.* New York: Simon and Schuster, 1994.

Bruchac, Joseph. *Roots of Survival: Native American Storytelling and the Sacred.* Golden, CO: Fulcrum Publishing, 1996.

Cave, Alfred. *Prophets of the Great Spirit: Native American Revitalization Movements in Eastern North America.* Lincoln: University of Nebraska Press, 2006.

Deloria, Barbara, Kristen Foehner, and Sam Scinta, eds. *Spirit and Reason: The Vine Deloria, Jr. Reader.* Golden, CO: Fulcrum Publishing, 1999.

Harrod, Howard L. *The Animals Came Dancing: Native American Sacred Ecology and Animal Kinship.* Tucson: University of Arizona Press, 2000.

Johnston, Basil. *The Manitous: The Spiritual World of the Ojibway.* St. Paul: Minnesota Historical Press, 2001.

Martin, Joel W. *The Land Looks After Us: A History of Native American Religion.* New York: Oxford University Press, 2001.

Pratt, Scott L. *Native Pragmatism: Rethinking the Roots of American Philosophy*. Bloomington: Indiana University Press, 2002.

Sweet, Leonard I., ed. *The Evangelical Tradition in America*. Macon, GA: Mercer University Press, 1997.

Treat, James, ed. *Native and Christian: Indigenous Voices on Religious Identity in the United States and Canada*. New York: Routledge, 1996.

Vecsey, Christopher. *Traditional Ojibwa Religion and Its Historical Changes*. Philadelphia, PA: The American Philosophical Society, 1983.

War and Conflict

Akwesasne Notes. *Voices from Wounded Knee: In the Words of the Participants*. 3rd printing, Mohawk Nation: Akwesasne Notes, 1975.

Anderson, William L., ed. *Cherokee Removal: Before and After*. Athens: University of Georgia, 1991.

Andrew, John A., III. *From Revivals to Removal: Jeremiah Evarts, the Cherokee Nation, and the Search for the Soul of America*. Athens: University of Georgia Press, 1992.

Aquila, Richard. *The Iroquois Restoration: Iroquois Diplomacy on the Colonial Frontier, 1701–1754*. Lincoln: University of Nebraska Press, 1997.

Bachman, Ronet. *Death and Violence on the Reservation: Homicide, Family Violence, and Suicide in American Indian Populations*. New York: Auburn House, 1992.

Beal, Merrill D. *"I Will Fight No More Forever:" Chief Joseph and the Nez Perce War*. Seattle: University of Washington Press, 1963.

Calloway, Colin G. *The American Revolution in Indian Country: Crisis and Diversity in Native American Communities*. New York: Cambridge University Press, 1995.

Cave, Alfred. *The French and Indian War*. Westport, CT: Greenwood Press, 2004.

Cave, Alfred. *Lethal Encounters: Englishmen and Indians in Colonial Virginia*. Westport, CT: Praeger, 2011.

Cave, Alfred. *The Pequot War*. Amherst: University of Massachusetts Press, 1996.

Churchill, Ward. *A Little Matter of Genocide: Holocaust and Denial in the Americas from 1492 to the Present*. San Francisco, CA: City Light Publishers, 2001.

Cook-Lynn, Elizabeth. *Anti-Indianism in Modern America: A Voice from Tatekeya's Earth*. Chicago: University of Illinois Press, 2001.

Danziger, Edmund Jefferson. *Great Lakes Indian Accommodation and Resistance during the Early Reservation Years, 1850–1900*. Ann Arbor: University of Michigan Press, 2009.

Decker, Peter R. *"The Utes Must Go" American Expansion and the Removal of a People*. Golden, CO: Fulcrum Publishing, 2004.

Fine-Dare, Kathleen S. *Grave Injustice: The American Indian Repatriation Movement and NAGPRA*. Lincoln: University of Nebraska Press, 2002.

Garrison, Tim Alan. *The Legal Ideology of Removal: The Southern Judiciary of Native American Nations*. Athens: University of Georgia Press, 2002.

Greene, Jerome A., ed. *Lakota and Cheyenne: Indian Views of the Great Sioux War, 1876–1877*. Norman: University of Oklahoma Press, 1994.

Hampton, Bruce. *Children of Grace: The Nez Perce War of 1877*. New York: Henry Holt, 1994.

Harvard Project on Indian Economic Development. *The State of the Native Nations: Conditions under U.S. Policies of Self Determination.* New York: Oxford University Press, 2008.

Heidler, David S., and Jeane T. Heidler. *Indian Removal.* New York: W. W. Norton and Company, 2007.

Holm, Tom. *Strong Hearts, Wounded Souls: Native American Veterans of the Vietnam War.* Austin: University of Texas Press, 1996.

LeBlanc, Steven A. *Prehistoric Warfare in the American Southwest.* Salt Lake City: University of Utah Press, 1999.

Lepore, Jill. *The Name of War: King Philip's War and the Origins of American Identity.* New York: Knopf, 1998.

Morningstorm, J. Boyd. *The American Indian Warrior Today: Native Americans in Modern U.S. Warfare.* Manhattan, KS: Sunflower University Press, 2004.

Nielsen, Marianne O., and James W. Zion, eds. *Navajo Nation Peacemaking: Living Traditional Justice.* Tucson: University of Arizona Press, 2005.

Parkman, Francis. *The Conspiracy of Pontiac and the Indian War after the Conquest of Canada.* Vol. 1, *To the Massacre at Michillimackinac.* Lincoln: University of Nebraska Press, 1994.

Rice, Glen E., and Steven A. LeBlanc, eds. *Deadly Landscapes: Case Studies in Prehistoric Southwestern Warfare.* Salt Lake City: University of Utah Press, 2001.

Sando, Joe, and Herman Agoyo, eds. *Po'Pay: Leader of the First American Revolution.* Santa Fe, NM: Lear Light Publishing, 2005.

Secrest, William B. *When the Great Spirit Died: The Destruction of the California Indians, 1850–1860.* Sangar, CA: Word Dancer Press, 2003.

Smith, Andrea. *Conquest: Sexual Violence and American Indian Genocide.* Cambridge, MA: South End Press, 2005.

Utley, Robert M., and Wilcomb E. Washburn. *Indian Wars.* Boston, MA: Houghton Mifflin Company, 2002.

Wearn, Phillip. *Return of the Indian: Conquest and Revival in the Americas.* Philadelphia, PA: Temple University Press, 1996.

Weaver, Jace. *Turtle Goes to War: Of Military Commissions, the Constitution and American Indian Memory.* New Haven, CT: Trylon and Perisphere Press, 2002.

Williams, Robert A. *Linking Arms Together: American Indian Treaty Visions of Law and Peace, 1600–1800.* New York: Oxford University Press, 1997.

Web Resources

American Indian College Fund
http://www.collegefund.org/

American Indian Social Studies Curricula
http://www.marquette.edu/library/archives/Special_Collections/education.shtml

American Indians of the Pacific Northwest Collection
http://content.lib.washington.edu/aipnw/

Ethnic Heritage: American Indian
http://www.cr.nps.gov/history/categrs/etnc3.htm

First Nations History
http://www.tolatsga.org/Compacts.html

Indian Affairs: Laws and Treaties
http://digital.library.okstate.edu/kappler/intro.htm

Indian Affairs: Tribal Directory
http://bia.gov/WhoWeAre/BIA/OIS/TribalGovernmentServices/TribalDirectory/

Indian Country Today Media Network
http://indiancountrytodaymedianetwork.com/

Indian Territory Division of the Oklahoma Archives
http://www.rootsweb.ancestry.com/usgenweb/ok/nations/

Indians of North America
http://www.csulb.edu/colleges/cla/departments/americanindianstudies/

National Museum of the American Indian
http://nmai.si.edu/about/

National Native American Graves Protection and Repatriation Act
http://www.cr.nps.gov/nagpra/index.htm

Native American Heritage: National Archives
http://www.archives.gov/research/native-americans/index.html

Native American Legal Resources
http://www.law.ou.edu/native/

North American Indians: Books to Start With: Smithsonian
http://www.si.edu/Encyclopedia_SI/nmai/reading-northamericanindians.htm

Records of the Bureau of Indian Affairs
http://www.archives.gov/research/guide-fed-records/groups/075.html

Teaching with Documents: Memorandum Regarding the Enlistment of Navajo Indians: National Archives
http://www.archives.gov/education/lessons/code-talkers/

Treaties Between the United States and Native Americans
http://avalon.law.yale.edu/subject_menus/ntreaty.asp

Tribal College Journal
http://www.tribalcollegejournal.org/

Tribal Directory
http://www.bia.gov/WhoWeAre/BIA/OIS/TribalGovernmentServices/TribalDirectory/

United States Department of the Interior Indian Affairs
http://www.bia.gov/index.htm

Index

421

About the Editors

Gary Y. Okihiro is a professor of international and public affairs at Columbia University. He is the author of *Pineapple Culture: A History of the Tropical and Temperate Zones,* and *Island World: A History of Hawai'i and the United States*, as well as the *Encyclopedia of Japanese American Internment* (Greenwood, 2013).

James E. Seelye Jr., is an assistant professor of history at Kent State University. A specialist in American Indian history and a student of Alfred A. Cave, he earned his PhD from the University of Toledo.